Volume 2 of *Thunderstorms: A Social, Scientific, and Technological Documentary*

Thunderstorm Morphology and Dynamics

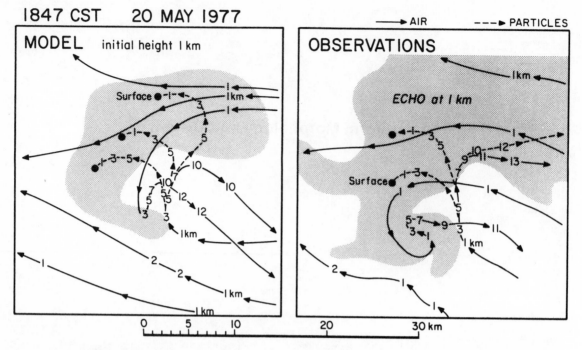

Detailed observations on airflow in supercell tornadic storms can be substantially simulated by numerical models. This figure represents a storm that occurred at Del City, Okla. Solid lines indicate air trajectories in the model (left) and as defined by observations (right) with two Doppler radars of the National Severe Storms Laboratory; dashed lines represent the trajectories of precipitation packets. Integers along the trajectories represent heights in kilometers. The shaded area in the model includes the region with model rainwater content ≥0.5 kg at model time, 2 hours after initialization with a warm thermal. The shaded area in the observations includes the region with radar reflectivity factor ≥30 dBZ. A striking feature of the observations, verified in the model, is that air rising in the updraft turns clockwise or anticyclonically with height, even though the streamfield of the updraft and its immediate environment shows cyclonic rotation. This appears to be an effect of the clockwise turning of the winds with increasing height in the storm environment. The precipitation trajectories illustrate transport away from the originating updraft into downdrafts on north and west sides of the storm on paths that curve cyclonically along their descending branches. The accumulation of rain on the back side of the storm provides substantial negative buoyancy through water loading and evaporation, and thereby drives the downdraft circulation. (After J. B. Klemp, R. B. Wilhelmson, and P. S. Ray, 1981, *J. Atmos Sci.* 38:1558–80; see also Chaps. 7 and 15 in this volume.)

Thunderstorm Morphology and Dynamics

Second Edition, Revised and Enlarged

Edited by Edwin Kessler

University of Oklahoma Press
Norman and London

BY EDWIN KESSLER

On the Distribution and Continuity of Water Substance in Atmospheric Circulations (Boston, 1969)

(Editor) *Thunderstorms: A Social, Scientific, and Technological Documentary*, 3 vols. (Norman, 1981–82)

(Editor) *The Thunderstorm in Human Affairs*, 2d ed. (Vol. 1 of *Thunderstorms: A Social, Scientific, and Technological Documentary*), (Norman, 1983)

(Editor) *Thunderstorm Morphology and Dynamics*, 2d ed. (Vol. 2 of *Thunderstorms: A Social, Scientific, and Technological Documentary*), (Norman, 1985)

Library of Congress Cataloging-in-Publication Data
Main entry under title:

Thunderstorm morphology and dynamics.

   (Thunderstorms—a social, scientific, and
technological documentary; v. 2)
   Includes bibliographical references and index.
   1. Thunderstorms.   I. Kessler, Edwin.   II. Title.
III. Series: Thunderstorms—a social, scientific, and
technological documentary (2d ed., rev. and enl.);
v. 2.
QC968.T48   1983 vol. 2   363.3'492 s [551.5'54]   85–8450
ISBN 0–8061–1936–5 (alk. paper)

The paper in this book meets the guidelines for permanence and durability of the Committee on Production Guidelines for Book Longevity of the Council on Library Resources, Inc.

First edition published 1981 for the U.S. Department of Commerce by the U.S. Government Printing Office, Washington, D.C. Second edition copyright © 1986 by the University of Oklahoma Press, Norman, Publishing Division of the University. Manufactured in the U.S.A.

Contents

Contents

Preface to the Second Edition

The preparation and first appearance of this book were a project of the National Severe Storms Laboratory and its parent organization, the Environmental Research Laboratories, in the National Oceanic and Atmospheric Administration, U.S. Department of Commerce.

For this edition, in addition to correcting a few typographical errors in the first edition and clarifying some passages, we have added to the content, updating where practicable. Chapters 5, 6, 7, 13, and 15 have some notable additions, chapter 10 has been expanded considerably, and chapter 8 has been revised and expanded to present a global perspective on tropical convection. An index has also been added.

We acknowledge with much appreciation the support of the National Center for Atmospheric Research, sponsored by the National Science Foundation, which has provided funds for the typesetting of this second edition.

I thank authors and reviewers for attention to many details and substantial improvements. Reviewers who have newly contributed to this edition include R. P. Davies-Jones, R. Houze, D. K. Lilly, D. L. MacGorman, S. Nelson, R. Rotunno, W. D. Rust, and F. Sanders. J. Kimpel has been a great help in graphic arts. I particularly thank Lindsay Murdock and Patricia Peterson for their remarkable editorial services in the first edition and am grateful for the support of friends and colleagues along the sometimes tortuous path to publication of this work.

EDWIN KESSLER

National Severe Storms Laboratory
August, 1984

Preface to the First Edition

This second volume of a comprehensive three-volume work presents our understanding of the form and distribution of thunderstorms and of their associated physical processes: thermal, dynamical, hygrological, and electrical. This work was begun in 1976, but chapters were completed at different times between then and now. Therefore, some are more current than others. All have been reviewed by their authors during 1981, though not necessarily revised; all are deemed accurate at time of publication. The latest date in the references for a chapter is usually indicative of the currency of the chapter content.

There is some overlap in the subject matter of different chapters in this and other volumes. Some topics are accordingly discussed more than once, and occasionally with somewhat varying conclusions. We have not generally objected to this, but instead believe that statements of diverse authoritative viewpoints should help apprise the reader of the real state of the science, and should help him toward his own conclusions or further study. Since cross references of related materials within this volume are not always given, the reader should examine the detailed Table of Contents for indications of related discussions. A good intermediate textbook may be helpful for background and derivation of some basic equations.

Although this publication is specialized and rather voluminous, it does not present all current significant knowledge on its subject. Indeed, that seems an unrealistic goal. The text does show that much has been learned during the three decades since the Thunderstorm Project.

I thank the authors for their cooperation in submitting their works and participating in the rather lengthy editorial process. I also thank reviewers Robert P. Davies-Jones, Carl E. Hane, Stanley L. Barnes, Charles F. Knight, Douglas K. Lilly, Roland List, David Rust, Joseph Schaefer, Roger Smith, William Taylor, Conrad Ziegler, and others anonymous. I am grateful to the staff of the Environmental Research Laboratories, Publication Services Division, Boulder, Colo., and for strong support and assistance, I thank my secretary, Barbara Franklin, and my wife, Lottie Menger Kessler.

Finally, I would acknowledge the optimism, brilliance, and great good humor of the late Frank Ludlam. The life and work of Frank Ludlam and of his wife, Jean, are shining examples for all people.

EDWIN KESSLER

Norman, Oklahoma
November, 1981

Thunderstorm Morphology and Dynamics

Figure 1.1. A population of cumulus clouds, seen from about 18 km over Oklahoma.

1. Introduction

Frank H. Ludlam

1. The Meteorological Role of Cumulus and Cumulonimbus

The atmosphere is almost transparent to sunshine, and most of that which passes through is absorbed at the Earth's surface. At terrestrial temperatures, however, the radiation into space of the absorbed energy is mainly in the invisible infrared, and in the lower atmosphere is hindered by water vapor in concentrations that make it almost opaque. Consequently, outward passage of the energy demands that the atmospheric temperature decrease rapidly with height. The saturated vapor concentration, which is an effective limit to the actual atmospheric-vapor content, also decreases rapidly with temperature; accordingly at some modest height between 10 km (in high latitudes) and about 16 km (in low latitudes) the vapor content becomes so small that it no longer has major significance and the stratosphere is entered. In the lower stratosphere the temperature is nearly constant with height, under more subtle controls. Beneath it, below an often remarkably sharp boundary called the tropopause, lies the moist troposphere in which upward transport of energy by radiation is continually assisted by convection.

This convection, which is responsible for most kinds of weather, divides the troposphere into regions of upward and downward motion. In the former, when air rises more than about a kilometer above the surface, vapor condenses, and clouds and perhaps rains form. In the latter, which are generally the more extensive horizontally, the remaining water soon evaporates; these are mainly regions of few clouds and sunny weather. The convection and hence the forms of cloud are of three principal kinds.

a. Small-Scale Convection

Small-scale convection is also called cumulus convection, from the small heap clouds that commonly form in it. The individual clouds are several kilometers apart and have dimensions of up to a kilometer or two, usually insufficient for shower formation. These fair-weather clouds are produced by heating the air in contact with warm land and water. They occupy vast areas in great populations, especially over the oceans in tropical regions and where cool air in higher latitudes flows towards warmer water, and also overland during sunshine (Fig. 1.1). Individual clouds are short-lived (that is, the convective circulations producing them are not uniform and steadily maintained), and the population contains many small clouds, only some of which ever become large. Over irregular land it is obvious that the largest clouds develop towers among clustered small clouds associated with some ground features that concentrate and intensify the ascent of air, such as areas that are particularly warm by virtue of their composition, low albedo, or high elevation. Inside the taller clouds the air rises at a few meters per second and is warmer than the clear surrounding air by a few tenths of a degree Celsius, a value consistent with a heat flux into the lower atmosphere at a rate set by the rate of surface warming.

b. Cumulonimbus Convection

Following the formation of showers, perhaps stimulated by relief from the weight of condensed water or release of latent heat of fusion during its freezing, the buoyancy, vigor, and size of cumulus towers are often greatly enhanced, and the clouds become cumulonimbus, or thunderclouds. The depth of the convection increases, often suddenly, from a few kilometers to the whole depth of the troposphere (Fig. 1.2). In low latitudes scattered cumulonimbus and more or less organized systems of cumulonimbus (including the tropical cyclones) represent the agency by which convection extends through the upper troposphere. In higher latitudes they occur only incidentally, and often fail to reach the tropopause, as details in large-scale convection.

c. Large-Scale Convection, Manifest as Cyclones and Anticyclones

The geometry of the Earth ensures that (on the average) in high latitudes less solar energy arrives over a unit of area of the Earth's surface than in low latitudes, where the Earth more directly faces the Sun. On the other hand, the emission of radiation into space depends mainly upon the temperature at which the high troposphere contains the last significant traces of water vapor, a temperature almost independent of latitude. Accordingly, the emission is almost the same everywhere: less than income in low latitudes and more in high latitudes, so that maintenance of the same mean temperatures in all latitudes implies that there is a mean trans-

Figure 1.2. Neighboring cumulonimbus towers with extensions of anvil cloud. (Photographed over Oklahoma on 26 May 1973 by Peter Sinclair.)

port of heat from low to high latitudes. This is effected partly by flow of warm ocean waters toward the poles but mainly by convection of heat poleward within the troposphere itself. In this large-scale convection, air warmed near the surface in low latitudes (by cumulus convection) streams toward the poles and arrives in high latitudes at high levels, producing deep but almost horizontal layered sheets of cloud (and rains) on its way (air leaving the surface layers in higher latitudes shares in the upward and poleward motion in and near the cloud belts but does not rise as high). Return flows of cool air descend slowly as they move waveringly into lower latitudes; in their upper levels they are mainly cloudless, but in their lower levels they encounter the cumulus convection, which restores their original warmth and moisture.

The ascent of air into higher latitudes, which produces the extensive belts of cloud, a few hundred kilometers across but much greater in length, is associated with the major cold fronts and cyclones, of which there are several at any one time in a hemisphere. The ascent is accompanied by horizontal accelerations which produce the narrow jet streams of middle latitudes. The descent of air typically takes several times longer than the ascent, and may not be completed until a large part of a hemisphere has been traversed, with several meanders through neighboring cyclones and anticyclones, in the predominantly westerly flows of middle latitudes. During this descent the high speeds attained in the jet streams are gradually lost.

2. Cumulonimbus Regimes

It is natural to classify cumulonimbus clouds according to the principal meteorological regimes in which they occur.

Foremost among these is the regime of tropical convection, in which the warm sunshine over land, and especially over hilly ground not far from the ocean where the air is moist, causes strong convection and thunderclouds nearly every afternoon. In these clouds, which being often widespread and numerous are not especially vigorous, the ascent speed of air reaches values not much more than 10 m s^{-1} in the upper parts. The clouds reach up to near the tropopause, and their frozen upper parts spread into the anvil shape typical of mature thunderclouds. They produce intense, thundery rains that moisten and chill the warm ground. In this way the convection becomes quenched locally, and the individual clouds are short-lived (lasting less than an hour). The frozen anvil-shaped parts are more persistent, and fresh clouds continually grow from neighboring sites, so that the anvil residues may accumulate to occupy a large fraction of the sky before evaporating slowly overnight. Similar clouds occur over the warmest parts of the tropical oceans during both day and night.

Cumulonimbus clouds that develop in middle latitudes, where winds associated with cyclones lead cool air rapidly toward warmer waters, are typically both smaller and less vigorous, not usually reaching above the middle troposphere. They invade inland regions, where sunshine raises the ground temperature to the oceanic values, but usually disappear quickly inland during the dark hours. These cumulonimbus do not play any essential role in the heat economy of the extratropical latitudes, which is dominated by the cyclones and anticyclones.

In consequence of the great thermal inertia of the oceans, this large-scale convection and a temperature gradient between low and high latitudes are maintained throughout the year (in midsummer the income of solar radiation is briefly nearly the same between the tropic and the pole). However, in consequence of the greater intensity of sunshine in middle-latitude summer, the cumulonimbus regime of low latitudes extends poleward across the continents in this season. The location and intensity of the cumulonimbus are then determined not only by topography but even more strongly by position with respect to large-scale (cyclonic) convection. Remarkably, a combination of favorable factors of both kinds leads to occasional growth of exceptionally severe thunderstorms. These severe local storms are accompanied by large hailstones and squalls (or even tornadoes) of a violence hardly ever attained in tropical regimes. They are prevalent in particular regions downwind of high ground, notably the Midwest of the United States, and pose serious problems by the hazards they bring to air transport, and especially because of the damage they inflict on crops and buildings.

3. Some Thunderstorm Theories and Phenomena

Over the last century an impressive quantity of observational data about thunderstorms over land has been gathered. In earlier times it had already been recognized that there is an obvious distinction between the ordinary thunderstorm of moderate intensity and short duration, the so-called air-mass storm, and the severe local storm. The latter is distinguished not only by its violence but also by its persistence over several hours and perhaps throughout the night, by its habit of traveling up to several hundred kilometers from its source, and by its association with frontal zones of strong horizontal temperature gradient and strong winds aloft. The persistence of the severe storm in these strong winds was long a puzzle, for it seemed likely that the winds must interfere with development of strong storm updrafts to the great heights observed (at first visually and more recently by radar). Because of the need to recognize the conditions in which thunderstorms develop, and in particular those in which they may become severe, simple theories were constructed to relate the likelihood of afternoon storms to conditions aloft observed during soundings made the previous morning.

a. The Parcel Theory of Convection

An important theory is based on the assumption that at least in the interior of thunderclouds air ascends adiabatically (without transfer of heat or mass across air parcel boundaries), losing any condensed water vapor, after beginning its rise in the state anticipated to be produced by the day's sunshine near the ground (this state is very difficult to infer theoretically, but in practice is forecast on the basis of experience or the trend observed during previous days). The assumption is evidently not useful for predicting growth of cumulus clouds, for in their interior the temperature is observed to be substantially less than that which would be realized by the condensation of vapor during adiabatic ascent from the cloud base. Moreover, it usually takes no account of the possibility for release of the latent heat of fusion during

freezing of cloud water at temperatures below 0°C. However, the assumptions employed are practically the simplest possible to make, and have the advantage that at any level the temperature of the cloudy air depends only on the state of the air when its ascent began. Further, apparently reliable measurements occasionally made inside the lower parts of large thunderclouds indicate that the assumptions are not unrealistic for the purpose of inferring a buoyancy for the cloudy air (that is, a temperature difference between the interior and the outside of a thundercloud), provided that this buoyancy is large (corresponding to temperature difference of at least several degrees Celsius). Complications owing to the weight of cloud water and variations of vapor content from cloud to environment can, in these circumstances, probably be overlooked without serious error.

According to the simple parcel theory of convection, the air accelerates upward under its buoyancy and acquires a maximum speed at the so-called equilibrium level, where the temperature of the cloud first decreases to become equal to that in its surroundings. On occasions of tall thunderclouds this level is usually near the tropopause. Above it the cloud air becomes colder than its surroundings and decelerates under a negative buoyancy before eventually coming to rest at some higher level, usually identified with that likely to be reached by the extreme tops of the thunderclouds.

On occasions of air-mass thunderstorms the maximum temperature excess of the cloudy air attained during its ascent is less than several degrees Celsius, and the cloud tops are observed barely to reach the equilibrium level. Probably, therefore, the air inside the clouds does not ascend adiabatically but, like the air in cumulus, suffers a mixing with surrounding clear air that substantially reduces its buoyancy. However, cloud tops in severe storms much more nearly correspond to the maximum predicted by the parcel theory, or even somewhat exceed it. It is tempting to infer that at least a proportion of the air ascends adiabatically, attaining the states predicted by the parcel theory. Nevertheless, it has to be admitted that no direct observations conclusively show this, and laboratory experiments on the rise of a limited volume of buoyant fluid (a "thermal") have shown that the maximum velocity attained in the interior is not associated with the region of greatest buoyancy. Therefore, thunderstorm observations must be interpreted with caution. In spite of this, the simple parcel theory remains a valuable reference. In numerical simulations of thundercloud evolution, diffusion can be allowed to lead to departures from adiabatic motion, but there is as yet no sound theory for diffusion.

A prime requirement for a theory of cumulonimbus convection is that a diagnostic sounding of the current state of the atmosphere shall indicate with confidence whether solar warming of the lowest layer, or some other process, will lead to development of cumulonimbus clouds and, if so, what will be the intensity of their drafts. It has to be admitted that proof of the simple parcel theory has been restricted to the demonstration that a necessary but not a sufficient condition for appearance of cumulonimbus is that the sounding shall show over a large depth of the troposphere a state

Figure 1.3. A long belt of cumulonimbus over the central United States, seen from the satellite GOES-3 (the most prominent clouds are groups of anvils). The view extends from northern Oklahoma (lower edge) to the Great Lakes (upper right). The cloud belt and accompanying squall line were associated with a cold front, which was followed by an incursion of much drier air and a large area of cloudless skies. Data shown in the photograph were collected at 1505 CST, 6 May 1975, 58 min after the data shown in Vol. 1, Chap. 8, Fig. 8.11.

of conditional instability. This is a lapse of temperature with height which exceeds that characteristic of the adiabatic ascent of saturated air (the "saturated adiabatic"). In this circumstance the atmosphere can be said to be unstable with respect to cloudy convection, for cloudy air displaced upward acquires a buoyancy that accelerates it, at least until the air has reached the equilibrium level of the theory. However, although a state of conditional instability is always observed to precede and accompany thunderstorms, it is also a common state on the more numerous occasions when clouds form but fail to grow beyond the size of small cumulus. Evidently on these occasions some organizing mechanism is absent, so that individual volumes of cloudy air remain small and subject to such a degree of mixing with their surroundings that the adiabatic ascent envisaged by simple theory is far from attained, even in the cloud interiors. It often seems that the state of deep conditional instability is not a requirement for the development of cumulonimbus convection but rather a product of its previous occurrence on preceding days or in neighboring regions. In forecasting practice, soundings are inspected to confirm that conditional instability is present, and decisions are made on other, more empirical and less specific grounds about whether it is likely to be realized.

These are about the only procedures possible in situations where the mild air-mass storms are likely to arise, and the instability is only marginal and is relieved virtually as it is generated. In other situations the instability is suppressed and for several days confined to a shallow layer of cumulus convection. In these circumstances a large amount of potential energy, represented largely by water-vapor content, may be stored in this shallow layer and eventually, after several days, be suddenly available for cumulonimbus convection of the severe kind, by the intervention of a process of intermediate ("meso") or large ("synoptic") scale. This frequently happens in particular regions and results in the severe local storms of cumulonimbus systems lying above frontal zones (Fig. 1.3). The preceding soundings show a moist lowermost layer capped by a warm layer of unusually dry air, above which the atmosphere again becomes conditionally unstable. If a deep layer is lifted in a meso- or synoptic-scale system, both the dry warm air and the lowermost moist layer cool, but the latter less rapidly as clouds form or thicken and latent heat of condensation is released. The dry air becomes relatively cool, and eventually the whole troposphere can enter a state favorable for upward growth of clouds into cumulonimbus. Its original state is then said to be one of convective instability. Experience shows this state to be characteristic of frontal situations in which the most violent thunderstorms develop, and much research has endeavored to identify the meso- or large-scale systems responsible for their formation, with limited success. It is still a matter of debate whether there are any important mesoscale systems for initiating storms that are independent of topographically induced circulations, whose effectiveness is difficult to recognize because their intensity and location depend strongly on several variables, such as

precise direction and stratification of the general airstream, moistness of the ground, and time of day and season.

b. The Downdraft

Dry air found in the lower middle troposphere on occasions of convective instability can be cooled by evaporation of rain or hail, often sufficiently to allow it to accelerate downward and reach the surface. Thereby the possibility arises that the severe thunderstorm becomes organized not only to raise potentially warm air but also to effect a more complete and efficient overturning of a deep layer of the troposphere. That this does happen is revealed by a low wet-bulb temperature in cool squalls that spread out from beneath severe storms: it can be shown that air in such squalls must have descended from levels above cloud base. Transfer of cloud water from updraft to downdraft can evidently occur only if the former leans over the latter, and there is often visible evidence of this in the shape of the cloud base (forming an arch around the squall) and its rearward-tilted lower surface.

The cool squall has an additional importance in lifting the layers into which it advances, thereby producing the kind of mesoscale system required to release the convective instability; once a severe storm has been formed, it provides a mechanism for its own maintenance and can travel away from its source. According to some tentative theory, it is envisaged that the downdraft and the updraft can compose a steadily sustained couplet ("supercell") of much greater efficiency than the ordinary impulsive convection. However, it has to be recognized that in consequence of the larger particle size the evaporation of water in a downdraft can virtually never be complete or as efficient as its condensation in an updraft; the conditions under which the water can be used to maintain the pair as a fitting and long-lasting couplet have yet to be determined, but the wind shear must play an important (and at first unsuspected) role in allowing transfer of water between the drafts.

Air in the layer below cloud base is the updraft source. However, being unsaturated, it too can be cooled by evaporation, although not as significantly as air in the upper dry layer. Nevertheless it too can contribute to the downdraft, and the configuration of the storm may be such that it reaches the surface immediately behind the wind-shift line of the squall front. Here it may be lifted forcibly to share in the updraft and become positively buoyant again above the (rather lower) level at which it becomes saturated and forms cloud. Such a process may be important if, during its course, the spin implied by the original shear of the wind in the vertical becomes twisted into the horizontal, for this initially strong spin is possibly concentrated below a strongly accelerating updraft into the violent rotation of the tornado. The tornado certainly develops below freshly growing cloud near the wind-shift line, and it is a difficult problem to account for its intense spin: this seems too great to be derived simply from concentration of the spin of horizontal winds in the broad frontal zone within which the squall line develops.

c. The Configuration of Drafts: Microphysical Aspects

In almost any theory of very large hail in severe storms, it is difficult to suppose that hail growth can be completed in the short time spent by air in a strongly accelerating updraft. Air enters cloud base with a relative speed of about 10 m s^{-1}, reaches speeds comparable with the fall speeds of the stones (40 m s^{-1} or more) in the upper troposphere, and streams rapidly away from the storm in the outflow of anvil cloud. The total time spent in the strong updraft and available for the growth of hail is therefore less than about 20 minutes. According to microphysical theory of cloud-droplet growth following freezing or the growth of ice crystals in the upper parts of the cloud, the time available is sufficient only for the production of hailstone embryos of millimetric size. It would therefore be expected that virtually all such precipitation would be blown forward out of the storm, that few particles would be available for generation of a downdraft, and that none could continue growth to a large size. It seems more probable that hailstone embryos are grown in the cumuliform clouds containing lesser updrafts formed on flanks of the principal storm cloud. They find their way at midlevels into the strong updrafts, either because there is a wind component taking them in this direction or because the strong updraft location is transferred sideways during propagation of the main storm across the general wind.

The nature of the configuration of drafts (their relative arrangement and the shape and definition of their interface) has not yet been adequately explored. The drafts must have an important bearing on several aspects of the storm: its ability to preserve a coherent form, its efficiency in redistributing momentum as well as heat upon the large scale, and the efficiency with which it converts condensed water into precipitation that can reach the ground. There is some evidence that the last varies between wide limits, being almost zero in some arid regions and frequently rather smaller in many severe storms than in lesser storms and showers. This kind of consideration becomes all-important in the theory of the suppression of large hail by artificial provision of more numerous embryos, especially since there is the daunting possibility that elimination of the bigger stones might lead also to elimination of stones large enough to reach the ground after melting, and thereby to removal of beneficial rain. Much more work needs to be done to relate microphysical aspects of thunderstorms to their more general characteristics.

4. Modern Techniques and Outlook

Among the modern techniques of observation that are providing greatly improved and more detailed information on thunderstorm structure are aircraft reconnaissance (mainly outside clouds) and, especially, use of pairs of Doppler radars to map the form of airflow in regions containing precipitation (and radar echo). The latter depends upon the approach of storms within convenient range; the data are of unparalleled abundance and resolution and provide unrivaled insight on the three-dimensional airflow and on the generation of rotation responsible for tornadoes.

With this abundance of information and recognition that storms have an evolution in time as well as an essentially three-dimensional structure in space, the analytical theory of thunderstorm structure has become confined to suggesting the most economical and significant ways in which numerical models can be used to simulate and explore storm structure. Because of their dynamical complexity these models have necessarily to rely on some simple parameterizations of processes on space scales of less than about 1 km, including the microphysical processes of the formation, freezing, aggregation, shattering, and melting of the cloud particles. Examination of the generation and separation of electrical charge that accompanies these processes has also had to be postponed, although it is their effectiveness which has given the thunderstorm its name (moreover, it has not been important to include the electrical among the thermodynamic transformations, because energetically it is comparatively trivial).

In summary, we observe recent impressive advances in observational technique and theoretical modeling. These have revealed the thunderstorm as a phenomenon demanding simultaneous attention to processes at work on a great range of scale—from the microscopic concerned with cloud particles, to the metric scales expressing friction and mixture on the kilometric cloud scale, and the divergence of particle path and air path, further to the mesoscale governing cloud formation and regeneration, and finally to the synoptic scale providing the setting in which the whole grand thunderstorm machine works and propagates. In this light it is wonderful that modern and effective observational and computational technique allows progress to continue, though not with the pace one would wish, for the problem as a whole must be among the most formidably complex that science has to offer.[1]

---

[1] Editor's note: An excellent general reference is Frank H. Ludlam's *Clouds and Storms* (Pennsylvania State University Press, University, Pa., 1980). We observe that speculative comments presented above by Dr. Ludlum have found support in subsequent observational and theoretical work, as described elsewhere in this volume.

2. Thunderstorm Climatology

Arnold Court and John F. Griffiths

1. Introduction

Thunderstorms are cloud masses from (or in) which electrical discharges create thunder. The cloud is almost always a cumulonimbus, in which individual cells produce rain, often copious, and sometimes hail, strong winds, and even tornadoes. Cells develop successively, but their sum, the individual thunderstorm, seldom lasts longer than 2 hours, although a procession of thunderstorms may cause thunder for half a day or longer. A space of about 30 km (20 mi) between the mesoscale systems that spawn thunderstorms in certain tropical and subtropical regions has been suggested by Henry et al. (1966).

Individual cells of a single storm, and separate storms in a line or cluster, can be identified readily by radar and from the air. They soon may be tracked continuously from satellites. From underneath, observers cannot tell how many separate cells and storms contribute to the towering clouds, rain, hail, lightning, and thunder that they report. Hence the basic material of thunderstorm climatology is not the frequency and duration of individual thunderstorms but the number of days (or hours) on which thunderstorms occur.

Even these data may not be correct: "By international agreement a 'thunderstorm day' is defined as a local calendar day on which thunder is heard, . . . regardless of the actual number of thunderstorms" (WMO, 1953). Some observers, however, may misunderstand and report the number of distinguishable thunderstorms in a month. Such a misunderstanding might explain the average of 322 thunderstorms per year sometimes credited to Bogor (formerly Buitenzorg), Indonesia, which is discussed in Sec. 3 below.

Because audibility is the criterion by which a thunderstorm day is defined, the noise level around a weather station influences the number of thunderstorms detected and reported. At modern observing stations at busy U.S. airports, where automatic remote-recording instruments permit the observer to remain indoors much of the time, thunder may not be heard as often as at smaller stations in quieter surroundings. However, lightning can be seen readily from airport control towers, and operators can alert weather observers; at many airports the weather is reported directly by the tower personnel.

No levels of thunderstorm intensity are recognized for U.S. climatic tabulations, but airways observations from 1935 to 1947 distinguished between light, moderate, and heavy (severe until 1941). The three categories differ in lightning frequency (occasional, frequent, incessant), rain (light, moderate to heavy, heavy), and wind (<30, <40, >40 mph). Since 1947, although the three classes are still used, both light and moderate thunderstorms have been reported as T, heavy as $T+$ (Baliles, 1958). Tabulations of thunderstorms reported according to these rules on hourly airways observations have provided data on thunderstorm hours, rather than days, but this source of information was curtailed in 1964, when archiving on magnetic tape was reduced to every third hour.

Almost all lightning, and hence thunder, comes from cumulonimbus clouds, the true thunderstorms. However, a very few flashes and consequent peals of thunder emanate from poorly developed clouds, just enough to give subpolar stations slightly more thunderstorm days than the actual number of true thunderstorms. Another consequence of the definition (day with thunder) is that a midnight thunderstorm causes 2 days to be counted. The pronounced nocturnal maximum in thunderstorm occurrence in the central United States, discussed in Sec. 2c below, inflates the number of thunderstorm days reported there.

Hail falls frequently in some part of every continent except Antarctica (Gokhale, 1975), and some success in reducing its incidence has been claimed in a few places. Efforts have relied on sound waves from cannon fire or explosions, or on silver iodide or other ice nuclei introduced by artillery, rockets, aircraft, or plumes from the ground. Successful or not, these activities have increased the publicity and reporting of hail, and hence the knowledge of its distribution in time and space.

Hail larger than snow pellets and graupel is classified primarily by size, the length of the longest axis, as compared with familiar objects. The names used have become fairly standard, with some exceptions, but their numerical definitions tend to vary, especially between English and metric usage (Paul, 1968). Typical diameters are designated as follows:

mm:	5	10	20	30	50	60
	shot	pea	grape	walnut	golf ball	hen egg	tennis ball
in:	¼	½	¾	5⁄4	2	5⁄2

True hail may be considered pea size or larger and large hail greater than ¾ in (19 or 20 mm) (Pautz, 1969) or 1 in (25 mm) (Paul, 1968).

The largest hailstone recorded in a substantiated report, 1.9 kg (4.2 lb), fell in Kazakhstan, USSR, and one weighing 0.97 kg (2.1 lb) fell near Strasbourg, France, in August 1958 (U.S. Army Engineer Topographic Lab., 1974). The United States record is held by a 0.76-kg (1.67-lb) stone 45 cm (17.5 in) in circumference that fell near Coffeyville, Kans., in September 1970. Reported weights of almost 4.5 kg (10 lb) in China, about 4 kg (9 lb) in Hungary, and 3.4 kg (7.5 lb) in India, if true, probably were for groups of hailstones clustered or frozen together. Hailstones lying a meter or more deep on the ground have been reported many times; generally, such falls consist of pea to walnut size and represent drifting by wind or concentrations from roofs or hillsides. Hailstorms usually cover an area less than 1 km² (0.4 mi²), but more than 44,000 km² (17,000 mi²) were affected by a storm in November 1913 (Bureau of Meteorology [Australia], 1929).

Hail statistics are of two kinds: reports at regular weather stations, which can sample only a small fraction of the total land area exposed to hail, and insurance claims of crop damage, which are rare after harvest. Hail frequency at a point (weather station) must be increased as much as 15 times, perhaps 100 times, to estimate hail occurrences over the area from which thunder is heard—generally a circle with 15- to 30-km radius, or a 1,000- to 2,000-km² area. Almost 800 voluntary observers distributed over 2,500 km² (1,000 mi²) around Pretoria and Johannesburg reported hail on 79 days per year, whereas Pretoria reported hail on only 5 of its 69 thunderstorm days (Carte, 1967).

These and other limitations on gathering the basic data of thunderstorms and hail must be considered in using the statistics of days with thunder and with hail to develop thunderstorm and hail climatologies, first for the United States, then for the world.

2. United States Thunderstorm Climatology

a. Maps

Thunderstorms occur in all parts of the 50 United States but with widely varying frequency and intensity. Rather weak storms occur very infrequently in Alaska and only two or three times a year in the Pacific Northwest. Large but not very violent thunderstorms occur on more than one-fourth of all days in part of Florida, and very severe storms develop locally in the eastern half of the conterminous United States several times a year.

Thunderstorm distribution in time and space of the conterminous United States (Table 2.1) has been mapped and discussed more than a dozen times in the past 80 years. Harrington (1894, chart xxiii) mapped the occurrences of *individual* thunderstorms from 1884, after which "the record of thunderstorms was kept uniformly at all stations." Henry (1906, plate xxvii, pp. 74–75) mapped all reported *days* with thunderstorms from 1874 to 1903. These older reports

were rejected by Alexander (1915, 1924, 1935), who accepted data only from 1904 onward for monthly and annual thunderstorm day maps covering one, two, and three decades. These maps were copied in many places, including the *Atlas of American Agriculture* (Kincer, 1922, Fig. 81) and Humphrey's book (1920, p. 328; 1929, pp. 313–14). The number of reported thunderstorm days increased greatly after the definition change in 1893 from "thunder with rain" to "thunder with or without rain" (Humphreys 1914, p. 353; 1920, p. 328; 1929, pp. 313–14). "The annual number of thunderstorm days reported per station since 1903 is almost double the number per station from 1880 to 1890."

Alexander's annual 1904–23 map was used by Gregg (1930) and redrawn by Brooks et al. (1936) for the North American thunderstorm day map in the *Handbuch der Klimatologie* (Ward and Brooks, 1936, Sec. J, Part 1). It was also the basis of the thunderstorm day map in *Climate and Man* (USDA, 1941), ostensibly for 1899–1938, the book's standard period. In the most intensive study of thunderstorm climatology thus far, Shands (1945) extended Alexander's work to cover four decades, 1904 to 1943. Most differences between his annual map and that of *Climate and Man* were explained by erroneous data in the earlier map. Many of Shands's maps were redrawn by Visher (1948, 1954) and later reprinted in various textbooks.

But the warnings of Alexander, Humphreys, Shands, and later Baliles (1958) have been ignored by their agency, which tabulates, publishes, and maps thunderstorm days for each station for its entire period of record, beginning in 1871 for the half-dozen oldest. These inhomogeneous figures, routinely presented in *Local Climatological Data* and elsewhere, have been used for several official publications. Although recognizing that definition changes caused more thunderstorms to be recorded after 1894, the Climatological Services Division (1952) used figures for the entire period of record at 266 stations for monthly and annual maps; the annual map has been copied in at least three textbooks. The same data provide by far the longest records in the WMO worldwide tabulation (WMO, 1953). Annual maps using all data through 1955 were prepared by Schloemer (1956), through 1964 by Environmental Data Service (1966), and through 1969 by Baldwin (1973); the EDS map was condensed and simplified for the *National Atlas* (USGS, 1971), and both the EDS and the Baldwin maps have been used for various NOAA publications. No thunderstorm map appears in the *Climatic Atlas of the United States* (Baldwin, 1968).

In contrast, the maps offered here (Figs. 2.1–2.3), like their immediate predecessor (Court, 1974), are for a recent period only, covering 25 yr, 1951–75. The 1951–70 data come from the hail and thunderstorm pages of the station record books, photocopied by the National Climatic Center. For 186 stations, data for the remaining 5 yr were extracted from the annual issues of *Local Climatological Data*; such material was not available for 19 stations, marked in Table 2.1, which consequently have data for only 20 yr. Only stations with complete data for 1951–70 were used, eliminating many that closed or no longer tallied thunderstorms because of reduced hours of operation. The 25-yr (or 20-yr)

Table 2.1. Mean Number of Days with Thunderstorms, 1951–75, by Months, Years, and Half Years
(† = 1951–70 only; winter = Oct.–Mar., summer = Apr.–Sept.; 0.00 < * < 0.5)

	Jan.	Feb.	Mar.	Apr.	May	June	July	Aug.	Sept.	Oct.	Nov.	Dec.	Year	Wint.	Sumr.
Birmingham, Ala.	1.8	2.3	4.4	5.2	6.5	8.5	11.8	9.3	3.8	1.0	1.8	1.4	57.8	12.6	45.3
Mobile, Ala.	2.0	2.2	4.5	4.7	6.7	11.8	17.8	14.2	7.4	1.8	1.8	2.4	77.4	14.7	62.6
Montgomery, Ala.	2.0	2.3	5.0	5.5	6.7	9.3	12.0	9.4	3.9	1.3	1.6	2.0	61.2	14.2	46.9
Flagstaff, Ariz.	*	*	0.5	1.4	2.6	3.7	16.0	16.6	6.8	2.3	0.6	*	50.4	4.0	47.0
Phoenix, Ariz.	*	0.7	0.7	0.6	0.6	1.0	6.1	7.8	3.2	1.2	0.8	*	23.2	3.8	19.3
Tucson, Ariz.	*	*	*	0.9	1.0	2.6	14.9	13.8	5.2	1.6	*	*	41.4	3.0	38.4
Winslow, Ariz.	*	*	*	1.1	1.9	2.8	11.2	11.0	5.0	1.5	*	*	35.7	2.6	33.1
Yuma, Ariz.	0.0	*	*	*	*	*	1.5	2.2	1.2	0.6	*	*	7.1	1.4	5.7
Fort Smith, Ark.	1.1	1.5	5.0	7.0	7.7	7.8	7.6	6.1	4.4	3.1	2.4	1.6	55.4	14.7	40.7
Little Rock, Ark.	2.0	2.4	4.7	6.4	6.7	7.6	9.4	6.2	3.8	2.8	2.6	1.8	56.2	15.7	40.2
Bakersfield, Calif.	*	*	*	*	*	*	*	*	*	*	*	0.0	2.4	0.9	1.5
Eureka, Calif. †	0.9	0.8	*	*	*	*	*	*	*	*	0.6	0.9	4.7	3.8	0.8
Fresno, Calif.	*	*	0.8	0.6	0.6	0.6	*	*	0.7	0.5	*	*	5.7	2.6	3.1
Long Beach, Calif.	*	*	*	*	*	0.0	*	*	*	*	*	*	3.5	2.0	1.5
Los Angeles, Calif.	*	*	*	*	*	*	*	*	*	*	*	*	3.4	1.9	1.5
Oakland, Calif.	*	*	*	0.5	*	*	*	*	*	*	*	*	2.4	1.1	1.2
Red Bluff, Calif.	*	0.7	1.2	1.2	1.2	1.5	0.8	0.8	0.6	0.6	*	*	9.4	3.2	6.2
Sacramento, Calif.	*	*	*	*	*	0.0	0.0	0.0	0.0	0.0	0.0	0.0	1.0	0.6	*
San Bruno, Calif.	*	*	*	*	*	*	*	*	*	*	*	*	2.0	1.4	0.8
San Diego, Calif.	*	*	*	*	*	*	*	*	*	*	*	*	2.2	1.4	0.8
San Francisco, Calif. †	*	*	*	*	*	*	*	*	*	*	*	*	2.2	1.3	1.0
Santa Maria, Calif. †	*	*	*	*	*	*	*	*	0.6	*	*	*	2.5	1.0	1.4
Stockton, Calif.	*	*	*	*	0.0	0.0	*	0.0	0.0	0.0	0.0	0.0	0.6	*	*
Alamosa, Colo.	0.0	0.0	*	1.3	5.2	6.5	11.6	11.6	4.5	0.7	*	0.0	41.6	1.0	40.7
Colorado Springs, Colo.	0.0	*	*	2.0	8.6	11.6	17.2	13.2	4.8	0.8	*	0.0	58.7	1.2	57.5
Denver, Colo.	0.0	0.0	*	1.2	6.0	9.7	9.8	6.9	3.2	0.8	*	0.0	38.2	1.0	36.8
Grand Junction, Colo.	*	*	0.9	1.6	3.9	4.7	7.2	7.3	4.8	1.5	*	0.0	32.4	3.0	29.4
Pueblo, Colo.	0.0	0.0	*	1.1	5.7	7.7	11.1	8.8	2.2	*	0.0	0.0	37.0	*	36.5
Bridgeport, Conn.	*	*	0.7	1.7	2.4	4.1	4.9	3.8	1.8	0.7	*	*	21.1	2.4	18.7
Hartford, Conn.	*	*	0.6	1.3	2.5	4.7	5.2	4.4	2.4	0.8	*	*	22.8	2.4	20.4
Wilmington, Del.	*	*	1.2	2.4	4.0	6.1	6.3	6.0	2.4	0.9	0.6	*	30.8	3.5	27.1
Washington, D.C.	*	*	1.2	2.5	4.6	5.6	6.2	5.3	2.1	0.9	*	*	29.3	2.9	26.4
Apalachicola, Fla.	1.5	2.6	3.4	2.6	4.4	8.5	14.4	14.8	8.2	1.6	1.4	1.8	65.5	12.4	53.0
Daytona Beach, Fla.	1.0	2.0	3.1	3.3	8.2	13.2	17.0	15.3	8.0	3.4	1.1	0.9	76.4	11.5	64.9
Fort Myers, Fla.	0.6	1.5	2.2	3.0	7.6	15.8	23.0	22.0	14.6	4.4	1.1	0.8	96.4	10.6	85.8
Jacksonville, Fla.	0.7	1.6	2.4	3.2	6.2	10.2	15.0	13.0	6.3	2.0	*	1.0	62.0	8.1	53.9
Key West, Fla.	0.8	1.6	1.5	1.6	4.4	10.1	12.5	13.7	11.6	4.3	0.8	0.9	63.8	9.9	53.9
Lakeland, Fla. †	1.1	2.1	3.0	3.8	8.5	15.7	21.9	20.9	12.8	3.4	1.2	1.1	95.6	12.0	83.5
Miami, Fla.	0.8	1.4	1.7	2.5	7.0	13.1	15.6	15.8	11.5	5.0	1.2	0.6	76.0	10.6	65.4
Orlando, Fla.	1.0	1.7	2.4	3.0	7.6	13.5	18.6	16.7	8.7	2.6	1.0	0.9	77.7	9.6	68.1
Tallahassee, Fla.	1.6	2.2	4.1	4.4	8.4	13.6	19.9	17.1	8.5	2.0	1.5	1.5	84.6	12.8	71.8
Tampa, Fla.	0.8	1.7	2.4	2.7	5.7	14.0	21.5	21.3	12.2	2.8	1.3	1.2	87.5	10.1	77.4
West Palm Beach, Fla.	0.8	1.6	2.1	3.2	7.5	13.8	15.9	16.1	11.4	4.9	1.2	0.7	79.1	11.2	67.8
Athens, Ga.	1.5	1.4	3.4	4.3	6.2	9.0	12.8	8.6	2.9	0.8	1.2	0.7	53.0	9.0	43.8
Atlanta, Ga.	1.4	1.7	3.6	4.1	5.5	7.9	10.8	7.2	2.4	0.9	0.9	0.8	47.2	9.2	38.0
Augusta, Ga.	1.0	1.6	2.9	4.1	6.6	9.8	13.8	10.2	3.9	1.0	0.9	0.6	56.4	8.0	48.4
Columbus, Ga.	1.4	2.0	3.8	4.5	6.2	9.1	13.5	9.6	3.3	1.0	1.0	1.3	56.7	10.4	46.2
Macon, Ga.	1.4	2.0	3.2	4.3	6.4	9.1	14.0	9.9	3.4	0.8	0.8	1.0	56.4	9.2	47.2
Savannah, Ga.	1.1	1.0	3.0	3.8	7.8	10.4	15.9	12.7	6.0	1.4	*	*	64.1	7.4	56.6
Boise, Idaho	*	*	0.5	0.6	2.5	2.8	2.4	2.2	1.2	0.7	*	*	13.4	1.8	11.6

Table 2.1. *Continued*

	Jan.	Feb.	Mar.	Apr.	May	June	July	Aug.	Sept.	Oct.	Nov.	Dec.	Year	Wint.	Sumr.
Lewiston, Idaho†	0.0	*	*	1.0	2.0	2.7	3.5	2.7	1.1	*	*	0.0	13.6	0.6	13.1
Pocatello, Idaho	0.0	*	*	0.6	3.4	4.8	5.8	5.3	2.4	0.6	*	*	23.5	1.2	22.3
Cairo, Ill. †	1.5	1.9	3.3	5.5	7.0	8.1	7.7	5.4	3.5	2.1	1.5	1.1	48.7	11.6	37.1
Chicago (Midway), Ill.	*	*	2.6	4.7	5.2	7.5	6.7	5.3	4.1	1.8	0.9	0.6	40.0	6.6	33.4
Moline, Ill.	*	0.5	2.1	5.2	7.0	7.9	8.5	6.6	4.9	2.6	1.0	0.5	47.3	7.1	40.1
Peoria, Ill.	0.7	0.6	2.6	5.7	7.1	8.4	8.0	6.8	5.2	2.5	1.1	0.6	49.3	8.2	41.1
Rockford, Ill.	*	*	1.8	4.4	5.6	7.8	7.9	5.4	4.7	2.3	1.1	*	41.9	6.0	35.9
Springfield, Ill.	0.6	0.8	2.6	5.7	7.2	8.6	8.7	7.0	5.3	2.2	1.4	*	50.4	8.0	42.4
Evansville, Ind.	1.1	1.2	3.8	5.0	5.9	7.1	7.6	4.8	2.9	1.9	1.4	0.6	43.2	10.0	33.2
Fort Wayne, Ind.	*	0.6	2.6	4.6	5.6	7.6	6.7	5.6	3.8	1.6	0.9	*	40.2	6.3	33.9
Indianapolis, Ind.	0.8	0.7	3.0	4.9	6.8	7.3	7.6	6.1	3.2	1.8	1.0	*	44.0	7.8	38.0
South Bend, Ind.	*	*	2.1	4.6	4.7	8.0	7.9	6.0	4.0	2.1	0.8	*	40.9	6.0	35.2
Dubuque, Iowa†	*	*	1.7	4.4	6.2	7.9	8.1	6.6	4.4	3.0	1.2	*	44.4	7.0	37.5
Des Moines, Iowa	*	*	2.0	4.6	7.4	9.6	7.9	7.4	5.2	2.7	1.2	*	49.4	7.1	42.2
Sioux City, Iowa	*	*	1.2	3.8	7.6	9.3	8.6	7.6	4.9	2.0	*	*	46.0	4.3	41.8
Concordia, Kans.	*	*	1.6	5.6	9.2	11.4	10.6	9.1	6.5	2.7	0.9	*	58.2	6.0	52.3
Dodge City, Kans.	*	*	1.1	3.6	7.9	11.1	10.9	9.4	4.7	2.0	0.7	*	52.2	4.6	47.6
Goodland, Kans.	*	*	0.5	2.1	7.3	10.6	11.5	8.2	4.0	1.3	*	*	46.2	2.6	43.6
Topeka, Kans.	*	0.7	2.1	6.0	9.4	9.9	9.2	8.0	6.3	3.5	1.4	*	57.2	8.3	48.9
Wichita, Kans.	*	0.8	2.2	5.1	8.9	10.0	8.3	7.6	6.0	3.3	1.2	*	54.1	8.1	46.0
Lexington, Ky.	0.7	1.1	2.8	4.7	6.4	8.2	10.0	6.5	3.0	1.7	1.1	*	46.7	7.8	38.9
Louisville, Ky.	0.8	1.2	3.2	4.7	6.4	7.3	8.4	6.3	3.1	1.8	1.2	0.5	44.8	8.7	36.2
Baton Rouge, La.	2.0	3.3	4.1	4.8	6.0	8.7	15.4	11.8	7.0	1.8	2.1	2.6	69.7	15.8	53.7
Lake Charles, La.	2.5	3.2	3.6	4.5	6.9	8.1	14.0	12.4	7.0	2.9	2.4	3.1	70.6	17.7	52.9
New Orleans, La.	1.6	2.7	3.4	3.8	5.6	9.2	15.4	12.7	7.2	1.8	1.6	2.4	67.4	13.6	53.8
Shreveport, La.	2.0	2.8	5.1	5.9	6.5	6.9	7.3	6.2	4.0	2.3	2.8	2.2	53.8	17.0	36.8
Portland, Maine	0.0	*	*	*	1.8	4.0	4.4	3.5	1.4	0.6	*	*	17.2	1.6	15.6
Baltimore, Md.	*	*	0.9	2.4	4.0	5.9	5.9	5.1	2.2	0.8	*	*	28.0	2.5	25.5
Boston, Mass.	*	*	*	1.1	2.0	3.6	4.3	3.5	1.7	0.6	*	*	18.3	2.0	16.2
Worcester, Mass.	*	*	*	1.0	2.8	4.2	5.1	3.8	1.7	0.8	*	*	20.5	1.9	18.6
Alpena, Mich.	*	0.0	*	2.6	4.2	6.2	7.0	5.8	4.3	1.7	*	*	32.9	2.7	30.1
Flint, Mich.	*	*	1.4	3.2	4.2	6.4	6.4	5.8	3.5	1.7	0.9	*	34.1	4.6	29.4
Lansing, Mich.	*	*	1.5	3.6	4.2	6.8	6.3	5.8	3.4	1.5	0.9	*	34.7	4.6	30.1
Marquette, Mich. †	*	0.0	*	1.1	3.7	6.3	5.5	5.1	3.5	0.9	*	*	26.7	1.6	25.1
Muskegon, Mich.	*	*	1.6	3.7	4.7	6.6	6.6	6.3	5.2	2.5	0.9	*	39.0	6.0	33.0
												*			
Sault Ste. Marie, Mich.	*	*	0.7	1.6	3.2	6.0	5.7	5.6	4.1	1.8	0.7	*	29.6	3.5	26.2
Duluth, Minn.	*	*	0.5	1.6	3.9	6.7	8.7	7.8	3.9	1.5	*		35.2	2.6	32.6
Internat'l Falls, Minn.	0.0	0.0	*	0.8	3.3	7.0	9.4	7.1	4.0	1.1	0.0	0.0	33.0	1.4	31.6
Minneapolis, Minn.	*	0.0	0.8	2.7	5.2	7.7	7.6	6.4	4.0	1.8	*	*	36.5	3.3	33.5
Rochester, Minn.	*	*	1.2	3.1	6.4	8.6	7.5	6.8	4.7	2.3	0.8	*	41.8	4.7	37.1
Jackson, Miss.	2.2	3.0	6.0	5.5	6.8	8.6	12.0	10.4	4.7	1.6	1.9	2.4	65.2	17.1	48.1
Meridian, Miss.	1.8	2.7	4.2	5.5	5.6	7.0	11.2	8.7	4.2	1.4	1.6	2.1	56.1	13.8	42.3
Columbia, Mo.	0.7	0.8	3.3	6.6	8.3	9.3	8.8	6.9	5.1	2.9	1.3	0.8	54.8	9.8	45.0
Kansas City, Mo.	*	0.8	2.2	5.8	7.4	8.4	7.6	6.5	5.2	3.3	1.1	0.6	49.3	8.3	40.9
St. Louis, Mo.	0.7	0.8	2.9	5.7	6.7	7.8	7.1	5.9	3.7	1.8	1.6	0.7	45.5	8.6	38.9
Springfield, Mo.	1.1	1.3	3.7	6.2	8.0	9.0	7.8	7.4	5.8	3.1	1.6	1.1	55.9	11.8	44.1
Billings, Mont.	*	*	*	0.9	4.0	7.4	6.3	5.8	2.0	*	0.0	*	26.9	0.5	26.4
Great Falls, Mont.	*	*	*	0.6	3.1	6.0	6.3	5.4	1.4	*	*	*	23.7	0.8	22.7
Havre, Mont.	0.0	0.0	*	0.5	2.1	4.9	5.6	5.2	1.3	*	0.0	0.0	20.0	*	19.7
Helena, Mont.	*	*	*	0.8	3.6	6.8	8.7	7.8	1.6	*	*	*	30.1	0.9	29.4
Kalispell, Mont.	0.0	*	*	0.9	2.8	5.5	5.1	4.9	2.1	*	*	0.0	22.0	0.8	21.2
Missoula, Mont.	*	0.0	*	*	2.9	4.9	6.1	5.5	2.0	*	*	0.0	22.5	0.5	22.0

Table 2.1. *Continued*

	Jan.	Feb.	Mar.	Apr.	May	June	July	Aug.	Sept.	Oct.	Nov.	Dec.	Year	Wint.	Sumr.
Grand Island, Nebr.	0.0	*	0.8	3.8	7.7	10.2	9.3	8.2	5.5	1.7	*	*	48.1	3.3	44.7
North Platte, Nebr.	0.0	*	0.8	2.8	7.0	11.2	10.6	8.7	4.5	1.4	*	0.0	47.3	2.6	44.7
Omaha, Nebr.	*	0.5	1.2	4.2	7.5	9.4	7.6	7.9	5.0	2.5	1.0	*	47.2	5.6	41.6
Scottsbluff, Nebr.	0.0	0.0	*	1.6	7.7	11.7	10.6	7.2	3.7	*	0.0	*	43.3	0.7	42.6
Valentine, Nebr. †	0.0	0.0	*	2.1	6.8	10.3	10.5	8.8	4.3	1.0	*	0.0	44.1	1.2	42.8
Elko, Nev.	*	*	*	1.1	3.2	3.6	5.2	4.4	1.3	*	*	*	19.7	1.5	18.7
Ely, Nev.	*	*	*	0.8	3.9	5.3	8.1	8.8	2.6	0.9	*	*	31.8	2.2	29.6
Las Vegas, Nev.	0.0	*	*	*	1.0	1.2	4.8	4.8	1.5	0.6	*	*	15.0	1.3	13.8
Reno, Nev.	0.0	0.0	*	*	2.2	2.6	4.0	3.0	1.2	*	0.0	0.0	13.8	*	13.4
Winnemucca, Nev.	0.0	*	*	0.7	2.1	2.9	3.0	2.8	1.3	0.6	*	*	13.7	0.9	12.8
Concord, N.H.	*	*	*	0.8	2.2	4.0	5.4	3.9	1.6	0.6	*	*	19.1	1.0	18.0
Atlantic City, N.J.	*	*	1.1	2.2	3.3	4.5	6.0	4.7	1.6	0.9	0.6	*	25.7	3.5	22.1
Newark, N.J.	*	*	0.7	1.6	3.5	4.8	5.7	4.4	2.2	0.8	*	*	24.9	2.7	22.2
Trenton, N.J.	*	*	1.4	2.2	4.4	5.8	6.6	5.9	2.6	1.1	0.6	*	31.5	4.2	27.3
Albuquerque, N.Mex.	*	*	0.7	1.2	3.4	4.3	10.8	10.3	4.4	2.0	0.6	*	38.2	3.7	34.5
Albany, N.Y.	*	*	0.5	1.0	3.4	5.6	6.7	4.6	2.1	0.7	*	*	25.6	2.0	23.5
Binghamton, N.Y.	*	*	0.8	2.3	4.0	6.7	7.0	5.6	2.7	1.2	*	*	31.1	2.8	28.3
Buffalo, N.Y.	*	*	1.2	2.5	3.0	5.0	5.4	6.2	3.2	1.8	1.4	0.6	30.8	5.5	25.3
New York (La Guardia), N.Y.	*	*	0.9	1.7	3.4	4.5	5.5	4.6	2.5	0.8	*	*	24.8	2.6	22.2
Rochester, N.Y.	*	*	0.8	2.4	3.6	5.4	6.1	5.6	2.5	1.2	*	*	28.5	2.9	25.6
Syracuse, N.Y.	*	*	0.8	1.9	3.4	5.7	7.0	5.5	2.6	1.0	0.6	*	29.5	3.2	26.2
Asheville, N.C.	*	0.9	2.4	3.4	6.6	8.2	11.3	9.7	3.1	1.1	*	*	47.8	5.5	42.2
Cape Hatteras, N.C.	0.9	1.6	2.0	3.3	6.2	6.2	9.2	9.2	3.5	2.4	1.4	1.0	47.0	9.4	37.6
Charlotte, N.C.	0.6	1.0	2.0	3.5	5.4	6.6	9.7	7.3	2.6	0.8	0.6	*	40.8	5.5	35.0
Greensboro, N.C.	0.6	0.7	1.6	3.4	6.2	7.6	9.8	8.4	2.8	1.0	*	*	42.9	4.6	38.2
Raleigh, N.C.	*	0.9	2.0	3.8	6.0	7.0	11.0	8.3	3.2	1.4	0.7	*	45.2	5.9	39.2
Wilmington, N.C.	*	1.0	2.0	3.6	5.1	7.4	10.9	9.5	3.6	1.4	0.7	0.5	46.2	6.1	40.2
Bismarck, N.Dak.	0.0	0.0	*	1.0	4.0	9.0	8.7	7.5	2.4	*	*	0.0	33.1	0.5	32.5
Fargo, N.Dak.	0.0	0.0	*	1.3	3.7	7.6	8.4	6.5	3.1	0.8	*	*	31.6	1.1	30.5
Williston, N.Dak.	0.0	0.0	0.0	0.7	1.9	6.7	7.2	4.6	1.5	*	0.0	0.9	22.6	*	22.6
Akron, Ohio	*	*	2.2	4.0	6.0	7.7	7.9	6.0	3.0	1.6	0.6	*	40.3	5.4	34.7
Cincinnati (Abbe), Ohio†	1.0	0.6	2.5	4.9	5.9	7.2	7.9	5.8	2.9	1.7	1.0	*	41.7	7.3	34.5
Cleveland, Ohio	*	0.6	1.8	3.9	4.9	6.6	5.7	5.2	3.1	1.6	1.1	*	35.2	5.6	29.4
Columbus, Ohio	*	0.6	2.1	4.5	6.4	7.8	8.2	6.4	3.1	1.4	0.8	*	42.1	5.7	36.4
Dayton, Ohio	0.6	0.5	2.4	4.4	6.4	7.0	7.3	5.8	2.8	1.6	0.6	*	39.8	6.0	33.8
Toledo, Ohio	*	0.5	2.0	4.2	5.5	7.7	7.6	5.8	3.4	1.3	0.7	*	39.3	5.1	34.2
Youngstown, Ohio	*	*	1.7	3.7	4.9	7.1	6.6	5.8	2.8	1.4	0.7	*	36.0	5.1	30.8
Oklahoma City, Okla.	0.6	1.2	3.0	5.6	8.5	8.8	6.6	6.5	4.6	2.9	1.2	0.7	50.2	9.5	40.6
Tulsa, Okla.	0.7	1.0	3.1	6.5	8.6	7.7	6.2	6.0	5.2	2.5	1.2	1.0	49.6	9.4	40.1
Burns, Oreg. †	0.0	*	*	0.6	2.3	3.1	2.6	2.5	1.3	*	*	0.0	13.1	0.6	12.5
Eugene, Oreg.	*	*	*	*	0.6	0.8	*	0.6	*	*	*	*	4.5	1.2	3.3
Meacham, Oreg. †	0.0	0.0	*	*	2.2	2.5	2.1	2.6	0.9	*	*	0.0	10.9	*	10.6
Medford, Oreg.	0.0	*	*	0.6	1.6	1.9	1.3	1.1	0.9	*	0.0	*	7.9	*	7.4
Pendleton, Oreg.	0.0	*	*	0.5	1.5	1.8	1.6	1.7	0.9	*	*	*	8.3	0.7	8.2
Portland, Oreg.	*	*	0.6	0.9	1.2	1.0	0.7	1.0	*	*	*	*	6.9	1.7	5.2
Salem, Oreg.	*	*	*	0.6	0.8	0.6	0.7	0.9	0.7	*	*	*	5.4	1.2	4.2
Allentown, Pa.	*	*	0.7	2.3	4.2	6.1	7.0	6.1	3.3	0.8	0.7	*	31.9	3.0	29.0
Harrisburg, Pa.	*	*	0.9	2.7	4.8	6.2	6.5	5.4	3.2	0.7	*	*	31.5	2.7	28.8
Philadelphia, Pa.	*	*	1.0	1.8	4.0	4.9	5.1	4.9	2.1	0.6	0.6	*	25.7	2.8	22.8
Pittsburgh, Pa.	*	*	1.7	3.7	5.3	6.9	6.9	5.6	2.9	1.4	*	*	35.8	4.5	31.4
Scranton, Pa.	*	*	0.8	2.2	3.7	6.1	7.6	5.2	2.8	0.9	*	*	30.8	2.9	27.6
Block Island, R.I. †	*	*	*	1.3	1.8	2.1	3.7	3.3	1.2	0.9	0.6	*	15.6	2.2	13.4

Table 2.1. *Continued*

	Jan.	Feb.	Mar.	Apr.	May	June	July	Aug.	Sept.	Oct.	Nov.	Dec.	Year	Wint.	Sumr.
Providence, R.I.	*	*	0.6	1.3	2.4	3.7	4.6	3.6	1.8	0.7	0.8	*	20.0	2.6	17.4
Charleston, S.C.	0.8	1.2	2.1	2.8	6.0	10.2	12.9	11.6	4.8	1.1	0.6	*	54.4	6.1	48.3
Columbia, S.C.	0.8	1.6	2.8	3.4	5.9	9.1	13.5	9.6	3.9	1.2	0.6	*	52.8	7.4	45.4
Greenville-Spartanburg, S.C.	0.8	1.3	2.8	3.4	6.1	7.9	11.2	7.5	2.9	1.4	0.6	0.5	46.5	7.5	39.0
Huron, S.Dak.	*	0.0	*	2.6	5.7	9.0	9.3	7.8	3.4	1.3	*	*	39.8	1.8	38.0
Rapid City, S.Dak.	0.0	0.0	*	1.2	5.5	9.9	11.4	8.1	3.0	*	0.0	*	39.5	*	39.1
Sioux Falls, S.Dak.	0.0	*	0.6	2.7	6.2	9.3	9.3	8.0	4.8	1.7	*	*	43.0	2.8	40.3
Bristol, Tenn.	*	0.8	2.1	3.6	7.0	8.1	9.5	7.7	3.1	1.0	*	*	44.2	5.0	38.9
Chattanooga, Tenn.	1.4	2.0	3.7	4.8	6.8	8.8	10.8	9.0	3.4	1.4	1.2	0.6	54.0	10.4	43.6
Knoxville, Tenn.	1.0	1.4	3.1	4.7	5.7	7.7	9.6	6.7	2.9	1.4	0.9	0.6	45.5	8.4	37.2
Memphis, Tenn.	2.1	2.4	4.7	6.8	6.4	6.9	8.4	6.4	3.5	1.7	2.1	1.8	53.2	14.8	38.5
Nashville, Tenn.	1.4	1.7	4.7	5.8	7.4	8.4	10.2	8.2	4.0	1.6	1.5	1.3	56.2	12.2	44.0
Abilene, Tex.	0.5	1.0	2.6	5.2	7.6	5.6	4.7	5.1	3.5	3.0	1.2	0.5	40.6	8.8	31.7
Amarillo, Tex.	*	0.5	1.1	3.0	8.0	9.2	9.6	8.4	3.2	2.0	0.6	*	45.8	4.4	41.4
Austin, Tex.	0.9	1.8	2.3	4.4	6.2	4.6	4.0	5.2	4.1	2.8	1.4	1.2	38.9	10.3	28.6
Brownsville, Tex.	*	0.7	*	2.0	3.1	2.7	2.0	3.8	4.1	1.9	0.6	*	22.1	4.3	17.8
Corpus Christi, Tex.	0.8	0.8	1.2	2.2	4.4	3.4	2.4	3.9	5.3	2.4	1.0	0.6	28.4	6.8	21.6
Dallas (Love), Tex. (51-72)	0.9	1.7	3.2	5.9	6.0	4.9	3.5	3.9	3.2	2.4	1.9	0.7	39.0	10.7	27.3
El Paso, Tex.	*	*	*	0.7	2.1	4.0	9.3	9.7	3.6	1.7	*	*	32.4	3.0	29.3
Fort Worth, Tex.	0.9	1.8	3.9	6.3	6.8	6.0	5.0	4.8	3.8	2.7	1.6	1.1	45.1	12.0	32.8
Houston, Tex.	1.5	2.2	2.5	4.3	6.3	6.6	10.6	10.0	7.2	3.5	2.0	1.8	58.6	13.7	44.9
Lubbock, Tex.	*	*	1.6	3.0	7.9	8.1	7.0	6.4	4.0	3.0	0.7	*	42.2	6.2	36.4
Midland, Tex.	*	*	1.1	2.8	6.2	5.5	6.0	5.6	3.1	2.1	0.7	*	34.2	4.8	29.3
Port Arthur, Tex.	2.2	3.0	3.1	4.0	6.0	7.1	13.5	11.8	6.7	2.6	2.4	2.4	64.8	15.5	49.1
San Angelo, Tex.	*	0.6	1.9	4.4	6.9	4.5	3.8	5.0	3.8	2.4	0.9	0.5	35.1	6.7	28.4
San Antonio, Tex.	0.8	1.3	1.8	3.8	6.3	3.9	2.8	4.2	4.2	2.3	1.5	0.8	33.6	8.6	25.1
Victoria, Tex.	0.8	1.2	2.4	3.5	5.6	5.4	6.3	8.1	6.8	3.0	1.6	0.9	45.5	9.8	35.6
Waco, Tex.	1.2	2.0	3.2	5.8	7.2	5.2	3.9	4.5	4.0	2.9	1.8	1.2	42.9	12.4	30.5
Wichita Falls, Tex.	0.9	1.4	3.0	5.6	9.3	7.1	5.8	5.7	4.0	3.0	1.6	1.0	48.4	10.9	37.5
Milford, Utah †	*	*	*	1.5	3.3	3.7	9.3	10.7	4.2	1.2	*	*	35.2	2.6	32.6
Salt Lake City, Utah	*	*	1.1	1.3	4.8	5.8	6.5	7.6	3.8	1.6	*	*	34.0	4.2	29.8
Burlington, Vt.	*	0.0	*	0.7	2.5	5.9	6.8	5.6	2.2	0.7	*	*	25.3	1.5	23.8
Lynchburg, Va. †	*	*	1.3	2.6	5.4	6.5	9.0	7.7	2.6	1.0	*	*	37.1	3.5	33.7
Norfolk, Va.	*	*	1.6	2.8	4.9	5.6	8.2	7.1	2.9	1.4	0.5	*	36.3	4.9	31.6
Richmond, Va.	*	*	1.6	2.5	4.9	6.2	8.2	6.3	2.8	1.1	0.6	*	35.3	4.2	30.9
Roanoke, Va.	*	*	1.2	3.2	6.0	7.3	9.3	7.4	3.0	1.2	*	*	39.6	3.3	38.2
Olympia, Wash.	*	*	*	0.6	*	*	*	0.9	0.6	0.6	*	*	4.9	1.6	3.4
Seattle-Tacoma, Wash.	*	*	*	0.7	1.0	0.6	0.6	0.8	0.7	*	*	*	6.6	2.2	4.4
Spokane, Wash.	*	*	*	0.6	1.4	2.6	2.2	2.4	0.6	*	*	0.0	10.5	0.6	9.8
Walla Walla, Wash. †	0.0	*	*	1.1	1.8	2.2	1.8	2.3	1.0	*	0.0	0.0	11.3	0.9	10.5
Yakima, Wash.	0.0	*	*	0.5	1.1	1.5	1.6	1.0	0.7	*	0.0	0.0	6.6	*	6.4
Charleston, W.Va.	0.6	0.9	2.0	4.4	6.9	7.2	9.4	6.4	2.8	1.0	0.6	*	42.6	5.4	37.1
Parkersburg, W.Va. †	0.6	0.6	1.9	3.7	6.0	7.7	9.0	6.5	3.0	1.5	1.0	*	42.0	6.2	35.8
Green Bay, Wis.	*	*	1.2	2.6	4.6	7.3	6.8	5.6	4.1	2.4	0.6	*	35.2	4.7	31.0
La Crosse, Wis.	*	*	1.4	2.9	6.0	8.3	7.3	6.5	4.5	2.3	0.5	*	40.4	5.2	35.5
Madison, Wis.	*	*	1.8	3.8	5.7	7.4	7.4	6.7	4.6	2.0	1.0	*	41.4	5.7	35.6
Milwaukee, Wis.	*	*	1.4	3.9	4.4	6.8	6.7	5.2	3.6	1.6	1.0	*	35.7	5.0	30.7
Casper, Wyo.	0.0	*	*	1.0	6.2	8.3	9.0	5.9	2.7	*	*	0.0	33.9	0.8	33.1
Cheyenne, Wyo.	0.0	*	*	1.4	7.7	11.2	13.0	9.4	4.0	0.7	*	0.0	47.6	0.9	46.7
Lander, Wyo.	0.0	0.0	*	0.6	4.0	7.0	9.3	6.4	2.8	*	*	0.0	30.6	*	30.2
Sheridan, Wyo.	0.0	*	0.0	0.7	4.2	9.2	9.0	6.9	2.6	*	0.0	0.0	33.1	0.5	32.6

Table 2.2. Number of Thunderstorm Days in Primary and Secondary Maximum Regions on Various Maps, with Source and Period and Numbers of Stations

Source	No. of stations	Period	Primary maximum		Secondary maximum	
			Region	No.	Region	No.
Harrington (1894)	*	1884–92	Southeast U.S.	>40	none	
Henry (1906)	—	1875–1903	Central Fla.	55	W. Missouri	50
Alexander (1915)	200	1904–13	Tampa, Fla.	93	Santa Fe, N.Mex.	78
Alexander (1924)	185	1904–23	Tampa, Fla.	94	Santa Fe, N.Mex.	73
Alexander (1935)	150	1904–33	Tampa, Fla.	94	Santa Fe, N.Mex.	72
Brooks et al. (1936)	150	1904–33	Tampa, Fla.	>90	N. N.Mex.	>70
USDA (1941)	200	1899–1938	Tampa, Fla.	>80	N. N.Mex.	>60
Shands (1945)	217	1904–43	Tampa, Fla.	>90	N. N.Mex., s.Colo.	>60
Climatological Services (1952)	266	1871–1951	Central Fla.	>90	N.E. N.Mex.	>60
Schloemer (1958, unpublished)	240	1871–1955	Tampa–south	101	Raton, N.Mex.	75
EDS (1966)	—	1871–1964	Central Fla.	>100	Colorado Rockies	>70
Baldwin (1973)	235	1871–1969	Tampa–south	>100	Raton, N.Mex.	>70
Court (1974)	261	1953–62	Tampa–south	>100	Raton, N.Mex.	>50
Court (this chapter, Fig. 2.3)	207	1951–75	W. central Fla.	96	Colorado Springs	59

*Apparently about 100 stations. Map is for number of thunderstorms, not number of days.

monthly means were combined into means for the year and for the summer (April–September) and winter (October–March) half years, which are given in Table 2.1 and mapped.

Other sources of thunderstorm climatology, in addition to numbers of days, have been the times of first and last thunder, formerly kept at first-order stations, and tallies of thunderstorms on hourly airways reports. Beginning times, 1906–25, were used by Gregg (1930) and Shands (1945, 1948), and reported hourly occurrences by Rasmusson (1971) and Wallace (1975) for the United States; Rasmussen's (1971) map is reproduced as Fig. 1.1a in Vol. 1, p. 4; Crichlow et al. (1971) estimated worldwide hourly thunderstorm probabilities by seasons by applying diurnal variation derived from Shands (1945) to the WMO tabulations (WMO, 1953).

b. Distribution

"Thunderstorms are most frequent in Florida and the Mississippi and lower Missouri Valleys, the average annual number being from thirty-five to fifty," Greely (1888, p. 241) wrote almost a century ago, before the phenomenon had been mapped. His location statement is still valid, but his numbers, possibly appropriate for thunder with rain, must be doubled to apply to thunder days with or without rain.

The locations of the primary and secondary maxima of thunderstorm days, and their numbers, on a dozen maps prepared from 1894 onward, are given in Table 2.2. On each, west-central Florida is shown as having the most thunderstorm days. Tampa, the leading site on the maps of Alexander and Shands, was not used for the Climatological Services Division (1952) map, on which Daytona Beach was the leading site, with 93 days.

Lakeland, between Tampa and Daytona Beach, appears to have the most thunderstorm days on subsequent representations. It is the highest point (66 m) in peninsular Florida,

80 km from the Gulf of Mexico and 110 km from the Atlantic Ocean, and it is under the usual summer influence of convergence of air from the two coasts. During the first 12 yr of operation, the station averaged 101 thunderstorm days per year (Schloemer, 1956); by 1965 the 24-yr average was an even 100. For another 10 yr, until observing hours were reduced in 1975, the Lakeland station, which was in the business district of a city of 40,000 people (not an airport), continued to report thunderstorms, but these reports have not been published since 1964. The 1951–70 mean used here is 95.6, slightly less than the 25-yr figure for Fort Myers. In each recent year, Lakeland's thunderstorm day total has been surpassed by more than a dozen other places. During the first 12 yr, 1951–62, Lakeland averaged 103 thunderstorm days, during the second, 1963–74, only 81. Listed year by year, 1970–75, the most thunderstorm days were reported (Fig. 2.4) by Tallahassee (87, 98), Lake Charles (97), Tallahassee (105), Orlando (103), and Tampa (113). From 1971 to 1975, Tampa had the highest average, 95 thunderstorm days per year, closely followed by Tallahassee with 94.6.

Even more erratic and questionable has been a secondary maximum somewhere in the southern or central Rocky Mountains. On early maps Santa Fe, N.Mex., was the western leader, with 78, 70, 72, and 66 on Alexander's and Shands's maps. But the Santa Fe station (2,137 m MSL) was replaced in 1938 by Albuquerque, 517 m lower and less thundery. A station established at Raton, N.Mex. (1,944 m), in 1944 and suspended 1954–55, had a 10-yr average of 75 on Schloemer's map and also 75 after 19 years, after which reporting stopped. Clayton, N.Mex. (1,515 m), also opened in 1944, had an 18-yr average of 54 when reporting stopped because of reduced hours of operation in 1964. Both these stations appear on previous maps, but not in Figs. 2.1–2.3.

After four years of study in the northern Rocky Moun-

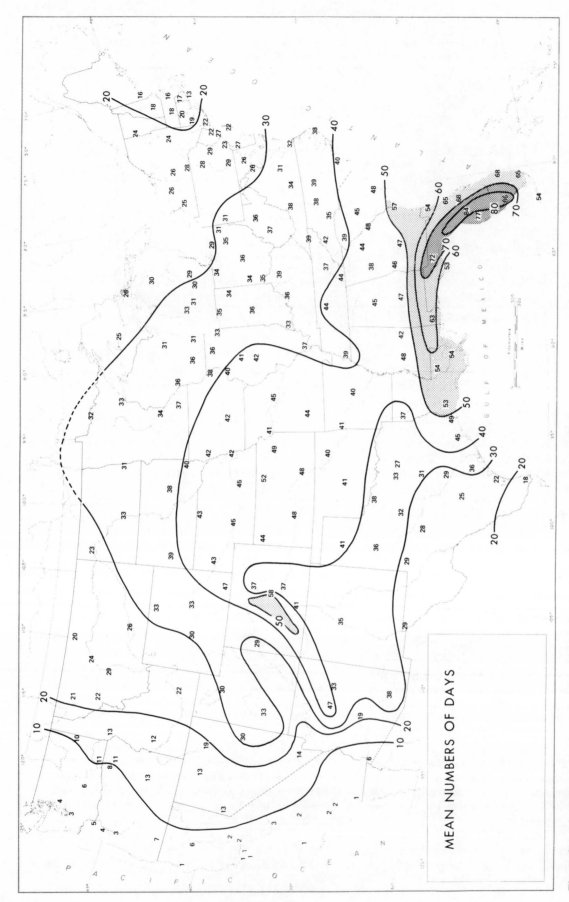

Figure 2.1. Mean numbers of days with thunderstorms during summer—April to September—1951–75.

MEAN NUMBERS OF DAYS

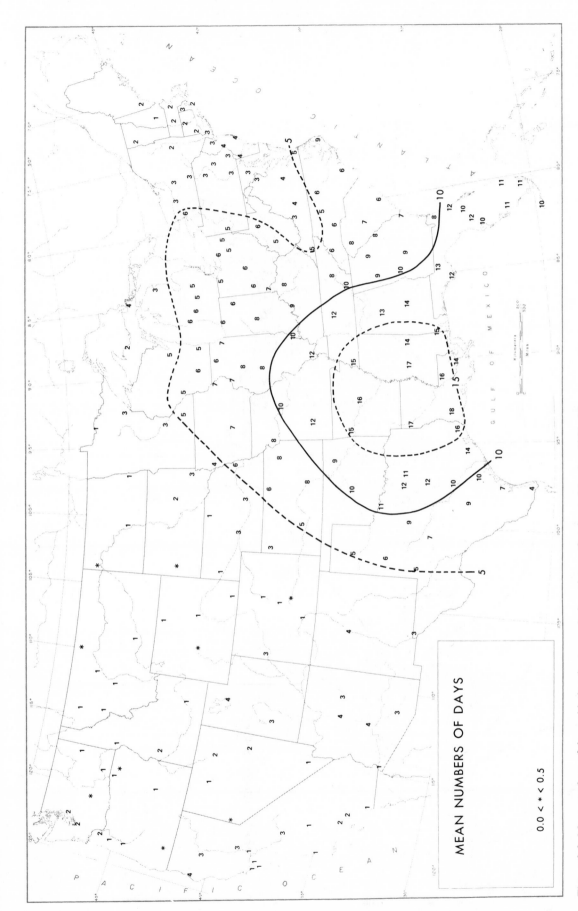

Figure 2.2. Mean numbers of days with thunderstorms during winter—October to March—1951–75.

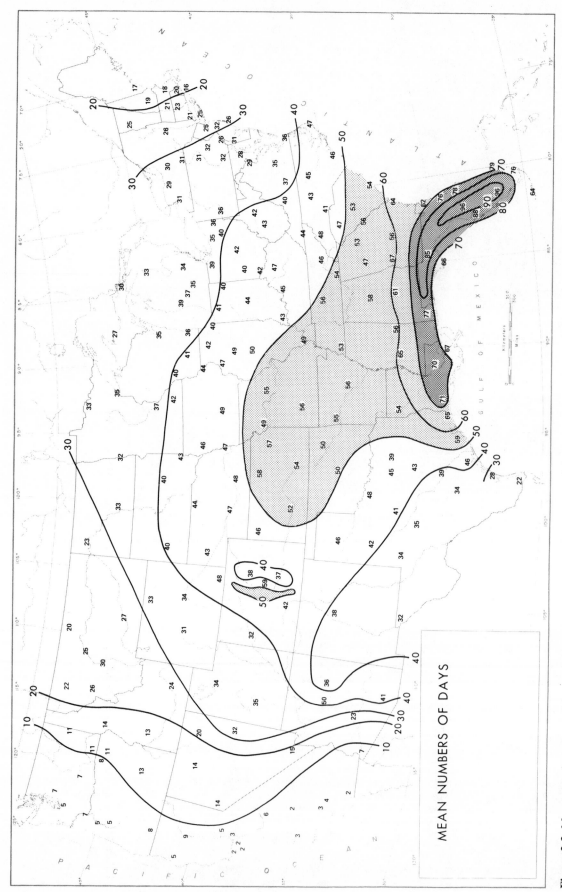

Figure 2.3. Mean annual numbers of days with thunderstorms, 1951–75.

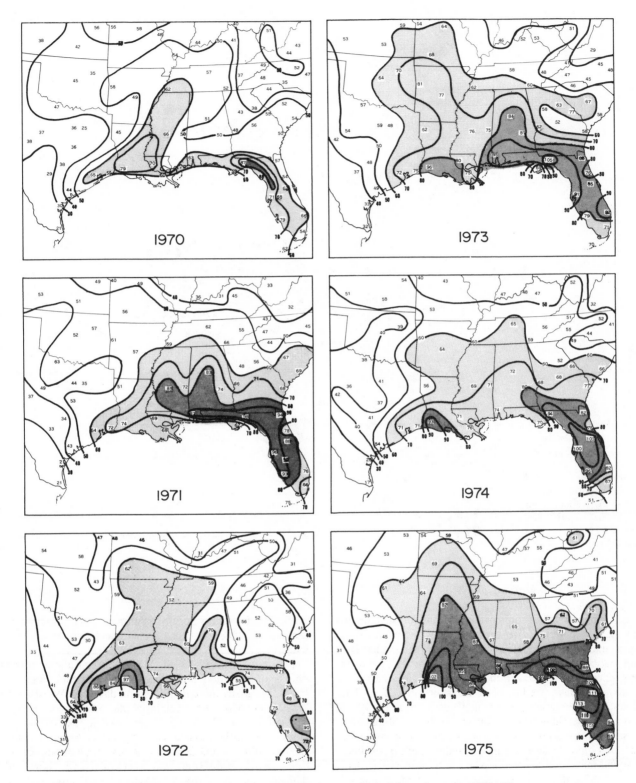

Figure 2.4. Annual numbers of thunderstorm days in the southeastern United States by years, 1970–75.

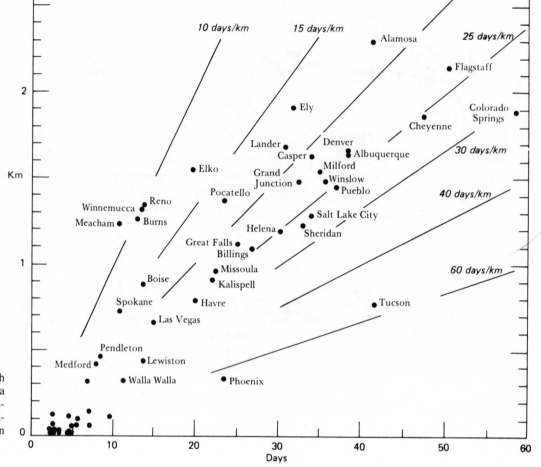

Figure 2.5. Variation with station elevation above sea level of mean annual number of days with thunderstorms in the western United States, 1951–75.

tains, Gisborne (1927) commented that "the forested mountain areas experience two or three times more electrical storms than the low country where most of the Weather Bureau stations are situated." The number of thunderstorm days reported at stations in the 11 western states increases by about 20 days per kilometer elevation (Fig. 2.5). The rate of increase varies from about 10 days/km in the Great Basin to more than 30 days/km in the Rocky Mountains. Possibly storms on distant mountains can be observed more readily at higher places and their thunder carefully awaited, or sound may be attenuated less at lower atmospheric density, or the ambient noise may decrease with elevation. Whatever the reason, this effect may explain the old Santa Fe and Raton figures, and the 1951–75 average of 57.5 thunderstorm days at Colorado Springs, 1,880 m above sea level; Denver, 100 km to the north and 260 m lower, has 36.8, and Pueblo, 60 km to the south and 440 m lower,

36.5. The Colorado Springs station is much closer to the mountains, which also are higher there than at the other sites.

Flagstaff, Ariz. (2,139 m MSL), through the combined effects of elevation and closeness to the San Francisco Peaks, has many more thunderstorm days than Winslow, 80 km east and 650 m lower, or other places in Arizona or New Mexico. In Figs. 2.1 and 2.3, increased number of thunderstorm days in the mountains is suggested. Summer hourly reports from 294 military and National Weather Service stations, mostly with 10 or more years of record, show well-defined maxima of storm frequency in extreme southeast Colorado, in western Arizona, and from Florida along the southeast Atlantic coast and the Gulf coast westward to near Houston, Tex. (Rasmusson, 1971).

Although thunderstorm activity generally decreases poleward from the tropics, in south Texas the trend is reversed.

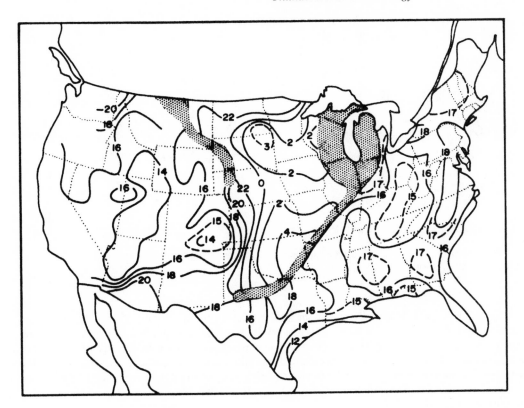

Figure 2.6. Hour (local mean time) of maximum frequency of thunderstorms, June to August (Rasmusson, 1971).

Annual numbers of thunderstorm days increase northeastward along the Gulf Coast from 22 at Brownsville to 46 at Victoria and 65 at Port Arthur.

c. Timing

Summer afternoons are the usual times for thunderstorms over land. In some parts of the United States the storms are most likely in winter, and elsewhere more frequent at night than during daylight (Trent and Gathman, 1972). In the lower Mississippi Valley summer thunderstorms are less frequent than in Florida, but the center of winter thunderstorm activity is in Louisiana and Mississippi (Fig. 2.2). Harrington (1894) noted this pattern, and it appears on the monthly maps of Alexander (1915, 1924, 1935), Shands (1945), and the Climatological Services Division (1952).

Thunderstorms are more frequent in winter than in summer along the Pacific Coast from southern California to southeast Alaska, where they occur occasionally with the synoptic-scale storms of that area's rainy season. Between 1951 and 1975, Sacramento had no thunder in the summer half year, whereas eight mainland Alaska stations, outside the panhandle, had none in winter. Summer is the dominant season for thunderstorms inland. In California the percentage of annual thunderstorm days occurring in the winter half year varies from 34, 37, and 46 at Red Bluff, Bakersfield, and Fresno in the Central Valley, to 56 at Los Angeles and Long Beach, 64 at San Diego and San Francisco, and 83 at Eureka, 180 km west of Red Bluff. At Annette Island, at the southeast tip of Alaska, the percentage is 61, but at

Juneau and farther northwest summer storms dominate. In Hilo, Honolulu, and Lihue the winter percentages are 75 to 80.

More complex, and hence the subject of much more discussion, is the diurnal pattern of thunderstorms. Gregg (1930) discovered that nighttime thunderstorms are more frequent than daytime ones over much of the Great Plains. He offered a table of the annual percentage of thunderstorm occurrences by 3-h periods at 59 stations during 20 years and mapped these for 6-h and 12-h intervals (6 A.M. to 6 P.M., noon to midnight). "In parts of Wisconsin, Minnesota, the Dakotas, Nebraska, Iowa, Missouri, and Kansas . . . with extensions to . . . Oklahoma and Texas, more thunderstorms occur at night than during the day: 30% to 40% from 6 P.M. to midnight, and 20% to 30% from midnight to 6 A.M." (Gregg, 1930, p. 220).

Gregg's discussion, which did not appear in the first (1925) edition of his *Aeronautical Meteorology*, was noted in the second as "largely based on a manuscript paper by the author," with no further details about the nature of the data used. Gregg became chief of the Weather Bureau in 1934, and died 14 September 1938. A few years later, Shands obtained for use in compiling *Thunderstorm Rainfall* a manuscript tabulation by Gregg of the hour of thunderstorm beginning, i.e., in which thunder was first heard, at 192 stations, mostly for 1906 to 1925 but some for as few as 7 years. Without mentioning Gregg's analysis of the data for 59 of the stations, Shands (1945, 1948) tabulated and mapped them by season and 6-h periods.

In the southeastern United States, except for the immedi-

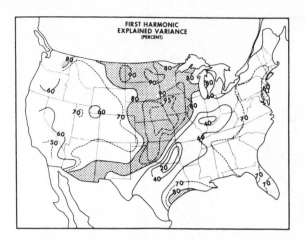
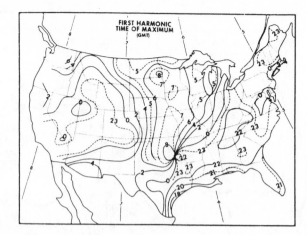

Figure 2.7. Variance of hourly numbers of thunderstorm reports, June–August, explained by first (diurnal) harmonic (left), and its time of maximum (right) (Rasmusson, 1971).

ate coasts, and over most of the western mountains and plateaus (Shands, 1945, Fig. 85), more than half of all thunderstorms began between 1200 and 1800 LST. Less than 30% started in eastern Kansas and Nebraska, southeastern South Dakota, western Iowa, southern Minnesota, and western Wisconsin. The same region, with extensions to upper Michigan, most of Wisconsin, northern Illinois, most of Missouri and Oklahoma, and north-central Texas, had just as many beginning between midnight and 0600. In summer (June–August) an average of eight thunderstorms (Shands, 1945, Fig. 92), or 31% to 50% of the summer total (Shands, 1945, Fig. 89), began during the first 6 hours of the day from Wichita to Kansas City to Sioux City.

A nighttime maximum in summer thunderstorms around Kansas City can be discerned on the small diagrams of thunderstorm diurnal variation in midseason months, 1936–39, at 60 full-time stations (Smith and Thom, 1941). Rasmusson (1971) found that "the hour of maximum thunderstorm activity" in summer (June–August) advances "eastward from the high plains to the Mississippi Valley" (Fig. 2.6). The first harmonic (Fig. 2.7) accounted for 80% to 90% of the total variance of the diurnal variation in thunderstorm frequency over the Great Plains in summer, and the second harmonic most of the rest. In the phase of this first harmonic "an early afternoon maximum is found over most areas of the mountain west," where more than 70% of the variance is explained, but the maximum comes later to eastward, after midnight in the Missouri Valley. Throughout the southeastern United States summer thunderstorms are most frequent in late afternoon.

Similar analysis of the same airways data (Wallace, 1975) shows that the region in which the phase of the first harmonic comes between 2100 and 0300 includes the Texas Panhandle, Oklahoma, and all states on the north and northeast, from eastern Montana to lower Michigan. Elsewhere afternoon (1500 to 1800) is the average time. Crow (1969) showed that convective activity in Colorado begins at 1600 to 1800 from Pueblo to Fort Collins and moves eastward at

about 60 km h, reaching the Wichita-Concordia line about 0100 to 0300. Summer precipitation has "maximum frequency in late afternoon over the front range of the Rockies and the Black Hills, and becomes later and later eastward to around midnight over the Plains and on east to the Mississippi" (National Weather Service, 1977).

d. Consequences

Lightning kills more than 100 people annually (Zegel, 1967) and is blamed for several hundred more deaths arising in part from lightning-caused fires, lightning-frightened drivers, and lightning-struck electric lines (Weigel, 1976). The geographical distribution of such fatalities is not closely parallel to that of thunderstorms, because fatalities depend on population density and activity, and time of thunderstorm occurrence; tractor drivers and golfers sheltered under trees are frequent victims.

Lightning also sets forest and brush fires, primarily in the western United States, especially when the rain accompanying the thunderstorm is scanty or has evaporated completely while falling. Of the annual average (1966–75) of more than 100,000 wildfires in the 48 conterminous United States, 9% were caused by lightning and were responsible for 10% of the burned area; in Alaska, 43% of the fires were lightning-caused, and they burned 82% of the 855,878 acres consumed (Table 2.3). Three-quarters of all recent forest and brush fires in Arizona and New Mexico have been caused by lightning, and more than half in Idaho and Montana; these have been responsible for more than half the area burned in those and other western states (Figs. 2.8 and 2.9). Lightning-caused fire incidence does not parallel thunderstorm incidence, because fuels must be dry enough to be ignited. In the northern Sierra Nevada of California, for example, thunderstorms are most common in May, but they start more fires in September, after the forests have gone 4 or 5 months without rain (Court, 1960).

Thunderstorm rain is an important part of the water bud-

Table 2.3. Average Annual Number of Wildfires and Areas Burned, 1966–75, with Corresponding Numbers and Percentages for Lightning-caused Fires Only †

(0.0 < * < 0.5; 0.00 < # < 0.05)

Station	Number of fires			Acres burned		
	Lightning	Total	%	Lightning	Total	%
Ala.	56	6,887	0.8	828	127,542	0.6
Alaska	178	415	42.8	702,273	855,878	82.1
Ariz.	1,502	2,091	71.8	29,369	47,867	61.4
Ark.	46	3,416	1.3	530	89,047	0.6
Calif.	1,628	7,604	21.4	11,497	138,182	8.3
Colo.	395	1,253	31.5	3,184	25,955	12.3
Conn.	1	550	0.2	4	1,487	#
Del.	*	38	0.5	*	390	0.1
Fla.	670	7,461	9.0	15,917	240,140	7.8
Ga.	217	10,007	2.2	1,312	49,422	2.7
Hawaii	*	41	0.7	221	12,215	1.8
Idaho	1,056	1,576	67.0	74,965	137,389	54.6
Ill.	*	220	#	1	5,630	#
Ind.	*	374	#	2	6,334	#
Iowa	*	208	0.1	1	3,978	#
Kans.	60	1,491	4.0	852	70,421	#
Ky.	3	1,992	0.2	48	35,300	0.1
La.	14	6,084	0.2	196	70,210	0.3
Maine	83	507	16.3	52	2,088	2.5
Md.	2	579	#	6	1,814	#
Mass.	20	6,191	0.3	25	7,611	0.3
Mich.	26	1,169	2.2	69	8,778	0.8
Minn.	24	1,218	2.0	179	56,230	0.3
Miss.	17	6,450	0.3	251	84,380	0.3
Mo.	8	3,054	0.3	128	39,786	0.3
Mont.	700	1,181	59.3	24,130	31,606	76.3
Nebr.	103	1,001	10.2	5,010	52,468	9.5
Nev.	241	505	47.8	17,857	35,675	50.1
N.H.	13	559	2.4	6	430	1.4
N.J.	3	1,471	0.2	7	9,070	0.1
N.Mex.	845	1,097	77.0	18,931	43,184	43.8
N.Y.	28	790	3.6	58	4,236	1.4
N.C.	30	4,151	0.7	1,154	68,490	1.7
N.Dak.	6	66	9.9	198	2,475	8.0
Ohio	4	983	0.4	7	4,502	0.1
Okla.	9	989	0.9	368	62,128	0.6
Oreg.	1,408	2,873	49.0	36,238	59,590	60.8
Pa.	12	1,285	0.9	275	8,976	3.1
R.I.	1	599	0.1	3	1,167	0.2
S.C.	44	4,956	0.9	1,581	56,424	2.8
S.Dak.	201	750	26.8	8,464	27,768	30.5
Tenn.	10	3,313	0.3	66	29,647	0.2
Tex.	22	1,681	1.3	901	36,627	2.5
Utah	342	729	46.9	22,602	25,666	88.1
Vt.	5	127	4.0	2	323	0.8
Va.	21	1,967	1.1	189	9,336	2.0
Wash.	446	2,006	22.2	21,322	34,514	61.8
W.Va.	8	1,426	0.6	160	33,169	0.5
Wis.	27	2,101	1.3	89	7,468	1.1
Wyo.	247	586	42.2	11,675	23,257	50.2

† Based on "Forest Fire Statistics," 1966 and 1967 and "Wildfire Statistics," 1968–75, published annually by Forest Service, USDA, Division of Cooperative Forest Fire Control through 1973, Cooperative Fire Protection Staff Group thereafter.

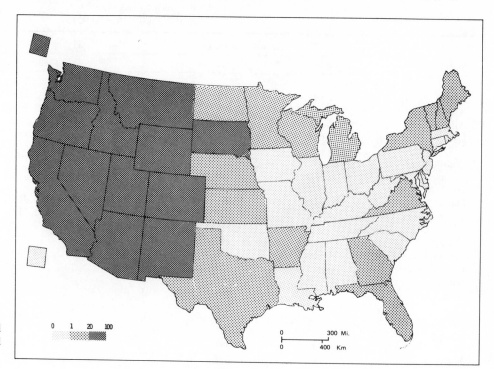

Figure 2.8. Percent of all forest and brush fires in United States caused by lightning, 1966–75.

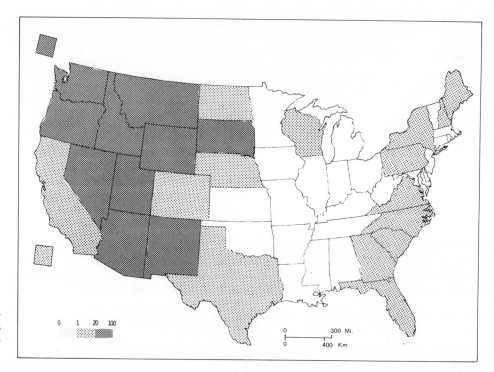

Figure 2.9. Area burned by lightning-caused wildfires, 1966–75, as percent of total area burned by forest and brush fires.

get throughout central and eastern United States. A single thunderstorm 50 km across leaving a conical pile of rain 3 cm deep at the center deposits almost 10 million metric tons of water. "Whenever the Midwest lacks summer thunderstorms, it receives too little rainfall for corn to thrive" (Visher, 1948, p. 336). Over most of the eastern United States at least half the annual precipitation comes in thunderstorms (Changnon, 1957). Wet summers have more thunderstorm days than usual, dry summers fewer (Shands, 1945). Extreme rainfall almost always comes from thunderstorms.

Hail of all sizes is most frequent in northeastern Colorado and southeastern Wyoming (Fig. 2.10), but large hail,

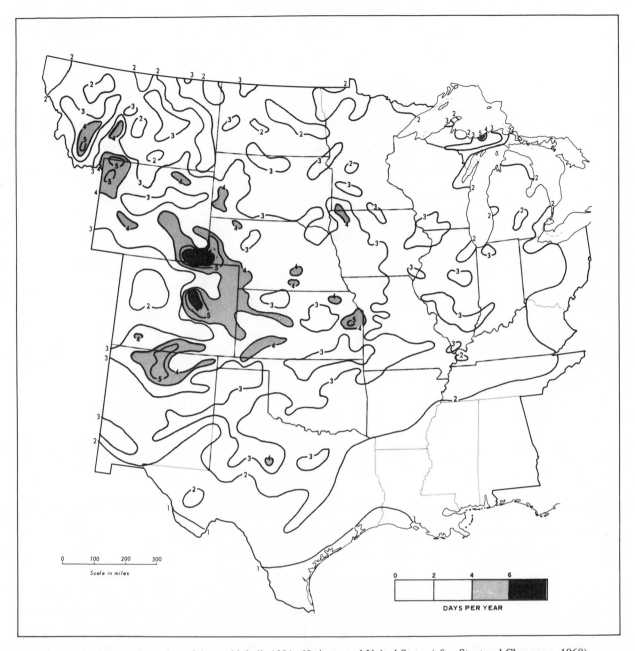

Figure 2.10. Mean annual number of days with hail, 1901–60, in central United States (after Stout and Changnon, 1968).

more than 19 mm (¾ in) in diameter, is most common some 600 km on the southeast, in central Oklahoma and Kansas (Fig. 2.11); a similar map appears as Fig. 1.6 in Vol. 1, p. 11. This is also the region of maximum tornado incidence (Fig. 2.12). Figure 2.10 is from an atlas of hail distribution, for each month and year for 1901–60, based on data from 1,285 first-order and cooperative stations in 17 states (Stout and Changnon, 1968); it has been extended to the whole country, using only first-order stations, by Changnon (1977). The large-hail and tornado maps were prepared from a tally of reports from observers of all kinds, including newspaper accounts and aircraft pilots (Pautz, 1969), during 15 years, 1953–67. Similar data for 1955–70 permitted Skaggs (1974) to draw monthly maps and an annual map showing maximum incidence (per 100 km² per 16 years) in north-central Oklahoma. This region has about 16 annual occurrences per 26,000 km² of large hail and tornadoes. Kessler and Lee (1978) have indicated that the center of tornado threat lies a few hundred kilometers ESE of the center of tornado frequency.

Numbers of reported tornadoes have increased dramatically since 1916, when regular tabulation began, and espe-

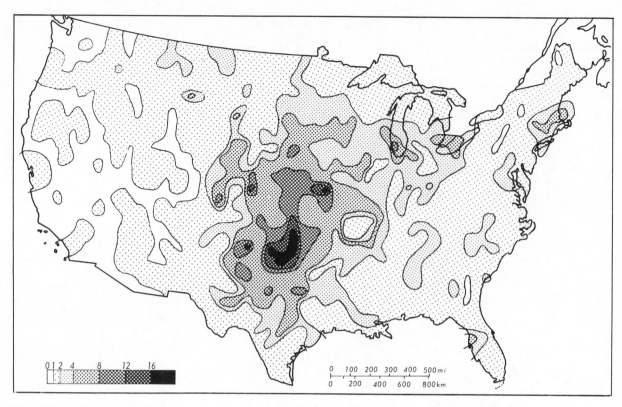

Figure 2.11. Mean annual incidence of large hail (>19 mm) per 26,000 km², 1955–67 (Court, 1974). Similar data appear on Fig. 1.6 in Vol. 1, p. 11.

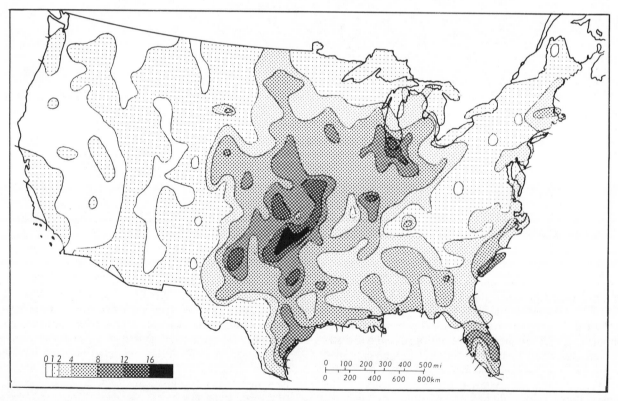

Figure 2.12. Mean annual tornado incidence per 26,000 km², 1955–67 (Court, 1974). This map is more detailed than the map of area-normalized incidence by state shown as Fig. 1.4a in Vol. 1, p. 8.

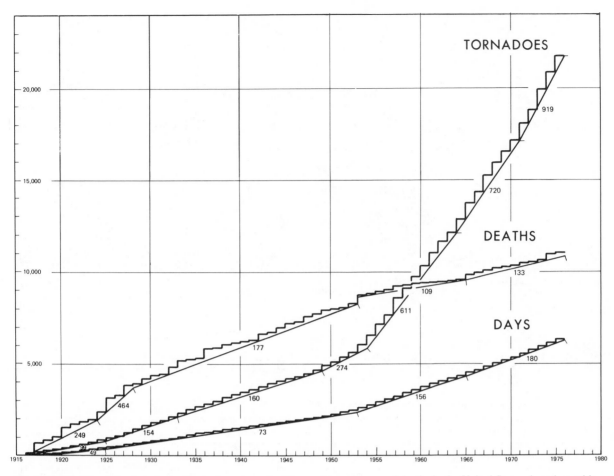

Figure 2.13. Cumulative numbers of tornadoes, tornado days, and tornado-caused deaths in the United States, based on table compiled by Vigansky (1975).

cially since 1955, when the National Severe Storms Forecasting Unit was established in Kansas City (Court, 1970). The number of tornado days, however, has increased much less, and the reported number of tornadoes per day has increased steadily from two in 1920 to five in 1975 (Fig. 2.13).

Changnon (1973) found that thunderstorm days reported at four major cities in the northeastern United States decreased 15% to 20% from one 35-yr period, 1901–53, to the next, 1936–70. Smaller decreases were found in the Midwest, and just east of the Rocky Mountains only Denver (the largest city) had many fewer thunderstorm days in the second 35-yr period. Three Gulf Coast cities (Tampa, New Orleans, Houston) had moderate decreases, but Miami had 4% more thunderstorm days in the second period, and Honolulu 2% more. The decrease could not be attributed to observational procedures, and only part seemed possibly to be caused by large-scale climatic fluctuations; urban atmospheric pollution was suggested as a possible cause.

In a largely unpolluted part of the country, southeastern Arizona, both annual maximum thunderstorm rainfall and total summer rainfall at eight stations, each with data for more than 70 yr, showed no trends in amount, variance, or autocorrelation, and hence were adjudged to be weakly stationary (Mills and Osborn, 1973).

3. World Thunderstorm Climatology

a. Global Distribution

The global distribution of thunderstorms is rather complex, but the influence of certain controls is visible. The frequency generally tends to decrease in the colder seasons. There are relationships, although not perfect, with topography, land-sea configuration, air-mass movements, and airflow on all scales. Figures 2.14–2.16 show that thunderstorms are most frequent at low latitudes, where the atmosphere's low layers are heated mostly by contact with warm ground or water and thereby conditioned for an overturning process essential to thunderstorms.

The annual pattern of thunderstorm days (Fig. 2.14) is complicated but can be interpreted using the controls partially enumerated above. Frequency is related, somewhat tenuously, to rainfall amounts. Air-mass movements to land

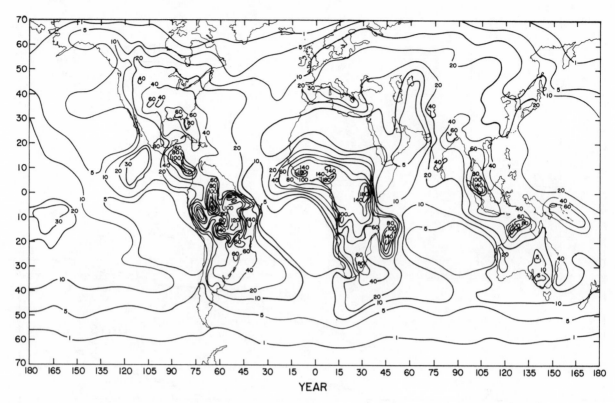

Figure 2.14. Annual number of thunderstorm days (WMO, 1953).

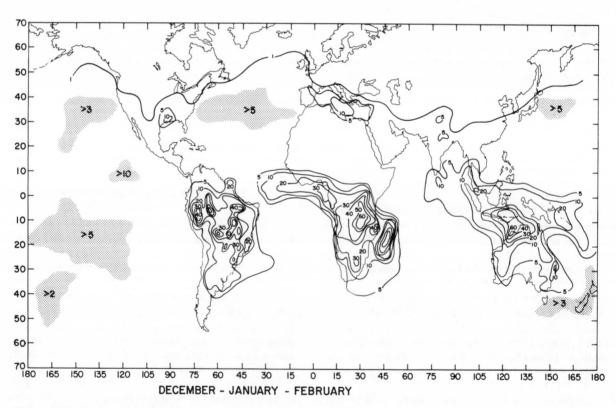

Figure 2.15. Number of thunderstorm days, December–February (WMO, 1953).

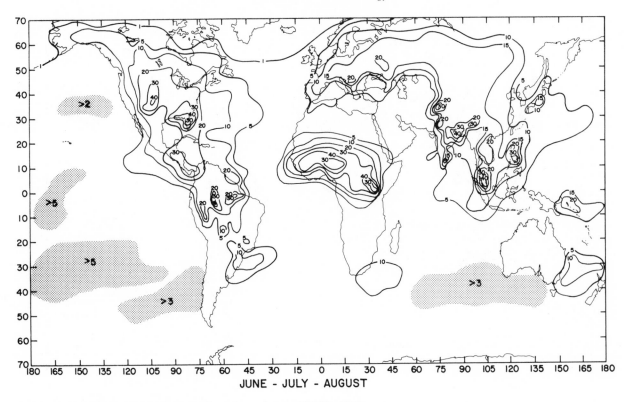

Figure 2.16. Number of thunderstorm days, June–August (WMO, 1953).

from warm bodies of water are often associated with high frequency, especially if topographic influences are also present. Large differences of thunderstorm frequency and daily cycle are produced by local variations of land and waters; equatorial islands tend to be sites of intense convection during afternoons.

Europe and Australia have few seasons with more than 20 thunderstorm days annually (Fig. 2.14). In Asia, only in the southeastern sector and around Bangladesh does the frequency exceed 60. South America and Africa vie for the most thunderstorm-prone continent. The pattern is intricate over central South America; there as elsewhere additional data and examination of physical factors should contribute insight into causes. The tropical oceanic regions around latitudes 20° north and south, regions of semipermanent high pressure, are relatively free from thunderstorms.

In the Northern Hemisphere winter (December–February) relatively few thunderstorm days occur north of 10° N (Fig. 2.15). The only important exceptions are in the southern United States, around New Orleans (Fig. 2.2), and in the central Mediterranean, where about 10 thunderstorm days are reported. In the Southern Hemisphere the location of the intertropical convergence zone dominates the pattern, although warm onshore winds and topography are also important, as in eastern Australia.

In the northern summer (June–August) the region south of 10° has few thunderstorm days (Fig. 2.16). The only exceptions are over the relatively warm ocean areas that are

occasionally affected by cold air-masses from farther south. Outside the tropics, in only a few areas does the high-sun period not yield the most thunderstorm days. The major exceptions are (1) the central Mediterranean (Sicily, Malta); (2) the Tasman Sea between Australia and New Zealand; (3) the Indian Ocean south of Madagascar; and (4) the Pacific coast of North America (see Fig. 2.2). Locations of many places mentioned in the text are shown in Figs. 2.17, 2.18.

In these areas interacting contrasting air masses of the low-sun (winter) season produce more thunderstorm days than do the oceanic convective patterns of summer.

Central Africa and Indonesia have long been considered to have the world's greatest incidence of thunderstorms, with recent data tending to give the dubious honor to Africa. Bogor, Indonesia, is sometimes cited as averaging 322 thunderstorm days per year, 1916–19. However, the average was 151 in 1941–57, and the number per year was between 4 and 41 from 1953 to 1962 (U.S. Army Engineer Topographic Labs., 1974). The figure 322 may actually be the annual number of individual thunderstorms, not days.

An absolute maximum of annual thunderstorm days of approximately 250 to 260 was proposed by Portig (1963), who used statistical curves in his analysis. The accepted record is 242 thunderstorm days per year, recorded over a 10-yr period at Kampala, Uganda (0°20′ N, 32°36′ E), just north of Lake Victoria. In this area, as often elsewhere in the equatorial regions, local influences are very strong. Thus many of the thunderstorms are heard only at Kampala

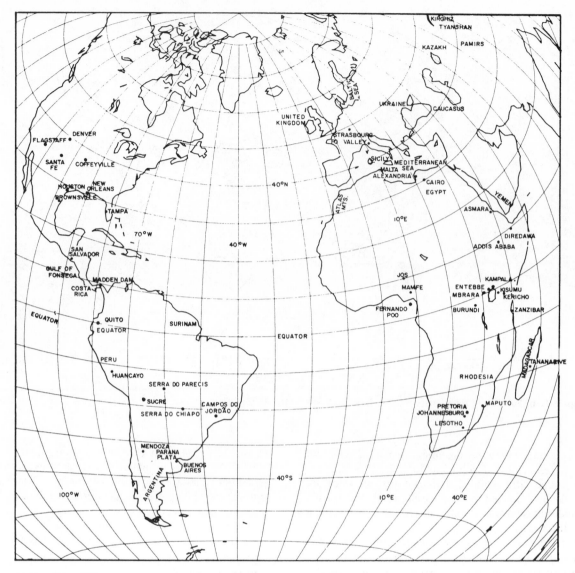

Figure 2.17. American, African, and European sites mentioned in text.

and do not reach the town; Mbarara, on the west side of Lake Victoria, experiences only seven thunderstorm days per year. In this area there is also a remarkable local variation of daily storm cycle, probably controlled by a lakeland breeze effect (Lumb, 1970). This is illustrated by the hourly distribution of storms at Entebbe, about 30 km southwest of Kampala, and at Kisumu, on the northeast edge of Lake Victoria (Fig. 2.19).

Not many places around the world report 200 or more thunderstorm days annually. A list of these, together with their seasonal distribution, is given in Table 2.4. The record numbers for Central America, Australia, Europe, and the USSR are given for comparison. The figures are taken from *World Distribution of Thunderstorm Days* (WMO, 1953) and *World-Wide Airfield Summaries* (U.S. Naval Weather

Service, 1969). Mamfe, Cameroon, has the record mean of 30 thunderstorm days in a single month and 81 in 3 consecutive months.

b. Regional Distribution

The continent of Africa has the greatest number of thunderstorm days (Fig. 2.14 and Table 2.4). More than 100 are recorded annually over about 20% of the land area in a belt from West Africa to the highlands of East Africa, and in western Madagascar. Frequencies of less than 5 are rare. Proximity to large bodies of warm water is important.

In southern Africa the highest frequency (about 90) is found on the eastern high plateau, especially over Lesotho. In the Malawi-Zimbabwe-Zambia area thunderstorms are

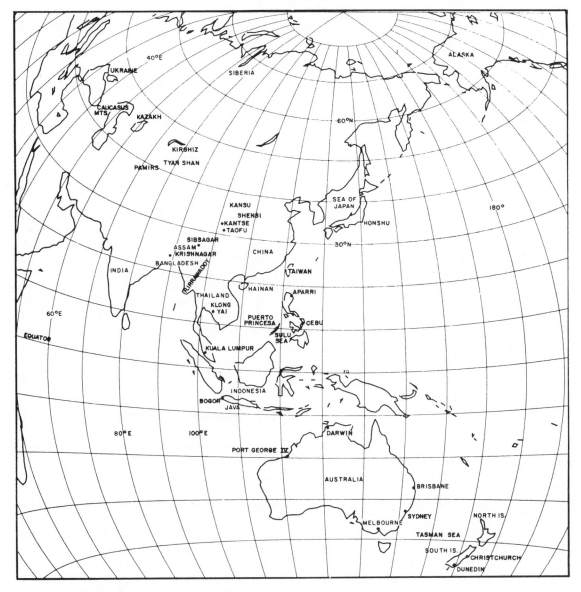

Figure 2.18. Asian, Australian, and New Zealand sites mentioned in text.

often associated with upper troughs. The cool upper air meets warm moist northeasterly flow at the surface, so frequent thunderstorms result, their number reaching more than 125 per year in some areas. In Madagascar about half the yearly total is recorded in summer (December–February).

In winter (June–August) thunderstorms are very rare, although air-mass interactions spawn occasional outbreaks at the southern extremity of the continent. In eastern Africa some pronounced gradients are noted. For example, Zanzibar has 61 days per year, but at nearby Pemba the incidence is less than 5; also in Uganda, there is the previously quoted contrast of Kampala (242) and Mbarara (7). In the Ethiopian highlands, occurrences average 80 to 100 days annually, but in the east, around Diredawa, this is reduced to less than 25. In the northern province of Eritrea, at Asmara,

the median duration is about 7 hr during July. Thunderstorm incidence in West Africa is generally associated with the well-known squall or disturbance lines that usually start about 330 to 550 km (210 to 350 mi) south of the Intertropical Convergence Zone and travel westward. The thunderstorms typically occur when topographic effects are added (Garnier, 1967).

In Australia the maximum frequency, around 100 thunderstorm days annually, occurs near Darwin, in the northwest; Port George IV reports an average of 27 in December alone (Table 2.4). At the other end of the scale some locations in New South Wales, South Australia, and Tasmania have averages of fewer than 5 (Gentilli, 1971). The east coast generally reports 20 to 40 thunderstorms a year, about twice the values from the west coast. Maximum frequency

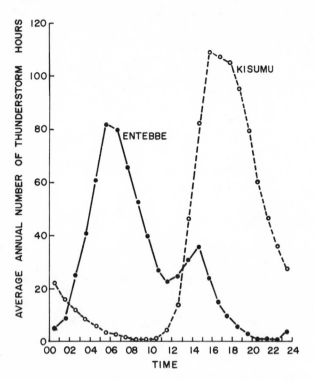

Figure 2.19. Average distribution of thunderstorm hours during the day for Kisumu (Kenya) and Entebbe (Uganda) (Lumb, 1970).

is usually in summer (November–February), except in the southwest, where more than 50% occur in May through August.

In New Zealand the frequency increases from east to west and generally with altitude (Maunder, 1971). On the west coast of South Island averages are around 15 to 25 thunderstorm days annually, but in other areas, such as Christchurch and Dunedin, the number is only 3 or 4. The frequency is highest in winter in the north and west of North Island, with a summer maximum in most of the remainder.

In Southeast Asia, although part of Java, Indonesia, is reported to hold pride of place for the maximum number of thunderstorm days, the visual reporting used there makes direct comparisons doubtful. The area with a better-substantiated large number of thunderstorm days is Malaysia, where Kuala Lumpur reports 180 annually, with 9 or more in every month, rising to a maximum of 21 in April; many station totals exceed 150. The interplay of two monsoonal patterns contributes to the large number reported in this essentially marine climate. Farther west the numbers decrease; Klong Yai, Thailand, records 159 thunderstorm days per year, with 20 each in June and July. In India, totals above 100 are very rare; Krishnagar (108) and Sibsagar (108) are unusual. Thunderstorms in the north of India and in west Pakistan are sometimes severe, with large hail, strong winds, and even tornadoes, especially during the northern spring (transition to wet monsoon). Elsewhere in India thunder is a frequent

accompaniment to excessive rains. Very few thunderstorms occur in the season of low sun (October–February).

In the Philippines the number of thunderstorms decreases rapidly from 80 days per year on the east coast to fewer than 20 in the western Sulu Sea. The seasonal distribution also shows a distinct change (Fig. 2.20), with Aparri as typical of the eastern stations, Cebu of the central, and Puerto Princesa illustrating the western area (Flores and Balagot, 1969). Figures 2.19 and 2.20 indicate large local variation common to areas where variable topography and irregular land and water masses coincide with characteristically weak regional control.

On Taiwan the west has the most thunderstorm days, around 35 to 45 annually, and 8 to 10 monthly in June through August. On the eastern side of the island the numbers are approximately halved. Thunderstorms are infrequent during winter months. According to Watts (1969), a publication by the Central Weather Bureau of China shows frequencies of thunderstorm days about twice those given in the WMO (1953) publication, ranging from about 100 in Hainan and decreasing northeastward to fewer than 20 a year. The length of the thunderstorm season is related to the annual frequency, with very few occurrences between mid-October and mid-February.

In the USSR the highest frequency occurs in the Caucasus, where thunderstorms occur on 20 to 40 days per year. In the higher areas and the Armenian Plateau this average increases to more than 50, but eastward, toward the Caspian Sea, the mean value is less than 10. The period May to August has the greatest frequency.

In central Asia thunderstorms are infrequent, for the lower air is too dry and the upper air too stable. Averages run from about 5 to 25 days, with May to July or August being most favorable for thunderstorms. Around the eastern Pamirs and Tyan Shan most of the annual rainfall is associated with thunderstorms. Central Kazakhstan is the transition region between the predominance of the early and midsummer thunderstorms in northern Kazakhstan and western Siberia and the predominance of the late-winter and early-spring cyclonic storms of central Asia.

Over much of the European USSR thunderstorms occur from 40 to 80 hours per year. One study showed that 50% of the thunderstorms were associated with cold fronts, 22% with warm fronts, and 28% with single air masses. The month of maximum frequency is generally July, with six to eight occurrences. Figure 2.21 actually shows the mean annual duration of thunderstorms, a value related to the more commonly used thunderstorm days. The Arctic and Pacific fringes have very few thunderstorms, and only areas in the Caucasus and western Ukraine have more than 100 thunderstorm hours annually (Lydolph, 1977).

Over most of Europe thunderstorms are relatively infrequent; only some Mediterranean locations report as many as 30 annually. In Scandinavia few places have more than 10 thunderstorm days in a year, with only 2 or 3 in the mountains and the Arctic. The storms are most frequent in the summer months but can occur with frontal passages at any time. In the British Isles central England averages between

Table 2.4. Stations with More Than 200 Thunderstorm Days Annually or with Highest Number for Selected Areas

Station	Jan.	Feb.	Mar.	Apr.	May	June	July	Aug.	Sept.	Oct.	Nov.	Dec.	Total
Kampala (Uganda) 0°20' N, 32°36' E, 1,310 m	15	15	19	22	22	20	19	23	23	25	22	17	242
Bunia (Zaire) 1°34' N, 30°13' E	17	10	17	16	18	18	16	26	27	28	19	16	228
Kamembe (Rwanda) 2°27' S, 28°54' E, 160 m	23	22	23	26	20	7	5	5	16	24	25	25	221
Bandung (Indonesia) 6°54' S, 107°34' E	24	24	23	22	20	10	5	12	11	21	22	24	218
Calabar (Nigeria) 4°57' N, 8°21' E, 60 m	11	11	19	25	25	23	15	9	18	25	23	11	215
Entebbe (Uganda) 0°02' N, 32°37' E, 1,150 m	14	13	15	17	18	18	19	19	19	20	18	16	206
Carauri (Brazil) 4°53' S, 66°54' W, 80 m	19	16	16	14	15	13	13	19	22	20	13	20	206
Mamfe (Cameroon) 5°46' N, 8°20' E, 120 m	6	6	21	26	30	25	13	10	20	27	16	1	201
Colón (Panama) 9°22' N, 79°54' W, 4 m	1	0	0	2	14	21	26	24	22	21	14	4	149
Port George IV (Australia) 15°25' S, 124°43' E	17	19	12	5	1	0	0	0	1	5	14	27	100
Aviano (Italy) 46°01' N, 12°35' E, 130 m	0	0	1	6	10	14	11	9	4	3	2	1	61
Yerevan (USSR) 40°08' N, 44°28' E, 900 m	0	0	1	6	11	12	7	5	4	2	0	0	48

10 and 20 days of thunder; very occasionally a series of thunderstorms can bring rainfall of more than 200 mm (8 in) in a day.

In France, the Low Countries, and much of central Europe thunderstorms become more frequent in April, as depressions from the southwest converge with northwesterly air streams. By June these interactions grow more severe and can lead to intense thunderstorms and hail. Maximum numbers of thunderstorms over Iberia occur in spring and early summer, but in late summer and early autumn they often form over the Mediterranean and move inland. In the usually "summer dry" Mediterranean instability thunderstorms over mountainous regions can bring more rain in summer than in winter, especially in Spain.

In South America, in the Argentine-Paraguay-Uruguay region the greatest thunderstorm frequency is in the mountainous areas and in the humid zone around Uruguay. Thunderstorms are most prevalent in summer, with relatively few in winter. The maxima are about 50 storm days per year with 8 to 10 in the most thunderstorm-prone months. In the Parana-Plata lowlands the maximum is about 40 thunderstorm days per year, with 4 or 5 as the maximum in a month.

A number of areas in Peru, Bolivia, and Ecuador have 100 or more thunderstorm days. For example, Quito (Ecuador) has 109 with maxima from March to May and October to November; Huancayo (Peru) has 106 with maxima from September to April; and Sucre (Bolivia) has 87 with maxima in October to January. These stations are all around the 3,000 m (10,000 ft) elevation. On Lake Titicaca storm activity is sometimes great, especially in the afternoon and early evening.

Areas of Brazil report the greatest frequencies of thunderstorm days in South America. Local heating triggers many severe storms, but convergence and, in the south, frontal activity play a role. In much of the eastern part of the country there are fewer than 20 thunderstorm days per year, some regions having fewer than 10 days. The frequency increases westward, reaching 80 to 130 over the Planalto Central, the Serras do Parecis, and Caiapos.

In the northern part of South America the seasonal distri-

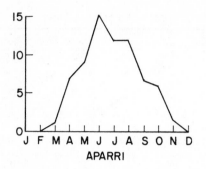
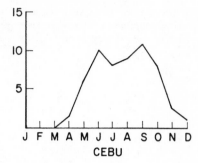
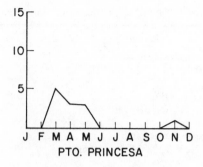

Figure 2.20. Mean monthly distribution of thunderstorm days for selected stations in the Philippines (Flores and Balagot, 1969).

bution changes with location in relation to the equatorial trough. With the trough on the south the coastal area has few thunderstorms. Surinam has an unusual thunderstorm referred to as *sibiboesie* (literally, "broom and forest," i.e., sweeping clean), in which windspeeds up to 30 m s (65 mi h) are recorded. These occur at any time when the trough is to the north, are triggered by surface heating, and bring a rapid drop in temperature of 6° to 8°C (11° to 14°F), relative humidity increases of up to 40%, but little rain, normally 10 mm (0.4 in).

For Central America and the Caribbean the many discrepancies noted in thunderstorm data make the statements unreliable (Portig, 1976). Two areas of maxima are suggested, one in the Gulf of Fonseca, on the Pacific Coast of Honduras (116 days per year) and one in the central Canal Zone (196 days at Madden Dam). San Salvador's figure of 115 is probably an underestimation. Portig remarks that smaller islands have fewer thunderstorms than do larger islands and that the southeastern part of the Caribbean experiences fewer storms than does the northwestern area. The period of maximum frequency in the northwest is from May to October and in the southeast from June to October with a definite peak in September. On some northeastern Caribbean islands stationary thunderstorms can produce very heavy rainfalls.

Thunderstorm climatic patterns over ocean areas have always been difficult to identify because of the paucity of truly representative oceanic data. Trent and Gathman (1972), studying the variation in the area of the world's oceans affected by thunderstorms at any one time, found, using more than 7 million synoptic ship observations, that the average thundery area is 202×10^4 km^2 with a diurnal peak of 240×10^4 km^2 during the period 1800 to 2400 GMT and a minimum of 167×10^4 km^2 during 0600 to 1200 GMT. The months with maximum probability of thunderstorms are June through August. Tekeuchi and Nagatani (1974) indicated that in the western Pacific the maximum thunderstorm activity is from midnight to early morning, the period when radiational cooling at the top of the cloud leads to instability. This finding probably holds true in many other oceanic regions.

c. Hail and Wind

The distribution of hail days is shown in Fig. 2.22 (Williams, 1973). Areas especially subject to hail are found in Africa. The plateau of western Kenya east of Lake Victoria is particularly affected; near Kericho, an important tea-producing area, as many as 80 hailstorms a year are reported; some localities average 10 incidents annually (Frisby and Sansom, 1967; Henderson et al., 1970). In a tea-growing area of 10,000 hectares (25,000 acres), 54 hail days were reported annually from 1950 to 1967; 51 days in August and September 1965 had hail on a dense reporting network. Elsewhere more than 5 hailstorms per year—a very large number—occur in regions of confluence or convergence of air masses, near high terrain, in some seasons. Such regions are around the Atlas Mountains, in Morocco; Addis Ababa, in Ethiopia; Tananarive, in Madagascar; Lesotho, in southern Africa; Toro, in Uganda; and Burundi. Little hail is reported along the African coasts; highlands normally report more hail than lowlands. However, an exceptionally heavy hailstorm hit Maputo (previously Lourenço Marques), in Mozambique, on 22 October 1977. It lasted for only 20 min with hailstones the size of baseballs and some as big as large grapefruit. Five people were killed, more than 100 were injured, and many houses were severely damaged. American observers present agreed that they had never seen such a storm in the United States. Jos, on the central Nigerian plateau, experiences three hailfalls annually compared with perhaps one in 2 or 3 years at lower elevations.

In South Africa hail is most frequent on the eastern high plateaus, around Lesotho. Extremely severe hailstorms in the Pretoria-Johannesburg area are comparable with those in the midwestern United States (Carte and Basson, 1970). The winter falls of the southwestern Cape Province are generally of graupel, or soft hail.

In Rhodesia about one-fourth of the stations report hail sometime during the year, with most noted in spring and early summer (October–December). November, the month when surface temperatures are near their maxima and upper lapse rates are steepest, generally has the severest storms, with stones occasionally reaching 15 to 20 mm (0.6 to 0.8 in) in diameter. At the other end of the continent, lower

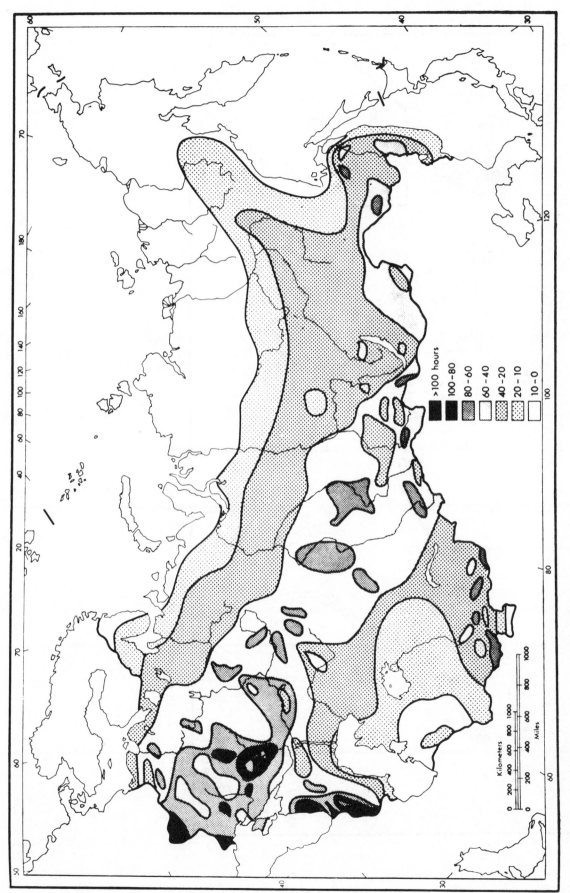

Figure 2.21. Mean annual duration of thunderstorms in the USSR (Lydolph, 1977).

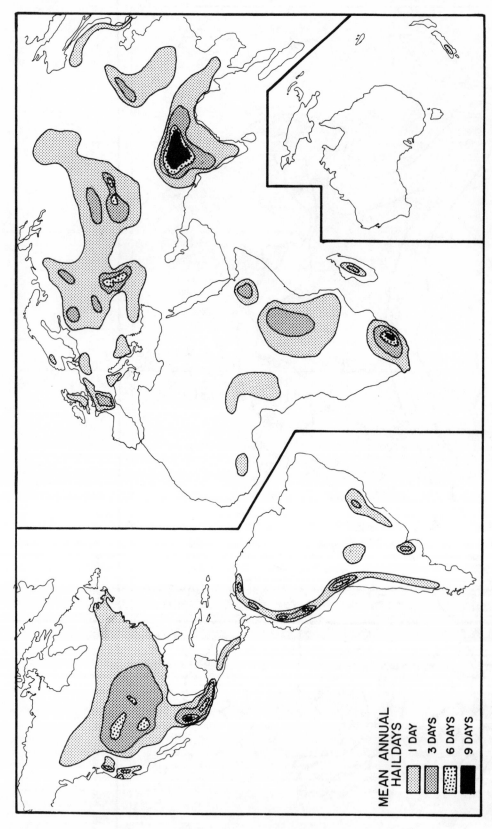

Figure 2.22. Mean annual frequency of hail at a point (Frisby and Sansom, 1967).

MEAN ANNUAL
HAILDAYS

I DAY

3 DAYS

6 DAYS

9 DAYS

Egypt can experience hailstorms during November and December, but most stations report an average of only two to seven instances per decade. Alexandria is an exception, with four to five incidents annually, and like Cairo it has reported stones 20 to 40 mm (0.8 to 1.6 in) in diameter.

In Australia the association between thunderstorms and hail is not very close, but some hailstorms cover large areas (Gentilli, 1971). Few hailstorms occur in the Australian tropics. Around Sydney and Melbourne such storms can occur in summer or winter; one in July 1931 caused damage of nearly half a million dollars in Sydney. As in many other areas of the world, certain areas or swaths seem much more prone to hail incidence than do neighboring regions. In December 1980, a very severe hailstorm hit a suburb of Brisbane, stripping many roofs and damaging or destroying numerous parked light aircraft.

New Zealand hail frequency decreases from south to north; regions exposed to the southwest show the greatest incidence (Maunder, 1971). In winter and spring cold fronts or instability showers can trigger hailstorms. Although some can be very severe, stone diameter rarely exceeds 20 mm (0.8 in).

Hail frequency varies appreciably in China; in the southeastern provinces, Taiwan, and the arid northeast it is almost unknown, whereas in Kansu and Shensi provinces it is recorded up to six times per year. As in most other regions topography is important, but elevation alone is not; both Kantse and Taofu are at 3,000 m (10,000 ft) and only 140 km (90 mi) apart, yet at Kantse hail is rare, whereas Taofu receives frequent, very intense hailstorms.

In the northeast India subcontinent the maximum average frequency of about one hailstorm annually is found in the foothills. In some areas as many as nine hailstorms have been reported in a year, and some very large hailstones probably occur in this region. The complex topography produces great variations over short distances. In the Irrawaddy delta of Burma the maximum frequency is during autumn (September–November), but in the northern hill stations it is from April to July or August (Ramdas et al., 1938). In the arid areas of southwestern Asia hail is rare, although occasional reports are received from the Yemeni highlands.

Few regions of the Union of Soviet Socialist Republics experience more than one or two hailstorms annually, and in the desert plains and the margins of the Arctic and Pacific, incidence is less than one in 2 yr. Maximum frequencies occur in the Caucasus and the mountains of Kirghiz; everywhere topography plays an important determining role. The relatively high frequency (4 or more days annually) in the fruit-producing area of the Caucasus is very serious, and many experiments in hail suppression have been tried. There hail sometimes lies for a couple of days (Sulakvelidze, 1969).

Lydolph (1977) has noted that in the plains of European USSR, the Caucasus, and the Asiatic area, the maximum hail occurrence is in May and June. However, where air masses move predominantly off warmer waters at certain seasons, the maximum is delayed until September to November along the Baltic and until November to January on the Georgia coast.

The winter hailstorms of Europe are associated with the moist polar air behind a cyclone. Although noted even in the Mediterranean, these are most frequent on the exposed west coasts of the northern latitudes. Some falls along the Norwegian coast are intense. In late spring and summer the hail associated with the well-developed thunderstorms is most frequent in lower latitudes. Where topographic influences are maximal, as in the Po Valley of Italy, vineyard owners have experimented with hail-suppression practices since the eighteenth century (Morgan, 1973; Papee et al., 1974). Extreme hail incidence in Europe from A.D. 1100 to 1400 has been studied by Weikinn (1967).

In Central America and the Caribbean hail is apparently rare, even in areas where thunderstorms are frequent. Portig (1976), who has many years' experience in this region, cites only a few cases, none severe. Stations in Costa Rica and Honduras report as many as two or three hailstorms per year, mostly from April to September.

In Brazil mainly the southeast is affected; Campos do Jordão (22°44′ S, 45°35′ W) at 1,655 m (5,550 ft) has two or three hailstorms a year. Parts of the Andean chain are likely to have many hailstorms, but data are sparse. In Peru and Ecuador stations above 3,000 m (10,000 ft) report annual averages of 10 or 11 hailfalls. In Argentina heavy damage is reported to crops in the provinces of Mendoza and Buenos Aires. The maximum frequency occurs in December and January (summer) in the late afternoon and early evening (Grandoso, 1966). Frisby and Sansom (1967) found insufficient data to draw isolines of hail distribution in this zone.

Tornadoes form in the most severe thunderstorms. These, in turn, can be part of an intense tropical cyclone—hurricane or typhoon. Hurricane Beulah, which hit Brownsville, Tex., in September 1967, spawned a record 115 twisters. Any area subject to hurricanes can expect associated tornadoes. Most tornadoes related to hurricanes are in the right-front quadrant, although they have occurred in every quadrant; one study indicated 5% in the left-rear quadrant. Basically, the tornado is not a phenomenon of the tropical areas, and some confusion can arise in parts of west Africa where the term is given to line squalls. For example, Santa Isabel, on the island of Fernando Póo, reports 28 tornadoes annually. Actually, in Africa tornadoes are normally sighted only in the area of The Rand, in South Africa.

Tornadoes are not unique to the United States. The comprehensive article by Fujita (1973) notes that tornadoes are frequently reported from Australia, Italy, Japan, New Zealand, the United Kingdom, and many other countries (Fig. 2.23). Rather surprisingly, the record number per unit area that he reports is held by the United Kingdom in 1966. However, the United States appears to have by far the greatest number of very large, intense tornadoes recorded worldwide.

As the observation network is increased, the frequency of tornado reports grows. In Australia the numbers went from about 10 per year in the period 1930 to 1960 to about 100

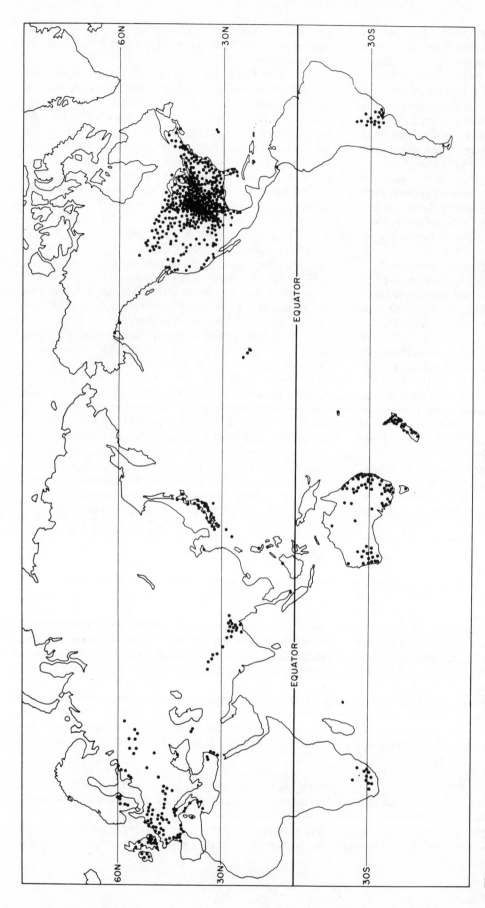

Figure 2.23. Density plot of tornadoes expected to occur in 4-yr period. Individual incidents in 1963–66. In the United States the number exceeds 2,600 (Fujita, 1973).

per year more recently. The seasonal distribution is uniform. New Zealand notes about 25 tornadoes annually, mainly from May to October in the western areas of the islands. In Japan, with 15 to 20 tornadoes annually, the main time of activity is in midwinter on the Japan Sea side of Honshu Island and in the summer (typhoon season) on the Pacific side.

In Europe the main tornado season is summer, but Fujita notes early winter maxima in England and the western Mediterranean. Tornadoes with maximum windspeeds in excess of 300 km h (187 mi h) are generally expected only in the United States and in a small area in the Bangladesh-Assam region.[1]

[1]Compilation of monthly, seasonal, and annual averages for the 207 U.S. stations was the work of Martha Berg and James Clubb. Figures 2.1–2.3 and 2.5 were prepared by Gregory Posely. Figure 2.4 was drawn by Dan Mullnix. Ron Young tabulated the wildfire data by states from annual Forest Service reports (Table 2.3) and drew the maps (Figs. 2.8, 2.9) of relative numbers of wildfires and area burned. Thanks are extended to Dorothy Lorenz for typing assistance and to Jackie Wilson for helping with the reference search on world thunderstorm climatology.

3. Thunderstorms at Sea

Frederick Sanders and John C. Freeman

1. Introduction

Although the extreme manifestations associated with land-based thunderstorms are seldom if ever observed at sea, the thundersquall with a wind field a few hundred miles long and 20 to 50 mi wide is a year-round hazard in many tropical areas and a hazard over oceans in both tropical and temperate latitudes. When the direct effects of wind on waves are reinforced by a pattern speed that greatly extends the duration of wind effects on wave packets, high waves, as well as wind, are particularly hazardous to small boats and offshore operations.

Ocean squall lines can be especially dangerous when they develop in areas where general weather conditions are good. Also, when bad weather of a persistent squall line or front is 10 to 20 hours in the offing, ocean surface activity can be seriously impacted by waves moving ahead of the storm area. Waterspouts, a milder relative of tornadoes, are much more common over sea than tornadoes are over land, and present an occasional hazard of slight areal extent to offshore structures and small boats.

2. Climatology of Oceanic Thunderstorms

a. Data Sources

Thunderstorms at sea are reported in routine observations at midnight GMT and every 6 h thereafter by ships, mainly in merchant-marine fleets. It is difficult to compare statistics from this source with thunderstorm data obtained from land stations. The latter sources are permanent and more or less evenly spaced, and their data include a count of days on which thunder is heard. In contrast, oceanic reporting locations generally are determined by population concentrations and major shipping routes rather than by systematic design.

Two compilations of maritime thunderstorm data are available: one produced by the National Climatic Center for the Naval Research Laboratory (NRL) (Trent and Gathman, 1972), comprising about 7 million observations taken from 1949 to 1963, and the other by the Meteorological Office of the United Kingdom and the Deutsche Wetterdienst for the World Meteorological Organization (WMO, 1956), comprising about the same number of observations made during an unspecified but presumably earlier period.

In the NRL sample, for each month and GMT observation time for each 10° square of latitude and longitude, computations show the percentage frequency of use of any synoptic-code number indicative of thunder and/or lightning at the time of observation or within the preceding hour (synoptic code ww = 13, 17, 29, or 91–99; these numbers correspond to thunderstorm observations described by international code (U.S. Weather Bureau, 1968, Table 4). In the WMO publication (WMO, 1956), estimated numbers of thunderstorm days (local calendar days on which thunder is heard) are given for each month without stratification by Greenwich Mean Time (denoted GMT or Z) but for each 5° square, as obtained from percentage frequencies of observation of thunder and of thunder and lightning (t and $t + l$ in the Beaufort notation). For the present study these numbers of days have been converted back to percentage frequencies by applying the formula used originally by WMO:

$$n = 12 \times \left[30 - 30(1 - p) \left(1 - \frac{p}{1.25} \right)^{23} \right]$$

where n is the annual number of thunderstorm days and p is the percentage frequency of observations of thunder. For comparison with the NRL results, the data for the 5° squares were combined to conform with the 10° squares used in the NRL sample before application of the formula. Annual percentage frequencies from each of these data sets appear in Fig. 3.1.

b. World Distribution

The WMO and NRL patterns of thunderstorm frequency are similar; values in the NRL sample were higher because they include observations of lightning alone, which were evidently excluded from the WMO data. The patterns agree best in the North Atlantic and the Mediterranean, for which both samples contain large numbers of observations. For the North Pacific the NRL pattern is generally regarded as more reliable, whereas for the North Indian and all southern oceans the WMO patterns are probably better. Considerable smoothing of the NRL data was required in the Southern Hemisphere because of erratic variation from square to

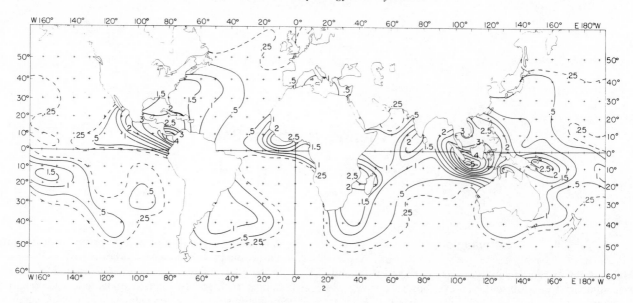

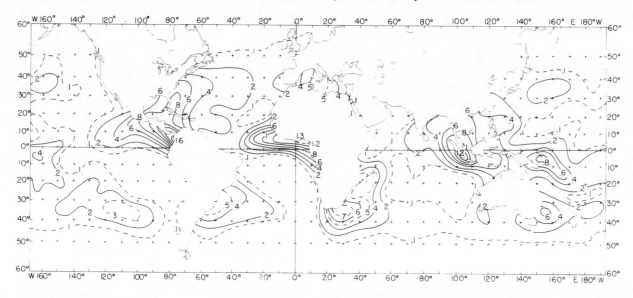

Figure 3.1. Percentage frequencies of thunderstorms and/or lightning in surface observations from (above) the NRL sample with solid isopleths at intervals of 0.5% and (below) the WMO sample with solid isopleths at intervals of 0.2%.

square owing to data deficiency. Poleward of latitude 60° the NRL data indicate mean frequencies of about 0.05%, but no stratification appears useful, either by geographical position or otherwise, because few observations are available, and few thunderstorms occur there.

Thunderstorms are most frequent over oceans in the deep tropics, with major activity near Panama and adjacent portions of Ecuador and Colombia, over the Gulf of Guinea near the African coast, and adjacent to western Indonesia and Malaysia. A center of activity nearly equal in strength just east of New Guinea extends as a ridge of relatively high frequency east-southeastward across the South Pacific into middle latitudes, ending within 1,000 miles of South Amer-

ica. This ridge parallels a major band of mean cloudiness shown on photographs taken from satellites. In the North Atlantic and the North Pacific high thunderstorm frequencies roughly parallel the Intertropical Convergence Zone (ITCZ) at 5° latitude, extending some 50° of longitude west from the coasts of Africa and South America.

Relative minima of thunderstorm frequency occur between 10° and 30° latitude in the trade-wind belts in the eastern and central parts of all oceans except the North Indian, where a minimum occurs in the northwest portion. These minima approach zero in all the southern oceans; the minimum is least pronounced in the North Atlantic. In both hemispheres these regions of low frequency lie over and

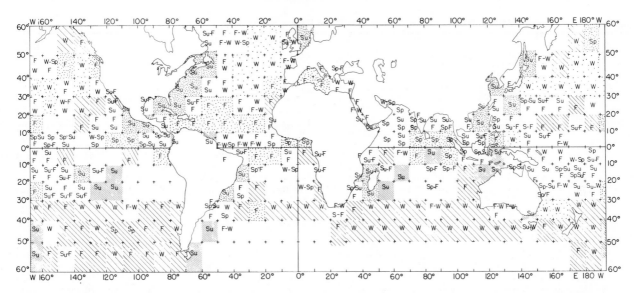

Figure 3.2. Seasons of maximum frequency of thunderstorms for each 10° square for which a determination could be made. *W* represents winter, *Sp* spring, *Su* summer, and *F* fall; the upper determination is from WMO data and the lower from NRL data. In dotted squares both data samples indicate the same season of maximum frequency. In hatched squares one of the samples indicates a maximum season, and the other does not. In unlettered squares neither source indicates a maximum season.

west of cold ocean currents. Toward the equator frequencies decrease in the western Atlantic and Indian oceans and in the central Pacific.

At most ocean longitudes a secondary maximum of thunderstorm frequency occurs in lower middle latitudes, poleward of the subtropical ridge of high pressure; from there thunderstorm frequencies decrease poleward to low values. In the westernmost North Atlantic and North Pacific there is no secondary maximum. The frequency decreases slowly but monotonically poleward along the Gulf Stream and Kuroshio, and the values are higher, latitude for latitude, over the Gulf Stream. Mediterranean frequencies are intermediate between values over the Gulf Stream and the Kuroshio, and are relatively high for the latitude.

In each of the southern oceans a middle-latitude center of high frequency is located at or near the east coast of the adjacent continent. All these maxima lie over warm ocean currents: the Brazil in the Atlantic, the Agulhas in the Indian, and the Australian in the Pacific. Unlike maxima in the Northern Hemisphere, these middle-latitude maxima are clearly separated from tropical maxima. An equatorward extension of high frequencies is located in the western South Indian Ocean between Madagascar and the African mainland. The middle-latitude maximum in the eastern South Pacific represents a merger of the ridge of high frequency that extends eastward from Australia and the ridge that extends east-southeastward from New Guinea.

c. Seasonal Variation

Both data samples were examined to determine the season of maximum thunderstorm frequency. Figure 3.2 shows the

results for squares in which the number of observations was considered adequate and the seasonal variation of activity was judged sufficiently pronounced.

Poleward of 30°, the latitude of the subtropical belt of high pressure in both hemispheres, the seasons of maximum frequency, with few exceptions, are winter and, to a lesser extent, fall, the opposite of typical seasonal variation over land. The most systematic deviations in the middle-latitude oceanic patterns occur in the western North Atlantic and North Pacific, where the summer maximum characteristic of the adjacent continent prevails.

It is doubtful that these cold-season thunderstorms result from synoptic-scale lifting of tropical air, although such lifting is almost certainly most vigorous in the western portions of these oceans, where air-mass contrasts are strongest and cyclogenesis is most frequent, especially in winter. Synoptic-scale data suggest that most of these cold-season thunderstorms occur in modified polar air which has been destabilized to a relatively great depth by a long passage over relatively warm water, without the marked descent or subsidence that occurs in association with a pronounced upper-level trough. Over the extreme western portions of the North Atlantic and North Pacific the cold winter outbreaks of continental air are intensely heated by the sea, but the unstable layer remains too shallow to permit deep convection and thunderstorm development. The fall maximum in the eastern Pacific and Atlantic and in the Mediterranean probably results from the vigorous autumn cyclonic activity in those longitudes, where planetary-scale upper ridges tend to develop often during the winter season, suppressing deep convection.

In the Southern Hemisphere polar air from Antarctica

Table 3.1. Groups of 10° Squares for Which Observations Are Assumed to Be Taken at Nominal Values of Local Civil Time and 6-hour Intervals Thereafter

Group 1 0020 (41,482)*		Group 2 0100 (37,482)*		Group 3 0140 (109,395)*		Group 4 0220 (89,585)*		Group 5 0300 (154,297)*	
° Lat.	° Long.	° Lat.	° Long.	° Lat.	° Long.	° Lat.	° Long.	° Lat.	° Long.
0–10 N	170–180 W	0–10 N	160–170 W	20–30 N	60– 70 W	10–20 N	50– 60 W	0–10 N	40– 50 W
10–20 N	170–180 W	10–20 N	160–170 W	30–40 N	60– 70 W	20–30 N	50– 60 W	10–20 N	40– 50 W
20–30 N	170–180 W	20–30 N	160–170 W	0–10 N	150–160 W	30–40 N	50– 60 W	20–30 N	40– 50 W
30–40 N	170–180 W	30–40 N	160–170 W	10–20 N	150–160 W	0–10 N	140–150 W	30–40 N	40– 50 W
40–50 N	170–180 W	40–50 N	160–170 W	20–30 N	150–160 W	10–20 N	140–150 W	40–50 N	40– 50 W
0–10 S	170–180 W	0–10 S	160–170 W	30–40 N	150–160 W	20–30 N	140–150 W	50–60 N	40– 50 W
10–20 S	170–180 W	10–20 S	160–170 W	40–50 N	150–160 W	30–40 N	140–150 W	0–10 N	130–140 W
20–30 S	170–180 W	20–30 S	160–170 W	0–10 S	150–160 W	40–50 N	140–150 W	10–20 N	130–140 W
30–40 S	170–180 W	30–40 S	160–170 W	10–20 S	150–160 W	0–10 S	140–150 W	20–30 N	130–140 W
40–50 S	170–180 W	40–50 S	160–170 W	20–30 S	150–160 W	10–20 S	140–150 W	30–40 N	130–140 W
10–20 S	80– 90 W	10–20 S	100–110 E	30–40 S	150–160 W	20–30 S	140–150 W	40–50 N	130–140 W
20–30 S	80– 90 W	20–30 S	100–110 E	40–50 S	150–160 W	30–40 S	140–150 W	0–10 S	130–140 W
30–40 S	80– 90 W	—	—	—	—	40–50 S	140–150 W	10–20 S	130–140 W
40–50 S	80– 90 W	—	—	—	—	—	—	20–30 S	130–140 W
10–20 S	90–100 E	—	—	—	—	—	—	30–40 S	130–140 W
20–30 S	90–100 E	—	—	—	—	—	—	40–50 S	130–140 W
10–20 S	0– 10 E	—	—	—	—	—	—	0–10 N	130–140 E
20–30 S	0– 10 E	—	—	—	—	—	—	10–20 N	130–140 E
30–40 S	0– 10 E	—	—	—	—	—	—	20–30 N	130–140 E

*Numbers of observations for the first nominal LCT for each square group are given in parentheses.

must travel a long over-ocean trajectory before reaching middle latitudes at all longitudes except about 50° to 70° W, where the Palmer Peninsula and South America may prevent deep heating. Here a summer maximum occurs similar to that observed in the Northern Hemisphere. This maximum, and other deviations from the winter-fall maxima in southern middle latitudes, may be an accidental result in a relatively small sample of observations.

In the trade-wind latitudes, between 10° and 30°, summer and fall are the preferred seasons for thunderstorm development in both hemispheres; north of the ITCZ thunderstorms are most frequent in the fall, as are tropical cyclones. In the southern trade-wind latitudes storms develop more often in summer for reasons that are not clear. As shown in Fig. 3.2, this summer maximum occurs mainly in areas adjacent to the continents and in Madagascar, all regions of high summer frequency of thunderstorms. The summer maximum region in the central Pacific lies on the equatorward side of the major band of cloudiness and high thunderstorm frequency. Perhaps large-scale lifting in this zone, which is most pronounced in summer, encourages release of potential instability in the tropical air, but the resulting thunderstorm maximum could hardly be deduced from first principles.

In deep tropical latitudes within 10° of the equator we find a surprisingly pronounced dominance of thunderstorm frequency from March through May. This dominance is especially strong in the eastern Pacific, the eastern Atlantic, and the Indian, the regions where sea temperatures are warmest. Newell (1979) has discussed the importance of this maximum in the Indian Ocean for the global energy budget. In these longitudes, moreover, satellite cloud photography indicates that during these months a secondary ITCZ tends to develop south of the equator, in addition to the pronounced one on the north.

d. Local Diurnal Variation

We have attempted to determine the local diurnal variation of ocean thunderstorms. Trent and Gathman (1972) presented evidence from the NRL sample that such storms are nocturnal. However, they examined only a small part of the data, and the data were for the occurrence of thunder and/or lightning. Observations of lightning alone show a nocturnal maximum because lightning can be seen at a much greater distance in darkness, especially if extensive thunderstorm-produced cirrus cloud layers are present to act as reflectors and if the background light level is low, as it is at sea.

In the NRL sample a separate count was made of only those observations in which synoptic-code *ww* values 91–99 were used. These codes imply precipitation at the station at the time of observation and thunder at the time of observation or within the hour before. Thus in this subset all reports of lightning alone, and some of thunder, were excluded. Two obvious difficulties remained. The frequencies were much lower after exclusion. Further, in a given 10° square, observations were made at only four local civil times (LCT's), if we attribute all observation locations in a square to its center position and all observing times to the conventional GMT's. The latter device is almost certainly sound, and the former seems unavoidable, although not ideal.

Data from all open-ocean squares were merged according to the nominal LCT of the square. Squares that impinged on continents or large islands were excluded since the diurnal variation might reflect the late-afternoon or other maximum characteristic of coastal regions. The latitude and longitude boundaries for each square in each of the nine square groups, with the first nominal LCT after midnight, are listed in Table 3.1. The raw percentage frequencies for each of the 36 nominal LCT's are given in Fig. 3.3. The wide scatter,

Table 3.1. Continued

Group 6 0340 (81,947)*		Group 7 0420 (91,876)*		Group 8 0500 (80,716)*		Group 9 0540 (38,628)*	
° Lat.	° Long.	° Lat.	° Long.	° Lat.	° Long.	° Lat.	° Long.
0– 10 N	30– 40 W	0– 10 N	60– 70 E	0– 10 S	70– 80 E	0– 10 S	80– 90 E
10–20 N	30– 40 W	10–20 N	60– 70 E	10–20 S	70– 80 E	10–20 S	80– 90 E
20–30 N	30– 40 W	0– 10 S	60– 70 E	20–30 S	70– 80 E	20–30 S	80– 90 E
30–40 N	30– 40 W	10–20 S	60– 70 E	30–40 N	10– 20 W	0– 10 S	0– 10 W
40–50 N	30– 40 W	20–30 S	60– 70 E	40–50 N	10– 20 W	10–20 S	0– 10 W
50–60 N	30– 40 W	0– 10 N	20– 30 W	50–60 N	10– 20 W	20–30 S	0– 10 W
30–40 S	30– 40 W	20–30 N	20– 30 W	0– 10 S	10– 20 W	30–40 S	0– 10 W
0– 10 N	120–130 W	30–40 N	20– 30 W	10–20 S	10– 20 W	0– 10 N	90–100 W
10–20 N	120–130 W	40–50 N	20– 30 W	20–30 S	10– 20 W	0– 10 S	90–100 W
20–30 N	120–130 W	50–60 N	20– 30 W	30–40 S	10– 20 W	10–20 S	90–100 W
0– 10 S	120–130 W	0– 10 S	20– 30 W	0– 10 N	100–110 W	40–50 S	90–100 W
10–20 S	120–130 W	10–20 S	20– 30 W	0– 10 S	100–110 W	0– 10 N	170–190 E
20–30 S	120–130 W	20–30 S	20– 30 W	10–20 S	100–110 W	10–20 N	170–190 E
30–40 S	120–130 W	30–40 S	20– 30 W	20–30 S	100–110 W	20–30 N	170–190 E
40–50 S	120–130 W	0– 10 N	110–120 W	30–40 S	100–110 W	30–40 N	170–190 E
0– 10 N	140–150 E	10–20 S	110–120 W	40–50 S	100–110 W	40–50 N	170–190 E
10–20 N	140–150 E	0– 10 S	110–120 W	0– 10 N	160–170 E	0– 10 S	170–190 E
20–30 N	140–150 E	10–20 S	110–120 W	10–20 N	160–170 E	10–20 S	170–190 E
—	—	20–30 S	110–120 W	20–30 N	160–170 E	20–30 S	170–190 E
—	—	30–40 S	110–120 W	30–40 N	160–170 E	—	—
—	—	40–50 S	110–120 W	40–50 N	160–170 E	—	—
—	—	0– 10 N	150–160 E	0– 10 S	160–170 E	—	—
—	—	10–20 N	150–160 E	10–20 S	160–170 E	—	—
—	—	20–30 N	150–160 E	20–30 S	160–170 E	—	—
—	—	30–40 N	150–160 E	30–40 S	160–170 E	—	—
—	—	40–50 N	150–160 E	—	—	—	—

which makes the result hard to interpret, is caused by the substantial variation in mean thunderstorm frequency among the various square groups (see Table 3.2). Note the especially anomalous high value in group 3 that reflects the large number of observations and high frequency of thunderstorms in the western North Atlantic. Table 3.3 lists mean percentage frequencies for each ocean area. The relatively high and low frequency in the North and South Atlantic, respectively, and the small number of observations in the southern oceans in the NRL sample are apparent.

To make the diurnal variation clearer, the frequency for each LCT for each square group was expressed as a percentage of the mean frequency for that group. These percentages are plotted on the graph in Fig. 3.3. Despite some remaining variability, probably caused by peculiarities of the data sample, frequencies are below average through the daylight hours. Above-average frequencies occur from about 1 h after mean sunset until about 1 h after sunrise. The broad maximum appears to peak at about 140% of average, 2 or 3 h after midnight. During the daytime frequencies are about 70% of average. The diurnal range is much smaller than that shown by Trent and Gathman (1972) because data for lightning unaccompanied by thunder are excluded from our sample.

Since land-breeze convergence effects near coasts are excluded, and since no diurnal process related to the microphysics of cloud electrification comes to mind, the most plausible explanation for the nocturnal maximum in open-ocean thunderstorms is long-wave radiative cooling of cumulus cloud tops during the night. Since such cooling cannot be appreciable through a deep layer of air above the

tops, the daytime minimum must result from a daytime capping of the cloud tops in deeply convective situations by an atmospheric layer only slightly stable for moist adiabatic processes (see Chap. 4). This inference is supported by the increase in frequency immediately after sunset, not long after the total radiative balance at the cloud tops presumably becomes negative.

e. Comparison of Oceanic and Coastal Thunderstorm Frequencies

World maps of thunderstorm frequency (e.g., WMO, 1956) indicate generally higher frequency over land than over sea. Almost all major centers in tropical latitudes are over land, and in middle latitudes the summer maximum over the continents is stronger than the winter maximum over the ocean.

Two explanations could account for differences between convection over continents and that over coastal regions, one based on the intensity of convection and the other on the idea that the mechanism of cloud electrification is less efficient over the ocean than it is over land. Although there is no unanimity about some important details, there is consensus (e.g., Mason, 1972) that the ice phase plays a crucial role in the electrification of almost all thunderstorms, although Moore et al. (1960) have provided some counterexamples (see Chap. 13). If the second explanation is accepted, one must argue that there is less ice in oceanic cumulus than there is in continental cumulus when other things are the same. The only evidence for this argument is the apparently greater precipitation efficiency of oceanic clouds attributable to a smaller density of condensation nu-

Table 3.2. Mean Percentage Frequencies of Thunderstorms for Square Groups

	Square Group								
	1	2	3	4	5	6	7	8	9
Mean pct. freq.*	0.067	0.062	0.156	0.090	0.086	0.086	0.078	0.071	0.081

*ww = 91–99.

Table 3.3. Mean Percentage Frequency of Thunderstorms and Number of Observations for Open-Ocean Areas

Ocean area	Mean pct. freq.*	No. of observations
North Atlantic	0.155	1,424,423
South Indian (20°–140° E)	0.117	6,831
Western South Pacific (140° E–170° W)	0.104	11,552
Western North Pacific (100°–180° E)	0.095	463,834
Eastern North Pacific (80°–180° W)	0.066	688,928
Eastern South Pacific (70°–170° W)	0.059	59,707
North Indian (30°–100° E)	0.059	13,598
South Atlantic (70° W–20° E)	0.022	63,757

*ww = 91–99.

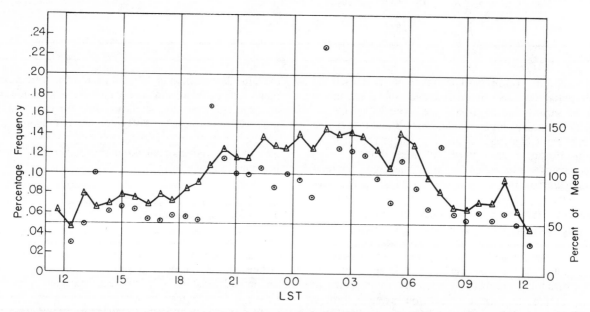

Figure 3.3. Local diurnal variation of frequency of thunderstorms from NRL data. Circled dots indicate raw values for the appropriate group of 10° squares. Dots enclosed in triangles represent percentages of diurnal average frequency for the appropriate square group.

clei and, therefore, larger cloud particles. Perhaps the residence time of a supercooled cloud droplet in an oceanic cumulus is too short to permit the extensive ice and graupel formation thought to be crucial to powerful electrification (see Chaps. 13 and 16). On the other hand, differences in convective intensity can be attributed to differences in the potential instability of an air mass, given the much faster response of land to the seasonal and diurnal variations in the surface radiation balance and different rates of transfer of heat (and moisture) to the overlying lower atmosphere.

Although we favor an explanation based on convective intensity (i.e., air more unstable over land), study of the change in thunderstorm frequency between locations on the shore or very close to it and on adjacent oceanic squares is indicated to assess cloud electrification as an explanation. If electrification efficiency is mainly responsible, then a drop in storm frequency should almost always occur between land and adjacent sea. This test is not conclusive since differences in surface heating at the coast can be large because of the sea breeze, for example. However, the sea-breeze circulation is shallow and probably plays a more important mechanical than thermodynamical role in convection. But the time scales of the explanations are different: the one for creation of potential instability is long compared with the one for individual cloud electrification.

To seek possible effects of cloud electrification, the WMO sample was examined for differences in annual average thunderstorm frequency between coastal and adjacent maritime locations (WMO, 1953, 1956). If the differences in percentage frequency, after averaging station-to-station variation over short distances, appeared to be less than 0.1, no significant difference was considered to exist. Results of this comparison appear in Fig. 3.4. Perhaps the most striking aspect of the comparison is the large extent of coast where no significant difference exists, both in the trade-wind belts and in the middle latitudes. This circumstance does not favor the cloud-electrification explanation.

Thunderstorm frequencies are decidedly lower over water than they are over land in extensive regions in the tropics: in Central America south of 15° N, along the east coast of South America from 10° N to 5° S, along the west coast of Africa over the same range of latitudes, on the east coast of that continent from the equator to 10° S, along the west coast of India, and on the central north coast of Australia. In all these regions, however, the prevailing wind is onshore during the season of high thunderstorm frequency over land, and it is tempting to attribute the increased activity to increased surface heating as the maritime tropical air comes ashore.

Near and poleward of 30° N the regions of increased frequency over land, along the Gulf Coast and southeast coast of the United States, and along the European coast from Portugal to Norway are likewise regions of onshore flow during the summer thunderstorm season.

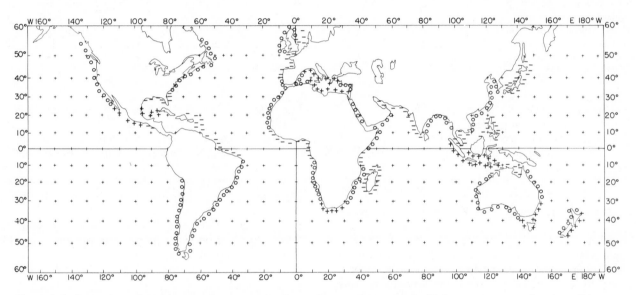

Figure 3.4. Comparison of thunderstorm frequency over the sea (in near-shore waters) with frequency at coastal stations. Zero indicates no significant difference; plus and minus indicate higher and lower frequency over the sea.

Mountainous islands within or outside the tropics have markedly increased thunderstorm frequencies: Japan, the Philippines, Madagascar, and the windward and leeward islands of the Caribbean. Enhanced surface heating and orographic lifting of the low-level air are major causes. The rugged Malay Peninsula behaves like a mountainous island, but the equally mountainous islands of Indonesia are an anomaly since coastal stations report significantly fewer thunderstorms than do ships offshore. This circumstance is hard to explain and may be attributable to Indonesian reporting practices.

An additional tropical anomaly is found along the coasts of Mexico between 15° and 25° N. Here thunderstorm frequency is lower at coastal stations than it is over the waters offshore. Reporting practice does not seem to be a factor,

however, because inland stations with frequencies higher than those offshore can easily be found.

Probably the strongest evidence for the convective explanation, however, is in the central Mediterranean, where thunderstorm frequencies are higher over the sea than they are on the coast. These storms, as pointed out earlier, appear to be associated with strong heating of early cold-season outbreaks of polar air over the relatively warm water. Other comparable regions where enhanced thunderstorm activity offshore appears to be attributable to oceanic heating are the coast of South Africa between 15° and 30° E, the southeast coast of Australia and Tasmania from 30° S, and perhaps the east coast of New Zealand (although here orographic descent of the westerlies may be an important factor).

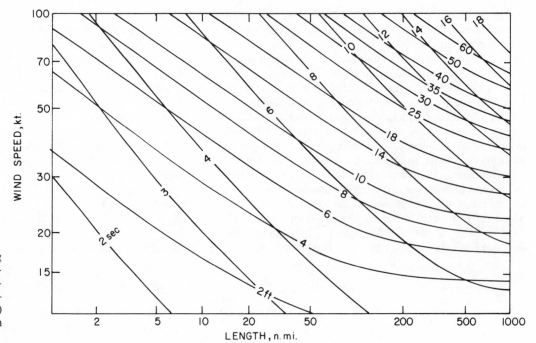

Figure 3.5. Forecasting curves showing wave periods and heights as a function of windspeed (ordinate) and fetch (abscissa) (modified from chart in Bretschneider, 1967).

On the whole, the evidence supports the idea that less frequent thunderstorm activity over the sea compared with frequency over land is attributable mainly to absence over sea of the intense potential instability produced over land by heating of an already warm, moist lower atmosphere.

3. Some Phenomenology in Marine Thundersqualls

Conditions produced by a squall line at sea are similar to those produced over land: high wind, lightning, whirlwinds (called waterspouts), and hail. In tropical seas waterspouts accompanying thunderstorms occur much more frequently than do tornadoes in thunderstorms on land. However, the average waterspout is weaker than are most reported tornadoes. Waves are an additional hazard of the sea squall; moving thunderstorms generate waves much higher than one would expect from a stationary storm of the same extent and windspeed. Lightning strikes the surface of the sea less frequently and usually less intensely than it strikes the ground in storms on land.

a. Wind Gusts

A common feature of thunderstorms is the leading gust front, usually associated with the storm downdraft; the highest wind gusts usually occur ahead of rapidly moving storms and are a threat to small boats. They are also a matter of utmost concern while sensitive cargoes such as liquefied natural gas are being loaded or transferred. In general, the downdraft in a thunderstorm at sea is smaller and weaker than that in the giant or supercell thunderstorms of the midwestern United States (see Chaps. 7–9). Thus the control-

ling or friction-free wind (at 100m) in thundersqualls at sea is weaker than that in extreme cases on land. However, the wind profile in the surface layer depends on the surface roughness. Thus the rougher the surface, the smaller the percentage of the 100-m wind that occurs at 5-to-10-m altitude. At sea, 30% to 50% of the 100-m wind occurs near the water surface, compared with values of only 10% to 25% over irregular land masses and urban areas. A 50-kn wind at 100 m results in a 15-to-25-kn wind over water and 5-to-13-kn wind on land (the peak surface gusts would be about 50 kn in both cases).

b. Waves in a Squall Line

Squalls carry high waves that move with the traveling field of winds. If an unwary forecaster were to glance at a typical squall line with its 15-to-30-mi width of high windspeeds, he might apply rules for large storm systems and forecast waves lower than those that are actually to occur. For example, a typical method used in computing wave heights and periods involves using two parameters: windspeed and fetch. A windspeed for the area in question is found by using surface maps and predicted changes in the weather pattern, and measuring the fetch, the distance over which these winds travel in an approximately straight line. Once the windspeed and fetch for the forecast period are determined, the Bretschneider chart (Fig. 3.5) is used to find the wave height and wave period. These winds are assumed to blow throughout the forecast period. Figure 3.5 shows a wave height of 4 ft and a period of 4 s for a wind of 20 kn over a fetch of 30 mi.

However, the waves in a moving squall line are much larger than are the waves observed from similar but station-

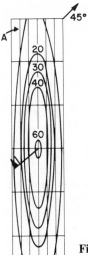

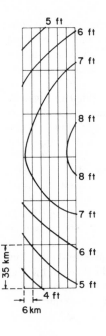

Figure 3.6. Model squall-line wind field. All winds are southwest winds. The pattern velocity is toward the northeast.

Figure 3.7. Approximate distribution of significant wave heights for the pattern in Fig. 3.6, moving northeast at 12.5 kn, the velocity that maximizes the waves at location *A* in Fig. 3.6. The wave pattern travels with the wind pattern.

ary wind fields implied in Fig. 3.5. One reason for this is the movement of the squall line. The total time history of the wave is the most important factor in wave forecasting. The wave must be watched as it moves along in order to develop an accurate wave forecast.

c. Wave Spectra in a Squall Line

Wave-spectrum calculations help the wave forecaster in a situation such as a squall line, where traditional forecasting methods do not accurately apply. A wave spectrum is a mathematical description of the distribution of the square of the wave height (wave energy) with frequency.

In concept, wave-spectrum forecasting is a simple process; each directional component of the total wave energy and frequency is computed separately, taking into account effects of wind, wave velocity, shoaling, and friction. The magnitudes of the directional components are developed and combined in a computer program to create a wave spectrum that describes the partial wave energy from each direction and the resultant wave height.

The significant wave is calculated by statistical methods from the wave spectrum and has been found to be nearly equal to the average height of the highest one-third of the waves; this corresponds closely to the wave height reported by an experienced ship officer or quartermaster. Where individual waves are observed during a time period characterized by 5-ft significant waves with 10-s periods, for example, one 8.5-ft wave occurs per hour, and four 7.5-ft waves occur per hour at any one observing point.

The computer program for wave spectrum developed by the Institute for Storm Research is based on physical concepts proposed by Pierson et al. (1966). The ISR program has been used with the model squall line wind field shown in Fig. 3.6 to compute wave spectra for a location at point *A*, for a range of pattern velocities. In this particular ex-

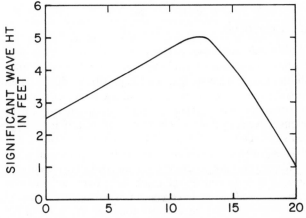

Figure 3.8. Significant wave heights at location *A* in Fig. 3.6, as a function of the speed of the wind pattern toward the northeast.

ample, with the forecast location (point *A*) in the upper-left corner of the wind field, the only directional fetches that affect the computation of the significant wave are from south-southeast to south-southwest. Although the model winds are uniformly from the southwest, the largest waves at point *A* come from the south-southwest. The velocity of the wind pattern toward the northeast influences the waves as indicated in Figs. 3.7 and 3.8. The highest waves at point *A* are produced in the model when the pattern velocity is about 12.5 kn, and the distribution of significant wave heights throughout the pattern in this case is shown in Fig. 3.7 (the 12.5-kn pattern speed, which produces the highest waves at point *A* is not the speed that generally maximizes the waves elsewhere). Note that the significant waves downwind from the maximum winds are up to 8 ft high. This means that a 12-ft wave is expected every 12 min and a 15-ft wave every hour. The eastward displacement of the wave maximum from the wind maximum means that for the assumed pattern velocity of 12.5 kn the waves outrun the winds and the largest waves would be encountered in advance of the strongest winds.

The mechanics of wave generation implicit in Figs. 3.7 and 3.8 involve magnification of wave heights by the moving wind field as a result of certain wave components remaining under the wind field for long periods of time. The wave period that receives maximum energy from the wind increases with the wind speed. The group velocity increases with the period. Therefore, the faster the wind, the faster the pattern velocity must be to magnify the waves most. That is, the pattern velocity for maximum magnification increases with windspeed, and, of course, the maximum waves also increase with windspeed.

Wave action during squalls is responsible for damage and loss of life during oil operations along the coast of the Gulf of Mexico. The surprising magnitude of the waves accompanying some storms causes damage and death during routine operations that could ordinarily be carried out safely during "normal" thunderstorms.

d. Waterspouts

Whirlwinds over water (waterspouts) extend from the water surface to a growing cumuliform cloud (for a more technical discussion of waterspouts, see Chap. 10). In the Northern Hemisphere most of these whirlwinds rotate cyclonically (counterclockwise). They generally occur in tropical regions in weak cyclonic circulations, particularly in the Florida Keys (Golden, 1974a, 1974b). Under anticyclonic conditions, subsidence inhibits waterspout development.

Waterspouts are generally less than 10 to 20 m in diameter, smaller than tornadoes, although large ones are occasionally observed. Most have condensation funnels, although the vortex may not be visible throughout the waterspout's length. The cloud and water droplets constituting the visible funnel are produced by adiabatic cooling and condensation as inward-spiraling moist air is drawn upward.

From the air a waterspout vortex first appears as a light-colored disk on the sea surface within a dark patch. The appearance of darkness is thought to be caused by the presence of capillary water waves, produced by the outer vortex flow; the light spot indicates a central reflective sea surface little disturbed by winds. Since the dark spots cannot be seen from the sea surface, the average lifetime of waterspouts is probably longer than generally reported, for instance, the 14.6 min for funnel events recorded at Key West, 1958–67.

The dark ring sometimes becomes a spiral as the waterspout develops. As tangential windspeeds exceed about 40 kn, a ring of sea spray forms near the spiral's epicenter and circulates helically upward. When the vortex is overtaken by a rain shower or even a downdraft of rain-cooled air, the vortex is disrupted and generally decays within 1 to 3 min.

Small waterspouts generally do little damage and reveal a bit of nature's intriguing response to the presence of warm,

moist, unstable air. However, strong ones, like tornadoes on land, can be destructive, and they occasionally move ashore.

4. Case Studies

a. A Thunderstorm System in the Atlantic Ocean

On the evening and night of 21–22 June 1970, a series of severe thunderstorms that had developed earlier just inland over New Jersey and Chesapeake Bay moved rapidly eastward to encounter a fleet of sailing yachts participating in the biennial race from Newport, R.I., to Bermuda (Sanders, 1972). The general surface analysis for 0000 GMT, 22 June, is shown in Fig. 3.9. To judge from the patterns of sea-level isobars and mean isotherms for the layer from 1,000 mb to 500 mb (represented by the thickness lines for that layer), a weak synoptic-scale lift was present, caused by warm advection over the position of the fleet, just north of the Gulf Stream. One line of thunderstorms swept through the fleet about 1 h before this time, and another struck about 9 h later (for detailed discussion of thunderstorms in the synoptic setting see Chap. 5).

Details of the passage, as reported by competing craft, appear in Figs. 3.10 and 3.11, affording a unique mesoscale view of the structure of these systems. Several boats were dismasted by the squalls and the accompanying high waves. Many crew members commented on the severity of the lightning, although only slight damage resulted from strikes. Detailed surface analyses are given in Fig. 3.12, and mesoscale analyses of sea-level pressure, superposed on the scope photography from Atlantic City radar (ACY), are shown in Fig. 3.13. The storms moved from the coast to the position of the fleet at speeds greater than 50 kn and lost little intensity, though they passed over sea surface temperatures insufficiently warm to provide destabilization directly to the systems. They were able to maintain great intensity some 200 mi offshore from the instability provided over land.

Systems of this sort, in addition to thunderstorms developing over the Gulf Stream, produce the large thunderstorm frequencies in the western North Atlantic, as shown in Fig. 3.1 and discussed in Sec. 2 above. While damaging to small craft, as we have seen, such systems are not generally damaging to large ships; these suffer more from waves driven by strong sustained winds.

b. A Squall Line in the Gulf of Mexico

Offshore operations sensitive to high waves take place off all coasts of North America. Many operations (e.g., diving, anchor adjustment, and delicate construction) require that wave heights be less than 5 ft during the whole operation, since higher waves expose personnel to hazards such as the danger of being washed overboard. Therefore, careful monitoring of conditions leading to squall-line formation is vital to the safety of offshore operations. For such monitoring, the forecaster can use surface weather observations, weather-radar summaries, and satellite pictures. Use of

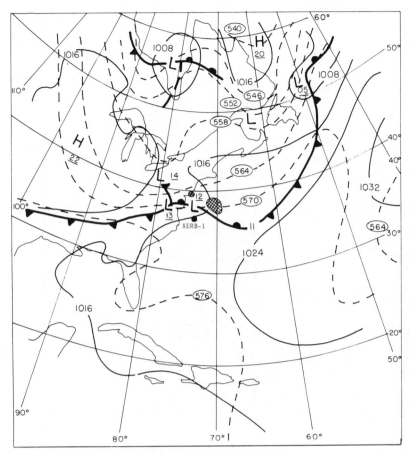

Figure 3.9. Analyses produced at the U.S. National Meteorological Center for 0000 GMT on 22 June 1970. Solid lines are sea-level isobars at intervals of 8 mb, and dashed lines are isopleths of thickness of the layer from 1,000 to 500 mb, at intervals of 60 m. The hatched area represents the approximate position of the racing fleet. The circled × represents Atlantic City (ACY).

these is discussed below for a squall line in the Gulf of Mexico on 7 January 1979.

In the surface analyses shown in Fig. 3.14, the thin solid lines are isobars at intervals of 4 mb, and the isopleths enclosing the squall line on the 0600 GMT chart indicate deduced windspeeds in knots. The prefrontal squall line began forming just before 0500 GMT on 7 January 1979 (2300 CST, 6 January) off the Louisiana coast with a low cell centered in central Louisiana and an associated cold front extending S-SW to just south of Brownsville, Tex.

Since reports of weather from Gulf waters are sparse, radar and satellite data are vital for preparing advisories to offshore workers. Figure 3.15 shows a series of plotted radar summaries taken from the Gulf Coast region. The squall line was first identified just south of Louisiana in the radar reports of 0535 GMT. The squall line continued to move through the Gulf of Mexico ahead of the cold front during the next 2 h.

Figure 3.16 is a series of infrared satellite pictures taken from 0532 to 1631 on 7 January 1979, corresponding to the surface maps and radar summary charts. The infrared picture contrasts temperature differences. The higher clouds and cloud tops are colder. The greater the number of differing shades in the photograph, the colder and higher are the cloud tops within the center. The satellite data show the main shower activity in the southeast quadrant of the low-

pressure area. The heaviest activity, identified by the light-gray areas that are within the large dark regions, coincides with the location of the squall line most clearly identified by radar (use of satellite data for thunderstorm analysis is discussed in Vol. 3, Chap. 12).

Wind velocity and wave height after 0500 GMT began to increase rapidly as the low cell slowly deepened with northwesterly flow behind the front and southeasterly flow ahead of it. Even as early as 0300 GMT, as expected from earlier weather charts (not shown), offshore oil rigs in the Ship Shoal region of the Gulf of Mexico began to encounter rough seas and heavy rain. During normal conditions offshore rigs with jack-up capability operate a few feet above the water level. In rough seas rigs are usually raised to a level at which they are relatively unaffected by waves. At 0500 GMT the crew of a rig at Ship Shoal Block 120 was forced to cancel operations and jack up to 9 ft above average sea level. One rig in this location received extensive damage in the squall line. At 1145 GMT work was still held up pending good weather. In the South Pelto region a moving rig began to experience high winds and 6-ft seas at 0700 GMT and had to be stabilized back onto the bottom. Around that time 7- to 10-ft seas were reported in the East Cameron, Vermillion, Eugene Island, and Ship Shoal regions of the Gulf of Mexico (see Fig. 3.14).

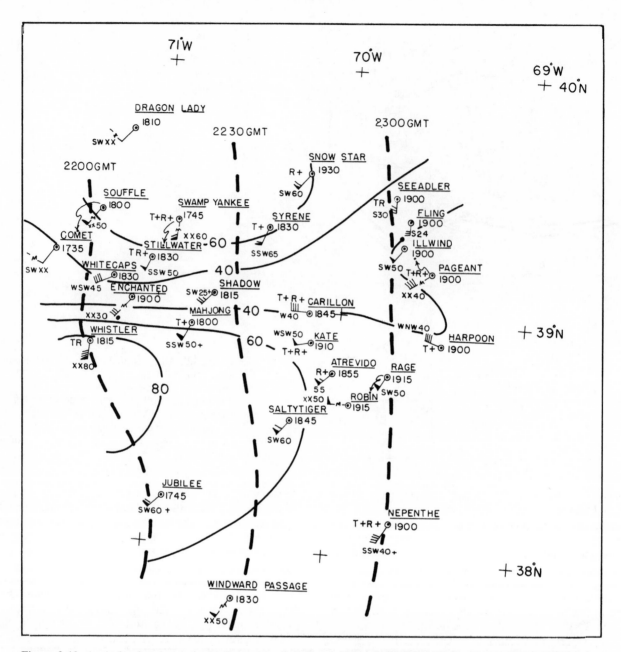

Figure 3.10. Analysis of peak gust in the first series of squalls on 21 June 1970. Solid lines are isotachs at intervals of 20 kn. Dashed lines are isochrones of the peak gust at intervals of 30 min. Yachts are identified by name. Peak velocities reported by yachts are plotted in the conventional manner. The reported time of squall (EDT) is at right of the station circle representing position of yacht. Reports of thunder (*T*) or rain (*R*) (+ indicating heavy intensity) from each yacht are plotted left of the station circle.

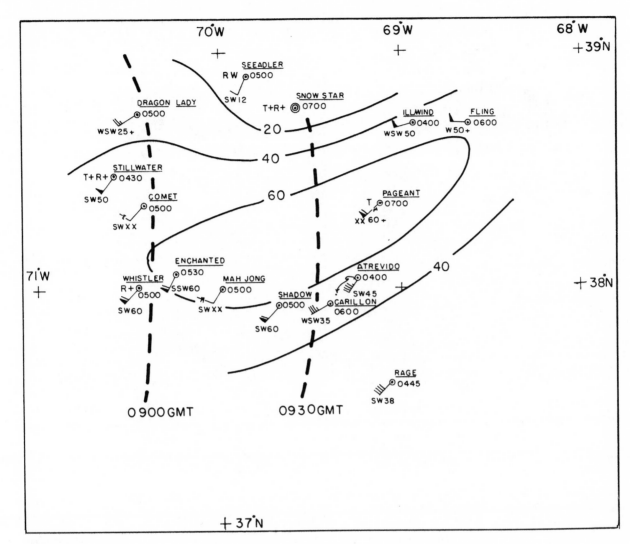

Figure 3.11. Analysis of peak gust in the second series of squalls on 22 June. See legend below Fig. 3.10 for explanation of symbols and letters.

53

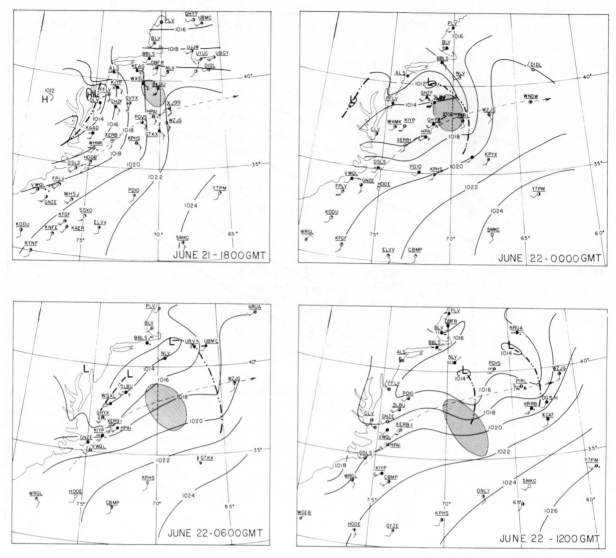

Figure 3.12. Surface analyses of the west-central Atlantic Ocean, 21–22 June 1970. Solid lines are isobars, labeled in millibars. Dash-dot lines represent the leading edges of squall lines. The thin dashed line is the mean June position of maximum current in the Gulf Stream. Ships are identified by radio call sign; winds and present and past weather are plotted in the conventional manner. The hatched area represents the approximate position of the racing fleet.

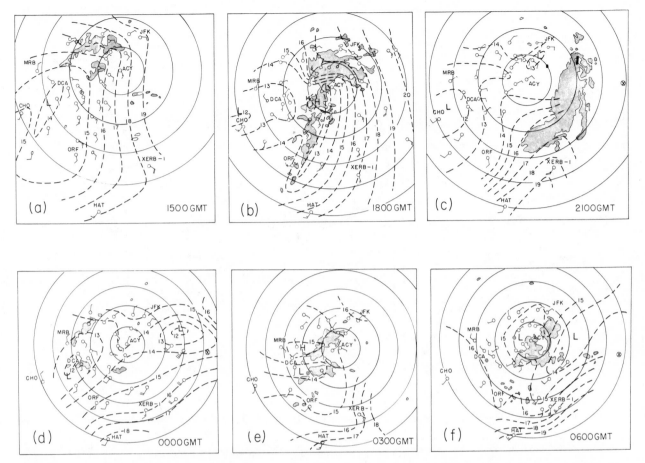

Figure 3.13. Mesoanalyses of sea-level pressure at 3-h intervals, 21–22 June 1970, superimposed on echoes observed by the WSR-57 radar at Atlantic City (ACY). The radar photograph nearest the nominal time of the 3-h surface observations is used. Circles indicate range at intervals of 50 mi. Dashed lines are sea-level isobars at intervals of 1 mb. Locations for orientation are J. F. Kennedy Airport, New York City (JFK); XERB-1 buoy; Martinsburg, W. Va. (MRB); and Washington National Airport, Washington, D.C. (DCA). The circled ×'s show the approximate centroid positions of yachts reporting squalls.

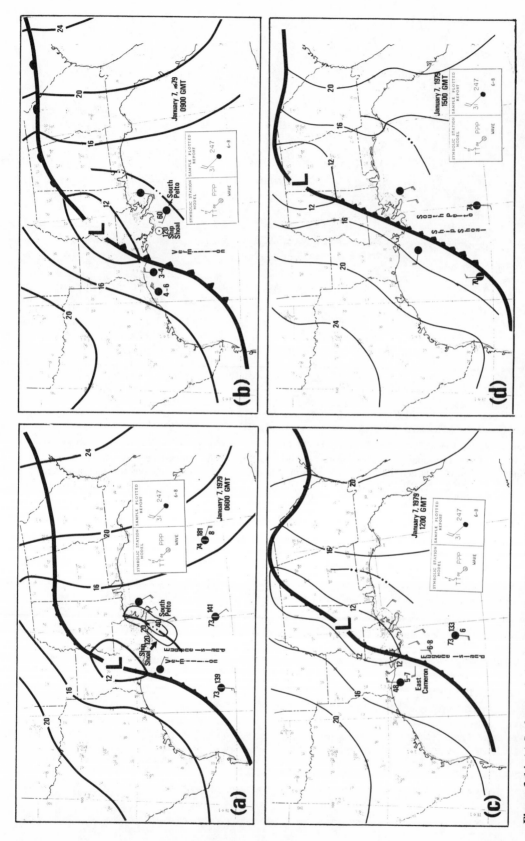

Figure 3.14. (a) Surface analysis of weather conditions for 7 January 1979, at midnight CST (0600 GMT). The squall line (—·—·—·—) precedes the cold front by more than 100 nmi. Estimated isotachs based on radar-echo speeds are included near the squall line. (b) Surface analysis for 3 h later (0300 CST, 7 January 1979). The squall line has advanced in an easterly direction. (c) Surface analysis for 0600 CST. Offshore reports indicate seas up to 8 ft. (d) Surface analysis for 0900 CST. As the low cell over northern Alabama moves northeast away from the coast, the squall line advances eastward more rapidly.

56

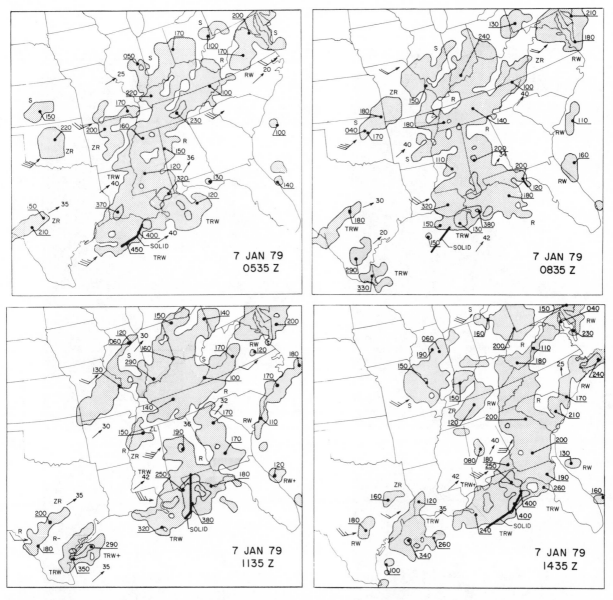

Figure 3.15. Weather-radar summary charts at 3-h intervals from 2335 CST (0535Z), 6 January 1979, to 0835 CST (1435Z), 7 January 1979. Shaded areas are regions of stronger intensity; echoes are moving northeast at about 40 kn.

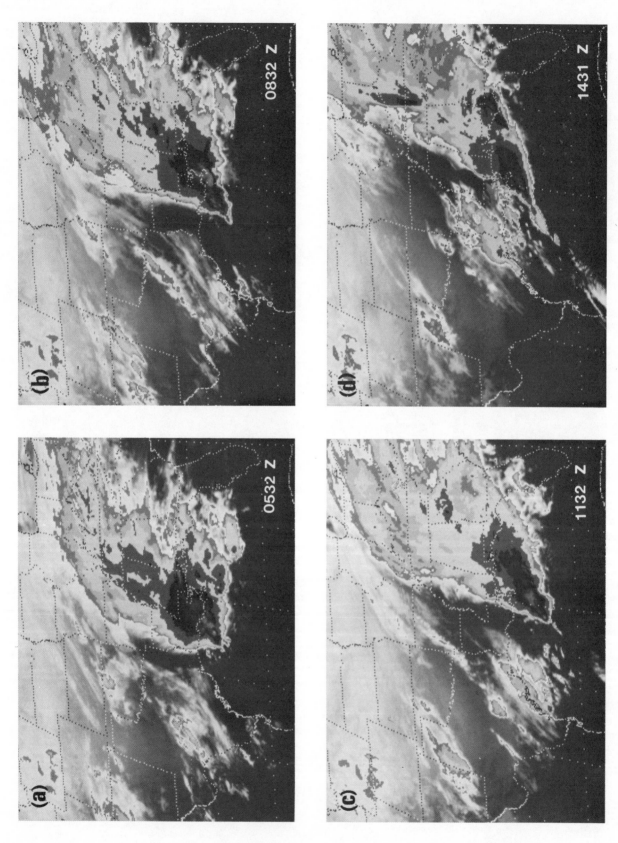

Figure 3.16. Infrared satellite photographs of the frontal activity as it passes eastward across the Gulf Coast. The most intense parts of the storm are the lightest-gray areas.

4. Basic Thunderstorm Energetics and Thermodynamics

Grant L. Darkow

1. Introduction

The thunderstorm or cumulonimbus is the ultimate growth stage in the cumulus-cloud family. Cumulus clouds, beginning with fair-weather cumulus, are the visual products of natural convection, i.e., air currents of rising warm air, predominantly vertical. By fairly localized vertical air currents the atmosphere redistributes its mass and energy within the convectively overturning layer to achieve a more stable density stratification.

Insight into the energetics of the massive and complex cumulonimbus-cloud system can be gained by first considering processes leading to the formation and development of the smaller and simpler convective cloud, the fair-weather cumulus. Considerable cumulus activity is closely tied to the diurnal cycle of solar heating. Solar radiational energy is absorbed at the Earth-atmosphere interface and converted to other energy forms. A portion of the absorbed solar energy is transferred to the air in contact with the ground in the form of sensible (measurable with a thermometer) heat energy. This addition of sensible heat energy to the lower layers of the atmosphere causes the familiar increase in surface temperatures from shortly after sunrise through early afternoon on a sunny day.

A less obvious but equally significant energy input into the lower atmosphere occurs simultaneously at the Earth-atmosphere interface when a portion of the absorbed solar energy is used to convert liquid water to water vapor. During the phase change of 1 gram of liquid water to water vapor, approximately 2,500 joules or 600 calories of heat energy are absorbed into the vapor phase. This energy of vaporization is also called the latent heat energy of the air, a term particularly appropriate here since it is not detectable by ordinary thermometry but may be converted to sensible heat at some later time and place. The conversion of latent energy to sensible heat takes place when the water vapor condenses into liquid cloud droplets. This energy-conversion process, the realization of the latent heat, plays a critical role in the development of convective clouds.

Masses or parcels of this heated and moisture-enriched air near the surface that become slightly less dense than the surrounding air begin to ascend as buoyant bubbles or plumes. The ascent of the air by Archimedean buoyancy in-

troduces other energy forms and energy-conversion processes. Increasing elevation is associated with an increase in geopotential energy. Movement introduces a component of kinetic energy to the air's total-energy content. These energy changes result from conversions from other energy forms and work done on the parcel by its environment. The complexities and consequences of the variety of possible energy transformations to the process of convective-cloud initiation and development are best approached by examining mathematical expressions of the principle of energy conservation.

2. Total Energy and Its Conservation

The total energy, E_T, of a unit mass of air may be expressed as

$$E_T = c_p T + gz + Lq + \frac{V^2}{2}, \qquad (4.1)$$

the sum of specific enthalpy, or heat energy processed at constant pressure; geopotential energy, or energy associated with elevation; latent energy explained in Sec. 1, and kinetic energy, or energy of motion. In Eq. 4.1, c_p is the specific heat of air at constant pressure; T the absolute, or kelvin, temperature; g the gravitational acceleration; z the height of the parcel above some reference-datum plane such as sea level; L the latent heat; q the specific humidity, or mass of water vapor per unit mass of moist air; and V the scalar velocity of the unit mass of air.

Our air parcel may move to different altitudes, and the pressure, airspeed, and vapor content may change, but in the absence of frictional forces, exchanges of mass with its surroundings, and other outside influences, the total energy remains unchanged along the air parcel trajectory. In many practical cases we can write $q = q_s$ to refer to a saturated condition that is maintained as condensation or evaporation proceeds (see Betts, 1974, for discussion of factors neglected by this approach).

3. Static Energy

The first three energy terms ($c_p T + gz + Lq$) in the total-energy expression, Eq. 4.1, have been called *static energy*, E_s, by Krietzberg (1964), *moist static energy* by Betts

(1975), *total heat content* by Riehl and Malkus (1958), and the *sigma function* by Kiefer (1941). The kinetic-energy term, $V^2/2$, is less than 0.5 J g^{-1} for speeds less than 30 m s^{-1}. The sum of the other three terms is of the order of 300 to 400 J g^{-1} within the troposphere. The contribution of the kinetic energy to the total energy content may be ignored without introducing an error of more than a few tenths of a percent. In fact, the uncertainty introduced into the determination of total energy content of an air sample in the real atmosphere by the acknowledged uncertainties in measurement of air temperature, height, and water-vapor content are greater than that contributed by entirely neglecting the kinetic-energy term. Thus to good approximation,

$$E_T \cong E_S = c_p T + gz + Lq, \qquad (4.2)$$

or, in differential form,

$$\frac{dE_T}{dt} \cong \frac{dE_s}{dt} \cong \frac{d}{dt}(c_p T + gz + Lq) = 0, \quad (4.2a)$$

and upon integration along the parcel trajectory,

$$E_s = (c_p T + gz + Lq) = \text{const.} \qquad (4.2b)$$

Although the contribution of kinetic energy to the total energy content is neglected at this point, to facilitate analysis of the major energy transformations, the kinetic energy of cloud air and its environment plays a critical role in the convective process. The kinetic-energy distribution within the cloud influences the rate of precipitation growth, the deposition of precipitation, the generation of vortex motion, etc. The kinetic energy of the cloud environment and its vertical variations influence the form of convective clouds, their speed and direction of travel, and the formation, intensity, and direction of motion of thunderstorm downdrafts and associated surface winds.

4. Parcel Process Temperature Lapse Rates

As mentioned in Sec. 1 above, the initiation and continued vertical ascent of convective elements depend mainly on the parcel remaining less dense than its environment. Air density depends on temperature, pressure, and water-vapor content of the air. The pressure of an ascending air parcel adjusts to very nearly equal environmental pressure. The density deficit between the parcel and its environment at any particular level is therefore directly proportional to how much warmer and more moist the parcel is than its immediate environment. Since water vapor is lighter than air, it makes moist air slightly less dense than completely dry air at the same pressure and temperature. The water vapor contribution to decreased density, though small, is important in the convective process, where small density differences yield important vertical accelerations. This effect is discussed in more detail below, but let us first examine the factors that contribute to the maintenance of temperature differences between the parcel and its environment. The temperature difference between the parcel and its environment and its

variation with height depend on two independent factors. One factor, the manner in which the environmental temperature varies with height, is dependent on the past history of the air at various levels, and over any one point can be known precisely only through measuring the vertical temperature profile or sounding. The other factor is the manner in which the parcel changes its temperature with changes of elevation and pressure.

In contrast to the variation of environmental temperature with height, the changes of the ascending parcel temperature with height are restrained by the conservation of energy expressed in Eq. 4.2b. We refer to these temperature changes as *process temperature changes*.

Let us first consider an unsaturated parcel of air that is not exchanging mass or energy with its environment. The process is then an *unsaturated adiabatic process*.

a. The Unsaturated Adiabatic Process Lapse Rate

If the parcel is initially unsaturated and remains in an unsaturated state, the water vapor mass content of the moist air or specific humidity, q, remains constant. For these conditions Eq. 4.2b reduces to

$$(c_p T + gz) \cong \text{const.} \qquad (4.3)$$

The sum of specific enthalpy and geopotential energy remains constant. An increase of height and potential energy, gz, is associated with a like decrease in specific enthalpy, $c_p T$. Differentiation of Eq. 4.3 with respect to height, z, yields

$$\left(\frac{dT}{dz}\right)_{\text{unsat}} \cong -\frac{g}{c_p}. \qquad (4.4)$$

Both g and c_p may be considered constant. The appropriate specific heat is that of moist air containing q grams of vapor per gram of moist air. Specific-humidity values in the atmosphere are observed to be consistently less than 2.5×10^{-2}. The specific heat at constant pressure of moist air, c_{p_m}, may be expressed in terms of the specific heat of completely dry air, c_{p_d}, and the specific humidity, q, as

$$c_{p_m} = c_{p_d}(1 + 0.81q). \qquad (4.5)$$

For q of the order of 2.5×10^{-2} or less,

$$c_{p_m} \cong c_{p_d} = 1.00 \text{ J g}^{-1} \text{ K}^{-1}. \qquad (4.6)$$

The approximation is accurate to 98% or better. In all subsequent developments the effect of water vapor on the specific heat of the air will be neglected, and c_p will be interpreted to be the specific heat at constant pressure of dry air. Similarly, the contribution of the mass of the water vapor to the total mass of the moist air will be neglected, and the small difference between the gas constant for dry air and that for moist air will be neglected.

For $g = 9.8 \times 10^2$ cm s^{-2} and $c_p = 1.00$ J g^{-1}K^{-1}, the unsaturated adiabatic process temperature change is -9.8 K km^{-1}. The temperature of unsaturated air decreases at this rate during ascent and increases at the same rate during descent regardless of its initial temperature and height. The unsaturated adiabatic process temperature lapse rate (or the dry adiabatic lapse rate) is

$$\Gamma_d = -\left(\frac{dT}{dz}\right)_{\text{unsat.}} = \frac{g}{c_p}.$$

An air parcel undergoing such a process is shown in Fig. 4.1.

b. Potential Temperature

It is also convenient to divide the sum of the specific enthalpy and geopotential by c_p to yield a quantity, θ_G, with the units of temperature so that

$$\theta_G = T + \frac{g}{c_p} z. \qquad (4.7)$$

This temperature may be called the *geopotential temperature* of air. Physically it represents the temperature that an air sample at arbitrary initial values of temperature T and height Z would achieve after unsaturated adiabatic descent to $z = 0$. Note the θ_G is uniquely determined by the initial values of T and z and is conserved for unsaturated adiabatic ascent and descent. The unsaturated adiabatic process curves on a T versus z diagram are therefore isolines of θ_G and may be so labeled. The graphical representation of θ_G is shown in Fig. 4.1.

Although the definition above, couched in a framework of energy concepts, is acceptable and conceptually convenient, a more rigorously conservative property, the potential temperature, θ, is widely used in meteorology because of the importance of pressure as a meteorological coordinate:

$$\theta = T\left(\frac{1,000}{p}\right)^{R/c_p},$$

where R is the gas constant for dry air. Physically θ is the temperature a sample of air would have if brought to a pressure of 1,000 mb during an unsaturated adiabatic process.

c. The Saturated Adiabatic Process Lapse Rate

Ascending air that is initially unsaturated cools until its specific humidity represents a saturated condition. The height at which this first occurs is the adiabatic or lifting condensation level. Any additional cooling tends to produce supersaturation within the parcel. However, observations in both the free atmosphere and the laboratory show that practically all water vapor in excess of that required for saturation immediately condenses into liquid cloud droplets. Although the mass of water vapor condensing is extremely small compared with the total mass of the moist air, the latent energy of condensation released to the air as sensible heat is significantly large. The cooling rate of ascending saturated air is slower than the unsaturated adiabatic rate in proportion to the rate of condensation.

The temperature changes experienced by a saturated parcel undergoing adiabatic expansion and remaining in a saturated state are governed by the conservation of total energy. From Eq. 4.2b under saturated conditions, $q = q_s$, we have

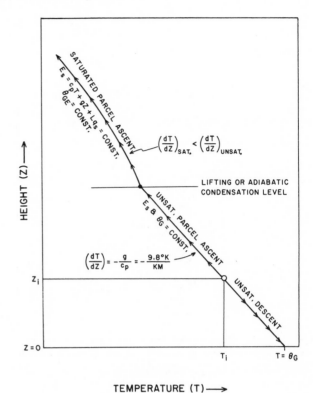

Figure 4.1. Parcel of air undergoing unsaturated adiabatic ascent and descent from initial conditions of T_i and z_i. Above the lifting condensation level the parcel is saturated and follows a saturated adiabatic process temperature lapse rate. $\theta_G = T_i + (g/c_p) z_i$.

$c_pT + gz + Lq_s = $ const. Differentiation with respect to height yields

$$c_p\left(\frac{dT}{dz}\right)_{\text{sat.}} + g + \frac{d}{dz}(Lq_s) = 0. \qquad (4.9)$$

Since $d/dz\,(Lq_s) = d/dT\,(Lq_s)\,(dT/dz)_{\text{sat.}}$, Eq. 4.8 yields

$$(dT/dz)_{\text{sat.}} = \frac{-\dfrac{g}{c_p}}{\left[1 + \dfrac{1}{c_p}\dfrac{d(Lq_s)}{dT}\right]} = \frac{(dT/dz)_{\text{unsat.}}}{\left[1 + \dfrac{1}{c_p}\dfrac{d(Lq_s)}{dT}\right]}. \qquad (4.9)$$

Although L decreases slightly with increasing temperatures, q_s increases exponentially with increasing temperature in such a way that the term

$$\frac{1}{c_p}\frac{d(Lq_s)}{dT}$$

is always positive. This term can assume values approaching 2 at the high temperatures, pressures, and specific-humidity values occasionally encountered near the Earth's surface, but it diminishes to negligibly small values at the very low temperatures found in the upper troposphere.

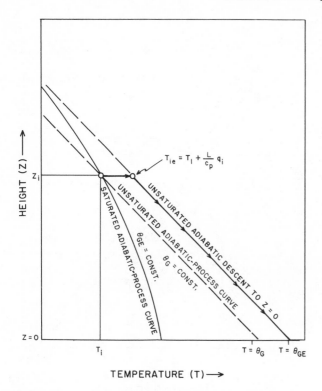

Figure 4.2. Schematic representation of the determination of equivalent geopotential temperature, θ_{GE}, for a parcel with arbitrary initial conditions of T_i, z_i, $q_i \cdot \theta_{GE} = \theta_G + (L/cp) \, q_i$.

Thus the saturated adiabatic process lapse rate varies from approximately one-third of the unsaturated lapse rate, or roughly 3 K km^{-1}, to an upper limit of 9.8 K km^{-1} within the normal range of atmospheric conditions. A typical value associated with conditions found at the base of fair-weather cumulus in tropical air is about 5 K km^{-1}, or one-half the unsaturated adiabatic lapse rate. With the onset of condensation at the lifting or adiabatic condensation level the process lapse rate of an ascending parcel is substantially reduced, and the reduction is highly dependent on the moisture content of the air at that level.

A parcel undergoing a saturated process during ascent above its lifting condensation level is shown in Fig. 4.1. A parcel undergoing descent and remaining saturated because of evaporation of liquid cloud droplets within the parcel also follows this process curve and becomes warmer at the saturated adiabatic process rate until all of its liquid content has evaporated. Subsequent descent and warming then proceeds at the unsaturated adiabatic rate. A descending saturated parcel maintained in a state of saturation because of evaporation of rain passing through the parcel also warms at essentially the saturated adiabatic rate. The sensible heat and water mass introduced into the parcel by the falling rain makes the process nonadiabatic (diabatic), but the related corrections are small and may be neglected in most practical applications. Evaporation of rain accounts for the

cold-air outflow associated with precipitation shafts or rain areas of many storms.

During the saturated adiabatic process the static energy of a parcel remains constant during changes of temperature, height, and water-vapor content. During the unsaturated adiabatic process the static energy of a parcel is also constant since $(d/dt)(Lq) = 0$. Thus static energy is conserved during both the unsaturated and the saturated adiabatic processes and serves as an excellent tracer of any particular sample of air.

d. Equivalent Geopotential Temperature

Division of the static energy by c_p yields a quantity with units of temperature. This quantity may be defined as the equivalent geopotential temperature of the air, θ_{GE}, which differs from the more commonly used pseudoequivalent potential temperature, θ_{se}, in two respects. In θ_{GE} the latent heat is added to the parcel during an isobaric process to yield an isobaric equivalent temperature, while in θ_{se} it is added to the parcel during saturated adiabatic expansion to zero pressure; in θ_{GE} the unsaturated adiabatic compression proceeds to the sea-level reference instead of to a reference pressure of 1,000 mb:

$$\theta_{GE} = \frac{E_s}{c_p} = T + \frac{q}{c_p} z + \frac{Lq}{c_p}. \qquad (4.10)$$

This equivalent geopotential temperature may be viewed as the temperature a sample of air initially at T, z, and q would have after conversion of its latent heat content (Lq) to sensible heat followed by unsaturated adiabatic descent to $z = 0$. Note that since $c_p \cong 1.00$ J g^{-1} K^{-1}, the numerical value of θ_{GE} in K equals the value of static energy in J g^{-1}. Equivalent geopotential temperature, like static energy, is conserved during the saturated adiabatic process. The saturated adiabatic process curves on a T versus z diagram are therefore also isolines of equivalent geopotential temperature and may be so labeled. Graphical determination of θ_{GE} is shown in Fig. 4.2.

During an unsaturated adiabatic process the mass of water vapor in the parcel is constant, and if the small variation of L with temperature is neglected, $(d/dT)(Lq) = 0$. Thus during both unsaturated and saturated stages the static energy, E_s, and the θ_{GE} are useful tracers of convective elements during their lifetimes.

5. Atmospheric Layer Stability

The susceptibility of a layer of air to convective overturning is largely a function of its density stratification. Before an examination of the probability of convective overturning, it is helpful to consider the conditions within a layer of air in static equilibrium with respect to the vertical.

a. Hydrostatic Equilibrium and the Hydrostatic Equation

In accordance with conservation of momentum, the vertical

acceleration of a unit mass of air is the sum of vertical-force components per unit mass acting on the air. For air in static equilibrium the vertical forces are the downward-directed force of gravity and the induced, vertically directed equal and opposite force with which we identify the decrease of air pressure with height:

$$\frac{1}{\rho} \frac{\partial P_h}{\partial z} = -g. \qquad (4.11)$$

In other words, Eq. 4.11 expresses a balance between downward-acting gravity and an upward-acting net pressure force that is equal to the weight of air within a vertical increment.

This relationship, when multiplied by ρ, becomes the hydrostatic equation. The notation P_h is used at this point to indicate the special condition of hydrostatic equilibrium. Integration of the hydrostatic equation from an arbitrary level z to the top of the atmosphere where $z = \infty$ and $P = 0$ yields the defining expression for hydrostatic pressure

$$P_h = g \int_z^{\infty} \rho \partial z. \qquad (4.11a)$$

Hydrostatic pressure at any level is therefore the weight of the entire air mass in a column of unit cross section above that level (variations of gravitational acceleration, g, with height are neglected in most meteorological applications; equation 4.11 can be derived from Eq. 4.11a, which can be used as the defining equation). Although departures from hydrostatic pressure are a necessary condition for vertical accelerations and convection, the departures of actual or total atmospheric pressure, P_T, in the atmosphere from hydrostatic pressure, P_h, are quite small even in the presence of significant vertical accelerations. The validity of this statement can be seen by considering orders of magnitude of terms in the vertical equation of motion for an inviscid fluid not in hydrostatic equilibrium:

$$\frac{dw}{dt} = -\frac{1}{\rho} \frac{\partial p}{\partial z} - g. \qquad (4.12)$$

For a parcel accelerating vertically from a velocity of 0 to 5 m s^{-1} in 1 km, $(dw/dt) \sim 10^{-2}$ m s^{-2}. Gravitational acceleration is of the order 10 m s^{-2}. Thus even for this very significant vertical acceleration the pressure gradient force term differs from the hydrostatic value, which by definition equals g, by only one part in a thousand, or 0.1%. This represents a departure of actual pressure from hydrostatic pressure of less than 1 mb (in tornadoes there is evidence that dw/dt may be of the same order as g in the surface layer; see Chap. 10).

An important utility of the hydrostatic equation for close approximation of pressure and pressure gradients in the real atmosphere stems from this condition of near hydrostatic balance in the atmosphere at nearly all times.

b. Nonhydrostatic Pressure Effects in Convection

In studies dealing with convection, the hydrostatic approx-

imation must be applied with care. Although departures from hydrostatic pressure are indeed very small, these small departures are entirely responsible for all vertical accelerations and vertical motion.

Total pressure, P_T, is the sum of the hydrostatic pressure, P_h, and some nonhydrostatic component, π, as follows:

$$P_T = P_h + \pi. \qquad (4.13)$$

Partial differentiation of Eq. 4.13 with respect to height z and division by $-\rho$ yields

$$-\frac{1}{\rho} \frac{\partial P_T}{\partial z} = -\frac{1}{\rho} \frac{\partial P_h}{\partial z} - \frac{1}{\rho} \frac{\partial \pi}{\partial z}. \qquad (4.13a)$$

The vertical component of the actual or total pressure gradient force is always expressible as the sum of the hydrostatic pressure gradient force plus the nonhydrostatic pressure gradient force. Substitution of Eq. 4.13a into the vertical component of the equation of motion yields

$$\frac{dw}{dt} = -\frac{1}{\rho} \frac{\partial P_h}{\partial z} - \frac{1}{\rho} \frac{\partial \pi}{\partial z} - g, \qquad (4.14)$$

but since, by definition,

$$-\frac{1}{p} \frac{\partial P_h}{\partial z} = g,$$

Eq. 4.14 reduces to

$$\frac{dw}{dt} = -\frac{1}{\rho} \frac{\partial \pi}{\partial z}. \qquad (4.15)$$

The vertical accelerations in an inviscid fluid are entirely caused by the vertical gradients of nonhydrostatic pressure. Equation 4.15 is in every respect equivalent to Eq. 4.12.

c. Vertical Accelerations of a Nonentraining Parcel

Consider a parcel of air of density ρ embedded in an environmental fluid of density ρ_e. Assume that the environmental air is in hydrostatic equilibrium. For the parcel the vertical equation of motion for an inviscid fluid is

$$\frac{dw}{dt} = -\frac{1}{\rho} \frac{\partial P}{\partial z} - g. \qquad (4.16)$$

In the environment the vertical equation of motion reduces to the hydrostatic equation

$$\frac{dw}{dt} = 0 = -\frac{1}{\rho_e} \frac{\partial P_e}{\partial z} - g. \qquad (4.17)$$

If the parcel pressure adjusts to the environmental pressure at all levels,

$$\frac{\partial p}{\partial z} = \frac{\partial P_e}{\partial z} = -g\rho_e.$$

Substitution of this expression into Eq. 4.16 yields

$$\frac{dw}{dt} = g\left(\frac{\rho_e}{\rho} - 1\right) = g\left(\frac{\rho_e - \rho}{\rho}\right). \qquad (4.18)$$

This buoyancy equation states that a parcel embedded in a

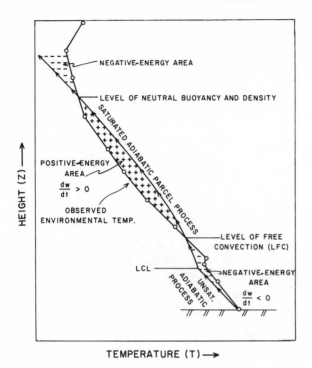

Figure 4.3. Positive- and negative-energy areas associated with the ascent of an initially unsaturated surface parcel.

denser fluid is accelerated upward in proportion to its density deficit. A parcel denser than its environment ($\rho_e < \rho$) is subject to a downward acceleration. Since

$$\frac{dw}{dt} = \frac{dw}{dz}\frac{dz}{dt} = w\frac{dw}{dz} = \frac{d\left(\dfrac{w^2}{2}\right)}{dz},$$

the relationship can also be interpreted in terms of changes of kinetic energy experienced by the parcel. Equation 4.18 can be converted to terms of temperature differences by applying the equation of state for an ideal gas to both the parcel and the environment and again allowing the pressures to be equal. For the parcel, $\rho = P/R_d T_v$, and for the environment, $\rho_e = P/R_d T_{v_e}$. T_v is the virtual temperature, i.e., the sensible temperature that would attach to the real moist-air sample when it has the same density as a sample of completely dry air at the same pressure. Substitution of these expressions for density in Eq. 4.18 yields

$$\frac{dw}{dt} = \frac{d\left(\dfrac{w^2}{2}\right)}{dz} = g\left(\frac{T_v - T_{v_e}}{T_{v_e}}\right) = gB, \quad (4.19)$$

where

$$B = \left(\frac{T_v - T_{v_e}}{T_{v_e}}\right) = \left(\frac{\rho_e - \rho}{\rho}\right),$$

the buoyancy factor. Of course, when the moisture contents of parcel and environment are nearly equal, sensible temperatures may be used in place of virtual temperatures.

Even if the environmental air and parcel are at the same temperature, difference in moisture content may yield a virtual temperature excess of the moist parcel air over the environmental air of the order of 1 K. This small virtual temperature excess, however, yields a vertical acceleration of the parcel of approximately 3 cm s^{-2}, adequate to produce an increase in vertical motion of 8 m s^{-1} if maintained through a depth of only 1 km.

Integration of Eq. 4.19 with respect to height from a level z_1, where $w = w_1$, to an arbitrary upper level z_2, where $w = w_2$, yields

$$\frac{w_2^2}{2} = \frac{w_1^2}{2} + g\int_{z_1}^{z_2} B(z)dz, \quad (4.20)$$

where the buoyancy factor is dependent on height z.

The integral in the last term of Eq. 4.20 is proportional to the area on a T-z diagram bounded by the process curve of virtual temperature for the parcel and the environmental virtual temperature plot between levels z_1 and z_2. If the parcel is warmer (rarer) than its environment, the area is referred to as a *positive-energy area*. Work is being done on the parcel by the environment to increase its kinetic energy. If the parcel is colder (denser) than the environment, the area between the curves is referred to as a *negative-energy area*.

Positive- and negative-energy areas for a parcel initially unsaturated at ground level and forcibly lifted through a lower negative-energy area are shown in Fig. 4.3.

d. Layer Stability Analysis by the Parcel Method

The hydrostatic stability of a layer of air with a particular temperature or density stratification can be estimated by parcel displacement analysis. With an energy diagram a sample of air within the layer is displaced vertically following the particular parcel process curve appropriate to its condition. After a small vertical displacement the parcel density is compared with that of the undisturbed environmental air at the same level. If buoyancy considerations indicate that the parcel would be accelerated back toward its original level, the layer is considered to be hydrostatically stable. If, on the other hand, the buoyancy force would cause the parcel to move farther away from its initial level, the layer is described as hydrostatically unstable.

In Fig. 4.4 it can be seen that for an unsaturated layer all environmental lapse rates, γ_e, less than the unsaturated adiabatic process lapse rate represent stable conditions. But if the environmental lapse rate exceeds 9.8 K km^{-1} (referred to as a superadiabatic lapse rate), any unsaturated parcel after displacement accelerates away from its original position, and the layer is considered to be hydrostatically unstable. Stability criteria for an unsaturated layer can, therefore, be expressed as comparisons of the observed lapse rates, γ_e, and the unsaturated process lapse rate, or alternately and equivalently in terms of the observed layer gradients of geopotential temperature $(\partial\theta_G/\partial z)_e$, as follows:

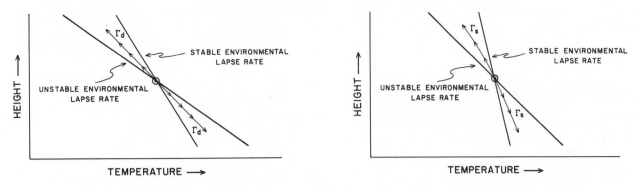

Figure 4.4. (Left) Unsaturated adiabatic parcel displacements. (Right) Saturated adiabatic parcel displacements.

Stable: $\qquad \gamma_e < \Gamma_d \quad$ or $\quad \left(\dfrac{\partial \theta_G}{\partial z} \right)_e > 0;$

Neutral: $\qquad \gamma_e = \Gamma_d \quad$ or $\quad \left(\dfrac{\partial \theta_G}{\partial z} \right)_e = 0;$

Unstable: $\qquad \gamma_e > \Gamma_d \quad$ or $\quad \left(\dfrac{\partial \theta_G}{\partial z} \right)_e < 0.$

If the layer and parcel are initially saturated, the appropriate parcel process lapse rate is the saturated adiabatic process lapse rate, Γ_s. The stability criteria for a saturated layer with an observed lapse rate, γ_e, or observed gradient of equivalent geopotential temperature, are as follows:

Stable: $\qquad \gamma_e < \Gamma_s \quad$ or $\quad \left(\dfrac{\partial \theta_{GE}}{\partial \theta} \right)_e > 0;$

Neutral: $\qquad \gamma_e = \Gamma_s \quad$ or $\quad \left(\dfrac{\partial \theta_{GE}}{\partial z} \right)_e = 0;$

Unstable: $\qquad \gamma_e > \Gamma_s \quad$ or $\quad \left(\dfrac{\partial \theta_{GE}}{\partial z} \right)_e < 0.$

A single set of layer-stability criteria can be formulated from a combination of the sets above with use of the fact that $\Gamma_d > \Gamma_s$:

Absolute stability: $\qquad\qquad \gamma_e < \Gamma_s;$

Conditional instability: $\qquad \Gamma_s < \gamma_e < \Gamma_d;$

Absolute instability: $\qquad\quad \gamma_e > \Gamma_d.$

For absolute stability or absolute instability the moisture content of the layer is irrelevant, but for conditional instability the moisture condition of the layer is critical. If a conditionally unstable layer is unsaturated, it is stable; if it is saturated, it is unstable. Conditional instability is characteristically observed through deep layers in maritime-tropical air.

An aspect of conditional instability of particular consequence to penetrative convection and thunderstorm activity is related to the different responses of a saturated layer to upward and downward displacements. Saturated air containing a typically small content (see Chap. 14) of liquid cloud water can descend in a saturated adiabatic manner for only a short distance before the liquid content is evaporated. Subsequent descent is then at the unsaturated adiabatic warming rate. Ignoring the evaporation of cloud droplets yields the approximation that saturated air follows an irreversible, pseudoadiabatic process in which the air ascends in a saturated adiabatic fashion but descends in an unsaturated fashion. Thus a saturated, conditionally unstable layer becomes unstable for upward displacements but is stable for downward displacements.

A consequence of this property is that release of this type of instability takes the form of strong saturated updrafts of limited areal extent surrounded by weak compensating subsidence of the stable environmental air over much larger areas. Intense downdrafts of large vertical extent are restricted to places in storm systems where evaporative cooling by heavy rain can maintain saturated descent.

e. Layer Stability Changes from Vertical Stretching

The temperature following any individual parcel in vertical motion changes very nearly in accordance with the process lapse rate appropriate to the parcel condition, saturated or unsaturated. Significant and rapid changes in layer lapse rate and stability can result if portions of the layer undergo differential vertical displacement. Such relative displacements are a consequence of horizontal mass convergence within the layer. Continuity considerations require the horizontal mass convergence to be associated with vertical divergence or stretching of the layer. For example, as the upper portion of an unsaturated layer ascends, it cools at the unsaturated adiabatic rate of 9.8 K km^{-1}. If at the same time the base of the layer descends (subsides), it becomes warmer at the same rate. If the initial lapse rate in the layer is less than the unsaturated adiabatic process rate, the lapse rate of the layer increases and its stability decreases, as is shown in Fig. 4.5. If the layer thickness is reduced by horizontal mass divergence, the layer lapse rate decreases markedly, and the stability of the layer increases. The same effect occurs in a saturated layer that remains saturated during lifting and vertical stretching as the top cools more rapidly than the layer base. These effects are also illustrated by Fig. 4.5. Thus horizontal convergence and resultant vertical diver-

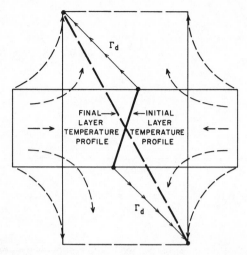

Figure 4.5. Increasing layer lapse rates in unsaturated air caused by vertical stretching of layer in association with horizontal convergence.

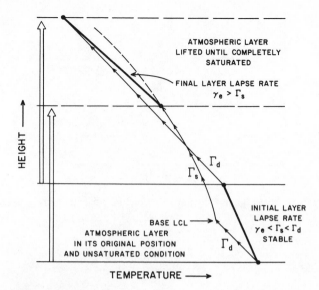

Figure 4.6. The lifting of a layer with potential convective instability to complete saturation. The original layer lapse rate displays absolute stability (i.e., $\gamma_e < \Gamma_s$), but lifting produces instability ($\gamma_e > \Gamma_s$).

gence or stretching are associated with decreasing stability and vice versa.

f. Potential Convective Instability

The stability of certain layers of the atmosphere can be decreased markedly through simple lifting if the layer has an appropriate moisture stratification. Consider a layer of air that is initially unsaturated but within which the base of the layer is closer to saturation than is the top. Upon lifting, both the top and the base of the layer initially become cooler at the unsaturated rate. The base of the layer, however, becomes saturated before the upper portion of the layer. Continued lifting now cools the base of the layer at the lesser saturated adiabatic process rate, while the top continues to cool at the unsaturated rate. Therefore, the layer lapse rate increases with increased lifting. In this manner absolutely stable lapse rates can be converted into conditionally unstable lapse rates. This effect is shown in Fig. 4.6, where the layer is lifted until it is entirely saturated. Then it possesses a lapse rate in excess of Γ_s and is unstable. Layers whose temperature and moisture stratification produce a lapse rate in excess of Γ_s when the layer is lifted to the saturated state are said to possess potential convective instability. Even before the entire layer becomes saturated, it is very likely that differential cooling of the top and bottom of the layer produces a condition in which parcels from the saturated base of the layer can be propelled by buoyancy in a saturated adiabatic fashion through the cooler and as yet unsaturated upper portions of the layer.

The existence of potential convective instability may be determined by examining the initial distribution of θ_{GE} or E_s within the layer before any lifting. If θ_{GE} or E_s decreases within the layer, there is potential convective instability. (The same criteria for potential convective stability exist in terms of vertical gradients of either pseudoequivalent po-

tential temperature or wet-bulb potential temperature.) The criteria for potential convective instability may be expressed as follows:

Potential convective instability: $\left(\dfrac{\partial \theta_{GE}}{\partial z}\right)_e < 0;$

Potential convective stability: $\left(\dfrac{\partial \theta_{GE}}{\partial z}\right)_e > 0.$

The reasons for this simple relationship between vertical variations in θ_{GE} of the layer in its original position and the realization of potential convective instability follow from the conservative nature of θ_{GE}. During both unsaturated and saturated rising motion, θ_{GE} values of the individual parcels within the layer are conserved. Saturated adiabatic-process curves are also isolines of θ_{GE}. When parcels in the base of the layer become saturated first and subsequently follow the saturated process curve that keeps them warmer (less dense) than parcels above, they must initially possess a higher θ_{GE} value.

The conversion of an atmospheric sounding, which is initially rather stable with a highly stable inversion layer, to an unstable sounding is shown in Fig. 4.7. Lifting is accomplished by a typical magnitude of horizontal convergence within the atmospheric boundary layer. It should be noted that the process is reversible if all condensate is retained as cloud. Similar values of low-level horizontal divergence with descent or subsidence of air aloft can convert an unstable sounding to one displaying considerable stability.

g. Latent Instability

The net energy that might be realized by the ascent of low-

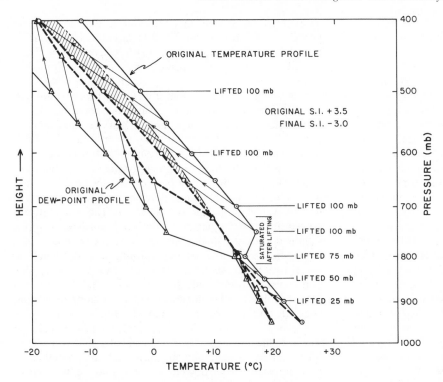

Figure 4.7. Destabilization of an initially stable sounding possessing potential convective instability caused by the lifting associated with horizontal convergence in the lowest 200-mb layer. The lifting and destabilization are those that would result from horizontal convergence of approximately 5×10^{-5} s^{-1} acting for 3 hours.

level air parcels through a specific observed environmental sounding is a measure of the latent instability of the sounding. The low-level air parcel follows the parcel process curve appropriate to its unsaturated or saturated condition. The parcel is assumed to be forcibly lifted if it initially enters a layer or layers where its parcel process rate causes it to be cooler (denser) than the environmental air. A low-level parcel undergoing such a process is shown in Fig. 4.3. There the lifted parcel is cooler than the environmental air from its level of origin, through its lifting condensation level, and up to the level of free convection (LFC), where the temperature of the now-saturated parcel equals environmental air temperature. Below the LFC the area between the parcel curve and the environmental sounding forms a negative-energy area. Above the LFC the parcel becomes warmer than the environmental air and ascends with increases of kinetic energy by buoyancy. The parcel continues to accelerate upward through the positive-energy area until its temperature (or density) once again equals that of the environment. According to nonentraining parcel theory, the parcel attains its maximum vertical velocity at this upper level of equal density. If ascent to this level is associated with an area of positive energy that exceeds the negative areas, the sounding is said to have latent instability. The degree of latent instability is considered to be proportional to the net-positive-energy area.

h. Stability Indices

Several stability indices are simple measures of hydrostatic instability. These stability indices are based on the layer-stability concepts discussed in Secs. 5a through 5g.

The first stability indices introduced yield a number proportional to the latent instability of the observed atmosphere through at least midtropospheric levels. These compare the temperature of a specified parcel of low-level air after lifting to the 500-mb level to the temperature of the undisturbed environmental air at the same level. The temperature excess in the midtropospheric levels is related to the size of the positive-energy area, the strength of the updraft, and the vertical accelerations experienced by cloud air penetrating to these levels. Among the more widely used stability indices of this sort are the Showalter Stability Index introduced by Showalter (1953), the Lifted Index suggested by Galway (1956), and the Best Lifted Index proposed by Fujita et al. (1970). These indices differ mainly in their specification of the parcel of low-level air considered to be representative of the updraft air. George (1960) suggested the K Index as a measure related to the probability of air-mass-type thunderstorm. The K Index considers the overall static stability of the 850-to-500-mb layer by simply subtracting the observed 500-mb temperature from the 850-mb temperature and the positive contribution of high moisture amounts at low levels by adding the 850-mb dew-point temperature. A possible buoyancy reduction of cloudy air parcels by evaporative cooling from entrainment of dry environmental air above the low-level moist layer is taken into account by subtracting the 700-mb temperature-dew-point depression. The Total Totals Index introduced by Miller (1972) also measures the bulk hydrostatic stability of the 850- to 500-mb layer by subtracting the observed 850-mb temperature from the 500-mb temperature. The positive contribution of high values of low-level moisture to midtropospheric parcel buoyancy is accounted for by subtracting the 500-mb environmental temperature from the 850-mb dew point.

The specification of data for the 850-mb, 700-mb, and 500-mb levels in the formulation of several of the indices above has been influenced by the routine availability of reported data at these "mandatory" upper-air levels. The corresponding heights are near 1,500, 3,000, and 5,500 m MSL, respectively. Slight modifications of these indices have been suggested that employ other levels or layer mean values, either observed or forecast. These modifications usually introduce more realism but sacrifice some of the ease and rapidity of calculation and objectivity of the originally suggested formulations.

The ultimate index or measure of latent instability is obtainable through a numerical or graphical calculation of the net-positive-energy area associated with parcel ascent. This can be done graphically by measuring the positive- and negative-energy areas between the parcel process curves and the plotted environmental sounding as discussed above and shown in Fig. 4.3. The calculation can also be made numerically through the finite difference integration of the integral in Eq. 4.20 in the form

$$E = R_d \int_{P_o}^{P_u} (T_{v_p} - T_{v_e}) d(lnP), \qquad (4.21)$$

where T_{v_p} is the virtual temperature of the ascending parcel, T_{v_e} is the observed environmental vertical temperature, P_o is the pressure at the level of origin of the ascending parcel, and P_u is the pressure at the top of uppermost positive-energy areas. Computations of this sort using the numerical techniques suggested by Prosser and Foster (1966) have been made routinely and tested operationally at the National Severe Storm Forecast Center of the National Weather Service. The net-positive-energy amount given by Eq. 4.21 is also referred to as the *convectively available potential energy* (CAPE); see, for example, Moncrieff and Miller (1976).

6. Energy Conversion Contributions of the Downdraft

The stability indices discussed above make allowances for the energy conversions and releases associated with the updraft branch of the convective storm. Normand (1946) called attention to the possible contribution of potentially cold air taken into the storm aloft to the total-energy conversions and maintenance of cumulonimbus systems. More recently many conceptual models of the quasi-steady-state severe-thunderstorm systems (Newton, 1950, 1963, 1966; Fujita, 1955, 1973; Browning and Ludlam, 1962; Browning, 1964; Fankhauser, 1971; Marwitz, 1972; Moncrieff and Green, 1972; and Fritsch, 1975) have reemphasized the importance of this downdraft branch of evaporatively cooled air to the intensity and continuity of the severe-storm system. It is possible to model the most intense portion or core of the downdraft air in a manner analogous to the nonentraining parcel methods used to describe the updraft core. As a first

approximation, assume that the coldest and most intense portion of the downdraft consists largely of lower mid-tropospheric environmental air that has been evaporatively cooled to its wet-bulb temperature by rain falling through it from a warm tilted updraft, or after entrainment into those portions of the cloud system containing precipitation. (A more realistic treatment is to assume the complete mixing of specified portions of environmental air and cloud air containing ample liquid water to bring the moisture to a saturated state. The resulting mixture has a static energy or θ_{GE} value equal to the mass weighted average of the two portions. The final temperature lies between the environmental wet-bulb and sensible temperatures.) During such a process the θ_{GE} value of the air is conserved. The evaporatively cooled air becomes negatively buoyant and descends in a saturated adiabatic manner as long as there is enough precipitation present to keep the warming air saturated. The parcel may reach the ground close to a saturated state. This rain-cooled downdraft air diverges horizontally at the surface, forming the thunderstorm gust front along its leading edge. If, on the other hand, the entire liquid-water content of the air is evaporated during descent, the parcel begins to warm at the higher unsaturated adiabatic rate while conserving its θ_{GE} value. This air may reach the ground as an unsaturated but cool downdraft, or it may be warmed to temperatures in excess of environmental temperatures at some distance aloft. The descending air is then decelerated rapidly and may reach an equilibrium level above the surface.

A profile of θ_{GE} typical of observed conditions in very unstable maritime tropical air is shown in Fig. 4.8. This profile is the average of 57 soundings made within 80 km of parent thunderstorms that produced tornadoes within 105 min after sounding release time. All soundings were released between 1700 LST and 1900 LST at various U.S. upper-air stations east of the Rocky Mountains. The surface air has the very high θ_{GE} values typical of the maritime tropical air over land during late afternoon. Above the surface layer the θ_{GE} values decrease markedly with increasing height and are least in the layer from 4 to 5 km aboveground. The strong decrease of θ_{GE} with height indicates a high degree of potential convective instability. The adiabatic-process curve for a nonentraining parcel originating at the surface is indicated. This parcel becomes positively buoyant where it crosses the plot of the saturated static-energy values ($c_p T + gz + Lq_s$) of the environmental air just below the 2-km level. At this height the level of free convection, the parcel, and the environmental air are at the same temperature, or, more precisely, the same virtual temperature. The static-energy content and the θ_{GE} value of the saturated parcel must therefore equal the saturated static-energy value of the environment. Above this level the air remains warmer than the environment until almost the 12-km level. The process curve for a downdraft parcel originating in the midtropospheric layer of minimum θ_{GE} is also indicated. This air reaches the surface with a θ_{GE} value about 16 K less than the value for the air that is replaced. If this air is still saturated, its sensible temperature is 10 K colder than the environment. Observational evidence that large quantities of outflow air from both individual thunderstorms and multithunderstorm complexes can reach the surface with the very low θ_{GE} values found only at levels 3 to 5 km aboveground has been given by Newton (1963), Zipser (1969, 1977), Fankhauser (1971, 1976), Darkow and Livingston (1975), and Betts et al. (1976).

The difference between the static-energy values in the updraft air and those in the downdraft air has been suggested as an energy stability index by Darkow (1968). An energy index using routinely reported pressure level data can be formed by subtracting the static energy of the 850-mb air from the value of the 500-mb level. A preferred modification to this index is to use average static-energy values in the lower 100 mb or 1 km as representative of the updraft parcel and the average values at 500 mb and 600 mb as representative of the midtropospheric minimum. This index is also a measure of the average potential convective instability in the layer from the surface to 500 mb.

The end result of the warm, moist updraft and the evaporatively cooled downdraft branches of the thunderstorm circulation is local stabilization of the atmosphere. Air of high total-energy content originally at low levels is propelled into the upper troposphere, mainly by buoyancy forces generated by latent-energy releases. Simultaneously, lower midtropospheric air of low total-energy content is cooled as it provides the latent heat of evaporation and descends to or very near the surface, creating a convectively stable stratification. The extent, in both space and time, of the cold-air production and stabilizing effect of multithunderstorm complexes such as squall-line systems has been well documented. Initial documentation was made through detailed mesoscale analysis of surface-station reports (see, for example, Fujita, 1955, 1959). More recently geosynchronous satellite observations such as those presented by Purdom (1973, 1976) give vivid visual evidence of the impact and extent of this outflow air. Although thunderstorm outflow air is normally characterized by convective stability, its boundaries and particularly its leading edge produce enhanced forced lifting of warm, moist low-level air in its path, with generation of new thunderstorms. Figure 4.9 demonstrates this process as viewed from the GOES-1 geosynchronous satellite.

7. Parcel Temperature Change Rates for a Saturated Process with Entrainment

Nearly all developments and discussions in this chapter have been made within the simplifying concept and assumption of nonentraining parcel dynamics. It is known, however, from both laboratory and atmospheric observations, that a saturated convective cloud element ascending in a cooler environment mixes with or entrains a portion of that environmental air. The turbulent mixing process reduces parcel buoyancy because of two effects. The mixing of cooler environmental air lowers the parcel temperature as the parcel gives up sensible heat to warm the entrained air. The parcel is also cooled as it provides the latent heat of evapo-

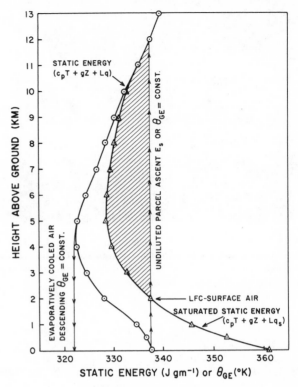

Figure 4.8. The average of the observed profiles of static energy, $c_p T + gz + Lq$ (open circles), and the saturated static energy, $c_p T + gz + Lq_s$ (open triangles), associated with 57 upper-air soundings made in areas of subsequent severe-thunderstorm development. The process curve followed by a surface parcel while ascending in a nonentraining adiabatic (either unsaturated or saturated) manner to the 12-km level is shown by a vertical arrowed line. The process curve followed by a parcel of air originally at the 4½-km level while descending to the surface as an evaporatively cooled downdraft is shown by a vertical arrowed line. The cross-hatched area indicates the layers in which the parcel is less dense than its environment and is therefore positively buoyant.

ration required to bring the entrained air to a saturated state at its final temperature through the evaporation of some of the liquid water content of the parcel. The impact of these additional energy conversions on the process temperature change of the ascending parcel may be determined by imposing the principle of conservation of total energy on the mixture.

Consider a saturated parcel of cloud air of mass M, temperature T, and specific humidity q_s. The cloud air ascends a distance dz while entraining an incremental mass of environmental air, dM, with a cooler temperature T_e and a lower specific humidity q_e. The sensible heat energy supplied by the cloud air in warming the entrained environmental air from its initial temperature T_e to a final temperature T is $c_p(T - T_e)dM$. The energy supplied by the cloud parcel in the form of the latent heat of evaporation required as the initially unsaturated entrained air is brought to a saturated state by the evaporation of cloud droplets is $L(q_s - q_e)dM$. During this same time the cloud's air parcel is ascending,

Figure 4.9. GOES-1 satellite visible imagery for 26 May 1975, 2102 GMT at left, 2232 GMT at right (after Purdom, 1976). A mesoscale high-pressure area produced by thunderstorm outflow air covers much of Arkansas, eastern Oklahoma, and extreme northeastern Texas. The boundary of this outflow air is clearly defined by the arc of small cumulus clouds (A–B–C). The outflow air triggers new thunderstorm activity at point A, beginning about 2100 GMT.

expanding, and cooling, with other energy conversions within the parcel. The increase in the parcel potential energy is $Mgdz$. The change in enthalpy of the parcel is $Mc_p dT$. As the parcel rises, expands, and cools, the water vapor content required to maintain saturation, q_s, diminishes. Water vapor in excess of that required for saturation condenses into cloud droplets, releasing the latent heat of condensation to the cloud air. The associated decrease in the latent-energy content of the air is $Md(Lq_s)$.

Assume that the resulting uniform mixture of cloud air and entrained environmental air may be treated as an isolated system. Further, the energy content and energy changes of the liquid water content of the system are ignored in this development because of their comparatively small size. The principle of conservation of energy implies that the energy given up by the cloud air to warm and saturate the entrained air equals the net sum of the changes of the various energy forms of the air, or

$$-c_p(T - T_e)dM - L(q_s - q_e)dM$$

$$= M[c_p dT + gdz + d(Lq_s)].$$

Considering a unit mass of cloud air (dividing by M) and dividing by the height increment yields

$$c_p(T - T_e)\frac{1}{M}\frac{dM}{dz} - L(q_s - q_e)\frac{1}{M}\frac{dM}{dz}$$

$$\cong c_p\left(\frac{dT}{dz}\right)_{\text{ent.}} + g + \frac{d(Lq_s)}{dz}, \qquad (4.22)$$

where "ent." represents the process lapse rate of a parcel that remains saturated while entraining environmental air.

Expressing

$$\frac{d(Lq_s)}{dz} = \frac{d(Lq_s)}{dT}\left(\frac{dT}{dz}\right)_{\text{ent.}}$$

and making use of the expression for the nonentraining saturated process rate, $(dT/dz)_{\text{sat.}}$, found in Eq. 4.9, yields

$$(dT/dz)_{\text{ent.}} \cong (dT/dz)_{\text{sat.}}\left\{1 + \frac{1}{g}\left(\frac{1}{M}\frac{dM}{dz}\right)\right.$$

$$\left. \times [c_p(T - T_e) + L(q_s - q_e)]\right\}. \qquad (4.23)$$

This particular expression of the entrainment-process temperature change rate in terms of the nonentraining-process change multiplied by the nondimensional factor within the braces is convenient for demonstrating the effects of entrainment in both a qualitative and a quantitative manner. For a parcel entraining cooler and dryer air, all the terms within the braces are positive. Since $(dT/dz)_{\text{sat.}}$ is a negative quantity, the saturated entrainment-process temperature change rate will be more negatiave. In terms of process lapse rates, we may state that the process lapse rate of an entraining saturated parcel is always greater than the process lapse rate of a nonentraining saturated parcel. The increase in the process lapse rate of an entraining saturated parcel over that of a nonentraining saturated parcel depends on the size of three factors: the mass entrainment rate ($[1/M]\,[dM/dz]$), how much cooler the environmental air is than the parcel, and how much dryer the environmental air is than the parcel.

Substitution of typical values for the difference between parcel and environmental temperatures and specific humidities shows that parcel cooling resulting from the latent-heat exchange term, $L(q_s - q_e)$, is normally much larger than the cooling resulting from the sensible-heat-transfer term. A saturated parcel at the 700-mb level (approximately 3 km) with a temperature of 11°C, entraining environmental air at 10°C and a relative humidity of 70%, will experience a latent-heat loss in bringing the entrained air to a saturated state that is 10 times the sensible-heat loss involved in warming the environmental air. Even if the environmental air in this example were initially saturated, the latent-heat loss would still be 2.5 times the sensible-heat loss.

The total impact of the entrainment effects is also directly proportional to the rate of mass entrainment. Observations in the atmosphere and laboratory indicate considerable variations in the size of this term, depending on the size of the convective element. The entrainment rate is observed to decrease with increasing size of the convective element ranging from values of 100% per km of ascent for cumulus clouds with a diameter of 1 km (Stommel, 1947) to values of 10% to 50% per kilometer of ascent for medium-sized cumulonimbus clouds with diameters of 10 to 15 km (Byers and Braham, 1949). The observed inverse relationship between entrainment rate and convective-element size appears physically reasonable when one considers that entrainment is dependent on exposed surface area, which varies with the square of the radius, while the entrained mass is distributed through the volume and mass of the element, which varies with the cube of the radius.

Entrainment rates appropriate to the parcels ascending in the updraft and downdraft cores of large thunderstorms have not been measured. Observations of the conservation of the thermodynamic variables such as static energy, equivalent potential temperature, and wet-bulb potential temperature in the cores of such systems imply, however, a near-negligible impact from entrainment. Thus the modeling of the thermal behavior in terms of nonentraining-parcel dynamics is a reasonable first approximation for storm cores. Effects of mixing on vertical-transport processes are highly significant, however, in most cases.

The simplified treatment of the entrainment process given above has not addressed some of the known complexities of entrainment as observed in the real atmosphere and in the laboratory. It is known that the total entrainment process involves a variety of size scales ranging from the small-scale turbulent elements within and immediately adjacent to the convective cloud to the much larger-scale organized inflow into the cloud referred to as "dynamic entrainment" by Murray (1970). Simpson et al. (1980) presents more thorough discussions of the importance of these scale variations to the total entrainment process.

The portion of the convective cloud experiencing significant impact from the entrainment process is also variable. Squires (1958), Paluch (1979), and Emanuel (1981) have emphasized preferential entrainment of environmental air at the cloud tops as opposed to lateral entrainment. This entrained and evaporatively cooled air forms downdrafts which penetrate deep into the clouds and may at times be intense enough to emerge from the base of the cloud.

Additional insight into the complexities and impacts of the entrainment process can be found in later chapters in this book, in particular in Chap. 15, where the mathematical simulation of convection is discussed.

8. Concluding Remarks

In this introductory treatment of the energy transformations of the thunderstorm various simplifying assumptions and approximations have been made. In addition, a number of physical processes known to be of importance in the energetics of the thunderstorm have been omitted from the discussion. The reason for these simplifications and omissions to this point is twofold.

First, it is the intent of this chapter to present, particularly for the nonmeteorologist, the normally dominant factors involved in the energy transformation process of the thunderstorm system. Second, the discussions in this chapter present a conceptual framework within which the more detailed treatments found in subsequent chapters may be set.

Some physical processes, other than the entrainment effects discussed in Sec. 7, known to contribute to vertical accelerations and effective buoyancies of convective elements apart from simple parcel theory are discussed below.

a. Compensating Environmental Changes

In parcel theory we have assumed that the air in the environs of the convective element is unresponsive and unaffected by the presence and passage of the convective element. Some compensating settling or subsidence of the environmental air surrounding convective elements is a necessary consequence of mass continuity. The subsidence is observed to occur on a variety of scales ranging from a small-scale turbulent cascade of evaporatively cooled air immediately adjacent to the cloud to large-scale gentle sinking and associated adiabatic warming in the more distant environment. Fritsch (1975) describes these effects in considerable detail.

b. Pressure Variations Within Parcels

Simple parcel theory assumes that the parcel pressure at all levels is that of a hydrostatically stable environment. This assumption is particularly inadequate for large convective elements, where even casual observations of the air movement within the element indicate the presence of significant horizontal pressure variations. This assumption is not made in the mathematical modeling discussed in Chap. 15.

c. Cloud and Precipitation Water Loading

Simple parcel theory ignores the impact of the weight of condensed water on the upward acceleration of parcels. The mass of suspended liquid water, cloud droplets, and precipitation contributes a downward-directed accelerating force of gm_1, where m_1 is the mass of condensed water per unit mass of air. The addition of this term to the thermal buoyancy term in Eq. 4.19 yields

$$\frac{dw}{dt} = gB - gm_1 = g(B - m_1) = gB^*, \quad (4.24)$$

where B^* is the effective buoyancy accounting for liquid-water loading. Observations of water content show a range from a few tenths of a gram per kilogram in small clouds to several tens of grams per kilogram in cumulonimbus clouds. A water content of 5 g kg^{-1} is sufficient to completely counteract the buoyancy caused by a virtual temperature excess of 1°C in the parcel. This is discussed further in Chap. 14.

d. Aerodynamic, or Form, Drag

Any blunt-shaped object moving through air experiences a decelerating drag force dependent on its size, shape, and velocity relative to the fluid. *Form drag* is independent of an additional drag caused by the frictional interaction between the object and the ambient air, discussed as entrainment, or mixing, drag below.

Form drag is a consequence of a slight nonhydrostatic pressure buildup on the forward or upwind positions of the object. The resulting pressure excess is called dynamic pressure. Maximum dynamic pressure occurs at locations where the impinging air is brought to rest or stagnation. Stagnation pressure values equal

$$\rho \, \frac{V_r^2}{2},$$

where V_r is the undisturbed relative-velocity component normal to the surface of the object in an upwind direction. For air with a relative velocity of the order of 10 m s^{-1}, the associated stagnation pressures are 0.5 mb, a small but significant departure from hydrostatic pressure. Dynamic pressure deficits of the same order of magnitude exist on the sides and downwind portions of the object. The integrated effect of these dynamic pressure variations over the surface of the object is to create a net pressure force in the relative downstream flow direction and to move the environmental air out of the path of the rising parcel.

For an upward-moving convective element with a relative velocity with respect to the ambient air of w, the form drag equals $-C_D(w^2/r)$, where C_D is an aerodynamic drag coefficient that takes into account the shape or form of the object and r is the element radius. The decelerating force per unit mass caused by form drag can be added to upward-accelerating force caused by effective buoyancy, B^*, in Eq. 2.24 to give

$$\frac{dw}{dt} = gB^* - C_D\frac{w^2}{r}. \qquad (4.25)$$

e. Entrainment, or Mixing, Drag

A buoyant convective element, whether it is an isolated bubble or an essentially continuous plume, entrains environmental momentum as it entrains the ambient heat, moisture, and mass discussed in Sec. 7. Mixing of nearly motionless environmental air into the convective element slows upward motion below that calculated from buoyancy considerations alone. This effect is called *entrainment*, or *mixing, drag*.

Various approaches have been used to model and evaluate the consequences of momentum mixing and mixing drag. Not only does this momentum mixing affect the upward acceleration on buoyant parcels, but it also affects the lateral momentum of the cloud air and contributes to the tilting of

cumulus clouds growing in an environment with wind shear (see, for example, Malkus, 1952). Most current efforts are centered in the type of numerical modeling discussed in Chap. 15.

Insight into the nature of the decelerating impact of momentum entrainment may be gained by considering the example of a convective element entraining environmental air of zero vertical velocity. Newton's second law expressing the conservation of the vertical momentum of the system is

$$\frac{d(Mw)}{dt} = \Sigma F_z, \qquad (4.26)$$

where ΣF_z is the sum of the vertical components of all real forces acting on the system in which both the vertical velocity, w, and the mass, M, are time-dependent. Expansion of the vertical-momentum-change term and division by mass M yields

$$\frac{dw}{dt} + \frac{w}{M}\frac{dM}{dt} = \Sigma \frac{F_z}{M}. \qquad (4.26a)$$

Since

$$\frac{dM}{dt} = \frac{dM}{dz}\frac{dz}{dt} = w\,\frac{dM}{dz},$$

Eq. 4.26a may be written

$$\frac{dw}{dt} = \Sigma \frac{F_z}{M} - \left(\frac{1}{M}\frac{dM}{dz}\right)w^2. \qquad (4.26b)$$

The last term on the right expresses the decelerating effect of momentum entrainment. Assuming, on the basis of atmospheric and laboratory observations, that the mass entrainment factor, $(1/M)\,(dM/dz)$, is inversely proportional by a factor k_m to the radius of the convective element, the entrainment-drag term may be expressed as

$$-\left(\frac{1}{M}\frac{dM}{dz}\right)w^2 = -\frac{k_m w^2}{r}. \qquad (4.27)$$

Adding this term to Eq. 4.25 yields

$$\frac{dw}{dt} = gB^* - k_l(k_m + C_D)\frac{w^2}{r}, \qquad (4.28)$$

where k_l, k_m, and C_D are constant factors of proportionality. This form of the equation of motion for an entraining spherical vortex was developed by Levine (1959).

f. Vertical Acceleration Resulting from Dynamic Pressure Interactions Between Storm and Environment

Aircraft observations of the updraft air flowing into the base of thunderstorms (Maurwitz, 1972; Foote and Fankhauser, 1973) have shown instances in which the updraft air is colder than the environmental air at the same level. The upward acceleration of this cooler, negatively buoyant air at these levels and elsewhere within the storm is explicable in terms of vertical variations in nonhydrostatic dynamic pressures. These dynamic pressures arise largely out of interactions between the horizontal-flow components of the storm air and the environmental air, as described in more detail in Chaps. 5 and 6.

As airstreams of contrasting horizontal momentum, such as the low-level thunderstorm outflow air and environmental low-level air, converge, dynamic-pressure excesses may reach values equal to the stagnation pressure,

$$\rho \frac{V_h^2}{2}.$$

V_h is the relative horizontal velocity of approach of the air. Stagnation pressures for $V_h = 10$ m s^{-1} are of the order of 0.5 mb. Integration of Eq. 4.15 shows that a decrease in the vertical of nonhydrostatic dynamic pressures of only 0.5 mb in the first kilometer above ground level is sufficient to accelerate neutrally buoyant air to an upward velocity of 10 m s^{-1} at the top of that layer. Newton and Newton (1959) have explained the preferential growth of new cells on the right-front flank of existing thunderstorms in terms of this forced lifting caused by dynamic pressure gradients. They show that the effects of vertical gradients in dynamic pressure can be combined with buoyancy considerations by modifying Eq. 4.19 to read

$$\frac{dw}{dt} \approx g\left(B + \frac{\partial \pi_D}{\partial p}\right), \tag{4.29}$$

where

$$\frac{\partial \pi_D}{\partial P}$$

is the vertical variation of dynamic pressure with total pressure. It can be seen from Eq. 4.29 that an upward decrease of 1 mb in dynamic pressure through a layer of 100-mb pressure thickness is equivalent to a parcel temperature excess of 2.5° to 3.0°C, depending upon environmental temperature.

5. Thunderstorms in the Synoptic Setting

Stanley L. Barnes and Chester W. Newton

1. Introduction

This chapter concerns the large circulation systems that bring about the general conditions necessary for thunderstorm occurrence. In temperate latitudes these systems include migratory cyclones and anticyclones, characteristically 1,000–2,000 km across, and the connected upper-level waves in the generally eastward circumpolar flow. Such "synoptic-scale" systems, whose lifetimes range from days to a week, can be analyzed with use of routine synoptic surface observations (typically 100–200 km apart over many continental regions) and upper-air soundings (300–500 km apart). In subtropical latitudes the oceanic anticyclones, much larger in scale and often semistationary for long periods, particularly in summer, are important because their winds transport moist tropical air into continental regions, where the main thunderstorm activity takes place.

In addition to the role played by these circulations in carrying heat and moisture horizontally over long distances, their associated regions of organized ascending and descending motions contribute to thunderstorm development. These motions affect the vertical stratification of temperature and water vapor in ways that lead to selective occurrence of convective storms in restricted regions. Moreover, migratory cyclones and anticyclones of temperate latitudes develop in regions of pronounced *vertical shear*, variation of horizontal wind with height. Shear influences the particular form taken by a thunderstorm, generally differentiating severe storms from the more common and less intense "air-mass" thunderstorms, and to a large degree shear controls precipitation processes (see Chap. 7).

Thunderstorms are an important part of the atmosphere's machinery for redistributing the excess heat and moisture that enter from the Earth's surface. With increased understanding of the physical processes by which thunderstorms interact with their environment, we can anticipate increased reliability both in forecasting the larger-scale developments that set the scene for convective action and in predicting the general area, intensity, and time of convection. Greater understanding of convective storm "feedbacks" and other subsynoptic-scale processes will be essential for proper treatment of energy transfer processes in numerical models employed to predict the evolution of synoptic-scale circulations.

2. Thunderstorms in Relation to Broad-Scale Circulations

Since the buoyancy that drives thunderstorm updrafts is derived from heat released by condensation of water vapor drawn from the lower layers, the wind patterns near the Earth's surface are most relevant in determining the regions where thunderstorms are most prevalent. Downdrafts, which depend upon the properties of air in the middle troposphere (see Chaps. 4 and 9), must be considered in connection with the dominant types of storms in a given region and season.

a. World Thunderstorm Frequencies and Prevailing Winds

Figure 5.1 shows streamlines of prevailing winds at the surface and the three main regions of thunderstorm activity for the solstitial seasons. Streamlines, simplified to show main features, are based on McDonald (1938) over oceans and mainly on analyses by Mintz and Dean (1952) and Riehl (1954) over land. Semipermanent high-pressure centers are denoted by H, and the mean intertropical convergence zone is shown by a line of circles. Zigzag lines show (generally on seaward sides of mountain ranges) the approximate regions where terrain rises above 1.5 km and presents a barrier to the flow of moist air in low levels. The regions shift seasonally between the hemispheres. Largest oscillations are over the monsoonal region of Southeast Asia–Indonesia–Australia and over the Americas, where the continents are separated by oceans. A smaller migration is observed over Africa. Thunderstorms predominate in regions where the prevailing currents flow over land after long traverses over warm tropical oceans, evaporation from which enriches the water vapor content of the low-level air. Over extratropical Eurasia direct penetration of marine tropical air is inhibited by the west-to-east-oriented mountain ranges extending almost unbroken from southern Europe to China. The main source of water vapor for summer thunderstorms is the moderately warm North Atlantic or, in the eastern part, monsoonal flow from the West Pacific.

Thunderstorms are much more common over land areas adjacent to the western than eastern sides of the oceans in subtropical and temperate latitudes. This distribution arises from two principal aspects of the broad-scale circulations of

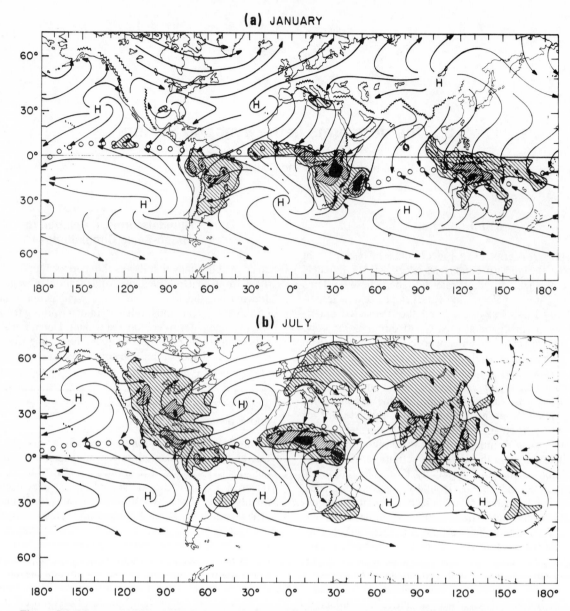

Figure 5.1. Mean streamlines in (a) January and (b) July and regions of most frequent thunderstorms. Outer hatching denotes average of more than 10, inner hatching more than 30, and innermost blacked-in regions more than 50 thunderstorm days during December–February and June–August (WMO, 1953; see Chap. 2 for more detailed distributions).

the subtropical oceanic highs. One is that poleward-moving air on their west sides has experienced long trajectories over tropical waters. Second, systematic rising motions characterize the westernmost portions of anticyclones, while their central and eastern sides are typified by sinking motions. Thus dry air, brought downward on the eastern sides of the highs and heated by compression, overlies a generally shallow layer of marine air. On the western sides, where systematic upward motions contribute to cooling, the atmosphere is generally more unstable.

b. Some Regional and Seasonal Variations of Thunderstorm Type

Within the broad-scale regions of thunderstorm activity in Fig. 5.1, certain subregions are subject to different kinds of storms. In discriminating climatologically favored storm types, one appropriate criterion is whether, with the airmass structure characteristic of a given region and season, thunderstorms can produce vigorous downdrafts. This distinction is meaningful in two ways. First, strong winds near

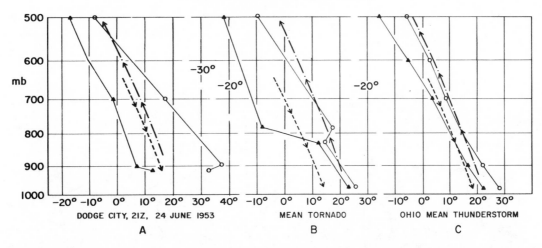

Figure 5.2. Soundings for types of air masses in which thunderstorms form over North America: (*A*) typical of high plains or desert regions (Beebe, 1955); (*B*) preceding tornadoes over Oklahoma and neighboring states (Fawbush and Miller, 1953); (*C*) on thunderstorm days in July and August 1947 over Ohio (Byers and Braham, 1949). Solid lines show temperature (right) and dew point (left). Dashed-dotted lines show moist adiabats corresponding to properties of lowest 100-mb layer in each case, yielding updraft temperatures above condensation level if this air rises without mixing with surroundings. Dashed lines are moist adiabats corresponding to 600- to 700-mb layer, yielding temperature of downdraft if it were saturated (see text).

the Earth's surface, blowing outward from a storm, result from spreading of a downdraft as it approaches the ground, under the influence of higher pressure associated with cold air beneath the storm. Second, evaporation of cloud water into a downdraft diminishes the amount of precipitation reaching the ground. As discussed by Normand (1938, 1946), Desai and Mal (1938), and Byers and Braham (1949), the production of a downdraft as a cold sinking current depends primarily upon the availability in the middle troposphere of potentially cool, dry air into which, upon its ingestion into a storm, significant evaporation can take place (see Chap. 4).

Three distinctive types of air-mass structure associated with thunderstorms are illustrated in Fig. 5.2.

Type A: With low humidity at all levels, high cloud bases and extensive virga are typical; a minority of shower clouds whose downdrafts descend all the way to the ground produce very strong, gusty winds, often dust-raising.

Type B: With a rich water vapor source in lower levels and dry air in middle levels into which condensed water can be partly evaporated to produce a well-developed downdraft, thunderstorms can produce both heavy precipitation and strong winds.

Type C: With moist air through a deep layer of the lower and middle troposphere, the evaporative potential is modest, and the wind gusts that accompany the onset of showers are typically nonviolent.

These archetypes are defined simply for the sake of discussion, and it should be emphasized that air-mass structure

at a given place varies widely depending upon the influence of synoptic disturbances. Nonetheless, certain types tend to dominate, and these vary regionally within each of the major areas of thunderstorm activity.

In the United States, the structures in Fig. 5.2 are most characteristically observed (*A*) over the high plains, the desert Southwest, and the western plateau, (*B*) in the central states east of the high plains, particularly in connection with cyclones in spring, and (*C*) over the Midwest and eastern states in summer. Type A, in which the downdraft can be much cooler and denser than the environment through a deep layer, is potentially capable of producing the most vigorous downdrafts and violent winds (Fawbush and Miller, 1954), while type *C* is most benign in this respect. In each case the downdraft temperature shown is the minimum attainable through evaporation; therefore, comparisons are valid in only a relative sense. Theoretical calculations (Kamburova and Ludlam, 1966; Das and Subba Rao, 1972) indicate that ordinarily the evaporation of water drops cannot keep pace with compressional heating in a fast downdraft, which is thus likely to be subsaturated with a lapse rate between moist and dry adiabatic. With type *A* soundings, strong surface winds are commonly observed even when there is little or no surface rain. In such cases (Krumm, 1954) intense evaporation takes place in the upper part of the subcloud layer; the air thus chilled, even though warming dry adiabatically during further descent, is still colder than its environment. The rate of cold-air production beneath a storm is proportional to the water evaporated, and the ratio of evaporated rain to the surface rain generally increases with the height of the cloudbase (Fujita, 1959).

In Fig. 5.2 the separation between saturated adiabats for the updraft and downdraft is a measure of the difference of

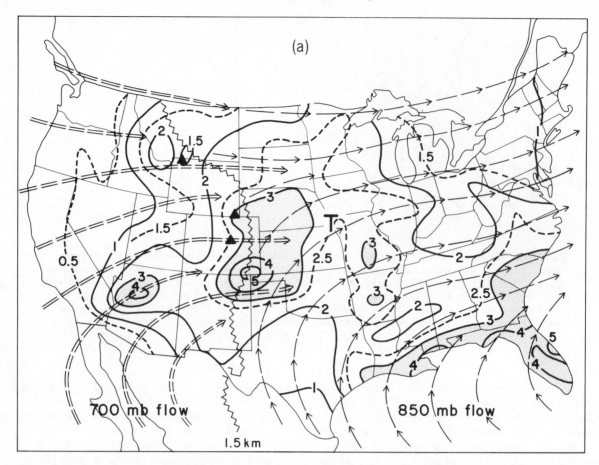

Figure 5.3a. Mean thunderstorm frequency in June–August, in percent of hours with thunderstorms reported (Rasmusson, 1971). Triangles show locations where hail frequency exceeds 90 days in a 20-yr period, for the 3-mo season, with greatest frequency in June (Stout and Changnon, 1968). The approximate location of maximum tornado frequency during this season is indicated by *T* (Fawbush et al., 1951). The zigzag line is the smoothed 1.5-km terrain contour east of the Rocky Mountains. Superimposed mean streamlines in July, of 850-mb flow over the central and eastern United States and 700-mb flow over the mountainous West, are based on wind-direction analyses by Crutcher (1959).

wet-bulb potential temperature[1] (θ_w) between near-surface and midtropospheric levels. A small difference suggests relatively thorough mixing in the vertical, which in type *A* results from intense surface heating producing a nearly dry-adiabatic lapse rate, and in type *C* from the cumulative effect of moist convection which, in an air mass of this kind, is readily set off day after day by surface heating. Sounding B is distinguished by a large lapse from the high

---

[1] Defined as the temperature an air parcel would have if cooled from its initial state adiabatically to saturation and thence brought to a pressure of 1,000 mb by a saturation-adiabatic process. θ_w (see, e.g., Hess, 1959, pp. 62–63) is a conservative property for an air parcel that does not exchange heat with its environment (by radiation, conduction, or mixing with air that has different θ_w). The processes involved are treated in Chap. 4, in terms of the differently defined but physically analogous quantity "equivalent geopotential temperature" θ_{GE}. The process curves (dashed) in Fig. 5.2 correspond to moist adiabats, along which θ_w is constant. In each case the θ_w at the level of origin of an air parcel prescribes its temperature if it is kept saturated, as a result of condensation in the updraft, or evaporation of droplets into the downdraft.

θ_w of the lower layer of moist air to the low θ_w of the overrunning dry air. Even in mean conditions (Fig. 5.3a) moist air from the Gulf of Mexico is overrun by dry air heated over the western plateau of the United States and Mexico. This condition makes the region east of the Rocky Mountains especially susceptible to the type *B* air-mass structure that, as discussed in Sec. 4d, peculiarly favors the generation of extreme instability and severe storms (Showalter and Fulks, 1943; Fulks, 1951).

India-Pakistan-Bangladesh and West Africa are other examples. During the summer monsoon (Fig. 5.1b) the Gangetic Plain and Brahmaputra Valley are covered by a deep layer of moist air with, even on the average, higher humidity than the type C sounding in Fig. 5.2. Thus abundant showery rain is characteristic, with modest evaporation. During this same season thunderstorms ("Andhis") over the desert northwest, where air-mass type A predominates, are characterized by little surface rainfall, pronounced evaporation, and strong dust-raising winds.

In the coastal region of North Africa from Nigeria westward, during the peak of the monsoon, the moist air is deep (type C), and rainy but nonviolent convection is typical. Farther north, the moist current becomes shallower, overlain by dry Saharan air (with an easterly jet stream in the upper troposphere). The θ_w is high in lower levels and low in the middle troposphere (type B), conducive to downdraft generation. Westward-moving "disturbance lines" that form in this region (Hamilton and Archbold, 1945) are essentially similar to squall lines of middle latitudes, with showers and strong surface winds.

A marked seasonal change of thunderstorm character is observed over the Gangetic Plain and neighboring hill provinces. Wet and relatively windless storms typify the monsoon months, and violent "nor'westers" occur in the same region in spring. During premonsoon periods, when the region is invaded in lower levels by moist tropical air from the Bay of Bengal, this is overrun by dry, potentially cool air associated with the westerly jet stream in the high troposphere; type B thunderstorms develop with the passage of disturbances in the upper westerly current (Ramaswamy, 1956).

c. Thunderstorms over the United States in Relation to General Airflow

Over the United States in summer (Fig. 5.3a), two distinct maxima of thunderstorms are evident, associated with different physiographical domains. One is over the southeastern states, dominated by the west side of the Atlantic subtropical anticyclone. Although intrusions of tropical air are progressively more sporadic farther north in connection with the passage of disturbances, during summer the southern states are persistently overrun by low-level air flowing directly from the Gulf of Mexico or the tropical Atlantic. By virtue of its rich moisture content, this maritime tropical (mT) air has high θ_w and is marginally unstable, and convective clouds readily ensue from afternoon heating of the near-surface layers.

The second region of most frequent thunderstorms is over the Rocky Mountains and the high plains on their east. As noted earlier, in the westernmost states thunderstorms are suppressed by subsidence on the east side of the oceanic subtropical anticyclone. In addition, low-level moist air from the Pacific (which has low θ_w owing to its passage over the cool California current) is largely prevented from penetrating inland by the coastal ranges. However, during the summer monsoon extensive thunderstorms result from intermittent surges of mT air that enter southern Arizona and California from the Gulf of California and the tropical Pacific, notably when dying tropical cyclones are present off the northwest coast of Mexico but also with lesser disturbances (Rasmusson, 1967; Hales, 1974; Brenner, 1974). More generally, the airflow that nourishes thunderstorms over most of the mountainous west arrives from the Pacific in westerly or southwesterly currents (Fig. 5.3a) that are not part of the humid marine layer but rather overlie it. The moisture content of this Pacific air is relatively low, but

heating during passage over the western plateau increases its θ_w in the lower 1–2 km above mean terrain level in midsummer to values nearly comparable with that of mT air. Afternoon thunderstorms regularly begin over the higher mountain ranges and may drift over neighboring valleys or plains before dissipating.

Considering the relatively low humidity and the elevated terrain, convective cloud bases are much higher (above sea level) over the western states than over the middle and eastern states. Within the transition zone of the high plains, the occurrence and character of thunderstorms (or other cloud systems) depend strongly upon the direction of low-level airflow on a given occasion, since it is only with winds having an easterly component that air with high moisture content can spread over the high plains. For example, near the eastern face of the Rockies in Colorado the cloud base is typically above 4,500 m (above sea level) in Pacific air from the west but commonly lowers to 2,500–3,000 m or so following a cold-front passage with onset of easterly winds, particularly in spring.

In stark contrast to the predominant afternoon thunderstorms over the mountainous West and over the southern and eastern states is a nocturnal maximum over a broad region from the Great Plains to the Middle West (Fig. 5.3b). Several processes may contribute to this. Organized vertical motions connected with cyclones and fronts (Sec. 4), or triggering by mesoscale phenomena (see Chap. 6), may initiate or prolong convection at any time of day or night in individual situations. Mountain thunderstorms tend to remain over the higher peaks during the day but drift away after solar heating weakens. Karr and Wooten (1976) found that the favored time for radar echoes over the mountains west of Denver was 1400–1600 MST, with maxima (of generally decaying storms) successively later to the east and maximum occurrence at the Kansas border at 2000–2200 MST. Organized convective systems such as squall lines and mesoscale Convective Complexes (see Chap. 6) form preferably in mid- to late afternoon but owing to their self-propagating nature commonly persist for 6–12 h or longer. Thus such storms originating over the Great Plains contribute to late-evening and early-morning occurrences at locations considerably to the east.

An important factor that contributes to the nocturnal maximum in Fig. 5.3b is the prevalence of strong southerly low-level jet streams (Bonner, 1968) upstream from this general region (Fig. 5.4). These jets are generally strongest somewhat after midnight (Blackadar, 1957; Hoecker, 1963), when also, on the average, horizontal convergence in lower levels over the middle and north-central states is more pronounced than during daytime (see Chap. 6). Southerly low-level jets, a feature physically most favored over the westward-rising terrain of the plains states (Means, 1954), increase in strength when cyclones approach this region from the west or develop in the lee of the Rockies (Djurić and Damiani, 1980). As discussed in Sec. 4b–c, they have important influences not only on the field of horizontal convergence and vertical motion but also on the destabilization of the air masses. These features may either influence the

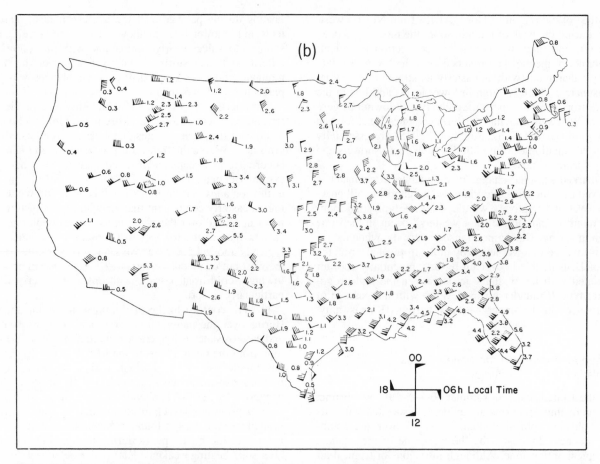

Figure 5.3b. Times of most frequent thunderstorms in the June–August period, plotted according to the orientations at the bottom. Numbers indicate percent of hours with thunderstorms. Barbs indicate "normalized amplitude" of the diurnal cycle, defined as the amplitude of the first harmonic divided by the 24-h mean. A full barb represents 10%, and a pennant 50%. For example, a normalized amplitude of 50% would mean, if higher harmonics were absent, that the probability of thunderstorms at the time of the maximum is 1.5 times, and at the time of the minimum 0.5 times, the 24-h mean. Very large values indicate a strong peak with marked suppression of the activity during the opposite half of the day (Wallace, 1975).

formation of nocturnal convection locally or enhance the persistence of convective systems that, as noted above, form farther west and pass through the region at night.

Rasmusson (1971) provides maps of the first and second harmonics of the diurnal variation of thunderstorms (see Chap. 2). The first harmonic explains 95% of the variance over the central nocturnal thunderstorm region, and 65%–70% over most of the regions dominated by afternoon thunderstorms. In a belt extending northeastward from central Texas, a transition zone (Fig. 5.3b) where there are significant numbers of both early-morning and afternoon thunderstorms, the second harmonic explains 20%–50% of the variance.

The nocturnal thunderstorm maximum is not identified with the preferred times for severe-weather phenomena. In the general region concerned, both tornadoes (U.S. Weather Bureau, 1956; Kelly et al., 1978) and severe wind gusts (Walters, 1975) are most frequent in late afternoon and

early evening, and heavy rain (Wallace, 1975) is most frequent in the early morning. These features presumably reflect mixed storm types in the region: violent thunderstorms influenced strongly by surface heating and night storms associated with dynamical processes mentioned above, which, according to Means (1944), typically have high cloud bases. In the cooler months (Wallace, 1975) nocturnal thunderstorms prevail over the eastern half of the United States, except in parts of the Gulf states.

3. The Synoptic Disturbance as Host to Organized Convective Systems

In many areas, such as the southeastern states, "air-mass" showers and thunderstorms caused mainly by daytime heating occur somewhat randomly over broad regions when the flow pattern resembles the mean flow (Fig. 5.3a). The mi-

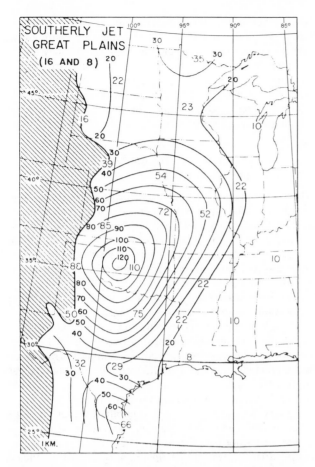

Figure 5.4. Frequency of southerly low-level jets observed mostly during summer, at 0600 CST during a 2-yr period (Bonner, 1968). Numbers at individual stations correspond to occasions where low-level maximum was 16 m s⁻¹ or greater, decreasing to 8 m s⁻¹ or less at a higher level.

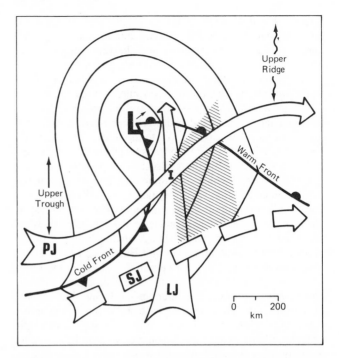

Figure 5.5. Idealized sketch of a middle-latitude, synoptic-scale situation especially favorable for development of severe thunderstorms. Thin lines denote sea-level isobars around a low-pressure center with cold and warm fronts. Broad arrows represent low-level jetstream (*LJ*), polar jet (*PJ*) in the upper troposphere, and subtropical jet (*SJ*) at a somewhat higher level in the upper tropical troposphere. The *LJ* advects moisture-rich air from subtropical regions to provide the basic fuel for convection. Severe storms (hatched area) are most likely to start near point I and, during the ensuing 6 to 12 h, as the surface cyclone moves northeastward (arrow) and the upper trough amplifies, gradually shift toward the east while building southward. The subtropical jet is not always present, but when it is, upper-level divergence is enhanced, and squall lines between the two upper jets become particularly intense. Other thunderstorms may occur outside the hatched region but most often are less intense. Severe thunderstorms also occur with many variations on this basic theme.

nority of storms that reach severe proportions, with exceptionally vigorous updrafts and downdrafts, large hail, violent surface winds, and/or tornadoes, occur primarily under special circumstances conditioned by traveling synoptic disturbances. Outbreaks may be initiated by disturbances at any time of day or season, sometimes when surface heating is not an immediate factor.

Differences in synoptic conditions associated with thunderstorms have long been recognized. For example, Humphreys (1914) distinguished "heat" thunderstorms in situations with weak horizontal winds, "cyclonic" thunderstorms in the southeast quadrants of cyclones where the wind veers with height and differential advection (Sec. 4) is important, and "trough" thunderstorms (in modern terms, forming near cold fronts). He also observed that "tornadic" thunderstorms are associated with differences of the wind currents at higher and lower levels (vertical shear) and illustrated updraft-downdraft circulations similar to those described in Sec. 3b.

We discuss features of synoptic disturbances that gener-

ate thunderstorm outbreaks, and illustrate some simple aspects of thunderstorm environment interactions. Preexisting subsynoptic-scale disturbances resulting from earlier thunderstorms, and the dryline discontinuity between continental and maritime tropical air masses (Rhea, 1966), other favored sites for thunderstorm formation, are discussed in Chap. 6.

a. General Features of a Synoptic Disturbance

Following an examination of features common to tornado situations, Fawbush, Miller, and Starrett (1951) identified those whose concurrence (Sec. 5) leads to generation of extreme thermal instability and its release in violent storms in specific regions of limited extent. Composite features are sketched in Fig. 5.5 in relation to a cyclone type commonly associated with widespread outbreaks of severe thunderstorms. The discussion in this section is highly generalized to bring out fundamental physical interactions; the structures of synoptic disturbances and the relations of severe storms to them vary greatly in individual situations.

In middle latitudes cyclones evolve downstream from wave troughs in the upper tropospheric polar jet stream (*PJ*) associated with the zone of temperature contrast between large-scale cold and warm air masses. Where a source of moist, warm air exists to the south, the commonly present low-level jet (*LJ*) can transport it rapidly northward in the warm sector of the cyclone. This process increases the low-level θ_w, which determines the temperature of rising saturated air (Sec. 2b), and thereby contributes to make the air mass potentially more unstable. The region east of the trough in the *PJ* is characterized by horizontal wind divergence in upper levels, with ascending motions in the troposphere beneath (Bjerknes and Holmboe, 1944). These rising motions (with typical maximum values on the order of 10 cm s^{-1} in the middle troposphere near the wave inflection) contribute to cooling in upper levels and thus to thermal instability. They also increase the depth of the moist layer and correspondingly the amount of water vapor available for condensation, and in some cases they lift air to its saturation level, initiating convection.

Frequently the subtropical jetstream (*SJ*) is present at a higher level south of the *PJ*. Unlike the *PJ*, the *SJ* is associated not with marked horizontal temperature contrasts in the lower troposphere but with strong vertical shear in the high troposphere. The core of the *SJ* generally is not strongly evident at the same level as the *PJ*, but its presence is often seen as a secondary windspeed maximum or as a broadening of the polar jet maximum toward the south.

Typically, severe storms first break out somewhere near intersection *I* (Fig. 5.5), where the *PJ* crosses over the *LJ* (Beebe and Bates, 1955). The center of vigorous convective activity (often in the form of a squall line composed of successively generated thunderstorms, which may extend partly north of the warm front) usually advances relative to the cold front, propagating in a generally southeastward direction. This development is in response to several influences: the storms tend to develop into the moisture source on their right flanks (Sec. 3d), the upper wave amplifies, and the jet advances southeastward. A broad zone of upper-level divergence is generally present in the diffluent zone between the *SJ* and the *PJ*. Whitney (1977) illustrates five situations comprising 16 days of severe-storm outbreaks, in which the *SJ* marked the southernmost locale of severe-weather activity (although not of cumulonimbus). In these cases severe storms developed first at or near a surface front and nearly beneath the *PJ*, sweeping across the diffluent zone between the *PJ* and the *SJ* as described above, and "most severe storms developed under the direct influence of the subtropical jet stream."

The predilection of severe-storm formation near *I* is essentially caused by the combination of quicker low-level moisture and heat transport by the *LJ* into this region than into regions to the east and west, and high-level divergence inducing upward motions most pronounced near the *PJ*.

Storms that form in this region exist in an environment with strong vertical wind shear, whose influence distinguishes them from storms that develop in weak shear. They tend to be more highly organized, with circulations partly driven by buoyancy (vertical accelerations), as are all thunderstorms, and partly by horizontal motions derived from the environmental winds that make the storms peculiarly effective thermodynamically.

b. Interactions Between an Organized Convective System and Environmental Flow

The significance of vertical shear for processes of an organized convective system is illustrated in Fig. 5.6, a vertical section through a squall line. The component of wind toward the right (the direction of squall line advance) increases upward. For present purposes it suffices to consider only this component; the three-dimensional structure of storms is treated in Chap. 7.

Dominant features of the circulation are an updraft canted toward the rear of the storm from its locus of entry in low levels on the advancing side and a downdraft originating in the middle troposphere that moves forward through the storm, underrunning the updraft. With this arrangement water condenses in the updraft, forming precipitation particles which fall out of the updraft and into the downdraft branch, wherein their partial evaporation chills the air as is necessary for descent. The downdraft diverges in lower layers partly toward the advancing side, where it manifests as the gust front (see Chap. 9). These features, namely, a cooperative condensation-evaporation cycle that is efficient owing to the arrangement of the drafts and regeneration of the updraft as the downdraft undercuts warm air at the advancing gust front, account for the self-sustaining nature of squall lines and large thunderstorms once precipitation has been initiated (Harrison and Orendorff, 1941; Newton, 1950; Fujita, 1955; Browning and Ludlam, 1962).

This configuration of drafts has been demonstrated by analyses of balloon soundings during storm passages (with high values of θ_w in slanting updrafts and low values in downdrafts; Henderson, 1971) and by Doppler radar observations of similar velocity fields when viewed along a transect through the central updraft and downdraft of a storm (Kropfli and Miller, 1975; see Chap. 7).

Calculations show that in a vigorous updraft of large diameter the vertical transfer of horizontal momentum effectively counteracts external forces exerted by strong winds in upper levels penetrated by the updraft (Newton and Newton, 1959; Hitschfeld, 1960; F. C. Bates, reproduced in Newton, 1966). Barnes (1970) suggests that a small excess hydrostatic pressure gradient owing to the warmer updraft column may also contribute to the counteractive forces that allow the updraft to resist deformation. Wind measurements of balloons released into updrafts show a strong tendency for conservation of the horizontal momentum of the low levels from which the air rises (Davies-Jones and Henderson, 1975). Considering this inertia, canting of an updraft opposite to the wind shear (Fig. 5.6) is accounted for by horizontal movement of a storm (Bates, 1961). The up-draft at a given time represents the locus of end points of trajectories of air parcels that have successively risen from the subcloud layer. Thus the upper portion, air that started its ascent earlier, lags the foot of the updraft, which has in the meantime advanced. Dependence of updraft form upon storm movement is illustrated in a case study by Chisholm (1973). On the basis of radar evidence he concluded that during the first phase of a storm, while it was "anchored" to the Alberta foothills, low-level air entered on its west side, and the updraft tilted in a downshear direction. Later, when the storm moved eastward with appreciable speed (in an environment with easterly winds in lower levels), the intake moved to the east side of the storm, and the updraft was canted in an upshear direction.

Air that enters the downdraft branch in middle levels, with a component of velocity exceeding the speed of the squall line, partly conserves its momentum and moves forward through the cloud system (Fig. 5.6). In one isolated thunderstorm radar-tracked chaff released directly upwind entered the storm in middle levels, while neighboring packets moved around it and exhibited circulations similar to flow around a columnar obstacle (Fankhauser, 1971). Fankhauser concluded that the airstreams passing around the flank and partly converging on the lee side are subjected to intense evaporation of small precipitation particles and cloud debris eroded from the active convective column. This supports Browning's (1964) view that the downdraft of a severe storm is substantially fed by midtropospheric air that is evaporatively chilled while streaming beneath the anvil, as well as by ingestion on the upwind side as in Fig. 5.6 (see Chap. 7). It seems likely that the latter dominates in a squall line since, in contrast to an isolated storm, the penetration of dry middle-level air to the downwind side would be rendered difficult owing to partial blocking of the airflow by neighboring cells, especially if there is extensive cloud between them.

Vigorous downdrafts have been measured by aircraft penetrating the higher levels of severe storms. These are, however, inferred to be separate from the lower-tropospheric downdraft, probably being air that has penetrated the tropopause in a strong updraft, become colder than the environment, then accelerated downward (Fig. 5.6). On thermodynamic grounds it is unlikely that downdrafts of this kind can descend to low levels; rather, air that has originated in an updraft remains aloft, passing into the expanding anvil of the storm (Newton, 1966). For a contrary view related to "downbursts" whose velocities in low levels greatly exceed ordinary downdrafts, see Fujita and Byers (1977).

Estimates of the water budget for a 20-km segment of the squall line (corresponding to an individual large thunderstorm) are based on wind and water-vapor observations (Fig. 5.6). The intake of water vapor into the updraft was about 9 kt s^{-1} (kilotons per second), and about 1 kt s^{-1} of water and water vapor (perhaps an underestimate) flowed out in the anvil eventually to evaporate in upper levels; 3 kt s^{-1} evaporated into the downdraft branch, and 5 kt s^{-1}

reached the ground as precipitation. These values and estimates for a few other cases suggest, for squall lines and large thunderstorms, a value of about 0.5 for the *precipitation efficiency* (*PE*), or ratio of surface precipitation to water flux into the updraft (Newton, 1968). Thus a large portion of the water condensed to furnish heat to drive the updraft is reevaporated to drive the downdraft. The above PE value seems most typical, but PE decreases with an increase of vertical shear (Marwitz, 1972b; Foote and Fankhauser, 1973). Also, as noted in Sec. 2, the dominance of downdrafts as part of thunderstorm circulation (reflecting the evaporation that occurs) differs according to the type of air mass in which the storm forms.

In summary, the environment characteristic of synoptic disturbances, with pronounced vertical wind shear, influences embedded convection in two main ways. One is to organize it into slantwise, rather than vertical, branches that mutually interact in an efficient thermodynamical-mechanical process. The second is that the huge quantities of moist and dry air necessary to supply the circulation branches are fed continuously to the storm by the relative horizontal winds. Both aspects confer a self-regenerative character, and some squall lines, beginning near the western side of and sweeping eastward through a tongue of moist, unstable air, do not perish until they encounter more stable air on the eastern side. Since such an unstable tongue is often associated with a synoptic disturbance such as the one shown in Fig. 5.5 that (usually) also moves eastward, the potential lifetime of the convective system is enhanced by this movement of the host disturbance.

Squall lines take various forms, ranging from a well-defined line of intense storms to broad cloud systems (upwards of 100 km wide) with embedded thunderstorms, generally of lesser intensity. In these broader systems, which may be associated with cold fronts or may be found in the warm air mass ahead of them, the overall character of the airflow and θ_w distribution is similar in kind to that shown in Fig. 5.6, with shallower slopes of the ascending and descending branches, commensurate with the greater widths of the cloud systems. Examples based on serial rawinsonde ascents are given by Newton (1950, 1963) and, with notably distinctive features and physical interpretations, by Sanders and Paine (1975), Sanders and Emanuel (1977), and Ogura and Liou (1980).

Although an extensive squall line is the most highly organized kind of efficient convection, other forms are common. In a given synoptic system several squall lines of restricted length and varied shape may be found forming and dissipating at different times. Massive multicellular clusters are also common, sometimes coexisting with squall lines and individual "supercell" storms.

c. Storm Type in Relation to Vertical Wind Shear

Within a potentially convective atmosphere, the vertical distribution of wind shear is a likely primary factor in determining storm type. Browning (1964, 1968; see Chap. 7) concludes that environmental flow continuously veering

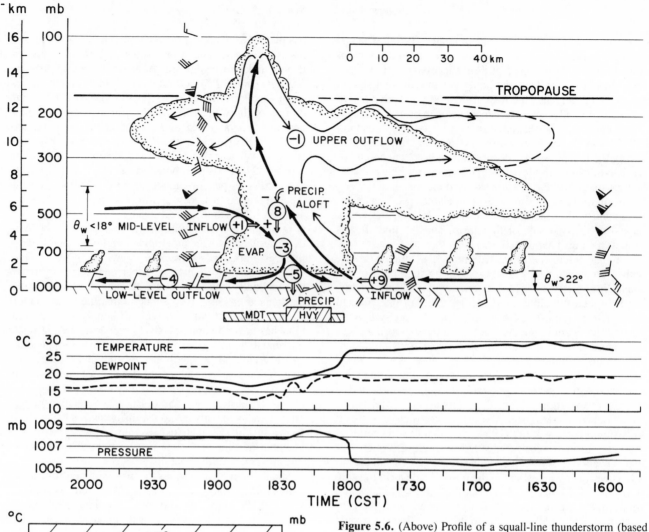

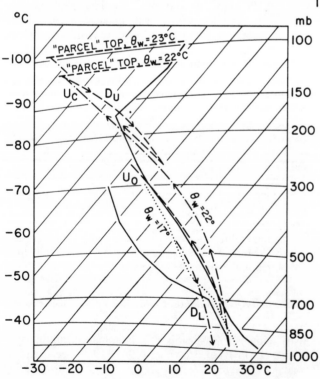

Figure 5.6. (Above) Profile of a squall-line thunderstorm (based on a series of radar observations, fivefold vertical exaggeration) as it passed Oklahoma City on 21 May 1961. The turret top (which fluctuated with time) is shown at the greatest height achieved. Winds (full barb, 5 m s⁻¹, pennant, 25 m s⁻¹) are plotted relative to the squall-line orientation, a shaft pointing upward being from 225°, parallel to the squall line. In a sounding behind the storm, the balloon passed through the anvil outflow, and the winds shown are not representative of the environment. Schematic arrows indicate the main branches of the airflow relative to the squall line that was moving toward the right at 11 m s⁻¹. On the right dashes outline the supposed air plume; the radar-detected cloud plume, at lower elevations, consists of small precipitation particles that have partly fallen out of the air plume while drifting downwind from the storm core. Encircled numbers show components of the water budget for a single storm occupying a 20-km portion of the squall line (kilotons per second, rounded). At the bottom are shown surface temperature, dew point, and pressure.

(Left) A sounding representative of the environment before the passage of the squall line. Dashed curves represent (U_C), the temperature in the core of the updraft protected from entrainment; (D_U), the temperature in the upper-level downdraft (which, upon spreading outward from the top of the updraft, is exposed to mixing with the environment); (U_O), the temperature in the outer fringe of the updraft, exposed to entrainment; and (D_L), the approximate temperature of the downdraft originating in the middle troposphere if it were saturated (redrawn from Newton, 1966).

84

Table 5.1. Thermodynamic Stability and Wind-Shear Parameters for Certain Well-Documented
Multicelled and Supercelled Storms (After Marwitz, 1972a)

Case study	ΔT_{500} (°C)*	Veering in subcloud layer (deg)	Mean subcloud wind (deg/m s^{-1})	Mean wind surface– 10 km (deg/m s^{-1})	Storm motion (deg/m s^{-1})	Cloud- layer shear (10^{-3} s^{-1})
Multicelled Storms						
Browning and Ludlam (1960)	+1	160	150/08	210/21	225/18	2.5
Chisholm (1966) 18 July 1964	+4	40	240/07	235/26	250/12	—
Chisholm (1966) 21 July 1964	+4	−90	250/06	230/17	250/10	—
Alhambra storm 12 July 1969	+2	30	020/03†	245/11	300/09	2.0
Rimbey storm 16 July 1969	+4	30	150/04	240/11	240/11	2.0
Benalto storm 17 July 1968	+3	45	150/04	265/07	305/09	1.5
Sylvan Lake storm 25 July 1968	+6	80	010/04	275/13	315/16	2.0
Carstairs storm 17 July 1969	+4	120	250/03	265/15	295/12	4.0
Butte storm 11 July 1970	+7	10	140/06	235/16	310/07	4.5
Supercelled Storms						
Browning and Donaldson (1963)	+4	50	180/17	230/27‡	255/10	2.5
Browning (1965)	+8	80	190/13	225/25	270/10	4.0
Haglund (1969)	+5	60	200/13	265/25	280/14	2.5
Marwitz and Berry (1970)	+9	90	190/10	250/17	285/14	4.5
Grover storm	+5	60	160/11	250/15	320/09	4.0

*Excess over environment temperature, for an updraft parcel, at the 500-mb level.
†Reported as 30 m s^{-1} in Marwitz's tabulation; we assume that the digits were transposed.
‡Marwitz's tabulation indicates a mean wind direction of 260° for this right-moving storm; recomputed as 230° from his Fig. 13.

with height through the storm-bearing layer is most conducive to producing the "supercell" thunderstorm, i.e., a
large, long-lived (up to several hours) storm consisting of
one quasi-steady updraft–downdraft couplet that is generally capable of producing the most severe weather (tornadoes and giant hail). From studies of Alberta hailstorms
and other published cases, Marwitz (1972a) suggests that
the cloud layer shear controls the class of thunderstorm,
which he divides into three principal categories: (1) supercell, (2) multicelled, and (3) severely sheared. He characterizes by magnitude and distribution the wind shear associated with each storm type (Table 5.1). For supercell
storms, winds are strong (>10 m s^{-1}) in the subcloud layer,
where the shear is mostly due to wind veering with height;
in the surmounting cloud layer wind shear is mostly due to
speed changes, with moderate shear values of 2 to 4 × 10^{-3}
s^{-1}. Multicelled storms (those having multiple updraft-
downdraft couplets which successively develop and decay)
occur in a similar shear structure, but winds in the subcloud
layer are weaker (<10 m s^{-1}). Severely sheared storms encounter shear (averaged through the cloud layer) exceeding
5 × 10^{-3} s^{-1} and little subcloud direction shear.

This classification of storm types is tentative (based on a
few case studies), but it points out the important role that
wind shear plays in determining storm type, when other
conditions are also favorable for the development of severe
thunderstorms.

This point has been illustrated in a study (Barnes and
Nelson, 1978) of two severe thunderstorms occurring 7
hours apart in the same area of Oklahoma. Early in the period the storms produced hail and strong surface winds
(nontornadic) and exhibited radar structures similar to supercelled storms, but they were smaller and shorter-lived (2 h)
than typical supercells. Later the storms grew larger and became tornadic and longer-lived (more than 5 h). The principal reasons for the change in storm character during the
period were determined from 40 environmental soundings
obtained within 50 km of the storms: a trend toward greater
convective instability, increased depth of the low-level moist
layer, and a change in the distribution of vertical wind
shear. A complicated shear structure was found in the vicinity of an early storm (hodograph *A* in Fig. 5.7), where shear
vectors changed from 295°/12 × 10^{-3} s^{-1} in the 1.5–3-km
layer to 180°/13 × 10^{-3} s^{-1} in the 3–4.5-km layer. A later

supercelled tornadic storm experienced more favorable shears in these layers: $265°/9 \times 10^{-3}$ s^{-1} and $270°/4 \times 10^{-3}$ s^{-1} (hodograph F). Both storms experienced subcloud winds exceeding 10 m s^{-1} and large net shear in the cloud-bearing layer ($4-5 \times 10^{-3}$ s^{-1}), placing them at the upper limit of Marwitz's classification for supercelled storms versus severely sheared storms.

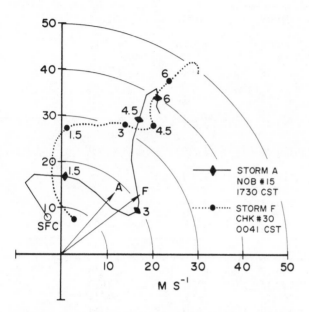

Figure 5.7. Environmental wind hodographs for two severe thunderstorms occurring within a 7-h period in Oklahoma. Different vertical-shear structures relative to the two storms (A and F) contributed to making storm A small and short-lived and making storm F large, long-lived, and tornadic. Labeled arrows show storm velocities (Barnes and Nelson, 1978).

All these results point to the conclusion that differences in storm type and intensity may depend as much upon the three-dimensional details of the flow in which they are embedded as upon the thermodynamic structure of that air. Further study is necessary to establish firmly the role of wind shear and other parameters in determining storm type. Differences in characteristics that distinguish supercelled from multicelled storms are often a matter of degree rather than kind. Even supercelled storms contain a fine structure believed to be somewhat analogous to a multicelled-storm structure (Nelson and Braham, 1975; Browning and Foote, 1976; Lemon, 1976). Also, classification in relation to wind shear is sometimes muddled, since a storm may quickly change from multicell to supercell, as in the Wokingham storm (Browning and Ludlam, 1962), or large single-celled storms may coexist with nearby clusters of smaller cells. Weisman and Klemp (1982) have recently obtained model simulation and case-study results which suggest that storm type is strongly dependent upon the ratio of buoyancy to vertical wind shear.

d. Movement of Storms in Relation to Environmental Wind

The Thunderstorm Project (Byers and Braham, 1949, pp. 108–14) found that radar echoes (of small air-mass storms) generally move with the direction and speed of the mean wind in the layer up to 6 km, although storm speed tended to be slower than wind speed when the latter was strong. By contrast, the tracks of larger and more vigorous storms typically deviate substantially (up to 60° or so) from the direction of the mean wind in the cloud layer.

In the warm sectors of cyclones, where convective storms are common, the wind usually veers with height (Fig. 5.5). In this circumstance most large thunderstorms move in a direction that deviates toward right of the vector mean wind in the layer occupied by the storm, as in Table 5.1. With such storm movement (for example, from the west) the more southerly winds in low levels have a component into the right flank of a storm. This feature was interpreted by Brooks (1946) as influencing storm movement by preferential growth of new convection on the right side, which intercepts a continuing supply of water vapor borne by the winds relative to the storm. Browning (1964) distinguishes between "discrete" propagation by cell growth and "continuous" propagation that sustains the updrafts of persistent individual storms.

As demonstrated by Newton and Fankhauser (1964), deviation from the mean-wind direction is greatest for storms with large diameters, the enhancement of low-level relative wind by rightward movement being consistent with a greater demand to replenish the water loss by precipitation from large-area, quasi-steady storms. More rarely, large storms (often paired with right-moving storms from which they separate) deviate toward left of the mean-wind direction (see Chaps. 7 and 15). Characteristically, in contrast to the large, rightward-deviating storms that move more slowly than the tropospheric mean wind, left-movers migrate very rapidly, a condition necessary to intercept an adequate supply of water vapor (Fankhauser, 1971). Weickmann (1953, 1964) appears to have been the first to elaborate the principle that strong vertical shear nourishes large thunderstorms because they migrate through an air mass in such a way that the relative horizontal winds sustain the huge appetites of their drafts.

Occasionally anomalous storm movements are observed which do not conform to these mean-wind relationships. Fritsch and Rodgers (1981) report a severe storm whose motion was perpendicular to the 500-mb wind and conclude that orography and other mesoscale influences were dominating. Zehr and Purdom (1982) and Weaver (1979) note the strong influence upon storm generation and propagation of convergences at mesoscale boundaries (e.g., sea-breeze fronts and outflows from preexisting thunderstorms; see Chap. 6), particularly where these intersect one another. Weaver also cautions that the movement of the severe portion of a storm, which may be controlled by such features and is most significant for storm warnings, can be very different from the movement of the radar-echo centroid for the storm as a whole.

Squall lines are sometimes composed of aligned single-cell storms and, on other occasions, lines of cell clusters. New storms form most frequently on the right-hand end of a squall line (with respect to its direction of motion); old storms die out on the left-hand end (Stout and Hiser, 1955; Newton and Newton, 1959). In a multicellular cluster individual cells move somewhat toward right of the mean wind, and the cluster more so, owing to favored formation of new strong cells on its right-rear flank, as a result of which clusters also move more slowly than their cells (Newton and Fankhauser, 1975). Thus on three scales, those of large individual storms, multicellular clusters, and the much more extensive squall lines, convective storms tend to move toward right of the vector mean wind, when the wind veers with height, as is most characteristic.

If a squall line is oriented at a large angle across the flow, the duration of its passage is likely to be brief; torrential rainfall rates may occur during passage of some cells, but on the whole the precipitation will be distributed over a broad swath. On the other hand, if the squall-line orientation is close to the direction of mean flow, successive storms (forming on the upwind end, as noted above) may pass over a given location and result in excessive cumulative rain amounts. This situation characterized the 10 most severe rainstorms in Illinois during a 10-yr period, an average of 5 successive rain bursts occurring at locations of greatest rainfall (Huff and Changnon, 1964).

4. Synoptic-Scale Dynamics in Relation to Thunderstorm Development

In Sec. 2b distinctions were made between the types of air masses in which thunderstorms form. It was noted that the air in summer is persistently moist and marginally unstable over extensive regions (Fig. 5.2, type *C*), so that daytime heating alone suffices to start convection. Latent-heat release in widespread and abundant shower clouds warms the middle troposphere, and the downdrafts cool the lower troposphere, preventing great instability.

Contrasting with this is the type of air-mass structure (type *B*) in which (if the lower layer is sufficiently humid) convection might be set off but whose depth is restrained by the temperature inversion capping the moist layer. Deep convection, penetrating through the middle and upper troposphere, may not be possible at all from daytime heating alone if the inversion is strong (especially if extensive cloud forms beneath it, diminishing solar heating), or the onset of deep convection will be delayed if the inversion is weaker. Thus the temperature and water-vapor content (or θ_w) can progressively increase in lower layers, with generation of potential instability until the restraint upon lower-level convection is removed, and violent overturning takes place (Fulks, 1951).

In Sec. 2b emphasis was placed on the significance of dry air aloft for the production of downdrafts, but another comparative feature worth noting is the effect upon updrafts. Entrainment of air through the sides of a cloud diminishes its buoyancy (see Chap. 4), an effect more sensitive to the dryness of the ambient air than to its temperature (Austin, 1951). In most situations, as in Fig. 5.2, type *B*, middle- and upper-tropospheric air is dry. The rate of entrainment, however, appears to be inverse to cloud diameter. Heights achieved by some storm turrets penetrating the stratosphere suggest interior moist adiabatic conditions (Roach, 1967; Chisholm, 1973), as confirmed by balloon observations in updrafts (Barnes, 1970; Davies-Jones and Henderson, 1975), indicating that the effect of entrainment is mostly on the sheath of a large-diameter updraft core (Newton, 1966). These features suggest that a minority of severe cumulonimbi that attain large diameter gain advantage over their smaller neighbors and that the intensity of these survivors depends upon the potential instability of the air mass, in agreement with forecasting experience.

In this section we discuss in less-than-complete detail the processes by which synoptic-scale circulations generate great instability, the circumstances responsible for an air-mass structure that inhibits premature onset of deep convection, and the mechanisms that bring about the final release in violent convection. These are in part diabatic and in part dynamic, that is, related to the field of motion. The relative importance of diabatic and dynamic influences varies in individual instances. It should be understood that diabatic influences are important for severe-storm cases as well as for ordinary air-mass convection, as shown by the late-afternoon and evening preference for severe storms that is pronounced in some regions, notably the great plains–Midwest, and less marked in others, such as the southeastern states (House, 1963). On the other hand, in many instances, soundings a few hours before tornadoes and hailstorms show structures for which convection could not be released by available amounts of solar heating (Fawbush and Miller, 1953), and there is clear evidence (Beebe and Bates, 1955) that dynamic influences modify the structure so as to make deep convection possible.

a. Wind and Temperature Structure of a Cyclone

The general features of a cyclone were shown in Fig. 5.5; here we discuss further how the wind, pressure, and temperature distributions are interrelated (for more complete treatments see, e.g., Petterssen, 1956, Chap. 12; Haltiner and Martin, 1957, Chaps. 11–13).

Except near the ground, where frictional effects are pronounced, the wind may to a first approximation be represented by the geostrophic wind, V_g, an expression of balance between the horizontal pressure gradient force and the Coriolis force (an apparent force owing to the Earth's rotation; see Chap. 15) when the airflow is unaccelerated:

$$V_g = \frac{1}{\rho f}\left(\frac{\partial p}{\partial n}\right)_z = \frac{g}{f}\left(\frac{\partial Z}{\partial n}\right)_p, \qquad (5.1)$$

where ρ is air density; f is the Coriolis parameter $2\Omega \sin \phi$, where Ω is the rate of Earth rotation and ϕ is latitude; p is pressure; g is gravity acceleration; and Z is geopotential height above sea level. The horizontal direction, n, is defined locally to be along the gradient, in the direction of

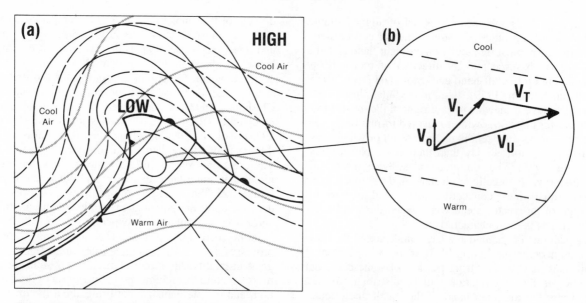

Figure 5.8. (a) Schematic of extratropical cyclone as depicted by height contours (heavy solid lines) of 1,000-mb surface and its relationship to upper-tropospheric flow represented at 300-mb surface (light contours). Height difference (thickness; dashed lines) between the isobaric surfaces is related to horizontal distribution of density, or equivalently mean temperature, in the layer. Relationship of lower and upper winds (assumed geostrophic) and thermally induced shear is shown by inset (b). Thermal shear vector, $\mathbf{V}_T$, has warmer air toward the right-viewed downshear. Surface winds blow across contours under the influence of frictional drag with Earth's surface and in the direction of lower pressure.

low-to-high pressure mapped at a given height (Z) above sea level (middle expression), or toward greater geopotential height mapped on an isobaric surface (right-hand expression). Technically, geometric and geopotential heights differ slightly because of the equator-to-pole variation in gravity. The defining relationship is $9.80\,Z \equiv gz$, where g, local gravity, is in SI units. For simplicity, we shall treat them synonymously.

Equivalence of the middle and right-hand expressions above (see, e.g., Hess, 1959, p. 188) follows from the hydrostatic relationship

$$\frac{\partial p}{\partial z} = -\rho g. \qquad (5.2)$$

Considering this equivalence, it is convenient for present purposes to portray the low-level circulation of a cyclone (Fig. 5.8a) in terms of height contours at the 1,000-mb isobaric surface rather than by the usual sea-level isobars. In the Northern Hemisphere, the geostrophic wind blows parallel to the contours with greater heights toward right of the wind direction and, according to Eq. 5.1, the geostrophic windspeed is greatest (at a given latitude) where the contours are closest together. Equation 5.1 is defined for straight-air trajectories, but appropriate modification for centripetal acceleration can be incorporated to arrive at an expression suitable for curved flow, the so-called gradient wind (Hess, 1959, Chap. 12); for a given windspeed the contours are farther apart in anticyclonically curved flow and closer together in cyclonically curved flow than in straight flow. As illustrated by spreading of the upper-level contours from

trough to downstream ridge in Fig. 5.8, this is the most common configuration (see examples in Sec. 6). This feature accounts for the horizontal divergence in upper levels downstream from upper-tropospheric troughs (Bjerknes and Holmboe, 1944). Locally, the directions of the geostrophic and gradient winds are the same. For simplicity, we shall henceforth express concepts in terms of the geostrophic wind, keeping in mind the modifications necessary for curved flow.

Near the Earth's surface, frictional retardation changes the balance of pressure gradient and Coriolis forces such that winds generally blow at an angle across contours toward lower height. Thus surface winds around the cyclone in Fig. 5.8a can be characterized as blowing from south in the warm sector (see Fig. 5.8b, where V_L is the low-level geostrophic wind and V_0 is the surface wind), from west and northwest in the cold air west of the low-pressure center, and from east and southeast in the cold air east of the center.

The closed circulations of extratropical cyclones and anticyclones, near the ground, give way to wavelike perturbations in the middle and upper troposphere, as in Figs. 5.8a and 5.13, which show contours at, for example, the 300-mb isobaric surface (about 10 km). This characteristic change of contour pattern with height is related to the horizontal variation of density. If $h = (z_U - z_L)$ is the "thickness" between isobaric surfaces at an upper level U and lower level L, the geostrophic shear through the layer ($\mathbf{V}_T = \mathbf{V}_U - \mathbf{V}_L$) can be written, analogous to Eq. 5.1, as

$$V_T = \frac{g}{f}\frac{\partial h}{\partial n}. \qquad (5.3)$$

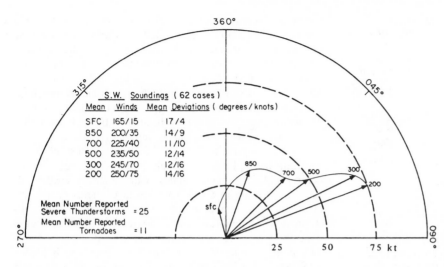

Figure 5.9. Mean proximity hodograph for 62 cases of severe thunderstorms under southwesterly flow aloft (after Maddox, 1976). Differential advection in 850- to 300-mb layer, as indicated by shear vectors (lines connecting heads of wind vectors), contributes to destabilization of air mass (see Table 5.2).

According to Eq. 5.2, the thickness is proportional to the pressure difference (a constant, since two isobaric surfaces are considered) and inversely proportional to the density of the layer. Density is inversely proportional to virtual temperature (the temperature a dry-air sample would have to have in order for its density to be the same as a given moist-air sample at the same pressure; with an error of less than 2%, we may use the actual air temperature instead) so that thickness lines correspond (approximately) to isotherms of mean air temperature in the layer. Accordingly V_T is referred to as "thermal wind": Eq. 5.3 states that the wind change with height is proportional to the temperature gradient (and, as in Eq. 5.1, is strictly valid only for straight, steady flow). In the Northern Hemisphere the vector thermal wind has warmer air toward the right.

The relation of thickness lines to a polar-front cyclone is illustrated by Fig. 5.8a, with large values of h (warm air) to the south and low values to the north of the fronts. Figure 5.8b shows the low-level geostrophic wind V_L, the shear vector $\mathbf{V}_T$, and the upper-level geostrophic wind V_U at the warm-sector location indicated in Fig. 5.8a.

b. Local Static Stability Change by Differential Advection and Vertical Motion

A cyclone produces an unstable stratification of energy in its warm sector primarily through the mechanism of differential advection. Typically, low-level southerly winds advect warm, moist air northward; at the same time upper-level winds may bring progressively colder air over the same region.

Figure 5.9 (Maddox, 1976) is a composite wind hodograph of 62 different synoptic situations associated with the development of severe thunderstorms under southwesterly flow aloft. In Sec. 4a the thermal shear vector was related to the horizontal distribution of mean temperature in the sheared layer, with warm air to the right of the shear vector. It is convenient to consider the mean potential temperature,

$\bar{\theta}$, of a layer, rather than temperature itself (the two being proportional since isobaric layers are involved). Applying the hydrostatic relationship in Eq. 5.2, the equation of state, $p = \rho R_d T$, and the definition of θ (Chap. 4), Eq. 5.3 takes the form

$$C f V_T = \frac{\partial \bar{\theta}}{\partial n}, \qquad (5.4a)$$

where

$$C = \left(\frac{1000}{\bar{p}}\right)^{R_d/c_p} [R_d ln(p_L/p_U)]^{-1}, \qquad (5.4b)$$

and is constant for a given isobaric layer. Here $R_d = 287.04$ J kg^{-1} K^{-1} is the gas constant for dry air, $c_p = 1,005$ J kg^{-1} K^{-1} is specific heat, and pressure p is expressed in millibars.

Excluding low levels affected by friction, and assuming that the winds at other levels are geostrophic or nearly so, the horizontal temperature gradient can be judged from the hodograph. Thus in Fig. 5.8b there is warm-air advection in the entire layer between levels L and U. This is also true for each individual layer in Fig. 5.9, but in different degrees.

The local change of potential temperature can be written

$$\frac{\partial \theta}{\partial t} = -\mathbf{V} \cdot \nabla\theta - \frac{dp}{dt}\frac{\partial \theta}{\partial p} + \frac{d\theta}{dt}, \qquad (5.5)$$

where the right-hand terms represent the effects of horizontal advection, vertical motion, and diabatic temperature change owing to combined influences of radiation, condensation or evaporation, and turbulent mixing. We first consider only the advection term, which can be written from Eq. 4 as

$$\frac{\partial \theta}{\partial t}_{adv.} = -V_n \frac{\partial \theta}{\partial n} = -C f V_n V_T, \qquad (5.6)$$

where V_n is the component of wind normal to the shear vector $\mathbf{V}_T$ in a layer (consistent with the earlier convention for n, V_n is negative when directed toward left of V_T).

Applying Eq. 5.6 to Fig. 5.9, the thermal advection is

Table 5.2. Stability Change in Lower Middle Troposphere Associated with Advection Alone (Eq. 5.6), for Maddox (1976) Southwest Mean Wind Sounding (Fig. 5.9)

	850–700 mb	700–500 mb
$C(10^{-10} \text{ m}^2 \text{ s}^{-2} \text{ K}^{-1})$	1.93	1.20
$V_T \text{ (m s}^{-1})$	8.70	6.50
$V_n \text{ (m s}^{-1})$	18.00	14.10
$(\partial\theta/\partial t)_{\text{adv.}} \text{ (K h}^{-1})$	+1.10	+0.40
$\bar{p} \text{ (mb)}$	771	591
$z \text{ (m) corresponding to } \bar{p}$	~2,250	~4,300
$(\partial/\partial z)(\partial\theta/\partial t)_{\text{adv.}} \text{ (K km}^{-1} \text{ h}^{-1})$		−0.34
Coriolis parameter $f = 10^{-4} \text{ s}^{-1}$		

large in the 850- to 700-mb layer through which the wind veers strongly, small in the 700- to 500-mb layer, and again larger in the 500- to 300-mb layer. Thus differential advection of temperature in the various layers increases the instability of the lower troposphere and the stability of the upper troposphere. For the 850- to 500-mb layer, the stability change based on (geostrophic) differential advection alone is estimated in Table 5.2. To illustrate the potential for stability change, consider θ initially distributed as in the U.S. Standard Atmosphere, where the θ increase upward in the middle troposphere is about 4 K km^{-1}. With destabilization at the computed rate, a dry adiabatic lapse rate would be reached in only 12 hours (in the absence of other processes).

In individual thunderstorm situations, differential advection may be very unlike that indicated in Fig. 5.9. In Fig. 5.7 the hodographs suggest very rapid advective warming in the 1.5- to 3-km layer, cooling in an intermediate layer, and negligible temperature advection at higher levels. Although the use of a hodograph for estimating differential advection is generally justified for large-scale flow, caution should be exercised when the flow is changing rapidly with time or when mesoscale disturbances are present, because of significant departures from geostrophic wind associated with their calculations. Examples of ageostrophic contributions to differential advection are found in Uccellini and Johnson (1979), and a case study by Kocin et al. (1982) indicates that ageostrophic components can become significant over periods as short as 3 to 6 h.

The additional influence of vertical motion on stability change must also be considered. As noted earlier, in the general region from an upper-level trough to the downstream ridge (Fig. 5.8a) there is upper-tropospheric divergence. Associated with this is general horizontal convergence in the lower troposphere, with ascending motions ($dp/dt < 0$) that reach maximum values somewhere in the middle troposphere. Since the atmosphere is statically stable ($\partial\theta/\partial p < 0$), rising motions in an unsaturated environment contribute to cooling (see Chap. 4). With small vertical motions near the ground and in the high troposphere, the general effect would be to destabilize the lower and stabilize the upper troposphere. Thus in the warm sector of a cyclone the effect of vertical motions upon gross stability change will ordinarily reinforce the influence of dif-

ferential advection as discussed above. This is true only as a generalization; cooling associated with upward motions is not necessarily greatest in the middle troposphere, depending upon the correlation of distributions, with height, of vertical motion and $\partial\theta/\partial p$ (see, e.g., Fig. 5.31). Diabatic effects may also significantly influence the local temperature.

Means (1944) explained the nocturnal maximum of thunderstorms (Sec. 2c) in terms discussed above. From hodographs of the mean wind during summer months and an expression analogous to Eq. 5.6, he found greatest advective warming in the layer of air below the 3-km level over the central and north-central states, with generally weaker advective warming in the 3- to 5-km layer. Thus on the average for the summer months differential advection contributed to maintain an unstable stratification. The region concerned is remarkably coincident with that of predominant night thunderstorms in Fig. 5.3b, over which Means established that low-level advective warming is very much stronger near and after midnight than in the afternoon. Since over a long period of time the local temperature changes slowly, he concluded that, in terms of Eq. 5.5, advective warming must be counteracted mostly by cooling owing to upward motions. These findings are consistent with the variation of low-level convergence associated with diurnal oscillations of the low-level jet (Chap. 6).

c. Potential Instability Generation in Relation to Flow Patterns

In Sec. 4b differential advection was diagnosed in terms of the wind structure and its effect on static stability at a given locality. Here we shall examine the process from the perspective of the moving, evolving synoptic disturbance in terms of airflow trajectories over periods of time, such as those between successive weather maps. We also consider the additional requirement that adequate water vapor in the lower layers be available so that condensation can result from lifting or turbulent mixing.

As noted earlier, the temperature achievable in cloud updrafts is prescribed by the θ_w of the low-level air, which depends on both its temperature and its moisture content. Local moisture change can be expressed by an equation analogous to Eq. 5.5 with q (specific humidity) in place of θ. Rather than discussing these fields separately, it will be convenient to consider θ_w itself. We shall consider only the changes of air-mass structure associated with quasihorizontal flow, for this purpose treating θ_w as a conservative quantity that follows the air motions. In reality, in the planetary boundary layer θ_w has a significant diurnal variation owing to radiative temperature change, and in lesser degree to exchange of water vapor with the Earth's surface and with the overlying atmosphere. These variations should properly be taken into account.

In portraying gross stability change, it suffices to consider properties at two levels, as suggested by Miller (1955). A commonly used and simple measure of potential stability is the Lifted Index, LI (see Chap. 4). This is defined as $(T'_5 - T_5)$, where T_5 is 500-mb temperature and T'_5 is the

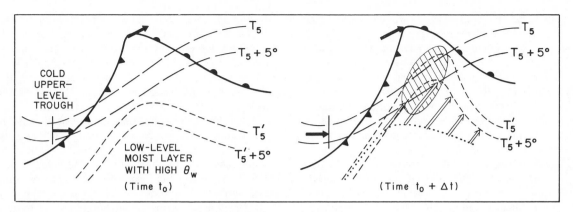

Figure 5.10. Schematic illustration of differential advection. Heavy lines, surface fronts; long dashes, a pair of isotherms T_5 at the 500-mb level, related to a surface cyclone and upper-level trough moving eastward as shown by thick arrows during the time interval between the sketches. Short dashes, successive positions of isopleths of wet-bulb potential temperature in the low-level moist layer, labeled in terms of T_5' achieved upon ascent to the 500-mb level with condensation. Hatched region indicates where, at the later time, $T_5' > T_5$ and the intervening layer is potentially unstable (adapted from Newton, 1963, Fig. 2).

temperature achieved by a parcel rising moist-adiabatically from lower levels and having the mean θ_w of the lowest kilometer.

T_5 and T_5' are sketched at two successive times in Fig. 5.10, depicting a combination of cooling aloft as a cold upper-level trough advances eastward, and northward advection of low-level air with high θ_w (or T_5') that can generate a new region of potential instability. This evolution regularly occurs over the Great Plains region when developing cyclones, or cold fronts from the Pacific, move eastward and draw moist and warm air northward from the Gulf of Mexico. In advance of such systems, as noted earlier, southerly low-level jets characteristically intensify. Under their influence tongues of *mT* air can advance rapidly, for example, with a moderate windspeed of 15 m s^{-1}, from the Gulf Coast to central Oklahoma in 12 h. Appreciable diurnal changes of windspeed can take place (typically an increase of about 6 m s^{-1} from midafternoon to early morning, according to Bonner [1968]), so that advective changes of stability can proceed rapidly during night hours (Means, 1944).

The general importance of low-level advection in generating or maintaining instability is indicated by Porter et al. (1955), in a study of 171 squall lines that formed in regions of maximum moisture in a variety of synoptic patterns. In practically 100% of the cases, warm-air advection was present at the 850-mb level in the region of squall-line formation, and squall lines persisted only as long as they remained in a region of warm advection (Means, 1952).

The process sketched in Fig. 5.10 quite regularly contributes to destabilizing the air in warm sectors of cyclones. However, depending upon such factors as the strength of the southerly current, the nearness of the source of moist air with high θ_w, the eastward speed of movement of the cyclone circulation (which affects the persistence of the low-level air current over a given locality), and the movement of the upper cold trough, a condition of actual instability may

or may not be achieved. Moreover, a condition of potential instability ($T_5' > T_5$) may be reached without ensuing deep convection, owing to inhibiting factors discussed below. Nonetheless, the general effectiveness of the process is attested by the finding (Fawcett and Saylor, 1965) that 80% of the "Colorado cyclones" (initially having stable and relatively dry air masses) forming in February through April during a 5-yr period developed severe thunderstorms as they moved eastward and drew *mT* air from the Gulf of Mexico into their circulations.

d. Suppression of Convection and the Generation and Release of Extreme Instability

As noted earlier, the generation of extreme instability seems to depend upon a prior condition that prevents overturning of an air mass by deep convection of ordinary intensity. Inversions of the kind in Fig. 5.2, type B, are favored over certain regions owing to combinations of physiographic circumstances. Their existence "plays an important part in the mechanism of the instability line, because it provides a 'cap' under which the temperature and moisture may increase until, combined with any cooling aloft, the vertical instability is sufficient for vertical convection" (Fulks, 1951).

Inversions capping the lower moist layer are commonly present some hours earlier but are insignificant at the time and site of severe storms (Beebe, 1958). A dominant mechanism for vitiating such an inversion is ascending motion, as described by Beebe and Bates (1955). In the example of Fig. 5.2, type B, lifting of less than 100 mb with cooling of the dry air in the inversion layer at an adiabatic rate would eliminate this restraint. Although such lifting may take place by various mechanisms, modification of this kind over a broad area commonly occurs in the region of ascending motion in advance of an extratropical cyclone and the accompanying upper-level trough and jet stream (Sec. 3a). As discussed by Beebe and Bates, the divergence and vertical motion fields associated with localized wind maxima on the jet stream are also important (see Sec. 4f and Chap. 6).

Considering the limited lateral extent of influence of a synoptic disturbance, the area containing a capping inversion may be only partly eradicated. Thus it is not unusual, for example, for an outbreak of severe storms over Kansas and Oklahoma to accompany the passage of a disturbance, while only suppressed convection occurs over parts of Texas where potential instability (in terms of air properties in the lower moist layer and the middle troposphere) is present, but dynamical influences are too feeble to set it off. This condition is significant for the intensity of convection farther north, since a southerly low-level current will, during its passage over heated ground, increase in θ_w while approaching the region where convection is realized.

Thus it is important to consider not only the local processes but also the atmospheric structure and air movements in three dimensions. Detailed examination of conditions for severe storms have been carried out in these terms by Carlson and Ludlam (1968), employing isentropic charts[2] to establish air trajectories.

An instructive example, taken from Carlson and Ludlam, is given in Fig. 5.11. This shows a springtime cyclone over the Rocky Mountains (the pronounced southward distortion of the 1,000-mb contours, differing from the usual structure of a cyclone, is associated with the orography of this region). Isotherms of potential temperature θ at screen level (about 1.5 m above the ground) show highest values over the elevated arid plateau of Mexico. Here, owing to intense surface heating, a deep layer of relatively dry air exists with a near-adiabatic lapse rate, as in Fig. 5.2, type A.

Isentropic charts in the middle troposphere (Fig. 5.11b), and at levels not shown, indicate southwesterly airflow from the Mexican plateau over the south-central United States. A heated, dry "Mexican plume" thus overruns the moist "trade wind" (mT) air entering this region as a southerly current over the plains east of the mountains. (The θ_w of mT air from the Gulf of Mexico exceeds that of the overlying plume, but its θ is very much lower.)

The vertical structure of the atmosphere over the plains is hence determined by the airflow in various layers whose properties are conditioned by regional physiography. Thus over central Texas (Fig. 5.11c), the presence of the Mexican plume is clearly shown by a strong inversion near 800 mb, surmounted by a layer up to about 550 mb wherein the lapse rate is nearly dry adiabatic. At higher levels, with airflow more from the west, air properties correspond to the upper troposphere over the Pacific. Farther north in Oklahoma (Fig. 5.11d moist mT air is overlain by drier air (between about 800 mb and 550 mb) whose potential temperature is appreciably lower than that at corresponding levels in Fig. 5.11c. Isentropic trajectories show that the air in this intermediate layer had passed over the desert Southwest from the Pacific.

Altus, Okla., was thus near the transition zone indicated by streamlines in Fig. 5.11b, south of which air originating in the tropics is heated to form a well-developed Mexican plume, and north of which the air in intermediate levels (although also traversing a heated plateau) enters from the Pacific, where it is initially cooler. Correspondingly, Carlson and Ludlam (1968) point out differences in the ease with which convection can be released in neighboring regions, depending on the past trajectories of airflow overlying them. They demonstrate similar effects of a heated "Spanish plume" upon convection in southerly flow over England and western Europe and note related physiographic influences in other severe-storm regions.

The processes are examined further in a detailed synoptic analysis and numerical experiment by Anthes et al. (1982), and in case studies by Carlson et al. (1983). In two examples the "mixed layer lid" is identified as the Mexican plume; in another, as heated air from the arid southwestern United States. In either case, confluence of the midlevel airstreams, as in Fig. 5.11b, results in a well-defined lateral edge of the lid. Deep convection becomes possible where "underrunning" takes place; i.e., in the region west or north of this edge where high-θ_w mT air, emerging from beneath the lid, underruns the cooler Pacific airstream. In this region potential instability is generated by differential advection as in Fig. 5.10, with the additional important feature that this instability can be readily set off by ascending motions where the lid is absent. The above studies present evidence that underrunning is enhanced by low-level isallobaric flow transverse to the lid edge (flow with a component toward the region of most rapidly falling pressure). This was attributed, in some instances, to pressure changes induced by migratory upper-level jet streaks (Uccellini and Johnson, 1979).

e. Moisture Supply in Relation to Advection and Convergence Fields

Advection and convergence in synoptic circulations supply water vapor to sustain convective systems, but not necessarily at the same rate at which the moisture is consumed. The water budget in a given region may be expressed

$$\frac{\partial S}{\partial t} = E - P - \int_0^{p_0} \nabla \cdot q\mathbf{V} \frac{dp}{g}, \qquad (5.7a)$$

in which

$$S = \int_{z_0}^{\infty} q\rho dz \equiv \int_0^{p_0} q \frac{dp}{g} \qquad (5.7b)$$

(subscript 0 denotes the Earth's surface) is water vapor storage in an atmospheric column over a unit area, P is rate of

---

[2]Charts on specified constant-θ surfaces, the potential temperature θ being nearly conserved over moderate periods of time, in the absence of condensation and at levels high enough above ground so as not to be influenced by surface heating and cooling. Isentropic surfaces slope upward from regions of warm air toward cold air (as seen on an isobaric chart). Thus lower pressure on an isentropic surface denotes its elevation over a cold air mass. Streamlines directed from high- to low-pressure contours generally indicate ascending airflow, although time changes in the distribution of isentropic contours must also be taken into account. These relationships, illustrated in Figs. 5.26 and 5.27, are further described in footnote 3, p. 107.

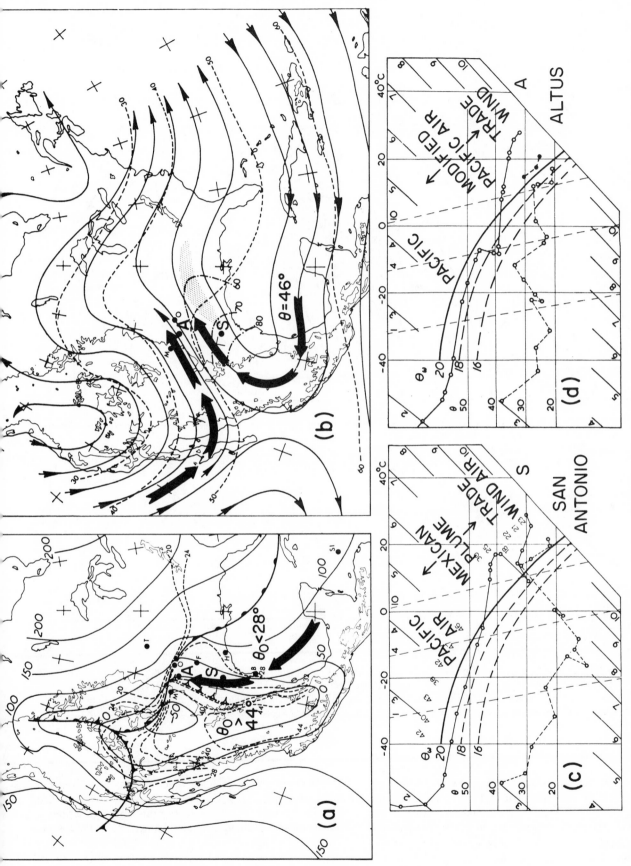

Figure 5.11. At 1800 CST, 4 May 1961: (a) 1,000-mb contours (in meters) and surface potential temperature θ (4°C interval, dashed). (b) Isentropic relative-flow chart for θ = 46°C: isobaric contours (dashed) are in tens of mb. (c) Temperature and dew-point sounding at San Antonio, Tex., plotted on a tephigram: vertical lines, isotherms (in °C); horizontal lines, dry adiabats (θ in °C); curved lines, moist adiabats (θ_w in ° C); isobaric levels are in hundreds of mb (windspeeds in knots to right of sounding curves). (d) Sounding at Altus, Okla., in vicinity of predominant severe weather. In (c) and (d) principal layers of air are identified according to the text description by Carlson and Ludlam (1968), the source of the figures. Heavy arrows are added to maps to emphasize main air trajectories.

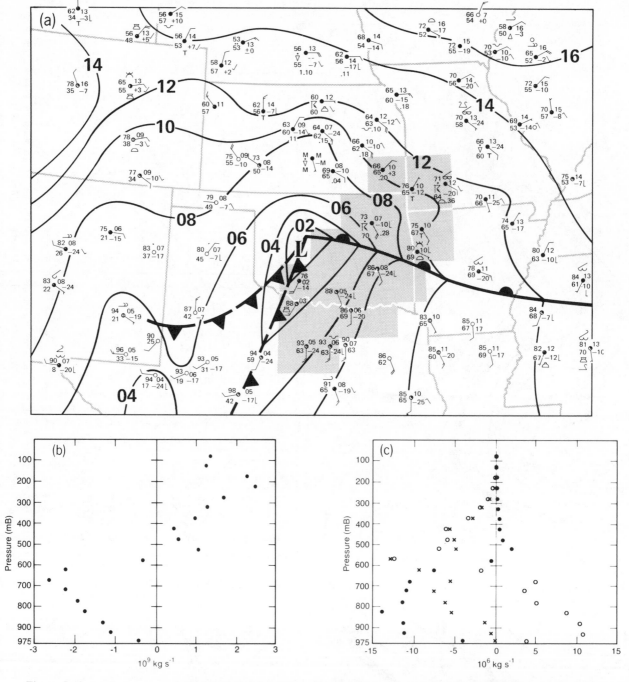

Figure 5.12. (*a*) Surface map at 1800 CST, 21 May 1961, with sea-level isobars (mb in excess of 1,000) and fronts. (*b*) Synoptic-scale mass divergence for various layers in the budget volume, over the shaded area in (*a*). Layers are 50 mb thick except for the 25-mb surface layer. (*c*) Moisture divergence for various layers in the budget volume. Filled circles indicate horizontal moisture divergence; open circles, vertical moisture divergence; crosses, total moisture divergence (after Fritsch et al., 1976).

precipitation at the ground, E is rate of evaporation from the Earth's surface, and **V** is horizontal wind velocity. The last right-hand term represents the horizontal convergence of water vapor into the region. Properly, both this and the storage term should include condensed water (cloud droplets and precipitation within the air column) (Kessler, 1969).

In calculations of large-scale water budgets these contributions are omitted because measurements of condensed water are not available. Their neglect is probably not serious in slowly changing situations, although Bradbury (1957) found suggestive evidence that appreciable quantities of water in the form of cloud droplets "may remain in suspension for

Table 5.3. Summary of Water Budget at 1800 CST, 21 May 1961*

Layer above Surface	Moisture flux (kt s^{-1}) Convective	Moisture flux (kt s^{-1}) Synoptic	Ratio of synoptic-scale influx to precipitation, % (Precip. = 150 kt s^{-1})
Surface–850 mb	—	30	18
Surface–700 mb	280	60	43
Surface–550 mb	(300)	80	55

* Abstracted, with rounding off, from tables in Fritsch et al. (1976). Note: "Synoptic" refers to moisture convergence into stippled area in Fig. 5.12a; "convective" is estimated moisture consumption by storms within the area (parentheses indicate downdraft flux included), and last column gives the ratio of synoptic-scale moisture convergence to the precipitation, for various layers above the surface.

several hours before being released as precipitation." On the scale of convective clouds the liquid-water contributions clearly cannot be neglected (McNab and Betts, 1978).

The last term of Eq. 5.7a may be written in the component forms

$$-\int_0^{p_0} \nabla \cdot q\mathbf{V} \, \frac{dp}{g} = -\int_0^{p_0} q\nabla \cdot \mathbf{V} \, \frac{dp}{g} - \int_0^{p_0} \mathbf{V} \cdot \nabla q \, \frac{dp}{g}, \tag{5.8}$$

showing that water-vapor supply could result either from horizontal mass convergence or from advection when the water vapor content of the air is greater on the upwind than on the downwind side of a region. The two processes commonly cooperate, as when southerly winds ahead of a cyclone become superimposed on a marked gradient of moisture, such as is normally present from the Gulf of Mexico northward, and at the same time low-level convergence causes the moist layer to become thicker. Conditions for abundant rainfall are then enhanced both by augmentation of water vapor available and, through the contribution of greater vapor content to θ_w, by increased potential instability for convection.

By Gauss's divergence theorem, Eq. 5.7a may be written in the alternative form

$$\int_A \left[(P - E) + \frac{\partial S}{\partial t} \right] dA = \int_L \int_0^{p_0} qv_n \, \frac{dp}{g} \, dL, \tag{5.9}$$

where v_n is the inward-directed component of air motion normal to curve L circumscribing an area A. This form is convenient when one is concerned with overall budgets over a region rather than the detailed distribution within it. The right-hand term expresses vapor flux across a vertical wall surrounding an atmospheric volume. With conservation of water mass, this must be balanced by the water flux $(P - E)$ across the Earth's surface, together with the change in amount of water stored within the volume. Fankhauser (1965; see Palmén and Newton, 1969, pp. 406–408) found close correspondence between water vapor convergence and observed rainfall in an extensive slow-moving squall line, when the local increase of water vapor storage was taken into account. Convergence of water vapor was greatest near the ground, decaying to zero at 700 mb.

According to Eq. 5.9, precipitation may also occur partly at the expense of water storage in the atmosphere. This was

demonstrated by Fritsch et al. (1976) in an analysis of the synoptic-scale water budget of the cyclone (Fig. 5.12a) with which the squall line portrayed in Fig. 5.6 was associated. Radar analyses showed broad precipitation areas mainly north of the warm front with tops generally below 9 km, and there were segments of squall lines in the warm sector (where tops to 15–17 km were reported) and also embedded in the cloud system north of the warm front. At the time of Fig. 5.12a the main convective activity was slightly east of the cyclone center; 6 hours later the squall line, about 600 km long, had moved 300 km ahead of the cold front in its northern part.

Maximum horizontal mass and moisture convergence in the lower troposphere occurred over northeastern Oklahoma–southeastern Kansas, where also the ascent at 500 mb was greatest. For the shaded region in Fig. 5.12a, area-integrated mass and moisture divergences in various layers are shown in Figs. 5.12b–c. Figure 5.12c also shows the vertical divergence of moisture flux and the three-dimensional flux of moisture into each layer, indicating maximum accumulation of water vapor in the middle troposphere.

Based on the moisture budget for an individual squall-line storm (Fig. 5.6) and an estimated 32 such cells in the budget volume, Fritsch et al. compared the air and water fluxes in the convective storms with their calculations from synoptic data. The results, partly summarized in Table 5.3, indicate that the net water fluxes in the embedded thunderstorms greatly exceeded the flow of moisture into the volume. Further, the estimated surface rainfall for the whole system was 150 kt s^{-1}, while the synoptic-scale moisture convergence was 80 kt s^{-1}, or about half the precipitation rate.

From these results Fritsch et al. concluded that "convective transport rates may be strongly related to the existing potential buoyant energy [degree of instability], rather than to the rate at which energy is generated by the large scale at the time of convection." This view is compatible with the diurnally varying nature of convective systems, which may, for example, develop in midafternoon and precipitate heavily for 12 hours, partly being supplied by concurrent moisture convergence and partly consuming the water vapor stored in the region. The decrease of water vapor storage is in turn consistent with the way air is processed by a squall line, as in Fig. 5.6. A squall line ingests the layer of moist air ahead of it, precipitates part of the water condensed (with a lesser part augmenting cloud water aloft), and disgorges on its rear side downdraft air less rich in water vapor (see example in Newton, 1950). Thus a squall line, sweeping over a broad swath during its lifetime, effectively replaces the moist layer with a shallower layer that has, level for level, up to 20–30% less water vapor content. As discussed by Fritsch et al., during quiescent periods between convection episodes the water vapor storage can be recharged by synoptic-scale advection and horizontal convergence processes.

f. Vertical Motions Associated with Jet-Stream Wind Maxima

It was noted earlier that divergence exists in the general region from a trough to the downstream crest in a upper-tropospheric wave. In a sinusoidal wave maximum upper-level divergence (with rising motions beneath) is located about midway between trough and ridge. Its intensity (Palmén and Newton, 1969, p. 144) is greatest for waves with short lengths and large amplitudes and large windspeed in the jet stream. These generalizations are based on a waveform with unchanging windspeed along the direction of the current. The presence of distinct wind maxima, alternating with weaker winds along the jet stream, significantly alters the distribution of upper-level divergence outlined above.

An important dynamical factor is associated with the approach of a jet maximum over the warm sector of a developing cyclone. Development here means the rate of production of absolute (geostrophic) vorticity near sea level. This is synonymous with a reduction in the central pressure of the cyclone (deepening) and a corresponding increase of the associated pressure gradients (intensification). Standard meteorological textbooks approach the subject of pressure change mechanisms with viewpoints ranging from heuristic (Hess, 1959, Chap. 14) to empirical (Haltiner and Martin, 1957, Chap. 19) to theoretical (Petterssen, 1956, Chap. 16). All explanations are traceable to a fundamental concept proposed by Dines (1912, 1919), which maintains that regions in the lower atmosphere characterized by mass convergence must be surmounted by regions of mass divergence in order to explain the usual small magnitudes of observed pressure change at the ground. Said in another way, there must be (at least) one level in the atmosphere where divergence changes sign, i.e., a level of mass nondivergence (LMND). Thus, over level terrain, the mass change in a vertical column extending from the Earth's surface will depend upon the sign of the net mass divergence in that column.

The local mass change is conveniently expressed as the height tendency of a constant-pressure surface:

$$\left(\frac{\partial z}{\partial t}\right)_p = -\frac{1}{\rho g} \int_0^p \nabla \cdot \mathbf{V} \, dp - \mathbf{V} \cdot \nabla z + w, \qquad (5.10)$$

which can be derived from the equation expressing mass continuity in a pressure coordinate system (e.g., see Haltiner and Martin, 1957, pp. 318–19). Unfortunately, three-dimensional mass divergence cannot be calculated from synoptic charts because horizontal mass divergence (the first right-hand term) is largely compensated by vertical mass convergence (expressed by the last term, if $w = 0$ at $p = 0$), a quantity not directly observable. Furthermore, advective mass changes (second right-hand term), which are relatively easy to estimate from synoptic data, are at least an order of magnitude smaller than either horizontal or vertical divergence.

Now we resort to a simple, oft-used model of divergence associated with a jet maximum to provide further insight to storm development. A factor to remember in the following is that air flows through the jet maximum (windspeeds exceed the rate of movement of the maximum center). Because of this, the forces acting on air parcels entering and exiting the jet maximum are unbalanced with regard to the mass distribution as represented by the geostrophic wind. Air parcels, in the absence of frictional forces, tend to conserve their momentum. Thus air entering the jet-maximum region, where the pressure gradient is greatest, will be moving slower than the geostrophic value (subgeostrophic winds) and will tend to accelerate. Air moving out of the maximum region results in supergeostrophic winds and will tend to decelerate.

Coriolis force is proportional to the actual windspeed and is directed toward the right of the motion. Therefore, in the exit region of the jet maximum, Coriolis force is temporarily greater than the pressure gradient force, with the result that exiting air will be deflected toward higher pressure (contours). Since the amount of deflecting force is proportional to the windspeed, the amount of mass moved across the contours will be greatest near the jet-stream axis, resulting in a pattern of divergence and convergence.

Consider $\mathbf{V} = \mathbf{V}_g + \mathbf{V}_n + \mathbf{V}_s$, where $\mathbf{V}_n$ is the component of the "ageostrophic wind," $\mathbf{V}_{ag}$, which is directed across contours and represents the direction difference between $\mathbf{V}$ and $\mathbf{V}_g$. The other component of $\mathbf{V}_{ag}$ is $\mathbf{V}_s$, which is directed along contours and represents the speed difference between $\mathbf{V}$ and $\mathbf{V}_g$. For the present discussion only the cross-contour component, $\mathbf{V}_n$, is relevant.

Figure 5.13 schematically shows an upper-level (e.g., 300-mb) jet maximum approaching a surface cyclone that lies in the jet's left-front quadrant (1) viewed along the direction of flow (*s* direction). Bjerknes (1951) shows that the cross-contour component of wind V_n along an isentropic surface is related to the actual wind V and its geostrophic component V_g by

$$V_{n,} = \frac{V \frac{\partial V_g}{\partial s} + \frac{\partial V_g}{\partial t_\Theta}}{f - \frac{\partial V_g}{\partial n}}. \qquad (5.11)$$

For simplification, we will consider that the mass field represented by the geostrophic wind varies only slowly in time, in relation to the magnitude of the other terms. In the model depicted by Fig. 5.13, the diffluent exit region of the jet

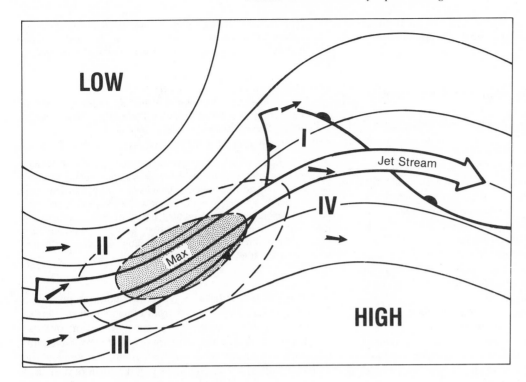

Figure 5.13. Schematic of the polar jet windspeed maximum along the jet axis and its influence upon vertical motion distribution in entrance and exit regions (the air moves faster than the propagation speed of the maximum center). Because of accelerations acting on air as it leaves jet maximum, winds have component from quadrant I to quadrant IV, inducing in those quadrants upper-level divergence and convergence, respectively, which give rise to upward motion in I and downward motion in IV that tend to enhance or suppress convective motions in those respective quadrants.

maximum is of main concern. Relative to the *n*-direction, V_g is maximum along the jet-stream axis and decreases at a diminishing rate toward both the high- and the low-contour sides of the jet. A profile of V_g plotted versus *n* has a somewhat bell-shaped curve. South of the jet axis, $\partial V_g / \partial n > 0$ and reaches a maximum value at the inflection point of the profile, which, of course, varies from case to case but always lies some distance from the jet axis. Thus the denominator in Eq. 5.11 is minimum and positive provided $\partial V_g / \partial n < f$, as is normally so. Also in the exit region, $\partial V_g / \partial s < 0$ and since $V > 0$, $V_n < 0$, meaning that the cross-contour component of flow is from quadrant I to quadrant IV. Since the denominator in Eq. 5.11 is minimum at the southern inflection of the $V_g - n$ profile, V_n is maximum negative at the same point. Thus in the exit region quadrant IV tends to be characterized by convergence, and quadrant I, including the jet axis, by divergence. Under this regime mass moves (isentropically) across contours toward higher values. Through Dines's compensation some other layer of the atmosphere must exhibit the inverse of this divergence pattern. Stratospheric air above the jet is inhibited from responding because of its extreme stability. Tropospheric air reacts more easily, producing an indirect circulation of rising motion in quadrant I and sinking motion in IV. A similar argument can be developed for the entrance region (quadrants II and III), except that here the mass at upper levels moves from high to low (i.e., northward), and descent occurs in II, while ascent occurs in III. Again, this analysis applies strictly for straight parallel flow. Curvature and the normal diffluence of streamlines in the exit region

(confluence in the entrance region) modify the described effects somewhat, and each case should be analyzed as to its own characteristics.

Uccellini and Johnson (1979) explain in greater detail the dynamics of this mass-momentum adjustment and its relationship to lower-level jet streaks. A more detailed explanation of similar circulations in relation to the low-level jet and a schematic diagram are also found in Chap. 6. The polar jet-stream circulation is superimposed upon the more general ascending-descending motions associated with the wave-flow patterns described earlier. Whether the air in IV actually descends (subsides) on the scale suggested by analysis of the jet exit region depends largely on the magnitude of the other causes of vertical motion, from both larger- and smaller-scale factors. Nonetheless, experience indicates that the passage of an upper jet maximum through a longer wave trough and its subsequent approach over the warm sector of a cyclone tend to enhance the upward motion in quadrant I and may contribute importantly to the release of potential instability.

McNulty (1978) has undertaken a quantitative empirical evaluation of divergence patterns associated with jet maxima and finds that upper-level divergence is indeed found in the forward-left quadrant (I) of a jet exit region and, when superimposed over low-level, conditionally unstable air and low-level convergence, gives rise to severe-thunderstorm episodes. It is not surprising then that one of the empirical rules used to forecast the location of severe-storm outbreaks (e.g., Porter et al., 1955) is that the initial convection near the intersection of the polar-jet axis and the cold front or, if dry surface air has invaded the region ahead of the front, at the intersection of the jet axis and the western boundary of the moist low-level air.

5. Some Aspects of Thunderstorm Forecasting

Forecasting thunderstorms is intimately tied to the general synoptic-scale forecast, and requires skill and experience at interpreting the present state of the atmosphere and anticipating where and when the causative elements will come together. This can be as simple a matter as analyzing an early-morning sounding from the area of concern to determine whether the atmosphere is conditionally unstable, how much moisture is available, and whether the expected diurnal heating will be sufficient to release the instability. These are the basic factors (e.g., see Petterssen, 1956, Chap. 25) involved in forecasting air-mass thunderstorms such as those that occur almost daily in summer over broad areas of the middle-latitude continents.

Forecasting severe thunderstorms is a far more complicated process; the difficulty seems inversely related to the anticipated strength of the associated synoptic disturbance. This is suggested by the greater success achieved in forecasting tornadoes in major outbreak situations than for those with fewer tornadoes (Pearson and Weiss, 1979). The likelihood of a major outbreak is less difficult to forecast because the large-scale conditions that cause rapid cyclogenesis are rather well understood, are usually quite visible in routine upper-air data long before the events transpire, and are synonymous with the factors known to be important in preparing the atmosphere for severe convection. On the other hand, convection associated with weaker synoptic systems can be just as intense, although generally not as widespread, and seems to be triggered by mesoscale disturbances that are neither as well understood nor as closely observed as are the larger-scale systems. Generally, severe-storm forecasts are made for areas on the order of 60,000 km^2, about one-third the size of most midcontinent states, and 1 to 6 h in advance of the anticipated development. Although tornadoes occur with preferred mean values of temperature, dew point, wind, and derived quantities at the surface and at various levels aloft in a given season, the statistical spread is appreciable (David, 1976; Williams, 1976). Hence this information is in itself inadequate for specific forecasts, and synoptic-dynamic processes must be considered.

The special conditions connected with severe thunderstorm outbreaks were introduced into forecasting procedures by Fawbush et al. (1951). They found that

tornado situations developed when, and only when, the synoptic situation was characterized by the following conditions:

1. A layer of moist air near the earth's surface must be surmounted by a deep layer of dry air.
2. The horizontal moisture distribution within the moist layer must exhibit a distinct maximum along a relatively narrow band (i.e., a moisture wedge or ridge).

3. The horizontal distribution of winds aloft must exhibit a maximum of speed along a relatively narrow band at some level between [3 and 6 km], with the maximum speed exceeding [18 m s^{-1}].
4. The vertical projection of the axis of wind maximum must intersect the axis of the moisture ridge.
5. The temperature distribution of the air column as a whole must be such as to indicate conditional instability. [The effect of radiative heating of the lower layers is implicit.]
6. The moist layer must be subjected to appreciable lifting. . . .

Synoptic situations preceding tornado development are often characterized by presence of the above conditions but in separate areas. The forecasting problem is then usually limited to determining whether or not the air motion is, or will be, such as to bring the different favorable areas to coincidence. . . . In all cases examined, at least four of the six conditions have been fulfilled 12 h prior to the outbreak of the storm, the remaining ones becoming satisfied by the time of the outbreak.

It may be noted that the synoptic conditions preceding flash floods (as distinguished from other manifestations of severe weather) may differ significantly from some of those listed above. In particular, prolonged heavy convective rainfall tends to be associated with very high dew points at the surface (also, as above, frequently in the form of a distinct moist tongue) but, in addition, with moist air in the middle troposphere (Maddox et al., 1979). Heavy rainfall (generally from mesoscale convective clusters) occurs with a variety of synoptic situations, in which the surface pressure and flow patterns may be weakly developed. An advancing middle-level short-wave trough often helps trigger and focus thunderstorm activity, but this may be associated with relatively weak winds aloft.

Forecasters at the National Severe Storms Forecasting Center and at the Air Force Global Weather Central have developed several diagnostic tools to assist them in ascertaining the factors associated with storm outbreaks. Seldom do all of these factors appear together with equal clarity, which makes severe-storm forecasting one of the most demanding exercises in weather prediction. The essential empirical techniques can be found in the technical literature (U.S. Weather Bureau, 1956; House, 1963; Miller, 1972) and are summarized with additional references in Vol. 1, Chap. 8, of this series. Computer processing and analysis play an increasing role. Automated analyses and objective probability predictions are essential for rapid assimilation of the huge quantities of observations that must be considered by the forecaster. In this section we shall briefly mention some recent developments in objective forecasting and, without any attempt to be exhaustive, some further synoptic considerations. In particular, the preceding sections were focused on generalizations about severe weather in relation to idealized cyclones; here some important variations will be noted.

a. Objective Forecasts

Recent developments in objective thunderstorm forecasting

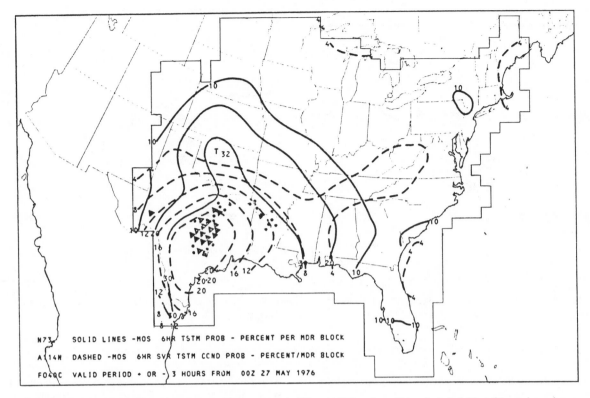

Figure 5.14. Computer-drawn map of thunderstorm probability (solid) and conditional probability of tornadoes, large hail, or damaging winds (dashed). The probabilities are valid for areas of roughly 6,000 km² during the 21- to 27-h interval following 0000 GMT initial time, or ±3 hours from 0000 GMT the next day. Observed tornadoes (solid triangle), hail (solid circle), and damaging winds (solid square) are indicated (courtesy National Weather Service, Techniques Development Laboratory).

have come from two areas of meteorological research. Investigators at the National Weather Service (NWS) Techniques Development Laboratory have developed thunderstorm-probability forecast techniques using screening regression methods that include the conditional probability that the thunderstorms will be severe. A medium-range (12–36 h) forecasting model uses radar data, climatology, and statistics output from current synoptic-scale numerical model predictions prepared twice daily at the NWS National Meteorological Center (Reap and Foster, 1975). These operational probability guidance forecasts, covering the eastern two-thirds of the continental United States, are objective and have proved valuable aids in drawing attention to the general areas in which severe storms are expected to develop (Fig. 5.14). A similar model incorporates hourly surface reports for short-range (2–6 h) prediction of thunderstorm and severe-weather activity (Charba, 1975, 1979).

Parameter predictors are objectively selected for these statistical forecast models on the basis of their association with the overall probability of the event. Interestingly, for the 12- to 36-h forecasts, the predictors chosen for the general thunderstorm forecast model are those that have been used subjectively by forecasters for decades:

1. A sufficiently moist atmosphere below 3 km that becomes convectively unstable in response to large-scale lifting.
2. A climatologically favorable location.
3. A boundary-layer convergence zone such as a front or pressure trough to aid vertical motion.

Additional parameters selected for the conditional probability of severe thunderstorms are low pressure in a region climatologically favorable for severe thunderstorms, warming owing to temperature advection, conditional instability, synoptic-scale upward motion, relatively strong vector wind shear, and a large westerly mean-wind component in the lower troposphere (below 500 mb).

The second effort toward improving severe-thunderstorm forecasting is in the research stages. It involves the development of fine-scale numerical prediction models that use parameterizations of both the initiation of convection and its influence upon the general synoptic-scale systems (e.g., Perkey, 1976). A comprehensive review of such models is given in Anthes (1983). These models are at present experimental; results to date indicate that there will be a significant improvement over current techniques when new data

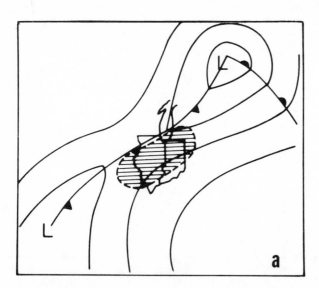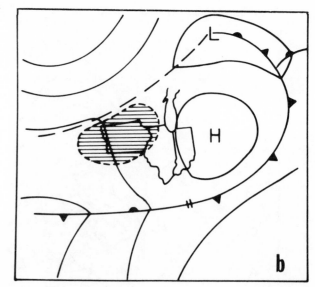

Figure 5.15. Typical surface pressure and frontal patterns for severe-thunderstorm outbreaks under northwesterly flow aloft. Of the cases studied during a 14-yr period, 20% were type 1 (a) and 28% were type 2 (b) (Johns, 1977).

Table 5.4. Oklahoma and Iowa Tornadoes Grouped by Quadrant from Which Tornado Moved*

Quadrant	Number	Percent
Southwest	474	69
Northwest	195	28
Other	17	3
All	686	100

*Data from Notis and Stanford (1973, 1976) include for Oklahoma 525 cases from 1959 to 1974, and for Iowa 161 cases from 1959 to 1971.

sources can be assimilated (e.g., higher-resolution soundings and satellite information).

b. Severe-Storm Outbreaks Under Northwesterly Flow Aloft

Most severe-thunderstorm outbreaks occur with the general large-scale synoptic distributions described earlier. However, it has long been known that a significant fraction of severe-weather events occurs with other synoptic-scale configurations (Galway, 1958). A study of Iowa and Oklahoma tornadoes (Notis and Stanford, 1973, 1976) showed that, of the tornadoes occurring from 1959 to 1971 for which sufficiently complete documentation exists (161 Iowa cases, 525 Oklahoma cases), about two-thirds are associated with synoptic conditions characterized by southwesterly flow aloft, while nearly one-third are associated with northwesterly flow aloft in response to which the storms move southeastward rather than northeastward (Table 5.4). The direction of tornado movement was found to be highly correlated

with the 500-mb flow direction; tornadoes occurred over a wide range of 500-mb windspeed with modal values near 25 m s^{-1} for northeast-moving tornadoes and 18 m s^{-1} for southeast-moving tornadoes, and longer paths were significantly correlated with stronger winds aloft.

Johns (1982) presented a 16-year analysis of the diurnal, seasonal, and geographical frequencies and characteristics of severe-storm outbreaks associated with northwesterly flow (NWF). An outbreak was defined as 20 or more clustered severe-storm events (tornado, hail >19 mm in diameter, or surface wind >25 m s^{-1}) or eight or more reports subsuming multiple events, with the time between events not to exceed 3 h.

NWF outbreaks often begin just south of a quasi-stationary front (Fig. 5.15a) or just south of a SW–NE–oriented pressure trough (Fig. 5.15b), and in either case a considerable distance (more than 500 km) from the surface center of low pressure and ahead of a southeastward-moving short wave embedded in general northwesterly flow on the west side of a larger-scale, long-wave trough (Fig. 5.16). Moisture is supplied by southerly flow from the Gulf of Mexico, either in the surface layer or just above a shallow polar air mass. These conditions do not represent a departure from the basic physical structure of the atmosphere described earlier as conducive to severe-storm development. The environment is conditionally and convectively unstable, as one might expect in view of the June–August annual peak for this storm type (Fig. 5.17).

With a pronounced midafternoon peak in beginning times, the average duration of an outbreak is 8–10 h. Confirming an observation by Miller (1972) that NWF outbreaks are likely to repeat during several successive days, serial occurrences (no more than two days apart) accounted for 71% of all cases. Most series involved two or three outbreaks, but in two cases there were eight or more.

The geographical distribution in Fig. 5.18 indicates that the region from eastern Nebraska to Ohio is most susceptible to severe-storm outbreaks in northwest flow, in contrast to the earlier (May) Oklahoma-Kansas maximum for all tornadic storms (see Chap. 2; also Maddox, 1976, Fig. 2). The pattern is broadly similar to that of SE-moving tornadoes, at least one of which occurs with most NWF outbreaks. Figures 5.17 and 5.18 are consistent with the general northward shift in tornado activity as summer progresses, a fact that is undoubtedly linked to the summer migration of the polar jet stream to higher latitudes, as well as the increased low-level moisture content requisite for instability.

The frequency of NWF cases that produce fewer than 20 severe events is, of course, greater than that indicated by Figs. 5.17 and 5.18. Tornado outbreaks (six or more) occurred with only 20% of NWF severe-weather outbreaks (whose dominant characteristic is violent straight-line winds). Maddox (1976) finds that tornado outbreaks most commonly occur with 500-mb southwesterly winds, whereas severe-storm outbreaks without tornadoes most commonly occur with winds from a westerly quadrant, biased toward the northwest. This is not to say that tornadoes themselves do not move from westerly or northwesterly directions. On the contrary, they frequently do move from those directions when the parent thunderstorm deviates markedly to the right of the environmental mean wind. But these storms most generally occur when that mean wind is from the southwest rather than the northwest.

c. High Plains Eastern-Slope Thunderstorms

Severe weather in the form of heavy rain occasionally invades the high-plains region just east of the Rocky Mountains, but under considerably different synoptic circumstances than mentioned so far. Details and illustrations of such an episode are presented by Hoxit et al. in Vol. 1, Chap. 2, of this series. The general synoptic features associated with these storms (Maddox et al., 1978) are as follows:

1. In the middle and upper troposphere a long-wave trough is situated over the western United States with a ridge line oriented NW–SE just east of the high-plains region, resulting in light S–SE upper winds (<10 m s⁻¹).
2. A short-wave trough (often quite weak) approaches the threat area from the southwest.

At the surface a slow-moving or stationary polar front lies just south of the threat area, with high pressure toward the northeast producing upslope flow from the southeast.

High moisture content (10–15 g kg⁻¹) is present in the polar air mass, and the prestorm soundings are typically a mixture of types *B* and *C* in Fig. 5.2).

Although general thunderstorm activity along the eastern slope usually follows the development of such a pattern, in-

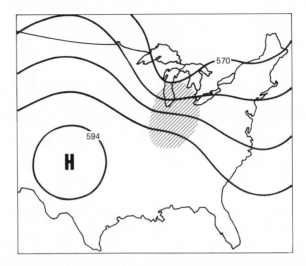

Figure 5.16. A schematic of typical upper-air flow (500-mb contours; units are dekameters) associated with severe-thunderstorm outbreaks under northwesterly flow. The shaded area in advance of the short-wave trough is the region most likely to produce thunderstorms (after Johns, 1977).

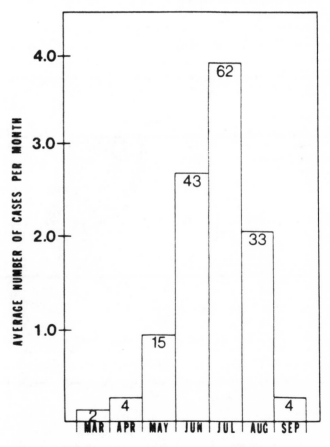

Figure 5.17. Frequency of northwest flow outbreaks by month, with total number of NWF outbreak cases per month indicated, 1962–77 (Johns, 1982).

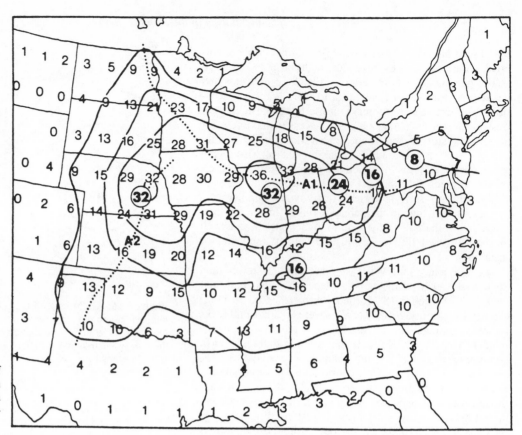

Figure 5.18. Total number of NWF outbreaks occurring in 2° latitude-longitude tessera in the 16-year period 1962–77 (Johns, 1982).

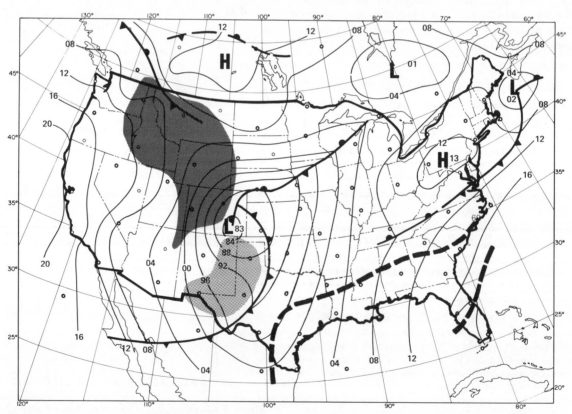

Figure 5.19. Surface analysis, 1800 CST, 2 April 1974. Heavy dashed lines, 60°F isodrosotherm (dew-point isoline); light solid lines, isobars at 4-mb intervals; dark shading, area of precipitation; light shading, area of blowing dust or blowing sand (from Hoxit and Chappell, 1975).

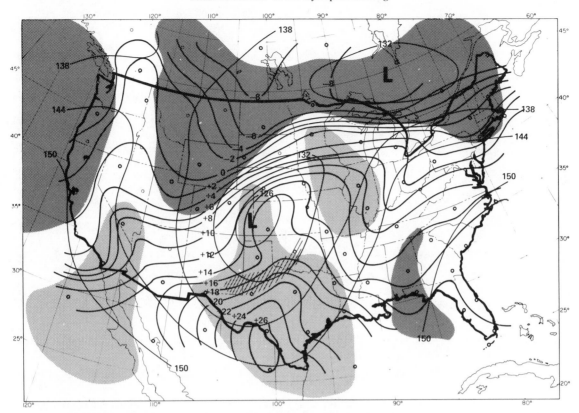

Figure 5.20. 850-mb analysis, 1800 CST, 2 April 1974. Contours, 60-m intervals; isotherms, 2°C intervals; light shading, dew-point depression > 20°C; dark shading, dew-point depression < 5°C; hatched, windspeeds > 50 kn (from Hoxit and Chappell, 1975).

tense storms often develop in connection with orographic and other mesoscale features. Once triggered, the storms move quite slowly in the weak upper flow and, being continually fed by the moist upslope flow, can produce tremendous rainfall (250–400 mm) in a relatively short time.

6. An Illustrative Case of Severe-Thunderstorm Development

The widespread occurrence of severe thunderstorms on 3 April 1974 east of the Mississippi River has been labeled the "outbreak of the century," and although it is atypical in the number of tornadoes produced, its synoptic-scale development is classic and an excellent example of the concepts presented in this chapter. The analyses presented here are, for the most part, the work of Hoxit and Chappell (1975). Review of this case with emphasis on its social impact is presented in Vol. 1, Chap. 3.

a. The Developing Synoptic Scene

By the evening of 2 April 1974, an already intense extratropical cyclone was moving eastward out of the high plains of Colorado (Fig. 5.19). Because of an intrusion of dry polar air into the Gulf coastal area only 12 hours before, the western branch of the Atlantic subtropical anticyclone had not as yet had sufficient time to advect the supply of moisture from the Gulf necessary to produce widespread thunderstorm activity ahead of the cyclone. At the surface, the 60°F isodrosotherm (about 11 g kg^{-1} mixing ratio) had advanced northward into the coastal states, but the moist layer was relatively thin. Mixing ratios over Texas were only 3–5 g kg^{-1} at 850 mb (Fig. 5.20).

The now-modified polar air mass lay over most of the states bordering the Ohio River and the New England states. Continental polar air over the northern plains was being drawn into the cyclone's circulation (Fig. 5.19), while dry air was rapidly pushing eastward across the southwestern states behind a cold front of Pacific origin. Strong southwesterly winds (hatched area in Fig. 5.20) were creating dust storms in New Mexico and western Texas (lightly shaded area in Fig. 5.19).

Key elements in the rapid development of this storm system were a strong (140-kn) polar jet maximum (Fig. 5.21) that propagated rapidly southeastward from the middle Pacific Coast, and strong cold-air advection (Fig. 5.22) that contributed to rapid height falls (about -100 m [12 h]$^{-1}$) at

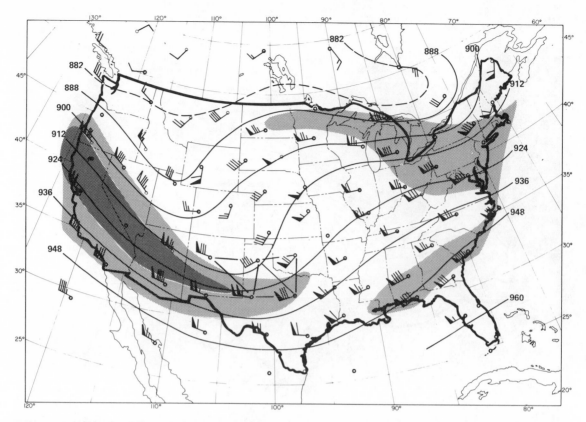

Figure 5.21. 300-mb analysis, 1800 CST, 2 April 1974. Contours, 120-m intervals; light shading, windspeeds 80–120 kn; dark shading, > 120 kn (from Hoxit and Chappell, 1975). Three triangles in the jet exit region over Texas, Oklahoma, and New Mexico indicate areas for which divergences were calculated (see Fig. 5.23).

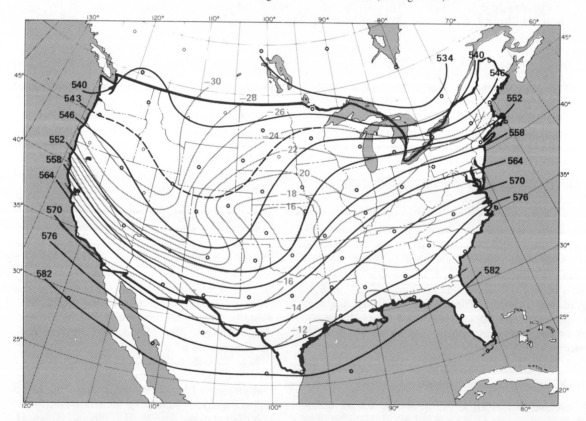

Figure 5.22. 500-mb analysis, 1800 CST, 2 April 1974. Contours, 60-m intervals; isotherms (light lines), 2°C intervals. Contribution of intense cold-air advection in Texas Panhandle and adjacent regions to developing cyclone is analyzed in Sec. 6a (Hoxit and Chappell, 1975).

300 mb in northwestern Texas and the adjacent regions and corresponding sea-level pressure falls of 8–10 mb.

The symptoms of cyclone development are much easier to identify than are the exact causes, which are often a complicated mixture of factors, many of them unobservable. Nonetheless, insight into the physical processes at work in the Texas Panhandle is revealed by a computation using Eq. 5.10.

Using the principles developed in Sec. 4f, it is convenient to consider only the mass change in a tropospheric layer, because our data do not extend to the top of the atmosphere. We approximate the differential height advection by the advection of thickness owing to the layer mean wind. Thus the equation for local thickness change follows from differencing two equations such as Eq. 5.10 applied to the respective pressure layers:

$$\frac{\partial(\delta z)}{\partial t} = \frac{1}{\rho g}\int_{p_2}^{p_1} \nabla \cdot \mathbf{V}\, dp - \bar{\mathbf{V}} \cdot \nabla(\delta z) + \delta w. \qquad (5.12)$$

We apply the equation of state and the hydrostatic relationship to represent the first right-hand term of Eq. 5.12 as

$$\frac{1}{\rho g}\int_{p_2}^{p_1} \nabla \cdot \mathbf{V}\, dp = \frac{R_d \bar{T}}{g}\, ln\,(p_1/p_2)\overline{\nabla \cdot \mathbf{V}} = \delta z \overline{\nabla \cdot \mathbf{V}}.$$
$$(5.13)$$

An approximation of the mean divergence in the triangular area with Albuquerque, N.Mex., and Amarillo and Midland, Tex., as vertices was obtained using a method suggested by Bellamy (1949). Divergences were calculated at the levels indicated in Fig. 5.23 based on the reported winds from 1,828 to 9,144 m. Layer average divergence, obtained by trapezoidal integration, was 4.0×10^{-5} s^{-1} (0.14 h^{-1}), making the value for the first right-hand term in Eq. 5.12 29 cm s^{-1} (1.04 km h^{-1}). This is also the magnitude of δw (subsidence) required to compensate the horizontal mass divergence in the layer.

The second right-hand term of Eq. 5.12 was evaluated on the basis of graphical addition and subtraction (Saucier, 1955, Chap. 5) of the 850-mb and 300-mb contour maps (Figs. 5.20 and 5.21). The results yield estimates of mean geostrophic wind and thickness distribution; $V_g = 26.5$ m s^{-1} and $\nabla(\delta z) = 60$ m (3° lat.)$^{-1}$ in the New Mexico–west Texas area. This strong cold-air advection was decreasing thickness at more than twice the rate observed for the preceding 12 h: -17.2 m h^{-1} versus -6.7 m h^{-1} average for the three stations.

The numerical imbalance in Eq. 5.12 determined by these computations suggests that differential subsidence, radiative warming, and eddy heat transport in the 850-to-300-mb layer may have been offsetting as much as 60% of the observed advection cooling in the area. Limitations and uncertainties in the data and analyses prevent a more thorough look into the processes that were contributing to cyclogenesis in this case.

b. The First Convection is Forced, but . . .

These events occurred before the atmosphere east of the Pacific front had become convectively unstable. Analysis of

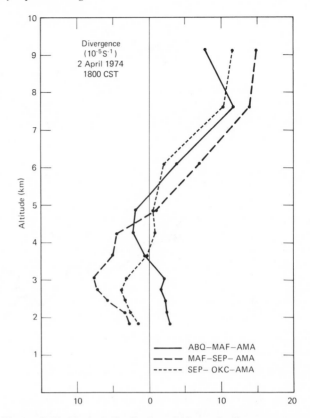

Figure 5.23. Vertical distribution of kinematic divergence computed from winds reported at levels indicated by dots for the three triangular areas shown in Fig. 5.21. Average terrain altitude for each area is indicated by the horizontal lines at the bottom, which also identify the divergence profiles.

the 1800 CST Lifted Index (*LI*; see Chap. 4 for definition) indicated that in general the atmosphere below 500 mb would not release convective energy (*LI* > 0; Fig. 5.24) without additional help. A destabilizing factor was present at this time in the form of the vertical circulation induced by the rapidly advancing Pacific front. Divergence computations in the vicinity of the front in northwest Texas and southwest Oklahoma revealed strong low-level convergence surmounted by even stronger divergence at the jet-stream level (Fig. 5.23). In the Midland-Stephenville-Amarillo area, $w = 17$ cm s^{-1} (0.6 km h^{-1}) at 5 km, while in the area southwest of Oklahoma City, $w = 6$ cm s^{-1} at 4 km. Because of the discontinuity (the front) in the lowest layers, we may be confident that the calculated divergence values, while real, are only symptomatic of the actual magnitudes that must have been occurring with the front on a smaller scale. Within 2 h after these observations a squall line developed in central Oklahoma and moved into Arkansas and Missouri during the night. However, only isolated severe weather occurred as a result of this first episode of convective activity.

c. . . . an Unstable Situation Rapidly Develops . . .

By the following morning (0600 CST, 3 April 1974), condi-

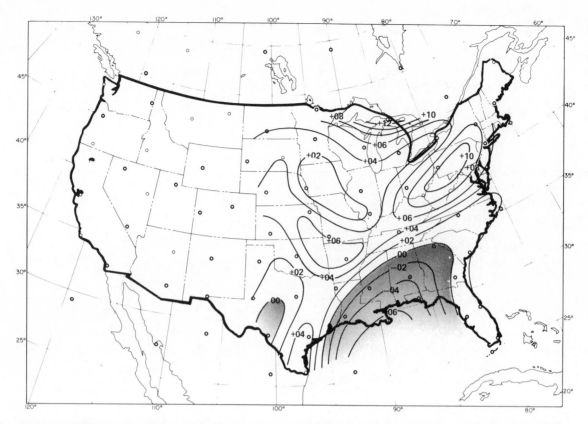

Figure 5.24. Lifted Index analysis, 1800 CST, 2 April 1974. Negative values (shaded) indicate air with potential for convective overturning (Hoxit and Chappell, 1975).

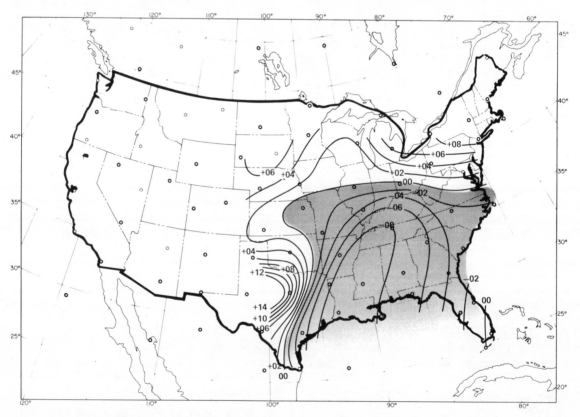

Figure 5.25. Lifted Index analysis, 0600 CST, 3 April 1974. Negative values (shaded) indicate air with potential for convective overturning (Hoxit and Chappell, 1975).

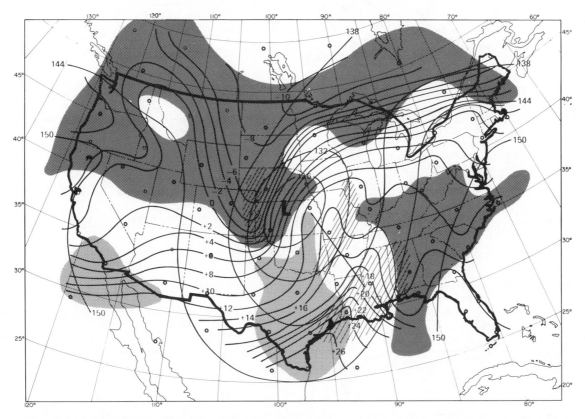

Figure 5.26. 850-mb analysis, 0600 CST, 3 April 1974. Contours, 60-m intervals; isotherms, 2°C intervals; light shading, dew-point depression > 20°C; dark shading, dew-point depression < 5°C; hatched, windspeeds > 50 kn. Line from Topeka, Kans., to Boothville, La., shows location of cross-section analysis presented as Fig. 5.27 (from Hoxit and Chappell, 1975).

tions had changed dramatically. The atmosphere over the entire southeastern United States had become conditionally unstable (Fig. 5.25), principally through the northward advection and deepening of the surface moist layer. A low-level jet (*LJ*) that had developed at 850 mb in the Louisiana-Mississippi region (Fig. 5.26) appeared to be an extension of the polar jet along isentropic surfaces (Fig. 5.27).[3] The altitude of this LJ is found to be coincident with the top of an inversion separating the lower moist air from dry air above. Uccellini and Johnson (1979) show that such jets can form as an induced response to the cross-contour mass adjustments in the exit region of a polar jet maximum as discussed in Sec. 4f. The exit region of the polar jet had by this time passed through the upper trough and was moving northeastward (Fig. 5.28). A branch of the subtropical jet from

southern Mississippi to Georgia had strengthened and was contributing to a broad region of upper-level diffluent flow over most of the area surrounding the lower Mississippi and Ohio rivers. Synoptic-scale kinematic vertical motions (Fig. 5.29; calculated by Hoxit and Chappell [1975], by a different method from that mentioned above) indicated two broad zones of activity: one extended from Nebraska to a maximum over Iowa and on through Wisconsin and Michigan; the other extended from Arkansas and Louisiana eastward to the Atlantic Coast. The contemporaneous radar depiction map (Fig. 5.30) indicated in the northern zone mostly rain showers from clouds whose tops were less than 35,000 ft (11 km). Thunderstorms whose tops were less than 43,000 ft (13 km) were scattered over the southern zone, while the most intense storms (tops over 15 km) were developing over Illinois.

Conditions in the area east of the Mississippi River were ripe for a major convective development. Only a capping inversion (Fig. 5.31) prevented the widespread release of the tremendous instability generated by the synoptic-scale developments. Throughout the day the inversion was lifted and weakened by the large-scale ascent in that region (Fig. 5.29). The cyclone, deepening and intensifying during the day, advanced from Kansas to Iowa and in its wake pulled

[3] Figures 5.26 and 5.27 provide an example of the relationships described in footnote 2: at 850 mb air at Topeka, Kans. (TOP in Fig. 5.27), is colder than air near Jackson, Miss. (JAN), by about 7°C, and the cross section reveals the 306 K isentrope slopes upward from 850 mb at Jan to above 600 mb at TOP. Height contours in Fig. 5.26 represent also geostrophic streamlines and are seen to have components toward TOP, implying ascent along the low-level isentropic surfaces, especially between JAN and Little Rock (LIT); see also Fig. 5.31.

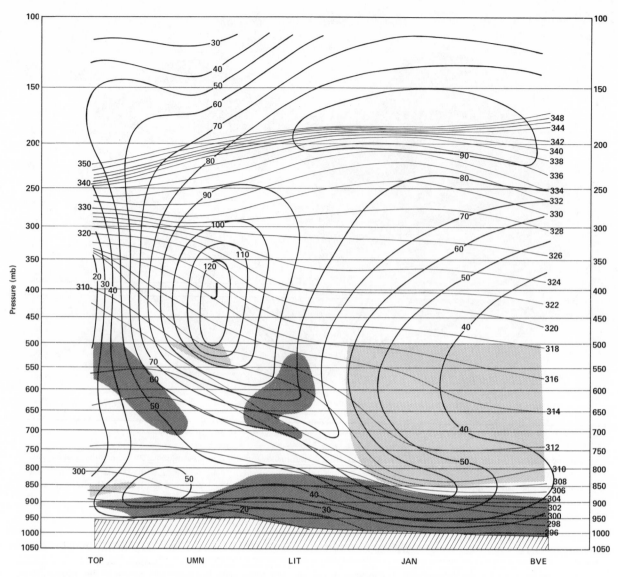

Figure 5.27. Vertical cross section from Topeka, Kans., through Monette, Mo., Little Rock, Ark.; and Jackson, Miss., to Boothville, La., 0600 CST, 3 April 1974. Heavy lines, windspeeds at 10-kn intervals; light lines, isentropes at 2-K intervals; light shading, dew-point depressions >20°C; dark shading, dew-point depressions <5°C (Hoxit and Chappell, 1975).

subfreezing temperatures southward into the Great Plains. Meanwhile, record-breaking warm temperatures developed in a broad area surrounding Huntington, W.Va., but receding cool air remained trapped in the valleys of the Appalachian Mountains. Low-level moisture continued its advance into the Ohio Valley, and dry air above the capping inversion pushed from Arkansas into western Kentucky. By 1800 CST the polar-jet exit region moved from its morning location over eastern Oklahoma (Fig. 5.28) to Indiana, while the LJ (Fig. 5.26) extended itself from Alabama to western Ohio.

d. ... and Triggers Three Tornadic Squall Lines

By late afternoon of 3 April, in a location more than 200 km ahead of the Pacific front, three tornadic squall lines developed in a 400-km-wide area from Mississippi to Michigan (Fig. 5.32), some containing thunderstorms whose tops reached above 17-km altitude. In Vol. 1, Chap. 3, of this series, Abbey and Fujita describe the damage and social consequences produced by some of the more than 140 tornadoes spawned by these thunderstorms during their rapid northeastward movement (at speeds up to 30 m s^{-1}).

Interestingly, the Appalachian region mentioned above experienced few tornadoes, and there were none in West Virginia. Several factors may have contributed to this fortunate circumstance. First, the squall lines reached those areas after sunset, and rapid cooling of the surface layers over the still-cold ground (early April) would have dimin-

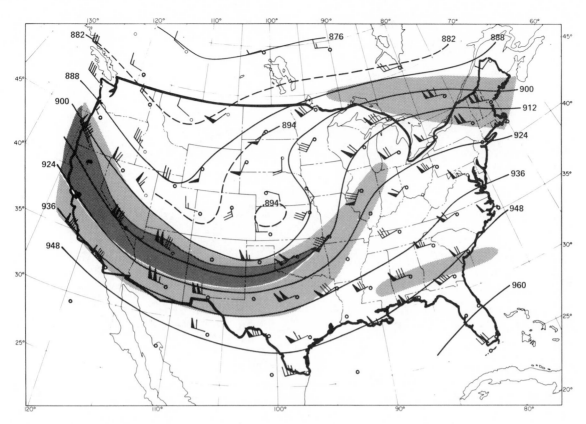

Figure 5.28. 300-mb analysis, 0600 CST, 3 April 1974. Contours, 120-m intervals; light shading, windspeeds 80–120 kn; dark shading, >120 kn (Hoxit and Chappell, 1975).

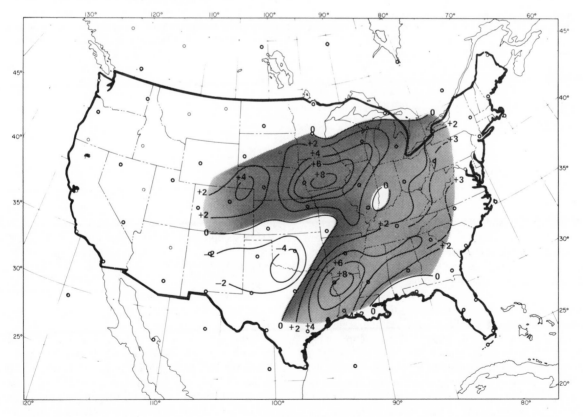

Figure 5.29. Kinematic vertical motions (cm s⁻¹), 0600 CST, 3 April 1974, at 675 mb (Hoxit and Chappell, 1975).

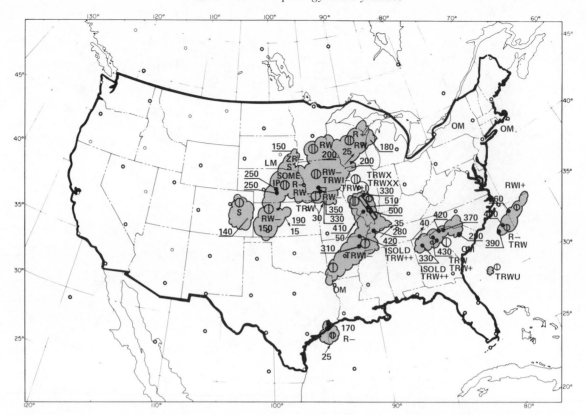

Figure 5.30. Radar summary, 0525 CST, 3 April 1974. Echo tops are in hundreds of feet; group motions (arrows) are in knots. *TRW*, thunderstorm; *RW*, rain shower; *R*, rain; *ZR*, freezing rain; *S*, snow. Intensity is indicated as heavy (+) or light (−) and increasing (+) or decreasing (−) following letters designating precipitation type. Coverage is indicated by circles with vertical bars: one bar, scattered (≤50%); two bars, broken (>50%). Thunderstorms are isolated (ISOLD) in the southern states, while a squall line (double line) has developed in southern Illinois (Hoxit and Chappell, 1975).

ished the energy supplied the updrafts. Second, the record warm temperatures in eastern Kentucky and adjacent regions of Ohio and West Virginia were associated with a region of subsiding air (at −2 cm s⁻¹) indicated by kinematic vertical motion analysis (not shown here, but appearing earlier over southern Illinois in Fig. 5.29). This subsidence is consistent with the circulation induced in the exit region of the polar jet (quadrant IV in Fig. 5.13). Although the imposed circulation did not entirely suppress convection in the area (Fig. 5.32), it may well explain the reduced intensity of the storms there. Finally, the polar air trapped within the mountain valleys should have offered some degree of insulation from the storm circulations above by virtue of its considerable negative buoyancy. Even if entrained into an updraft because of existing vertical pressure gradient per-

turbation (see Davies-Jones and Henderson, 1975; Marwitz, 1973), its coolness would tend to diminish the energy of the updraft. This is not to say that vortices (funnel clouds and weak tornadoes) cannot develop in cool surface air (see Cooley, 1978), but that damaging tornadoes are not as likely to occur with such conditions.

By the following day (4 April), the cyclone and accompanying jet were entering Canada well north of the unstable air along the Atlantic seaboard. The southward-advancing polar air mass had overtaken the Pacific front and removed the convective potential from the area west of the Appalachian Mountains. Nonetheless, squall lines redeveloped ahead of the polar front from Virginia to Florida and generated about 20 tornadoes, but these were not as severe as those that had occurred the previous afternoon.

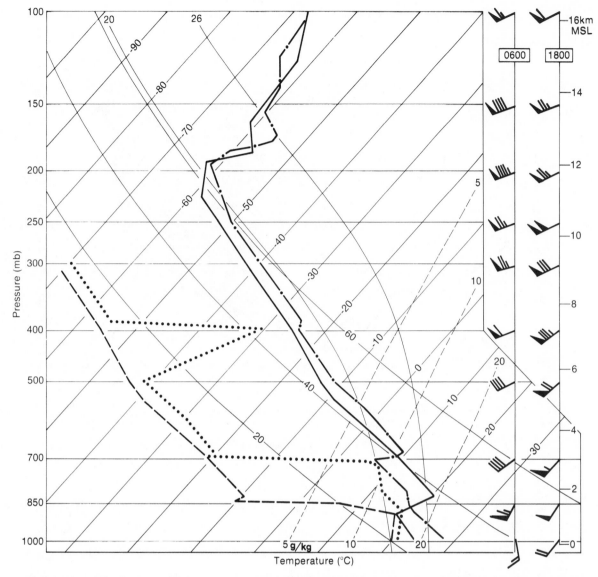

Figure 5.31. Temperature, dew point, and wind soundings for Jackson, Miss., at 0600 CST (solid and dashed lines) and 1800 CST (dot-dash and dotted lines), 3 April 1974. On this skew-*T* diagram, 5, 10, and 20 g kg^{-1} mixing ratio lines slope toward the upper right; 20°, 40°, and 60°C dry adiabats curve concavely toward the upper left; convex curves are 20° and 26° C moist adiabats.

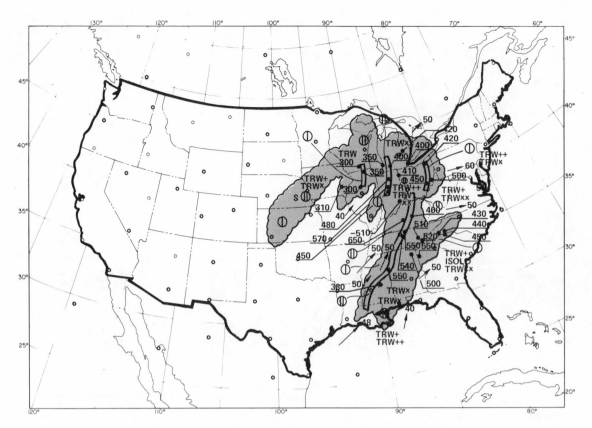

Figure 5.32. Radar summary, 1735 CST, 3 April 1974. See Fig. 5.30 for explanation (Hoxit and Chappell, 1975).

6. Thunderstorms and Their Mesoscale Environment

Joseph T. Schaefer, L. Ray Hoxit, and Charles F. Chappell

1. Introduction

The previous chapter discusses synoptic-scale processes associated with thunderstorms. Here we are primarily concerned with the relationship of smaller-scale features to thunderstorms and generally limit discussions to the meso-β and meso-α scales. The mesoscale is subdivided into meso-γ (2–20 km), meso-β (20–200 km), and meso-α (200–2,000 km) scales (Orlanski, 1975). The meso-β scale characteristic length is comparable with that of an organized convective storm system or squall line. Processes operating on this scale both trigger and concentrate convection (Newton, 1963). Further, it is mostly through meso-β-scale processes that synoptic-scale energy is transmitted down to the thunderstorm (Newton and Newton, 1959) and through which thunderstorms in turn modify the large-scale flow (Fritsch, 1975). Examples of meso-α-scale features include upper-level short waves and low-level jets. These scale processes play an important role in developing the conditionally unstable environment and producing vertical motion fields that release this instability.

Because of the broad scope of mesoscale meteorology, this discussion is limited to midlatitude, continental thunderstorm conditions. It is over these parts of the globe that mesoscale observations are most readily available. Accordingly, theories on the small-scale dynamical mechanisms which cause thunderstorm initiation, growth, decay, and interaction are most applicable there. Thunderstorms at sea are examined in detail in Chap. 3. Similarly, tropical thunderstorms are highlighted in Chap. 8. Both chapters include discussions of synoptic and mesoscale phenomena.

2. Mesoscale Phenomena Priming the Environment for Organized Convection

a. Upper-Level Wind Maxima

Organized convection generally occurs in an environment where the winds increase with height. The fastest velocities are typically restricted to narrow horizontal bands (jet streams) at altitudes higher than 6 km. The patterns of horizontal divergence and convergence associated with these jet streams produce organized vertical air currents. These currents serve two functions. First, they redistribute the heat and moisture content of the atmosphere. In cloud-free areas of upward vertical motion, low-level air rises and cools adiabatically. This air arrives at higher levels cooler and denser than the air originally at that level. Thus the atmosphere is driven toward thermodynamic instability (Beebe and Bates, 1955). Second, the upward motion brings air parcels to condensation. When these processes happen over a limited region, the potential for strong thunderstorms is enhanced (Beebe, 1958). Structural details in the jet stream (jet streaks) have been postulated as one localizing mechanism (House, 1959; McNulty, 1978).

For years meteorologists debated whether wind shears at the jet-stream level were synoptic-scale (Reed and Danielson, 1959) or mesoscale (Berggren, 1952). Recent aircraft data indicate that jet maxima are indeed mesoscale phenomena. The cross-stream shear is concentrated in zones approximately 100 km wide (Shapiro, 1976). The length of a speed maximum appears to be about one order of magnitude greater than its width (Palmén and Newton, 1969). Windspeeds in the jet maxima average 65 m s^{-1} (Riehl et al., 1952, pp. 776–79). Such speeds, typically faster than can be explained by a simple balance of the pressure gradient and Coriolis forces, are called *supergeostrophic* (for a discussion of geostrophic balance see any standard dynamic meteorology text, e.g., Holton, 1972). The wind maxima normally propagate downstream at approximately 20 m s^{-1}. Thus air flows through a wind maximum, and mesoscale convergent-divergent patterns are created.

The horizontal dimensions of an area of supergeostrophic winds determine whether it is synoptic or subsynoptic (synoptic scales are those well represented by the standard networks of meteorological observing stations, approximately the meso-α scale and larger). For large wind perturbations, the wind field adjusts to the pressure field, and the system is synoptic. However, for small features, the wind field dominates and drives the pressure into balance (Bolin, 1953, Okland, 1970); such systems can be thought of as subsynoptic. The separation between these two regimes occurs at the Rossby radius of deformation, the distance a wave in the atmosphere can travel without being markedly affected by the Earth's rotation. For middle latitudes, the Rossby radius of deformation is on the order of 1,000 km (Haltiner, 1971).

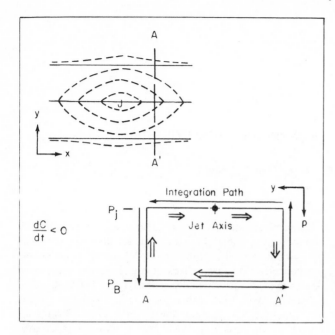

Figure 6.1. A plan view of an isotach maximum (upper left) and its induced secondary circulation along axis A–A'.

Thus near a jet streak, the horizontal-pressure distribution normally adjusts to the wind field. This adjustment generates motion transverse to the basic flow direction.

The inviscid equations describing horizontal motion are

$$\frac{du}{dt} = f(v - v_g) \qquad (6.1)$$

and

$$\frac{dv}{dt} = -f(u - u_g), \qquad (6.2)$$

where, parallel to the basic flow, u is the actual wind component and u_g is the geostrophic wind component. Normal to the basic flow, v is the actual wind component, and v_g is the geostrophic wind component; f is the Coriolis parameter, $2\omega \sin(\phi)$, where ω is the Earth's angular velocity of rotation; and ϕ is the latitude. The derivative is a "total derivative" following an air parcel in motion.

As an air parcel enters a speed maximum, $u < u_g$ and a positive transverse flow ($dv/dt > 0$) is created. However, as it exits, the wind is supergeostrophic, $u > u_g$, and a negative transverse flow ($dv/dt < 0$) is induced. These transverse winds set up a vertical circulation as indicated schematically in Fig. 6.1.

Technically, circulation is the precise measure of the average wind tangent to a closed curve; mathematically,

$$C = \oint \mathbf{V} \cdot d\mathbf{r}, \qquad (6.3)$$

where $\mathbf{V}$ is the vector wind and $\mathbf{r}$ is a vector parallel to the curve. Counterclockwise motion is defined to be positive. As shown by Cahir (1971), this formula can be used for analytic study of jet-streak-induced motions. Equation 6.3

is applied to a plane transverse to the jet-streak, and the line integral is transformed to a surface integral by application of Green's theorem, yielding

$$\frac{dC}{dt} = \oint \frac{d\mathbf{V}}{dt} \cdot d\mathbf{r} = \iint \nabla \times \frac{d\mathbf{V}}{dt} \cdot \mathbf{i}\, dA$$

$$\simeq -\iint \frac{\partial}{\partial p}\left(\frac{dv}{dt}\right) dp\, dy, \qquad (6.4)$$

where $\mathbf{i}$ is a unit vector normal to the area. Substituting Eq. 6.2 into Eq. 6.4 and assuming a constant Coriolis parameter yields

$$\frac{dC}{dt} \simeq -f \int_{y_1}^{y_2} dy \int_{p_J}^{p_B} \frac{\partial}{\partial p}(u_g - u)\, dp. \qquad (6.5)$$

Thus the development of the circulation depends on the vertical shear of the ageostrophic wind.

If the lower boundary of integration (p_B) is positioned at a level where the wind is geostrophic, Eq. 6.5 reduces to

$$\frac{dC}{dt} \simeq f \int_{y_1}^{y_2} (u_g - u)_J\, dy, \qquad (6.6)$$

where J indicates the integration is at jet level. In the jet-streak exit region in Fig. 6.1, $dC/dt < 0$, and the acceleration of the circulation is thermally indirect with upward motion in the cold air on the cyclonic side. In the inflow region, the circulation is reversed, $dC/dt > 0$, and rising occurs on the anticyclonic side.

Cahir developed a two-dimensional, time-dependent numerical model to simulate these vertical circulations and applied it to data collected before the famous Palm Sunday tornado outbreak (11 April 1965). The wind perturbation generated a narrow band of low- and midlevel upward vertical velocity concentrated within approximately 250 km north of the jet axis (Fig. 6.2). This region was where a major thunderstorm system (and tornadoes) developed.

The lower portion of the circulation induced by a jet maximum aloft often appears in the form of a narrow jetlike wind band. This lower-level jet flows nearly perpendicularly to its high-level parent. A study of the dynamics of this type of jet indicates that the concentration of momentum into a narrow band is the kinematic response of the atmosphere to pressure changes caused by the buildup and depletion of mass by the circulation as it propagates with the jet maximum (Uccellini and Johnson, 1979). This type of lower-level jet is often observed in the environment before organized thunderstorm activity (Kocin et al., 1982; Moore and Squires, 1982).

b. Boundary Layer Processes

1. Low-Level Jets: A diurnal oscillation in boundary layer wind velocity is common during the summer over continental areas. Its amplitude is typically 2–3 m s^{-1} (Hering and Borden, 1962), the maximum winds having a southerly component occurring between 0000 and 0300 local time (Bonner, 1968; Hoxit, 1975). Physiographic effects can

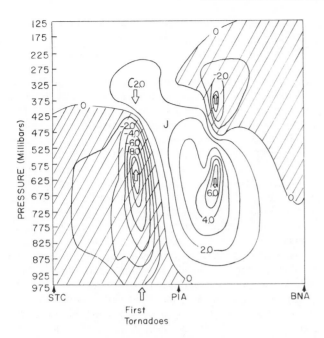

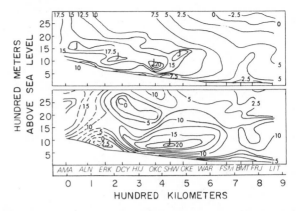

Figure 6.3. Vertical cross sections through low-level jet stream. Top: 1800 CST, 30 May 1961 (after Hoecker, 1963); Bottom: 0000 CST, 31 May 1961. Horizontal axis runs from Amarillo, Tex. (AMA), to Little Rock, Ark. (LIT). Isotachs are of the southerly wind component in meters per second.

Figure 6.2. Jet-stream-induced circulation numerically inferred from Palm Sunday (11 April 1965) data. Points along the horizontal axis correspond to St. Cloud, Minn. (STC), Peoria, Ill. (PIA), and Nashville, Tenn. (BNA). Contours are vertical-velocity isotachs in meters per second (after Cahir, 1971).

enhance these southerly low-level winds on the mesoscale and produce a two-dimensional core of high-velocity flow within the lowest 2 km of the atmosphere (Wexler, 1961; Bonner and Paegle, 1970; Hoxit, 1973). This low-level jet is both physically and dynamically different from that previously discussed, viz., the low-level transverse circulation induced by an upper tropospheric jet streak (Uccellini, 1980).

Boundary-layer low-level jets are frequently observed along the western portions of the Great Plains (Means, 1954) and can be quite strong, often greater than 25 m s⁻¹ (Bonner et al., 1968). The maximum wind core is normally within 500 m of the ground. Little is known about the spatial dimensions of the low-level jet stream, but data from special observational networks suggest a width of about 600 km. During daytime hours, the windspeed decreases, and the jet stream may degenerate into several narrow bands, often less than 200 km wide (Fig. 6.3; Hoecker, 1963). A strong, horizontal, west to east pressure gradient to the lee of the Rocky Mountains with a sustained flow of air northward from the Gulf of Mexico generally occurs with this phenomenon (Bonner, 1966).

In addition to causing mesoscale changes in thermal stability through differential advection, the low-level jet stream and its associated convergence fields are thought to influence generation of nighttime thunderstorms (Sangster, 1958). Nocturnal nonfrontal thunderstorms in the Midwest are typically associated with a low-level jetstream whose axis is oriented N–S or NE–SW (Pitchford and London,

1962). Frictional effects make theoretical determination of the divergence field accompanying the low-level jet stream much more complicated than for the upper-level jet stream (Schaefer and Doswell, 1980). However, by compositing observations, it has been empirically found that the most probable region of upward vertical motions greater than 1 cm s⁻¹ is in the jet exit region (Bonner et al., 1968; Fig. 6.4).

One common explanation of the low-level jet is that it is simply an inertial oscillation in the wind field, i.e., a cyclic variation caused directly by the Earth's rotation (Blackadar, 1957). The period of such an oscillation is

$$T = \frac{\pi}{\omega \sin \phi}.$$

Under inertial conditions, a speed minimum will change into a maximum in one-half of this period and then return to a minimum after a whole one. Thus, at San Antonio, Tex. (29.5° latitude), the wind completes a cycle in approximately 24 hours, and a noon subgeostrophic wind becomes supergeostrophic about midnight.

To show this, assume that the geostrophic wind is constant with time and that winds are horizontally uniform, and combine Eqs. 6.1 and 6.2 (using complex variables; see Schaefer, 1973) to give

$$\frac{\partial W}{\partial t} = -ifW, \qquad (6.7)$$

where

$$W = (u - u_g) + i(v - v_g). \qquad (6.8)$$

Then integration of Eq. 6.7 yields

$$W = W_0 e^{-ift}, \qquad (6.9)$$

where W_0 represents the initial ageostrophic wind. The solution (Fig. 6.5) indicates that the magnitude of the ageo-

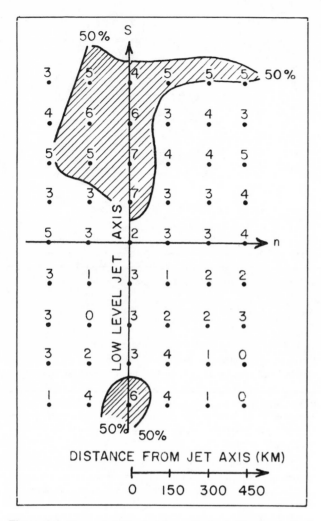

Figure 6.4. The probability that the vertical velocity at an individual point is greater than 1 cm s^{-1}. Numbers at points are the number of times (from a possible ten) the air is rising at a rate greater than 1 cm s^{-1} at 2.5 km above sea level. Within shaded areas probability exceeds 50% (after Bonner et al., 1968).

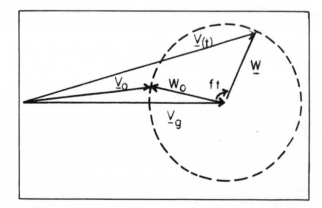

Figure 6.5. Inertial oscillation induced by ageostrophic winds.

strophic wind remains constant, and its direction rotates around a circle during a pendulum day.

However, true inertial motion can occur only in a frictionless atmosphere. Near the Earth's surface, within the planetary boundary layer, turbulent dissipation must be accounted for in the motion equations. It is usually assumed that turbulence is proportional to the wind gradient. This proportionality can be expressed in terms of an eddy viscosity. Typically, eddy viscosity decreases through the middle and upper portions of the boundary layer (O'Brien, 1970). It is also a function of the thermal stratification and undergoes a diurnal variation. During the day, the eddy viscosity at a given level is generally larger than it is at night (Wu, 1965). Buajitti and Blackadar (1957) incorporated these concepts into a numerical model of the low-level jet. Their results show that a frictionally modified inertial oscillation contributes significantly to producing a low-level nocturnal wind maximum, but it cannot account for the observed amplitude and shape of the diurnal wind fluctuation.

Another explanation of the low-level jet is that it arises from a diurnal variation of the geostrophic wind over the moderately sloping terrain east of the Rocky Mountains. During the afternoon, air adjacent to the ground is warmer than air farther removed from the surface. When the terrain slopes, a horizontal temperature gradient and a corresponding pressure gradient arise, causing a southerly geostrophic wind (Sangster, 1967). After dark, a low-level convergence develops as radiationally cooled air moves downslope (Bleeker and Andre, 1951). Holton (1967) showed theoretically that the diurnally oscillating pressure gradient force causes a maximum in the low-level flow approximately 9 hours after maximum heating. However, this theory cannot account for the three-dimensional, jetlike structure of the wind maximum.

Bonner and Paegle (1970) formulated a theoretical model that included both a temporally varying eddy viscosity and a spatially and temporally varying geostrophic wind, giving a much more realistic wind variation (Fig. 6.6). This model suggests that the primary cause of the low-level jet is the diurnal variation of the eddy viscosity. The secondary influence of a temporarily varying geostrophic wind greatly magnifies and modulates the induced inertial oscillation.

As a further expansion, a two-dimensional numerical model over a sloping terrain that allows spatial as well as temporal variations of eddy viscosity has been developed by Chang (1976). This model develops a diurnal wind oscillation that is greatest about 500 mb above the surface. However, the speed of the low-level jet varies with the terrain slope. This again suggests the modulating role of the diurnally varying geostrophic wind generated by the terrain profile.

The low-level wind maximum can be explained, but the mechanism that concentrates it into a jet stream is not well established. Wexler (1961) considered the low-level jet stream to be an atmospheric analog to the Gulf Stream. Both occur in geophysical fluids flowing from the southeast. Westward motion is blocked by topography and forced northward. In a column of air moving northward, f increases. Conservation of potential vorticity, $[(f + \zeta)/D =$ constant], requires that the vertical component of relative vorticity, $(\zeta = \partial v/\partial x - \partial u/\partial y)$, decrease and/or the thickness of the column D increase. If the fluid depth is approximately constant and the horizontal shear of the westerly wind component $(\partial u/\partial y)$ is negligible, the southerly component is forced to increase as the flow approaches the mountains from the southeast; i.e., $\partial v/\partial x$ becomes increasingly negative. Since the geostrophic wind some distance from the Rockies remains constant, a supergeostrophic wind is generated over the sloping terrain. This theory, however, does not account for the diurnal characteristics of the low-level jet stream.

As an alternate mechanism, consider a geostrophic wind parallel to the terrain contours. Frictional retardation causes an ageostrophic boundary layer flow toward lower pressure, either ascending or descending the slope. If the air moves upslope, it expands adiabatically, and rising motion off the surface occurs. This mechanism is called *Ekman pumping over sloping terrain* (Iwashima and Yamamoto, 1974) and can create vertical velocities of several centimeters per second. These velocities are independent of those caused by a horizontally nonuniform geostrophic wind (normal Ekman pumping; Holton, 1972). Accompanying these vertical motions, the ageostrophic wind intensifies in a horizontally limited region. During the day the boundary layer becomes quite thick, and significant ageostrophic winds extend to relatively high altitudes. In the evening the boundary layer stabilizes, and the eddy viscosity decreases, leaving the large ageostrophic flow. It is hypothesized that this flow goes into an inertial oscillation and rotates anticyclonically, forming the low-level jet stream.

The numerical model of Chang (1976) shows this effect (Fig. 6.7). At 1800 LST, a 5-m s⁻¹ ageostrophic upslope wind exists, but no southerly low-level jet stream is apparent. Eight hours later the upslope wind has decreased, and a low-level jet (> 20 m s⁻¹) has developed. Paegle and Rasch (1973) found terrain slope the greatest single factor contributing to concentration of the nocturnal wind maximum into a low-level jetstream. The potential vorticity effect in air forced northward by the Rocky Mountains is apparently of lesser, but not negligible, importance. It increases the amplitude of the diurnal oscillation 10% to 20%.

The low-level jet stream is neither a necessary nor a sufficient condition for thunderstorm activity, but it provides a plausible explanation for the summertime nocturnal thunderstorm maximum over the Great Plains (Wallace, 1975). The organized convergent region in the downstream portion of the low-level jet stream increases statistically the likelihood of nocturnal thunderstorm development in a region where it actually occurs. Also, the low-level jet stream rapidly transports air with high potential wet-bulb temperatures (θ_w) northward from the Gulf of Mexico and enhances convective instability, thus increasing thunderstorm potential.

2. Variations in Temperature and Moisture: A low-level inversion is a typical feature of an environment supportive

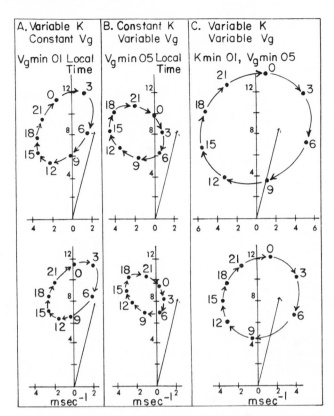

Figure 6.6. Hodographs of wind variations from (A) variable viscosity and constant geostrophic wind, (B) constant viscosity and variable geostrophic winds, and (C) variable viscosity and variable geostrophic wind. Upper diagrams are for 32.5° latitude; lower, for 37.5° latitude. Altitude is 500 m; times are CST. Oscillations in geostrophic wind and eddy viscosity are phased to give minima at 0500 and 0100 CST, respectively. Arrow denotes initial geostrophic wind (after Bonner and Paegle, 1970).

of organized convection (Showalter and Fulks, 1943). The inversion serves an important function by providing a lid that retards the release of convective activity, allowing the moisture content and temperature of the boundary layer to increase without altering that of the overlaying free atmosphere (Fulks, 1951).

The diurnal variation of turbulence that influences the low-level jet is also partly responsible for the formation of this inversion. Turbulence that gives rise to momentum diffusion also transfers heat. This heat transport can be considered in terms of an eddy thermal conductivity. While thermodynamic stability influences the relationship between the eddy conductivity and the eddy viscosity, both generally increase and decrease in concert (Businger et al., 1971). The nocturnal decrease of the eddy viscosity in midportions of the boundary layer coincides with a decrease in the eddy conductivity. The downward flow of sensible heat is impeded. This, in combination with radiational cooling of the near-surface air, forms or strengthens a thermal inversion in the region immediately above the low-level jet.

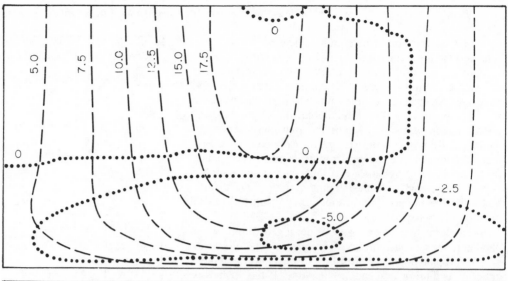

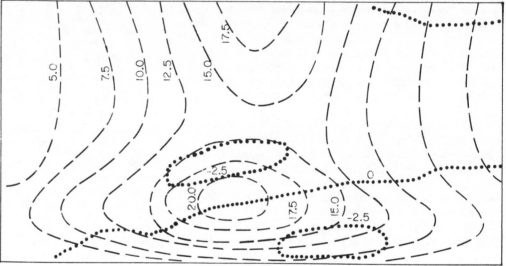

Figure 6.7. Low-level jet generated by numerical model simulating Ekman pumping over sloping terrain (upper: 1800 CST; lower: 0200 CST following day). Dashed lines are isotachs of southerly component; dotted lines are isotachs of westerly components (after Chang, 1976). The horizontal axis stretches for 1,000 km normal to the mean terrain contours. The vertical dimension covers the lowest 4.2 km above the ground.

The warm air beneath the inversion is usually very moist. Water-vapor mixing ratios decrease markedly through the inversion, and the overlying free atmosphere is often quite dry. On a fine scale, the base of the inversion (Fig. 6.8) is often higher than the level where the moisture starts its rapid decrease (Fig. 6.9). This height difference arises from entrainment of drier air through the inversion into the boundary layer (Schaefer, 1976). The magnitude of the difference appears to be related to vertical variations in the horizontal moisture advection (Mahrt, 1976).

Differences in the structure and depth of the thermal boundary layer and the moist layer can influence convection character. For example, a parcel in a weakly developed updraft originating near the surface may suffer substantial entrainment just below the base of the thermal inversion and arrive at the inversion with a lower moisture content than it initially possessed. Thus the instability of the parcel in a stronger, larger, and possibly rotating updraft is better protected from entrainment (Ward, 1967; Simpson and Dennis, 1974) and reaches the inversion base with its initial convective instability intact.

3. Mesoscale Phenomena Localizing Convection

a. Solenoidal Circulations

In addition to priming localized areas for organized thunderstorm activity, mesoscale circulations often focus the actual release of the atmospheric thermal instability. One of the best examples is a solenoidal circulation, an organized vertical circulation driven by density and pressure differences associated with a temperature gradient. These gradients are often caused by topographic features. In this broad category of circulations are land-sea or land-lake breezes, mountain-valley winds, and urban-heat islands. When the environment is primed for convection, the upward vertical velocities associated with such circulations can trigger thunderstorms.

Sea breezes have been observed and used for human purposes for more than two millennia. The Athenian general Themistocles took advantage of a sea breeze to destroy the Persian fleet at the Bay of Salamis during the fifth century B.C. (Plutarch, A.D. 100). The leading edge of the sea breeze,

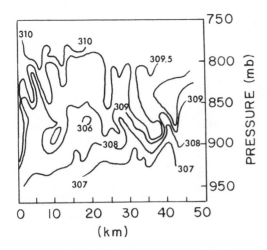

Figure 6.8. Isopleths of potential temperature (K) along an inversion surface measured from airplane over western Oklahoma on 19 April 1961 (after Staff, NSSP, 1963).

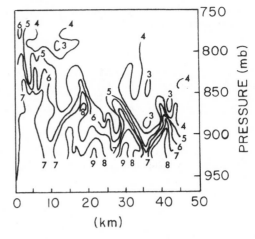

Figure 6.9. Isopleths of mixing ratio (g kg^{-1}) corresponding to Fig. 6.8 (after Staff, NSSP, 1963).

the sea-breeze front, coincides with a narrow zone of surface layer convergence, upward vertical velocities, cumuliform clouds, and often thunderstorms.

The development of a sea breeze begins shortly after dawn, when the land along a coast becomes warmer than the adjacent water. This occurs because solar heating of a substance is concentrated at its surface. Heat is conducted downward much more rapidly in water than in soil, so air in contact with land is heated much more rapidly than that over the sea. Pressure is lower at low altitudes in warm air than in cold air, and a pressure gradient from sea to land is created. In response, the air near the surface flows from sea to land. A combination of surface convergence and heating causes the air to rise over the land. Near the top of the boundary layer the vertical motion leads to adiabatic cooling and an increase in the pressure over the land relative to the pressure at the same level over the water. This produes a weak flow seaward several hundred meters above the surface. As the thermal contrast between land and water intensifies during the day, both intensity and dimension of circulation increase, reaching a maximum during the late afternoon.

In the evening, the land cools, the temperature gradient vanishes, the circulation weakens as a result of friction, and motion finally ceases. As the land continues to cool during the night, a seaward temperature ascendant is established, and the circulation reverses. A land breeze forms and goes through a similar cycle. As the circulation progresses, the wind at a given coastal station turns clockwise with time as the winds are acted upon by the Coriolis force (see Eqs. 6.1 and 6.2).

Observational studies of the Texas coast sea breeze (Hsu, 1969) show that it is best developed at about 1500 local time, when the mean onshore breeze has a velocity of 6 m s^{-1}, with the return flow averaging 3 m s^{-1} (the land breeze circulation has comparable wind velocities). Convective showers are most likely to occur in the area of strongest con-

vergence about 1 or 2 hours later. Low-level winds along coastlines are usually affected by the sea breeze, even when large-scale synoptic influences are present.

Many features of the sea-breeze circulation can be exemplified by considering an onshore component of the wind, (u), and the vertical velocity, (w), controlled only by pressure gradient forces and skin friction parameterized by the Guldberg-Mohn coefficient (Haurwitz, 1947):

$$\frac{du}{dt} = -\frac{1}{\rho}\frac{\partial p}{\partial x} - Ku, \qquad (6.10)$$

and

$$\frac{dw}{dt} = -\frac{1}{\rho}\frac{\partial p}{\partial z} - Kw - g, \qquad (6.11)$$

where ρ is the density, g is the gravitational acceleration, and K is the coefficient of friction. When these winds are averaged around a closed curve in the x–z plane, the time rate of change of circulation, C (see Eq. 6.3), is

$$\frac{dC}{dt} = -\oint \frac{dp}{\rho} - \oint g\,dz - KC. \qquad (6.12)$$

The solenoidal term, $\left(-\oint \frac{dp}{\rho}\right)$, is of special meteorological interest. It expresses the fact that warmer air moves toward lower pressure while cooler air moves toward higher pressure. If one superimposes lines of constant pressure (isobars) and lines of constant density (isopycnics), the solenoidal term is proportional to the number of times the lines intersect within the curve of integration. The more intersections within the curve, the stronger the tendency for a circulation to develop. The second integral on the right vanishes identically since g is a single-valued function of z. The final term expresses the dissipative role of friction.

Density can be replaced by pressure and temperature (T) by using the ideal-gas law,

$$p = \rho RT,$$

where R is a constant determined by the molecular composition of air. Substituting into Eq. 6.12 yields

$$\frac{dC}{dt} = \oint RT \frac{dp}{p} - KC. \qquad (6.13)$$

For the circuit shown in Fig. 6.10, the time rate of change of the mean velocity ($\bar{u}$) becomes

$$\frac{d\bar{u}}{dt} \simeq R \ln\left(\frac{p_0}{p_1}\right)(\bar{T}_L - \bar{T}_S)/2(h + L) - Ku, \qquad (6.14)$$

where $\bar{T}_L$ and $\bar{T}_S$ are the mean temperatures between levels P_0 and P_1 over land and sea, respectively. The simplest approximation of the land-sea temperature difference is that it is a periodic function of time:

$$R \ln\left(\frac{p_0}{p_1}\right)(\bar{T}_L - \bar{T}_S)/2(h + L) \equiv A \cos \omega t, \qquad (6.15)$$

where A is the amplitude of the forcing function and ω is the Earth's rotation rate. Combining the last two equations and integrating yields

$$\bar{u} = ce^{-Kt} + \frac{A}{K^2 + \omega^2}(\omega \sin \omega t + K \cos \omega t). \qquad (6.16)$$

This result can be easily verified by differentiation. Since the wind should be calm when there is no temperature differential ($A = 0$), the integration constant, c, is zero.

According to Eq. 6.15, the maximum temperature difference occurs at $t = 0$. From differentiation of Eq. 6.16, it is seen that the maximum speed occurs when

$$\omega^2 \cos \omega t - \omega K \sin \omega t = 0.$$

Thus the time increment, Δt, between the maximum temperature differential and the speed maximum is

$$\Delta t = \left(\frac{1}{\omega}\right) \tan^{-1}\left(\frac{\omega}{K}\right). \qquad (6.17)$$

Observations indicate that the friction coefficient is approximately 5×10^{-5} s^{-1}, giving a Δt of about 3 h.

While the theoretical solution can be expanded to show the effects of the Coriolis force and to give vertical velocity as a function of both space and time (Defant, 1951), a true sea-breeze simulation requires a more adequate specification of the frictional forcing and the land-sea temperature contrast. Numerical techniques are better suited to this task. Pielke (1973) has developed a three-dimensional numerical model of the Florida sea breeze. A sample of the vertical velocities produced by the model and the corresponding radar observations of convective activity are shown in Fig. 6.11. The importance of the sea breeze as an organizer of convection is evident.

Mountain-valley winds are similar to the sea breeze. The solenoids that drive this circulation arise from the tem-

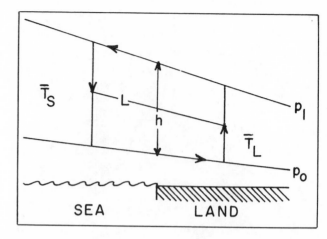

Figure 6.10. Schematic of sea-breeze circulation.

perature difference between air heated over the inclined mountain slopes and the air at the same altitude over adjacent valleys. This temperature difference causes rising air along the slopes during the day and a reverse downslope flow at night. A numerical model of this phenomenon showing its relationship to thunderstorm genesis has been developed by Orville and Sloan (1970).

Topographic features are not necessary for the development of a solenoidal circulation. Differential surface heating is the primary ingredient. This can be caused by a variety of mechanisms. For instance, areas of early-morning overcast clouds heat much more slowly than regions with clear skies. When two such locales are juxtaposed, the resultant midday surface-temperature differences drive circulation (Sun and Ogura, 1979). At times the upward portions of this circulation induce thunderstorm formation (Weiss and Purdom, 1974).

In a more speculative realm, it is possible that large urbanized complexes produce a localized solenoidal circulation that acts as a trigger for convection. The presence of even a moderate-sized city produces a sizable "heat island." Between 1967 and 1970, Columbia, Md., grew from a farming community with a population of about 200 to a town of more than 10,000. Temperature measurements indicated a nocturnal warm anomaly greater than 3°C developed over the new town (Landsberg and Maisel, 1972). This warm urban air is juxtaposed with cooler rural air and gives rise to a solenoidal field.

In support of this hypothesis, tetroon data indicate that organized upward vertical velocities exist over cities (Angell et al., 1973). Further detailed low-level wind studies in St. Louis, Mo., show that a convergent flow exists in the proximity of the urban area (Ackerman and Appleman, 1974). Precipitation statistics indicate that a 25% average increase in summer rain and greater percentage increases in thunderstorms and hail were observed downwind from the St. Louis urban complex during 1971–74 (Changnon et al., 1976).

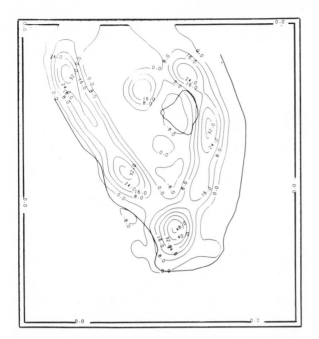 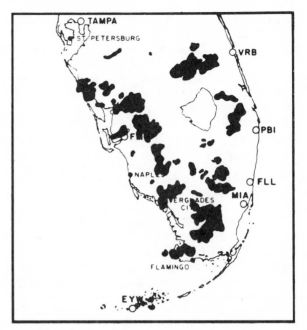

Figure 6.11. Comparison of vertical velocities (cm s^{-1}) produced by numerical simulation (left) and observed radar-echo coverage (right) (after Pielke, 1973).

b. Boundary Layer Instabilities

The mean height of the low-level inversion typifying the organized thunderstorm environment lies within the first 1.6 km above the ground (Fawbush and Miller, 1954). The inversion surface undergoes rapid mesoscale fluctuations (Fig. 6.8). Aircraft data suggest that these are stationary waves or rolls that nearly parallel the low-level flow (Staff, NSSP, 1963). Various types of dynamic instability may account for this phenomenon.

A thermally unstable boundary layer with little vertical variation of wind direction but a vertical gradient of horizontal windspeed exhibits a phenomenon called *convective Ekman layer instability* (Kuettner, 1971). The observed stable stratification in the boundary layer during most of the day seems to rule out this mechanism for most atmospheric cases.

If a boundary layer exhibits a linear increase of speed with height, *parallel instability* can arise (Lilly, 1966). This instability is caused by an interaction between inertial (Coriolis) and frictional (viscous) forces. However, this effect is most active when the ratio of the inertial to the viscous forces (Reynolds number) is lower than that commonly observed in the atmosphere.

When the vertical profile of horizontal windspeed possesses an inflection point, nonviscous *inflection point instability* can exist (Brown, 1972). An inflection point corresponds to an extremum in the vertical profile of horizontal vorticity ($\partial w/\partial x - \partial v/\partial z$ or $\partial u/\partial z - \partial w/\partial x$, where w is the vertical component of the velocity). An air parcel displaced past this point is forced to a position compatible with its initial vorticity but on the other side of the extremum. This

instability is effective for weakly stratified fluids, those in which the ratio of energy generation by buoyancy to energy dissipation by turbulence (the Richardson number $\{Ri = [g/\overline{\theta}] \, [\partial\theta/\partial z] \, / \, [\partial s/\partial z]^2$, where s is the windspeed, θ the potential temperature, and $\overline{\theta}$ is its mean value$\})$ is less than 0.25.

Resonance between incipient instabilities and internal wave motions is still another possible cause for inversion fluctuations. This interaction develops in regions of large wind shear and appears as amplifying waves. This mechanism can be quite effective in fluids with a high static stability (Kaylor and Faller, 1972).

These are just four of many possible causes of the observed banding along the top of the inversion surface. All these theories predict spacing between rolls of 3 to 10 km with an orientation roughly parallel to the mean boundary layer wind (LeMone, 1973). The meteorological significance of these bands is largely unknown. However, the preferential structuring of upward vertical velocity in bands across the boundary layer and the frequent development of organized thunderstorm systems into squall lines possibly reflect an interaction between these organized boundary layer convective currents and other mesoscale processes in the free atmosphere. For example, a modified form of parallel instability can account for several features of the squall lines associated with the 3 April 1974 tornado outbreak (Raymond, 1978).

c. The Dryline

The *dryline* is a mesoscale feature, with its own associated vertical circulation. A dryline is a narrow, almost-vertical zone, across which a sharp moisture gradient occurs at the Earth's surface. In the afternoon, a dew-point temperature change of 15°C in 2 km across a dryline is not uncommon, but there is no measurable systematic density discontinuity associated with it (McGuire, 1962). The air exhibits a nearly adiabatic lapse rate on the dry side, while an inversion "caps" the moisture on the other side.

Even though the dryline is often not colocated with the zone of maximum surface convergence, it serves as a focus for convecting activity. A band of cumuliform clouds is typically located over it. Some of these clouds can develop into strong thunderstorms that propagate away from the dryline. After this occurs, another cloud band may develop along the dryline (Fig. 6.12). This implies that the cloud line is a direct result of dryline presence (Schaefer, 1973).

One possible mechanism for driving the dryline circulation arises from the dependence of air density on its heat and moisture content. This joint dependence actually allows diffusion to destabilize the flow and cause potential energy to be transformed into kinetic energy. One example is thermohaline convection in the oceans, where convective cells arise from a diffusively driven interaction between the salt and heat contents of seawater. A density decrease with height in a multipropertied fluid does not guarantee hydrodynamic stability, because diffusion may reorder the constituents, releasing the potential energy stored in the individual components. If the two properties have different diffusivities, linear theory can be used to show the development of organized convective currents (Turner, 1973). However, even if the diffusivities (or eddy diffusivities) are identical, instabilities can occur when the constituent relationship for density is nonlinear. This process is referred to as *nonlinear biconstituent diffusion*.

In the atmosphere, air density is directly related to the virtual potential temperature (θ_V), a nonlinear combination of heat and moisture content:

$$\theta_V = \theta\left(\frac{1 + q/0.622}{1 + q}\right) \simeq \theta(1 + 0.608q), \qquad (6.18)$$

where θ is the potential temperature and q the mixing ratio of water vapor. If diffusion is the only physical process considered and eddy coefficient theory is assumed, statements of the first law of thermodynamics and conservation of moisture are simply

$$\frac{\partial\theta}{\partial t} + \mathbf{V} \cdot \nabla\theta = K\nabla^2\theta \qquad (6.19)$$

and

$$\frac{\partial q}{\partial t} + \mathbf{V} \cdot \nabla q = K\nabla^2 q, \qquad (6.20)$$

where t is time, $\mathbf{V}$ the vector velocity, and K the eddy diffusivity is assumed constant and equal to the eddy conductivity. Combining Eqs. 6.19 and 6.20 through Eq. 6.18 gives the time rate of change of the virtual potential temperature:

$$\frac{\partial\theta_V}{\partial t} + \mathbf{V} \cdot \nabla\theta_V = K\nabla^2\theta_V - 1.216K\nabla\theta \cdot \nabla q. \qquad (6.21)$$

In the absence of motion, Eqs. 6.19 and 6.20 are simply diffusion equations and yield an exponential decay of any nonlinearities in the initial field. However, the virtual potential temperature, Eq. 6.21, contains an additional contribution that is a direct result of the nonlinear density relation. With time, each component configuration changes at a rate determined by its own distribution and independent of that of the other component. Virtual potential temperature (density) changes at a rate proportional to the scalar product of the constituent gradients. Even if the virtual potential-temperature field is initially uniform, it cannot maintain its spatial uniformity except in the trivial case when both density constituents are independent of position. Thus in a nonlinear multipropertied system, diffusion acts to create density irregularities.

Schaefer (1975) developed a numerical model that incorporates this effect with the motion equations. The model demonstrates that, with typical dryline conditions, nonlinear biconstituent diffusion is capable of generating upward vertical velocities greater than 10 cm s^{-1}. The maximum upward motion occurs immediately over the dryline. Further, the secondary circulation induced by the dryline helps maintain the sharpness of the moist-dry interface itself against the smoothing action of linear diffusion.

Since the dryline represents the edge of the capping low-level inversion, vertical differential advection can cause moist boundary layer air to flow out from beneath this lid. This causes rapid destabilization and favors explosive storm development (Carlson et al., 1983). Such a flow bringing moist air across the dryline often appears to be augmented by the low-level jet which develops in response to the presence of an upper-level wind maximum (Carlson et al., 1980).

The motion of the dryline is quite complex. Portions of the dryline may be moving eastward while other parts are quasi-stationary. During synoptically quiescent conditions, vertical mixing and the general decrease of the surface elevations from west to east over the Great Plains account for much of the observed motion (Schaefer, 1974).

After dawn, boundary layer mixing starts as surface temperatures rise in response to insolation. West of the dryline, any nocturnal radiational inversion is rapidly replaced by an adiabatic lapse rate. Since the depth of the moist layer increases eastward from the dryline, the heat input required to erase the capping inversion increases in that direction with a corresponding delay of inversion breakdown. Parallel to the dryline, the surface elevation is approximately constant (as is the inversion height), so that the amount of heating required to break the inversion is also nearly uniform in this direction. When the needed amount of heat has been absorbed, the low-level moist air mixes with the dry air aloft. The surface dew-point temperature drops rapidly, and the dryline "leaps" eastward to a position where no appreciable mixing between air masses has occurred.

As insolation continues, surface temperatures rise. Since the diurnal temperature range is greater in dry air than in moist air (Haltiner and Martin, 1957), the rise is most rapid west of the dryline. Afternoon temperatures are slightly higher in the dry air than in the moist. However, in the after-

Figure 6.12. Satellite photograph of a dryline in eastern Kansas and central Oklahoma at 2101 GMT, 29 March 1979. Note the strong thunderstorms that have moved eastward off the dryline, but the continued presence of the cumuliform cloud band along it.

noon the virtual temperature on both sides of the dryline is about the same since the contribution from the excess sensible heat in the dry air is compensated by that owing to the large water-vapor content on the moist side.

In the evening, the dry air cools rapidly, a nocturnal inversion forms west of the dryline, and vertical mixing of momentum is inhibited, leading to decreasing and backing low-level winds in the dry air. The slower temperature decline in the moist air provides for nearly steady flow east of the dryline. A net easterly wind component develops across the dryline and carries it westward. As cooling continues, the dry air becomes denser than the moist air so that it can no longer be easily displaced by the moist air. From this time until insolation again induces eastward motion, the dryline remains nearly stationary.

Nonuniform dryline motion is due to irregular terrain and heating rates. Numerical experiments confirm this interpretation and also demonstrate the adequacy of horizontal advection by the strong ageostrophic winds in the moist boundary layer to the east to force a westward retreat of the dryline during the evening (Chang, 1979).

The basic motion is modulated by a daytime increase in the westerly boundary layer winds west of the dryline (Lanicci and Carlson, 1983). This increase is caused by the downward mixing of high-velocity upper-level momentum to the surface in the deep, nearly adiabatic layer west of the dryline (Sasaki, 1973, Danielsen, 1975). This deep momentum mixing typically occurs in mesoscale packets and causes the dryline to bulge (Tegtmeier, 1974). These bulges appear as perturbations along the dryline which enhance or detract from the dryline's quiescent motion (McCarthy and Koch, 1982).

Not only does the occurrence of a dryline bulge influence dryline motion, but it also acts as a focus for convective activity (Sasaki and Tegtmeier, 1974). It appears that the downward flux of momentum creates localized areas of convergence and divergence which propagate into the moist air east of the dryline in a wavelike manner (Koch and McCarthy, 1982). These convergence areas are often precursers of extreme convection (Livingston, 1983).

Although the dryline is not a geographically universal feature, it is observed over many parts of the globe. Drylines frequently occur during the spring over the Great Plains region of the United States. From 1966 to 1968, a dryline was present in that region on more than 41% of the days in April, May, and June (Schaefer, 1973). Drylines are also a significant feature during the premonsoon months in India (Weston, 1972). In central west Africa, the intertropical convergence zone often acts like a dryline (Eldridge, 1957). In the Southern Hemisphere, drylines have been reported in Brazil (Chu, 1975). All of these features are often associated with thunderstorm activity.

d. Frontogenetic Circulation

Basically, fronts are synoptic-scale phenomena. The temperature gradients, horizontal wind shear, and horizontal divergence are most extreme near the ground, becoming rather diffuse above the lowest kilometer. However, a front is not a substantial (i.e., material) surface; air is entrained through the frontal zone giving rise to pockets of air having different characteristics. The structure of a frontal zone contains mesoscale detail (Sanders, 1955).

The process of frontogenesis is quantized with the frontogenetic function (F), which measures the temporal rate of change of the gradient of a scale property (S) within an air parcel. Mathematically, that is:

$$F = \frac{d}{dt} \left| \nabla_2 S \right| \qquad (6.22)$$

where d/dt is the total derivative taken following a parcel in motion and $|\nabla_2 S|$ is the modulus of the horizontal gradient of S. Following Miller (1948), consider a rectangular coordinate system (x, y) oriented with the y axis along the gradient of S so that there is no variation in the x direction (i.e., the x axis parallels the front). Eq. 6.22 can then be expanded as

$$F = \left(\frac{\partial}{\partial t} + v\frac{\partial}{\partial y} + w\frac{\partial}{\partial z}\right)\left(\frac{\partial S}{\partial y}\right).$$

With some algebraic manipulation this becomes

$$F = \frac{\partial}{\partial y}\left(\frac{\partial S}{\partial t} + v\frac{\partial S}{\partial y} + w\frac{\partial S}{\partial z}\right) - \frac{\partial w}{\partial y}\frac{\partial S}{\partial z} - \frac{\partial v}{\partial y}\frac{\partial S}{\partial y}, \qquad (6.23)$$

or contracting back into a total derivative,

$$F = \frac{\partial}{\partial y}\left[\frac{dS}{dt}\right] - \frac{\partial w}{\partial y}\frac{\partial S}{\partial z} - \frac{\partial v}{\partial y}\frac{\partial S}{\partial y}. \qquad (6.24)$$

If S is considered as potential temperature (θ), the first term on the right represents diabatic effects.

By ignoring this term, the resulting equation is

$$F \sim -\frac{\partial w}{\partial y}\frac{\partial \theta}{\partial z} - \frac{\partial v}{\partial y}\frac{\partial \theta}{\partial y}, \qquad (6.25)$$

demonstrating that frontogenesis will occur if there is a tilting forced upon the isentropic surfaces either by a horizontal gradient of vertical velocity or by a confluent (deforming and/or converging) action of the base flow upon any existing thermal gradient.

Sawyer (1956) and Eliassen (1962) theoretically demonstrated that a circulation in the cross-frontal plane must coexist with frontogenesis. This circulation is purely ageostrophic (Shapiro, 1981) and is much weaker than the nearly geostrophic base flow of the free atmosphere. It arises from the requirement that a horizontal nondivergent flow must have a secondary vertical circulation to remain in both hydrostatic and geostrophic balance. This secondary flow becomes a significant factor when the ratio of inertial forces to the coriolis force (Rossby number, $Ro = U/fL$, where L is a characteristic length of the flow and U is a characteristic velocity) grows to approach unity (Gidel, 1978). Thus

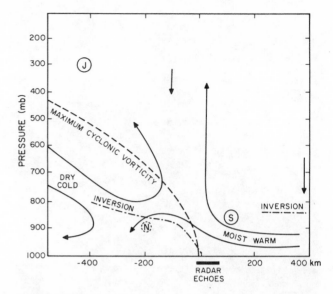

Figure 6.13. Schematic of frontogenetic circulation analyzed by Ogura and Portis (1982). The dot-dashed line connects the position of the maximum horizontal surface temperature gradient to the inversion behind the front. The jet stream is indicated by J, the postfrontal northeasterly boundary layer flow maximum is located by the N, and the prefrontal southwesterly low level jet is shown by S.

frontogenetic effects are most likely to occur in regions of nearly geostrophic (i.e., nondivergent) midlevel flow which exhibit strong deformation and/or vorticity. Clouds associated with upper-level deformation zones are common and have a rather unique signature in satellite imagery (Weldon, 1979). These deformation clouds often produce significant precipitation (Scofield et al., 1982).

Simplified versions of the thermohydrodynamic equations which drive atmospheric flow can be solved analytically (Stone, 1966; Hoskins and Bretherton, 1972) to show frontogenesis. Essential observed characteristics of frontogenesis are illustrated by such models. The relative importance of the various physical processes can be shown, but quantitative results cannot be diagnosed (Blumen, 1980). More detailed physics can be incorporated into numerical simulations (Williams 1967; Ross and Orlanski, 1978). Such studies indicate that forces and physical processes in the boundary layer such as friction (Keyser and Anthes, 1982) and surface heat and moisture fluxes (Benjamin and Carlson 1983) play a significant role in creating the mesoscale structure observed in fronts.

The significant two-dimensional features of one cold frontal zone have been summarized by Ogura and Portis (1982). As shown by their schematic (Fig. 6.13), the circulations associated with frontogenesis are complex. Since the forcing for the circulations is centered on the vorticity maximum, the vorticity maximum axis is indicated. Also shown are the low-level inversions and the frontal zone. Related portions of the polar jet stream, its induced southwesterly low-level jet and a postfrontal northerly flow maximum are also shown for completeness. A thermally indirect circulation existed ahead of the front. This created an inversion in the prefrontal air mass, effectively limiting moisture to the low levels. A direct circulation behind the front assisted the formation of the postfrontal inversion. A gliding (overrunning) of prefrontal air over the cold dome with an eventual mixing through the frontal surface occurred. Strong upward vertical motion was positioned immediately above the front's surface position. This ascending flow was a major factor in thunderstorm development along the front (note the zone of radar echoes indicated under the schematic).

While Fig. 6.13 illustrates the complexity of frontal circulations, frontal characteristics are really three-dimensional and vary significantly in different synoptic situations. For example, Newton (1950) presents a dramatically different situation where the low-level upward vertical velocity is concentrated ahead of the frontal zone. Numerical experiments indicate that the temperature, moisture, and horizontal and vertical winds induced by frontogenetic circulations are typically distributed in cellular patterns (Ross and Orlanski, 1982). This structure is reflected in the mesoscale organization of subsequent thunderstorms. There are indications that the strength and location of thunderstorm development can be related to the strength of the frontogenetic forcing (Berry and Bluestein, 1982).

e. Prestorm Mesoscale Pressure Systems

Strong thunderstorms often develop in association with low-pressure systems having diameters up to a few hundred kilometers. For example, Magor (1971) selected 60 tornado days at random and found that 55% of 195 reported tornadoes occurred within 100 km of a mesoscale low-pressure area. Mesolows may appear as perturbations on fronts. However, at times they are found in advance of well-defined squall lines. Often mesolows are a result of dynamic processes associated with upper-level short wave troughs and exist before the onset of convection. The attendant circulations and convergence-divergence fields help focus and trigger thunderstorm development.

One consistent explanation for the development of a mesolow on a front is a small-scale analogy to classic synoptic-scale baroclinic instability theory. The mathematical treatment of this notion is intricate and is not covered here. The essential ingredient for synoptic-scale baroclinic development is positive differential vorticity advection across a layer of veering geostrophic winds (Petterssen, 1956). The scale of the disturbance that develops is inversely proportional to the vertical wind shear (baroclinity) and directly related to the mean thermodynamic instability of the environment. For a given shear, smaller wavelengths are preferred as the thermodynamic stability decreases (Gall, 1976). For synoptic-scale applications, maximum growth rate occurs for wavelengths of about 2,500 km.

On the mesoscale, the theory of baroclinic instability has not been fully developed. Assumptions necessary to treat the phenomenon analytically, such as a constant Richardson number, are not valid on the mesoscale (Charney, 1948). Computational problems have precluded the numerical treatment of the instability for very small waves. However, diagnostic studies show that mesoscale systems derive much of their energy from baroclinic conversion and that, before major convection begins, the energy generation associated with a frontal mesolow is confined to low levels (Kung and Tsui, 1975). This is consistent with the synoptic-scale theory that shows that progressively smaller wavelengths grow in shallower layers.

Indications are that for mesoscale lows the vertical shear vector of the horizontal wind points toward decreasing upward vertical velocities (Doswell, 1976). This alignment is consistent with warm-air advection ahead of the region of maximum upward vertical velocity. Such warm advection induces surface pressure falls and may be partly responsible for the development of the mesolow. However, as the maximum vertical velocity becomes superposed over the mesolow, a "self-limiting" process commences. This occurs when the adiabatic cooling associated with upward motion in a thermodynamically stable environment becomes strong enough to counteract advective warming and further surface pressure falls cease (Palmén and Newton, 1969). Thus mesoscale lows do not become strong enough to make a significant contribution to the climatological energy budget of the general circulation.

f. Gravity Waves

If a parcel is vertically displaced in a stable atmosphere, buoyancy forces tend to restore it to its initial position. Because of three-dimensional continuity, vertical motion at one point induces divergence and vertical velocities at other points. Thus a wave, driven by buoyancy, is created. Since the forces of buoyancy are due to gravity, such waves are called *gravity waves* (Atkinson, 1981). While wave amplitude, period, and propagation velocity are mainly controlled by buoyancy, inertial and frictional forces as well as baroclinic effects are important. Many gravity-wave classifications exist, depending on the relative importance of these various forces. One important and distinctive feature of gravity-wave motion is that upward vertical velocity occurs in concert with rising pressure (for a mathematical analysis see Gossard and Hooke, [1975]).

A rigorous linear theory of gravity waves in a moist stratified atmosphere close to saturation has been developed by Einaudi and Lalas (1975). Their analytical treatment indicates that gravity waves are potentially capable of producing vertical motions strong enough to cause condensation and thus force thunderstorm activity. One potential gravity-wave source is the jet stream (Mastrantonio et al., 1976). Several modes of gravity waves are excited by this phenomenon, and some propagate energy and momentum toward the Earth's surface. Several problems exist with theoretical linear gravity-wave models. Although they adequately describe the form that the disturbance initially takes, later stages require nonlinear processes not included in the theory.

For gravity waves to be of meteorological significance, it

is necessary for them to propagate horizontally without rapidly transmitting their energy to great heights. It can be theoretically shown that this requires more than a low-level inversion (Lindzen and Tung, 1976). Rather, a thermally stable lower troposphere must be bounded above by a region of minimal stability that reflects vertically propagating energy. Further, there must be a level in the upper region where the wind velocity is approximately equal to the phase speed of the trapped wave. Thus gravity-wave activity is most notable when there is strong wind shear aloft and stability in the lower troposphere (Gedzelman and Rilling, 1978). Typically these conditions occur when a frontal or dryline inversion is present. It has been proposed that the bulges observed along the dryline are caused by gravity waves (Koch, 1982).

There is a long record of empirical studies of gravity-wavelike phenomena in the atmosphere (e.g., Goldie, 1925). Brunk (1949) followed a sequence of four waves from the Mississippi River eastward to the Atlantic Coast. These pressure pulsations apparently were initiated by strong thunderstorms. Their passage was accompanied by strong rainfall and gusty winds. Many other works have shown that rainfall rates increased and thunderstorms intensified with the onset of rising pressure associated with such waves (Uccellini, 1975; Miller and Sanders, 1980).

Presently the role of gravity waves in thunderstorm initiation is nebulous. Uccellini (1975) observed apparent gravity waves using routine surface weather observations. The waves had an amplitude of 1.5 mb, a period of 3 h, a wavelength of 500 km, and a propagation velocity of 40 m s^{-1}. These waves propagated along a low-level inversion and not only reinforced existing convectivity, but also seemed to trigger new storms. Miller and Sanders (1980) studied a day when a ten-packet gravity wave traversed a region of extreme thermodynamic instability. They found that, while convection was enhanced when it was overtaken by a gravity wave, the thunderstorms were not caused by the gravity wave.

Inertial-Symmetric Instability

A stable atmosphere which exhibits significant vertical shear of the horizontal wind is subject to symmetric instability where perturbations grow by drawing energy from the kinetic energy of the mean flow. If under such conditions local regions of negative potential vorticity develop through viscous or diabatic processes, a special form of this instability, inertial instability develops. This instability produces vertical circulations which appear as roll vortices oriented parallel to the mean shear (Emanuel, 1979).

Negative potential vorticity is most likely to occur on the anticyclonic side of a jet stream. Under typical conditions, theory indicates that the rolls should have a horizontal spacing of about 100 km and produce a strong enough low-level convergence to support convection (Emmanuel, 1978). It has been suggested that such rolls can act as a thunderstorm trigger (McGinley and Sasaki, 1975).

4. Convective Feedbacks to the Mesoscale

The preceding sections discuss how various mesoscale processes can initiate deep convection. Similarly, thunderstorms can significantly modify the mesoscale. This interaction between the thunderstorm scale and the mesoscale is not well understood and poses some of the most interesting and important problems in meteorology. Nonlinear interactions in the form of up- and downscale feedbacks are possible among the cloud scale, the large mesoscales, and even the synoptic scale.

a. Vertical Circulations and Thermal Changes near Convective Clouds

The upward transport of mass and moisture in organized thunderstorms may be several times larger than the amount of mass and moisture supplied by the synoptic-scale circulations. For a region containing a squall line, Fritsch et al. (1976) computed mesoscale upward transport approximately five times larger than that supplied by the synoptic scale. Therefore, downward mass and moisture transport must also occur in these mesoscale circulations (Gray, 1973). The definition of the scale of these compensating downward motions (Fritsch, 1975) remains a major problem and a barrier to understanding the evolution of organized convection.

As precipitation develops and begins to fall from the cloud region, evaporational cooling (Fujita, 1959) and the drag imparted to the air by falling rain or hail combine to produce strong moist downdrafts (Takeda, 1965). When the downdrafts reach the surface, the air spreads out, forming the well-known thunderstorm outflow. Calculations by Newton (1966) indicate that mass transport in these moist downdrafts is only slightly more than one-half of that in the thunderstorm updrafts. Johnson (1977), in a study of afternoon convection over south Florida, also found that moist downdrafts were not sufficient to balance the mass transport in the cloud updrafts—especially during the early afternoon, when convective activity was increasing. Within a few storm diameters around the visible cloud boundaries, downward countercurrents with velocities up to a few meters per second are found (Sinclair, 1973). This descent is dry adiabatic; yields localized regions of warm, dry air (Feteris, 1961; Cunningham, 1959); and undoubtedly represents a further compensation for the storm updrafts.

Moist downdrafts and local countercurrents represent cloud scale and smaller mesoscale circulations and reflect immediate atmospheric response to the strong convective updraft. They are usually manifested by vertical velocities on the order of several meters per second and can be easily observed and measured.

In addition, downward mass flux is often prevalent in larger mesoscale regions of general subsidence. Near organized tropical convection, these subsidence regions contain relatively warm dry air that extends downward into the boundary layer (Zipser, 1969; 1977). Middle- and upper-level sinking with horizontal dimensions of 100–200 km has also been observed over western Europe (Feteris, 1968). These circulations develop during the early stages of convection and extend upward into the lower stratosphere. Subsidence downwind of intense squall lines over the central United States has been documented by Hoxit et al. (1976). Magnitudes of the sinking typically range upward to around 2 m s^{-1}.

These three mechanisms by which downward fluxes can occur, i.e., moist downdrafts, cloud scale countercurrents, and mesoscale subsidence, are depicted in Fig. 6.14. Since some of the downward compensation occurs on a horizontal scale larger, by an order of magnitude or more, than the scale of the active updrafts, it is proportionately weaker and aggravates the problem of measuring all the convectively driven circulations.

It is important to recognize that these vertical circulations are associated with thermodynamic changes. In the moist downdraft-thunderstorm outflow region, the lowest few hundred meters of the atmosphere are cooled about 3°–10°C. Dry adiabatic descent in the regions of local countercirculations and general subsidence is usually most pronounced in the upper troposphere and both warms and dries the environment. These processes combine to create an increased static stability in the environment. Moist downdrafts are a direct result of evaporative cooling. In regions surrounding clouds, dry adiabatic subsidence occurs. This is the mechanism that enables thunderstorms to fulfill their dynamic mission of stabilizing their environment (Lopez, 1973). Thus the release of latent heat in the storm updrafts provides greater buoyancy and enhances the updrafts, which in turn drive the compensating downward circulations in the environment.

b. Dynamic and Kinematic Responses to Convection

(1) Mesohigh-Pressure Systems: Overall, a net warming of the environment caused by latent heat release by thunderstorms must occur. Under certain conditions this can contribute to synoptic-scale cyclone development (Tracton, 1972). More often, these thermal changes lead to dynamic responses in the form of mesoscale wind and pressure systems. The meso-, or bubble, high is the best-documented mesoscale system produced by deep convection. The existence and evolution of these systems have been vividly portrayed in analyses by Fujita et al. (1956). Midtropospheric air, cooled by evaporation, is transported downward into the boundary layer. This produces a cold dome of air near the surface, higher surface pressure, and strongly diverging winds. Initially, this thunderstorm outflow is much like a density current. The leading edge of the outflow, the gust front, lifts the preexisting warm air, frequently triggering new thunderstorms and propagating the convection. A gust front is often identifiable by a distinctive "arc cloud" signature in satellite imagery (Gurka, 1976).

The low-level outflow from a single large cumulonimbus may cover more than 5,000 km^2. Outflow from several storms may merge to form a squall-line gust front with a trailing mesohigh several hundred kilometers in length. The

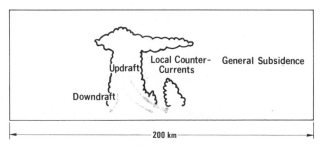

Figure 6.14. Schematic presentation of the vertical circulations associated with deep convective clouds.

excess surface pressure is typically 2–5 mb. However, the system is very shallow and is usually confined to the lowest kilometer of the atmosphere. These large mesohighs often develop anticyclonic circulations and may persist for several hours after the initiating thunderstorm activity ceases. During the slow decay of such a system, local areas of low-level convergence and lifting along the gust front provide a favored location for the initiation of new and often severe convection (Purdom, 1976). This is especially true if the outflow boundary intersects another convergence zone, such as a cold front or dryline (Miller, 1972). At other times, warm, moist air overrunning a slow-moving or stationary mesohigh may produce a quasi-steady mesoscale convective system with attendant heavy rains and occasionally disastrous flash flooding. The favored region for development of new convection is shown schematically in Fig. 6.14.

(2) Convectively Forced Mesolow Pressure Systems: Surface pressure troughs or mesolows often form in response to strong convective activity. On the cloud scale, a small surface low is often found beneath the updraft region (Charba and Sasaki, 1971). These pressure perturbations have a nonhydrostatic component related to the acceleration of air parcels within the updraft (Marwitz, 1973).

Larger mesoscale surface lows, called *wake lows*, often develop to the rear of the mesohighs. These low-pressure systems, typically 50–400 km, are essentially hydrostatic. Therefore, the mean temperature of an atmospheric column is warmer in this region of lower pressure. This warming can result from one mechanism or a combination of processes, i.e., advection of warmer air into the region, modification of rain-cooled air by surface heating, or localized subsidence behind the organized convection.

Also, larger mesoscale surface lows in advance of the updraft areas are associated with organized thunderstorm activity (Fig. 6.15: Magor, 1958, 1959). These low-pressure systems probably result from strong localized warm-air advection and/or adiabatic warming in mesoscale subsidence regions (Hoxit et al., 1976). The pressure perturbation in these mesolows is typically somewhat less than that in mesohighs but extends through a greater depth of the atmosphere.

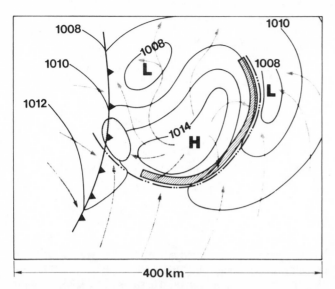

Figure 6.15. Schematic example of mesoscale surface pressure systems and streamlines. Included is a mesolow in advance of the convection, a "bubble" or mesohigh in the area of precipitation and/or thunderstorm outflow, and a "wake" low to the rear of the mesohigh. A squall line (————··————··————··) and a cold front (▼▼) are also shown. Favored areas for new cloud development are hatched.

(3) Upper-Level Perturbations: Low-level horizontal momentum is transported in the updraft region to the middle and upper portions of the cloud. Since organized thunderstorms tend to form in an environment with moderate-to-strong vertical shear in the horizontal winds, there is usually a significant difference between the horizontal momentum of the updraft and the environment. Although turbulent mixing along the cloud edges acts to destroy these differences, the updraft core retains much of the low-level momentum (Davies-Jones and Henderson, 1975). Therefore, the storm partly blocks and diverts the environment flow around the updraft (Fankhauser, 1971).

In the upper troposphere or lower stratosphere, cumulonimbus clouds become negatively buoyant; i.e., the temperatures inside the clouds are colder than in the surrounding environment. Therefore, both mixing and evaporation cool the environment, and a mesoscale high-pressure area may form in the tropopause region near the active convection. The outward-directed pressure gradient affects the environmental winds, reducing the upstream velocities while increasing the flow downstream. This phenomenon was first documented by Fujita and Bradbury (1969). In areas of organized convection, such upper-level perturbations extend over areas several hundred kilometers on a side. An example of the general changes at slightly lower levels where the clouds are still positively buoyant is shown in Fig. 6.16. Strong convective activity over the lower Mississippi and Ohio valleys resulted in significant warming between the subtropical and polar jets. As a result, the thermal gradient and windspeeds associated with the polar jet intensified. In

addition, there appears to be a general increase in the speeds downstream of the convection, while the reverse is true upstream. Ninomiya (1971a, 1971b) has also documented cases with similar changes in the thermal and wind fields at upper levels. In general, strong convection warms the troposphere in the 700- to 250-mb layer, and cools it above 250 mb.

Kinetic-energy generation and dissipation in regions of organized thunderstorms occur at a much faster rate than in middle-latitude cyclones (Tsui and Kung, 1977). While much of the generated energy is dissipated in the immediate region of convection, upscale feedback to the synoptic scale does occur, as shown in Figs. 6.15 and 6.16. Calculations by Fuelberg and Scoggins (1978) also document this upscale transfer of energy.

c. Convective Responses to Larger Mesoscale Circulations

One of the most interesting possibilities concerning the interaction of convective storms and their environment is that changes in the environment brought about by convection may themselves tend to enhance and organize the convection. At first this appears to be inconsistent with the stabilizing effect of compensating vertical circulations, but we have already given an example of this effect. The moist downdraft cools and stabilizes the boundary layer beneath a thunderstorm. However, the lifting along its boundary tends to destabilize the atmosphere and trigger new convection. New cells grow and eventually produce their own precipitation and downdrafts. This cycle may be repeated several times and convection propagated downwind by this process.

Subsidence downwind (ahead) of existing thunderstorms may contribute to organizing and intensifying the convection. Initially, the subsidence suppresses the downwind convective activity by slightly reducing the available buoyant energy and, in some instances, by enhancing the low-level inversion. At the same time, the adiabatic warming produces a low-level pressure trough or mesolow in advance of the convection. Winds will respond to this changing pressure (isallobaric) field and flow toward the trough. Ahead of this region, low-level divergence may be produced, and low-level cloudiness often dissipates. Between the region of pressure falls and the gust front, the isallobaric wind increases the boundary layer convergence of mass and moisture, enhancing the potential for convective activity. As shown in Fig. 6.17, subsidence downwind followed by arrival of the outflow from convection upstream contributes first to a capping, then to a sudden, forced release of convective instability. These processes represent a kind of meso-dynamic instability, where the convective feedbacks create mesoscale wind and pressure systems that enhance and organize the convection.

Sanders and Paine (1975) and Sanders and Emanuel (1977) have found evidence of another type of feedback process. Detailed analyses of organized convection over the National Severe Storms Laboratory network in Oklahoma revealed the existence of a mesoscale "updraft-downdraft"

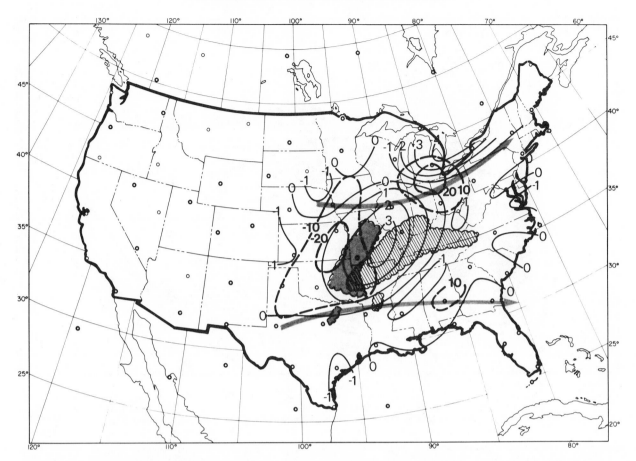

Figure 6.16. Analysis of 6-h changes in upper-level winds and temperature, 0000–0600 GMT, 25 April 1975. Solid lines are 300- to 250-mb mean temperature changes. Dashed lines are 250-mb windspeed changes. Heavy arrows indicate jetstream location. Radar echoes at 0000 GMT are shaded; radar echoes at 0600 GMT are hatched (based in part on special rawinsonde data obtained during the National Aeronautics and Space Administration AVE IV experiment).

couplet. They interpret the downdraft as being driven by evaporation of cumulus clouds in the middle troposphere and attribute the persistence and organization of the convection to the existence of the mesoscale sinking.

d. Mesoscale Convective Complexes

Convective feedback to mesoscale and perhaps even synoptic scale systems is epitomized by the Mesoscale Convective Complex (MCC). An MCC is defined as a quasi-circular conglomeration of thunderstorms having a cloud-top area larger than 100,000 km² and persisting for more than 6 hours (Maddox, 1980a). MCC's are prolific rain producers, but hail and tornadoes may also be associated with them (Maddox and Dietrich, 1981).

A typical MCC develops from several individual thunderstorms in an area where midlevel warm-air advection is creating a mesoscale region of upward vertical motion (Maddox 1983). These storms cause a midlevel region of anomalous warming and an associated low-pressure area. A mesoscale reaction to this occurs in the form of an elevated layer of inflow. Concurrent with this midlevel development, the surface outflow air of individual storms merges to create an intense mesohigh. The result of these two processes is an intensification of convection along the gust front. As the storms saturate their immediate environs, a warm core structure with a moist adiabatic lapse rate becomes evident. A large midtropospheric upward circulation develops and forces a mesohigh at upper levels with anticyclonic outflow. Once in existence, an MCC can maintain itself for several days, although it may undergo diurnal variations in intensity.

Dissipation typically occurs when the flow of warm, moist air to the complex is disrupted. This can occur when the surface cold dome becomes so extensive that the surface convergence zone is displaced far away from the cloud area or when the system moves into an environment hostile to convection (Maddox et al., 1980).

Maddox (1980a) documented 43 MCC's over the central United States between March and September 1978. Typically, the first thunderstorms developed during the afternoon with convective complex organization appearing in early evening. Satellite imagery (as in Fig. 6.18) indi-

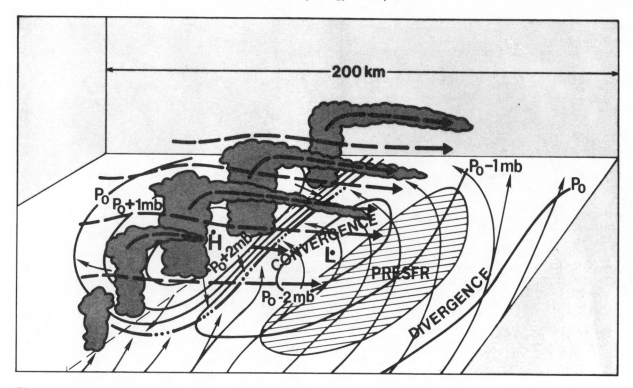

Figure 6.17. Three-dimensional squall-line model including upper-level streamline (dashed), surface pressure perturbations (thick solid lines); region of rapidly falling pressures (hatched); surface streamlines (thin solid lines); and squall line or gust front (————···————···————). Cirrus anvils were drawn as narrow plumes so that surface features could be illustrated.

Figure 6.18. Enhanced infrared satellite imagery showing a typical MCC centered over eastern Kansas and western Missouri at 1500 GMT, 22 June 1981. Interior black, gray, and white contours indicate colder infrared temperatures and higher cloud tops.

cates that most systems grow to their maximum size after midnight.

The effect of MCC's on the large-scale environment can be quantitatively evaluated by using numerical-scale separation techniques (Maddox, 1980b). Mature complexes are often associated with upper-level mesoscale regions of pronounced cooling, high pressure, and strong anticyclonic outflow. Unexpected MCC development can lead to large forecast errors. In one spectacular case, remnants of an MCC that formed on 17 July were still affecting the weather on 22 July (Bosart and Sanders, 1981). The upscale feedback from convective complexes may affect the subsequent evolution of weather systems.

5. Summary

We have presented an overview of the complex scale interactions involved in mesoscale meteorology. In the spectrum of atmospheric events, the mesoscale occupies an intermediate position where observations have been limited. Most observations have been taken on the much larger synoptic scale, where regional weather patterns are established, or the much smaller cloud scale, where actual weather occurs. This lack of mesoscale data makes much of what has been said speculative and open to modification by further research.

The role of the mesoscale in modulating the large-scale environment is qualitatively understood. Much of the physics involved in conditioning localized areas for convective storm development is also known. However, the transfer of this knowledge into useful forecast techniques is far from complete. Methods of parameterizing cloud processes into mesoscale numerical models and maximizing the information content of meteorological data need further development. We must also improve techniques for retrieving and using quantitative data from satellite observations.

Less is known about triggering mechanisms. With few notable exceptions, actual events that release the atmosphere's potential instability can be only hypothesized. Gravity waves are prevalent in the environment, but their significance has not been established. The hydrodynamic principles controlling the development of mesoscale pressure systems are nonlinear and thus not resolvable by standard techniques. Many modes of instability are exhibited on the mesoscale, but their pertinence to actual weather development must be determined.

Study of feedback from smaller scales to the mesoscale is still in its infancy. In a global sense, thunderstorms stabilize the atmosphere, but the geometric configuration of the heat redistribution controls storm intensity and even future storm development. Warming owing to latent-heat release can assist synoptic-scale cyclone development. Midlevel cooling owing to evaporation from storm clouds can further destabilize the adjacent atmosphere. It remains to be learned under what circumstances these effects provide key energy inputs to developments on the mesoscale.

7. Morphology and Classification of Middle-Latitude Thunderstorms

Keith A. Browning

1. Thunderstorm Cells

The dynamical building block of a thunderstorm is the cell. A *cell* is a compact region of relatively strong vertical air motion (many meters per second). The usual way of identifying the overall extent of cells is by visual observations of cumuliform turrets during early stages of their evolution before the development of precipitation and, thereafter, by radar observations of the associated volumes of precipitation. Cells defined in these two ways are not quite collocated, and it is often necessary to make clear which is being referred to.

Most thunderstorms are composed of short-lived units of convection, referred to as *ordinary cells*. At any given time such storms consist of a succession of ordinary cells at different stages of evolution. The Thunderstorm Project (Byers and Braham, 1949) was the first successful attempt to obtain definitive observations using radar and aircraft, and it identified three stages in the evolution of ordinary cells (Fig. 7.1): cumulus, mature, and dissipating.

The cumulus stage in cell development is characterized by updrafts throughout. They cause the cell to grow upward as entrainment of drier ambient air takes place across its boundaries. As the cell builds up, a large amount of moisture condenses, and precipitation particles grow. The precipitation begins descending, and an associated downdraft starts to develop.

The mature stage is characterized by precipitation reaching the ground. An updraft and downdraft coexist side by side, the downdraft being best developed in the lower portions of the cloud. The downdraft brings cold air in the rain area toward the ground, where it produces a diverging pool of cold air. The leading edge of the cold air forms a micro–cold front, characterized by an abrupt change of temperature and wind and an increase in pressure (see Chap. 9). New cells tend to develop above this outflow.

The cell enters the dissipating stage when the updraft is replaced by a downdraft. This spreads throughout the entire cell and then weakens and disappears. At the same time the cold dome of downdraft air near the surface subsides, and the winds decrease.

The lifetime of an individual cell averages about an hour, during which time it may travel 20 km or so in the direction of the upper winds in which it is embedded. A storm consisting of a sequence of such cells may, however, persist for several hours.

The kind of storm studied in the Thunderstorm Project was the common variety of thunderstorm often referred to as an *air-mass storm*. In the presence of the favorable vertical distribution of temperature, humidity, and wind velocity encountered in some frontal regions, a much more vigorous unit of convection known as a *supercell* may develop (Browning, 1964). Although supercells are rather uncommon, they are important because they are responsible for a disproportionate amount of severe weather, especially damaging hail and tornadoes (Nelson, 1976; Nelson and Young, 1979).

A supercell can be recognized by certain characteristic visual and radar features, described in Sec. 5b. Perhaps its most basic distinguishing feature is a circulation that is not only large and intense but also virtually steady state, with updraft and downdraft coexisting to each other's advantage for a long period (30 min or more). Essentially the supercell is a prolonged version of the mature stage of an ordinary cell, in which the updraft-downdraft couplet takes on a stable configuration. It is probably best to regard ordinary cells and supercells as archetypal extremes of a spectrum of dynamical steadiness. According to this view, the supercell would be equivalent to a series of ordinary cells following one another in rapid succession. However, supercells, with their rotating updrafts and large vaults (see below), may appear to differ from ordinary cells in kind as well as in degree.

Ever since Browning and Ludlam (1962) put forward the notion of a steady thunderstorm cell, there has been controversy about the reality of the steady-state hypothesis (e.g., Battan, 1980). Some individual supercells unquestionably do propagate continuously and at a rather uniform velocity, with only minor fluctuations in dimensions and intensity over periods long compared with the time taken for air to pass through them. Nevertheless, the existence of fine-scale fluctuations in the structure of supercells is stressed by many workers (e.g., Nelson and Braham, 1975; Barge and Bergwall, 1976; Warner, 1981); thus, to be precise, one should refer to supercells as quasi-steady. Of course, the apparent steadiness of a storm cell does depend on the resolution of the observations, and high-resolution observations do reveal a good deal of substructure, but our realization of this should not be allowed to obscure the fact that there can

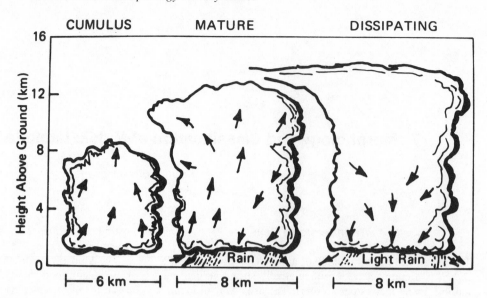

Figure 7.1. The three stages in the life cycle of an ordinary thunderstorm cell, as derived by the Thunderstorm Project (Barnes, 1976, after Byers and Braham, 1949).

be very real differences in the degree of steadiness of ordinary cells and supercells. It is believed that supercells can indeed be treated as truly steady insofar as much of the essential physics is concerned.

2. Thunderstorm Propagation and the Distinction Between Steady-State Storms and Persistent Impulsive Storms

The nature of an individual thunderstorm complex is determined by the number, type, distribution, and mode of propagation of the cells from which it is built. Some storms contain only one kind of cell. Others contain a mixture of ordinary cells and supercells either simultaneously or at different times. Several storm categories are given in Fig. 7.2. A unicellular storm may consist of a single ordinary cell of short duration or a supercell of long duration. The former are generally weak. The latter are often intense and are commonly referred to simply as *supercell storms* (e.g., Chisholm and Renick, 1972; Marwitz, 1972a; Browning and Foote, 1976). Multicell storms and line storms consist of a number of cells, with successive cells usually forming on the right flank (occasionally on the left) as viewed along the direction of travel of the storm. Sometimes a multicell storm consists of a mixture of ordinary cells and supercells; very rarely, all the cells may be supercells. More often, however, the individual cells are all ordinary. The main dichotomy, then, is between what are generally referred to as supercell storms and multicell storms. The distinction is not always easy to apply; for example, Foote and Wade (1982) and Foote and Frank (1983) show that some storms display attributes of both classes.

As shown schematically in Fig. 7.3, a multicell storm propagates in a discrete way (Browning, 1962; Marwitz, 1972b; Newton and Fankhauser, 1975). Such a multicell storm may be "persistent" in the sense that at any time there

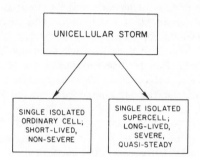

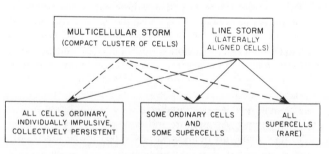

Figure 7.2. A simple classification of thunderstorm types. The primary classification relates to the basic cell type—either supercell or ordinary cell. A secondary classification applies to the entire storm complex, describing it as a unicellular, a multicellular, or a line storm.

is always at least one cell within it that is active. However, the storm propagates discontinuously, or impulsively, so that no individual cell achieves a quasi-steady circulation. On the other hand, in the limiting case of a supercell storm, the updraft may occupy the entire envelope in Fig. 7.3, which then propagates steadily as a whole.

Marroquin and Raymond (1982) show that a simple lin-

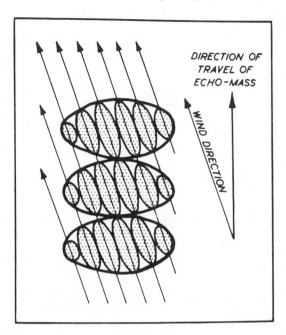

Figure 7.3. Formation of new cells on the right flank of a multicell thunderstorm and their eventual decay on the left flank, causing the whole storm to travel to the right of the winds (Browning and Ludlam, 1960).

earized convective overturning model predicts the propagation velocity of ordinary thunderstorms quite well but fails to predict the deviant motion of supercells. In the Northern Hemisphere the direction of propagation of a supercell is usually to the right of the winds at most levels (left in the Southern Hemisphere); however, the motion can occasionally be to the left of the winds. This gives rise to two kinds of supercells: severe right-moving (SR) supercells (Browning, 1964) and severe left-moving (SL) supercells (Hammond, 1967). The motion of supercells is discussed further in Sec. 5.b.

3. General Properties of the Circulation in and near Thunderstorms

a. The Inflow Toward the Updraft

In a traveling thunderstorm, regardless of whether it is composed of ordinary cells or a supercell, the updraft generally enters at the front or side rather than from the rear. An example of a multicell storm fed from the front is shown in Fig. 7.4. The characteristic presence of rising cloud towers at the rear of most storms (Byers and Battan, 1949) is not inconsistent with front feeding, since air entering at the front at low levels may penetrate to the rear of the storm as it rises to higher levels (Browning and Ludlam, 1962; Newton, 1966). "Back-feeder" storms occur when the location of successive updrafts is anchored to the topography. Thus slow-moving thunderstorms over mountain ranges and foothills may have their primary inflow area along the trailing

edge behind the precipitation core (Henderson and Duckering, 1970), but if they move away from the hills, the main updraft moves to the front of the storm (Cooper et al., 1969; Marwitz et al., 1969; Chisholm, 1973). The level of origin of air entering the updraft is generally quite low. Occasionally the inflow may be as deep as 2 or 3 km, but the updraft core is usually fed by air from the kilometer closest to the ground (e.g., Fig. 7.4).

A characteristic feature of the inflow in the more intense thunderstorms is a small region of low pressure (mesolow) beneath the updraft core. The associated surface pressure anomaly can be -0.5 to -1.5 mb (Fujita, 1963; Foote and Fankhauser, 1973; Barnes, 1974; Ellrod and Marwitz, 1976; Barnes, 1978). At cloud base it is probably even more (Bonesteele and Lin, 1978). Although the surface pressure anomaly normally associated with the mesolow is small compared with the $+4$-mb anomaly frequently associated with the downdraft-induced mesohigh, it nevertheless gives rise to considerable acceleration and confluence in the inflow toward the updraft. According to Grandia and Marwitz (1975), increments in horizontal velocity of 5 to 10 m s^{-1} are common in the inflow, with 15 m s^{-1} being an extreme value. Heymsfield (1978) reports an increment of 18 m s^{-1}.

Air originating near the ground ascends smoothly and virtually unmixed to cloud base in the main inflow region of most storms. Potential temperature (θ) and specific humidity (q) are therefore conserved and can be used as tracers (Marwitz, 1972a). Figure 7.5 shows measurements from an aircraft traversing an updraft at cloud base. These measurements, which are probably typical of intense storms, show that the updraft core at cloud base is characterized by a maximum of q but a minimum of θ; the virtual temperature at cloud base is often as much as 2°C lower than that in the environment (Marwitz, 1973; Davies-Jones, 1974; Davies-Jones and Henderson, 1975; Grandia and Marwitz, 1975). This is caused by the updraft drawing on air near the ground from a boundary layer in which θ increases with height and q decreases with height (see Sec. 4a). If thermal buoyancy were the only vertical force, it would be impossible to account for the maintenance of updrafts characterized by negative buoyancy below cloud base. As Grandia and Marwitz (1975) and Bonesteele and Lin (1978) point out, this difficulty can be resolved by taking into account the effect of nonhydrostatic pressure perturbations.

b. Vertical Air Velocity Within the Updraft

Entrainment of dry environmental air into the updraft has an inhibiting effect on the updraft in cumulus clouds, but it can, to a first approximation, be neglected in the cores of the broad updrafts associated with some thunderstorms. Even in developing cumulus congestus clouds there tends to be a region of moist adiabatic ascent toward the upshear side of the updraft (Heymsfield et al., 1978). Thus a rough estimate of the upper limit of the updraft velocity can be obtained from moist adiabatic parcel theory. Newton (1968), for example, has estimated that virtual-temperature excesses of 1°, 3°, and 5°C averaged over the depth of the tro-

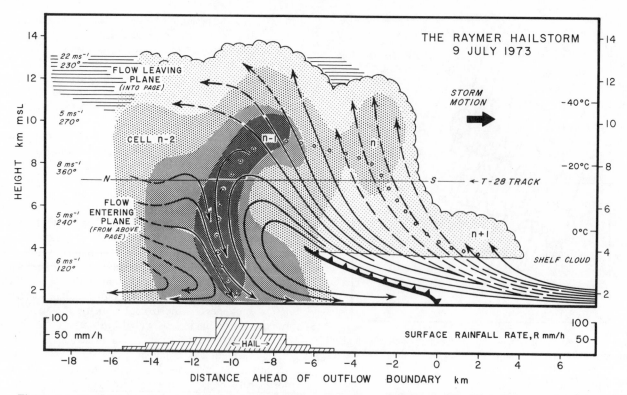

Figure 7.4. Descriptive model of a multicell thunderstorm in northeastern Colorado, showing a vertical section along the direction of travel of the storm. Thick lines: smoothed streamlines of flow relative to moving storm; lightly stippled shading: extent of cloud; darker grades of shading: radar reflectivities of 35, 45, and 50 dBZ; open circles: trajectory of a hailstone during its growth from a small particle. Right: temperature scale: temperature of a parcel lifted from the surface. Left: velocities: environmental winds relative to the storm based on soundings behind the storm. The model can be regarded as an instantaneous view of a typical structure with four different cells ($n + 1$, n, $n - 1$, and $n - 2$) at different stages of evolution, or it can be regarded as showing four stages in the evolution of an individual cell (Browning et al., 1976).

posphere would give rise to maximum updraft velocities at tropopause level of 28, 49, and 63 m s^{-1}, respectively. Chisholm (1973) has used a modified form of parcel theory that allows for the effect of water loading by an adiabatic water content, assuming the condensed water to be carried with the updraft. He estimated maximum updrafts from 14 to 69 m s^{-1} for 29 hailstorms in Alberta. Vonnegut and Moore (1958), Malkus (1960), and Saunders (1962) have calculated the vertical velocities at tropopause level required to produce different amounts of penetration above that level, again assuming adiabatic ascent. They show that, for typical values of static stability in the lower stratosphere, a vertical velocity of about 20 m s^{-1} is required for every 1 km of penetration. Penetrations of cloud tops 1 to 3 km above the tropopause are common for severe thunderstorms, and very occasionally penetrations of 5 km occur. If one were to believe the predictions of parcel theory, this would indicate vertical velocities of up to 100 m s^{-1} (Donaldson et al., 1960; Roach, 1967). None of these estimates, however, takes into account nonhydrostatic pressure gradients, which may diminish the updraft velocity substantially in regions of strong positive buoyancy (Schlesinger,

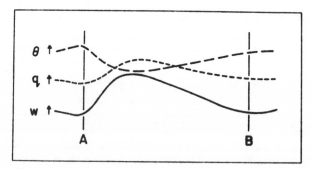

Figure 7.5. Profiles of potential temperature (θ), specific humidity (q), and updraft velocity (w) as measured at cloud base during a flight beneath a northeast Colorado supercell from one side (A) to the other (B) (Marwitz, 1972a).

1975). Loading by any large accumulations of precipitation would also reduce the updraft velocity.

Actual measurements of updraft velocity have been made by many different techniques. At cloud base, aircraft measurements give typical values of between 2 and 6 m s^{-1}

136

(Wichmann, 1951; Auer and Marwitz, 1968; Cooper et al., 1969; Chisholm, 1973; Foote and Wade, 1982); occasionally updrafts at cloud base may exceed 10 m s^{-1} (Browning and Foote, 1976). At cloud-top levels the rate of rise of radar-echo tops and visible cloud turrets have led Ludlam (1959), Goyer (1970), and Renick (1971) to infer updrafts in excess of 20 m s^{-1}. There is a very extensive literature on in-cloud measurements of vertical velocity. Measurements using radar-tracked balloons, dropsondes and rawinsondes have given maximum vertical velocities ranging from 12 and 13 m s^{-1} in the studies of Sulakvelidze et al. (1967) and Bushnell (1973), respectively, to ~30 and 37 m s^{-1} in the studies of Cooper (1970) and Davies-Jones (1974). Radar-tracked chaff has given maximum updrafts of 14 m s^{-1} (Ellrod and Marwitz, 1976) and 9 to 27 m s^{-1} (Marwitz, 1973). Some of the most reliable measurements have been obtained from aircraft and sailplane penetrations: examples of maximum updrafts measured in this way are 10 to 15 m s^{-1} (Byers and Braham, 1949), ~30 m s^{-1} (Wichmann, 1951), 10 to 20 m s^{-1} (Sand, 1976), 23 m s^{-1} (Heymsfield et al., 1978), 26 m s^{-1} (Heymsfield and Musil, 1982), and 16 m s^{-1} (Dye et al., 1983). Reliable measurements have also been obtained from vertically pointing Doppler radar: examples of maximum updrafts measured are 20 m s^{-1} (Battan and Theiss, 1966), 20 m s^{-1} (Battan 1975), 18 m s^{-1} (Battan, 1980), and 10 m s^{-1} (Hauser and Amayenc, 1981). Further measurements of in-storm vertical velocities have been obtained from multiple Doppler studies: examples of maximum updrafts measured in these studies are 20 m s^{-1} (Kropfli and Miller, 1976), ~30 m s^{-1} (Brandes, 1977a), 25 to 40 m s^{-1} (Heymsfield, 1978), 12 m s^{-1} (Heymsfield, 1981), >35 m s^{-1} (Ray et al., 1981), 20 to 25 m s^{-1} (Knupp and Cotton, 1982a), 38 m s^{-1} (Miller et al., 1982), 50 m s^{-1} (Nelson, 1983), and 20 m s^{-1} (Miller et al., 1983).

Some of the updraft maxima referred to above were observed to occur at an altitude not far above cloud base and to decrease above that level (e.g., Sulakvelidze et al., 1967; Marwitz, 1973; Ellrod and Marwitz, 1976). This conflicts with the predictions of simple parcel theory, which in most thunderstorm situations would lead one to expect a maximum updraft velocity in the upper troposphere. On the other hand, most of the measurements by Doppler radar do indeed show that the vertical air velocity attains its highest value in the upper or middle troposphere. An example is shown in Fig. 7.6. Other examples are shown later in Figs. 7.7 and 7.9. The multiple Doppler studies can be expected to provide the most representative measurements of the vertical velocities because of their ability to sample a large proportion of the total storm volume every few minutes.

c. Lateral Extent and Shape of the Updraft

Most of the early data on the vertical extent of thunderstorm updrafts came from ordinary weather radar (e.g., Byers and Braham, 1949; Douglas, 1963; Donaldson, 1965); after beam-width errors are corrected, a rising echo top can be identified rather closely with the updraft top. The horizontal dimensions of the updraft are not always as easily identified on the basis of echo extent because precipitation is transported horizontally into neighboring regions. This problem does not apply near the top of freshly rising towers or where a quasi-steady echo extends above the level of the tropopause, and measurements of the lateral dimensions of the echo in these regions indicate updraft diameters ranging from 3 km for short-lived ordinary cells to 15 km for some long-lived supercells.

Aircraft flights by Auer and Marwitz (1968) just below cloud base in thunderstorms with hail have shown a wide range of updraft areas from 10 to 172 km^2; the average area was 63 km^2. In contrast, Cooper et al. (1969) found that the updraft area at cloud base was often less than 9 km^2 although they occasionally encountered traveling storms with updraft areas in excess of 80 km^2. Browning and Foote (1976) have presented aircraft and visual observations of a supercell in which the area of the updraft was as great as 200 km^2 both at cloud base and, judging from the diameter of the cloud dome, at tropopause level. Data on the lateral extent of updrafts in the middle troposphere have been provided by Sand's (1976) aircraft penetration; he reported updrafts of 10 to 20 m s^{-1} over distances of about 5 km. Similarly extensive regions of strong updraft have been observed in most of the multiple Doppler studies referred to in Sec. 3b. In the particularly intense supercell storm studied by Nelson (1983) a region of updraft exceeding 20 m s^{-1} extended almost continuously at middle levels for 20 km in a direction normal to the storm's direction of travel.

Kyle et al. (1976) have derived a composite average of the updraft profiles in the middle troposphere for storm cells in which the updraft was single-celled and greater than 8 m s^{-1} at that level. They found the profile to be approximately Gaussian in shape, with a width that increased from 2 to 3 km for an updraft maximum of 10 to 15 m s^{-1} to 4 to 5 km for an updraft maximum of 15 to 20 m s^{-1}. According to Auer et al. (1969), when the updrafts are traversed at cloud base in a direction normal to the direction of travel of the storm, the profile of vertical velocity tends to be more nearly that of a top hat as opposed to the Gaussian profile found by Kyle et al. Hart and Cooper (1968), Auer et al. (1969), Kyle et al. (1976), Ellrod and Marwitz (1976), and Nelson (1983) all report that the updraft dimension along the direction of storm motion tends to be less than that normal to this direction.

Some early descriptive models of cumulonimbus clouds visualized an essentially erect updraft; it is now recognized, however, that updrafts are often tilted. One of the first observationally validated models showing a tilted updraft was derived by Browning and Ludlam (1960, 1962). More recent multiple Doppler observations, such as those by Kropfli and Miller (1976), Foote and Frank (1983), and Nelson (1983), provide even more convincing evidence of a tilted updraft. Figure 7.7 shows the flow pattern relative to the storm in a section oriented along the direction of the storm's travel. As in the model derived by Browning and Ludlam, the main updraft is inclined in the upshear direction in the troposphere, the tilt decreasing with height; the downdraft

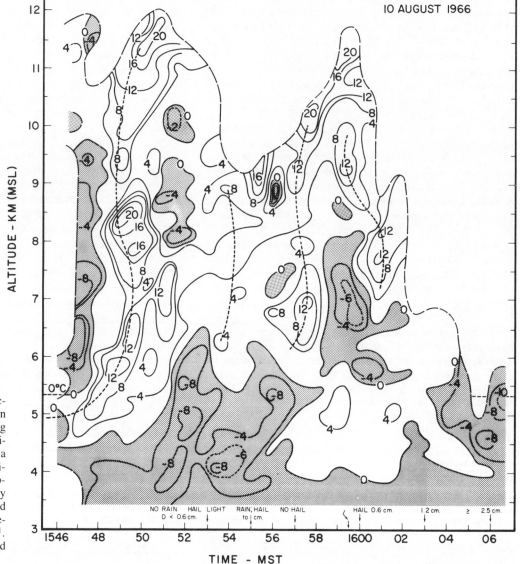

Figure 7.6. Time-height section showing detailed pattern of updraft velocity during passage of an intense multicell thunderstorm over a mountain in southeastern Arizona, as estimated using observations from a vertically pointing Doppler radar. Solid isopleths are of vertical velocity at intervals of 4 m s^{-1}. Downdraft regions are shaded (Battan, 1975).

beneath it is fed by dry and potentially cold middle-level air overtaking from the rear. Distinctly different results were obtained by Miller (1975) in a dual Doppler study of a weak thunderstorm. He found that, although the updraft was fed from the front of the storm at low levels, the tilt of the up-draft reversed from an upshear tilt to a downshear tilt at a very low level. Evidently no single model of the updraft configuration is going to fit all cases.

d. The Updraft as an Obstacle to Environmental Flow

There is a tendency for the vigorously rising air in an up-draft to change its horizontal momentum only slowly. This

led Newton and Newton (1959) to postulate that the updraft tends to behave like an obstacle, causing the environmental flow to divert around it. Of course, it does not do so at very low levels, where air enters it as a well-defined inflow. It cannot be considered to behave like a truly solid obstacle at any other level because its outer portions are eroded away by the environmental flow. However, it is suggested by Ra-mond (1978) that positive pressure perturbations at high levels within the updraft help to some extent to protect it against erosion. Also Lilly (1983) suggests that helicity re-duces the diffusing and dissipating effects of turbulence upon rotating updrafts within supercell storms (helicity is the product of the windspeed with the vorticity component

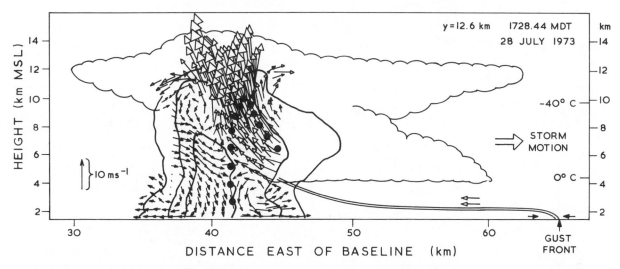

Figure 7.7. Flow pattern within vertical section along direction of travel of multicell thunderstorm in northeast Colorado, as inferred from dual Doppler radar data. Velocity vectors represent flow relative to the storm (scale is shown by the vertical 10 m s^{-1} vector). The solid contours represent radar reflectivity at 8-dB intervals. Approximate cloud outlines, gust front, and inflow measurements from a low-flying aircraft provide a context for the Doppler radar measurements. The chain of large dots represents the trajectory of a growing hailstone (adapted by I. Paluch and J. C. Fankhauser, of National Center for Atmospheric Research, from Kropfli and Miller, 1976).

along the streamlines; Lilly found that the flow in supercell updrafts is predominantly helical, i.e., the vorticity vector tends to be oriented along the streamlines; the suppression of turbulence is deduced theoretically). The analogy of the updraft as an obstacle appears to be a useful concept, especially for severe thunderstorms consisting of long-lasting supercells.

Observations of the wind field in the middle troposphere around supercells have been made using radar-tracked chaff (Fankhauser, 1971), using ground-based Doppler radar (Brown and Crawford, 1972; Heymsfield, 1976, 1978; Eagleman and Lin, 1977; Lemon et al., 1978; Klemp et al., 1981; Foote and Frank, 1983; and Miller et al., 1983), and using airborne navigational Doppler radar (Fujita and Grandoso, 1968; Browning and Foote, 1976). Observations show environmental air passing around the storm core and accelerating as it streams past (Fig. 7.8). A double vortex structure is often observed which may be partly due to the cyclonic shear on one side of the storm core and the anticyclonic shear on the other side where the environmental air is overtaking it (see also Sec. 3e). Radar observations of vortices being shed in the wake of severe thunderstorms have been interpreted as further supporting the view of the updraft behaving in some ways like a solid obstacle (Lemon, 1976a).

e. Rotation Within the Updraft

Tornadoes develop within regions of vertical vorticity that are associated sometimes with the sheared boundaries of updrafts, especially at the updraft-downdraft interface, and sometimes with rotation of the entire updraft. Most severe

tornadoes appear to be associated with rotating updrafts (see Chap. 10). Many updrafts, however, rotate without producing tornadoes.

Significant rotation of the updraft as a whole is confined mainly to supercells. The updraft in an SR supercell rotates cyclonically. Visual observations sometimes show cyclonic rotation of the main cloud base (Barnes, 1970) and occasionally also of the updraft column (Davies-Jones et al., 1976). The rotation is thought to account for the development of the characteristic radar hook echo (Sec. 5b) as precipitation particles descend within it (Browning, 1964). More strictly, according to Brandes (1977a) and Lemon and Doswell (1979), it is the interaction between a cyclonically rotating updraft and a downdraft that yields the hook shape. Evidence of cyclonic circulation extending to high levels within the updraft has been obtained in numerous Doppler radar studies of SR supercells (e.g., Burgess et al., 1975; Ray et al., 1975; Brandes, 1977a, b; Heymsfield, 1978; Lemon et al., 1978). The circulation appears to develop aloft and then descend toward the ground.

Anticyclonically rotating updrafts have been detected in SL supercells (Burgess et al., 1976; Knupp and Cotton, 1982a). Rotation of updrafts in opposite senses within SR and SL supercells has been simulated numerically by Wilhelmson and Klemp (1978).

Trajectory analyses show that the air rising through the updraft in an SR supercell may turn either cyclonically or anticyclonically. Heymsfield (1978) found that it turned cyclonically with height, but Klemp et al. (1981) and Foote and Frank (1983) found that individual air parcels turned anticyclonically even though the updraft as a whole was rotating cyclonically.

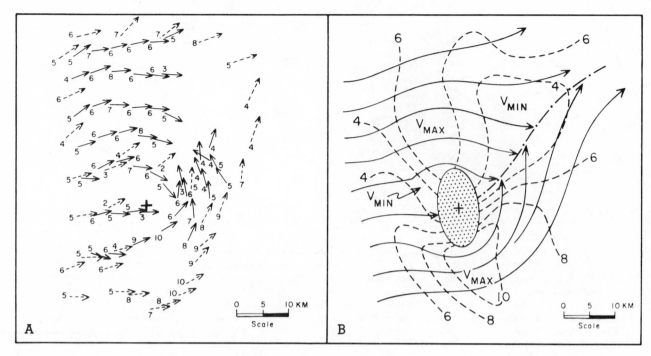

Figure 7.8. Thunderstorm updraft behaving as an obstacle to the environmental flow in the middle troposphere. (A) Composite 500-mb relative wind field around the thunderstorm centered on the cross, derived from aircraft measurements (dashed lines) and chaff displacement (solid lines). The vector magnitude (m s^{-1}) appears at the tail. (B) Synthesized streamline and isotach patterns based on winds in (A). The dash-dot line denotes the wake axis (Fankhauser, 1971).

The onset of rotation in an SR supercell and the development of a radar structure with hook echo occurs simultaneously with the onset of continuous propagation to the right of the winds (Browning, 1965b). Fujita and Grandoso (1968) have proposed that the rightward motion of these supercells is caused by the cyclonic rotation itself through the effect of the Magnus lift force. Although rightward cell motion and cyclonic rotation certainly develop hand in hand, we do not believe that the anomalous motion is a result of the rotation. Rotunno and Klemp (1982) suggest a way in which both the rightward motion and rotation can be generated together in an SR supercell. They show how dynamically enhanced vertical pressure gradients may promote rightward propagation in situations where the environmental wind shear vector veers with height.

The origin of cyclonic rotation within an updraft is attributable to the tilting of the horizontal component of vorticity in the inflow. As first proposed by Browning and Landry (1963) and Barnes (1970), the important component is that resolved *along* the direction of the relative inflow. The strong veer of the wind with height in the relative low-level inflow gives a component of vorticity along the mean inflow direction that can be as great as 10^{-2} s^{-1}. It is important to note that this component is measured *relative* to the moving storm cell; it therefore becomes larger after the onset of rightward cell motion, so that the anomalous motion of a supercell may in fact lead to increased rotation of the updraft rather than be the result of it.

The effect of differential cloud-scale vertical motions is that the horizontal component of vorticity *perpendicular* to the inflow direction is also tilted into the vertical (Schlesinger, 1975; Tootenhoofd and Klemp, 1983). This generates a vortex doublet with rotation of differing sense on opposite sides of the updraft, which may be difficult to distinguish observationally from the vorticity caused by environmental air blowing around the updraft. Horizontal convergence will stretch the vortex tubes and further increase the vertical component of vorticity. According to Rotunno (1981), this may account for the preferential intensification of one part of a vortex doublet at the expense of the other, so as to give rise to an essentially single-signed vortex.

f. Turbulence

Turbulence data are available from both aircraft and ground-based Doppler radar. Flights into the updrafts of intense thunderstorms show a qualitatively consistent pattern:

1. In the updraft at cloud base the flow is smooth (Wills, 1939; Wichmann, 1951; Piggott, 1955; Auer and Sand, 1966; Auer and Marwitz, 1968; Dennis et al., 1970; Marwitz and Berry, 1971; Marwitz et al., 1972). Foote and Fankhauser (1973) point out that the inflow tends to be smoother even than air measured at the same altitude well away from the storm.

2. In the updraft core in the middle and upper troposphere, there is light-to-moderate turbulence (Sinclair, 1969; Sand, 1976). This is consistent with air rising into an unstable region; any perturbation becomes amplified by the instability.

3. In the areas of high radar reflectivity bounding the updraft core, there is at least moderate and frequently severe turbulence both at middle-tropospheric levels (Sand, 1976) and in the upper troposphere (Burnham and Lee, 1969).

Doppler radar measurements obtained with low-elevation scans (Frisch and Strauch, 1976; Strauch and Merrem, 1976) have also indicated a close association of the region of most intense turbulence with the region of highest reflectivity in the middle troposphere. Frisch and Strauch showed that the turbulence was centered about the rather strongly sheared interface between the main updraft and downdraft. They measured variances caused by velocity fluctuations on scales smaller than 800 m exceeding 14 m² s⁻² within a volume with linear dimensions of 2 km. Although there was no direct evidence of an inertial subrange extending to these scales, they computed that, if this had been the case, the maximum energy dissipation rate, ε, would have been more than 3,000 cm² s⁻³, corresponding to severe turbulence. Doppler radar measurements by Knupp and Cotton (1982b) revealed very similar results for another severe thunderstorm: an estimated peak value of ε of 1,500 cm² s⁻³ occurred at midlevels in the vicinity of an updraft-downdraft shear zone. The updraft itself was very smooth at low levels, but buoyancy and wind shear acted together to generate turbulent eddies, some larger than 500 m, at middle levels.

Turbulence spectra have been derived by a number of workers from aircraft penetrations of storms. Steiner and Rhyne (1962), flying through the upper parts of severe thunderstorms, obtained a spectrum obeying a −5/3 law, which gave ε approaching 10,000 cm² s⁻³. Sand et al. (1974) and Heymsfield and Musil (1982) measured an ε of up to about 3,000 cm² s⁻³. Other measurements in large thunderstorms, summarized by MacCready (1964), give maximum values of ε in the range 1,000 to 5,000 cm² s⁻³. According to a number of aircraft flights at about the 5-km level reported by Summers et al. (1972), while ε in the average small cumulus is only of the order of 100 cm² s⁻³ or less, ε in large cumulus towers growing on the flanks of thunderstorms can be as great as 1,000 cm² s⁻³, i.e., comparable with that within the main thunderstorm updraft itself (see Vol. 1, Chap. 7).

The most extensive set of turbulence spectra measurements within thunderstorms has been reported by Kyle (1975). He analyzed data obtained by an aircraft penetrating 13 updrafts about 4 km above ground level. He categorized sections of the flights according to whether they were in clear air, an organized updraft, downdraft, or a region of disorganized motion. He derived mean values of spectral slope and, because the slopes were usually close to $k = -5/3$, he also derived the corresponding ε with the results shown in Table 7.1. A typical value of ε in thunderstorm updrafts was found to be 500 cm² s⁻³.

Table 7.1. Spectral Slope (k) and Energy Dissipation Rate (ε) in Different Parts of Thunderstorms in Northeastern Colorado*

Location	Average k	Average ε (cm² s⁻³)	Range of ε (cm² s⁻³)
Updraft	−1.63	500	27–1,730
Downdraft	−1.56	300	8–5,800
Unorganized	−1.50	110	1–1,000
Clear air	−1.34	~1	0–20

*Source: Kyle, 1975.

g. Some Properties of Downdrafts

Narrow downdraft zones have been observed at the boundaries of active cloud turrets (Ackerman, 1969), and broader zones of warm, dry downdrafts have been detected in the clear air surrounding the upper parts of severe storms (Sinclair, 1973; Fritsch, 1975; Hoxit et al., 1976). The strongest downdrafts, however, are usually encountered within the main precipitation fallout zones. The vertical velocity of these downdrafts varies widely, but they tend to be very roughly half as strong as the peak updraft velocity and to occur at lower altitudes (see, for example the Doppler radar studies by Battan, 1975; Kropfli and Miller, 1976; Heymsfield, 1978; Foote and Frank, 1983; Nelson, 1983). One of the strongest downdrafts observed so far (25 m s⁻¹) was reported by Nelson (1983) (Fig. 7.9). Downdrafts of about 15 m s⁻¹ have also been reported in the Doppler studies by Strauch and Merrem (1976), Heymsfield (1978), and Miller et al. (1982) and from aircraft penetrations by Heymsfield and Musil (1982).

The main dynamical importance of downdrafts is in their influence on the intensity and persistence of the overall circulation. As long ago as 1946, Normand recognized that a thunderstorm can "take advantage of the energy available from descending moist currents [and] that it may be organized to take in potentially cold air at the higher levels as

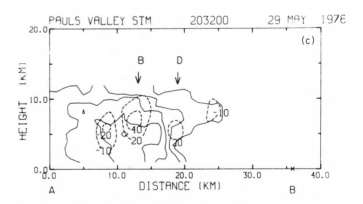

Figure 7.9. Vertical cross section through an intense supercell storm observed by triple Doppler radar. Solid lines are radar reflectivity at intervals of 5 dBZ. Dashed lines are vertical velocity in m s⁻¹. Note the 20 m s⁻¹ downdraft adjacent to the 40 m s⁻¹ updraft (Nelson, 1983).

well as potentially warm air at low levels." It is essential, as Ludlam (1963) pointed out, that the updraft should be inclined in such a way that the water condensed in the updraft can be precipitated into air with low wet-bulb potential temperature (θ_w). Once the precipitation has entered this cold air, it can produce a downdraft through evaporative cooling and melting as well as through its drag (Hookings, 1965; Kamburova and Ludlam, 1966). The evaporative cooling mechanism is not straightforward, however, because the small droplets that evaporate most easily have insufficient terminal fallspeed to penetrate far into the cold air. Haman (1973) therefore suggests that downdrafts are best maintained by evaporation of small droplets supplied by entrainment of cloudy air from neighboring updrafts. There is a certain range of entrainment rates for which this process is effective. Too small an entrainment will not provide a sufficient supply of small droplets; too large an entrainment may introduce too much warm air from the updraft, which will overcompensate the evaporative cooling.

The cold downdraft air diverges in all directions at the ground, where it gives rise to the well-known mesohigh (Fujita, 1963). Most of the downdraft air gets left behind the storm, but some of it initially flows ahead or at one side of the storm as a density current, giving rise to a sharp gust front. Although many thunderstorms consist of a sequence of short-lived cells, the density current produced by the cold outflow from their combined downdrafts tends to persist in a rather steady state, and this acts as an integrating and smoothing control on the impulsive-cell dynamics. Moncrieff and Miller (1976) suggest that if the propagation velocity of the density current is well matched to the propagation velocity of the overall cumulonimbus then a relatively steady circulation might develop. This view is supported by the finding of Auer et al. (1969) that the gust front associated with intense, quasi-steady thunderstorms is usually found 5 to 6 km ahead of the leading edge of the main precipitation core. When the gust front spreads much farther ahead of a storm, as in Fig. 7.7, the supply of boundary layer air to the main updraft is likely to be cut off, thereby leading to its decay.

There can be little doubt that the downdraft plays a crucial role in the organization of most thunderstorms and that theoretical models should take proper account of it. At the same time, however, we must not overlook the fact that a few thunderstorms are apparently able to become severe and fairly steady in the absence of a cold downdraft reaching the surface (e.g., Davies-Jones et al., 1976).

h. Downbursts and Microbursts

The term *downburst* has been introduced by Fujita (Fujita and Byers, 1977) to describe the exceptionally strong small-scale downdrafts which induce outbursts of damaging winds near the ground. Small downbursts are referred to as *microbursts* (Fujita, 1981). They have typical horizontal dimensions of a few kilometers or less and are thus almost an order of magnitude smaller than the overall downdraft region.

They present a major hazard to aircraft (Fujita and Byers, 1977; Fujita and Caracena, 1977). Emanuel (1981) suggests that they may be a manifestation of penetrative downdrafts generated where dry low-θ_w air overrides cloudy high-θ_w air near the foot of an updraft.

4. Factors Affecting the Severity of Thunderstorms

The severity of a thunderstorm can be judged in many ways. What we are concerned with here, however, is its dynamical intensity, which can be expressed in terms of the strength and lateral dimensions of the vertical drafts. Related to these criteria are other factors, such as the penetration of the updraft above tropopause level, the strength of the surface winds, and to some extent, the maximum hail size. Surface rainfall, on the other hand, is not always well correlated with dynamical intensity (Browning, 1977), nor is lightning frequency (Pakiam and Maybank, 1975). It is probably justifiable to think of the dynamical severity in many cases as being related to the degree of steadiness of the dynamical organization. Although steadiness is not so much the cause of the severity as a concomitant of it, it must contribute to the severity by promoting a dynamically efficient circulation.

It has long been recognized that severe thunderstorms are favored by strong convective instability, abundant moisture at low levels, strong wind shear usually veering considerably with height, and a dynamical lifting mechanism that can release the instability (Newton, 1963). We now examine the physical significance of these factors and introduce other factors that affect the severity and steadiness of the convection.

a. Thermodynamic Structure in the Vertical

The importance of strong convective instability, resulting from cold air aloft and high-θ_w air at low levels, is obvious. Examples given in Sec. 3b show how, on the basis of simple parcel theory, the updraft velocity would be influenced by the temperature excesses generated within the updraft aloft. According to Marwitz (1972a, b), all kinds of severe thunderstorms tend to be associated with temperature excesses of 4°C or more at 500 mb.

A little less obvious but nevertheless important for severe convection is the existence of a lid of warm dry air capping the boundary layer. This is illustrated in Fig. 7.10, which shows a mean sounding for air masses giving rise to thunderstorms severe enough to produce tornadoes. Fawbush and Miller (1953) found that the stable lid near 800 mb was also a feature of the environment for thunderstorms producing large hail. Air parcels lifted from the surface can be seen to acquire very large temperature excesses when lifted above the lid. As Carlson and Ludlam (1968) and Carlson et al. (1983) have emphasized, such a lid has the effect of inhibiting premature release of convective instability and enables a high θ_w to build up at low levels. This sets the stage for the development of vigorous deep convection when the air at

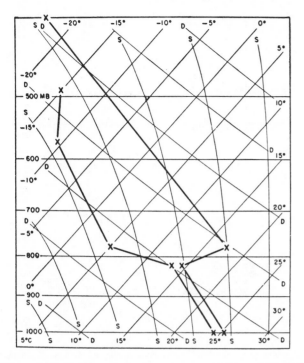

Figure 7.10. Profiles of mean temperature (right) and wet-bulb temperature (left), plotted on skew-T, log-p diagram, representative of the atmosphere in the vicinity of thunderstorms intense enough to have produced tornadoes. Data based on 75 cases in the United States (Fawbush and Miller, 1953).

low levels is subjected to large-scale ascent (e.g., ahead of a trough) or to mesoscale lifting (e.g., in association with a migrating upper-level jet streak, a dry line, a cold outflow from a neighbouring storm, or the topography). Vigorous convection is particularly likely to occur where the air at low levels flows out from under the lateral boundary of the lid, a process called *underrunning*.

Strong capping inversions are common in parts of the American Midwest, for example, where warm dry air from an elevated arid region overruns cooler but very moist air from the Gulf of Mexico. Even when a strong lid is not present, however, the boundary layer may still be influenced by vigorous entrainment of relatively dry warm air at its top associated with strong buoyancy generation of turbulence. Such a situation often prevails in northeast Colorado in the summer (Mahrt, 1975). As a result, the boundary layer there, which is typically 2 km deep in thunderstorm situations, is characterized by a weak increase in virtual potential temperature with height (except for the superadiabatic layer within 100 to 200 m of the ground) and a substantial decrease in mixing ratio with height. Thus it is quite usual on thunderstorm days for the air with the highest θ_w to be situated at the lowest levels despite the existence of slight static stability. Differential advection often further increases the vertical gradient of moisture near the ground. Together these factors cause the lifting condensation level and the convective instability to depend critically on whether a sur-

face value of moisture or a layer-averaged value is applicable. Established updrafts can transfer high-θ_w air from near the surface to cloud base with negligible modification by entrainment, in which case the near-surface value of mixing ratio is applicable. On the other hand, the initiation of fresh convection is likely to depend more on the average characteristics of the convectively stirred boundary layer. Thus the large lapse of mixing ratio offers a distinct advantage to established convection. By inhibiting the initiation of deep convection that might otherwise compete with any existing thunderstorm updraft, this helps an existing storm to remain intense and more nearly steady state. Boundary layer subsidence which is sometimes produced ahead of intense storms (Barnes, 1978) can have a similar effect.

b. Wind Shear and Veer

Another factor that appears to influence thunderstorm severity is the nature of the vertical wind shear. Figure 7.11 shows typical wind hodographs characterizing the environment of three different kinds of storms, as derived by Chisholm and Renick (1972) on the basis of their experience in Alberta. The weak-shear hodograph (a) is associated with short-lived thunderstorms consisting of a single ordinary cell. It is also probably representative of poorly organized multicell storms that do not become intense. The two strong-shear hodographs (b and c) are both characteristic of severe hail-producing thunderstorms, hodograph b representing well-organized multicell storms and hodograph c representing the more nearly steady-state supercells.

The importance of strong shear is that, for a storm cell traveling at the speed of the wind in the middle troposphere, the low-level air has a strong component of relative motion toward the approaching storm. This means that the magnitude of the inflow can be properly matched to the magnitude of the buoyant updraft. In the absence of suitable shear the inflow will be insufficient to sustain any vigorous updraft that might result from large thermal instability. These ideas have been expressed quantitatively by Moncrieff and Green (1972) in terms of a bulk convective Richardson number (Ri). They define Ri as the ratio of available potential energy produced by buoyancy to available kinetic energy produced by shear. They showed theoretically that a low value of Ri owing to strong low-level shear accompanying strong thermal instability favors maintenance of a vigorous and nearly steady-state convective circulation. The importance of this kind of Ri as a criterion for the possibility of development of a quasi-steady supercell storm is further supported by the work of Haman (1976, 1978).

Figure 7.11 shows that the hodograph for supercell storms does not differ significantly from that for well-organized multicell storms in the magnitude of the overall tropospheric wind shear. Thus strong tropospheric wind shear, although necessary for a persistent storm, is not the only factor that determines whether a steady-state supercell will develop (see also Marwitz 1972a, b). The most significant differences in the wind profile associated with supercell and multicell storms seem to be in the strength of the subcloud winds and the amount of veering with height, especially at low levels. According to Marwitz (1972a), the mean sub-cloud environmental wind associated with supercells is greater than 10 m s^{-1}, and its direction is backed by more than 60° with respect to the mean environmental wind. Allowing for the anomalous motion of supercells, the low-level inflow relative to such a cell may therefore be as great as 15 to 20 m s^{-1} in its far environment (Paul, 1973; Browning and Foote, 1976). As discussed elsewhere in this chapter, it is the veer of the wind at low levels that appears to be responsible for the rotation and anomalous motion of the updraft in supercell storms.

c. Precipitation

The development of precipitation has a major effect on the dynamics of thunderstorms. Both fallspeed differences of different precipitation particles and terminal fallspeed changes of a given population of particles can lead to accumulation of precipitation in certain parts of a storm. Although precipitation concentrations as high as 20 to 30 g m^{-3}, as proposed by Sulakvelidze et al. (1967), probably do not occur extensively (Kessler, 1969; Chap. 14), large volumes with concentrations of up to 10 g m^{-3} may be common. Drag produced by 4 g kg^{-1} of precipitation would have an effect equivalent to the negative buoyancy associated with a virtual temperature deficit of 1°C (Saunders, 1961). Such a mixing ratio corresponds to a concentration of only ~3 g m^{-3} in the lower troposphere and ~2 g m^{-3} in the upper troposphere. Thus water-loading effects can significantly impede an updraft or, alternatively, help sustain a downdraft. As noted in Sec. 3g, evaporation of the precipitation will further intensify a downdraft by chilling it. The generation of a strong downdraft in turn stimulates the development of an adjacent updraft, which may become intense, especially if the two can coexist side by side without mutual interference. Development of a severe thunderstorm therefore requires that the storm can become organized in such a way as to (1) minimize the accumulation of precipitation in the updraft and (2) facilitate the transfer of precipitation from the updraft where it is generated into adjacent downdrafts that can be fed continuously with dry and potentially cold air.

One way of minimizing water loading in the updraft is for the updraft to be inclined. Mathematical models such as those of Srivastava (1967) and Kessler (1969) suggest that in the case of an essentially vertical updraft of moderate intensity the development of high concentrations of precipitation is likely temporarily to convert the updraft into a downdraft; further development of precipitation accompanying regeneration of the updraft then repeats the cycle, and a pulsating circulation is produced resembling the succession of updrafts in an ordinary multicell storm. In an inclined updraft, however, the amount of water loading is decreased because the horizontal component of motion of the updraft air relative to the motion of the cell carries the precipitation across the updraft (see dotted trajectory in Fig. 7.7), and

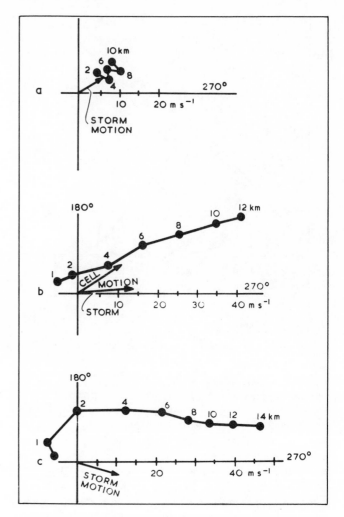

Figure 7.11. Typical wind hodographs representing environmental conditions accompanying different classes of Alberta hailstorms. Hodographs are representative of (a) ordinary single-cell storms producing very little hail, (b) well-organized multicell hailstorms, and (c) supercell storms (Chisholm and Renick, 1972).

this limits the residence time of particles within it (Kessler, 1975a). If the updraft is inclined in the upshear direction as shown schematically in Fig. 7.12, then the precipitation falling out at the rear can generate a strong downdraft, provided the shear enables cold, dry middle-level air to enter the downdraft region and sustain it.

Browning and Ludlam (1962) developed the concept of a combination of wind shear and a tilted updraft enabling the updraft and downdraft to be maintained continuously without serious interference, thereby enhancing the overall energy of a storm. However, Moncrieff and Green (1972) have since argued on theoretical grounds that it is dynamically impossible to sustain a steady circulation of this kind without a significant component of the circulation occurring in a plane at right angles to it. This implies that for a storm to be long lasting its organization must be essentially three-dimensional. That this is indeed sometimes the case is vividly illustrated in Fig. 7.13, which shows an updraft circulation in which the outflow aloft leaves the storm approximately at right angles to the inflow near the surface. When the inflow approaches the right flank of the storm, most of the precipitation falls out on the left flank (Sec. 5b). This gives rise to a stable side-by-side, updraft-downdraft couplet instead of the front-to-back, updraft-downdraft couplet portrayed in Fig. 7.12; however, the basic requirement for the water-loading effect to be transferred from the updraft to the downdraft is still fulfilled.

Another way of minimizing precipitation accumulation in the updraft is for the conversion of cloud water into precipitation to proceed inefficiently (Kessler, 1975b). One indication of this kind of inefficiency is the presence of what

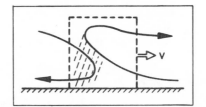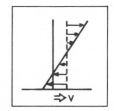

Figure 7.12. (Left) An idealized two-dimensional airflow configuration allowing precipitation generated within updraft to fall into and intensify underlying downdraft. Boundaries of the thunderstorm are represented by dashed square. (Right) A vertical profile showing the winds in the environment; the arrows represent winds relative to the storm traveling at velocity v (after Browning and Ludlam, 1962).

Figure 7.13. Well-organized, three-dimensional thunderstorm clouds over Alberta. Two storm cells can be seen; in each of them air approaches the updraft at low levels from the southeast (from the right side of the photograph) and leaves the storm within an anvil trailing toward the northeast (at the right and into the plane of the photograph) (reproduced by courtesy of the Alberta Research Council; similar photographs of the same storm are presented by Warner, 1976).

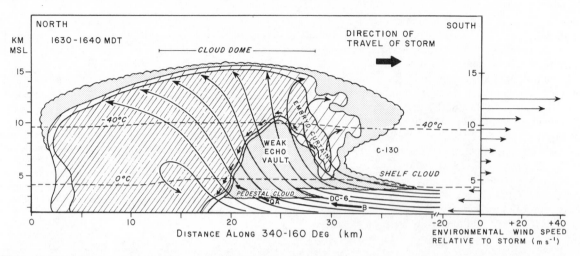

Figure 7.14. Vertical section through supercell thunderstorm in northeastern Colorado. The section is oriented along the travel direction of the storm, through the updraft core. Two levels of radar, reflectivity are represented by different densities of hatched shading. Areas of cloud devoid of detectable echo are shown stippled, the largest such area being the radar vault. The thin lines are streamlines of airflow relative to the storm based on aircraft measurements (thick arrows) and other observations. To the right of the diagram is a profile of the wind component along the direction of travel of the storm as derived from a sounding 50 km south of the storm. The short, thin arrows skirting the vault represent a limiting hailstone trajectory (Browning and Foote, 1976).

is known as a *weak-echo vault*, or simply *vault*. Because radar echo from a thunderstorm is caused by precipitation grown in an updraft, meteorologists for a long time tended to identify radar echo too closely with the actual updrafts, apparently forgetting that there is a lag between initial condensation in the updraft and development of radar-detectable precipitation. However, Browning and Ludlam (1962) and Browning and Donaldson (1963), noting a vault-shaped region of weak echo in the core of severe thunderstorms, interpreted such vaults as symptoms of intense updrafts. According to them, the updrafts in these vaults are so strong that, although they are filled with cloud, precipitation does not have time to form within them before the air in the updraft has risen to very high levels; any precipitation formed in weaker updrafts on the flanks of the vaults does not have any opportunity of penetrating into them.

Following these early observations, vaults have been observed by many researchers and with much better resolution (e.g., Fig. 7.14). According to Dennis (1971), vaults are common in the more severe storms in South Dakota. According to Chisholm and Renick (1972), they are also common in Alberta. Vaults are indeed a characteristic feature of supercell storms, but they do not occur to any significant extent within ordinary cells. Simultaneous observations by radar, aircraft, and stereophotography (Chisholm and Warner, 1969; Marwitz et al., 1969; Chisholm, 1970; Browning and Foote, 1976) have confirmed that vaults are accompanied by extensive updrafts at cloudbase, and radar observations of chaff (Marwitz, 1973) have shown that the updrafts observed at cloud base continue upward through the

full extent of the vault. Further evidence of this is provided by Doppler radar observations (e.g., Lemon et al., 1978; Foote and Frank, 1983). By contrast, however, in unsteady storms without vaults, it is not uncommon for the radar-echo intensity to reach maximum values within the updraft cores (e.g., Miller et al., 1983).

In the presence of a well-developed vault, such as that portrayed in Fig. 7.14, much of the cloud water is exhausted into the thunderstorm anvil as small ice crystals. Thus the overall precipitation efficiency, defined as the ratio of the surface-precipitation output to the water-vapor input, can be very low in vaulted supercell storms (Browning, 1977). According to Burgess and Davies-Jones (1979), the precipitation efficiency can also be very low in other kinds of intense storms which, although they do not fit the classical supercell storm model, appear to have strong updrafts in a region of very low radar reflectivity. Inefficient cloud conversion has important microphysical implications with respect to precipitation modification (Browning and Foote, 1976), but the point we wish to stress here is that the existence of an updraft core unencumbered by precipitation loading helps the updraft maintain an intense and quasi-steady organization (Kessler, 1974). It would be wrong to assert that this could be the sole cause of this kind of organization, for we must remember that it is because of the intense and relatively sustained nature of the updraft that a vault is able to develop in the first place. However it seems that we have here an important feedback mechanism that, along with rotation, helps make a supercell different from an ordinary cell to some extent in kind as well as in degree.

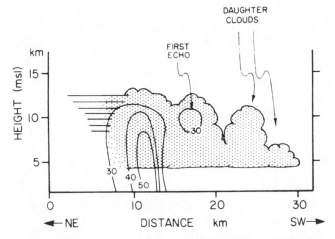

Figure 7.15. Cross section through typical multicell thunderstorm in South Dakota showing a sequence of evolving cells. Stippled shading: cloud; solid contours: radar reflectivity (dBZ) associated with precipitation. (Right) newly developing daughter clouds in which the precipitation has not had time to grow to radar-detectable sizes; (Left) mature cell with precipitation reaching the ground. In between, one of the daughter clouds has just developed its first radar echo aloft (after Dennis et al., 1970).

5. Conceptual Models of Thunderstorm Circulations

a. Multicell Storms

Ordinary multicell thunderstorms are characterized by the successive formation of more or less easily resolvable new cells, usually on the right flank of the storm. According to Dennis et al. (1970), these new cells appear as cumulus clouds, sometimes arranged in lines, extending up to 30 km from the mature cell (Fig. 7.15). They often develop out of a shallow cumuliform shelf cloud on the right flank of the storm and grow rapidly as they approach the main cumulonimbus cloud mass, merging within 10 to 40 min of their formation. A first radar echo, associated with the initial development of precipitation, usually appears in these clouds just before they merge with the main cloud mass, and the merger tends to be followed by a burst of heavy rain or hail reaching the ground. During Project Hailswath (Goyer et al., 1966), these developing clouds became known as *feeder clouds*. However, this term is misleading when applied to ordinary multicell storms, in the sense that the clouds to not *feed* the mature cloud but grow and *become* the mature cloud. Therefore we refer to them instead as *daughter clouds*. Use of the term *feeder cloud* should be restricted to the flanking lines of developing cumulus clouds that sometimes merge with and appear to intensify supercells (Lemon, 1976b). Figure 7.16a shows a succession of feeder clouds on the flank of a supercell storm. A structure more typical of a multicell storm is shown in Fig. 7.16b. For contrast the relatively smooth, dome-shaped updraft summit of a giant supercell storm is reproduced in Fig. 7.16c. The diameter

of a typical supercell dome where it penetrates the tropopause level is generally several times larger than the individual turrets in a multicell storm.

Chisholm and Renick (1972) have presented a model of the structure and evolution of an ordinary multicell storm based on their experience with combined visual and radar observations (Fig. 7.17). According to them, a typical rather intense storm of this kind contains two to four radar cells at any given time. New radar cells develop from cloud towers 3 to 5 km in diameter rising at 10 to 15 m s^{-1} (Renick, 1966; 1971) in a preferred region on the right flank (cell 3 at time 0 in Fig. 7.17). As the daughter cell grows and becomes the new storm center, the previous cell (cell 2 in Fig. 7.17) begins to decay while yet another (cell 4) forms. New cells continue to form in this way at roughly 10-min intervals, and each cell is identifiable on radar for 20 to 30 min. A total of 30 or more cells may develop during the lifetime of a storm.

The evolution of the vertical structure of one of the radar cells (cell 3) is depicted at the bottom of Fig. 7.17. The first echo appears in the upper troposphere about 10 min after the associated daughter cloud starts rising rapidly. The rapid intensification of this echo is interpreted as caused by the growth of graupel to millimeter sizes. Soon after the first echo appears, it develops an inverted, cuplike shape partly encompassing a weak-echo region (an incipient vault), which lasts only a few minutes before the entire echo descends to the ground and obliterates it. The weak-echo region is considered to be a region of moderately strong updraft. This may perhaps reach 20 m s^{-1} before water loading begins to have an effect.

The description of Fig. 7.17 applies to vigorous multicell thunderstorms that develop in the presence of moderate-to-strong wind shear (2 to 5 × 10^{-3} s^{-1}). In weaker shear the production of daughter clouds is likely to be less systematic in both space and time.

b. Supercell Storms

We restrict the discussion in this section to the structure of isolated supercells. The discussion can be generalized to apply to supercells adjoining other storm cells, although in such situations precipitation from one cell may enter the circulation of another (e.g., Browning, 1965c) and produce further complications.

In contrast with individual ordinary cells, which to a first approximation can be considered closed systems drifting with the mean winds, a supercell behaves as an open system that propagates continuously either to the left or to the right of the mean winds with a velocity that permits it to maintain a continuous circulation. According to Browning (1964; 1968), the circulation pattern in the SR supercell has a three-dimensional configuration of the form sketched in Fig. 7.18a. A hodograph of the winds typical of the environment of such a storm is shown in Fig. 7.18b. A comparison of Fig. 7.18a with Fig. 7.18b shows that the updraft air enters the SR supercell at low levels in the direction of

(a)

(b)

(c)

Figure 7.16. (a) Line of feeder clouds flanking a supercell storm east of Oklahoma City on 8 June 1974. The view is toward the south (photo by NSSL Storm Intercept Team). (b) Multicellular thunderstorm in northwest Texas on 31 May 1976. This storm produced large hail (photo by Steven Tegtmeier). (c) Supercell thunderstorm in northeastern Colorado on 21 June 1972. This storm produced giant hail and a tornado. The view is from a position 35 km west of the storm and shows the very large, smoothly shaped dome at the top of the storm (photo by G. B. Foote).

the low-level winds (L) and leaves within the anvil in the direction of the high-level winds (H). Precipitation falling out of the updraft descends mainly to the side of the updraft because of the strong winds overtaking from the right rear flank. Dry air with low θ_w from middle levels (M) approaches with a component from the right flank and carries this precipitation toward the left flank to form a downdraft there. The result is an SR supercell with a stable, side-by-side, updraft-downdraft couplet as referred to in Sec. 4c.

It is instructive to resolve the circulation pattern in Fig. 7.18a into two vertical planes, one along W–E and the other along S–N. The vertical circulation along W–E resembles that in Fig. 7.12, albeit with a "knot" in it. The vertical circulation along S–N, sketched in Fig. 7.18e, is similar to that found by Moncrieff and Miller (1976) for tropical

thunderstorms that propagate into the winds at all levels. The fact that supercells, the steadiest and most intense thunderstorms cells, are characterized by a propagating component of the kind depicted in Fig. 7.18e suggests that this is a specially favored mode of organization, corresponding to the organization that is best able to exploit the energy available from the latent-heat sources and sinks and the drag associated with the precipitation.

Figure. 7.19, derived from a recent triple Doppler study by Foote and Frank (1983), provides an example of the kind of organization in Fig. 7.18 (a and e). Ribbon A in Fig. 7.19 represents the flow through the strongest part of the updraft. Ribbon D represents the flow of air streaming around the leading edge of this updraft which becomes the strongest part of the downdraft. Together, ribbons A and D

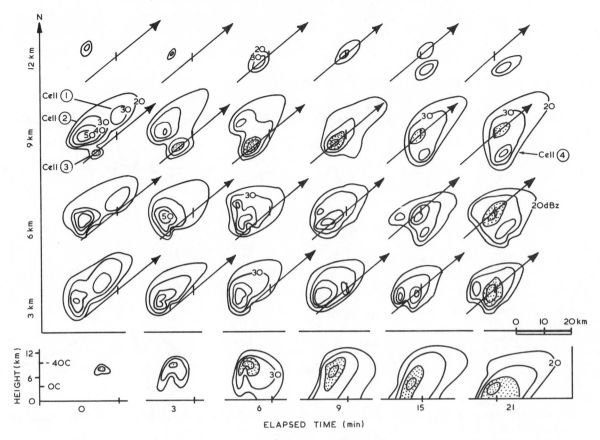

Figure 7.17. (Top) Horizontal radar sections through a multicell thunderstorm for four altitudes, at six times during the evolution of constituent cells. Reflectivity contours are at 10-dBZ intervals. Arrows depict the direction of cell motion and a geographical reference line for vertical cross sections appears at the bottom of the figure. Cell 3 is shaded to show the life history of an individual cell. (Bottom) Vertical radar sections of cell 3 (Chisholm and Renick, 1972).

correspond to the interlocking circulations depicted in Fig. 7.18 (a and e). The storm represented in Fig. 7.19, although essentially an SR supercell, did have some cellular substructure superimposed on the steady circulation. Even some more obviously multicellular storms apparently can exhibit a broadly similar organization (e.g., Miller, 1978).

A complicating feature of Fig. 7.19 is a second downdraft (ribbon E) behind the main updraft. According to Foote and Frank, however, the flow along the cyclonic streamline D was substantially stronger than that along E, a result which they consider to be general for right-moving storms. Lemon and Doswell (1979) also present evidence for a second downdraft, which they refer to as the rear-flank downdraft. Located more strictly on the right flank of right-moving storms, this downdraft tends to develop when the storm enters a late stage of development associated with tornadogenesis. Klemp and Rotunno (1983) too refer to the development of a second downdraft at this stage; however, they refer to a main storm-scale downdraft corresponding to that in Fig. 7.18 which began to wrap itself cyclonically

around the updraft, plus a second, much smaller scale, dynamically induced, so-called occlusion downdraft which forms near the circulation center.

An SR supercell travels to the right of and slower than the mean tropospheric winds (Fig. 7.18b). An SL supercell, on the other hand, travels to the left of and faster than the mean winds (Fig. 7.18d). As a result, the dynamical organization of an SL supercell (Fig. 7.18c) is a mirror image of that in Fig. 7.18a, although mirrored about the mean tropospheric shear vector (*HL*) rather than about the travel direction of the storm (Browning, 1968). Thus the locations of the updraft and downdraft are interchanged, and the inflows are toward the front of the storm rather than from the right flank.

Occasionally a severe storm splits into contiguous SR and SL supercells, which then follow highly divergent paths (Fujita and Grandoso, 1968; Achtemeier, 1969; Charba and Sasaki, 1971; Bluestein and Sohl, 1979). Using three-dimensional numerical models, Thorpe and Miller (1978), Klemp and Wilhelmson (1978a), and Wilhelmson and

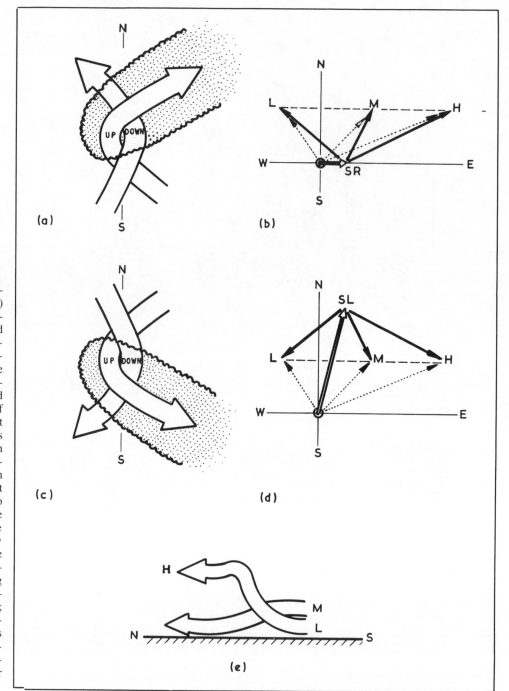

Figure 7.18. Dynamical organization of supercell storms. (a) The three-dimensional configuration of circulations associated with primary updraft and downdraft in an SR supercell. Although not shown explicitly, the downdraft diverges in all directions where it reaches the ground on the left (*North*) flank, some of the air flowing toward the right (*South*) flank, where it produces a gust front. The circulations in (a) are consistent with the hodograph (dashed line) in (b), in which the solid arrows represent environmental winds relative to the *SR* storm at low (*L*), middle (*M*), and high (*H*) levels of the troposphere. The storm velocity is represented by a double-line arrow. Figs. (c) and (d) are counterparts of (a) and (b), showing the circulation and environmental winds relative to an *SL* storm; winds relative to the ground (dotted arrows) are the same in (d) as in (b). Figure (e) shows the circulations in (a) resolved in a vertical section along *SN* (after Browning, 1964, 1968).

Klemp (1978, 1981) have found that such splitting may occur in the presence of strong low-level shear when a precipitation-induced downdraft divides the updraft of the preexisting storm. Numerical model studies of cell splitting by Schlesinger (1978, 1980) and Clark (1979) suggest that other dynamical factors leading to the entrainment of dry air may also be important.

Figure 7.18 depicts the simple situation of an environment with a unidirectional wind shear (i.e., end points of vectors **L**, **M**, and **H** are in a straight line). According to Klemp and Wilhelmson (1978b), either the SR or the SL supercell may be selectively enhanced if the environmental shear at low levels is not unidirectional. Thus, for example, when the wind hodograph turns clockwise with height as is

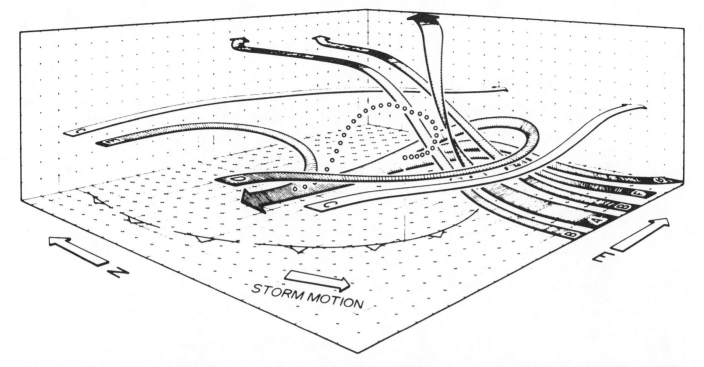

Figure 7.19. Major components of the airflow within an SR supercell as derived from triple-Doppler observations by Foote and Frank (1983). The strong updraft is depicted by the ribbon labeled *A*, which starts at low levels south-southeast of the storm, rises sharply in the storm interior, and leaves the storm toward the northeast to form the anvil outflow. On the flanks of the strong updraft the air rises more slowly (*B*) and penetrates farther to the rear of the storm before also turning to the northeast. In the middle levels there is a tendency for the westerly environmental flow to be diverted around the sides of the storm (ribbons labeled *C*), but some air also enters the storm and contributes to the downdraft (ribbons *D* and *E*). A contribution to the downdraft flux is also made by air originally at low levels southeast and east of the storm (ribbons *F* and *G*), which then rises several kilometers before turning downward in the vicinity of the echo core. The strongest part of the downdraft is represented by ribbon *D*. All the ribbons in this model represent streamlines of flow in a coordinate system relative to the storm which is moving toward the south-southeast as shown. The small circles indicate the possible trajectory of a hailstone.

usually the case, the development of the SR supercell is favored. A wind hodograph turning clockwise with height implies a relatively strong component of cold, dry middle-level (*M*) flow toward an *SR* storm but a relatively weak component of the middle-level airflow toward an *SL* storm. This favors the maintenance of the SR storm in two ways: (1) by increasing the flux of air capable of feeding the downdraft and (2) by displacing the precipitation and its associated downdraft farther away from the main updraft, thereby helping up- and downdrafts coexist without mutual interference.

Supercell storms display radar-echo patterns that are often strikingly similar from storm to storm (Browning and Ludlam, 1960, 1962; Browning and Donaldson, 1963; Browning, 1965a; Chisholm, 1970; Marwitz, 1972a; Renick et al., 1972; Nelson and Braham, 1972; Browning and Foote, 1976; etc.). The schematic model of an SR supercell in Fig. 7.20 shows the relation of the updraft to the radar echo (stippled), together with the cyclonically curving trajectories of the precipitation particles that account for the shape of the radar echo. A well-known feature of the echo pattern shown here is the vault, bounded on one side by a hook echo and on another by an echo overhang.

Air approaches the updraft initially beneath the echo overhang before rising within the vault. Part of this forward overhang contains particles several millimeters in diameter, some of which are believed to be destined to become hailstone embryos, and so it has been given the name *embryo curtain* by Browning and Foote (1976). The precipitation particles in the embryo curtain are thought to originate on the right flank of the main updraft near the upwind stagnation point (location *S* in Fig. 7.20), where the environmental flow aloft divides around the storm. Only a few of these particles may be able to enter the updraft core in a supercell. Browning and Foote have pointed out that this is important for the growth of hail; it is probably also important for the dynamics in that it helps prevent water loading in the updraft core.

The entry of precipitation into the updraft core is, according to Browning (1977), likely to be influenced by the angle α between the direction of the low-level inflow (*L*) and the direction of the middle-level environmental flow (*M*) relative to the storm in Fig. 7.18. If α is roughly 90°, and especially if the middle-level flow is strong, precipitation falling around the periphery of the updraft core may

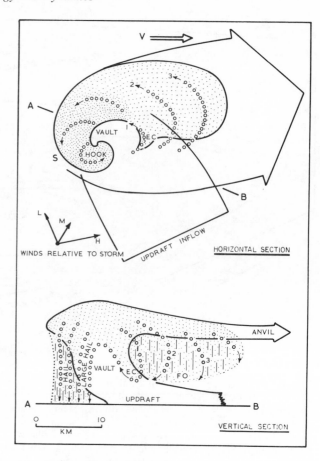

Figure 7.20. Horizontal and vertical sections illustrating relation of updraft to the radar echo in SR supercell storm. Solid curves: extent of the updraft air; dotted curves: trajectories of some precipitation particles accounting for the characteristic shape of the radar echo. Horizontal section: light and heavily stippled shading denotes extents of rain and hail in the lower troposphere respectively; AB oriented in the direction of the mean tropospheric wind shear, into which the updraft is inclined at low levels. Vertical section: broken vertical hatching denotes downdrafts with strong normal components of motion. Characteristic features of the echo pattern referred to in the text are the vault, hook, forward overhang (*FO*), and embryo curtain (*EC*) (redrawn from Browning, 1964).

spend insufficient time above the inflow to the updraft for much of it to be able to descend into a position from which it can be carried up into the updraft core, in which case a vault may be produced. If, on the other hand, α is very large and the inflow to the updraft approaches the front of the storm more nearly directly beneath the forward overhang, as in the case studied by Krupp and Cotton (1982a), then precipitation falling around the periphery of the updraft core can hardly avoid entering the inflow near the foot of the updraft, where the updraft is too weak to prevent the particles from penetrating all parts of it. Depending upon the degree of water loading and evaporative cooling below cloud base, the updraft then may or may not break down. Perhaps it remains fairly steady for a while to give what might be called an unvaulted supercell (Foote et al., 1975), or perhaps it reverts to an impulsively propagating multicell storm.

More research is needed to clarify the interaction of the storm dynamics with the three-dimensional precipitation trajectories. Because of their more nearly steady organization, it will be easier to carry out such studies for supercells than for multicell storms.

8. Tropical Convection

Yoshi Ogura

1. Introduction

The *Glossary of Meteorology* (1970) defines the thunderstorm as "a local storm invariably produced by a cumulonimbus cloud, . . . always accompanied by lightning and thunder, usually with . . . heavy rain." This definition emphasizes the electrical activity characteristic of these storms. Here, instead of the electrical phenomena, we consider the distribution, the thermodynamic structure, and the processes involved in the deep convective clouds and cloud systems that produce strong winds and torrential rains in the tropics, focusing on recent progress in observation and understanding. Among topics not treated substantially here are tropical cyclones (see Anthes, 1982), relationships among sea surface temperatures, convective cloud activity, and planetary scale circulations, and some features of thunderstorms over tropical land masses such as India.

Most of the solar energy intercepted by the Earth is absorbed in tropical regions. The tropics (from 30° N to 30° S) cover half the surface of the Earth and constitute the atmospheric boiler that not only produces tropical thunderstorms but also drives the global atmospheric circulation (Lorenz 1967).

Much of our recent knowledge of the structure and evolution of tropical convective systems has come from specially designed field observation programs. These programs include the Line Island Experiment (February–April 1967); the Venezuelan International Meteorological and Hydrological Experiments (VIMHEX) (June–September 1969 and June–September 1972); the GARP Atlantic Tropical Experiment (GATE) over the eastern Atlantic and the African continent (June–September 1974); the Winter Monsoon Experiment (MONEX) over southeast Asia (December 1978–February 1979); Summer MONEX during the summer of 1979 over the area extending from the east coast of Africa to southeast Asia; and the West African Monsoon Experiment (WAMEX) during the same summer over western and central Africa. The field programs of the last three monsoon experiments were undertaken concurrently with the First GARP (Global Atmospheric Research Program) Global Experiment (FGGE). Data from these programs and from satellite observations are the basis of new insights regarding the synoptic-scale and mesoscale disturbances and associated deep convection that produce heavy rain during the winter monsoon over southeast Asia and the summer monsoon over Asia and western and central Africa (Ramage, 1971; Riehl, 1979). We have learned more about easterly waves and upper tropospheric vortices, the two classes of generally distributed synoptic-scale disturbance that enhance precipitation in the tropics. We have acquired further details of the evolution and structure of the two major types of mesoscale convective systems in the tropics—squall and nonsquall cloud clusters.

a. Convective Regions in the Tropics

Figure 8.1 shows a schematic meridional cross section of the tropical ("Hadley") circulation. Three convective regimes are identified. The stratocumulus regime and trade cumulus regimes represent shallow convection, i.e., overturning with a vertical extent much smaller than the atmosphere's scale height. Shallow convection is a means by which heat and water from the ocean surface are distributed through the layer below the broad descending branch of the Hadley circulation. In the region of general subsidence of the air, a sharp inversion at the cloud top defines the upper boundary of a moist layer. Clouds in the stratocumulus regime may be dense enough to form a horizontally continuous layer of stratus or stratocumulus clouds. The clouds are typically organized, however, into units of mesoscale cellular convection (see Hubert, 1966; Agee et al., 1973; and Agee, 1982, for more detailed descriptions). The inversion gradually becomes higher and weaker as it extends equatorward and becomes the trade-wind inversion. In the trade cumulus regime, shallow, primarily nonprecipitating cumuli exist in the face of large-scale subsidence. Equatorward of this area is a regime of deep convection and cumulonimbus clouds known as the Intertropical Convergence Zone (ITCZ). The ITCZ, a prominent feature of the global atmospheric circulation, is roughly parallel to the equator and is especially pronounced over oceanic regions.

Deep convection is strongly variable on the large span of continents and oceans and at times even longer than years, and strong variations range downward in scale to a few kilometers and tens of minutes marked by individual cells in development and motion. The distribution of deep convection on these various scales is clearly shown by radiation measurements from satellites, since the cold high tops of con-

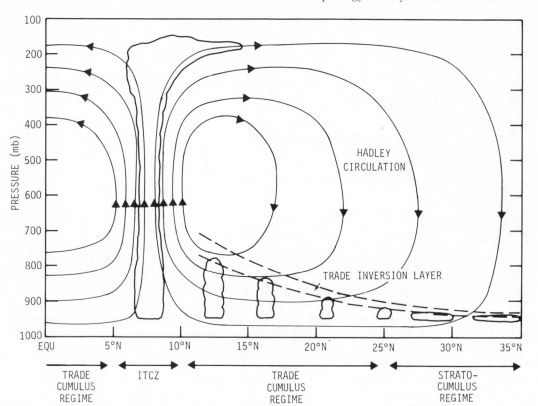

Figure 8.1. Schematic mean meridional cross section of the Hadley circulation.

vective clouds are weaker sources of outgoing infrared radiation observed at wavelengths to which the atmosphere is nearly transparent than is warm ground under clear skies. Figure 8.2 shows 3- and 4-year means of total outgoing infrared radiation (IR) measured in the window region (10.5–12.5 μm) by the NOAA scanning radiometer mounted on the polar-orbiting NOAA 4 satellite (Liebmann and Hartmann, 1982). In the low latitudes over the oceans, where surface temperature is only weakly varying, the convective cloudiness that identifies the ITCZ is closely associated with weak outgoing IR at these wavelengths.

In Fig. 8.2b several areas of strong convective activity can be identified in the Northern Hemisphere summer season, June–August. An outstanding feature is strong activity over the Indian subcontinent and Indonesia. Also, the ITCZ is visible in the Pacific between the equator and 15° N. Note that the convective activity is not uniform along the ITCZ; it is relatively strong over the eastern Pacific but weak over the central Pacific. The strong convective activity over Indonesia extends eastward along the ITCZ and also southeastward to form the South Pacific convergence zone (SPCZ). Another area of low IR identifies the ITCZ over Africa and the eastern Atlantic. A comparison of Fig. 8.2b with the percentage frequencies of thunderstorms and/or lightning in surface observations (Fig. 3.1 in this volume) shows reasonably good agreement between them. In the Northern Hemisphere winter season (December–February, Fig. 8.2d), the ITCZ in the northern Pacific disappears, and the low IR

area is centered over the maritime continental regions along the enhanced SPCZ.

b. Satellite Observations of Precipitation and Convection

Various new methods utilizing meteorological satellite data have been developed to monitor precipitation and deep convection. Our interest here is in techniques that are easy to apply to mapping global- or regional-scale rainfall in the tropics and have spatial and temporal resolution commensurate with various research requirements. The reader is referred to the survey by Barrett and Martin (1981) on this subject. An additional technique (Murakami, 1983) utilizes blackbody temperature measured with spatial resolution of ~5 km in the form of their mean value ($\bar{T}_{BB}$) and standard deviation (σ_B) within each 1° longitude-latitude square mesh. Murakami introduced the convective intensity index I_c defined by

$$I_c = \frac{\bar{T}_{BB} - T_{400}}{T_{tr} - T_{400}} \times 10 \qquad (8.1)$$

where T_{tr} and T_{400} are temperature at the tropopause height and the 400-mb level at each 1° square mesh, respectively. When no cloud-top heights exceed 400 mb, I_c is set to zero. When all cloud tops reach the tropopause level, I_c is 10. Empirically, I_c is set to zero wherever $\sigma_B < 5$ K.

Figure 8.3 shows the horizontal distribution of monthly

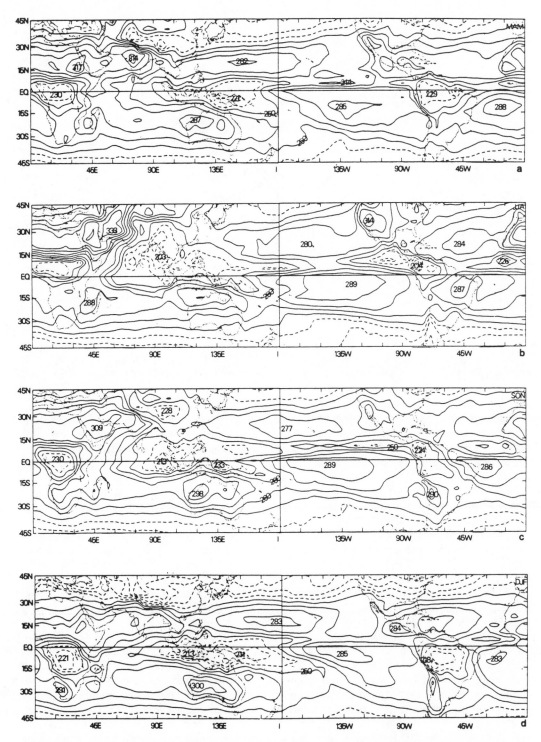

Figure 8.2. Outgoing infrared radiation as measured by satellite. Contours are at intervals of 10 W m^{-2}; Contours for 240 W m^{-2} and less are dashed. (a) Three-year mean for March, April, and May 1974–77. (b) Four-year mean for June, July, and August 1974–77. (c) Four-year mean for September, October, and November 1974–77. (d) Four-year mean for December, January, and February 1974–78 (Liebmann and Hartmann, 1982).

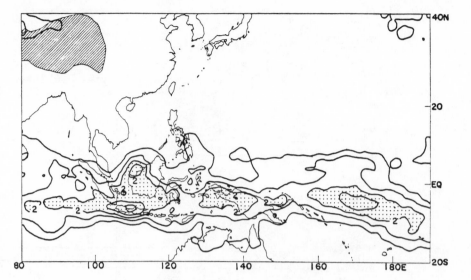

Figure 8.3. Horizontal distribution of monthly mean values of the convective intensity index for December 1978. Contours are at intervals of 0.5 units starting from 1, which correspond roughly to 10% of cloud tops reaching to the tropopause. Areas with values larger than 2 are shaded. Hatched area approximates the Tibetan Plateau above 3,000-m elevation (Murakami, 1983).

mean values of the convective intensity index defined by Murakami from satellite data. The major convective area in December 1978 is seen to have been aligned in the east-west direction along and to the south of the equator. Further, three local maxima of the index can be identified. One is located over the Indonesian islands around the Java Sea, including Sumatra, Java, and Borneo. The other two are located over New Guinea and in the South Pacific Ocean east of the Solomon Islands, apparently representing the northern tip of the SPCZ (Vincent, 1982).

Figure 8.4 illustrates a wind field typical of the vicinity of the ITCZ over the tropical Atlantic in the summer season in the Northern Hemisphere. The wind vectors are based on the motions of clouds (trade-wind cumulus at the lower level and filaments of cirrus from the tops of cumulonimbus clouds at the higher level) as viewed from the ATS III geosynchronous satellite in orbit at a fixed longitude over the equator. The shaded regions correspond to heavy cloudiness associated with deep cumulus clouds along the ITCZ. Wind in the lower troposphere has a component directed down the horizontal pressure gradient from the subtropical high-pressure belts toward the equatorial trough, a belt of minimum pressure that usually lies in the vicinity of the ITCZ. The northeasterly trade wind, which is simply a reflection of the quasi-geostrophic easterly flow around the southern flank of the subtropical high-pressure belt, is brought into juxtaposition with the cross-equatorial flow from the Southern Hemisphere at about 10° N. The reversal between the lower and upper troposphere flow over most areas is clearly visible in the figure.

Cumulonimbus clouds in the tropics are typically organized by synoptic-scale disturbances. Such organizations of the clouds are easily recognizable in satellite photographs as "cloud clusters" with horizontal dimensions of several hundred kilometers. The individual cloud clusters are relatively short-lived (½ to 2 days). However, as seen in Fig. 8.5,

cloud masses tend to move across the tropics westward, repeating dissipation, rebirth, and aggregation (see Sec. 5).

c. The Effect of Cumulus Convection on the Hadley Circulation

The importance of cumulonimbus clouds to the energy budget in the tropics was first stated by Riehl and Malkus (1958, 1961). As a measure of energy, consider the moist static energy (h) defined as

$$h = c_p T + gz + Lq, \qquad (8.2)$$

where c_p = specific heat of air at constant pressure, T = temperature, g = gravitational acceleration, z = geopotential height, L = latent heat of condensation, and q = specific humidity. Similar to wet-bulb potential temperature, h thus defined is conserved for moist adiabatic processes (see Chap. 4). Assuming zonal symmetry around the Earth, Riehl and Malkus (1958) considered the budget of h for the equatorial trough zone 10° latitude in width, dividing the atmosphere into two layers (Fig. 8.6). First, from wind measurements they computed the lateral low-level mass inflow and the upper-level mass outflow across the poleward boundary. Assuming no lateral flow across the trough-line boundary, this lateral flow pattern indicates the ascending motion across the 500-mb surface from the mass continuity consideration. Riehl and Malkus then calculated the heat budgets for each layer, using mean data for temperature and moisture, and estimates for radiative cooling rate and sensible and latent heat fluxes (Q_s and Q_e in the figure) from the Earth's surface. The computed horizontal heat flux in the low layer across the poleward boundary consisted of 1.15 units associated with the mean horizontal inflow, minus 0.17 units associated with eddy moisture flux. The result indicates that the deficit of 1.73×10^{15} cal s^{-1} in the upper layer has to be counterbalanced by the vertical

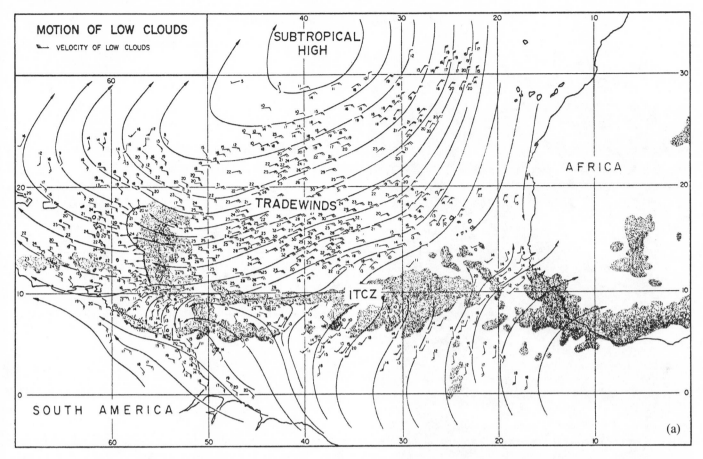

Figure 8.4. (a) Distribution of low-level cloud motions in the vicinity of the intertropical convergence zone at about 1500 GMT 14 July 1969. (b) Distribution of upper-tropospheric cloud motions and wind observations at about 1500 GMT 14 July 1969 (Fujita, 1971).

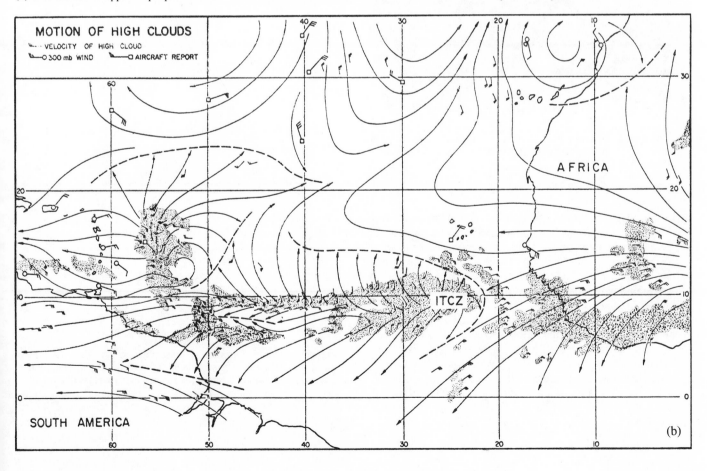

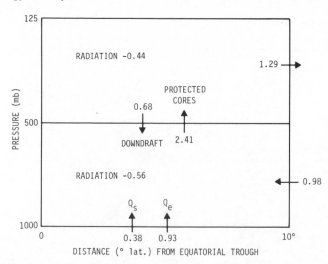

Figure 8.6. Heat budget for winter side of equatorial trough zone. Fluxes are in units of 10^{15} cal s^{-1} for 10° latitude belt (after Riehl and Malkus, 1958).

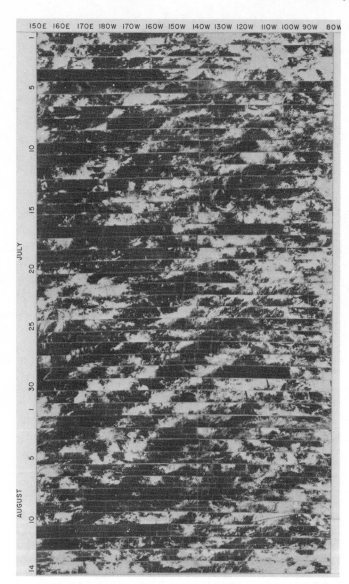

Figure 8.5. Time-longitude section of satellite photographs of 1 July–14 August 1967 for 5°–10° N latitude band in the Pacific (Chang et al., 1970).

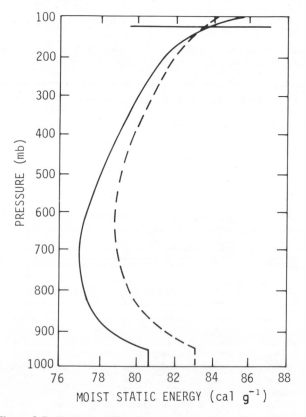

Figure 8.7. Vertical profiles of moist static energy. The solid profile is for 20° latitude from trough. Dashed profile is for trough zone itself. Solid horizontal line denotes mean position of tropopause (Riehl and Malkus, 1958).

heat transport across the 500-mb surface. If the mean vertical mass transport (M) in this equatorial belt is responsible for the vertical energy transport, the vertical heat transport (H) will be given by $H = M\bar{h}$, where $\bar{h}$ is the area-averaged heat content. Riehl and Malkus found that H thus estimated was significantly smaller than that required for the energy budget in the upper layer.

To explain this, the hypothesis that much of the mass flux must take place inside the "protected cores" of cumulonimbus clouds ("hot towers") was advanced. The basis of this hypothesis is provided in Fig. 8.7, which shows the vertical profiles of h in the trough zone itself and 20° poleward of it. Note that h has a minimum at about 750 mb. This indicates that a gradual, uniform, rising circulation, as envisaged in the Hadley circulation, would produce cooling rather than warming above the minimum *h*. The hot-tower hypothesis points to the giant cumulonimbus chimneys of tropical disturbances as the mechanism of ascent, vapor combustion, and upward energy pumping, whereby the air is imported from cloud bases to the upper troposphere with virtually undiluted properties of the high-energy subcloud layer.

From this consideration Riehl and Malkus estimated that $2.41 \times 10^{15}\,\mathrm{cal\,s^{-1}}$ of energy are transported upward through 500 mb by hot towers, accompanied by compensating downdrafts that transport $0.68 \times 10^{15}\,\mathrm{cal\,s^{-1}}$ of heat downward, as indicated in Fig. 8.6. This upward vertical transport of energy occurs in association with $18 \times 10^{13}\,\mathrm{g\,s^{-1}}$ of the undiluted upward mass flux through the 500-mb surface. If the protected towers ascend at 5 m s^{-1}, they occupy an area roughly 0.1% of the equatorial belt, 10° latitude in width. This means that the ascending branch of the Hadley circulation is concentrated in the very restricted regions of the towering clouds within tropical disturbances. Riehl and Malkus (1961) later applied the hot-tower concept to study of the energy budget for a hurricane. Riehl and Simpson (1979) repeated their calculations concerning structure and heat balance of the equatorial zone of low pressure with greatly enlarged observational material accumulated during 20 years. The new data confirmed the conclusions reached previously in most important aspects.

During the past 20 years mathematical formulations have been developed to represent the collective effect of cumulus convection on large- or synoptic-scale tropical circulations, and the complexity of different forms of cumulus organization has been better recognized. A concept of "conditional instability of the second kind" (CISK)[1] was introduced to explain the development of tropical disturbances such as hurricanes and some synoptic-scale waves observed in the tropical regions, taking into account some of these collective effects. Further, it has become clear that the deep-cloud activities are modulated by larger-scale meteorological fields. Research is being undertaken to investigate effects of large-scale circulation on the initiation, maintenance, and decay of organized convective systems and feedback effects of a cumulus cloud ensemble on the large-scale circulation.

2. Winter Monsoon over Southeast Asia

a. Synoptic Aspects of Cold Surges

During the Asian winter there is a strong, though intermittent, outpouring of cold air from the Siberian high, which converges over the equatorial "maritime continent" (Ramage, 1971) region of Malaysia, Indonesia, and the South China Sea to ensure very heavy rainfalls there (see Fig. 8.2). A cold surge in southeast Asia may be defined as a

[1] When the cooperative interaction between the cumulus convection and a large-scale perturbation leads to unstable growth of the large-scale system, the process is referred to as CISK (Ooyama, 1982).

sharp drop in surface temperature, an occurrence of a minimum temperature substantially below the seasonal average, a sudden freshening of the northerly or northeasterly monsoon winds, or a combination of these events (Chang et al., 1979).

T. Murakami (1980a, b) analyzed outgoing longwave radiation data obtained from NOAA polar orbiting satellites during the winter months in 1974–77 over the Asian monsoon region. Variations with prominent periods in the range 4–6 days and 15–30 days were identified. The latter were larger than the former. Disturbances in the former class were found to propagate westward in equatorial latitudes over the western North Pacific and the South China Sea in the winters of 1974–75 and 1976–77. In contrast, they propagated eastward (westward) in the area west (east) of about 130° E in 1975–76. These large year-to-year changes in phase propagation appear to be related to interannual differences in monsoonal surge activity near the East China Sea and Japan. The fluctuations of longer periods were very large over the Arafura Sea and Indonesian seas north and northwest of Australia, over the Philippines, and over the Bay of Bengal and the South Indian Ocean. Inverse relationships were observed between the changes at a reference point (10°S, 130°E, in the Arafura Sea) and over the Philippines, the western Pacific and Malaya, and the Bay of Bengal, suggesting southward propagation of perturbations along 100°–115° E from about 25° N to 20° S.

Ramage (1971) and Chang et al. (1979) are among those who have documented sequences of synoptic-scale events that lead to intensification of precipitating systems near the Equator. Chang focused on two cold-surge events that occurred between 4–6 and 10–11 December 1974 (Fig. 8.8). Figure 8.8a shows the cloud distribution in the pre–cold-surge situation at 0800 GMT, 3 December. At this time the cold front had just passed Hong Kong and is marked as the southern edge of the overcast that covers most of eastern and central China. Cloud groups CB1 and CB2 are near the equator. Superposition on a surface weather map shows that both CB1 and CB2 were associated with low-pressure centers (in Fig. 8.9 the cyclonic center associated with CB1 is labeled CB1). A line connecting CB1 and CB2 would be near the equatorial trough. Convection in CB1, along the northern edge of Borneo, was weak and scattered on 3 December, when CB2 was a much more intense and organized cloud cluster. CB2 was moving westward about 8° longitude a day, probably in association with the easterly waves (Chang et al., 1970) discussed in Sec. 5 below.

The cold front advanced southward very rapidly, and strong northeasterly winds prevailed over the South China Sea at 0600 GMT 6 December (Fig. 8.9). Cluster CB1 was intensified by the increased northeasterlies within 24 h of the first surge (6–7 December), while it was moving slowly northward. On 8 December it was temporarily weakened by an incursion of cold surface air along the coast of Vietnam but reintensified with sustained northeasterlies when surface air temperature again increased (9–10 December), as shown in Fig. 8.8b. In the meantime, cluster CB2 weakened. However, the second surge occurred as the cyclonic center that accompanied cluster CB2 was moving westward across the central South China Sea north of cluster C1. During 11–12 December the cyclonic center of CB2 intercepted the northeasterly surge and became intensified while blocking off the southward penetration of the northeasterly wind.

b. Observations of Winter Monsoon Convection

During the December 1978 field phase of Winter MONEX, three Soviet research ships were situated in a triangular array over the South China Sea north of Borneo (Fig. 8.10). On most of the days from 6 to 28 December, 6-hour soundings were taken at the ship sites. In addition a radar was installed especially for the Winter MONEX at Bintulu. It was observed that over the sea north of Borneo the general level of convective activity increased during monsoon cold surges and during the passage of westward-propagating near-equatorial disturbances. Convective activity decreased during monsoon lulls. Furthermore, radar and ship observations showed that the convection in that region underwent a remarkably regular diurnal cycle (Houze et al., 1981; Johnson and Priegnitz, 1981).

Figure 8.11 shows schematically the daily cycle of convection over the sea. Convection is typically initiated at about midnight with an offshore low-level wind. This wind meets the monsoonal northeasterly flow just off the coast, and the cloud system begins to form as a group of isolated cells (Fig. 8.11a). The convection continues to develop, and by 0800 LST it evolves into a mesoscale rain system consisting of a combination of deep cells and stratiform rain falling from a middle-to-upper-level anvil cloud (Fig. 8.10b). The precipitation area is often continuous over a horizontal distance of 200 km. When the sea breeze begins at about noon, the lower-level convergence and formation of cells cease, and the stratiform precipitation and anvil cloud slowly die out, though the upper level cloud continues to expand horizontally (Fig. 8.10c).

During the course of this diurnal cycle, the mesoscale precipitating system normally passed over the southern portion of the ship array shown in Fig. 8.10. The passage of three convective systems on 9–11 December over *Ak. Korolov* is illustrated in Fig. 8.12 (Johnson and Kriete, 1982). The rainfall episodes (identified from hourly surface data) are indicated by vertical lines in the lower portion of Fig. 8.12a; longer lines represent heavier rain. Each cloud system can be approximately visualized as being enclosed within the 80% relative humidity (stippled) region. As each system passed the ship, squall-type weather, with heavy rain, a surface wind shift, and sudden cooling (~2°C), normally occurred at its leading edge. At the rear of the rain area in each case is a region of warming in the lower troposphere of up to 2°C, with maxima near 800 mb. Drying is seen to accompany the low-level warming. However, the low-level drying and warming do not extend to the surface, and only light rain, if any, reaches the surface in this region. As shown below, these lower tropospheric features closely resemble those reported for mesoscale convective systems associated with tropical squall lines observed in other parts

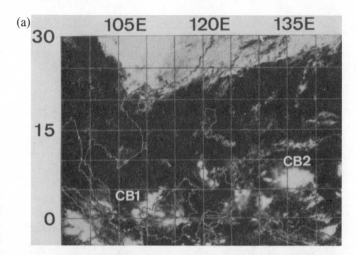

Figure 8.8. (a) NOAA-3 mosaic for 3 December 1974, centered near 0800 GMT; (b) NOAA-3 mosaic for 9 December 1974, centered near 0800 GMT. CB1 and CB2 denote convective cloud clusters (Chang et al., 1979).

of the tropical oceans (Fig. 8.12b is discussed in Sec. 8 below).

Concurrently with the radar and ship observations aircraft observations were carried out over the South China Sea during Winter MONEX and provided a unique data set. Warner (1981, 1982) analyzed data obtained during 10–12 December 1978, the period of the first cold-surge event in that month. He noted a striking similarity between clouds in the northeast monsoon flow and those in the northeast trade winds southwest of the east Pacific anticyclone (Malkus and Riehl, 1964). Stratus patches occurred upstream, related to subsidence. Near 10° N small cumulus gave way to congestus, and clouds increased in height downstream. The maximum cloud-top height reached 15 km in a cloud cluster observed over the ship array on 10 December (see Fig. 8.12). Churchill and Houze (1984) studied both the aircraft observations and the Bintulu radar data obtained on 10 December 1978. The aircraft penetration of three cloud clusters revealed microphysical differences between the convec-

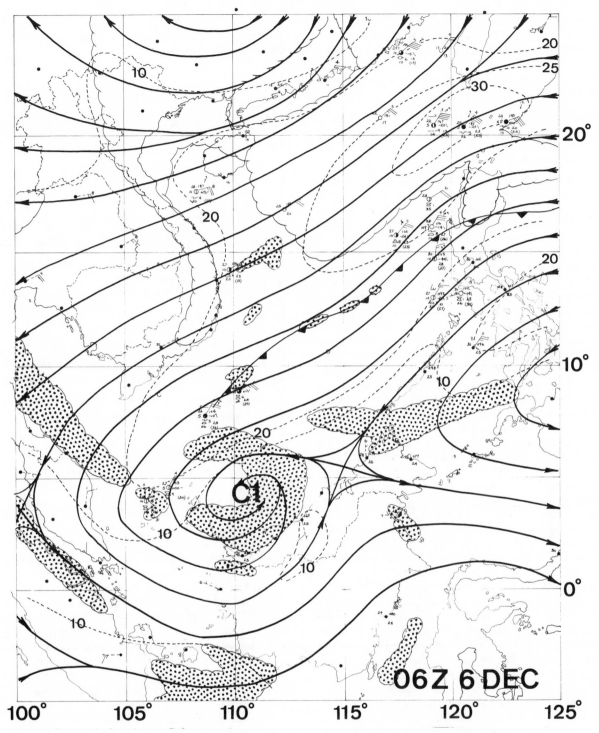

Figure 8.9. The 850-mb surface streamline and isotach analysis for 0600 GMT 6 December 1974. Solid wind vectors are surface reports; dashed vectors are 850-mb reports. C1 is the major cyclonic center. Nephanalysis of major cloudiness is included (Chang et al., 1979).

tive cells and the stratiform anvil regions. The cells were characterized by high particle concentrations, and ice particle growth was predominantly by riming. In the stratiform regions particle concentrations were lower, and ice particles grew by vapor deposition and aggregation (see also Chap. 16, Introduction).

3. Summer Monsoon over Asia

a. Arabian Sea Disturbances

The summer monsoon circulation over India and southeast Asia is broadly manifested as airflow northward to the great Asian landmass from the oceans bordering it on the south and east. In general, the onset of the monsoon is marked by a substantial increase in rainfall, but precise definition of onset may depend upon the meteorological variables that one wishes to emphasize. The summer monsoon "sets in" around the last week of May over India and its neighborhood and somewhat earlier over southeast Asia. The summer monsoon begins to diminish ("withdraw") from the Indian continent by the middle of September. There is a large interannual variability in the onset of the Asia summer monsoon, and the prediction of onset lingers as one of the major problems in tropical meteorology.

The field program of the Summer MONEX was undertaken in 1979. That year had an abnormally late monsoon. Figure 8.13 shows the motion fields during the month-long transition period (Krishnamurti et al., 1981). The preonset motion field at low levels (Fig. 8.13a) is characterized by a prominent anticyclonic circulation over the northern Arabian Sea and dry northwesterly flow over India. On 14 June a tropical disturbance developed on the northern side of the low-level westerly jet near the southern tip of India and started moving northward. Such a disturbance has been unofficially referred to as an "onset vortex" in recognition of its unique role in the onset phenomenon. The "official" onset of the monsoon was on 12 June over the southwestern coast of India. Between 12 and 17 June the onset vortex intensified and moved slowly northward, bringing with it monsoon rain along the west coast of India. By 17 June it had reached near-hurricane intensity (Fig. 8.13b shows the system at 850 mb one day later). Thereafter it moved northward to roughly 20° N and then west-northwestward toward the coast of Oman. The motion field during one postonset period (Fig. 8.13c) was characterized by the establishment of the strong low-level jet and the monsoon flow over most of the Indian subcontinent. During the last half of June torrential rains, amounting to 600–700 mm, fell in 10 days along the west coast of India, bringing the year's total to normal levels (Fein and Kuettner, 1980).

A linear stability analysis of the horizontally sheared monsoon current observed during the onset of Summer MONEX shows that superposed perturbations would grow as a result of *barotropic instability* (Krishnamurti et al., 1981).[2] The horizontal scale of the perturbation with maximum growth rate corresponds closely to the scale of the onset vortex. Mak and Kao (1982) extended the analysis of

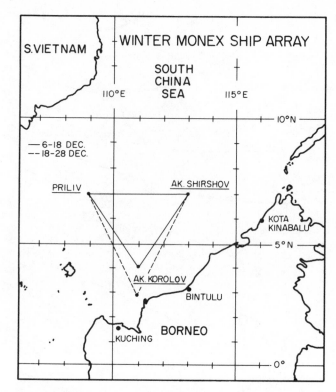

Figure 8.10. The Winter MONEX observation ship array during the December 1978 field phase (Johnson and Kriete, 1982).

Krishnamurti et al. by including the vertical shear. They found that, although barotropic instability is a major driving mechanism for the onset vortex, the mainly barotropic instability mechanism incorrectly predicts some aspects of the cyclogenesis.

The planning meeting of MONEX included midtropospheric cyclones (MTCs) as one of the scientific problems to be considered (International Council of Scientific Unions/ World Meteorological Organization [ICSU/WMO], 1976). MTCs have horizontal scale of 3,000 km and are generally found over the summer monsoon areas, including the northeastern part of the Arabian Sea, southern Indochina, and the South China Sea (early summer). MTCs either move very slowly westward or remain quasi-stationary for many days. The uniqueness of MTCs lies in their vertical structure. Although they are hardly detectable either at the Earth's surface or in the upper troposphere, they have a vigorous cyclonic circulation in the 700–500-mb layer. They usually have a pronounced warm core above the middle level and a slight cold core below that level. They are usually characterized by very intense convective and noncon-

---

[2] An instability arising from the particular distribution of the vertical component of vorticity that characterizes this current. Disturbances in a barotropically unstable current grow at the expense of the kinetic energy of the mean flow.

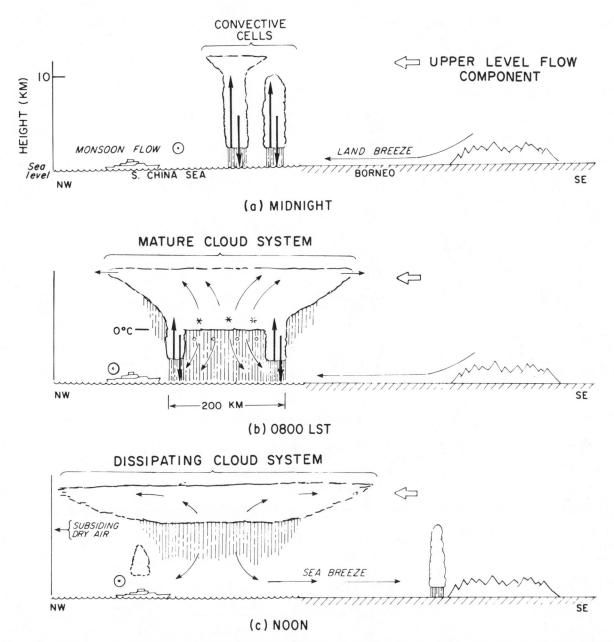

Figure 8.11. Development of a diurnally generated nonsquall cloud cluster off the coast of Borneo during Winter MONEX. Arrows indicate airflow. The circumscribed dot indicates the northeasterly monsoon flow out of the page. Outline arrows indicate the component of the typical east-southeasterly upper-level flow in the plane of the cross section. Heavy vertical arrows indicate cumulus-scale updrafts and downdrafts. The thin arrows show the mesoscale vertical circulation developing in middle to upper levels of stratiform cloud. The asterisks and small circles indicate ice above the 0°C level melting to form raindrops just below this level (Houze et al., 1981).

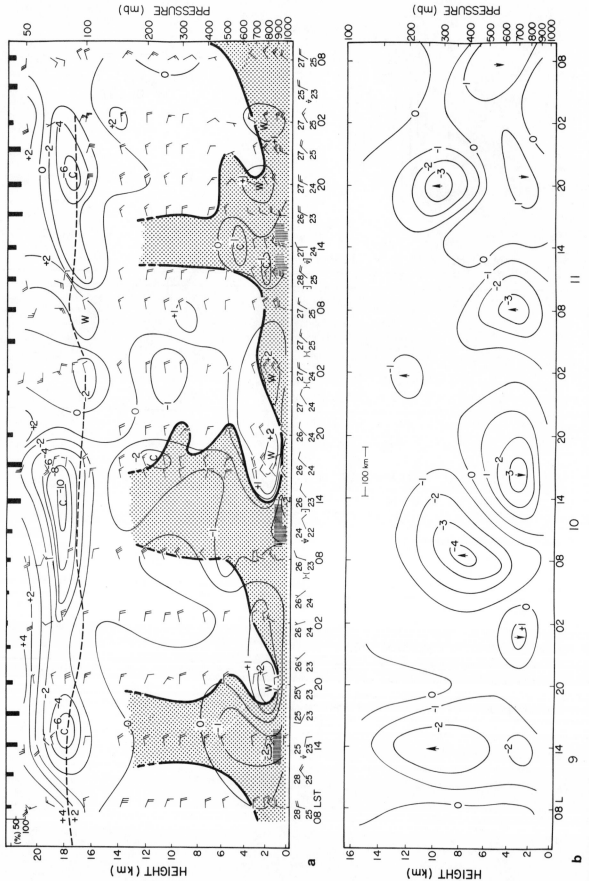

Figure 8.12. (a) Rawinsonde time series at *Ak. Korolov* for 9–11 December 1978. Stippling denotes periods of greater than 80% relative humidity. Closely spaced vertical lines near the surface indicate periods of rain at the ship, longer lines representing heavy rain. Solid contours are temperature deviations (K) from the 6–28 December mean; *C* and *W* denote cold and warm centers. Wind speeds are in m s⁻¹ (one half barb = 2.5 m s⁻¹ and one full barb = 5 m s⁻¹). The horizontal dashed line at ~18 km marks the tropopause. The bars at the top indicate the percentage of triangular area in Fig. 8.10 covered by bright IR satellite cloudiness (scale at upper left). (b) Vertical velocity in units of 100 mb day⁻¹ (≈1 cm s⁻¹ at 950 mb and 2 cm s⁻¹ at 400 mb) for the ship triangle. The distance scale represents the advective length scale based on ~6 m s⁻¹ movement of the mesoscale anvil cloud (Johnson and Kriete, 1982).

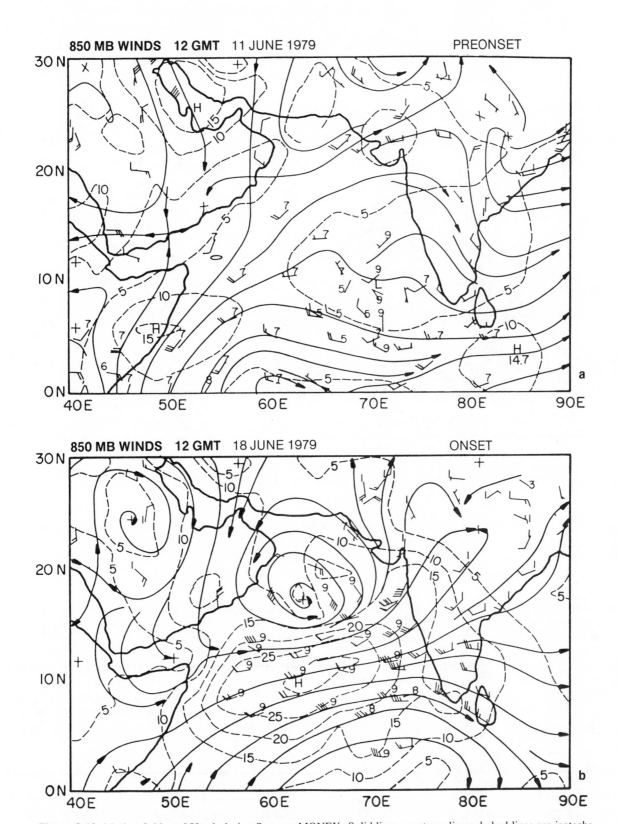

Figure 8.13. Motion fields at 850 mb during Summer MONEX. Solid lines are streamlines; dashed lines are isotachs (m s^{-1}). One full barb represents 5 m s^{-1}; a half barb, 2.5 m s^{-1}; and a solid triangle, 25 m s^{-1}. (a) Preonset of monsoon, 11 June 1979. (b) Onset of monsoon, 18 June 1979. (Krishnamurti et al., 1981; continued on p. 166).

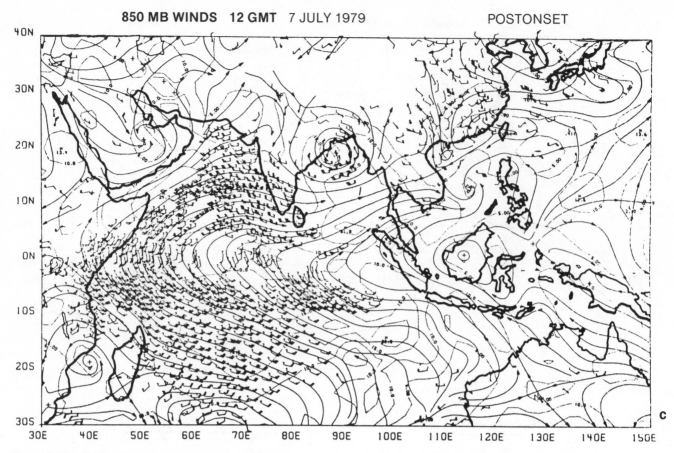

850 MB WINDS   12 GMT   7 JULY 1979   POSTONSET

Figure 8.13c. (c) Postonset of monsoon, 7 July 1979 (Krishnamurti et al., 1981).

vective rainfall rates. Rainfall amounts of ~20 cm in 24 h are not uncommon.

In the pre-MONEX period the best-documented MTCs may be those that developed over the west coast of India (Miller and Keshavamurty, 1968) and over Indochina (Krishnamurti and Hawkins, 1970). Mak (1975) developed a model that assumed a zonal flow component with uniform easterly vertical shear and a southerly flow component having a maximum value in the low troposphere. He showed that many characteristics of the most unstable wave in his model are comparable with the corresponding observed ones. His theory has been extended by Brode and Mak (1978) to include the effect of condensation.

Thus Mak envisions that the MTC that developed over the west coast of India had a baroclinic origin. On the other hand, as described above, the onset vortex of 1979 appears to have had a barotropic origin. Fein and Kuettner (1980) noted that the onset vortex of 1979 had some of the characteristics of the MTC during its initial stage. Mandel et al.

(1984) showed that the maximum kinetic energy of the onset vortex in 1979 resided between 900 and 700 mb during the period considered (16–18 June 1979). Further studies are needed to clarify similarities and differences in the structure and evolution of MTCs over various geographical locations.

With regard to convection associated with the onset vortex of 1979, Shin and Mak (1983) reported the result of their statistical analysis of data collected by the Electra aircraft of the National Center for Atmospheric Research (NCAR) on 16 June 1979. Uninterrupted 1-s resolution (~140-m resolution in distance) data were collected over the Arabian Sea on a constant midtropospheric level. The Electra completely encircled in a counterclockwise direction the well-developed onset vortex (shown in Fig. 8.13b as it was two days later). The time series of velocity components shown in Fig. 8.14 reveals much subsynoptic-scale fluctuation. It was found that the subsynoptic-scale vertical velocity field includes both distinct mesoscale and convec-

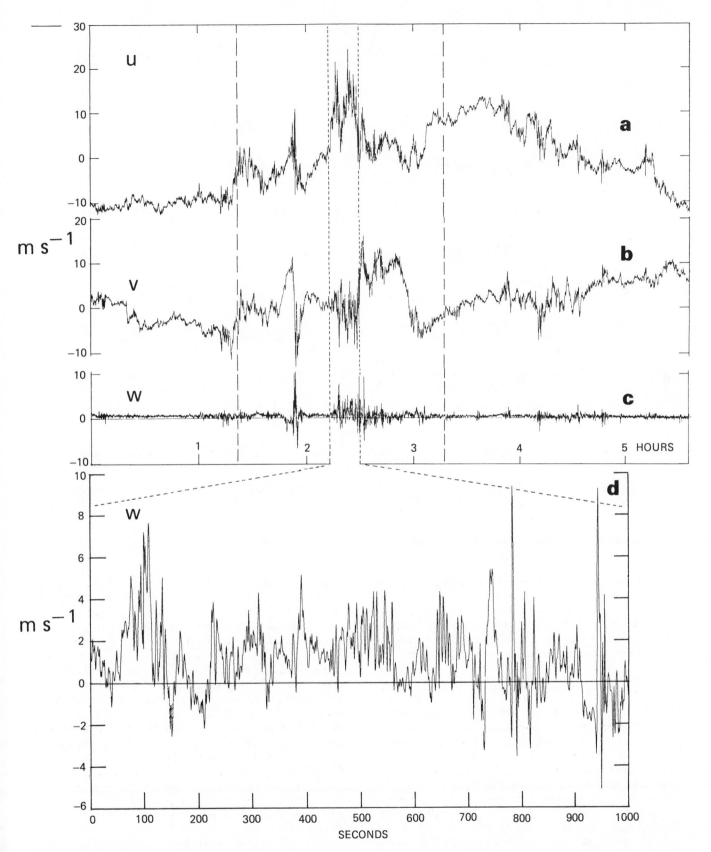

Figure 8.14. The time series of (a) the eastward u, (b) the northward v, and (c) the vertical w velocity component along the Electra's flight path over the Arabian Sea at the 500-mb level on 16 June 1979. The interval between the dotted lines is record I. (d) An enlarged plot of w in record I (Shin and Mak, 1983).

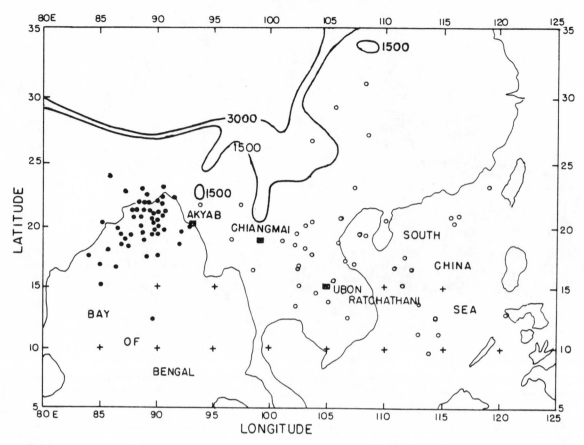

Figure 8.15. Locations of first appearance of a low or depression in the Bay of Bengal (filled circles) and locations of the associated 24-h isallobaric minimum on the first day it was detectable (open circles). Data are for July–August 1969–78. Heavy lines represent land elevation (*m*), averaged over 1° quadrilaterals (Saha et al., 1981).

tive scale components, with prevalent wavelengths about 30 km and 6 km, respectively. The updrafts were typically 1–3 m s⁻¹, and the downdrafts were about 1 m s⁻¹ at the 500-mb flight level. Notably, these magnitudes of updrafts and downdrafts are much smaller than those typical in thunderstorms in middle latitudes (see Sec. 8 for further discussion).

b. Bay of Bengal Cyclogenesis

During the period of southwest monsoon (June–September) about two low-pressure systems form each month over the northern part of the Bay of Bengal. These disturbances, commonly referred to as monsoon depressions, have in their mature stages a horizontal scale of 2000 km, and they move toward the west or northwest several degrees of longitude per day. They are accompanied by heavy precipitation and are important components of Indian weather (Rao, 1976; Sikka, 1977).

In a recent article, Saha et al. (1981) sought to determine whether all monsoon depressions form without any triggering from outside the bay or whether some of them develop around nuclei of disturbances that move in from outside.

Maps of 24-h changes of sea-level pressure during July and August over the 10-year period 1969–78 showed that 45 (87%) of the 52 monsoon depressions that formed in the bay were associated with preexisting disturbances coming in from the east. In 12 (23%) instances, the disturbance was associated with a typhoon or named tropical storm in the South China Sea; the remaining 33 (64%) were weaker systems originating over a broad region of land and sea. Figure 8.15 shows the locations of first appearance of the monsoon depressions, along with the locations of the associated 24-h isallobaric minima on the first day they were detected. It is seen that, although the origins of the isallobaric centers range as far north as central China and as far east as the Philippines, there is a preference for a region centered about 16° N, 103° E, which is in Thailand. Figure 8.16 shows the tracks of five tropical storms that had a direct association with monsoon depressions in the Bay during the period 1969–78.

Further, Saha et al. (1981) identified synoptic-scale wave disturbances that propagated westward across southeast Asia. They applied three different methods to determine wave characteristics: subjectively analyzed isallobaric maps,

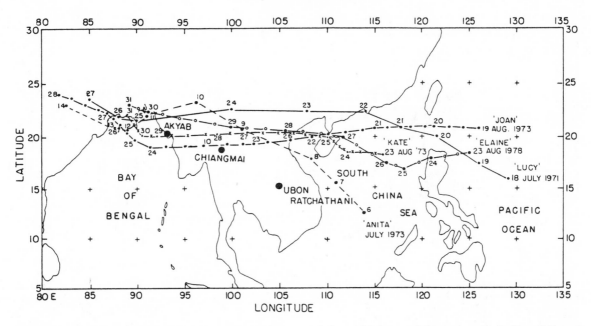

Figure 8.16. Tracks of five tropical storms that had direct associations with lows and depressions in the Bay of Bengal between 1969 and 1978 (Saha et al., 1981).

time sections at three stations, and objective lag cross correlation and power spectrum analyses. The wave characteristics thus determined vary slightly depending upon the methods applied. Generally, the periods they found tended to be in the range 4.3–5.1 days, with phase speeds of 5.1–6.7 m s⁻¹ and wavelengths of 2,100–2,500 km. In Sec. 5 these wave characteristics are compared with those observed in other parts of the tropical oceans.

In July 1979, during Summer MONEX, a well-defined depression was sampled by aircraft observations over the Bay of Bengal. This depression formed near the Burmese coast on 3 July and moved slowly (~2 m s⁻¹) westward, reaching the Indian subcontinent on 8 July. Several authors investigated the structure and evolution of this uniquely well observed depression. Nitta and Masuda (1981) and Sanders (1984) primarily used data from aircraft dropwindsondes and conventional upper-air soundings. Surgi (1984) used the FGGE Level IIIb data prepared by the European Centre for Medium Range Weather Forecasts; Warner (1984) primarily used aircraft flight level and dropwindsonde data to examine the central core structures of the depression on 7 July.

Figure 8.17 shows east–west vertical cross sections of selected meteorological parameters across the depression center observed on 7 July when the depression was at its mature stage (Nitta and Masuda, 1981). It is apparent from Fig. 8.17a and 8.17b that the maxima of both the perturbation meridional wind and vorticity are located below 500 mb. Figure 8.17c indicates a prominent doublet of ascent west and descent east of the depression center. The satellite imagery also shows cloudy areas located west and south of

the depression center. Although it is not clearly visible in Fig. 8.17, the depression sloped toward the southwest with height (Sanders, 1984; Warner, 1984). Fig. 8.17d shows a warm area at and east of the center, suggesting a warm core in the lower troposphere. This contrasts with earlier findings by Krishnamurti et al. (1975) and Godbole (1977), in which well-defined cold cores were present in the lower troposphere below an upper-level warm core. Nitta and Masuda attributed this difference to the later stage of development characteristic of the systems studied earlier.

What mechanism, then, is responsible for triggering a monsoon depression in the Bay of Bengal or enhancing a nucleus disturbance that moves in from an area outside? Shukla (1977, 1978) considered a combination of CISK-barotropic-baroclinic instability. Keshavamurty et al. (1978), Raman et al. (1978) and Goswani et al. (1981) argued that baroclinic instability cannot be the mechanism. Recently a differential approach by Lindzen et al. (1983) identified characteristics of barotropically unstable disturbances in the mean 500-mb zonal flows during July and August over the Bay of Bengal in reasonable agreement with observations. However, the growth rate of unstable disturbances was unrealistically small in the models. On the other hand, Sanders (1984) stressed baroclinic processes in the monsoon depression. He noted that the westerly flow at low levels with easterly flow at upper levels defines a vertical shear as large as 35 m s⁻¹ between 850 mb and 200 mb during the summer over the southern tip of the Indian subcontinent. From quasi-geostrophic theory he attributed ascent west of the depression center to warm-air advection. It is interesting that this situation is similar to easterly waves observed over the east-

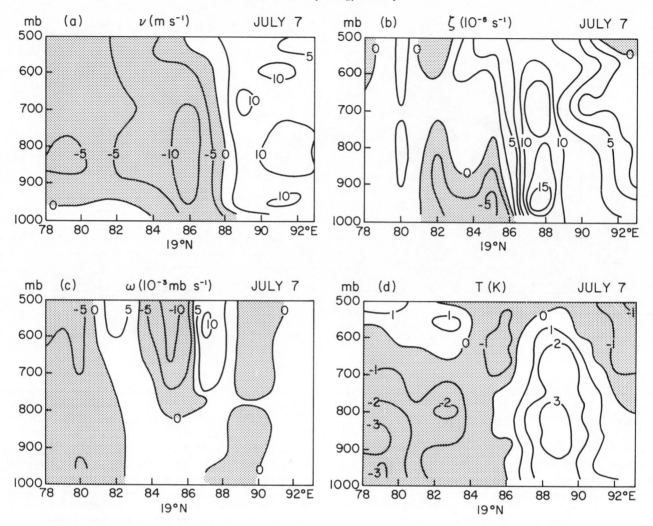

Figure 8.17. Longitude-height sections at 19° N across the center of a Bay of Bengal monsoon depression on 7 July 1979. (a) The meridional wind component. The shaded area denotes northerly winds. (b) Relative vorticity. Shaded areas denote negative vorticity. (c) Vertical velocity in pressure coordinates. Shaded areas denote rising motions. (d) Temperature deviation. Shaded areas denote negative deviations (Nitta and Masuda, 1981).

ern Atlantic (Sec. 5). Surgi (1984) studied the energetics of the depression and concluded that both the barotropic and baroclinic processes maintain the eddy kinetic energy of the depression, the former to a greater extent during the early development stage and the latter to a greater extent thereafter. This conclusion is similar to findings of Krishnamurti et al. (1983).

4. Summer Monsoon over Western Africa

A monsoon circulation is a major rain producer in western Africa. The following account of the west African monsoon and associated convective activity is based mainly on the work of Balogun (1981).

From May to September the thermal equator moves progressively northward and allows the very persistent moisture-laden Atlantic southeast trade winds to cross the equator, turn into a southwesterly current, and spread over the west African countries (Fig. 8.18). The moist current forms a wedge under the very dry northeasterly flow from the Sahara. The moist current contributes about 80% of the annual rainfall over the west African region.

The boundary zone between the moist and dry air masses is known to African meteorologists as the *intertropical discontinuity* (ITD). Fig. 8.19 shows the average monthly position (1959–71) of the ITD estimated along longitude 7° E for the different weather zones over Nigeria. Zone A lies north of the ITD and is completely devoid of convective activity. In zone B, which extends about 200 to 400 km south of the surface position of the ITD, convection is largely suppressed and precipitation is limited to light

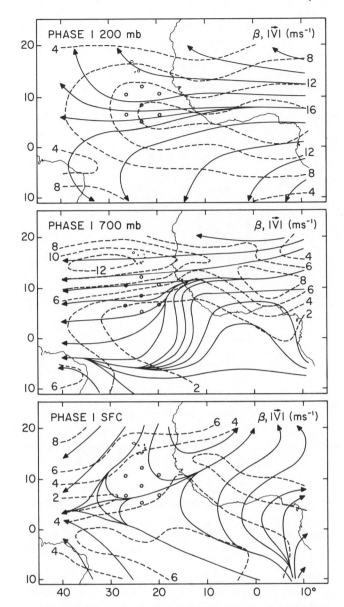

Figure 8.18. Streamlines (solid lines) and isotachs (dashed lines) for GATE Phase I at surface, 700 mb, and 200 mb over western Africa and the eastern Atlantic. Isotachs are in m s^{-1}. Circles represent GATE ship array (Vincent, 1981).

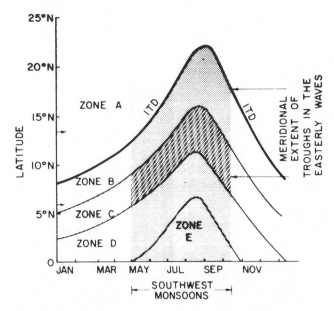

Figure 8.19. Average monthly meridional variation of the intertropical discontinuity at about longitude 7° E for the weather zones over Nigeria (Balogun, 1981).

showers. The most convectively active zone is zone C, a band about 300 to 500 km wide south of zone B. Zone C is characterized by intense thunder activity. Map analyses show that wind and moisture convergence are concentrated in this zone. It is also a breeding zone for squall lines and cloud clusters (see Sec. 7 below). In Sec. 5 it is also shown that the African wave activity was strongest in this zone during the GATE period (June–September). Zone D is characterized mainly by continuous light rain and drizzle with occasional moderate thunder activity. A relatively drier

zone *E* is characterized by light rain and rare thunderstorm activity.

Figure 8.20 shows the mean rainfall for the coastal and the inland areas over Nigeria. The marked rainfall minimum in the month of August in parts of the west African coast has been noted by many authors, including Hamilton and Archbold (1945); Ireland (1962); Obasi (1965); Ilesanmi (1971); Adedokun (1978); and Walker (1960). Although the minimum in rainfall is often emphasized, there is also a minimum in thunderstorm activity. Several explanations have been offered. One is that the south Atlantic subtropical anticyclonic system, which during the months of May–September moves northward so that its northern periphery extends to the coastal areas of west Africa, produces synoptic-scale downward motion over the area; this in turn inhibits vertical growth of clouds. Another explanation is that the upwelling process, well marked in the coastal waters in west Africa in August, leads to colder waters at the ocean surface, with corresponding stabilization of the lower atmosphere over the region. The effect of the "Walker circulation" has been invoked to explain the relative dryness of some parts of the west African coast.[3] It has been suggested that the west African coastal region is influenced by a descending branch of the Walker circulation system in August, which results in poor rainfall in parts of the region.

---

[3]The "Walker circulation" is a large-scale seesaw of atmospheric mass between the Pacific and Indian oceans in the tropics and subtropics. It operates on both seasonal and interannual time scales (Walker, 1924).

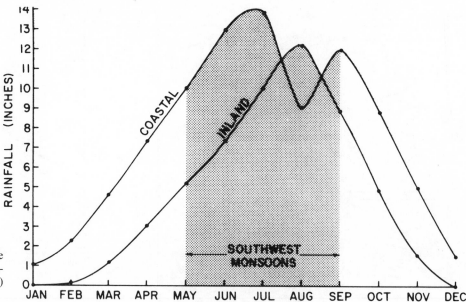

Figure 8.20. Mean rainfall for the coastal (coast to latitude 7° N) and inland (latitude 10° N to latitude 13° N) areas over Nigeria (Balogun, 1981).

5. Easterly Waves

Easterly currents in the middle and lower tropical troposphere are known to undergo wavelike perturbations that modulate deep convection and occasionally give rise to tropical cyclones (Anthes, 1982). These perturbations were first extensively described by Riehl (1945, 1954), who used data from the Caribbean area to describe their general features. Since then easterly waves in various parts of the tropical oceans have been much investigated with data from various sources and a variety of analytic methods. The reader is referred to the book by Riehl (1979) for early studies of easterly waves. Studies on easterly waves observed over the western African continent and the eastern Atlantic (now commonly referred to as "African waves") observed during GATE have been summarized by Reed (1978) and Burpee and Reed (1982).

Table 8.1 lists characteristics of easterly waves as determined by different investigators. Basically the table updates a list originally prepared by Saha et al. (1981). However, waves whose maximum amplitudes are in the upper troposphere or lower stratosphere have been excluded, even though their lower extensions may appear in the lower or middle troposphere.

a. Flow and Thermodynamic Structure

Figure 8.21 shows the flow and thermodynamic structure of African waves over the GATE ship array determined by Thompson et al. (1979) by applying a composite technique

to the GATE Phase III data.[4] In their composite technique, which was first applied by Reed and Recker (1971) to easterly waves over the western Pacific, the entire easterly wave was divided into eight categories. Category 4 marks the position of the 700-mb wave trough (denoted by *T* in Fig. 8.21) at the reference latitude. Category 8 marks the 700-mb ridge position (*R*); categories 2 and 6 are the position of the maximum northerly (*N*) and southerly (*S*) wind components, respectively. Intermediate categories are denoted by 1, 3, 5, and 7.

Figure 8.21a shows the deviation of the meridional wind component from its Phase III mean at each level. The perturbations are largest at 700 mb; there is a second maximum at 175 mb and a minimum near 300 mb. The upper-level perturbations are nearly out of phase with the lower. Figure 8.21b shows that the bulk of the troposphere has positive vorticity centered near the wave trough; this is capped by a layer of negative vorticity. Figure 8.21c shows that there are two maxima in the upward motion: one is located near category 3 (between *N* and *T*) at 750 mb and the other near category 4 (*T*) at 350 mb. The reason for this dual structure is not completely known. Thompson et al. (1979) suggested discrete multiple cloud populations: ahead of the trough a group of clouds reached the middle of the troposphere, resulting in a middle-level divergence, and another group of

[4]GATE had three intensive observation periods: Phase I (26 June–16 July), Phase II (28 July–16 August), and Phase III (30 August–19 September), all during 1974.

Table 8.1. List of Investigations of Characteristics of Waves in the Lower and Middle Tropical Troposphere in the Northern Hemisphere Summer Seasons

| Region | Investigators | Data | Wave characteristics | | | | |
| | | | Amplitude | | Period (days) | Phase speed (m s^{-1}) | Wavelength (km) |
			Pressure (mb)	Meridional component of wind (m s^{-1})			
Western Africa and eastern Atlantic	Carlson, 1969a,b	Surface and upper-air data, 1968	1.4	—	3.2	7	2,000
	Burpee, 1972	Upper-air data, 1960–64	—	1–2	3–5	12	4,000
	Reed et al., 1977	Upper-air data, GATE Phase III	—	5 at 700 mb	3.5	8	2,500
	Thompson et al., 1979	Upper-air data, GATE Phase III	—	4.5 at 700 mb	—	—	—
	Albignat and Reed, 1980	Upper-air data, GATE Phase III	—	1–4.5 at 850 mb	3.5	8.4	2,500
	Chen and Ogura, 1982; *and* Tai, 1980	Upper-air data, GATE Phase I	—	3.5 at 700 mb	3.5	12	3,600
		Upper-air data, GATE Phase II	—	3 at 700 mb	3.5	12	3,600
		Upper-air data, GATE Phase III	—	5 at 700 mb	3.5	8	2,400
Caribbean	Riehl, 1945, 1948, 1954	Sea-level pressure (SLP) and upper-air data, 1944	—	—	3–4	6.5	1,500–2,000
Eastern Pacific	Ogura and Tai, 1984	Upper-air data, 1979	—	4 at 850 mb	5–6	6–7	3,000~3,500
Western and central Pacific	Palmer, 1952	Wind at surface and aloft, 1946	—	—	3–4	5.5	1,650
	Rosenthal, 1960	Wind, 1956	—	—	4	—	—
	Wallace and Chang, 1969	Upper-air data, 1963 (including other parts of tropics)	—	—	4–5	8	3,000
	Chang et al., 1970	Wind, 1964	—	3 (central) 8 (western)	4–5 (central) 6–7 (western)	— —	— —
	Nitta, 1970	Upper-air data, 1962	—	—	4–5	14	5,000–6,000
	Reed and Recker, 1971	Upper-air data, 1967	—	3–4 at 800 mb	5	9	3,500–4,000
Southeast Asia	Saha et al., 1981	Surface pressure, 1971–73, 1977, 1978	3 (mb d^{-1})	—	4.3–5.6	5.2–6.7	2,100–2,500
India	Keshavamurty, 1973	Wind at 850 mb, 1967	—	—	5.6	—	2,200
	Bhalme and Parasnis, 1975	SLP gradient, 1961–70	—	—	5–6	—	—
	Krishnamurti and Bhalme, 1976	Nine selected parameters of monsoon system, 1957, 1967	—	—	4.5	—	—
	Murakami, 1976	Upper-air data, 1962	—	—	4–5	7	3,000

clouds reached almost to the tropopause. It is interesting to note that a similar dual structure of the vertical velocity has been observed in a mesoscale convective system over Oklahoma (Ogura and Chen, 1977). See Ogura (1982) for further discussion on the vertical velocity fields in mesoscale convective systems. Figure 8.21d shows a cold core below 600 mb and a warm core above it in categories 3 to 4. The formation of a cold core at low levels has been attributed to evaporative cooling (e.g., Riehl, 1954). This explanation seems questionable, however, in light of the recent observations of the structure of cloud clusters (Sec. 7 below). In Fig. 8.21e, a moist air tongue extends in categories 4 (T) and 5 (between T and S), reflecting the strong activity of deep convection in these categories. The precipitation rate was also found to have its maximum in category 3 in easterly waves over the western Pacific (Reed and Recker, 1971).

Wave motions during GATE Phases I and II were less organized and weaker than those during Phase III, and their structure was somewhat different from that shown in Fig. 8.21 (Chen and Ogura, 1982). In Fig. 8.22 the rainfalls estimated from satellite images by Griffith et al. (1980) and Woodley et al. (1980) are composited for each phase of GATE. In addition to the fact that the rainfall rate is different in different segments of African waves, Fig. 8.22 shows that the position of the confluence line shifted latitudinally with the passage of a wave in a systematic manner in Phase III (see also Frank, 1983). The confluence line formed when the northern hemispheric trade wind was brought into juxtaposition with the cross-equatorial southwesterly flow.

Figure 8.22 also shows that most precipitation occurred a few degrees south of the confluence line throughout the entire GATE period. This indicates that, even though the rain-

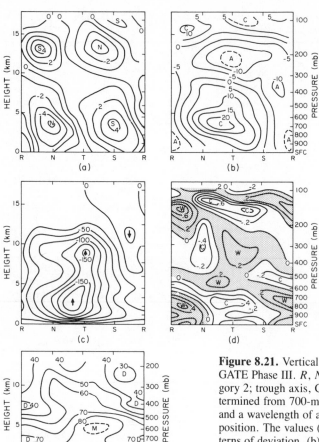

Figure 8.21. Vertical cross sections of wind components for African waves observed during GATE Phase III. *R*, *N*, *T*, and *S* denote ridge axis, Category 8; maximum northerlies, Category 2; trough axis, Category 4; and maximum southerlies, Category 6, respectively, as determined from 700-mb flow. The length of the abscissa represents a period of about 3 days and a wavelength of about 2,000 km. (a) Meridional wind component as a function of wave position. The values (m s^{-1}) at each level have been subtracted from the mean to show patterns of deviation. (b) Relative vorticity in units of 10^{-6} s^{-1}; *A* and *C* represent anticyclonic and cyclonic centers. (c) Vertical velocity in pressure coordinates; units 10^{-5} mb s^{-1} about 1 mb day^{-1}. (d) Vertical cross section of temperature deviation in K. (e) Moist and dry centers are denoted by *M* and *D* in this field of relative humidity (Thompson et al., 1979).

fall is unquestionably modulated by easterly waves, deep convection in the ITCZ occurs primarily in association with confluence of the low-level flows. Sadler (1975), in his pre-GATE study, pointed out that the major cloudiness was found to occur in the westerly flow on the south side of the surface confluence line in the region between the surface col and the African coast. Using the GATE data, Estoque and Douglas (1978) showed that the maximum rainfall was about 100 km south of the surface confluence line. A similar conclusion was drawn by Frank (1983).

McBride and Gray (1980) investigated the relative importance of various large-scale processes in controlling convection over three tropical oceans: the GATE region, the western Pacific, and the western Atlantic trade-wind region; the ITCZ forcing, measured in terms of the vertical velocity at the 850-mb level, was found to be −80, −30, and +10 mb d^{-1}, respectively. The wave forcing was taken to be equal to the difference in the 850-mb-level vertical velocities between the wave trough and the ridge. Its magnitude was estimated as ±30, ±20, and +15 mb d^{-1}, respectively. In Chen and Ogura's (1982) analysis of data over for the GATE ship array, the ITCZ forcing was defined as the

vertical velocity at the 800-mb level. Its magnitude averaged over the entire GATE period was found to be −130 mb d^{-1}. On the other hand, the averaged wave forcing at the 800-mb level was ±35 mb d^{-1}, qualitatively consistent with McBride and Gray's estimate.

b. Origin, Growth, and Decay

The horizontal distribution of the variance of the meridional wind, band-pass-filtered to include only fluctuations with periods of 3–4 days, is shown in Fig. 8.23 at the 600-mb level for the entire GATE area (Tai and Ogura, unpublished paper). According to Albignat and Reed (1980), the initial weak perturbations may originate as far east as the southern tip of the Red Sea (~45° E). The midtropospheric easterly jet is present over central and western Africa in association with the strong temperature gradient in the north-south direction in the summer season (see Fig. 8.17). Consequently, barotropic and baroclinic energies are continuously fed into the African waves while they travel westward over the African continent (Burpee, 1972, 1975;

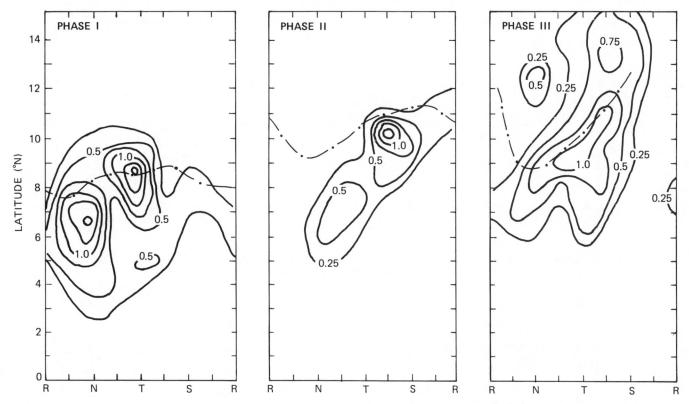

Figure 8.22. Latitudinal distributions of precipitation rate (mm h^{-1}) estimated from satellite data as a function of wave category (as in Fig. 8.21) for African waves observed over the GATE ship array. The dash-dotted lines indicate the position of the surface confluence lines (Chen and Ogura, 1982).

Mass, 1979; Thompson et al., 1979; Albignat and Reed, 1980). Figure 8.23 further shows that once waves leave their growth region and propagate westward across the Atlantic they decay nearly as rapidly as they grew. Nevertheless, some of them survive to reach the Caribbean area, as discovered earlier by Carlson (1969a,b) and others.

Data gathered during the FGGE year have permitted us for the first time to see the global nature of tropical disturbances. Figure 8.24 shows the result of a power spectrum analysis of winds over the eastern Pacific during the summer (June–August) of 1979 at 11.25° N and at 850 mb (Ogura and Tai, 1984) based on the Level IIIb data prepared by the European Centre for Medium Range Weather Forecasts. Both the zonal and the meridional wind components exhibit spectral peaks at periods of 3.5–6 days west of 100° W. Further statistical analyses show that these perturbations are associated with westward-propagating waves with wavelengths of 3,000–3,500 km and propagation speeds of 6–7 m s^{-1}. A composite analysis of these data shows that general features of the wave disturbances are similar to those found earlier over the western Pacific (Reed and Recker, 1971). The deep convective activity, inferred from satellite IR measurements, was also found to be modulated by wave disturbances in that it had the maximum intensity in wave

categories 3–5. (A second peak in the zonal wind component in Fig. 8.24a is centered at the period of 40 days, without the corresponding peak in the meridional winds. This peak may be related to the 40–50-day oscillations of the tropical atmosphere, first discovered by Madden and Julian [1971, 1972]. A discussion of this subject is beyond the scope of this chapter.)

Thus easterly waves have been identified during the Northern Hemisphere summer over many parts of the tropical regions: west Africa, the eastern Atlantic, the Caribbean Sea, the eastern and western Pacific (Fig. 8.5), southeast Asia, and India (see Table 8.1). However, an outstanding feature of these waves is that their amplitudes are substantially localized geographically. Mechanisms responsible for growth of easterly waves are not yet completely understood. Significant differences in the energetics between easterly waves over the western Pacific and African waves have been noted (Norquist et al., 1977; Reed, 1978; Thompson et al., 1979). African waves over the GATE ship array received their kinetic energy primarily through the barotropic conversion process, and, surprisingly, diabatic heating actually opposes the wave growth. On the other hand, in easterly waves over the western Pacific the large magnitude of eddy available potential energy is generated by diabatic heating and is con-

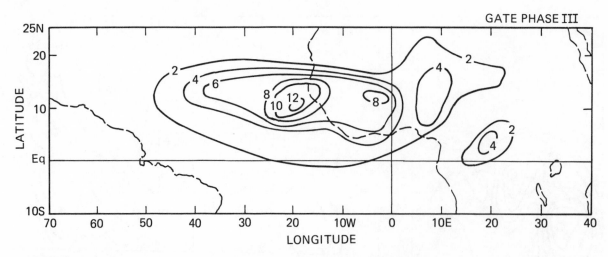

Figure 8.23. Horizontal distribution of variance of the meridional wind in m² s⁻² at 600 mb for the entire GATE area during GATE Phase III. Values are bandpass-filtered to include only perturbations with periods of 3 to 4 days.

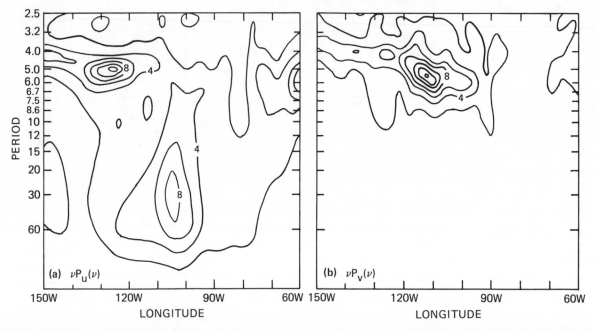

Figure 8.24. Longitudinal distribution of the power spectrum density ($P(\nu)$ multiplied by frequency ν for (a) the zonal wind and (b) the meridional wind at 850 mb and at 11.25° N for the period June–August 1979 over the eastern Pacific. Contours are at intervals of 2 m² s⁻² (Ogura and Tai, 1984).

verted to eddy kinetic energy. A small portion of this eddy kinetic energy is then converted to zonal kinetic energy (Wallace and Chang, 1969; Nitta, 1970).

6. Upper Tropospheric Vortices

Another distinct synoptic-scale disturbance that modulates deep convective activity in the tropics is the upper tropo-

spheric vortex associated with a cold low. Early studies on these disturbances have been summarized by Riehl (1979); they dealt mainly with the Caribbean area. Later, taking advantage of the increased quantity and quality of wind observations from jet aircraft platforms and satellite data, Sadler (1976, 1978) made case studies of tropical troughs over the mid- or western Pacific. His focus was on the possible role of these troughs in typhoon development.

The geosynchronous meteorological satellite has facili-

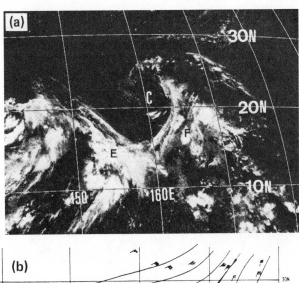

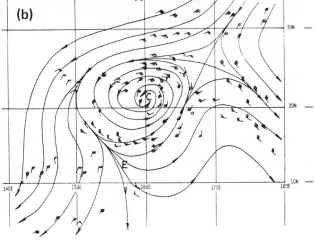

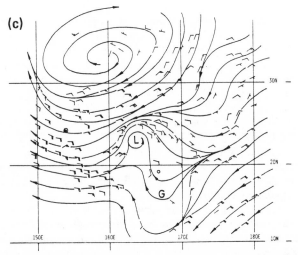

Figure 8.25. Data from the western Pacific Ocean at 00 GMT 21 July 1978. (a) Infrared imagery. (b) Upper-level streamline analysis based on satellite-derived winds. One full barb denotes 10 kn; a solid triangle denotes 50 kn. *C* is cyclonic circulation center; *E* is an active convective cluster. (c) Low-level streamline analysis. *L* is cyclonic circulation; *G* is anticyclonic flow area (Shimamura, 1981).

tated measurement of winds at upper and lower levels with good temporal and spatial resolutions (see Vol. 3 of this work). Shimamura (1981, 1982) studied four upper-tropospheric cold lows over the western North Pacific. In the example shown in Fig. 8.25, he traced a low center for about 8 days as it moved westward at an average speed of 4.5° longitude a day. The outstanding feature in the satellite image (Fig. 8.25a) is that the low center aloft (*C*) was cloud-free, encompassed by well-developed clusters (as *E* and *F*) in the south-to-east quadrants. Figures 25b,c show that cluster *E* was located in the region of the upper-level diffluence flow and considerably removed from significant surface features in the wind field. Cluster *E* eventually developed into a typhoon. This situation was similar to those discussed earlier by Sadler (1976, 1978). Cluster *F* was apparently associated with the low-level wave trough, east of the upper low center.

The low center passed near Wake Island. The time-height cross section shown in Fig. 8.26 gives a clear description of the flow and thermal structure near the low center. The bulk of the troposphere was filled by the cold low with 25 m s^{-1} winds at the top of the layer at 200 mb and topped by a marked warm core. This structure is remarkably similar to that depicted earlier by Erickson (1971) for a cold low observed over the Caribbean area. Figure 8.26 also shows that air was dry in the region from the low center on the west and moist on the east. The broad features of this cold low, including the cloudiness distribution relative to the low center, are also similar to those described by Carlson (1968) and common in other cold low events analyzed by Shimamura.

However, Shimamura also noted that the evolution of the upper tropospheric cold low and its relation to low-level disturbances varied from one event to another. In one case a low-level disturbance caught up with an upper cold low, which then became a warm core disturbance and eventually developed into a typhoon. In another case a low-level disturbance, which developed first several degrees east of an upper cold low, eventually developed into a typhoon. During its development, however, the upper low moved northwestward, clearly keeping its identity independent of the low-level disturbance. Shimamura noted the similarity of this event to that analyzed by Yanai (1961).

More work is needed to understand the physical processes that give rise to and maintain these upper-level cold lows and the interrelationships between upper- and low-level circulations.

7. Tropical Squall Clusters

In the tropics deep convective clouds are frequently organized to form "cloud clusters," which are defined as a group of cumulonimbus joined in their mature and dissipating stages by a common cirrus shield ~ 100 to 1,000 km in the horizontal (International Council of Scientific Unions/World Meteorological Organization [ICSU/WMO], 1970). Thus the clusters seen in satellite imagery resemble middle-latitude mesoscale convective complexes (MCCs, Maddox, 1980; see also Chap 6). Typically the cirrus shields of tropical cloud clusters are not as cold as required by Maddox's criteria for a middle-latitude MCC (Houze and Hobbs, 1982). However, Houze and Rapaport (1984) analyzed a squall line that occurred during GATE and found that the cloud shield associated with it easily satisfied Maddox's criteria in terms of both its horizontal dimension and its duration.

A special type of cloud cluster is the "squall line" or "squall cluster." As noted by Martin (1975) and Payne and McGarry (1977), squall clusters are evident in satellite imagery by their explosive growth, oval shape, very high brightness, and rapid propagation. Even though squall clusters occurred much less frequently than nonsquall clusters over the GATE ship array (Aspliden et al., 1976), squall clusters have attracted the interest of tropical meteorologists because of the well-defined structure and motion they possess.

The tropical squall line was first described as a distinct meteorological phenomenon by Hamilton and Archbold (1945). The first documentation of a tropical squall line observed during an organized field experiment was presented by Zipser (1969). Later Betts et al. (1976) investigated squall lines observed in VIMHEX, and Zipser (1977) presented results of a case study for a squall cluster that developed over the Caribbean area. GATE has provided an excellent opportunity to investigate in greater detail the evolution and structure of tropical squall clusters (Houze, 1977; Leary and Houze, 1979; Fortune, 1980; Gamache and Houze, 1982; Houze and Rappaport, 1984; and others).

Figure 8.27 shows schematically a typical cross section through a tropical squall cluster that was observed primarily by aircraft penetrations and supplemented by satellite data, radar data, surface meteorological data, and soundings (Zipser, 1977). The structure of a GATE squall cluster presented by Houze (1977) is similar to that shown in Fig. 8.27 in many respects. A cloud cluster is composed of several components in terms of vertical motions: convective-scale updrafts, convective-scale downdrafts, the mesoscale downdraft, and the mesoscale updraft. Convective-scale updrafts occur in the cumulonimbus elements making up the squall line. Just behind and below the sloping updraft of the squall line there is a concentrated downpour of heavy precipitation that contains a convective-scale downdraft. The air feeding the convective-scale downdraft comes from levels between 900 and 600 mb. When the convective downdraft air reaches the surface, it has a lower moist static energy (see Chap. 4) than the presquall boundary layer air. It spreads out, partly toward the front of the squall line system and partly toward the rear, in a thin layer 50–500 m above the surface. An extensive precipitating middle- to upper-level stratiform cloud shield, or anvil cloud, trails the squall line.

Recently Gamache and Houze (1982) determined the airflow around and inside a GATE squall cluster by compositing radar and wind observations. The result shows the mesoscale updraft in the anvil, thus confirming the earlier speculation of Leary and Houze (1980), who diagnosed an anvil updraft from the thermal stratification and horizontal wind in the anvil region of a tropical squall cluster. This result is also consistent with the net upward motion over large-

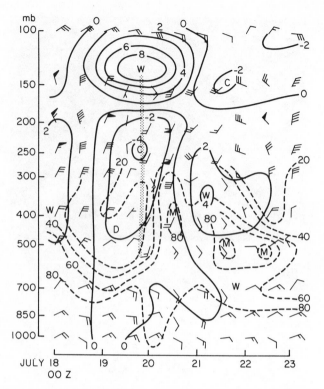

Figure 8.26. Time-height cross-section analysis for the Wake Island station for the upper tropospheric cold low shown in Fig. 8.25. Solid and dashed lines show temperature anomaly from the July monthly mean at this station in °C and relative humidity in percent, respectively. The shaded zone indicates the vertical axis of cyclonic circulation. *W:* warm; *C:* cold; *M:* moist; *D:* dry (Shimamura, 1981).

scale regions partly occupied by tropical squall clusters found by Frank (1978) and Ogura et al. (1979) in the mid- to upper troposphere. Middle-latitude squall lines similar to tropical squall lines also exhibit mesoscale anvil updrafts (Sanders and Paine, 1975; Sanders and Emanuel, 1977; Ogura and Chen, 1977; Ogura and Liou, 1980). Further, there is mesoscale updraft in the anvil cloud of Brown's (1979) numerical model. The maximum updraft in Gamache and Houze's (1982) tropical anvil was ~ 8 μb s^{-1}. The corresponding value for the middle-latitude squall line, estimated by Ogura and Liou (1980) by a similar composite technique, was ~ 30 μb s^{-1}, substantially larger than the tropical counterpart.

Below the anvil the air subsides over horizontal scales of 100–500 km. Figure 8.28 shows the thermodynamic structure of the tropical mesoscale downdraft documented by Zipser (1977). The warming and drying effects of subsidence are clearly indicated by a wide separation between temperature and dew point. The separation reaches its maximum near 900 mb (Fig. 8.12a also shows the warming at low levels). The warm dry air just above the surface air has about the same value of moist static energy as the air near the base of the anvil. Figure 8.29c shows the thermo-

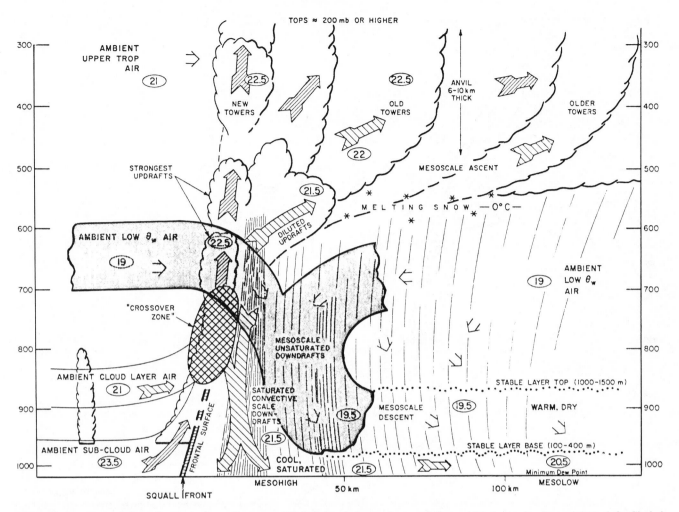

Figure 8.27. Cross section of a tropical squall system. All flow is relative to the squall line, which is moving from right to left. Circled numbers are typical values of wet-bulb potential temperature in °C (Zipser, 1977).

dynamic structure of the middle-latitude counterpart of the tropical mesoscale downdraft. The similarity between Fig. 28 and Fig. 29c is rather remarkable. Gamache and Houze (1982) estimated the magnitude of the maximum mesoscale downdraft for their tropical cluster at ~8 μb s^{-1}. The middle-latitude counterpart for Ogura and Liou's (1980) squall line was ~40 μb s^{-1}.

Figure 8.30 shows a typical life cycle of a tropical squall cluster observed during GATE (Houze, 1977). A line of convective precipitation appeared on radar at 1,000 GMT on 4 September 1974; only a small amount of cloud (detected by satellite) penetrated above the 12-km level. By 1,500 the squall cluster was in a mature stage; active convective cells were aligned to form the leading edge of the cluster, trailed by a considerable area of high cloud and light rain in a manner similar to that shown in Fig. 8.27. By 0445 on 5 September the convective line had almost disappeared, and the remaining precipitation was mainly light

rain falling from upper-level cloud, which itself was shrinking in size.

According to the statistical studies of Martin (1975) and Aspliden et al. (1976), squall clusters are most frequent over the African continent. Figure 8.31 shows the results of a case study by Fortune (1980) for a family of five squall lines that developed in series over the African continent. These squall clusters were initiated from groups of, or individual, cumulonimbus clouds identified in the figure as *A–C, D–F, G–H,* and *L*. Clusters *A–C* and *D–F* developed almost simultaneously and eventually merged. The resulting combined squall clusters appeared to trigger the development of the next cluster during its late stages, when it approached the developing cells *G–H*. In a similar way the squall that developed from *G–H* subsequently appeared to trigger two new squall lines, one to the south and one to the north, as it spread out and approached the cumulonimbus cells *K* and *L*. In their surface manifestations these squall

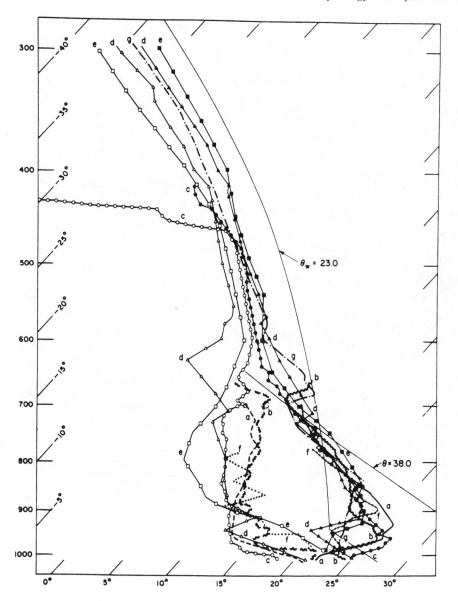

Figure 8.28. Characteristic soundings of temperature and dew point in tropical postsquall regions. (a) Mostly in rain; (b) behind leading edge and 50 km behind trailing precipitation; (c) behind trailing precipitation; (d) behind leading edge and 174 km behind trailing precipitation; (e) 50 km behind trailing precipitation; (f) postsquall; (g) postsquall (no dew point available) (Zipser, 1977).

lines resemble those of middle latitudes, though the tropical systems propagate toward the west.

8. Tropical Nonsquall Clusters

As noted in the preceding section, the overwhelming majority of cloud clusters over the GATE ship array consisted of nonsquall clusters. There is a large body of references dealing with GATE nonsquall clusters as well as squall clusters. The reader is referred to the review article on convection in GATE by Houze and Betts (1981).

Figure 8.32 shows the structure of a slowly moving (~3 m s^{-1}) convective band determined primarily by multiple

aircraft penetrations (Zipser et al., 1981). A comparison with Fig. 8.27 shows marked similarities between squall clusters and nonsquall clusters in many aspects of their structures. In Fig. 8.32 as in Fig. 8.27, at the leading edge there are well-defined mesoscale features that are 10–40 km in scale, quasi-two-dimensional, and persistent for several hours. The squall line is composed of convective scale updrafts 5 km or less in size with marked variability in all three dimensions. Behind the updraft zone, at the leading edge and below 3–4 km, is a broad descent zone that corresponds to the stratiform rain.

Nonsquall clusters have lifetimes of a day or less (Martin, 1975; Martin and Schreiner, 1981). The life cycle of a nonsquall cluster (Fig. 8.33), as described by Leary and Houze

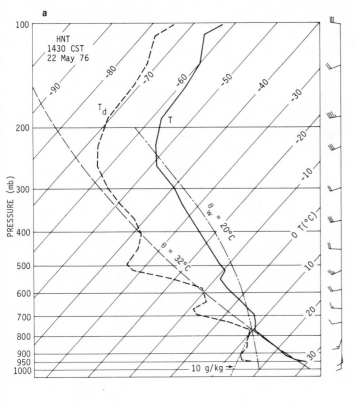

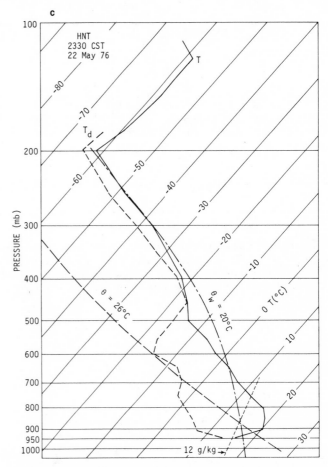

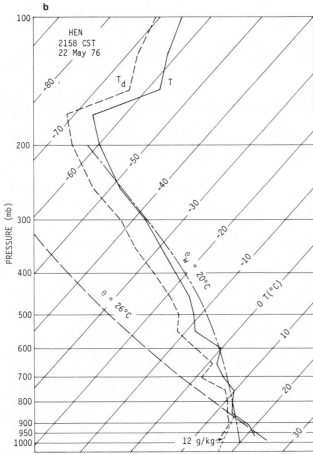

Figure 8.29. Characteristic soundings of temperature (*T*) and dew point (*T$_d$*) for the middle-latitude squall line that occurred on 22 May 1976 over Oklahoma. Selected dry (*θ*) and moist (*θ$_w$*) adiabats and mixing ratio (g/kg) have been added. One full barb for wind is 10 kn. (a) Observation in presquall regions from Hinton, Okla., at 1430 CST. (b) Observation in squall region from Hennessey, Okla., at 2158 CST. (c) Observation in postsquall regions from Hinton, Okla., at 2330 CST (Ogura and Liou, 1980).

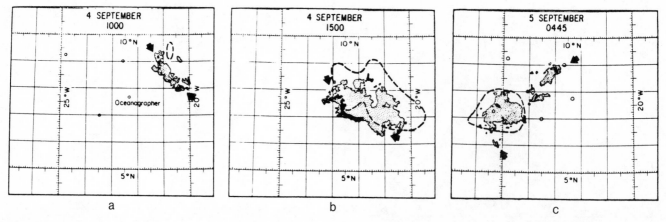

Figure 8.30. Life cycle of cloud and precipitation pattern associated with an equatorial oceanic squall-line system. Dotted region encloses low-level precipitation detected by radar. Black indicates regions of precipitation intensity in excess of 38 dBZ or 14 mm h⁻¹. Dashed line is satellite infrared isotherm for −47°C, which corresponds to the intersection of the upper-level cloud shield with the 11-km level. Arrows locate end points of squall line. Location of Research Vessel *Oceanographer* is indicated in *a*. Time is in GMT (Houze, 1977).

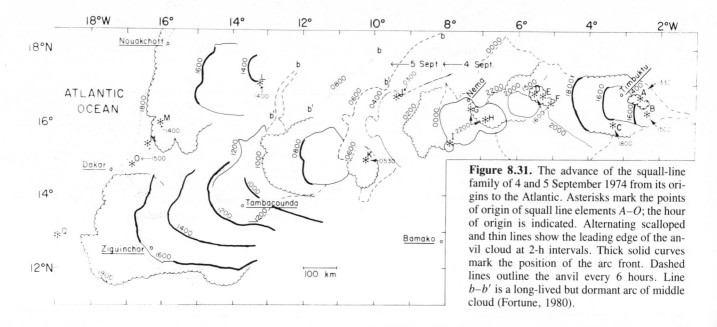

Figure 8.31. The advance of the squall-line family of 4 and 5 September 1974 from its origins to the Atlantic. Asterisks mark the points of origin of squall line elements *A–O*; the hour of origin is indicated. Alternating scalloped and thin lines show the leading edge of the anvil cloud at 2-h intervals. Thick solid curves mark the position of the arc front. Dashed lines outline the anvil every 6 hours. Line *b–b'* is a long-lived but dormant arc of middle cloud (Fortune, 1980).

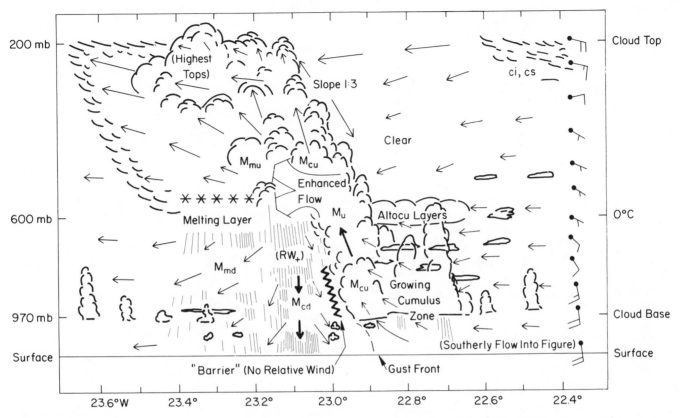

Figure 8.32. Cross section of a slowly moving tropical nonsquall cluster on 14 September 1974 over the GATE ship array (Zipser et al., 1981). System motion is left to right at 3 m s⁻¹. Arrows show relative winds.

(1979), is similar in many respects to that of a squall cluster and to that described for winter clusters in the South China Sea (Fig. 8.11). The formative stage of a tropical nonsquall cluster is usually identified with imposed synoptic or mesoscale convergence at low levels (Fig. 8.34), as in middle latitudes (Ogura and Chen, 1977; Ulanski and Garstang, 1978; and many others). The convergence may be associated with westward-propagating easterly waves, a confluence line in a larger-scale flow (Sec. 5), a downdraft outflow boundary from an old cloud (Sec. 7), or some other feature that intensifies convergence locally (Sec. 2b). The triggering of convection by low-level convergence is followed by the growth of several discrete cumulonimbus elements. As a consequence the rainfall is dominated by convective cells in the formative stage.

In the intensifying stage older convective elements grow and merge while new elements continue to form. This process gradually leads to a large continuous rain area composed of convective cells interconnected by stratiform precipitation of moderate intensity. The structure of this portion of a nonsquall cluster is similar to that of the anvil associated with a squall cluster. Indeed, Fig. 8.12b clearly indicates that mesoscale subsidence in the lower troposphere occurred on 10 and 11 December 1978 in the regions of warming and drying.

By the mature stage the stratiform component of the total precipitation can equal or surpass the convective component. The stratiform component continues to be strong into the dissipating stage, although both of the components gradually weaken. Many of these structural features of tropical clusters have been simulated by Soong and Chen (1984) with a two-dimensional cloud model. In the squall case Houze (1977) found that the integrated stratiform component accounted for 40% of the total rain, whereas in the nonsquall cases the stratiform rain accounted for 30% of the total for a GATE cluster (Leary, 1981) and 50% for a South China Sea cluster (Churchill, 1982). Similar results have been obtained for other squall clusters by Gamache and Houze (1983). Zipser et al. (1981) and Houze and Rappaport (1984) found essentially similar results for a nonsquall cluster.

Despite the similarities in their evolution and structure, the nonsquall and squall clusters in GATE exhibited differences in appearance, motion, and other aspects of their structures. In appearance nonsquall clusters did not possess the distinctive oval cirrus shield or arc-shaped leading edge characteristic of squall clusters (Houze and Betts, 1981). Squall clusters traveled faster than nonsquall clusters. The typical propagation speed of squall lines over the GATE area was 15 m s⁻¹ (Aspliden et al., 1976). The speed of the squall lines documented by Fortune (1980) was as high as 25 m s⁻¹. As a consequence, squall clusters had no "steer-

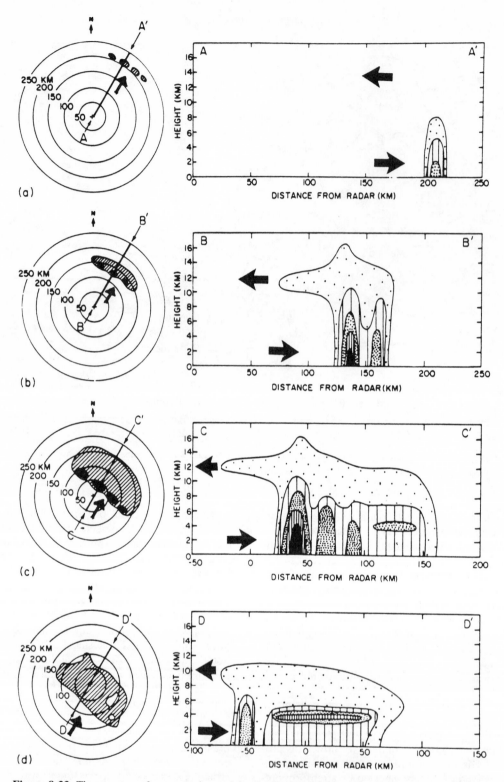

Figure 8.33. The structure of a mesoscale precipitation feature as viewed by radar in (right) horizontal and (left) vertical cross sections during its (*A*) formative, (*B*) intensifying, (*C*) mature, and (*D*) dissipating stages. The outside contour of radar reflectivity is the weakest detectable echo, and the inner contours are for successively higher reflectivity values. Heavy arrows on horizontal cross sections indicate direction of the low-level winds. Arrows on vertical cross sections indicate directions of the low-level and upper-level winds relative to the feature (Leary and Houze, 1979).

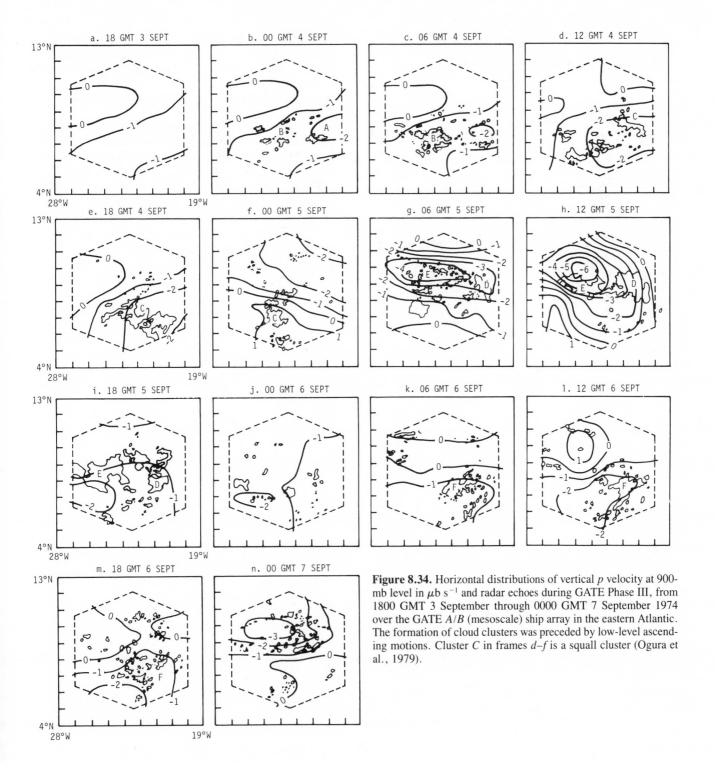

Figure 8.34. Horizontal distributions of vertical p velocity at 900-mb level in μb s^{-1} and radar echoes during GATE Phase III, from 1800 GMT 3 September through 0000 GMT 7 September 1974 over the GATE *A/B* (mesoscale) ship array in the eastern Atlantic. The formation of cloud clusters was preceded by low-level ascending motions. Cluster *C* in frames *d–f* is a squall cluster (Ogura et al., 1979).

Table 8.2. Vertical Velocities of Updraft and Downdraft Cores at 4.5-km Altitude, from Different Data Sets

	Vertical velocity (m s^{-1})		
	Thunder-storm Project (Byers and Braham, 1949)	Hurricanes (Gray, 1965)	GATE (Zipser and LeMone, 1980)
Median updraft core	6.3	3.8	2.9
Strong (10%) updraft core	11.8	6.7	5.0
Median downdraft core	5.8	3.4	1.8
Strong (10%) downdraft core)	10.0	5.8	2.9

Source: Zipser and LeMone (1980).

ing levels," and the relative winds were directed into the cluster at all levels, as shown in Fig. 8.27. Apparently the propagation of squall clusters was a combination of translation and a discrete propagation associated with formation of new cells at the leading edge of the squall clusters (Houze, 1977).

However, not all tropical squall clusters have the structure and propagation characteristics described above. This was demonstrated by Houze and Rappaport (1984) in their analysis of a GATE squall line. This squall line moved more slowly (~8 m s^{-1}) and without discrete jumps. There were a radar-echo overhang and a stratiform rain area ahead of the squall line as with many middle-latitude squall lines.

9. The Gust Front

Yoshi K. Sasaki and Thomas L. Baxter

1. Introduction

A thunderstorm gust front is the leading edge of the horizontal airflow resulting from the downdraft spreading at the ground; it is the downdraft's most dramatic manifestation. The gust front is the interface between warm, moist air in the thunderstorm environment at low altitudes and the cool, nearly saturated air of middle-level origin. Negative buoyancy propels descent of middle-level air as a substantial component of overall thunderstorm circulation. This negative buoyancy results principally from evaporation of precipitation that has fallen into dry, potentially cold air that is situated, through effects of wind shear, so that it receives precipitation from above. Negative buoyancy may also result from evaporation of cloud that formed in warm air and then mixed with dry air entrained from the near-storm environment, and also from the weight of condensation products accumulated in the warm, moist updraft. The descending current is deflected horizontally by the ground. The sum of all effects sometimes produces horizontal speeds exceeding 25 m s^{-1} in air behind the gust front; on rare occasions the airspeed approaches twice this value and may become extremely destructive.

Most of our quantitative information about gust fronts has been obtained from measurements collected during the late 1960s and the 1970s on instrumented towers. A 450-m tower in Oklahoma City has yielded the most comprehensive data, as reported by Charba and Sasaki (1971), Charba (1974), and Goff et al. (1977).

Recent attempts to correlate observational data on low-level gust front structure with data on other aspects of thunderstorm structure have used numerical simulation. Even though models of microphysical processes, i.e., the processes influencing development of cloud and precipitation from water vapor, and models of cloud-scale dynamics have improved, thunderstorm numerical simulations are still inadequate with respect to realistic depiction of gust front details.

2. Observations

Figures 9.1a–d are photographs in a time sequence showing the development of a gust front. In Fig. 9.1a, a rainshaft is visible on the right, with some trace near the center. In Fig. 9.1b, the gust front is beginning to outrun the thunderstorm. The location of the strongest wind is made visible by dust. A few minutes later (Fig. 9.1c), the distance of the leading edge of the dust from the rainshaft has doubled. Notice the greater depth of the dust layer just behind its leading edge. This characteristic feature is called a "head." In Fig. 9.1d, the gust front has left the thunderstorm far behind. It is not uncommon to find gust fronts many tens of miles from the thunderstorms in which they originate.

Figure 9.2 shows a gust front at one instant of time as seen on a modern Doppler radar. The display in Fig. 9.2a is a plan view of reflectivity, which increases with rainfall rate. In Fig. 9.2b there is the plan distribution of the radial component of velocity, i.e., the velocity component along the radar beam, coded at the right in meters per second. Along a line indicated by the arrows, the velocity component toward the radar (at the center of the circle) increases rapidly with radial distance. The line of rapid velocity change between the arrows is seen to lie at the leading edge of heavy precipitation shown in Fig. 9.2a. Subsequent to the time of these radar photos the gust front moves ahead of the precipitation area, as in Fig. 9.1.

Charba (1974) has provided a comprehensive analysis of a gust front. On 31 May 1969, a severe thunderstorm complex passed through a special high-resolution observation network in central Oklahoma operated by the National Severe Storms Laboratory. A well-defined gust front was documented by measurements at seven levels on the 450-m tower when the front was about 15 km outside the edge of the thunderstorm's radar echo, i.e., 15 km ahead of the storm's heavy-rain area. Charba combined these data with observations from surface stations, special radiosonde sites, and radar to study the structure of the gust front.

Figure 9.3, a vertical cross section of the thunderstorm outflow area, summarizes results of Charba's study. The cold outflow air forms a shallow layer with a distinct boundary zone separating it from the low-level warm air that it displaces. The windshift that precedes the gust surge is associated with the start of a marked pressure rise, probably produced by the ram effect of the cold air, and perhaps related also to a gravitational wave that propagates on a temperature inversion between 2 and 3 km above the ground. In the region from the windshift line to about 3 km behind it,

(a)

(b)

Figure 9.1. Time sequence of gust-front development 30 July 1976 near Cheyenne, Wyo.; (a) 1623 LST, (b) 1635 LST.

the windspeed is not great, but in this zone the wind shifts direction from south to west. In this zone warm air is vigorously ascending just ahead of the cold outflow.

The gust surge is the most prominent characteristic of the gust front; the surge occurs when the temperature is near its maximum. The surge is followed by increasing westerly and northwesterly winds, further rise of pressure, and rapidly declining temperature. Within the cold air mass, shown in Fig. 9.3, there is a second boundary or gust-front zone marking further wind shifts and pressure changes. Such irregularities in the cold airstream may be associated with fluctuations in updraft speed and precipitation production in the thunderstorm from which the outflow emanates, but are also natural consequences of wave-producing forces stimulated by the flow itself. The downdraft air flowing to the right (eastward) near the ground in Fig. 9.3 has a distinct "waving" behavior, rising ahead of each gust-front zone and descending behind it. There is a narrow band of very warm

air just ahead of the primary gust front and a similar band of relatively warm air ahead of the secondary one.

Areas of maximum turbulence illustrated in Fig. 9.3 are the low-level, narrow zone along the primary gust front and deeper zones upstream from each head formation. In Charba's gust-front case and most others, measurements of the equivalent potential temperature in the downdraft air indicate that most of the downdraft originates at altitudes between 3 and 8 km. A gust front substantially less intense than that studied by Charba is illustrated in vertical cross section in Vol. 1, Chap. 7, Fig. 7.20.

3. Computer Simulation of Thunderstorms

The gust front and the thunderstorm of which it is a part cannot be properly understood as separate entities. The convergence produced along the gust front often provides the

(c)

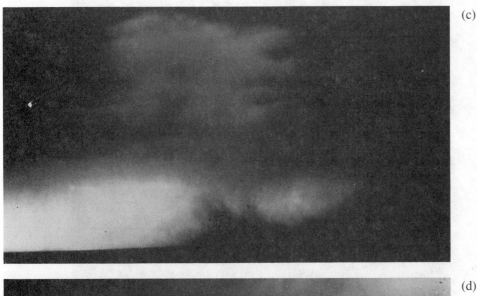

(d)

Figure 9.1. *Continued.* (c) 1638 LST, (d) 1641 LST (photos by Larry Newbarrer).

impetus for production of new cloud, either discretely or continuously, resulting in new updrafts or maintenance of existing storm updrafts. Since complete observations of the internal structure and evolution of thunderstorms are not available, we seek greater understanding through numerical modeling of known physical principles. Simulations, performed on high-speed digital computers, are complementary to observational studies: they include the detailed time evolution that the observations usually lack, they treat both the storm and its immediate environment, and they can simulate a variety of storm structures and evolutions in a controlled way with systematic variation of environmental or other parameters.

In general, realism in numerical simulations of the dynamics and interaction of a storm with its environment increases with the inclusion of more spatial dimensions. One-dimensional models suffer from their inability to take realistically into account environmental effects of wind shear and entrainment, and because precipitation products formed in

the updraft move only vertically in such a model. Two-dimensional modeling was initiated by Malkus and Witt (1959) in a study of dry convection. Moisture was introduced a few years later by Ogura (1963). The work of Kessler (1969) (see Chap. 14) in the microphysics of cloud and rain contributed to more comprehensive treatment of liquid water in models of the late 1960s and early 1970s.

Three-dimensional cloud and storm models were developed last because they require computers of large capacity and high speed. The physics of precipitation must be treated in a parameterized manner in these models, but confidence is much increased in three-dimensional simulations. Steiner (1973) used a shallow three-dimensional model to simulate dry convection and nonprecipitating clouds. More recently, as described in Chap. 15, there have been successes in modeling deep, precipitating convection with highly parameterized microphysical processes.

Simulation of gust fronts is possible in principle only in the two- and three-dimensional models. It should be empha-

(a)

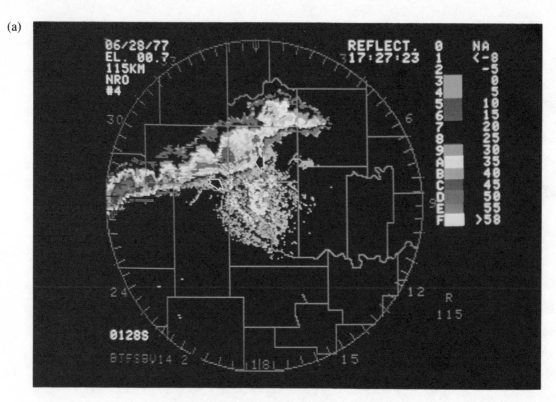

Figure 9.2. (a) Reflectivity display of 10-cm Doppler radar at Norman, Okla., 1727 CST, 28 June 1977. The circle marks a range of 115 km from the radar at its center. (b) Radial velocity display corresponding to (a). The location of a gust front is marked by arrows.

(b)

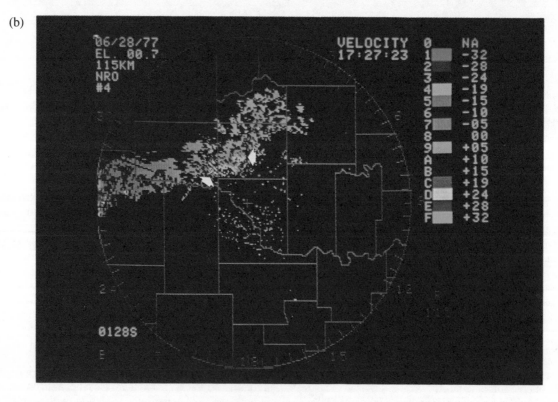

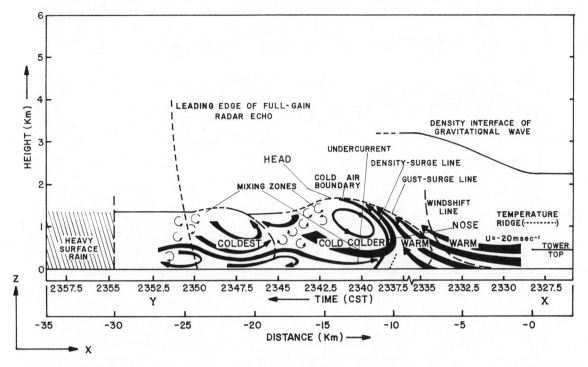

Figure 9.3. Composite schematic model combining features of analyzed and deduced structure of wind shift and gust front leading the squall line of 31 May 1969 (after Charba, 1974).

sized that these models treat the cold outflow and not details of the interface with warm air, as in the gust front illustrated in Fig. 9.3. This is because the actual transition from warm inflow to cold outflow air takes place over a distance of approximately 500 m, whereas the separation between grid points in these multidimensional models is a few hundred meters to several kilometers.

Figure 9.4 illustrates the resolution of the gust front in these models and shows several structures of gust fronts produced by cloud models. The squall-line airflow is indicated by vectors proportional to speed, and water content by a heavy line outlining the area of rain. Simulations were accomplished using the two-dimensional model of Hane (1973) with environmental soundings on two days when squall lines occurred in Oklahoma. In Fig. 9.4a there appear to be several weak gust fronts in the surface airflow ahead of the major area of updraft. These result from the spreading of air near the surface from downdrafts located in the lower 3 km above the surface. These downdrafts result from precipitation produced in areas of upward-moving air that move from right to left from the primary gust-front area to the area of major updraft. In contrast, Fig. 9.4b shows one gust front only, produced by a single strong downdraft from a somewhat more vigorous simulated storm. The major difference in conditions between these two cases is the larger magnitude of vertical shear in the environmental wind in Fig. 9.4b. Since the spatial resolution of the model in both cases is only 400 m, details of the interface between inflow and outflow air cannot be studied, but the relation of

outflow air to storm features and magnitude of outflow quantities appears realistic. For example, the temperature difference between outflow and inflow in this model is typically 6°–10°C, and the velocity of the outflow air relative to the ground is about 20 m s^{-1}.

Three-dimensional simulations have provided some insight into the relations of outflow air and gust front to the maintenance of existing convection and to the discrete development of new convection. Klemp and Wilhelmson (1978) demonstrated the relation of the gust front to selective enhancement of left- or right-moving storms. Miller (1978) discussed a simulation of a multicellular storm in which new storms form in succession along the gust front from a previous storm. Thorpe and Miller (1978) reported similar results using a somewhat different environmental wind profile. Wilhelmson and Chen (1982) described simulations that include the development of successive cells along a cold outflow boundary and compare their results with a Colorado storm that exhibited very similar behavior.

Considerable progress has been made in relating outflow air and, implicitly, gust fronts, to other storm features through use of multidimensional cloud models. It is clear that, besides being produced by the thunderstorm, the gust front often exerts important influence on the successive evolution and structure of the thunderstorm. Computer limitations do not allow explicit modeling of the detailed structure of the gust front (outflow boundary) as a part of cloud simulations. Modeling of these details has been accomplished through focusing on the gust front itself with thunderstorm

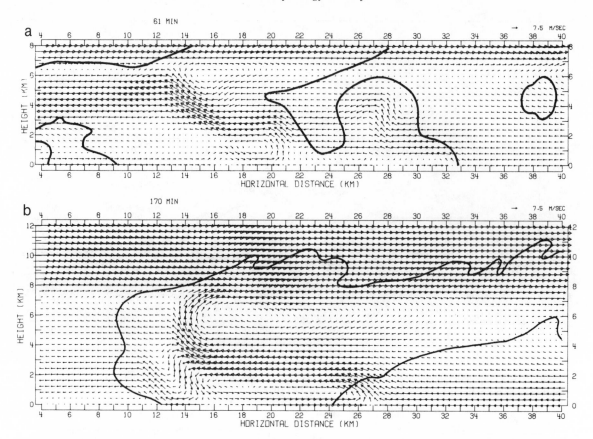

Figure 9.4. Vertical cross sections including a wind vector field and outline of rain area from two-dimensional numerical simulations of squall lines that occurred on (a) 19 May 1977 and (b) 22 May 1976 in Oklahoma. Note in the surface winds the periodic fluctuations in speed. Note the single strong downdraft and gust front in (b).

forcing specified; this approach is discussed in the following section.

4. Origin of the Gust Front

At least two mechanisms seem to be important for generation by thunderstorms of strong horizontal winds at the ground:

1. Downward transfer of entrained momentum from the strong environmental flow aloft. Descending rain-cooled air tends to carry the horizontal momentum that it had at its original level. Thus strong winds aloft are a significant predictive indicator of destructive potential.

2. The addition of kinetic energy to the air during its descent, by virtue of density differences.

In relation to item 2 above, since a parcel of rain-cooled air at the pressure of its environment has a density decrease-ment proportional to the temperature difference ΔT between parcel and environment, we can write

$$\frac{dw}{dt} = g \frac{\Delta T}{T}, \qquad (9.1)$$

where w is vertical velocity, t is time, g is the acceleration of gravity, and T is the average temperature. If the parcel descends without restraint by viscosity a distance $H = 5 \times 10^3 \, m$ while $\Delta T \sim 5$ K and $T \sim 250$ K, the time taken for its descent by simple mechanics is

$$t = \sqrt{2H \left/ \frac{dw}{dt}\right.} = 224 \text{ s},$$

and its vertical speed at the end of that time is

$$v = \sqrt{2H \frac{dw}{dt}} = 45 \text{ m s}^{-1}.$$

As the airstream is decelerated by the ground, the local pressure increases, and the horizontal gradient of that pressure causes the flow to be deflected into the horizontal plane.

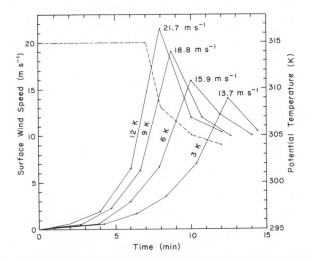

Figure 9.5. Surface windspeed as a function of time at a fixed point ($x = 9.7$ km) for the cases of different coolings. Each profile is labeled with the maximum surface windspeed and the corresponding maximum temperature decrease at $z = 500$ m. The dashed line depicts the surface temperature variation in the 12-K case (Mitchell and Hovermale, 1977).

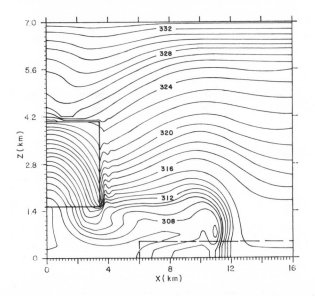

Figure 9.6. Potential temperature field (θ) after 12 minutes of simulation. Boxed area denotes region of fixed θ values. The subdomain enclosed by broken lines represents the entire cross section of Fig. 9.5. Contour values range from 306 to 333 K at 1-K intervals (Mitchell and Hovermale, 1977).

This process gives speeds that are somewhat too large, because the parcel theory neglects all responses of the environmental air to the parcel motion (see Chap. 15).

Another approach to estimation of horizontal airspeeds is given by Margules's (1905) process, which considers the environmental responses and treats the conversion of available potential energy to kinetic energy in a closed framework.

Consider the example of two air columns with adiabatic lapse rates, initially motionless and side by side, and at the same pressure level of 500 mb with a temperature difference of 5 K between the columns. Pressure forces arising from density differences produce motions tending toward a horizontal layering of the airmasses, with the warmer air on top. The decrease of potential energy in the layered configuration is equated to an increase of kinetic energy. If all the kinetic energy were converted to horizontal motion, then a windspeed of 12 m s^{-1} could result in both the warm and the cold air masses.

In an attempt to quantify the evolution of events leading to gust-front formation, Mitchell and Hovermale (1977), assuming that a large body of air in a thunderstorm has been cooled by evaporation, constructed a nonhydrostatic, dry, two-dimensional primitive equation model. An arbitrary, externally imposed, local cooling function neglects the detailed microphysics of evaporation but provides for the initiation and maintenance of a continuous cold downdraft. The model is slab symmetric, rather than axisymmetric; thus the downdraft is more properly viewed as a continuous line of downdrafts normal to the computational plane rather than an isolated downdraft. Ambient wind shear is not included, and computations are begun in a hydrostatically balanced rest state. The spatial resolution is 233 m horizontally and 175 m vertically with a time resolution of 0.35 s; thus at least some detail in the gust front can be examined. Certain features in the results do compare well with observed thunderstorm outflow.

Figure 9.5 shows the relationship between the temperature decrease by the middle-level cooling and the time variations of horizontal windspeed at the ground. When the cooling is 6 K, the horizontal windspeed can reach 15.9 m s^{-1}. Remember that the Margules process predicts 12 m s^{-1} windspeed with a 5-K temperature difference. The Margules process provides for equal distribution of the kinetic energy per unit mass throughout the entire two air columns. The numerical simulation allows more realistic distribution of the kinetic energy and momentum, which may cause stronger outflow windspeed near the surface in spite of surface drag.

Figure 9.6 shows the potential temperature field after 12 minutes of simulation. The evaporative temperature decrease was prescribed to be time-invariant over the small area outlined by the heavy solid lines in this figure. The subdomain enclosed by broken lines in the lower right corner corresponds roughly to the area scanned by the meteorologically instrumented TV tower when a gust front passed over on 31 May 1969, as analyzed by Charba (see Sec. 2). The unit of the x coordinate between the simulation and the observation is adjusted because of the difference in the gust-front movement, resulting in the model fields' being horizontally compressed compared with the observed fields. The analyzed temperature field for this case is shown in Fig. 9.7. Although the observational region overlaps only a small portion of the computational domain, the similarity between these two temperature fields is striking. The horizontal windspeed after 12 minutes of the numerical simula-

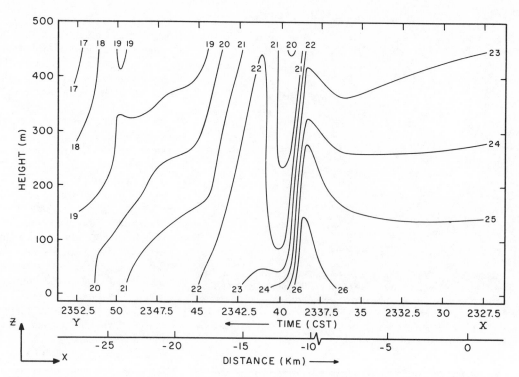

Figure 9.7. Temperature analysis for 31 May 1969. Contour values range from 17° to 26°C (Charba, 1974).

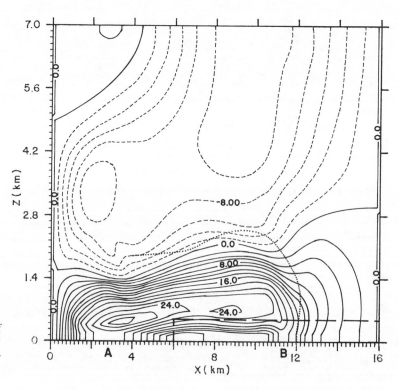

Figure 9.8. Horizontal windspeed after 12 minutes of simulation. Contour values range from −10 to 29 m s⁻¹ at intervals of 2 m s⁻¹. The dotted line is the 314 isentrope from Fig. 9.6 (Mitchell and Hovermale, 1977).

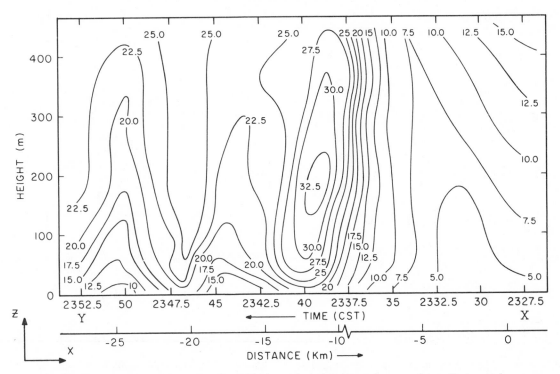

Figure 9.9. Windspeed analysis for 31 May 1969 in vertical plane normal to gust front. Contour values range from 5 to 32.5 m s^{-1} at intervals of 2.5 m s^{-1} (Charba, 1974).

tion is shown in Fig. 9.8. The isotach cross-section analysis done by Charba (1974) for the case of 31 May 1969, in the vertical plane normal to gust front, is shown in Fig. 9.9. The domain at the lower right corner of Fig. 9.8 bounded by the heavy broken lines is nearly equal to the entire domain of Fig. 9.9. The isotach patterns in these two domains are in fair agreement.

The natural processes simulated in the experimental and numerical models discussed above are manifested in Doppler radar data and in other data acquired from tornadic thunderstorms in Oklahoma on 8 June 1974, analyzed by Brandes (1977). Figure 9.10a shows some trajectories of air parcels relative to the severe storm. Observe that air moving northward from the southeast quadrant ascends from a height below 1 km to 1.3 km at the positions indicated by the open circles. One trajectory from the south shows rising motion followed by descending motion. On the west side of the storm, air at 2-km height moves northward, then turns southward, descends, and becomes involved in the core circulation. These trajectories can be somewhat understood in terms of the nearly instantaneous data shown in Figs. 9.10b and 9.10c.

The arrows in Fig. 9.10b represent the distribution of horizontal air velocity at an altitude of 1.3 km, relative to the motion of the storm. Wind shifts are denoted by the heavy lines, vertical air velocity (negative downward) is shown by the lighter dashed lines; these are 4-m s^{-1} contours. The light solid lines represent the radar reflectivity factor in dBZ; the isopleth labeled 50 represents a rainfall

rate of approximately 50 mm hr^{-1}. Note that the vertical velocity isopleths bearing -4 labels reside within the heavy-rain area. The descending air spreads southward and merges with low-level inflow air at a marked wind-shift line, where the inflow air ascends. Figure 9.10c shows that southward-moving air west of the circulation center extends much farther south at 0.3-km altitude than at 1.3-km altitude. This is indicative of the slope of the gust front, generally upward toward the north. The air at low altitudes southwest of the circulation center has clearly passed through the rain area, where it has been subject to cooling by evaporation of rain. Other data show that this air, which originated at about 2-km altitude and was dry and therefore potentially cold, was cooled about 6°C by evaporation of rain. The negative buoyancy thus induced was the major contribution to strong outflow at lower altitudes.

The storm process in this case is associated with a tornado at the heavy circle shown in Figs. 9.10b and 9.10c. The tornado circulation itself is of too small a scale to be manifested in detail in these figures, but the trajectories show a special influence of the tornado circulation near the storm core.

5. Concluding Remarks

Past studies have presented strong evidence to suggest that thunderstorm gust fronts develop when evaporatively cooled midlevel air descends, converting its potential energy to ki-

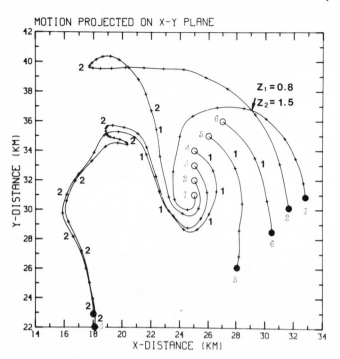

Figure 9.10a. Parcel trajectories in the Harrah, Okla., thunderstorm, 8 June 1974. Initial locations shown by dots and final locations (all at 1.3-km elevation) shown by open circles. Selected heights (km) indicated. Tick marks give locations at 2-min intervals (after Brandes, 1977).

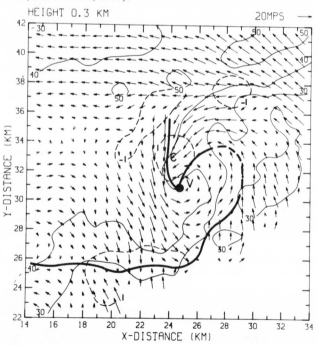

Figure 9.10b. Wind field at 1.3-km altitude synthesized from dual Doppler radar observations at 1553 CST. Vectors indicate storm-relative winds (scale at upper right), thin dashed contours are vertical velocity (m s⁻¹), and thin solid contours are radar reflectivity factor in dBZ. Heavy lines are wind-shift lines. A tornado was at the location marked by a solid circle (after Brandes, 1977).

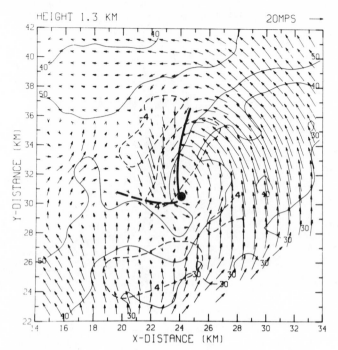

Figure 9.10c. Wind field, as in Fig. 9.10b, except for 0.3-km altitude. *C* and *V* represent centers of convergence and vorticity.

netic energy and carrying down the momentum entrained from aloft, and is deflected into horizontal flow by the ground. This conclusion is supported by observation of the wet-bulb potential temperature of the outflow air, which identifies this air with the midlevels. This conclusion is also consistent with the tendency of thunderstorm models to produce stronger downdrafts when evaporation is modeled more accurately and environmental flow is treated more realistically.

Numerical simulations have shown promise in aiding our understanding of both the details of gust-front structure and the two-way interaction of gust fronts with various thunderstorm features. One goal is to be able to run a full-cloud model with sufficient horizontal and vertical resolution in the boundary layer to depict details along the outflow boundary, and learn of the effects of the cloud upon the evolution of the gust front as well as the role that the gust front plays in initiation of new convection. Simulations from multidimensional cloud models have already revealed much information on the effect of thunderstorm outflow on the maintenance of the storm through discrete or continuous generation of new updrafts. Additional realism will be gained when we are able to take into account the structure of the storm environment more adequately than in the simplified forms now used. In the meantime, new observational tools are contributing to the stockpile of information.[1]

[1] This chapter was prepared under the sponsorship of National Science Foundation Grant No. ATM-7824892.

10. Tornado Dynamics

Robert P. Davies-Jones

1. Introduction

Of all atmospheric storms, tornadoes are the most violent. Maximum windspeeds in the most intense tornadoes probably lie in the range 110–125 m s^{-1} (250 to 275 mi h^{-1}). Because of their unpredictability and high-energy density, tornadoes represent an awesome challenge to the scientific observer and the would-be weather modifier. The engineer is fascinated with the tornado because of its ability to produce locally very high concentrations of mechanical energy (a crude estimate of the rate at which kinetic energy is produced in a tornado is 10^3 MW, based on my revision of Vonnegut's [1960] and Michaud's [1977] estimates). The eyewitness is awe-inspired by the often beautiful but fearsome spectacle of the fiendish whirlwind. Previous reviews pertinent to this chapter include those by Morton (1966), Davies-Jones and Kessler (1974), Golden (1976), Lewellen (1976), Lilly (1976), Davies-Jones (1976), Snow (1982), and Bengtsson and Lighthill (1982).

2. Definitions

A *tornado* is a violently rotating, tall, narrow column of air, averaging about 100 m in diameter, that extends to the ground from a cumuliform cloud. It is generally marked visually by a funnel-shaped cloud pendant from cloud base and/or a swirling cloud of dust and debris rising from the ground. The condensation funnel does not necessarily extend all the way to the ground, and may be obscured by dust. In rare cases a funnel does not develop. Virtually all tornadoes are associated with cumulonimbi, although they may form from lesser clouds that flank the thunderhead. A funnel cloud is identical to a tornado except that its circulation does not reach the ground.

A *waterspout* is essentially the ocean or large-lake counterpart of the land-based tornado. However, waterspouts are usually less intense and far more frequent than tornadoes and form readily from cumulus congestus cloud lines as well as from cumulonimbi.

Tornadoes, funnel clouds, and waterspouts are atmospheric examples of a general class of fluid flow called *vortices*. A vortex is a flow with a core of concentrated vorticity. Vorticity, a vector, is a measure of how fast local elements of fluid are spinning about their own axes. *Circulation* is the macroscopic measure of rotation in a fluid and, when no torques are acting, is conserved. Thus circulation is the fluid analog of angular momentum (note, however, that circulation is a scalar whereas angular momentum is a vector). Precise definitions of vorticity and circulation are given in Sec. 10 below.

3. Morphology, Life Cycle, Damage Patterns

Tornado funnels may assume various forms from a thin rope to a cylindrical or conical shape, to a thick, amorphous mass of black cloud in contact with the ground, to multiple funnels (Fig. 10.1). The funnel outline also varies considerably from sharp-edged to very ragged, suggesting that the flows in tornadoes may be either smooth or highly turbulent (the narrowest funnels are generally the smoothest). The funnel need not extend to the ground for intense damage to occur. Almost all tornadoes rotate cyclonically, but anticyclonic ones do occur (Burgess, 1976b; Fujita, 1977). Tornado films show that the flow visible on and just outside the funnel surface is nearly always spiraling upward.

The funnel undergoes considerable changes in size and shape during the tornado's life (Fig. 10.1). The tornado life cycle may be divided into five discrete but somewhat overlapping stages (Golden and Purcell, 1978a; Davies-Jones et al., 1978):

1. The dust-whirl stage, when the first signs of circulation are visible as dust swirling upward from the surface and/or a short funnel pendant from cloud base (damage is light).
2. The organizing stage, characterized by an overall downward descent of the funnel and increase in intensity of the tornado.
3. The mature stage, when the funnel reaches its greatest width and is almost vertical (damage is most intense).
4. The shrinking stage, marked by decreasing funnel width, increasing funnel tilt (usually the foot of the tornado lags behind its upper part so that the typical tilt is toward the northeast with height), and a narrowing damage swath (damage may still be severe, however).
5. The decay stage, when the vortex is stretched into a

Figure 10.1a. Examples of different tornado funnel types. See also Figs. 10.2, 10.18, 10.24, 10.29. Right: A smooth-walled funnel with cylindrical dust cloud, Enid, Okla., 5 June 1966, looking NW (ESSA photo by Leo Ainsworth).

Figure 10.1b. A thin funnel during the organizing stage of the 24 May 1973 Union City, Okla., tornado. The condensation funnel has not yet touched the surface, but debris is rising off the ground. Direction of view WNW (photo by S. Tegtmeier).

Figure 10.1c. Tornado in Fig. 10.1b in its mature stage. The funnel has reached its maximum size. Direction of view NW (photo by S. Tegtmeier).

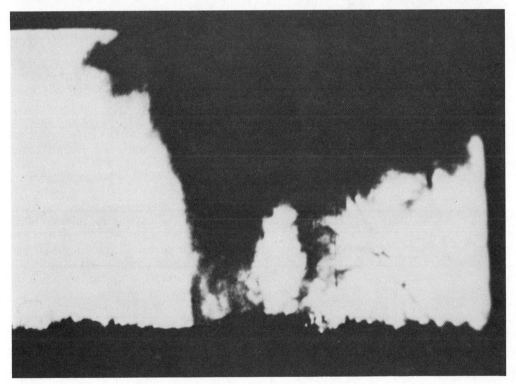

Figure 10.1d. A multiple-funnel tornado near Oshkosh, Wis., 21 April 1974. Direction of view WNW (taken from motion picture by D. Sennholz).

Figure 10.1e. The Union City tornado in its decay stage. The funnel has been drawn into a long, contorted rope shape. Direction of view ENE (photo by R. Gannon).

rope shape (by vertical wind shear or the effects of surface drag), and the visible funnel becomes greatly contorted before dissipating.

Most major tornadoes evolve through all five stages. Minor tornadoes, however, may abort in stages 1 or 2 or evolve through the sequence 1 → 2 → 5. Once a tornado enters its mature stage, its circulation usually stays in continuous contact with the ground through stages 3, 4, and 5. A few intense tornadoes decay abruptly by spreading out and becoming diffuse (Agee et al., 1976). The overall debris distributions along part of or the entire track often show few signs of circulation, and in some cases the damage could be mistakenly attributed to straight-line winds except for the well-defined long, narrow path. A motion picture of the Union City, Okla., tornado of 1973 showed that during the shrinking stage most of the debris was ejected far ahead of the tornado, even though the rotational wind-speeds greatly exceeded the translational speed (Davies-Jones et al., 1978). The damage survey showed that at this stage debris from known sources was strewn in a cone along the path. In contrast, signs of circulation were very evident

in the damage caused during the tornado's mature stage when the debris cloud was almost symmetrical. Obviously, the character of the flow near the ground changed markedly between stages 3 and 4 in this case. Another feature of the Union City damage was indications of strongly radial, low-level (lowest 1 m or so) flow into the vortex's center during the shrinking and decay stages.

Waterspouts undergo life cycles broadly similar to the evolution of tornadoes (Golden, 1974a, b). The first visible sign of a vortex is a *dark spot* on the sea surface. A short funnel pendant from the clouds may be present initially, or it may develop later in the dark-spot stage. Dark spots may occur in groups of two or more with one often dominating the others, which soon decay. The lifetime of the dark-spot stage is 1 to 22 min, and many never evolve further. Tracers dropped on the sea surface indicate that the dark spots are caused by rotation imposed from above.

The second stage, not always present, is the formation of *spiral patterns* on the sea (Fig. 10.2). Frequently only one major dark band (scale 150 to 1,000 m) emanates from a nearby shower. The cause of the surface darkening is not clearly understood but is thought to relate to variations in structure of sea surface waves. Smoke-flare observations show that the spiral band depicts a convergence line on the ocean surface and that regions of flow away from the vortex exist along the surface.

The next stage begins as the wind increases beyond a critical value (~23 m s^{-1}) and throws up a *ring of spray* from the surface. The funnel increases in size, tilts, and begins moving more rapidly along the surface as it is overtaken by the wind-shift line associated with the outflow from a neighboring shower. At the same time the spiral tightens.

The *mature stage* lasts 2 to 17 min and is characterized by peak winds, increasing tilt, and maximum forward speed of 3 to 8 m s^{-1} (15 m s^{-1} in extreme cases). The waterspout moves generally along a gently curved path. The spray ring evolves into a spray vortex, and the funnel sometimes has a double-walled structure (Fig. 10.2). Often the waterspout is not visible throughout from cloud to sea surface.

The *decay stage* lasts 1 to 3 min as the rain-cooled air finally overtakes the waterspout. By now the spiral pattern has disappeared, and the funnel becomes distorted and breaks up. During the decay stage a spiral rain curtain is sometimes seen. It lasts about 5 min and occasionally is intense enough to give a hook echo on radar.

4. Tornado-Parent Storm Relationship

The core of a tornado is two orders of magnitude smaller in horizontal dimension than a thunderstorm. The total energy and the circulation of the parent storm greatly exceed those of the tornado. Thus the theoretician is faced not with the problem of locating sufficient energy and circulation for the tornado but rather with explaining the processes operating during tornadogenesis that lead to singularly high energy density (energy per unit volume) and vorticity.

Figure 10.2. Waterspout over the Florida Keys on 10 September 1969. Note the double-wall funnel and the spiral pattern on the sea surface (NOAA photo by Joseph Golden).

The basic flow in a typical tornadic thunderstorm is as follows (Fankhauser, 1971; Atkinson, 1981; Houze and Hobbs, 1982; Chap. 7). Warm, moist air flows into the storm at low levels on its right [1] flank, rises in a rotating updraft at the right rear, and flows out of the storm in the anvil (Fig. 10.3). Environmental midlevel dry air, flowing around the updraft, is cooled by evaporating precipitation. As it sinks to the ground and spreads out, part of this rain-cooled air mass is drawn cyclonically around the updraft with a "pseudo-cold front" or "gust front" forming at its leading edge. As it advances, the front lifts the moist, potentially unstable air ahead of it, continuously regenerating the updraft. The passage of such a front is characterized by rapid cooling, abrupt pressure rise, and strong wind gusts. Be-

cause the environmental winds increase with height, another downdraft may develop on the storm's rear flank (Burgess et al., 1977). This subsidence seems to be associated with intensifying low-level updraft rotation and its attendant pressure reduction near the ground.

Tornadoes can be categorized into two groups, according to the absence (type A) or existence (type B) of a mesoscale parent circulation (3 to 9 km in diameter). The main subgroup of type A tornadoes forms on the gust front under the flanking line of new cells that continuously develop on the right rear flank of severe thunderstorms (Fig. 10.4). In this location Bates (1968) has seen a line of dust whirls with very tenuous connections to the base of the cumuli. Several vortices abort, but one or two may develop into tornadoes. At the time the vortex forms, the cloud tops overhead may be only 4 km, although the parent cloud usually adjoins taller clouds. These tornadoes can be a considerable distance (up to 20 km) from the rain shaft of the parent storm. Eddies up to 1 km in diameter are sometimes seen at cloud base in association with these tornadoes, but are too small and weak to be identified effectively by radar.

Tornadoes of the second type form from a cyclonically rotating mesovortex (mesocyclone, or tornado cyclone if the cell produces a tornado), which is linked spatially with the main updraft. Occasionally type A may evolve into type B. Severe tornadoes belong to type B. Mesocyclones were first discovered by Brooks (1949), who found that tornadoes were frequently embedded in small, low-pressure areas roughly 15 km in diameter. A pendant or hook forming on the right rear of an echo (see Fig. 10.5) often identifies mesocyclones on radar. The hook is caused by precipitation drawn into a cyclonic spiral by the winds, and the associated notch in the echo is caused by precipitation-free, warm, moist air flowing into the storm (Browning, 1964). The inflow is confined primarily to the lowest 3 km. The winds and temperature fields at low levels in a mesocyclone resemble the classic model of a middle-latitude cyclone (Fig. 10.6; Brandes, 1977). Significant cyclonic wind shifts are observed at the "pseudo-cold" and "pseudo-warm" fronts (the latter is the part of the gust front that is ahead of the wave apex in Fig. 10.3b). Tornadoes may form either at the apex of the wave or toward the edge of the mesocyclone, where the pseudo-cold front is a favored location. Mesocyclones occasionally persist for a few hours and may spawn several tornadoes. The tornadoes are steered by the larger-scale mesocyclone circulation in which they are embedded.

More than one tornado may be on the ground simultaneously. Tornadoes produced by the same storm constitute a tornado family. Fujita (1963) and Darkow (1971) have noted an approximate 45-min periodicity in the touchdown times of family members. Successive tornadoes may overlap in time by a few minutes but usually do not coexist. If the damage tracks of the tornadoes appear to form a wavy broken line, the family is classified as series mode (Fujita, 1974). In a parallel-mode family, the damage tracks are parallel arcs with each new tornado forming on the right side of its predecessor (Fig. 10.7). The parallel mode is subdivided

[1] As viewed along the direction of storm movement in the Northern Hemisphere. Southern Hemisphere storms are mirror images (i.e., right and left are transposed).

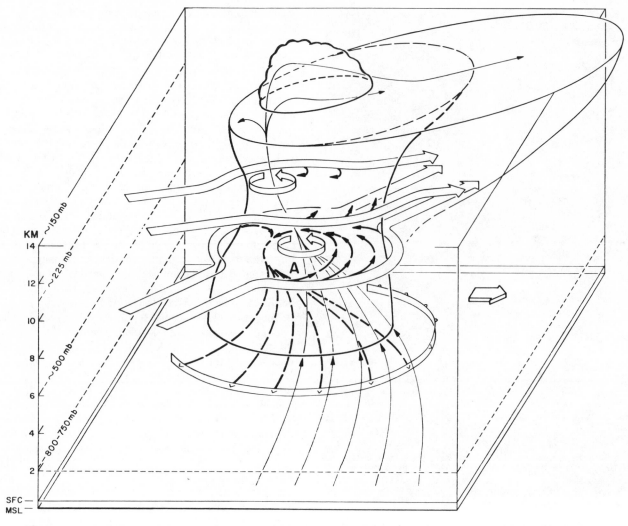

Figure 10.3a. Three-dimensional interpretation of interacting external and internal airflow associated with individual persistent great-plains cumulonimbus. The thin, solid inflowing and ascending streamlines represent the history of moist air originating in low levels (surface to ~750 mb). The heavy dashed streamlines trace the entry and descent of potentially cold and dry middle-level (700- to 400-mb) air feeding down-rushing and diverging downdraft. The surface boundary between the inflow and downdraft is shown as a barbed band. The internal circular bands signify net updraft rotation. The shape and orientation of the dividing external bands represent typical vertical shear and character of ambient relative horizontal airflow at middle (~500 mb) and upper (~225 mb) levels. The approximate pressure-height relationshhip is shown on the left-forward corner of the perspective box. The broad, flat arrow on the right represents direction of travel (after Fankhauser, 1971).

into left turn and right turn, according to the direction in which the paths curve. The rightward staggering of successive tornado paths is explained in Sec. 13 below.

Two mesocyclones may occur in such proximity that they rotate around each other (Brown et al., 1973; Fujita, 1974). The period of revolution is typically 1 h or more, and the mesocyclones usually decay before completing one revolution.

Mesocyclones may possess surface winds (other than those associated with embedded tornadoes) that are ex-

tremely damaging. An exceptionally strong mesocyclone that induced a pressure fall of 34 mb in 15 min (see Fig. 10.8) was estimated to contain windspeeds in excess of 50 m s^{-1} (Ward, 1964). Typically the maximum pressure deficit is about 5 mb, and the surface winds are moderate (roughly 15–20 m s^{-1}).

Fujita et al. (1976) have observed that tornadoes tend to form when the height of the storm top is decreasing. As shown in Fig. 10.3, warm updraft air overshoots its equilibrium level; penetrates the stratosphere, where it becomes

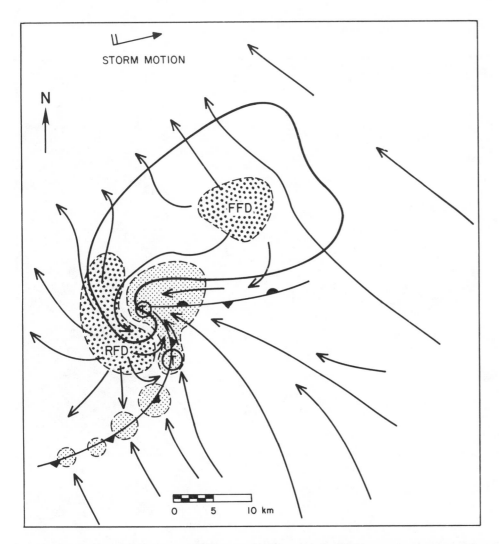

STORM MOTION

N

FFD

RFD

0   5   10 km

Figure 10.3b. Schematic plan view of a tornadic thunderstorm at the surface. The thick line encompasses radar echo. The thunderstorm wave-like "gust-front" structure is also depicted by use of a solid line and frontal symbols. Surface positions of the updraft are finely stippled; forward-flank downdraft (FFD) and rear-flank downdraft (RFD) are coarsely stippled, along with associated streamlines (relative to the storm). Likely tornado locations are shown by encircled T's. The major cyclonic tornado is most probable at the wave apex, while a minor cyclonic tornado may occur at the bulge in the cold front (southern T), which also marks the favored location for new mesocyclone. Anticyclonic tornadoes, if any, are found even farther south along cold front (adapted from Lemon and Doswell, 1979).

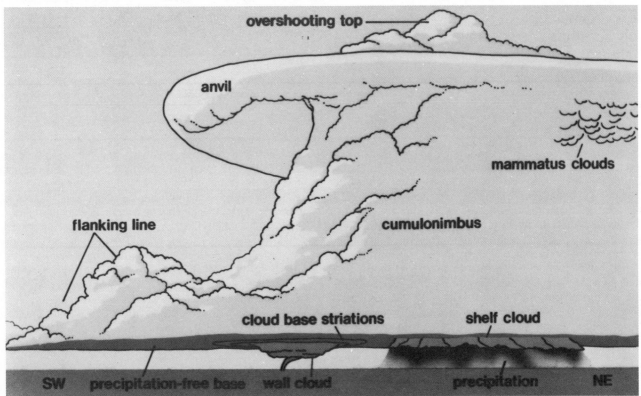

overshooting top

anvil

mammatus clouds

cumulonimbus

flanking line

cloud base striations

shelf cloud

SW   precipitation-free base   wall cloud   precipitation   NE

Figure 10.4. Composite view of a typical tornado-producing cumulonimbus as seen from the southeast. The horizontal scale is compressed (diagram by C. Doswell and B. Dirham).

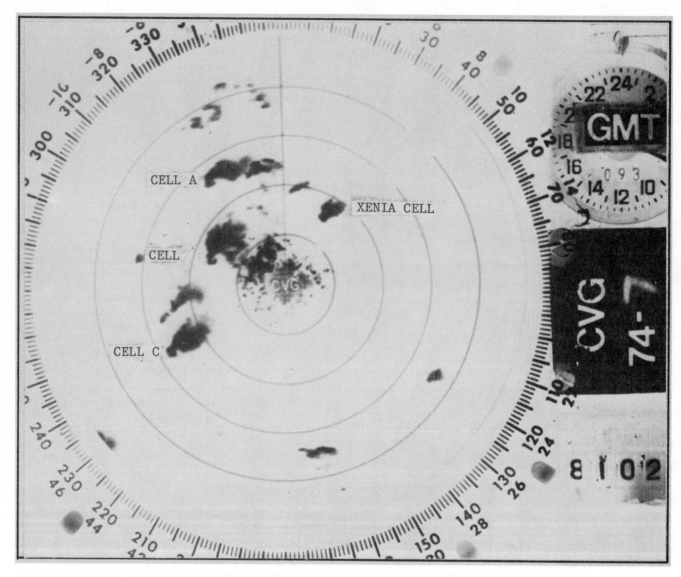

Figure 10.5. WSR-57 PPI radarscope showing four storms (A, B, C, and Xenia cells) displaying hook-echo configuration at reduced-gain setting (15-dB attenuation). WSR-57 radar, National Weather Service, Covington, Ky., 2019 GMT, 3 April 1974. Spacing between range circles is 46 km (NOAA photograph; Agee et al., 1975).

cooler than its surroundings; and sinks back down to its equilibrium level before flowing out in the anvil. The resulting cloudy dome (also called *overshooting top*), drawn in Fig. 10.4, is a transient phenomenon. Storm overflights have shown that intense tornadoes occur after the top has collapsed and is relatively flat. However, most collapsing tops are not associated with tornado formation, and not all tornadoes follow dramatic changes in the upper structure.

Visual observations (see Vol. 3, Chap. 2) have shown that major tornadoes generally form on the right-rear flank of the storm, adjacent to but outside the precipitation shaft (Fig. 10.4). Typically the tornado forms from a convective tower whose base is precipitation-free and lightning-free. The tornado is frequently situated near the surface wind-

shift line that separates inflowing and outflowing air and close to the intersection of the flanking line and the main tower of the cumulonimbus. The cloud towers in this region of the storm have sharply defined boundaries, suggesting strong updrafts. Presumably heavy rain does not fall around the tornado initially because the vortex is embedded in updrafts that are either strong enough to keep the precipitation suspended aloft or tilted so that most of the precipitation descends northeast of the tornado. Many tornadoes end their lives in rain. Large hail (golf-ball size and larger) often falls near the tornado, frequently just ahead and to the left (Agee et al., 1976). Cloud-to-ground lightning is most frequent close to the precipitation shaft but is rare in the tornado vicinity (Davies-Jones and Golden, 1975a, b). Exceptions to

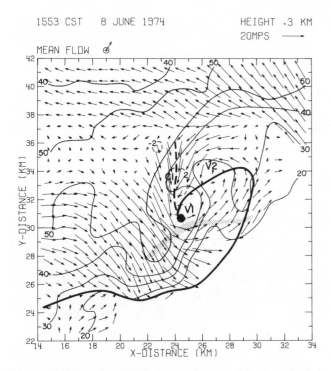

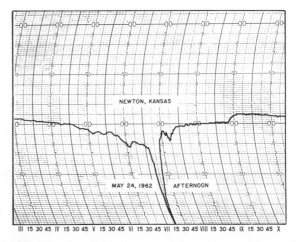

Figure 10.8. Surface pressure record of an intense tornado cyclone. Abscissa is time; ordinate pressure from 28 in. Hg in intervals of 0.1 in. (1 in. Hg equals 33.9 mb).

Figure 10.6. Low-level (300 m above the ground) horizontal wind field of a mesocyclone as mapped by dual Doppler radars. Arrow lengths are proportional to windspeed according to scale at upper right. The mean flow (upper left) at this level has been removed to accentuate the circulation. Solid contours pertain to radar reflectivity (dBZ). The heavy line is gust front; the damage path of a tornado (on the ground at this time) is stippled. North is toward the top of the figure (Brandes, 1977).

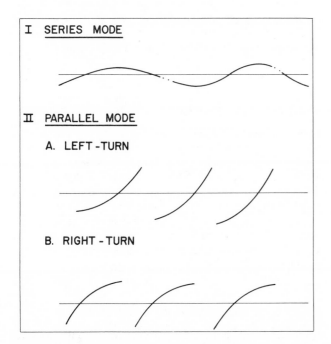

Figure 10.7. Damage path configurations for different types of tornado families (Agee et al., 1976).

these general rules occur. For instance, a few tornadoes are embedded in rain throughout their existence. Occasionally luminosity of an apparently electrical origin is noted in the funnels of nocturnal tornadoes (Vaughan and Vonnegut, 1976), and lightning discharges down the funnel itself have been documented (Davies-Jones and Golden, 1975a).

Often, the mesocyclone can be recognized visually by a cylindrical, rotating wall cloud (or discrete lowering of the cloud base 1–10 km in diameter) hanging from the base of the main tower, which may have spiral striations on its base or sides (Fig. 10.9; Fujita, 1960). Speeded-up photography has shown the main tower of a cumulonimbus rotating from its base to its anvil (Koscielski, 1967). Sometimes a low, tail-shaped cloud extends outward from the wall cloud to the east or north. Cloud material in the tail cloud streams into the wall cloud (Fujita, 1960). Very intense upward motions are observed on the forward sides of wall clouds. A major tornado is almost always suspended from a wall cloud until near the end of its life, by which time the wall cloud may have dissipated. Often gradual evaporation of cloud is observed in the wall cloud and main tower base on the rear and right sides of the tornado, forming a (relatively) "clear slot" (see Fig. 10.1c, left side). This observation is consistent with a developing, unsaturated, rear-flank downdraft (Burgess et al., 1977; Lemon and Doswell, 1979) and reveals that tornadoes form in strong vertical velocity gradients near the edge of their parent updraft and close to a downdraft. Tornado-parent storm relationships are discussed further in Sec. 13.

Although waterspouts also form from cumulonimbi, many form from lesser clouds. Golden (1974a, b) observed that most sightings in the Florida Keys are of multiple waterspouts and that these waterspouts tend to occur over very shallow water (less than 4 m deep) in building, cumulus-congestus cloud lines with one or two incipient showers.

205

Figure 10.9. The base of a rotating cloud at Fargo, N.Dak.) 20 June 1957, seen from the east. Note the wall cloud, the tail cloud, and the cyclonic striations (Fujita, 1960).

Parent circulations of these waterspouts are much weaker and smaller than mesocyclones. These waterspouts are akin to type A tornadoes. Sometimes cyclonic and anticyclonic waterspouts are present simultaneously in the same cloud line. At the time of waterspout formation the maximum and average cloud-top heights may be only 5 and 3.5 km. In the region of the cloud lines, aircraft measurements indicate mesoscale convergence and cyclonic vorticity, plus a super-adiabatic lapse rate in the lower half of the subcloud layer. Neighboring heavy rain showers are important in the production of waterspouts, which tend to form in strong updrafts just ahead of the leading edge of rain-cooled air. Note that maritime clouds develop showers far more rapidly than do continental clouds. Congestus over the ocean may produce rain before reaching the freezing level (Ruskin and Scott, 1974).

5. Tornado Statistics

Extreme variability characterizes tornadoes. Only 3% of the roughly 900 tornadoes that occur in the United States every year account for the mean annual death rate (~100 deaths) and most of the $200 million annual property losses (Galway, 1975). Most tornadoes are relatively weak and short-lived (1–2 min) and typically inflict damage to an area 2 km long and 50 m wide while moving from the SW at 15 m s^{-1} (Fujita and Pearson, 1973). In extreme cases, the path length may exceed 150 km, the width of the damage may be 3 km, the lifetime may exceed 1 h, and the translation speed may reach 30 m s^{-1}. Sixty percent of tornadoes move from the SW, and only 4% have a westward component of motion (Wolford, 1960). Anticyclonic tornadoes are rare, but their frequency has not been estimated reliably. At least 14 have been documented in recent meteorological literature. Wakimoto (1983) estimates that 1 in 700 is known to be anticyclonic.

Waterspouts also generally persist for only a few minutes, although they have been known to last for 1 h (Golden, 1973). Roughly 15% of waterspouts rotate anticyclonically. Waterspouts rarely attain the intensity of strong tornadoes.

Fujita (1971) has categorized tornadoes according to rough assessments of damage severity. Only 10% of tornadoes are intense enough to blow down walls of well-built houses. The Fujita scale has proved useful for climatological and risk assessment studies (Abbey, 1976).

6. Tornado Climatology

a. Geographical Distribution

Intense tornadoes occur more frequently in the central United States than anywhere else in the world. In the most susceptible areas, two to four tornadoes a year occur in a 10,000-km^2 area (Fig. 10.10). Mississippi and Alabama have a disproportionate amount of long-track tornadoes (Wilson and Morgan, 1971; Kessler and Lee, 1978).

Waterspouts are far more common than tornadoes and occur with a frequency greater than 400 per year per 10,000 km^2 in favorable locations such as the Florida Keys (Golden, 1977).

b. Seasonal Distribution in the United States

In the cold months tornadoes are generally confined to the southeastern states. The location of maximum tornado activity shifts northward with the jet stream and advancing

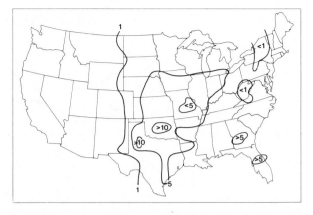

Figure 10.10. Average annual number of tornado occurrences per 10,000 mi^2, (26,000 km^2) 1953–75 (prepared by National Severe Storms Forecast Center; Abbey, 1976).

warm moist air through the central and into the northern plains states during spring and summer. May has the most activity, 20% of the annual number of tornadoes; January has the least, only 3% of the total.

Waterspouts are most common between June and September, when shallow coastal waters along the southeastern U.S. coast are warmest (Golden, 1973).

c. Diurnal Distribution in the United States

Tornadoes happen during all hours of the day, but 42% occur between 1500 and 1900 LST (Skaggs, 1968). This afternoon maximum reflects the role played by diurnal surface heating in destabilizing the atmosphere. Because they form most frequently over water that is shallow and thus subject to significant diurnal temperature change, waterspouts also occur predominantly between 1500 and 1900 LST (Golden, 1973). For a more comprehensive review of tornado statistics and climatology, see Abbey (1976) and Kelley et al. (1978). Galway (1977) and Novlan and Gray (1974) present climatological aspects of tornado outbreaks and hurricane-associated tornadoes, respectively.

7. Tornado Forecasting

Present forecast techniques identify the potential for widespread tornado outbreaks successfully but are less dependable in predicting isolated occurrences (Pearson and Weiss, 1979). Famous tornado outbreaks include the 148 tornadoes that occurred on 3–4 April 1974 (Fujita, 1974; Vol. 1, Chap. 3) and the 47 Palm Sunday tornadoes of 11 April 1965 (Fujita et al., 1970). Since tornado outbreaks in extratropical cyclones have a disproportionately high percentage of intense long-track tornadoes (Fujita, 1974), it is fortunate that these outbreaks are usually predicted successfully. Outbreaks of less intense though still damaging tornadoes also occur in the right-front quadrants of tropical cyclones

as they cross the American Gulf Coast. In 1967 Hurricane Beulah spawned 115 tornadoes in Texas (Orton, 1970).

Galway (1977) has identified three types of tornado outbreaks. A local outbreak is one confined to a circular area of ~3 × 10^4 km^2, lasting 5½ h. In a progressive outbreak the activity typically progresses eastward or northeastward over a 9½ h period, affecting several states. In a line outbreak, which lasts 8 h on average, the eastward progression is limited, but tornadoes occur in widely separated locations along a north-south axis at roughly the same time.

Present tornado forecasts, issued by the National Severe Storms Forecast Center in Kansas City, usually refer to tornadoes expected to develop 1 to 7 h after the forecast, in rectangular areas about 225 × 320 km (72,000 km^2). These forecasts are called "watches." About 40% of watches are verified, that is, are followed by tornadoes somewhere in the forecast box during the forecast period (Pearson and Weiss, 1979). The probability of one or more tornadoes occurring in a randomly selected 72,000-km^2 box in a 6-h period near the seasonal and geographical maxima of tornadoes is roughly 5%. Further evidence of the forecasters' skill in identifying the weather conditions associated with tornadoes is the statistic that 66% of fatalities occur inside or within 40 km of a watch area (Galway, 1975).

About 30% of tornadoes fall within forecast boxes (Pearson and Weiss, 1979). Most of the rest are isolated occurrences and are difficult to predict because the atmosphere is not sampled with sufficient spatial and temporal frequency. Upper-air data are collected routinely at 1200 and 0000 GMT from stations 400 km apart. These data are supplemented by finer resolution data (e.g., hourly surface reports, satellite photographs, radar reports) that are not quantitative enough to initialize a numerical model but do give the forecaster insight into how atmospheric conditions are changing.

The following conditions favor tornadoes (SELS Staff, 1956; Miller, 1972; see also Chaps. 5, 6 and Vol. 1, Chap. 8):

1. Abundant moisture in the surface layer to a depth of at least 1 km. Moisture and moisture flux are monitored by following surface dew-point changes and computing the horizontal convergence of moisture. The presence of a dry air mass at intermediate levels (with base at 1 to 2.5 km), providing the potential for strong downdrafts through evaporative cooling, is also favorable.

2. Deep conditional and convective instability, that is, large lapse rates of temperature and moisture through a great depth.

3. The presence of a stable layer or inversion. This acts to prevent deep convection from occurring until the potential for explosive overturning is established. By the time of tornado formation the inversion has been eroded locally (Beebe, 1958).

4. A mechanism to remove the stable layer. The most common mechanism is dynamic lifting with surface heating and warm-air advection below the inversion. Other possible mechanisms include lifting by terrain and by gravity waves. Dynamic lifting is strongest near thin zones of low-level

convergence such as fronts or drylines (dew-point fronts) and beneath regions of pronounced upper-level divergence. Typically, these features occur in combinations to provide sustained lifting through deep layers.

5. Moderate to strong winds that veer with height, with large values in a narrow horizontal band (jet stream) at altitudes above 6 km. Such winds are associated with transition zones between cold and warm air masses, where severe thunderstorms most frequently form (Fig. 10.11). Strong low-level vertical wind shear and a low-level jet (around 850 mb) are also conducive to tornadoes.

In special cases threat areas smaller than the standard box can be defined through examination of hourly surface charts and of satellite photographs. Magor (1959) and Sasaki and Tegtmeier (1974) have shown how the detection of small-scale disturbances in the surface pressure and wind fields can aid tornado forecasting. A favored location for tornadoes is on the northeast side of developing small-scale lows and on the moist side of dryline bulges. Since tornadoes sometimes occur at the intersection of the leading edge of cold-air outflow, emanating from a group of storms, and another boundary (e.g., front), satellite photography can be used to foresee such intersections and hence to give precise short-range predictions of tornado development (Purdom, 1976). However, real-time recognition of the situation is often difficult.

Soundings taken near the times and locations of hurricane tornadoes show moisture through deep layers with only slight buoyant instability and pronounced vertical wind shear at low levels (Novlan and Gray, 1974; Gentry, 1983). Hill et al. (1966) detected dry intrusions at intermediate levels aloft into the circulations of tornado-producing hurricanes. This dry air aloft and the low-level shear are the main similarities with the classical Great Plains tornado environment.

Cold-air funnels are associated with thunderstorms that form in deep cold-core, synoptic-scale lows (Cooley, 1978). These funnel clouds are smooth and narrow. Their parent thunderstorms are high-based and not particularly tall or intense. In rare cases when their circulations do reach the ground, cold-air funnels cause only minor damage, and the public should not be unduly alarmed when it is under cold-core lows because the potential for really severe tornadoes is absent.

No attempts are made to predict waterspouts. Strong baroclinicity and vertical wind shear, characteristics of the synoptic conditions under which tornadoes occur, are absent from the area over southern Florida during the waterspout season (June–September) (Golden, 1974b). Furthermore, the waterspout environment is also less unstable with a less pronounced dry layer at intermediate levels. Favorable waterspout conditions are high surface temperature (~31°C) and dew point (~23°C), conditional instability, and the imminent passage of a weak trough line in the lower mean flow (easterlies or westerlies). The shallow coastal water (only 1 m deep over wide areas) is propitious since, during the late afternoon, solar heating can raise its temperature to as high as 32°C.

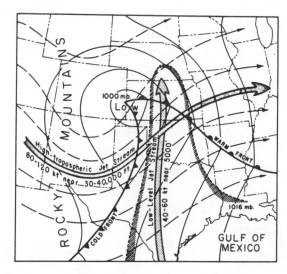

Figure 10.11. Schematic features of a severe-weather outbreak. Solid lines are sea-level isobars; dashed lines are streamlines of upper tropospheric flow; shading is the general area of moist tongue in lower levels associated with the region of potential instability (from C. Newton; cf. p. 81, Fig. 5.5).

8. Tornado Detection

Tornadoes are detected in various ways. National Weather Service offices receive reports of sightings by the general public and by trained spotters. After weighing the reliability of such reports, the local Weather Service Office may issue a tornado warning valid for one or more counties and for roughly 1 h. Observations by trained spotters are invaluable even in this age of remote sensors, because they still provide the basis for most warnings.

Warnings are also issued on the basis of radar observations. Hook-shaped echoes (Fig. 10.5) have been associated with tornadic storms, but unfortunately the correlation is far from perfect (Donaldson et al., 1975) Incidentally, the hook shape is indicative of rotation on the cloud scale, not the tornado scale. Other criteria exist for issuance of warnings based on the three-dimensional structure of radar echoes, and these are more reliable (Lemon, 1977).

The most promising detection device is the Doppler radar (Vol. 3, Chap. 10). This radar can measure the speed of precipitation targets toward or away from the radar antenna, as well as the reflectivity. Two types of vortex signatures are seen in the Doppler velocity fields (Burgess, 1976a; Brown et al., 1978). The vortical nature of the winds must be implied from shear patterns in the Doppler fields, since only one component of motion is measured.

The mesocyclone signature (Fig. 10.12) indicates a vortex with a core diameter of 3–9 km and maximum tangential velocities of 22 m s^{-1}. A bona fide mesocyclone must exhibit time and height continuity. Roughly 50% of identified mesocyclone signatures are associated with tornadoes,

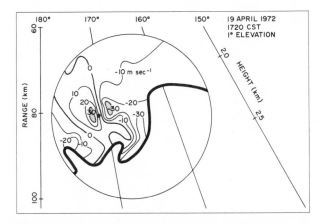

Figure 10.12. Single Doppler velocity field with mesocyclone signature at time of a tornado (black dot).

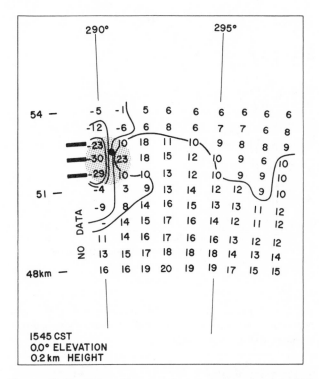

Figure 10.13. Union City tornadic-vortex signature (stippled) near the ground within the field of single Doppler mean velocities (m s^{-1}). Velocities are relative to TVS motion (10.0 m s^{-1} from 283°). Velocities away from radar are positive; those toward radar are negative. The dark dot is the surface-tornado position. Dark rectangles are relative sampling volume size. Azimuths and ranges are from the NSSL Doppler radar in Norman, Okla.

and the average lead time between mesocyclone identification and tornado touchdown is 20 min. The mesovortex is first detected at midlevels in the storm and with time extends toward the top and bottom of the storm. Most tornadoes (and all strong ones) occur in storms with mesocyclone signatures at 0° elevation. From 1972 to 1979 only 3 of the 143 mesoscale circulations detected at NSSL were anticyclonic, and all 3 failed to produce a tornado.

The tornadic-vortex signature (TVS; formerly known as GGS, i.e., *gate-to-gate shear*) is a small-scale, high-shear region associated with the tornado itself (Fig. 10.13). A true TVS must satisfy specified time and height continuity criteria. The radar beam is too wide to resolve a tornado core so that the TVS, or shear between two azimuthally adjacent sampling volumes, is ~5 × 10^{-2} s^{-1}, or roughly two orders of magnitude smaller than the maximum shear in a tornado. The TVS is first detected at midlevels and, like the mesocyclone, extends both upward and downward. It reaches cloud base coincident with funnel-cloud appearance and at low levels overlays the tornado damage track. In the Union City tornado the TVS tilted to the NNE with height (as did the tornado below cloud base) and was detected 23 min before tornado touchdown (Brown et al., 1978). This lead time is typical for strong tornadoes. Practically all TVS's are associated with tornadoes, but not all tornadoes are associated with detectable TVS's. The maximum ranges for mesocyclone signature and TVS recognition depend on circulation size and intensity and on radar antenna size. Because of their small, weak, shallow parent circulations, type A tornadoes are the most likely to occur without any indication on Doppler radar.

Another instrument used to detect tornadoes remotely is the *sferics detector* (Vol. 3, Chaps. 7 and 8; Taylor, 1975). This device is based on the correlation between the severity of storms and the rate of high-frequency electromagnetic emissions. During tests it was found that 80% of tornadoes within 70 km could be detected, but unfortunately the false-alarm rate was unacceptably high. Although only about 2% of nontornadic storms triggered the alarm, the high ratio

(100:1) of nontornadic to tornadic storms resulted in false alarms 7 times out of 10.

Despite much research, methods to identify tornadic storms from geosynchronous satellites are unproved operationally. Tornadoes generally occur after the collapse of the storm's overshooting top, but since this signature is not unique, it cannot be used for warnings (see Sec. 4). Other signatures are being developed, however, for satellite identification of severe thunderstorms (see Vol. 3, Chap. 12).

Another method of tornado detection involves correlating timely reports of major power-line breaks with radar (Shultz and Smith, 1972). Home barometric devices based on rapid pressure falls are inadequate, because only a few seconds elapse between the alarm and tornado passage.

9. Measurements of Tornado Parameters

The maximum windspeed and total pressure deficit are of extreme interest to engineers designing vital structures, such as nuclear-reactor housings, to withstand tornado passage. The magnitudes of these parameters, however, are not well known because tornadoes are difficult to intercept and

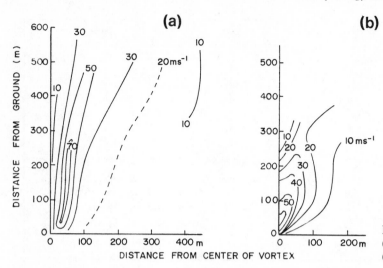

Figure 10.14. (a) Tangential and (b) vertical components (in m s^{-1}) of low-level velocities in 1957 Dallas tornado (after Hoecker, 1960).

extremely violent. Various methods, described below, have been used to estimate the windspeeds and other meteorological variables in tornadoes.

a. Photogrammetry

The motions of identifiable features (such as large debris, dust aggregates, and cloud tags) in close-range tornado motion pictures can be measured by use of photogrammetric techniques. Required knowledge is camera location, framing rate, a mapping of the damage track to determine the range from camera site to tornado, and azimuths and elevation angles of landmarks visible in the movie (Golden, 1976). The analysis measures directly those velocity components that are perpendicular to the camera's principal axis. If the camera axis is horizontal and the debris orbits are circular, then the tornado's vertical and tangential velocities can be deduced. However, this approach, employed by Hoecker (1960) for the 2 April 1957 Dallas tornado, assumes that the tracers perfectly delineate the airflow, whereas in reality solid debris (apart from fine dust) is centrifuged out of the vortex and settles. Hoecker applied a correction for fallspeed but not for centrifuging. Also, asymmetries in the flow caused by the vortex's tilt and other effects can bias the results. Hoecker's velocity fields (Fig. 10.14) were composited over 19 min of the tornado's lifetime, which is a long time for assumption of steady flow. Hoecker found a maximum tangential velocity of 75 m s^{-1} at a height of 70 m and a radius of 40 m, implying centripetal accelerations of 14 *g* (gravity). The maximum vertical velocity, 67 m s^{-1}, was located on the axis at a height of 40 m. The axial velocity decreased above this level to 0 near the tip of the funnel (300-m elevation). The results also indicated a narrow annular region of anticyclonic vorticity just outside the radius of maximum winds.

Given the tangential wind field just above the boundary layer, the maximum surface-pressure deficit can be computed cyclostrophically (defined in Sec. 15) and depends on air density and square of tangential velocity. For the Dallas tornado the lowest pressure was computed to be 60 mb below ambient (Hoecker, 1961). Hoecker also presented the geometrical configuration of the isobaric surfaces and the effect of changes in condensation pressure on funnel size and shape.

Motion pictures of several other tornadoes have also been analyzed. In the 17 April 1963 Kankakee, Ill., tornado, the maximum measured vertical velocity (80 m s^{-1}) was located more than 200 m from the axis and about 200 m above the ground (Goldman, 1965). Here the intense upward velocities are not confined to the core (i.e., to within the radius of maximum tangential winds). Golden and Purcell (1977) detected upward speeds of 60 m s^{-1} at 60 m above the ground in the 30 August 1974 Great Bend, Kans., tornado, implying upward accelerations of 3 *g* in the lowest 60 m. Rising motions decreased rapidly with elevation above 100 m. Another feature of the Great Bend tornado was a band of dust that flowed rapidly along the ground into the vortex. Speeds of 50 m s^{-1} were measured in this inflow. The presence of this dust band strongly suggests that low-level inflow into tornadoes is concentrated in a spiral jet rather than being axisymmetric.

In most tornadoes the highest measured tangential velocities were in the lowest 200 m. However, since tracers were frequently absent at higher elevations, this result may be regarded as tentative. In the 21 April 1974 Oshkosh, Wis., tornado, the highest rotational windspeeds were measured at, rather than below, cloud base (Blechman, 1975).

The Union City, Okla., tornado (24 May 1973) was filmed at close range in both its mature and shrinking stages (Golden and Purcell, 1978b). Maximum rotational windspeed decreased from 80 m s^{-1} in the mature stage to 65 m s^{-1} in the shrinking stage. The major difference between the two stages was the much smaller radius of maximum winds in the shrinking stage (25 m compared with 200 m), implying an order of magnitude decrease in circulation (Sec. 10).

Asymmetry in the vertical velocity fields around the funnel is frequently observed. Typically, cloud elements on the right-rear side of the tornado sink and evaporate, whereas fractus clouds, spiraling in toward the funnel on the left-front side, rise rapidly. This asymmetry seems to be associated partly with the tornado's tilt and partly with the slow intrusion of a rear-flank downdraft into the tornado's circulation (Lee et al., 1981).

Some large tornadoes for a time actually consist of several vortices (called *suction vortices*) in close proximity (Fig. 10.1d). Obtaining maximum windspeeds photogrammetrically is difficult because three basic motions are involved: the tornado's translation, the suction vortices' translation around the axis of the tornado, and rotation around the axes of individual suction vortices, which is the hardest to measure. For the 3 April 1974 Parker, Ind., multivortex tornado, Forbes (1976) obtained windspeeds in suction vortices of 127 m s^{-1} at 386-m elevation and 113 m s^{-1} at 150 m. On the same day a suction vortex in the Xenia, Ohio, tornado moved at 95 m s^{-1} (Golden, 1976). Maximum windspeeds in this tornado were undoubtedly higher, since motion around the suction vortex's axis was not measured.

Windspeeds at low levels in intense waterspouts attain tornadic values. Golden (1974a) has measured tangential velocities up to 85 m s^{-1} in the spray vortices of waterspouts. However, such high speeds occur very close to the axis (at roughly 10-m radius). Thus strong tornadoes differ from strong waterspouts not so much in extreme windspeeds as in circulation ($\sim 5 \times 10^4$ m^2 s^{-1} compared to $\sim 5 \times 10^{-3}$ m^2 s^{-1}). For more information on photogrammetric analyses of tornado movies, see Golden (1976), Forbes (1978), and Lee et al. (1981).

b. Ground Marks

Cycloidal marks, called suction marks (Fig. 10.15), are the most interesting and useful of the marks left by tornadoes crossing open fields (Fujita et al., 1970). Ground inspections reveal that they consist of short pieces of stubble laid in cycloidal rows about 15 cm high and 1.5 m wide. They are indicative of suction vortices rotating around the axis of the tornado, because the combination of straight line and circular motion yields a cycloidal path. The small pieces of debris are carried into the bases of these vortices by strong radial inflow very near the surface and are left behind in lines of litter trailing the vortices. A multivortex tornado passing through a city produces suction swaths of more intense damage. The suction vortices are particularly devastating because they locate maxima in the wind, pressure-deficit, and pressure-change fields.

The path of a suction vortex depends on the translation velocity of the parent tornado, the radial distance between the suction vortex and tornado axis, and the speed at which the suction vortex is moving around the tornado axis. The first two can be estimated from radar data and the observed size of the cycloidal loops, enabling the suction vortex's translation speed to be computed. Analyses of suction marks

have yielded speeds of 80 to 95 m s^{-1} (Fujita et al., 1970). These are low estimates of maximum windspeeds, because rotation around suction vortex axes is not taken into account. Analyses are complicated by difficulty in following single suction vortex paths because of erasure of part of the tracks by other vortices; in many cases the actual number of suction vortices is not clearly resolvable. Two to seven suction vortices may be present simultaneously. Suction vortices are transient, often dissipating before completing one revolution around the parent tornado's axis, with newly forming subvortices taking their place. Distances of suction vortices from their parent tornado's axis range from 50 to 300 m. The core diameters of suction vortices vary from 10 to 150 m. Three different types of multivortex tornadoes have been identified visually: (1) no central funnel, but several suction vortices of roughly equal size, made visible by condensation and debris, revolving around a common axis; (2) a central large funnel, with one or two smaller satellite funnels revolving slowly around it; and (3) a central funnel, with small-scale "dust" vortices embedded in the debris cloud. Types 2 and 3 can also give rise to suction marks; they differ from type 1 in that their vorticity is concentrated principally at the center of the system.

c. Direct Passages over Instruments

Anemometers are often blown away in tornadic conditions; when they survive, there is always the question whether they received the storm's full force. The highest value ever recorded was 67 m s^{-1} at Tecumseh, Mich., during one of the 1965 Palm Sunday tornadoes (Fujita et al., 1970).

Several recording microbarographs have been affected by tornadoes (Davies-Jones and Kessler, 1974). The largest pressure drop ever recorded with tornado passage, 22 mb, is small compared with theoretical values and, oddly, is less than the 34-mb pressure deficit recorded in the 1962 Newton, Kans., mesocyclone (see Fig. 10.8). Because pressure gradients are so intense in tornadoes, the low measured values may be attributed to instrument damping and sluggish response. Also, chances are slim that a microbarograph lies exactly in the path of lowest pressure. A 1953 Cleveland tornado passed within 200 to 700 m of nine barographs (Lewis and Perkins, 1953). The measured pressure profile was consistent with a potential vortex (defined in Sec. 10) of circulation 4.7 $\times$ 10^4 m^2 s^{-1}.

Since 1981 a specially designed, portable, instrumented package (TOTO; Bedard and Ramzy, 1983) has been placed in front of a few tornadoes (Bluestein, 1983). In spite of near misses, TOTO has not yet recorded a tornado passage.

d. Remote Sensing

An important tool for severe-thunderstorm research is the meteorological Doppler radar. This specialized radar measures the Doppler frequency shift caused by the component of radar target movement parallel to the radar beam. Two Dopplers spaced on a baseline 40 km or more apart and op-

Figure 10.15. Cycloidal ground marks left by the Anchor, Ill., tornado of 3 April 1974 (Fujita, 1974).

erated in unison are required to map two-dimensional flow patterns (e.g., Fig. 10.6), and three radars at the vertices of a triangle can detail three-dimensional flows.

At the National Severe Storms Laboratory two 10-cm wavelength, high-resolution pulsed Doppler radars are used (Wilk and Brown, 1975). Frequency shift information is recorded in separate sampling volumes, each one a truncated cone 150 m long, aligned along the 0.8°-wide radar beam. Both the mean velocity and the velocity spectrum are obtainable for each sample volume (see Vol. 3, Chap. 10).

The horizontal extent of a tornado core is smaller than the horizontal resolution of NSSL's Doppler radars. However, the maximum velocity within a radar sampling volume can be estimated by examining the velocity spectrum for that sampling volume (Zrnić and Doviak, 1975). Maximum windspeeds obtained by this method (up to 92 m s^{-1}) compare reasonably with photogrammetric values (Zrnić et al., 1977; Zrnić and Istok, 1980; Hennington et al., 1982).

Other instruments based on the same Doppler principle but portable may be used in the future to obtain windspeed measurements of tornadoes. These require close-range intercepts (Vol. 3, Chap. 2). The infrared Doppler lidar has the advantage of a narrow beam width but suffers from attenuation problems; it must be brought to within a few kilometers of the tornado to gain sufficient power return from the vortex. The lidar has already been used to obtain waterspout observations from an aircraft (Schwiesow et al., 1981;

Schwiesow, 1981). The maximum velocity detected by the lidar was 34 m s^{-1}. The waterspouts ranged from 4 to 50 m in core diameter. A 1-cm portable Doppler radar would have less angular resolution than a lidar, but its beam would not be as attenuated and would penetrate the tornado's dust cloud farther. Photogrammetry and Doppler techniques complement one another since the latter measures the line-of-sight velocity component and the former yields the transverse components.

e. Direct Probing

Because waterspouts are more frequent and can be approached more safely than can tornadoes, methods to introduce probes directly into tornadoes are field-tested first on waterspouts. From 1970 to 1974 a group from Purdue University attempted to measure pressure, temperature, humidity, and wind in waterspouts, using a specially designed drag body, which a light airplane towed diametrically through the vortices (Church and Ehresman, 1973). Because of many difficulties the measurements obtained were not completely satisfactory. One nagging doubt was whether the body passed through the periphery instead of the central core of the vortex. In a more recent experiment (Leverson et al., 1977) a small, highly stressed, instrumented aircraft was flown directly through the waterspout. The measurements indicated (1) tangential velocities up to 28 m s^{-1}, (2) pres-

tornado core occurs primarily through the lower part of the boundary layer and the corner region.

Vortices are destroyed by inflow from their ends. Vortex interaction with the lower surface places restrictions on low-level inflow. Aloft the vortex must terminate in a buoyant updraft (region IV), so that downflow into the core is also restricted (Morton, 1970). Large horizontal shears measured by Doppler radar suggest that the tornado sometimes reach great vertical extents (>10 km) (Brown et al., 1978; Lemon et al., 1982), although, presumably, the core spreads and tangential velocities decrease with height. However, in other cases the tornado signature disappears above 3 km (Brandes, 1981). Overall, the tornado generally tilts to the left of the storm-motion vector with height. The overall tilt is typically 25° from the vertical.

Since tornadoes must terminate somewhere aloft, they must spread laterally with height. Because of this spreading, the swirl and meridional (radial-axial) components of motion are coupled through the pressure field.

The different flow regions are discussed further by Morton (1970), Lewellen (1976), and Snow (1982). The reader is referred to Snow for a description of the vortex lines and flow characteristics in the various regions.

15. Theoretical Modeling

Theoretical treatments of vortices have generally been limited to axisymmetric, laminar flows in basically incompressible fluids. Most investigators have treated turbulent flows as if they were laminar by using a constant "eddy" coefficient of viscosity (which is several orders of magnitude larger than the molecular value for air to account for increased diffusion). Adiabatic changes of volume in the atmosphere are allowed for by substituting potential temperature, potential density, and a modified variable for temperature, density, and pressure in the equations. To simplify the equations, the Boussinesq approximation (that variations in potential density and potential temperature are relatively small and may be neglected except in the buoyancy term) is made. However, variations in potential density in the centrifugal-force term are important near a tornado's axis and should be taken into account. These assumptions limit us to the lowest 3 km of the atmosphere and to windspeeds of less than about 110 m s^{-1}. Latent-heat release and other effects caused by the presence of water substance are added complications that, although important, are not included here. Only axisymmetric vortex flows about vertical axes are considered. Equations for three-dimensional deep, moist convection are presented in Chapter 15.

The equations of motion, continuity, and heat transfer in cylindrical polar coordinates (r, θ, z) with velocity components (u, v, w) are

$$\frac{\partial u}{\partial t} + u\frac{\partial u}{\partial r} + w\frac{\partial u}{\partial z} - \frac{v^2}{r} - 2\Omega v$$

$$= -\frac{1}{\rho}\frac{\partial p}{\partial r} + \nu\left(\frac{\partial^2 u}{\partial r^2} + \frac{1}{r}\frac{\partial u}{\partial r} - \frac{u}{r^2} + \frac{\partial^2 u}{\partial z^2}\right), \quad (10.9)$$

$$\frac{\partial v}{\partial t} + u\frac{\partial v}{\partial r} + w\frac{\partial v}{\partial z} + \frac{uv}{r} + 2\Omega u$$

$$= \nu\left(\frac{\partial^2 v}{\partial r^2} + \frac{1}{r}\frac{\partial v}{\partial r} - \frac{v}{r^2} + \frac{\partial^2 v}{\partial z^2}\right), \quad (10.10)$$

$$\frac{\partial w}{\partial t} + u\frac{\partial w}{\partial r} + w\frac{\partial w}{\partial z} = -\frac{1}{\rho}\frac{\partial p}{\partial z} + \frac{gT'}{T_a}$$

$$+ \nu\left(\frac{\partial^2 w}{\partial r^2} + \frac{1}{r}\frac{\partial w}{\partial r} + \frac{\partial^2 w}{\partial z^2}\right), \quad (10.11)$$

$$\frac{1}{r}\frac{\partial}{\partial r}(ru) + \frac{\partial w}{\partial z} = 0, \quad (10.12)$$

and

$$\left(\frac{\partial}{\partial t} + u\frac{\partial}{\partial r} + w\frac{\partial}{\partial z}\right)T' + \frac{\partial T_a}{\partial z}w$$

$$= \kappa\left(\frac{\partial^2}{\partial r^2} + \frac{1}{r}\frac{\partial}{\partial r} + \frac{\partial^2}{\partial z^2}\right)T', \quad (10.13)$$

where the coordinate system is rotating with constant angular velocity, Ω (which, for atmospheric vortices, is the vertical component of the Earth's rotation rate), $P = p + \rho\Omega^2 r^2/2 - g\rho z$ is pressure, ρ and $T_a(z)$ are ambient values of density and temperature, T' is temperature deviation from T_a, and ν and κ are the eddy coefficients of viscosity and thermal diffusivity, usually assumed to be equal (note the difference between v and ν [Greek nu]).

We now consider analytical investigations of each of the flow regions described in Sec. 14. More detail is provided in the reviews by Hall (1966), Lewellen (1976), and Snow (1982).

a. Region I: The Core and Outer Flow

The following exact, steady-state solutions of these equations do not satisfy realistic boundary conditions but are nonetheless enlightening.

First, consider a homogeneous fluid (T_a = constant, T' = 0) in a nonrotating reference frame ($\Omega = 0$). The simplest solution is the combined Rankine vortex (see Sec. 10), where

$$u = w = 0,$$

$$v = \frac{\Gamma}{2\pi r} \quad \text{for } r > r_c,$$

and

$$v = \frac{\Gamma}{2\pi}\frac{r}{r_c^2} \quad \text{for } r \leq r_c. \quad (10.14)$$

The maximum tangential velocity, $v_{max} = \Gamma/2\pi r_c$, occurs at $r = r_c$, the core radius. This combination of inner solid-body rotation and outer potential-vortex flow satisfies Eq. 10.10 exactly except at the transition, $r = r_c$. This flow can be generated only by inserting a hollow, rotating cylinder into a fluid (Lugt, 1983).

Equations 10.9 and 10.11 reduce to cyclostrophic balance,

$$\frac{\partial P}{\partial r} = \frac{\rho v^2}{r}, \tag{10.15}$$

and hydrostatic balance,

$$\frac{\partial P}{\partial z} = -\rho g, \tag{10.16}$$

respectively. From Eqs. 10.14 and 10.15 we find that the axial pressure deficit owing to swirl is

$$\Delta p_\Gamma = \rho v_{max}^2, \tag{10.17}$$

and the largest radial pressure gradient,

$$\left(\frac{\partial p}{\partial r}\right)_{max} = \frac{\rho v_{max}^2}{r_c}, \tag{10.18}$$

is located at $r = r_c$. The combined Rankine vortex fits some measured tornadic-tangential flow profiles fairly well above the boundary layer (of course, the cusp at $r = r_c$ is smoothed out in actuality). Theoretically the radial pressure distribution at the top and bottom of the boundary layer should be very similar (except in the corner region), and hence we may use Eq. 10.18 to estimate the maximum rate at which surface pressure changes locally as a tornado moves toward a point at speed C. The resulting formula,

$$\left(\frac{\partial p}{\partial t}\right)_{max} = -C\frac{\rho v_{max}^2}{r_c}, \tag{10.19}$$

predicts that maximum rates of pressure fall are 10–100 mb s^{-1}.

The next simplest vortex-type solution to the equations is the Burgers (1948) and Rott (1958) "one-cell" vortex:

$$u = -ar,$$

$$v = \frac{\Gamma}{2\pi r}\left[1 - \exp\left(\frac{-ar^2}{2\nu}\right)\right],$$

$$w = 2az,$$

and

$$p(r, z) = p(0, 0) + \rho \int_0^r \frac{v^2}{r}\,dr - \frac{\rho a^2}{2}(r^2 + 4z^2), \tag{10.20}$$

where $2a$ (>0) is the (constant) horizontal convergence. The flow is driven by infinite excess pressure at $r = \infty$ or by infinite suction at $z = \infty$. Since u and v and the central pressure deficit are not functions of z, the streamlines in r–z planes are completely independent of circulation. This decoupling of the meridional and swirl flow is seldom achieved in reality, except in the limit of very small circulations. The controlling influence of a ground boundary layer on the flow is not represented, because only no-stress boundary conditions ($\partial u/\partial z = \partial v/\partial z = w = 0$) are satisfied at $z = 0$. Eddy viscous forces act only in the tangential direction and establish a core that rotates approximately as a solid body. The maximum tangential velocity, $v_{max} = 0.72\Gamma/2\pi r_c$, occurs at a radius $r_c = 1.12\sqrt{2\nu/a}$. The pressure deficit at the axis owing to circulation is $\Delta p_\Gamma = 1.68\rho v_{max}^2$.

Sullivan (1959) obtained a similar solution, but of a "two-cell" structure in which inner and outer "cells" are separated by the surface, $r_1 = 2.38\sqrt{2\nu/a}$. The axial-flow reversal (i.e., central downdraft) in this solution is not caused by the vortex flow since the swirl and updraft flows are decoupled. However, Morton (1969) demonstrated, for vortex flows that spread laterally with height, that the two flow components are closely coupled and that reversal should be expected, although the downdraft, driven by the downward pressure gradient force associated with the decrease in tangential velocity with height, may not reach the lower surface. One- and two-cell solutions are compared in Fig. 10.22. In a one-cell vortex fluid spirals in toward the axis and rises along it. In the two-cell case fluid spirals inward and upward in the outer cell, downward near the axis, and out and upward near the outer edge of the inner cell. Interestingly, the two flows are driven by the same axial pressure gradient, $-4\rho a^2 z$. For the same values of ambient convergence and circulation, the one-cell vortex has a smaller core, higher tangential speeds, and lower central pressure. Kuo (1966) found similar one- and two-cell solutions for vortices driven by latent-heat release in a conditionally unstable atmosphere. Kuo's model consists of two layers (subcloud and cloud). Saturation is maintained in the upper layer even in descending regions. Kuo's equations have the same form as Eqs. 10.9–10.13, with a modified equivalent potential temperature substituted for temperature to take latent-heat release into account. The large-scale convergence, specified as $2a$ in the Burgers-Rott and Sullivan solutions, is given by $\beta \equiv (-g\delta[lnT_a]/\delta z)^{1/2}$ in Kuo's solutions. With the equivalence, $\beta \equiv 2a$, Kuo's two-cell solution is similar to Sullivan's, but Kuo's vortex is more concentrated ($r_1 = 1.59[4\nu/\beta]^{1/2}$). Kuo's solution yields a maximum tangential velocity $v_{max} = 0.85\Gamma/2\pi r_c$ at a radius $r_c = 2.06(4\nu/\beta)^{1/2}$, and a circulation-associated central pressure drop $\Delta p_\Gamma = 1.14\rho v_{max}^2$. For Kuo's one-cell solution $v_{max} = 0.68\Gamma/2\pi r$, $r_c = 1.22(4\nu/\beta)^{1/2}$, and $\Delta p_\Gamma = 1.74\rho v_{max}^2$, and comparison with the Burgers-Rott results shows only small changes in numerical coefficients. These formulas are evaluated cautiously for a tornado by Davies-Jones and Kessler (1974).

In addition to previous criticisms of cylindrical vortex solutions, Kuo's two-cell vortex has another drawback: the downdraft in the center is cold—an unlikely circumstance, as explained in Sec. 13. All the above solutions predict that the radius of maximum tangential velocity is independent of circulation. This is a direct consequence of uncoupled meridional and swirl flows and conflicts with experimental observations (described in Sec. 16). Inviscid computations based on the realization that the convergent swirling flow cannot penetrate too close to the axis when only a finite amount of energy is available to drive the flow (because $v \propto r^{-1} \to \infty$ as $r \to 0$) correctly predict that the core radius of a turbulent vortex should increase with increasing circulation. This suggests that the inviscid interaction between swirl and

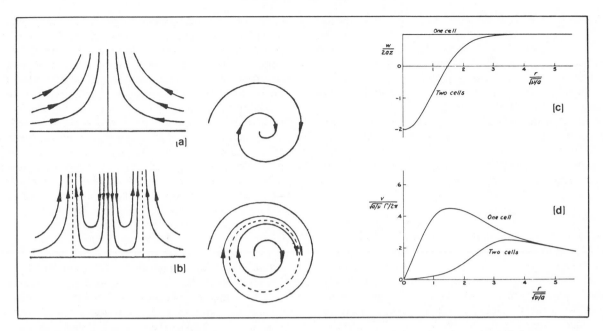

Figure 10.22. Sketches of projections of streamlines onto a vertical plane through the axis and a horizontal plane: (a) "one-celled" Burgers-Rott vortex; (b) "two-celled" Sullivan vortex. Velocity distributions as functions of radius: (c) axial velocity; (d) tangential velocity (Sullivan, 1959).

updraft may be more important than the balance between inward radial advection of angular momentum and its outward diffusion in determining the tornado's core size (Lewellen, 1976; Rotunno, 1977), especially since the turbulent transport of angular momentum may be inward (Sec. 9; Rotunno, 1978).

Long's (1958) solution and Morton's (1966) scale analysis of Eqs. 10.9–10.13, assuming a tall, thin, axisymmetric vortex that spreads slowly with height, demonstrated for the core region that (1) the cyclostrophic balance is valid, (2) vertical and tangential velocities are of the same order of magnitude while radial velocities are much smaller than either, and (3) swirling and updraft flows interact strongly. Lewellen (1976) concluded further that buoyancy in the core produced by latent-heat release in the funnel cloud is unimportant; the tornado must be driven from above by intense convection within the parent cloud (see also Smith et al., 1977).

A given solution for the vortex core may be unrealizable because the flow is unstable to small perturbations (see Davies-Jones and Kessler, 1974, for a concise introduction to this topic, including the analog with instability in stratified flows). Instability may lead to chaotic turbulence or to a new, highly ordered flow structure. Neglecting density differences and viscosity (which generally has a stabilizing effect), vortex flows of the type $u = 0$, $v = v(r)$, $w = 0$ are stable to axisymmetric disturbances if $\partial \Gamma^2 / \partial r \geq 0$, where $\Gamma(r)$ is the circulation, and unstable otherwise (proved mathematically by Rayleigh, 1916). The physical grounds for this "inertial" stability are given in Sec. 10. Vortex cores are inertially stable. Letting $w = w(r)$ in the analysis

leads to the conclusion that large radial shears in vertical velocity may be destabilizing (Howard and Gupta, 1962), perhaps explaining why some vortex cores are highly turbulent (Davies-Jones and Kessler, 1974), although breaking waves may be another reason (Rotunno, 1979).

Rayleigh (1916) also showed that the flow $u = 0$, $v = v(r)$, $w = 0$ is stable (may be unstable) to nonaxisymmetric perturbations with no axial dependence when the unperturbed vertical vorticity is (is not) a monotonic function of radius. This type of stability is known as *barotropic stability*. The one-cell vortex solutions given above are barotropically stable, but the two-cell vortices may be barotropically unstable since vertical vorticity is concentrated in an annular region of large shear between the cells. Such a region approximates a vortex sheet and thus might be expected to roll up into individual vortices when perturbed. Hence suction vortices may be the outgrowth of a barotropic instability (Davies-Jones and Kessler, 1974: Davies-Jones, 1976; Rotunno, 1978; Staley and Gall, 1979). Rotunno (1978) and Gall (1983) have shown that when three-dimensional perturbations and base state vertical velocity, $w = w(r)$, are admitted into the problem, the most unstable perturbation is always a helical one with negative pitch, i.e., in the opposite sense to the outer streamlines in Fig. 10.22b. Observations (Sec. 16) and Rotunno's (1982) numerical simulations reveal that suction vortices have a negative pitch, consistent with the stability analyses, and that they tend to be aligned with the local (helical) vortex lines of the azimuthally averaged flow. Rotunno (1978, 1982) also demonstrates that the perturbations transport angular momentum radially inward.

Another type of instability may be responsible for the unsteadiness and final decay of tornadoes after they have been stretched into a rope shape. At this stage the tornado does not retract into the clouds or diffuse outward. Instead, the funnel breaks up with clear gaps appearing at intervals along the funnel, as if an unstable wavelike disturbance has disrupted the flow. Widnall and Bliss (1971) have shown that a slender vortex containing axial velocity is unstable to long wavelength sinusoidal displacements of its center line.

The effect of density variations on stability has been treated by Leibovich (1969). As mentioned in Sec. 13, cold air in the core tends to destabilize the flow.

b. Region II: The Boundary Layer

Mathematical solutions for the boundary layer flow are extremely hard to obtain even for the simplest case, laminar (nonturbulent) flow beneath a potential vortex (Burggraf et al., 1971). Although tornado boundary layers are turbulent, laminar solutions probably yield the general flow characteristics. Inward radial velocities near the surface are of the same order as tangential velocities in region I. Penetration of boundary layer parcels closer to the axis may cause the maximum tangential velocity to be located in the corner region in spite of the angular momentum losses suffered by these parcels. Thus the maximum tangential velocity may be considerably higher than that predicted by cyclostrophic balance (Lewellen, 1976). The radial velocity maximizes in the lowest few meters. Next to the ground the flow may be strongly radial (Burggraf et al., 1971; Davies-Jones et al., 1978).

In the boundary layer solutions the vertical velocity in region I is initially unspecified and later computed from mass continuity. Weakly descending motion into the boundary layer is deduced in the outer portion of the vortex; within the core the boundary layer erupts upward in an intense jet in the corner region. These solutions, however, do not take into account free-stream convergence and vertical gradients, both of which may modify somewhat the above pictures of the flow.

Finally, it will be recalled from Sec. 10 that the boundary layer may exert considerable influence on the flow above it.

c. Region III: The Corner Flow

The corner region is extremely important because it joins the boundary layer with the core; unfortunately, it presents enormous theoretical difficulties. Some of its features have been discussed in the previous section. For weakly rotating updrafts the horizontal pressure gradient along the ground is adverse, and the outer flow separates from the surface and passes by the corner region, preventing the formation of a strong vortex near the ground (Rotunno, 1979). Stronger swirls lead to a favorable pressure gradient and elimination of the flow separation. As the swirl ratio (or overall ratio of swirl to updraft flow; see Sec. 16) is increased, the flow changes as depicted in Fig. 10.23. The vortex breakdown is particularly interesting (Hall, 1972; Leibovich, 1978). Vor-

tex breakdown refers to the abrupt change in the core structure of a vortex. There is a strong analogy between rotating and stratified flows (Davies-Jones and Kessler, 1974), with vortex breakdown as the counterpart of hydraulic jump. Upstream of (or below) the breakdown, the flow consists of a high-velocity, rapidly swirling jet. The core flow undergoes an abrupt transition to a new, larger diameter with lower axial and swirl velocities. Above the breakdown point, flow along the axis is reversed, turbulence levels are higher, and the central pressure deficit is smaller. Below the breakdown point, the flow is supercritical, i.e., inertia waves propagate only in the downstream direction, while above it the flow is subcritical, i.e., waves are able to progress upstream (but not past the breakdown). The upper flow may be axisymmetric or assume the form of a single or double helix (Sarpkaya, 1971). Breakdowns occur when the swirl ratio passes a critical value of order one. Laboratory investigations have shown that, although breakdowns may occur anywhere along the core, the corner region is a favored location. Sometimes the downstream flow becomes supercritical again with the subcritical flow confined to a bubble-shaped enlargement of the core. In such cases a second breakdown may occur downstream of the first. It is uncertain whether vortex breakdowns actually occur in tornadoes; however, photogrammetric data (Hoecker, 1960; Golden and Purcell, 1977; Sec. 9a) as well as funnel shapes (Fig. 10.24; Burggraf and Foster, 1977), strongly suggest that they do.

According to Maxworthy (1973), the vortex breakdown acts as a "buffer zone" through which incompatible upstream and downstream boundary conditions can be matched.

Rare observations of tornadoes with condensation filaments near the ground, which are unconnected to cloud base above, may be explained by postulating the presence of vortex breakdown, because lowest dynamic pressures occur below the breakdown point. At larger swirl ratios the central downdraft penetrates to the surface, and the breakdown is eliminated.

d. Region IV: The Top Layer

Because vorticity tends to be transported along streamlines, the tornado probably extends to near the top of its parent updraft. The dynamics of a concentrated vortex in a decelerating flow dictate that if the axial velocity surrounding the vortex is brought to rest then the flow along the axis should be reversed (Hall, 1966; Lewellen, 1976). Thus at the top of a swirling updraft (i.e., in region IV) there should actually be a secondary downdraft along the axis of rotation (Fig. 10.25). In Sec. 12 it was argued that a rotating updraft should not overshoot its equilibrium level; here we see that there may even be a visible crater at the top of a rotating storm if the parent updraft extends this high. Lilly (1976) suggested that the axial pressure gradient may force the warm, dry air all the way down to a low-level vortex breakdown. This process would lead to a hydrostatic reduction of

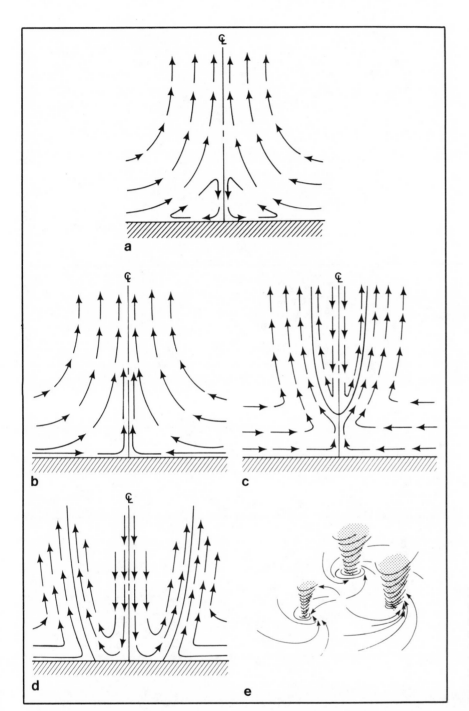

Figure 10.23. Effect of increasing swirl ratio on vortex flow. (a) Weak swirl—flow in boundary layer separates and passes around corner region; (b) one-cell vortex; (c) vortex breakdown; (d) two-cell vortex with downdraft impinging on ground (core radius increases rapidly with increasing swirl ratio); (e) multiple vortices. The connected CL indicates the centerline.

Figure 10.24. Photographs of Jordan, Iowa, tornado of 13 June 1976. (Above) Tornado with nearly conical funnel, looking WSW.

Figure 10.24. *Continued.* Tornado a short time later with bulge on visible core (photographs by Jim Bruzek; Burggraf and Foster, 1977).

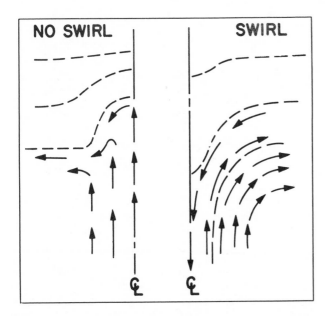

Figure 10.25. Qualitative effect of swirl on updraft capped by stable temperature stratification. Dashed lines are potential temperature isolines; arrows are direction of flow (Lewellen, 1976).

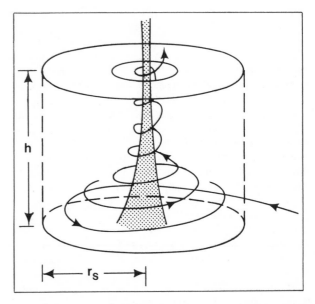

Figure 10.26. Flow in a vortex chamber. The fluid enters with a tangential velocity component, spirals inward, and exits axially at a smaller radius.

surface pressure and would allow tornadic winds below the breakdown to approach the thermodynamic limit described in Sec. 12. How far this downdraft extends is not known, but this process is an energy-consuming one, since the descending air warms dry-adiabatically and becomes increasingly buoyant.

16. Laboratory Simulations

Laboratory models aim to isolate the essential ingredients believed important for tornado maintenance while of necessity dramatically simplifying and idealizing the actual flow. Realistic-looking vortices can be produced easily in the laboratory with very simple equipment. All apparatuses work by concentrating vorticity (usually produced artificially) through convergence. No model can be expected to resemble the tornado in every respect, but attention must be paid to comparisons of the experiments and nature to discover whether the laboratory results are relevant. Appearance alone is insufficient to justify relevancy; model flows must also be geometrically and dynamically similar to tornadoes. In most cases vertical vorticity is supplied to the flow. Thus the experiments are more relevant to the actual flow structure of tornadoes than to their ultimate source of rotation (Sec. 13). Controlled experiments which model vortex formation by vertical drafts in a vertically sheared environment have been developed minimally owing to technical difficulties.

The two most common types of apparatus are the rotating tank and the vortex chamber. Rotating-tank experiments (Long, 1956; Turner and Lilly, 1963) are conducted in tall cylinders containing water placed on variable-speed rotating turntables. Meridional flow in the container is driven by withdrawing fluid from the axis at either the bottom or the top of the cylinder and readmitting it at the outer rim or by injecting buoyant fluid along the axis.

Vortices can also be produced in nonrotating tanks through amplification of the Earth's vorticity, if great care is taken to ensure that the fluid's relative vorticity is insignificant compared with the Earth's vorticity before the drain is opened and that the draining rate is sufficiently slow (Shapiro, 1962).

The vortex chamber (Fig. 10.26) is a cylindrical container with plane end walls. Fluid enters the apparatus at the curved wall with a tangential motion component, spirals radially inward, and is extracted axially through an end wall at some smaller radius. Alternatively, the meridional flow may be driven by buoyant convection.

The vortex chamber has been used extensively for both engineering and geophysical investigations. The flow is a function of r_s, h (both defined in Fig. 26), r_0 (the exhaust radius), $2\pi Q$ (the volume flow rate through the apparatus), $2\pi M$ (the circulation at the outer wall), and ν (the kinematic viscosity of the fluid). Only four independent nondimensional numbers exist: r_0/r_s; h/r_0 ($\equiv a$, the aspect ratio); $r_0 M/(2Q)$ ($\equiv S$, the swirl ratio); and $Q/(\nu h)$ ($\equiv N$, the radial Reynolds number). Physically, S is a measure of the ratio of the tangential velocity at the exhaust radius, r_0, to the mean vertical velocity, $\bar{w}$, through the exhaust. Another nondimensional number we refer to is Θ, the angle of inflow at the porous wall measured with respect to the radial (tan Θ $\equiv hM/Q$).

Most engineering studies have concentrated on flows with high swirl ratios, where the through flow is diverted into the end-wall boundary layers, and the lower boundary layer flow turns upward near the axis into the vortex core and exits through the exhaust.

In tornado simulators the swirl ratio should be much smaller, of order one (Davies-Jones, 1973). Most simulators work at Reynolds numbers high enough for the surface boundary layer and vortex core to be turbulent. When the flow is laminar, the core radius varies inversely as the square root of the circulation. In contrast, core radius increases with circulation for turbulent flow.

Ying and Chang (1970) found good agreement between boundary layer profiles of u and v measured in their vortex chamber and the theoretical profiles for the turbulent boundary layer beneath a potential vortex. The maximum inward velocity occurred very close to the ground. The boundary layer tangential velocity increased with height monotonically to its asymptotic free-stream value.

Ward (1972) pointed out that in tornadic thunderstorms the updraft producing the convergent wind field is an order of magnitude larger than the width of the tornado damage track (typically, 5 km versus 0.5 km). Also, the converging layer of warm, moist air supplying the thunderstorm may be no more than 2 km in depth. A tornado-producing rotating cumulonimbus cloud (tornado cyclone) seen at close range by the author supports Ward's statements. All the evidence suggests that this cloud outlined a large, intense updraft (~ 5 km in diameter), supplied by inflow ~ 1 km deep (Davies-Jones et al., 1976). The tornado was less than 100 m in diameter. Ward's model simulated the tornado flow field geometry more realistically than other models, because r_0/r_s could be varied from $\frac{1}{8}$ to $\frac{1}{2}$ and a from 0.25 to 2.7 (in other models the exhaust radius is small compared with the height and radius of the vortex chamber; however, there is no evidence for the existence of a sink of limited horizontal extent in the vicinity of tornadoes). Ward's model is unique in that it is capable of duplicating a wide range of tornadic vortices (Church and Snow, 1979).

Davies-Jones (1973) showed that the swirl ratio for tornado cyclones is of order one, as is the case for Ward's model. Since the swirl and aspect ratios of tornado cyclones lie within the experimental range, the model has bearing on tornadoes. Of course, the Reynolds number for the model was orders of magnitude less than tornadic values. Fortunately, the flow was relatively insensitive to the Reynolds number at the high Reynolds numbers used.

In Ward's tornado simulator (Fig. 10.27) an exhaust fan at the top created convective flow. Air flowed into a confluent zone through a rotating screen before entering the convective chamber, where it rose and exited the apparatus through a fine-mesh honeycomb. The intent was to model a rotating thunderstorm updraft, with its inflow concentrating ambient vertical vorticity near the axis. The inflow was confined to low levels in the apparatus because in severe-storm environments midlevel air is dry and offers resistance to vertical

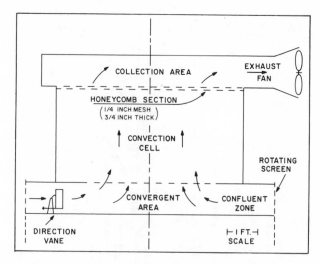

Figure 10.27. Vertical section of Ward's apparatus.

lifting. The honeycomb prevented fan-induced vorticity from entering the apparatus. It also removed the rotation from the outflow, thereby divorcing the vortex from the fan by distributing the pressure deficit relatively evenly over the top of the chamber and exposing the top of the vortex to overlying, nonrotating flow (as must be the case, although less abruptly, in the atmosphere). Because of this annulment of the central pressure deficit at the top, the axial flow was downward through the honeycomb. This downflow ended at an axial stagnation point below which the vortex core was laminar and upflowing (Fig. 10.28). Above the stagnation point the core was turbulent and bulged out. This transition is a vortex breakdown.

The swirl ratio, S, measures the relative strengths of circulation and forced convection. Davies-Jones; (1973) found that the turbulent-core radius, nondimensionalized by r_0, the updraft radius, was primarily a function of swirl ratio alone. For $S \lesssim 0.04$ no vortex formed. As the swirl ratio was progressively increased, the stagnation point descended down the axis until it reached the surface and the radius of the turbulent core increased rapidly from 0.01 r_0 to 0.3 r_0. For $a \lesssim 2$, the single-vortex flow underwent transition to a two-vortex configuration at some critical swirl ratio in the range 0.45 to 0.7 (depending on the Reynolds number). The vortices formed on opposite sides of the parent vortex near the radius of maximum tangential windspeed, and the pair rotated around the central axis at about one-half that speed, since each was in the velocity field of the other. Similar tornado pairs have been observed (Fig. 10.29). By further increasing the swirl ratio, three and four vortices were obtained, corresponding either to multiple tornadoes in a mesocyclone or, on a smaller scale, to suction vortices in a tornado (see Fig. 10.1e). The multiple vortices may be a manifestation of an instability (as discussed in Sec. 15a). They are wrapped around the central axis with a negative

Figure 10.28. Laboratory vortex enlargement associated with transition from laminar to turbulent flow.

pitch in agreement. with theory (Sec. 15a) and observations of type 1 multivortex tornadoes (Sec. 9b).

The model also featured a surface pressure profile characteristic of tornadoes. The high-pressure ring surrounding the core was explained by inflow deceleration giving rise to a local speed minimum. Barograph recordings of tornado and tornado cyclone passages often show such pressure peaks (Fig. 10.8). With increasing inflow angle the peaks disappeared because of increasing dominance of tangential over radial flow. An improved and larger version of Ward's model has been built at Purdue University, and a more precise description of the behavior of the model has been provided by Church et al. (1977, 1979), Church and Snow (1979), and Church (1982). For example, they documented asymmetries in the flow above the vortex breakdown with first a single and then a double helix appearing as the swirl ratio is increased. The helices were located between the leading breakdown and a second breakdown point downstream at moderate swirl ratios. This region is eliminated at higher swirls as the breakdown points reach the surface.

The Purdue investigators have made limited velocity measurements (Baker and Church, 1979) and extensive pressure measurements, both at the surface (Snow et al., 1980; Pauley et al., 1982) and aloft (Church and Snow, 1983). The peak windspeed in the core for turbulent vortices is roughly proportional to the mean vertical velocity through the updraft hole, $\bar{w}$. The azimuthally averaged surface pressure field has the following characteristics: The lowest pressure is at the center for one-celled vortices but is located in a ring off center for two-celled vortices, which have a slight local pressure maximum at the center. For fixed geometry and volume flow rate (but varying circulation), the largest radial pressure gradients are found in one-celled vortices, while the maximum pressure deficit, Δp, occurs for the value of swirl ratio, S_T at which the leading breakdown point (separating laminar and turbulent core flow) reaches the surface. As S increases beyond S_T, Δp decreases because the vortex core expands rapidly enough to overcompensate the increase in circulation. Although Δp increases once more at swirls beyond the transition to multiple vortices, the deficit never reaches the value attained at S_T. Varying the geometry and flow rate leads to the conclusion that Δp is roughly proportional to $\rho \bar{w}^2$. Pressure was also measured in the individual vortices when multiple vortices were present. The pressure deficits in the secondary vortices are two to three times greater than elsewhere in the parent vortex, but still less than the deficit at S_T.

The variation of central pressure with height was also investigated. For laminar vortices central pressure decreases rapidly with height near the surface and then becomes constant. The maximum pressure deficit (aloft), Δp_m, depends on the cube of circulation, since $\Delta p_m \sim \rho v_{max}^2 \sim \rho \Gamma^2 r_c^{-2}$ and $r_c \propto \Gamma^{-1/2}$ for laminar vortices. The strong upward pressure gradient force near the surface provides the upward acceleration for air in the corner region. At the surface p shows a slight decline with increasing Γ and is a factor of seven less than the pressure deficit aloft in the most extreme case. For vortices with a breakdown in the convergent area (see Figs. 10.27, 10.28) Δp decreases abruptly with height above the breakdown. The largest surface deficit is associated with the situation where the breakdown has just reached the surface, and in this case Δp declines rapidly with height. At circulations beyond this transition to a two-cell turbulent vortex at the surface, the surface deficit is less, but Δp declines little with height.

A parallel study showing how v_{max} depends on Γ would be valuable since Eq. (10.17) does not provide a reliable estimate of v_{max} for several reasons (e.g., ρw^2 makes a significant contribution to p for laminar vortices, and the core does not rotate as a solid in two-celled vortices).

The flow behavior in Ward-type chambers has been investigated theoretically by Davies-Jones (1973), Baker and Church (1979), Gall (1982), and Raymond and Kuo (1982). Valuable numerical simulations have been provided by Harlow and Stein (1974) and Rotunno (1977, 1979, 1982).

Using a different type of apparatus, Maxworthy (1972) demonstrated the importance of vortex breakdown and how the vortex flow can be disrupted by introducing perturbations. His work may suggest means of tornado modification.

Other experimenters have used convective rather than mechanical means to drive the meridional flow. Several experiments have shown that a vortex extending the whole depth of the apparatus can be driven by buoyancy forces acting at upper levels. Thus unstable air near the ground and condensation in the funnel are not necessary for tornado formation.

Figure 10.29. (Above) Laboratory vortex pair compared with (below) turbulent double tornado on 11 April 1965 at Elkhart, Ind. (lower photo by Paul Huffman, looking NW; Fujita et al., 1970).

The meridional circulation in Turner and Lilly's (1963) experiment was driven by the drag of rising gas bubbles released by dropping suitable nuclei in carbonated water. Thus buoyancy was produced by changes of phase in the fluid itself and so was akin to the release of buoyancy by condensation in the atmosphere. The life history of the model vortex bore some resemblance to that of tornadoes.

With a large number of nuclei and a large amount of gas in solution, the vortex was quite thick and regular, but as the nucleating agent dissolved or the gas supersaturation decreased, the vortex became slender, ropelike, and helical, with waves traveling down the core, much like the appearance of a tornado in its decay stage.

In Emmons and Ying's (1967) experiment, rotation decreased entrainment into a fire plume by an order of magnitude, thereby reducing the amount of oxygen available for combustion and giving rise to a greatly increased length of flame.

Dessens (1972) investigated the influence of surface roughness on laboratory vortices. He used very rapid rotation rates so that the flow was rotation-dominated. Comparison of rough and smooth "ground" experiments showed that roughness increased core diameter, boundary layer convergence into the vortex, and updraft speed but decreased tangential velocity, central pressure deficit, and (by implication) overall destructiveness. These findings agree with Golden's (1968) visual description of a waterspout crossing an island and with some numerical simulations (Bode et al., 1975).

Leslie (1977) found, using Ward's model, that the critical swirl ratio for transition to a greater number of vortices increases with greater surface roughness. Thus multivortex tornadoes are more likely to occur over smooth surfaces than over rough ones. In subsequent work Leslie (1979) found that in Ward's apparatus increasing surface roughness yielded smaller core diameters (contrary to Dessens's results). Pauley et al. (1982) found that surface roughness decreased the maximum pressure deficit in the Purdue chamber.

In summary, laboratory models have given insight into the types of vortices that occur, the flow and vortex diameter dependencies on external parameters such as swirl ratio, and the role of vortex breakdown. Davies-Jones (1976) and Maxworthy (1982) have presented more detailed reviews of this subject.

17. Numerical Simulations

Numerical vortex models have generally been restricted to axisymmetric simulations of laboratory experiments with closed flows (Leslie, 1971; Bode et al., 1975; Wilkins et al., 1974) or open flows (Harlow and Stein, 1974; Rotunno, 1977, 1979), or with convective processes of limited depth in a swirling atmosphere (e.g., Mal'bakhov and Gutman, 1968, 1972; Eskridge and Das, 1976; Smith and Leslie, 1978, 1979; Leslie and Smith, 1978, 1982). Typically the models have been developed in support of one or other of the theories discussed in Sec. 13 (see Lewellen, 1976, for a more in-depth review of numerical simulations).

Laboratory experiments with closed circulations are the simplest to model because of the well-defined boundary conditions. The choice of appropriate boundary conditions and initial conditions for open flows is crucial to the model's realism, because the outcome depends critically on the history of the flow. When attempting to model an actual tornado, the modeler may decide to simulate the whole vortex or just its lower regions. In either case, defining suitable boundary conditions for the sides and top of the computational domain demands considerable thought. A complication is that the tornado is not an isolated flow but is embedded in a thunderstorm, and we have limited insight into how the tornado and thunderstorm interact. Results also depend on choice of the numerical scheme and system of equations.

So far, although the models have revealed interesting features of vortex flows, none of them can realistically be claimed to model a tornado because of deficiencies in the equations or in the initial and boundary conditions. Most investigators have assumed constant eddy viscosity. Hence the effect of rotation in reducing entrainment into a jet is absent from their models. Lewellen and Sheng (1980) developed a model with a more sophisticated parameterization of turbulence. The maximum velocity in their model was located in the corner region.

Rotunno (1982) achieved the first successful simulation of the multiple-vortex phenomenon in an asymmetric simulation of Ward's vortex chamber. The peak tangential velocity in the multiple vortices was 20 to 30% higher than the maximum tangential velocity of the azimuthally averaged flow.

Numerical simulations of a mesocyclone, the parent circulation, have been achieved (Klemp and Wilhelmson, 1978; Schlesinger, 1978; Chap. 15). Modeling a three-dimensional cumulonimbus cloud (i.e., without assuming either line or axial symmetry) requires an advanced computer because of model size, the intricacies of deep compressible convection, and the complex interactions of dynamics, thermodynamics, and cloud physics. Model results have established that the tilting of horizontal vorticity into the vertical is an important rotation source for mesocyclones (see Sec. 11). Simulated storms compare favorably with observed storms under the same environmental conditions (Klemp et al., 1981).

Klemp and Rotunno (1983) used a "nested-model" approach to improve the resolution of the Klemp-Wilhelmson model in the mesocyclone region. The horizontal resolution was reduced by one-fourth to 250 m in the nested model, which, being of limited horizontal extent, derived its lateral boundary conditions from the coarser model. The smaller-domain model was run for 6 min in the life of the storm and produced a higher-resolution vorticity field which bore encouraging resemblance to observed storm features. The mesh is still not fine enough to resolve a tornado, however.

The success enjoyed by the three-dimensional models in simulating supercell storms in spite of an imperfect parameterization of turbulence is attributed to helicity by Lilly (1983). Helicity is the scalar product of storm-relative velocity and vorticity and is high in a supercell storm (where vertical vorticity and vertical velocity are positively correlated) and its environment (where the vorticity tends to be streamwise; Sec. 11). Helicity inhibits the normal cascade of energy from large scales to small scales and thus makes the numerical results less dependent on the parameterization of subgrid-scale turbulence.

Another use of numerical methods is in the so-called retrieval of thermo-dynamical and microphysical variables from Doppler-radar-observed wind fields. Given the wind field and appropriate boundary conditions, equations are solved numerically to obtain storm-scale fields of temperature, pressure, etc. More details of this technique are provided in Vol. 3, Chap. 13.

18. Outlook for Modification

Up to this point I have explained what is currently known about tornadoes and what kinds of projects are under way to increase our understanding. Vortices, in general, are poorly understood even though they are present in numerous engineering problems. In the atmosphere concentrated vortices appear to depend on unstable stratification and enhanced background vorticity for their creation and maintenance. This view is supported by observations of substantial vortices near erupting volcanoes and in large fires under favorable atmospheric stratification and wind shear (Morton, 1966; Church et al., 1980).

Too little is known about tornadoes at this stage to attempt to modify them; the entire sequence of events leading to their formation is still not understood, and their flow fields have yet to be described adequately. However, I shall close by describing some of the more practical modification possibilities (see also Chap. 16).

One proposal is based on the idea that vortices tend to weaken over rougher surfaces because of reduction of net low-level inflow. This theory is supported by some modeling results (see Sec. 16) and observations of waterspouts coming ashore. Waterspouts and tornadoes often break up on encountering cliffs. The base is arrested, while the upper part continues forward; the vortex is stretched longitudinally into a rope shape, becomes unstable, and dissipates (Hardy, 1971). Multivortex tornadoes may revert to single-vortex structures over rough terrain (Blechman, 1975). The 10 April 1979 Wichita Falls tornado contained multiple vortices over flat countryside on either side of the city but appeared to be a single large vortex as it passed over the rougher surface of the city. Artificial mounds and ridges might protect cities somewhat, but other significant observations indicate that intense tornadoes would penetrate

such defenses. For example, Fujita (1974) has documented a tornado that climbed a 500-m ridge and crossed a deep canyon, uprooting trees continuously. Baker *et al.* (1982) associated a sudden increase in surface roughness with a transient increase in a tornado's destructiveness.

Modification by cloud seeding is another possibility (Davies-Jones and Kessler, 1974). Through warm-cloud seeding, the growth of precipitation particles might be accelerated. A resulting accumulation of large particles would produce increased drag and intensify the storm's downdraft and low-level outflow. The spreading cool air might overtake the vortex and cut off its warm, moist inflow, thereby bringing about its premature demise.

Another suggestion is to produce a cirrus cloud deck artificially, using jet aircraft contrails (NOAA, 1974). The presence of the high clouds would reduce surface heating significantly and hence tornado potential. This method might eliminate some tornadoes, but not all, because many tornadoes, occurring after dark or under widespread overcast skies, do not require warming of the atmosphere's lowest layers.

Finally, the creation of a low-level disturbance (explosion) in the tornado core might permanently disrupt the vortex (Maxworthy, 1972, 1973; Chang, 1976). This technique, successful in laboratory simulators, might run into many legal as well as logistical obstacles if attempted in field experiments. Maxworthy (1972) also discusses the use of jets to produce boundary layer disturbances which would propagate inward and disrupt the core flow.

Any efforts to modify a severe storm having potential or actual tornadoes will obviously have to be carried out with extreme caution, and it would be wise to experiment first with waterspouts, which are less threatening and are more amenable to scientific studies. Actual attempts to modify menacing tornadoes are probably many years away. In the meantime, we should mitigate losses by seeking improved building codes and construction practices. Also we should continue researching the dynamics of tornadoes, their parent storms, and storm-environment interactions.

11. Hailfall and Hailstorm Characteristics

Griffith M. Morgan, Jr., and Peter W. Summers

1. Introduction

A severe hailstorm is, for most first-hand observers, a singular and memorable event. It is singular because in many places it hardly ever occurs, and it is rare even in the so-called hail belts. It is memorable because of the sudden transformation to a winter landscape in the middle of summer and because of the spectacular damage inflicted on crops and property by ice missiles up to several centimeters in diameter falling at speeds up to 45 m s^{-1}.

There are, however, several regions in the world where hail does occur regularly every summer with annual point frequencies of between 3 and 10 occurrences. These areas cover only a small fraction of the Earth's surface, but some of these are in prime agricultural areas, and the frequency and severity of hail often become determining factors in the success or failure of many farming operations. The two largest contiguous areas are in the Northern Hemisphere. One is in the upper Great Plains of North America, extending for more than 2,000 miles from the Canadian provinces of Alberta and Saskatchewan southward across the Dakotas, Nebraska, Colorado, and Kansas to Oklahoma and Texas. The other major region extends from southern France across Switzerland, southern Germany, northern Italy, Austria, Yugoslavia, Bulgaria, and Romania into vast areas of the Caucasus region in the USSR. In the Southern Hemisphere the main areas affected are Mendoza Province of Argentina and northeastern South Africa.

The regions with a high frequency of damaging hailstorms are thus mostly in middle latitudes and downwind of high mountain ranges. The ranges organize airflows both at lower levels and in the upper troposphere in a way that is frequently conducive to the formation and persistence of hailstorms.

Hail frequency drops off rapidly toward the poles. In the tropics thunderstorms are very frequent, but any associated hail occurs mostly at high elevations and only very rarely at low elevations. The true frequency of hail in the tropics is hard to ascertain owing to a paucity of observations (Frisby and Sansom, 1967). Although tropical thunderstorms are not nearly as serious agriculturally as those in middle latitudes, they can cause severe damage locally to sensitive crops such as tea, coffee, and tobacco.

Some west-coast areas of the world receive hail showers most frequently in spring. The hail is generally small (<1-cm diameter), often in the form of graupel or soft hail (see Huschke, 1959), but it can cause severe damage to fruit trees in the flowering or fruit-setting stage. Examples of regions with this problem are Washington, Oregon, and northern California and, in the Southern Hemisphere, Tasmania and North Island of New Zealand.

Annual crop losses caused by hail in the United States alone have been estimated at $685 million in 1973 prices (Boone, 1974). Conversion to 1978 prices and addition of hail losses in Canada indicate that total crop loss from hail in North America was about $1 billion annually in the late 1970s. Losses in Europe and Asia are probably of the same magnitude as those in North America.

Worldwide annual crop losses caused by hail represent about 1% of the total agricultural production. Losses caused by diseases, pests, or drought in any given year far exceed this amount. However, there is a very important psychological aspect of hail-incurred losses. Drought afflicts all farms over large regions more or less equally, but in hailstorms a few farms can suffer total loss while neighbors go unscathed. Thus a farmer's perception of hail and his reaction to hail suppression are based very much on personal experience, which leads to much of the controversy and emotionalism surrounding efforts at artificial hail suppression in many parts of the world.

Attempts to alleviate crop losses caused by hail have an interesting and colorful history (Morgan, 1973). The modern era of weather modification began with the discovery by Langmuir and Schaefer (Schaefer, 1946) that ice formation could be artificially stimulated in clouds (see Chap. 16), which led to a rapid expansion of research in cloud physics. The study of hail received special emphasis because of the large economic benefits that would accrue from successful hail suppression.

There are several other reasons for studying hail. There is, of course, the curiosity of natural scientists that has stimulated the study of interesting and important physical phenomena through the ages. Hailstones are clearly in this category. Hail is a form of precipitation, and its variation in time and space is one of the elements of the climate of a region. The detailed study of the structure and growth characteristics of individual hailstones, as described in Chap.

12, can give useful information about the environment in which hailstones form and grow in thunderstorms. Thus in a way they act as a sensor of conditions in a region where it is very difficult to obtain direct cloud microphysical measurements. Finally, hail is an important product of many thunderstorms, and measurements of hailfall amounts are essential for gaining a better description and understanding of the overall water budgets of thunderstorms.

Some of the more useful references covering the climatology of hail include Flora's (1956) classic, the first comprehensive description of hailfall observations in the United States and around the world. This work describes in great detail many spectacular hailfalls in terms of hailstone sizes, accumulated amounts, and the extensive crop and property damage that has been sustained in the United States, state by state, and many other places. Frisby and Sansom (1967) constructed a climatology of hail in the tropics from all available observations taken by the meteorological services. Changnon (1977) presents an in-depth description of the various spatial and temporal scales of hailfall using the data obtained from several mesoscale networks operated in recent years. Other useful works covering the broader aspects of hail are by Geneve (1961), Weickmann (1964), Chisholm and English (1973), Foote and Knight (1978), and Douglas (1963).

2. Characteristics of Hailstones

In Chap. 12, List provides a detailed physical description of the properties of individual hailstones and some insight into their growth characteristics. Such meticulous analysis can be done on only a small sample of stones preserved in a cold room. In contrast, this section describes the properties of hailstones deduced from large numbers of stones collected in several places around the world.

a. The Largest Possible Hailstone

Early accounts of the sizes of hailstones were uncritically accepted and became part of the lore of hailstorms. For example, Buist (Gibson, 1861) passed on a report of a hailstone in India "the size of an elephant." Another was "20 ft. in diameter." The authenticity and credibility of such reports must be seriously challenged, but the question of what is truly the largest hailstone ever to fall remains unanswered.

Approaching credibility is the hailstone that fell in 1925 in Germany and was reported by Talman (1936) to have measured 26 × 14 × 12 cm. Its weight was estimated from its dimensions as 2.04 kg. Flora (1956) gives many descriptions of large stones and spectacular hailfalls.

For many years the largest hailstone officially reported in the United States was one that fell at Potter, Nebr., on 6 July 1928. It had a circumference of 43 cm and weighed 680 g. This record was surpassed on 3 September 1970, when a stone weighing 766 g with a circumference of 44 cm fell at Coffeyville, Kans. (Fig. 11.1). Fortunately, this and several other stones were preserved and sent to the National Center for Atmospheric Research, Boulder, Colo., for analysis

Figure 11.1. The largest hailstone ever recorded in the United States. It fell at Coffeyville, Kans., on 3 September 1970. It weighed 776 g and measured 44 cm around its largest circumference (photo courtesy of NCAR).

(Ludlum, 1971). The best statement about the maximum possible size of a hailstone is still that made by Talman (1936): "Judging from the meager data we possess concerning the maximum violence of thunderstorm updrafts, it would seem that something less than five pounds is the extreme possible weight of a hailstone, while a two pound hailstone would deserve a place in a museum if it could be preserved there."

The largest stones are interesting curiosities, but their only scientific importance is related to the maximum updrafts required for them to grow; early-twentieth-century estimates of updraft strengths were based on the maximum stone sizes observed (see Humphreys, 1964, p. 360). When these huge stones fall they are usually few and far between and thus do not cause much crop damage; however, clearly they can damage property severely and have been known to kill people and animals. The much greater numbers of moderate-sized stones are significant to agriculture, and the cloud physicist is interested in the total spectrum of sizes.

b. Shapes and Appearance of Hailstones

Large hailstones sometimes have very unusual and curious shapes (see Chap. 12). Occasionally they can have long protrusions, giving the appearance of a dagger (Mossop, 1971; Briggs, 1968). More frequently large stones have less spectacular lobes. Most stones have a fairly uniform smooth appearance, and these are of most interest for understanding hailstorms. However, very few systematic studies have been

Table 11.1 Comparison of Shapes of Hailstones Collected in Canada and South Africa

Location	Sample size (no. of stones)	Shape classification groupings (%)			
		Cones	Spheres, oblates, prolates	Irregular	Miscellaneous (acorn, apple, raspberry)
Transvaal, South Africa, 1959–67	4,484	11.8	71.7	9.0	7.5
Transvaal, South Africa, 1965–69	1,423	15.8	57.1	11.7	15.4
Alberta, Canada, 1969	1,920	21.2	59.4	7.9	11.5

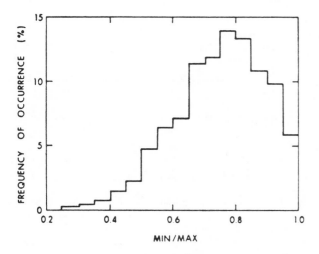

Figure 11.2. Frequency distribution of the ratio of the minimum over the maximum (min/max) diameters for a sample of 1920 hailstones collected in Alberta, Canada (Barge and Isaac, 1973).

made of the frequency of occurrence of the more common shapes because of difficulties involved in collecting, storing, transporting, and analyzing quantities of stones without any appreciable melting. The two largest such studies have been carried out in Alberta, Canada, and the Transvaal, South Africa.

The main motivation for studies by Carte and Kidder (1966, 1970) was to deduce the growth environment of hailstones from observed structural properties. Shape is one property that affects the falling mode, collection efficiency, heat exchange, and hence the growth rate of stones. They classified stones into spheroids, ellipsoids, apples, cones, and irregular shapes. The classification was done by visual inspection until 1965, when the lengths of the three principal axes of all stones were measured. The study in Alberta by Barge and Isaac (1973) was begun mainly to aid interpretation of data from polarizing weather radars. The classification types used were spheres, oblate spheroids, prolate spheroids, cones, irregulars, acorns, and raspberries. Because of the different classification schemes used in these two studies, a direct comparison of the data is not possible, but can be partly accomplished by grouping some of the types as shown in Table 11.1. The most remarkable aspect of the data in Table 11.1 is the similar percentages in each major classification in the two different geographical regions. In both regions more than half the stones collected were roughly spherical. The next most common shape was the cone, and in both regions cones occurred most frequently in the smaller-size categories. Other shapes, such as raspberry, acorn, and apple, occurred only occasionally, and the least frequent were the knobbly, irregular shapes.

Because the ratio of the two orthogonal components of the returned signal with a polarizing radar is related to the ratio of the axes of the reflecting hydrometeor, Barge and Isaac (1973) placed strong emphasis on the ratio of minimum to maximum dimensions of the stones (min/max). The frequency distribution of min/max for all the measured hailstones is shown in Fig. 11.2. The modal value of the ratio is between 0.75 and 0.79, and although the smallest value of min/max was 0.30, more than 80% of the values are between 0.60 and 1.00. This discussion has dealt with the complete ensemble of stones collected from many storms. However, the percentage of stones in the various shape categories can vary widely from storm to storm.

These studies should be extended to other regions and should use much larger samples because the shape as defined by the axial ratio is critically important in two ways. First, decreasing the axial ratio of an oblate hailstone from 1.0 to 0.8 increases the final mass achieved at the ground by a factor of 3. English and Warner (1970) showed this in modeling hailstone growth in a well-documented hailstorm that occurred over Montreal. Second, changing the axial ratio of wet, randomly oriented, oblate spheroids from 0.95 to 0.60 changes the amount of depolarization in the radar return by a factor of 100 (Atlas et al., 1953).

c. Hailstone Fallspeeds

The speeds at which hailstones fall greatly influence their damage potential. At times large stones make huge dents in automobiles and even pass right through very substantial materials such as asbestos cement roofing. Hailstone fallspeeds have long been a subject of interest for this reason and as indicators of how fast the air can be moving upward in the thunderstorms that produce them.

Hailstones, like raindrops, tend to fall at limiting speeds under the competing action of their weight and the drag of the air. As they grow (or melt), they tend to fall faster (or slower). For a given size they fall faster at high altitudes than near the ground, owing to reduced drag in less dense air. The fallspeed of a smooth sphere can be expressed in terms of its weight, w, its cross-sectional area, a, the drag coefficient, C_D, and the density of the air, ρ_a (a function of altitude), by equating the weight to the drag. This gives

$$v_t = \sqrt{\frac{2w}{C_D \rho_a a}}$$

When the mass is expressed as a function of the diameter, this reduces (at constant altitude) to $v_t = kd^{1/2}$. Wegener (1911) and Weickmann (1953) used the same form. The value of the drag coefficient for hailstones is a subject of controversy. It depends on the shape of the object (here spherical), its roughness, and the Reynolds number, a dimensionless parameter that determines the character of the flow around the object. Eng Young and Browning (1976) showed that for a wide range of Reynolds numbers (up to 10^5) the drag coefficient of simulated hailstones remained constant at about 0.6, a widely used value.

Various values for the densities of hailstones have been assumed, but measurements taken by Vittori and Di Caporiacco (1959) show that at the ground they are typically not much less than the pure ice value of 0.915 g cm^{-3}.

A very fascinating phenomenon takes place with large or rough spheres. The drag coefficient of a smooth or rough sphere is a function of its speed through the air. As the speed of the stone increases from zero, the drag coefficient is nearly constant at a high value over a wide range of speeds. At a critical threshold speed the drag coefficient lowers drastically over a narrow range of speeds. This was originally explained by Prandtl (1914) and is thoroughly discussed by Hoerner (1965). Bilham and Relf (1937) calculated the fallspeeds of smooth spheres using measurements of the drag coefficients and found that the fallspeed as a function of diameter is something like the schematic curve of Fig. 11.3.

Figure 11.3 illustrates that between diameters d_1 and d_2 (about 7 and 10.5 cm), a sphere falls stably at two markedly different speeds depending on whether it enters the supercritical regime. The transition from the lower to the upper curve might be caused by the stone's encountering a gust. Above d_2 all stones are in the supercritical region and fall at high speeds. Landry and Hardy (1970) dropped smooth and rough spheres from an airplane and tracked them with radar. They observed a smooth sphere of 7.5-cm diameter (near d_1) undergo the transition to the low-drag regime and then return to the lower-speed, high-drag regime. They found that roughened spheres fell mostly in the supercritical regime. Roughness has a dual effect: it increases the drag in the supercritical regime but moves the transition or double-valued region to lower diameters. This is shown as the dashed curve in Fig. 11.3. A smooth hailstone that becomes rough will actually begin to fall faster as it moves into the supercritical regime, but when an initially rough sphere begins to melt, fallspeed decreases sharply as the hailstone becomes wet and smooth (Willis et al., 1964).

The consequences of this transition phenomenon are these:

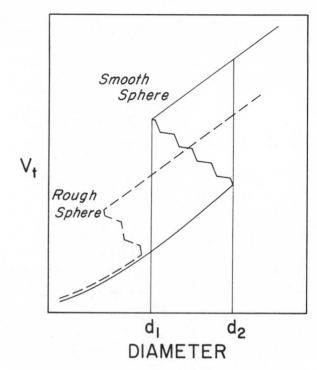

Figure 11.3. Schematic representation of the relationship between the terminal fall velocity of a hailstone (V_t) and its diameter (based on Bilham and Relf, 1937).

1. There is great uncertainty about the fallspeeds of large, rough hailstones because of the wide variability of their roughness and of air turbulence.

2. Because of the high fallspeeds above a diameter equal to d_2 of Fig. 11.3 (Bilham and Relf calculated velocities in excess of 100 m s^{-1} for smooth ice spheres), hailstones with diameters significantly greater than d_2 are unlikely.

3. Although the fallspeed of the Coffeyville, Kans., hailstone, the largest reliably documented hailstone yet recorded, was estimated by Roos (1972) at 43 m s^{-1}, it is not unthinkable that a smaller stone could fall even faster because of its individual roughness characteristics.

d. The Hardness of Hail

Not all hail reaching the ground arrives as solidly frozen ice. Some stones shatter on impact because of structural weakness caused by cavities of air or unfrozen water. Others are so soft that they can be picked up and squeezed like a sponge. The frequency of occurrence of such soft stones is of interest from several points of view.

First, some theories of hailstone growth predict a considerable amount of wet growth in which latent heat released by freezing of accreted water cannot be transferred from the growing stone fast enough to freeze all the liquid water. Such growth has been reproduced in a wind tunnel (List, 1961), and the mechanism is described in Chap. 12.

Table 11.2. Frequency of Occurrence of Different Liquid Water Contents in Hailstones Collected at Three Places in the United States and one in Africa*

Liquid water content (%)	Hailstone cases	
	Number	Percent
0	41	52.0
0–4	29	36.6
>4	9	11.4

*Gitlin et al., 1966.

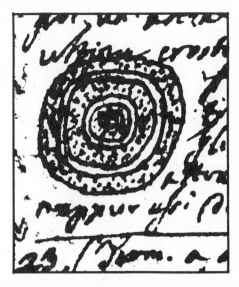

Figure 11.4. Drawing of a section of a hailstone from an original manuscript by Alessandro Volta in 1806.

Second, crop and property damage caused by soft, spongy hailstones is obviously less than that caused by hard hailstones of the same size. This leads to the third point: if stones could be made softer artificially by, for example, cloud seeding, there would be less crop damage.

Perhaps the most interesting and controversial aspect of hailstone hardness is related to a method of hail suppression that generates explosions within or near storm clouds. This technique has been used at least since the sixteenth century in Italy with artillery, since the nineteenth century with hail cannon, and more recently (since the late 1940s) with explosive rockets (Morgan, 1973). It was suggested by Vittori (1960) that generating such explosions could induce cavitation in the enclosed water pockets of hailstones. This in turn might cause large hailstones to shatter in the air or at least so weaken their structure that they might disintegrate on impact, thereby causing less damage (Sansom, 1966b). There is some experimental evidence of this weakening effect in laboratory tests (Vittori, 1960; Favreau and Goyer, 1967), although these claims are challenged by List (1963). Whether the range of effectiveness of such explosions in the free atmosphere is great enough to have any practical significance is open to question.

It is, of course, very difficult to ascertain the amount of unfrozen water in falling hailstones. The only quantitative measurements have been made with a mobile-calorimeter technique developed at the National Center for Atmospheric Research (Gitlin et al., 1966). Seventy-nine hailstones collected from nine hailstorms at four locations (Kericho, Kenya, Africa; Boulder, Colo.; New Raymer, Colo.; and Rapid City, S.Dak.) were analyzed. The unfrozen-water contents ranged from 0 to 16% (except for one suspect value of 55%) and were distributed as shown in Table 11.2.

Data from volunteer farmer observers in Alberta and South Africa have been analyzed by Summers (1968) and Carte and Basson (1970). In both cases a substantial fraction of the hailfalls was reported to contain some soft hailstones—over a 3-yr period from 1965 to 1967 in Alberta 47% of the reports indicated some soft hail, and over a 7-yr period in the Transvaal the frequency was 22%. In Italy soft hail appears to be rather rare. According to Prodi (1974), from 1968 to 1972 only 8% of the reports from the Po Valley indicated some soft stones, and only 2% indicated that all stones were soft.

e. Hailstone Embryos

Volta (1806) described the internal structure of hailstones (see Fig. 11.4). He found them to contain usually, in addition to an alternating series of clear and opaque rings, an opaque central nucleus that he labeled a snowflake, calling it the *embryo*, a term still in use. In some cases he found the opaque nucleus to be missing and believed the embryo must then have been a frozen raindrop. Kämtz in 1840 suggested that cirrus crystals were the embryos of hailstones.

There has been much recent attention to the importance of embryo type in understanding hail formation and in applying this understanding to hail suppression. Some numerical-model studies have shown that seeding to suppress hail may have different results, depending on whether the hail embryos are frozen, supercooled raindrops or graupel that have grown from snow crystals (Young, 1978; Nelson, 1976). From these models and other considerations it has been argued that when embryos form by the graupel process seeding may actually increase hail (Atlas, 1976).

The Soviet accumulation zone model and the suppression technique based upon it seem to require frozen-drop embryos (Sulakvalidze et al., 1967), as does the Swiss hail experiment that evolved somewhat later (Federer, 1978). Knight and Knight (1973) have shown that hail in northeastern Colorado grows primarily from graupel, and they have demonstrated an opposite tendency in Oklahoma and the South African lowveld, where hail embryos are more likely to be frozen drops (Table 11.3). Carte and Kidder (1970) have reported a higher frequency of graupel (rime) embryos, especially in the larger stones from storms in the Pretoria-Witwatersrand area of the South African highveld.

A change in embryo type as a function of size has been reported both by Carte and Kidder (1970) and by Knight

Table 11.3. Comparisons of the Hailstone Embryo Classification for Three Regions

Region	No. of stones analyzed	Size (cm)	Percent graupel*	Percent frozen drop*
Northeastern	2,306	≤2.5	86	8
Colorado†	155	>2.5	52	30
Oklahoma†	274	≤2.5	25	55
	381	>2.5	18	68
South Africa‡	954	≤2.5	30	54
South Africa lowveld	363	>2.5	6	82

*The balance of the 100% is made up of stones with indeterminate embryo type.
†Knight and Knight (1976).
‡N. C. Knight, personal communication.

Table 11.4. Percentage Frequency of Occurrence of Maximum Hail Size Within Specified Ranges per Observed Point Hailfall in Various Regions, Ranked in Order of Decreasing Frequency of Large Hail

Region	Maximum hail diameter (cm)		
	<1	1–3	>3
	Percent		
Northern India[a]	37	38	25
Southwestern France[b]	40	46	14
Northeastern Colorado[c]	33	60	7
Oklahoma[d]	49	43	7
Central Alberta[e]	49	45	6
Denver, Colo.[c]	44	52	4
New England[c]	60	36	4
Transvaal, South Africa[f]	54	43	3
Central Illinois[c]	70	27	3

[a]Brooks, 1944.
[b]Changnon, 1971.
[c]Paul, 1968.
[d]Nelson and Young, 1978.
[e]Wojtiw, 1975.
[f]Carte and Basson, 1970.

and Knight (1973), although Carte and Kidder have reported a predominance of graupel embryos in larger hailstones, and Knight and Knight have always observed that the percentage of frozen-drop embryos increases with increasing hailstone size in northeastern Colorado, Oklahoma, and the South African lowveld.

f. Contaminants in Hailstones

In addition to the nucleating particle, which causes the initial freezing of an ice crystal or condensation of a cloud droplet later to become the hailstone embryo, most hailstones contain material scavenged out of the atmosphere within or below cloud. Studies of ice nuclei, which are found in large numbers in hailstones, were carried out by Vali (1970) and Rosinski (1974). Vali found that when rain and hail were collected simultaneously the concentrations of nuclei, detected by freezing drops formed from the samples, were similar. When hailstones were sectioned (Vali, 1971), the concentrations of nuclei were fairly uniform except for the outermost layers.

The internal distribution of iron and chloride particles in hailstones was studied by Vittori et al. (1969) and Prodi and Nagamoto (1971) in attempts to learn about hailstone growth conditions. Insoluble particles ranging in size from the submicroscopic up to several hundred micrometers were found by Rosinski (1966). Fungi and bacteria have also been found in hailstones (Mandrioli et al., 1973). Hailstones have been discovered to contain insects (Knight and Knight, 1978), and a wide variety of even stranger objects such as frogs and fish has been reported (Fort, 1919).

Analysis of substances deposited in the atmosphere by atomic tests and scavenged by hailstones has provided better understanding of hail development. Blifford et al. (1957) analyzed 41 hailstones collected near Washington, D.C., and found the average beta activity of 11 melted stones to be 1.4×10^{-10} Ci (curies) ml^{-1}. Sectioned stones showed significantly more radioactivity in the core than in the outer layers, suggesting that the embryos formed in regions of relatively high fission product concentration. Jaffe et al. (1954) noted that deposition of fission products in thunderstorm rain and hail was greatly increased by recirculation of growing hailstones in contaminated air.

By comparing the concentrations of contaminants in hail with those found in concurrently collected rain, it is possible to infer something about the scavenging processes taking place. This was done for sulfur in the neighborhood of sulfur-extraction natural-gas plants in central Alberta by Summers and Hitchon (1973). They concluded that the main removal mechanism in convective clouds was in-cloud (rainout) rather than below-cloud (washout) scavenging and that convective storms were very efficient mechanisms for removal of air pollutants from the lower atmosphere because of the large volume of air processed by such storms.

3. Characteristics of Point Hailfall

a. Distributions of Hailstone Sizes

(1) Frequency Distributions of Maximum Hail Sizes: Because of difficulties in obtaining meaningful measurements of the total number of hailstones falling at a point, very few data are available on the size spectrum of hailstones. Most attention has been devoted to the more easily observed maximum hail size. Several comparative studies of the distribution of maximum hail sizes (Paul, 1968; Changnon, 1971) are summarized in Table 11.4 with additional data. These data are based on projects that lasted for several years, covered a substantial region, and relied on the estimates of observers. Large hail appears to occur most often in India in association with premonsoon squall lines, and records indicate that more people have been killed there than in any other country (Flora, 1956). In North America

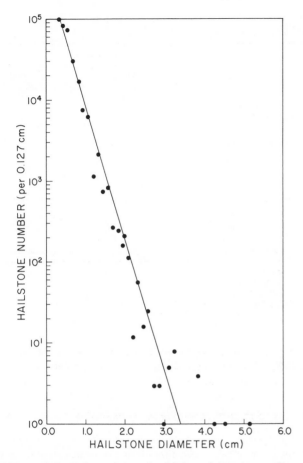

Figure 11.5. Hailstone size distribution giving the number of stones per 0.127-cm-diameter class interval as a function of diameter based on 3-yr data from a hailpad network in Alberta (original data courtesy of L. Wojtiw, Alberta Research Council.

the highest frequency of large hail occurs in the lee of the Rockies.

(2) Size Distributions at the Ground: The most extensive data on hailstone size distributions at the ground are available from hailpad networks operated in three locations in North America and one in France. These pads give the size distribution averaged over the duration of the storm. The most detailed set of data is from Alberta, where two networks were operated from 1974 to 1976 (Wojtiw and Lunn, 1977). The raw data were obtained and plotted for the large network, consisting of 500 stations over an area of 34,467 km² (Fig. 11.5). These data show a very good fit to the exponential probability density function, $P(\Delta d)$, of the form

$$P(\Delta d) = N_o \exp[-\lambda(d - d_{min})\Delta d], \qquad (11.1)$$

where Δd = size class interval, N_o = number constant, λ = slope of best-fit line to data, d = average diameter in class, and d_{min} = minimum stone diameter measured.

In Fig. 11.4 the equation for the exponential fit is

$$P(\Delta d) = 3.8 \exp[-3.8 (d - 0.25)\Delta d]. \qquad (11.2)$$

Table 11.5. Comparison of the Value of the Exponent λ Found by Fitting Exponential Probability Density Functions to Hailpad Data from Four Regions

Region	Period of data collection	λ
France	1975[a]	−4.2
Alberta	1974–76 large network[b]	−3.8
	1974–76 dense network[b]	−3.4
Illinois	1972–1974[c]	−3.4
	All 6 years (1967–68; 1971–72; 1973–74)[c]	−2.8
Northeastern Colorado	1972–74 (seeding experiment)[d]	−2.7
	1976[e]	−2.3

[a] Average of many individual spectra by Jean et al., 1976.
[b] Wojtiw and Lunn, 1977.
[c] Changnon and Morgan, 1976.
[d] Crow et al., 1976.
[e] NHRE 1976 data base.

By using the number of classes per cm and the total number of 1-ft² hailpads hit during the period, Eq. 11.2 can be transformed into

$$N_d = 132 \exp[-3.8 (d - 0.25)] \text{ m}^{-2} \text{ per 1-mm} \qquad (11.3)$$
class interval.

Data from all regions were fitted to an equation of the form of Eq. 11.3, and the value of the exponent λ was ranked in order of decreasing negative slope, as shown in Table 11.5. On the average a point hailfall in France has a smaller fraction of large hailstones than does a point hailfall in Alberta or Illinois, and the northeastern Colorado sample has the largest fraction of large hail (this is not in conflict with the ranking of Table 11.4, which shows France having a high frequency of larger stones; Table 11.4 deals with the single largest hailstone in any point hailfall; Table 11.5 treats the entire spectrum of sizes).

These time-averaged size point distributions, with the probability of hail occurrence, can provide useful quantitative data for the design of structures that are susceptible to damage from hail above certain threshold sizes. For example, photovoltaic solar-heating collector panels can be seriously damaged by large hail; widespread use of the panels would clearly require taking hailfall into consideration either in design strength or in estimation of life expectancy.

(3) Size Distribution Aloft: Size spectra at the ground must be known in order to develop hail-size damage functions, but another interest of the cloud physicist is the size spectra in the cloud. This is important for understanding and modeling the hail growth process and for estimating the radar reflectivity in cloud volumes containing hail. The radar reflectivity is proportional to the sum of the sixth powers of diameters and so is strongly controlled by the number of the larger hailstones.

Marshall and Palmer (1948) showed that raindrop size distributions are exponential and, further, that the magnitude of the negative exponent decreases as the precipitation rate increases. To test the applicability of these observations to hailstones, the first serious attempt to determine hailstone size distributions was made in Alberta (Douglas, 1963, 1965b). Samples were collected in wire-mesh baskets and preserved in a freezer by volunteer farmer observers, who carefully noted the duration of each hailfall. From 1958 to 1963 they obtained 67 usable samples, which were size-sorted by diameter in 1/8-in increments and counted. The distribution data thus obtained of sizes at the ground were not published but were used to generate distributions of sizes during descent, using a relationship between hailstone fallspeed and diameter and hailfall duration. The assumption had to be made that the distributions did not change with time during the fall, and Douglas found that all the distributions could collectively be described by the relationship

$$N_d = 10 \exp(-3.1d) \text{ m}^{-3} \text{ per mm size interval,} \quad (11.4)$$

where d is the diameter in centimeters (this is a revised version of an earlier equation and appears in Hitschfeld and Stauder, 1965, p. 47).

A large number of the individual samples appeared to be truncated versions of the collective distribution. Since the size distributions aloft are derived from point observations at the ground, the truncated distributions suggest that the parent population aloft was size-sorted (perhaps by wind shear) during the fall (Hitschfeld, 1971).

These size distributions obtained by Douglas were the only ones available for 10 years, until hailpads came into widespread use. More recently Federer and Waldvogel (1975) estimated some size distributions in a Swiss multicell hailstorm, using the same approach, but with time-resolved data from a hailstone disdrometer over a 13-min period. In this case they found that the mean spectrum could be represented by

$$N_d = 12.1 \exp(-4.2d) \text{ m}^{-3} \text{ per mm size interval.} \quad (11.5)$$

Thus the total number density aloft is similar to that found by Douglas, but the larger negative slope of the exponent indicates fewer large stones per unit volume.

The first actual measurements within a storm were made by the armored T-28 aircraft used in the National Hail Research Experiment, penetrating hail growth regions. The best data were obtained by use of a laser hail spectrometer on 21 July 1975 (Spahn and Smith, Jr., 1976). Sixteen representative 1-s size distributions were obtained during one penetration. Averaging all distributions gave a good exponential fit (correlation coefficient $r = 0.91$) with the value of the exponent $\lambda = -3.9$.

In summary, the observational evidence available to date clearly shows that hailstone sizes averaged over many samples fit an exponential distribution. Individual samples vary widely and in many cases appear to be truncated portions of a more general distribution. The value of the exponent λ lies between -2 and -4, but many more data would be re-

Table 11.6. Summary of Available Information Hailfall Duration at Various Locations Around the World

Location	Duration (min)		
	Median	Mean	Maximum
Bedford, England[a]	2	5–6	>30
New England[a]	3.4		25
Denver, Colo.[a]	5		45
Central Illinois[a]	5–7	5–9	
Northeastern Colorado[a]	10–15		
Central Alberta[b]	≥5	10	>40
Austria[c]		8–10	50
France[c]		5–10	90
Belgium[c]			20
Rostov region, USSR[c]		10	20
European part of USSR[c]		15	20–30
Northern Caucasus, USSR[c]		5–10	30
South Africa[d]	6	8	>24

[a] Paul, 1968.
[b] Wojtiw, 1975.
[c] Sulakvelidze, 1967.
[d] Carte and Basson, 1970.

quired to establish with any certainty the variability of N_o and λ and to determine whether there is any real systematic difference from one climatic region to another.

b. Duration and Continuity of Point Hailfall

(1) Duration: Hailfall at a point on the ground can last from a few seconds with a smattering of stones to more than an hour with several centimeters of ice burying crops. Descriptions of some spectacular falls are given by Flora (1956). Any particular hailfall is usually much briefer than the rain from the same storm. This suggests that the hail formation zone aloft is only a fraction of the total volume of a thunderstorm. Information on hailfall duration is available from several locations around the world (Table 11.6). There is a remarkable consistency from region to region; the mean value of hailfall duration is between 5 and 10 min, with one exception. The duration of hailfall at the ground is a direct function of the areal size of the hail-producing zone in a thunderstorm and the speed of motion of the storm. Since all the regions shown in Table 11.6 are in middle latitudes, the average storm motions are similar, and the similar durations therefore suggest that there is a universal average size to the hail-producing zone in thunderstorms.

There is a tendency for longer durations to be associated with larger hail size. Paul (1968) points out that the period during the peak of the hail season in Alberta with the greatest percentage of large hail also had the longest mean duration. The relationship between duration and size was investigated more quantitatively by Carte and Basson (1970). They showed that both the mean and the median hailfall durations increase with increasing maximum hail size. In fact, those falls containing stones >3 cm in diameter last about twice as long as those falls with no stones >1 cm. This suggests that the larger stones fall from larger hail-producing

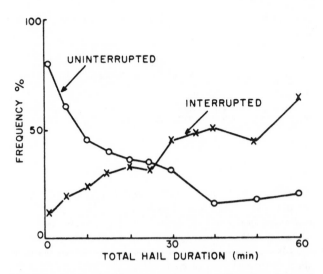

Figure 11.6. Relative frequency of reports of interrupted or continuous point hailfall as a function of total duration for the 17 main hailstorms in Alberta during the 1963 season (Douglas, 1965).

Table 11.7. Percentage Frequency of Reports Indicating Continuous Hailfall or a Given Number of Bursts

	Number of bursts						
	1 (continuous)	2	3	4	5	6	7
Alberta*	66	23	8	1.8	0.4	0.4	0.2
South Africa†	69	24	5	1.5	0.6	—	—

* Pell (1970), based on 2,066 reports, 1967–1968.
† Carte and Basson (1970), based on 7,803 reports, 1962–69.

cells, which on the average take longer to pass over a given point on the ground.

(2) Continuity: The preceding discussion treats duration as the total elapsed time from the onset of hail until its final cessation. However, a common characteristic of hailfall is unsteadiness. Hail often comes in short, intense bursts with intervening lulls, or even gaps. This intermittency is difficult to measure quantitatively without high-resolution recording instruments. In both Alberta and South Africa the farmers are asked to indicate the number of bursts of hail, and while the estimate is rather subjective, the large number of reports lends some credence to the statistical results.

In the first study of interrupted hailfall, Douglas (1965) analyzed data from the 17 major storms in Alberta during the 1973 hail season. The results, shown in Fig. 11.6, clearly indicate that the longer the duration the more likely it is that the hailfall will be interrupted. Pell (1967) tabulated 7,622 reports on interrupted hailfall in Alberta from 1964 to 1966 and found an almost-linear reduction in the probability of continuous hailfall with time, reaching 50% at 26–30 minutes. In other words, the probability was 50% that at least one interruption occurred during a hailfall that extended over 26–30 minutes.

The most comprehensive study of intermittency was carried out by Pell (1970), using 2,066 reports collected in Alberta during the 1967 and 1968 hail seasons. These reports provided unambiguous information on the number of hail bursts observed by farmers. Table 11.7 shows the percentage frequencies with which given numbers of bursts were reported, together with similar South African data extracted from Carte and Basson (1970). The two distributions are remarkably similar, suggesting that some fundamental characteristic of hailstorms is responsible. Pell (1970) developed a

statistical model in an attempt to explain these distributions. Using the work of Chisholm (1967) on the small-scale radar structure of Alberta hailstorms and the data from Byers and Braham (1949) to give typical cell sizes, spacing, and lifetimes, and assuming that the point intermittency is produced by the passage overhead of several cells, each producing continuous hail, Pell was able to generate modeled intermittency close to that observed.

4. Characteristics of Hailfall Patterns

a. Introduction

The fact that hail from one storm often covers a substantial area has been known for at least 200 years (Volta, 1806). Crop insurance data from the early part of this century have also given an indication of the extent to which damaging hail can cover large areas of the countryside. However, it was not until the establishment of hail-reporting networks, especially those in Illinois and Alberta, that quantitative information could be obtained on hailfall patterns. These patterns show up on all scales from the individual field to the whole of North America. A review by Changnon (1977) gives a full appreciation of scale effects in hailfall study.

b. Hailswaths

As hailstorms move along, they produce hail on the ground in areas that, although by no means completely covered with hail, can be readily grouped into entities that exhibit spatial and temporal coherence and are called *hailswaths*. The swath is the overall pattern of hail left by a single hail-producing thunderstorm, and can be as long as several hundred kilometers with a width of up to tens of kilometers.

One of the best early documentations of hailswaths was given by Prohaska (1907) for several storms in Austria on 6 July 1905. Most of the 12 swaths were 20 km or more wide, and 2 were more than 200 km long, lasting for 4 hr. Another example was the extremely severe storm that devastated central parts of Alberta Province, in Canada, on 23 July 1971. One storm laid down a swath 30 to 40 km wide over a distance of at least 320 km. Stones larger than walnuts were reported for half its length, and total damage to crops was estimated at $10 million (Summers, 1972).

Within the world's hail belts many hailswaths occur in a single season. A dramatic example of this took place in Alberta, which has one of the highest regional frequencies of hail in the world. Figure 11.7 records all the swaths containing hail ≥2-cm diameter that occurred in Alberta during the summer of 1975. Most swaths were short, with typical lengths between 30 and 80 km, but three were very long, in excess of 300 km. The direction of motion of the storms was varied, although most had a westerly component. The storms were concentrated in the area west of Red Deer (near the center of the map). Wojtiw (1975) produced similar yearly maps from 1957 to 1973, and the same general characteristics show up every year. From these maps Wojtiw determined the frequency distributions of swath lengths (Table 11.8). Such distributions, if they were available for other regions, would be useful statistics for comparative climatology.

c. The Hailstreak

Before the creation of the finer-scale networks, the hailswath was generally regarded as the basic surface hailfall pattern. Again from Alberta came the first quantitative description of the "patchiness" of the hailfall within a swath (Carte et al., 1963; Fig. 11.8). In the mid-1960s, Changnon (1970) discovered that what appeared from coarse measurements to be a single, albeit irregular, pattern, or hailswath, was often composed of several subareas of hailfall. These were called *hailstreaks*, defined as areas of hail continuous in space and time. The instantaneous-hailfall cells, which as they move along generate the hailstreak, are the intersection with the ground of individual *hailshafts*, coherent columns of hail falling below the cloud. Using point values of hail starting and ending times, derived from rain gages modified for the purpose, Changnon (1966) found that hailstreaks often overlapped, because some hailcells traveled over paths already traversed by another, giving rise to the intermittency in point hailfall discussed in Sec. 3b. A detailed summary of dimensions and properties of 760 Illinois hailstreaks based on 8 years of observations was presented by Changnon and Morgan (1976). From that summary one can picture the hailstreak as being produced by a hailcell moving at about 50 km h^{-1} (but at times as much as 100 km h^{-1}) over a period of typically 6 to 11 min (at times in excess of 15 min). Hailstreaks are frequently 5 to 10 km^2 in area and 1 to 2 km in width by 5 to 10 km in length. This prompted Changnon (1970) to give a more precise definition of a hailswath as "an enveloped area of hail comprising two or more hailstreaks separated by no more than 20 mi (32 km) during 12 hours or less."

It is difficult to define the patterns within hailstreaks with networks that can be deployed economically. Some idea of hailstreak features can be gained from examining crop damage, despite the difficulties in relating it to hail. Changnon and Barron (1971) explored the use of aerial photography for estimating crop damage and observed "swirl patterns,"

Table 11.8. Distribution of the Lengths of Hailswaths, Alberta, Canada, 1956–73*

	Hailswath lengths (km)				
	15–50	50–80	80–110	110–145	≥145
Average frequency (percent)	34.5	31.4	16.0	9.5	8.6

*Wojtiw, 1975.

which they attributed to gusts of wind enhancing the damage potential of the hail. Towery et al. (1976) noted very prominent *hailshadows*, areas of reduced crop damage to the lee of large obstacles, such as farmsteads and groves of large trees. The same effect occurred in soybean fields located just downwind of cornfields. The shadows extended downwind to a distance 10 times the height of the obstacles (a fact that must be considered in choosing sites of hail-measuring instruments), clearly ruling out direct interception of stones by the obstacles as cause of the reduced damage.

Another interesting observation stemming from the aerial photography is a phenomenon of striped patterns in the damage, called *hailstripes* by Towery and Morgan (1977). These were attributed to a strandlike structure in the hailshaft, exemplified in the Alberta hailstorm shown in Fig. 11.9. The stripes result when such a hailshaft pattern is blown across the fields by high winds (see Fig. 11.10). Mollo-Christensen (1962) described a mechanism that might explain the formation of these hailstrands. It is an instability phenomenon whereby an initial perturbation in the velocity, a small downdraft, occurs, causing forces that accelerate the hailstones toward the center of the downdraft. The increased concentration of hailstones there strengthens the downdraft, enhancing the effect. Random fluctuation in hailstone concentration could have caused the initial downdraft perturbation. Either kind of perturbation will tend to intensify.

Admirat (1973) reported finding organized distributions of hail within hailstreaks that he calls *hailcores*, where there is a correlation between the total number of stones and the size of the largest stone falling at a point. On the other hand, Carte and Held (1978) reported that they did not find such organized distributions in South African hailstorms. Special networks set up in southwestern Nebraska and Illinois in the United States were used to study the patterns within hailstreaks (Morgan and Towery, 1974). Hailpads set 100 to 200 m apart showed an irregular pattern of maxima and minima in the number of hailstones falling per square meter, with only slight evidence of any organization (Fig. 11.11).

d. Large-Scale (National) Hail Patterns

Viewed on a sufficiently large scale, hailfall patterns show much coherence. Thus the 4-day sequence of maps in Fig.

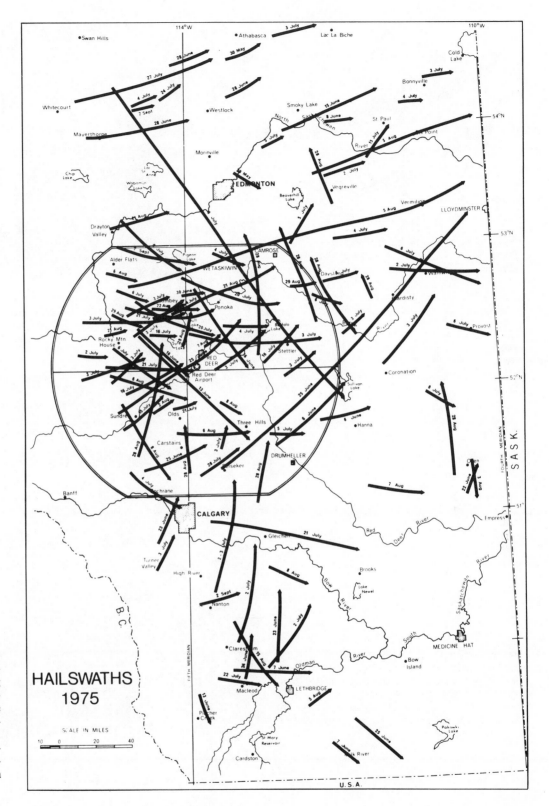

Figure 11.7. Map showing the location of all hailswaths in Alberta during the 1975 summer hail season, which produced some hail greater than 2-cm diameter (Diebert, 1976). The flattened circular outline encloses the operational area of the Alberta Hail Project.

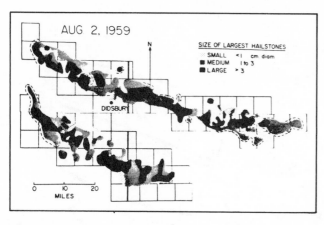

Figure 11.8. Map showing the patchiness of hailfall within two Alberta hailswaths, based on a large number of reports by farmers (Carte et al., 1963).

Figure 11.9. View of Alberta hailstorm showing strandlike structure in hail falling in left center of the photograph (photograph courtesy of B. L. Barge, Alberta Research Council).

Figure 11.10. Aerial photograph of hail damage near Champaign, Ill., taken 12 days after a storm on 29 June 1976. The print was made from a false-color infrared transparency. Note the well-marked hail-stripes in the damage pattern in the right and left center of the photograph (photograph courtesy of Country Companies).

Figure 11.11. Distribution of the total number of hailstones per square meter over a 1.6-km² network of hailpads in Illinois. The outer square represents the network boundary (Morgan and Towery, 1974).

Table 11.9. Hail Mass, Rain Mass, and the Hail-Rain Mass Ration (H/R) for 33 Haildays in Northeastern Colorado*

	Hail mass (10^7 kg)	Rain mass (10^9 kg)	H/R (%)
Average	12.6	6.35	1.8
Standard deviation	22.8	5.83	2.2
Highest value	111.9	27.80	10.7

*Crow et al., 1976.

812 thunderstorm traverses at altitudes between 6,000 ft (2,000 m) and 26,000 ft (8,600 m) MSL.

Where in the thunderstorm cloud is hail born, and where does it grow? Some light can be shed on these questions by studying the relationship of hail to other components and products of the complex system that produced it.

a. Hail and Rainfall

Hail-producing storms always produce rain as well. In fact, in terms of mass output, hail is a very minor product of a hailstorm. Crow et al. (1976) have given daily values of total rain and hail mass observed with the rain-hail network over an area of 1,600 km² in northeastern Colorado during 1972–74. From these one can calculate the ratio of hail-to-rain mass (H/R) for each hailday. Table 11.9 gives the average rain and hail masses and the average H/R ratio for the samples, along with some extremes and standard deviations.

The figures in Table 11.9 show that the hail output of a hailstorm is not likely to exceed about 10% of the total rain production in mass terms and is typically only a few percent. Similar estimates were arrived at by Strong (1974) for 17 storms in Alberta, and point estimates of H/R in France reported by Jean et al. (1976) are not inconsistent with these. Point ratios are more variable, of course; the maximum point value reported in the French study was 0.47. Occasionally hail without any rain has been observed to fall at a point.

Changnon (1970) classified hailstreaks as occurring in the center or on the right or left flank of their associated rain cells. Of 434 hailstreaks studied, 39% occurred along the center, 36% on the right, and 25% on the left. A study of 16 very damaging hailstreaks revealed that all occurred in the core of the rain cell. In fact, it is typical in Illinois for rain and large hail to fall at the same time. This is in contrast to some other areas, for example, Italy (Morgan, 1973), where large hail typically falls entirely outside the rain-cell area, usually to be followed by some rain and smaller hail.

Hail from a given storm tends to fall over a smaller area than rain, and a given rain cell can have more than one hailstreak associated with it. In Illinois, Changnon (1970) reported 259 hailstreaks associated with 93 rain cells in 1968, with as many as 9 hailstreaks being associated with a single rain cell. For 8 haildays in Languedoc, France (Jean et al., 1976), the ratio of the area covered by rain to that covered by hail varied from slightly less than 4 to more than 150 (the latter when rain fell over the entire network). Geneve (1961) reported observations that showed that as the peak storm

11.12 shows regular progression during an intense period of hail activity, each day of hail producing crop losses of more than $1 million. The shaded areas are counties that experienced loss, and the three levels of shading indicate the dollars in claims paid. The resolution by county obscures fine details of the pattern but enhances clarity of the large-scale organization. The losses occurred mostly in large county groups separated from each other by no-loss counties. The large groups of associated counties with hail loss show the effects of passage of large hail-producing systems. Some of these large systems are loosely associated with large, synoptic weather systems (fronts, low-pressure centers, squall lines), which have been drawn in for each day. Some are associated with certain types of topography, as in the Texas Panhandle–New Mexico region. Although there is a certain degree of systematic pattern within the hail-producing systems, counties with highest losses are rather localized.

5. Hailfall and Thunderstorm Features

Hail at the ground is only an occasional product of thunderstorms. Why do not all thunderstorms produce hail? Some argue that all do but that the hail usually melts before reaching the ground. This is not substantiated by the many aircraft penetrations of thunderclouds. Byers and Braham (1949) reported that hail was encountered on only 51 of

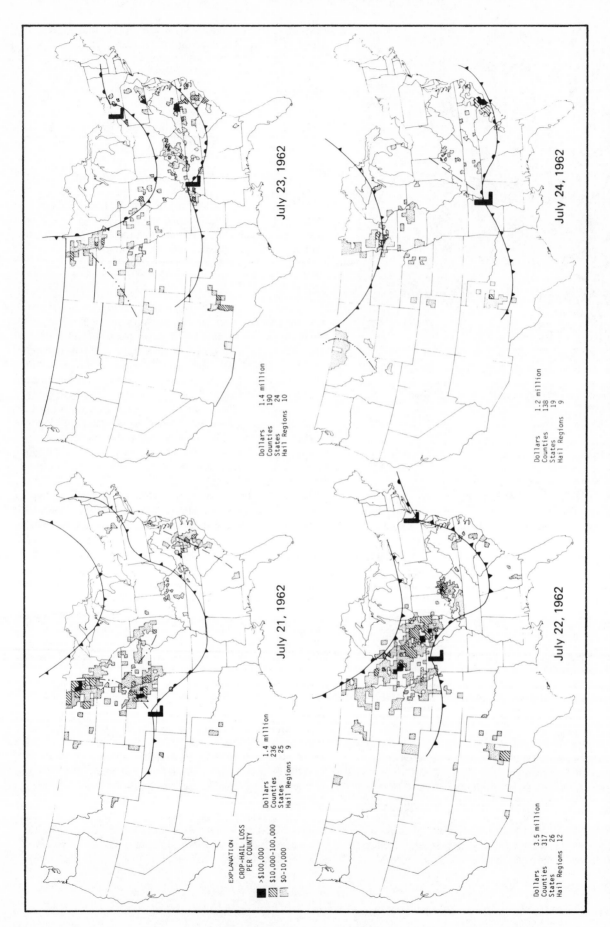

Figure 11.12. A 4-day sequence of maps showing the southeastward progression of hail damage in association with the movement of surface weather pattern (Changnon et al., 1977).

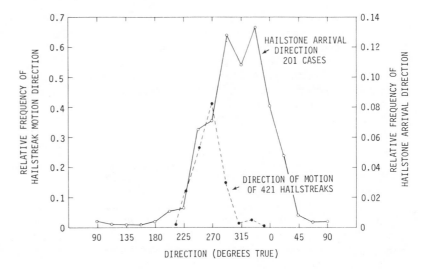

Figure 11.13. Frequency distribution of the direction of motion of hailstones arriving at the ground compared with the motion of the hailstreaks that produced the hail, as estimated from hailpad data in Illinois (Morgan and Towery, 1976).

rainfall intensity at a point increases, the probability of hail also occurring at that point also increases.

Some rain that falls from thunderstorms is undoubtedly melted hail. The notion that the very large, widely spaced raindrops, often the first to fall, are melted hailstones is very old (Volta, 1806). Attempts have been made to detect melted hail by measuring the temperature of rain (for example, Byers et al., 1959; Tomassini and Morgan, 1968). The results have never been quite clear, and Newton (1950) has shown that when a hailstone melts the resulting cold raindrop assumes the wet-bulb temperature of the air in such a short time that detecting drops with any other temperature is unlikely.

b. Hail and Thunderstorm Outflow

Hail does not always fall with strong winds, but the most damaging hailfalls are often accompanied by winds that increase the kinetic energy of impact of the stones. This is discussed in more detail in Vol. 3, Chap. 9. Changnon (1973) estimated that in Illinois 60% of hail occurrences are associated with significant wind. In a large sample from Italy, 61% of observations involved windblown hail (Vento and Morgan, 1976). Morgan and Towery (1976) have estimated the direction of arrival of hailstones from the dent orientations on hailpads. The distribution of these directions for 201 measurements made in Illinois in 1975 is shown in Fig. 11.13, along with the distribution of the orientation of 421 hailstreaks. These confirm a characteristic that had been previously noted in individual cases. The hailstreak orientations show a peak at about 270°; that is, the responsible hailcells tend to move from west to east. The hailstones tend to arrive from more northerly directions; that is, they are being blown across the cell to the right of its motion. The picture one gets from this is that the hail source aloft moves along the streak axis, releasing hail into a downdraft that blows across this track. This places the hail on the right side of the storm, or at least on the right of the downdraft air sources.

c. Hail and Lightning

Lightning ranks with hail as one of the most damaging and frightening phenomena accompanying thunderstorms. During the nineteenth century the two were closely linked in the public and scientific mind because of the wide acceptance of Volta's electrical theory of hail formation (1806).

A consequence of this nexus between hail and lightning was the spread through Europe and other parts of the world of thousands upon thousands of tall lightning rods, known universally by the French term *paragrêles*, erected especially for the prevention of hail. The theory behind this was that, since electrical forces were responsible for the suspension and growth of hailstones, discharging the cloud would stop the growth.

Sansom (1966a) reported that in Kenya there was markedly reduced lightning activity from damaging hailstorms compared with nondamaging storms. Table 11.10 shows the breakdown of 68 hailstorms by lightning frequency and the occurrence or nonoccurrence of crop damage. This shows that only 28% of damaging storms, as compared with 65% of nondamaging storms, were accompanied by lightning more frequent than one flash per 5 min. Sansom offered as an explanation the effect of the lightning-produced shock wave softening the hailstones. Hallett (1967) offered a microphysical explanation that linked the reduced lightning to the growth processes of the hail, thus proposing to exchange cause for effect. The question of relationship between lightning and hail is a very fundamental one and deserves further consideration in research.

There are no studies providing data on the position of lightning strikes in relation to the position of hailfall. This is an interesting question that would be amenable to field study. We can only pass on the general impression that in the high plains of the United States, where visibility is generally good and cloud bases high, cloud-to-ground lightning appears to occur just outside the precipitation shaft of thunderstorms. A Canadian study (Larson, 1973) has shown that in large thunderstorm (squall) systems most of the electrical discharges are not in the main centers of rain and hail activity but aloft in the rather stratified cloud at the rear of the squall line. This was first noted by Prohaska (1907).

d. Hail and Severe Weather

The largest hail is usually produced by the most strongly developed thunderstorms. For this reason hail is often accompanied by the other severe phenomena associated with thundery weather, such as tornadoes, severely damaging winds, and locally damaging rainfall. This association is often missed and, in fact, in the midwestern United States, where the most severe weather tends to occur in the spring, when most crops grown there are not yet susceptible to damage, hail that accompanies severe weather goes nearly unnoticed in relation to the attention received by tornadoes.

Changnon and Morgan (1976) prepared a calendar of convective weather events to serve as a basis for forecasting studies. This calendar listed, from March through October for 1967 to 1978, the daily occurrence of thunderstorms, rain, severe rainstorms ($\geq$10-cm depth of point rainfall), tornadoes, hail, and severe winds ($\geq$80 km h^{-1}) over a 67,840-km^2 area of central Illinois. The 56-mo period covered by the calendar included 42 days with tornadoes, 1,318 thunder and/or rain days, and 433 haildays. Hail occurred on 33% of the thunder-and-rain days.

It was found that 54 (at least 12%) of the days with hail also had tornadoes or heavy damaging rainfalls. This association is important because it provides background information essential for determining the impact of hail prevention experiments or operations on these other phenomena. Geographical variations in relationships between hail and severe weather are to be expected. Some of the more hail-prone areas, for example, the northern high plains of the United States, have relatively low tornado frequency.

e. Miscellaneous Phenomena Associated with Hailstorms

Most hailstorms occur with thunderclouds that have no distinctive coloration, but on some occasions observers report this as the most remarkable phenomenon associated with the storm they have experienced. The colors reported vary, pink and green being the most frequent. One of the authors, Griffith Morgan, performed a field survey of a very severe hailstorm that took place on 3 April 1974 near Bloomington, Ill. Giant, 7.5-cm diameter hailstones fell at many places from this hailstorm. Spectacular colors ranging from pink to green to yellow to red were reported from all sides of the storm cloud. In no way could they be attributed to sunset or sunrise effects; the storm took place shortly after local noon. Some of the accounts described the colors as "blackish yellow" or "reddish black." These colors, and es-

Table 11.10. Relationship Between the Number of Instances of Damaging and Nondamaging Hailstorms and the Interval Between Lightning Flashes in Kenya

	Interval between lightning flashes		
	$\leq$5 min	>5 min	No lightning
Number of damaging storms	11	13	15
Number of nondamaging storms	19	6	4

Source: Sansom, 1966a.

pecially green, are associated with tornado clouds. Residents of the midwest United States consider these anomalous cloud and sky colorations sure signs of some form of very severe weather. There appears to be no clear scientific explanation for these colors, in spite of numerous accounts in the literature of their occurrence.

At times one hears accounts of a remarkable low-lying dense cloud hugging the ground and assuming bizarre shapes caused by the wind that moves out ahead of the hailshaft. This was the case in a hailstorm whose characteristics were described by Towery and Morgan (1977). The phenomenon can appear to be a tornado and cause some concern to the observer. This cloud or fog is undoubtedly caused by the air being chilled below its dewpoint by the melting hail. Flora (1956) describes a South Dakota hailstorm, after which a heavy mist formed over the hail on the ground. This phenomenon is not common; probably a very large amount of hail is necessary to form a cloud that will endure any appreciable time.

On occasion various sounds are also associated with hailstorms. There are old accounts (Volta, 1806; Gibson, 1861) of crackling noises, coming from the hail-producing cloud and believed to be of electrical origin, that were compared to the sound of tons of walnuts pouring from the sky. Fishermen on Lake Garda, in Italy, have described a characteristic "hail roar" as hailstorms cross the lake (Ludlam, 1959). Some of the reported noises can be attributed to the action of wind and hail on trees and buildings.

f. Hail Formation and Growth Within Thunderstorms

It is important to know where in the thunderstorm cloud hail starts to grow, how it moves during its growth, and where, with respect to the moving cloud, it falls out. These are very difficult to pin down, and both theoretical and observational studies have achieved widely varying results.

(1) Theoretical Studies: Many attempts have been made to derive the growth trajectories of hailstones theoretically. A pioneering effort was that of Hitschfeld and Douglas (1963). Numerical models of convective clouds have been much exploited for this purpose. Most models to date have had only the vertical dimension, and most are steady state, though some describe the temporal evolution of the cloud. Gokhale and Rau (1969) used a steady-state model and inferred hail growing in the −4° to −30°C regions of the cloud. Dennis and Musil (1973) used a time-dependent formulation and reported that a hailstone's greatest growth would occur in the colder parts of the cloud, around −30°C. Bradley (1977) used a very similar model and deduced that the −30° to −58°C region as the important one.

Increasing the spatial dimensions of the model to two is a step toward realism and an opening to complexity. English (1969; 1973) developed a two-dimensional model of the air-flow and other properties of the severe-hailstorm updraft using observations presented by Chisholm (1969) and Warner (1969). Calculations of hailstone growth and trajectories in this model showed hailstones following high, arched trajectories from the embryo level (−5° and −15°C), peaking at the 7- to 8-km level in clouds where the −40°C level was from 7.3 to 10.1 km. Horizontal excursions of more than 6 km were inferred.

Three-dimensional airflow depicted by data from two or more Doppler radars that scan a common volume represents the most realistic description of the hailstone environment, since important advection effects and inferred cloud distributions are expressed in full detail, as discussed in Vol. 3, Chap. 13. Heymsfield *et al.* (1980) found that significant temporal and spatial variations of hail production were related to airflow evolution in a Colorado storm. The interaction of several cells individually providing favorable hail formation and growth environments is documented in that study as well as in an Oklahoma storm studied by Ziegler *et al.* (1983). A broad region of moderate updraft appears necessary to suspend hail aloft in the prime growth layer (Nelson, 1983).

The models applied to hailstorm studies by various researchers differ in many ways other than being one-, two-, or three-dimensional and being steady or time-dependent. The reader should consult Orville (1978) and Chap. 3 of this volume for a detailed review of progress and problems in the numerical simulation of hailstorm phenomena.

(2) Observations: The maximum frequency of hail encounters on the Thunderstorm Project (Byers and Braham, 1949) was between 10,000 and 15,000 ft (3 to 5 km) in Ohio, though hail was encountered at all altitudes up to 25,000 ft. In Florida the maximum frequency of hail encounters was at 16,000 ft. Maximum radar-echo top heights on the same project were 37,000 to 38,000 ft (12 to 13 km); in general only the lower two-thirds of the cloud was probed by the aircraft. The results suggest that hail is most frequent at midcloud levels.

Browning and Foote (1976) deduced from radar and other observations of the National Hail Research Experiment the hail-growth trajectories in a single supercell storm. They showed hail growth beginning (embryo stage) at altitudes between 5 and 10 km in a radar "hot spot" (probably a cumulus cell) on the right flank of the main updraft. During their growth the hailstones rose as high as 12 or 13 km (temperature below −40°C) and moved horizontally (relative to the storm) as much as 20 km from front to back.

In the Soviet Union (Sulakvelidze, 1967) radar evidence shows great geographical variability in the location of hail growth in the clouds. In the Alazan Valley (Georgian SSR), the accumulation zone (AZ), a zone of high liquid water content in which the Russian theories predict that hail grows, lies generally between 4 and 6.5 km above sea level. The AZ lies just above the level of the maximum in-cloud vertical velocity. Calculations using sounding data have shown that this velocity maximum can occur anywhere from 0° to −40°C. Radar measurements in the Alazan Valley show that the environment at the level of the cloudtops tends to be colder than −30°C. Radar and soundings have also shown that the temperature at the peak of the radar reflectivity profile, seen as the center of hail growth, can be from 0° to −36.4°C, with a modal value of −12° to −15°C. The zone tends to be from 3 to 7.5 km thick, most often 5.5 to 6 km. The temperature at the top of the zone, defined by the reflectivity being 10 dB less than the peak value, can be from −16.4° to −60°C, with a modal value of −36.3°C. The hail in these zones reaches the ground about 4–5 min after the zones appear. In the northern Caucasus and Transcausasus the "hail focus" lies, on the average, between 2.5° and −10°C, with an average temperature of −3.3°C at the maximum radar echo.

Battan (1975) analyzed Doppler radar observations of a mountain hailstorm and found evidence for hail at many levels in the storm, all the way to its top (near 12 km). He inferred growth during both ascent and descent of hailstones. Donaldson (1965) showed that the median height for the peak reflectivity in 37 hail cases in New England was about 7 km.

Attempts have been made to determine vertical trajectories of growing hailstones by analyzing the structure and isotopic composition of collected hailstones. Unequivocal interpretation of these studies is difficult (see Chap. 12), but the results may be indicative. Facy et al. (1963) performed early isotopic analyses, and Knight et al. (1975) and Macklin et al. (1977) have used the same techniques, considering also crystal structure and air-bubble sizes and concentrations. Knight et al. showed mostly simple trajectories but some indicating recirculation. Several large stones did not grow above the −25°C level. A comparison of hail trajectories inferred from isotopic analysis (Knight *et al.*, 1983) and a numerical model (Ziegler *et al.*, 1983) demonstrates encouraging agreement between the essentially independent structural-observational and numerical-physical models of hailstone evolution used by meteorologists during the mid-1980s.

Macklin et al. reported results indicating growth of a hailstone, mostly between −17° and −30°C, on an embryo that formed at around −30°C. Another grew at temperatures between −20° and −25°C on an embryo that originated somewhere between −10° and −15°C. The crystal analysis results for the giant Coffeyville hailstone suggested that it grew at temperatures slightly below −20°C, while the isotopic analysis indicated growth at temperatures slightly above −20°C.

These studies show that hail can form and grow at many

different locations and altitudes within thunderstorms. No doubt many of the differences can be accounted for by the different topographical and climatological regimes in which the studies were conducted. But the hope that one could find a single, all-encompassing theory of hail formation is rapidly fading. As more data become available, it seems more likely that there are several distinct classes of hailstorms in which the cloud microphysics and the storm dynamics interact in fundamentally different ways. These interactions are a focus of current hailstorm research.

6. Hailstorms and Their Environment

A discussion of the environment in which hailstorms take place must draw heavily on material that pertains to the more general area of severe-storm forecasting, covered in Chaps. 4–6 and Vol. 1, Chap. 8. Our attempt is to emphasize factors specifically applicable to hailstorms. We urge the interested reader to become acquainted with the amazing collection of experience and techniques in severe-storm forecasting presented by Miller (1972).

a. Hail and Surface Synoptic Features

When a weather forecaster analyzes a surface weather map, he tries to locate, by means of rather complex sets of clues in the data, certain features such as high- and low-pressure centers, fronts, and squall lines. In the mind of the analyst these features carry idealized distributions of weather phenomena. The approach and passage of a cold front, for example, is associated with a certain average sequence of weather events, and the timing of this sequence can be tied to the expected speed of the front. Forecasters have developed associations, albeit subjective, between hailstorms and these analysis devices that provide tools useful to forecasters and studies of hailstorm climatology (Huff, 1964).

Fawbush et al. (1957) determined that the percentage of hailstorms associated with fronts (including squall lines) for the entire United States varies from 37 in Arizona-Nevada to 100 in Mississippi. At Denver, Colo., Harrison and Beckwith (1951) and Beckwith (1960) have described hailstorms there as mainly post-cold-frontal phenomena associated with anticyclones north and east of Denver or with the western quadrants of nearby cold lows. Morgan (1973) noted that postfrontal squall formation was responsible for some of the heaviest hailstorms in the Po Valley of Italy, and this may be characteristic of areas to the lee of large mountains.

Vogel (1974) tabulated the synoptic features associated with all summer rain events over a large rain-hail network in St. Louis. Thirty-nine rain periods had hailstorms. Their distribution by synoptic type was determined by R. Grosh (personal communication) and is given in Table 11.11. Hail was most often associated with squall lines, then squall areas, cold fronts, and warm fronts. Together these four types accounted for 90% of the hail-producing periods. Fawbush et al. (1957) found 86% of Illinois hailstorms to be front-related.

Table 11.11. Frequency of Hail for Various Synoptic Types *

	Percent of the 39 hail-producing periods	Number of hail cases as a percent of total periods in the indicated category
Squall line	44	61
Squall area	21	19
Cold front	15	32
Warm front	10	57
Low	5	50
Stationary front	3	9
Air mass	3	2

*Changnon and Morgan (1976).

b. Hail and Thermal Stratification of the Atmosphere

Only a few thunderstorms produce hail that reaches the ground. Shands (1944) first pointed out that in the United States the regions of greatest thunderstorm frequency (Florida and the Gulf states) are also the regions of lowest hailstorm frequency. He also noted however, that in any one place years of high thunderstorm frequency are also years of high hail frequency. On the other hand, the ratio of hail to thunderstorm occurrence reaches a minimum at the time of the maximum occurrence of both hail and thunderstorms during the warmest months. Shands's explanation for this involved the lower average height of the zero isotherm in the spring as the determining factor. When the zero level is at high altitude, much hail melts before reaching the ground.

Appleman (1959) sought to explain the behavior of the hail-thunder ratio. He examined regimes of static air-mass instability in the Great Plains and the Gulf states and found essentially no difference. Citing also a study by Wood (1955) showing that the warmer the base temperature of the thunderstorm the greater the instability energy required to produce hail at the ground, Appleman restated the importance of the greater warmth of the lower parts of the Gulf Coast clouds in suppressing hail. The mechanism he favored to explain the hail-suppressing effect of warm cloud bases was derived from the large-droplet theory of hail formation that identifies the largest droplets entering the freezing zone of the cloud as the hail embryos. He speculated that when the warm part of the cloud is deep the largest droplets grow to fallout sizes and never enter the freezing region, and the cloud then produces only snowflakes and graupel in its colder regions. Pappas (1962) has based a hail occurrence (yes-no) forecast technique on Appleman's reasoning, and Grosh and Morgan (1975) have attempted to apply it to the interpretation of radar echoes.

Many studies have attempted to relate hail occurrence or nonoccurrence, and hail sizes, to upper-air thermodynamic soundings with the motivation of improving hail forecasting. The earliest index of instability for thunderstorm fore-casting was given by Showalter (1953); it is based on the difference between the temperature of a parcel of air lifted from the 850-mb (1,500-m) level to 500 mb (6,000 m) and the temperature of the 500-mb environment. Instability, or strong potential for storm development, is favored by warm, moist air at low levels being overlain by relatively cool air at midlevels. Over the years many other indices, mostly resembling the Showalter Index, have been developed, such as the Lifted Index (Galway, 1956), Boyden's Index (1963), and the Vertical and Cross Totals of Miller (1972). These are used in hail forecasting on the assumption that the greater the instability value (1) the greater the likelihood of thunderstorms, (2) the greater the probable strength of the thunderstorm, (3) the greater the likelihood of hail, and (4) the greater the probable size of the largest hail (Dan-ielson's [1978] discussion of the many inherent difficulties in hail prediction merits reading).

Miller (1972) includes two techniques based on thermal stratification that are directly focused on hail. One proposes that the probability of hail is greatest when the height of the *wet-bulb zero* (WBZ, the height above the ground at which the wet-bulb temperature equals 0°C) lies in a certain range. The height of the WBZ is seen as both the level at which falling hail begins to melt and the level of origin of the thun-derstorm downdraft. Morgan (1970) has shown, however, that the WBZ height is well correlated with the average mixing ratio in the lowest layers, another parameter used in thunder and hail prediction, so that the importance of WBZ to hail is unclear (Morgan studied these parameters at one location and did not consider the horizontal variation of WBZ). This problem of intercorrelation between parame-ters taken from soundings is very pervasive in the search for hail predictors.

The other hail technique presented by Miller is used to forecast the size of hail. It is based on a calculation of the velocity the updraft acquires through buoyance as it passes through the hailstone growth region, presumed to be in the $-5°$ to $-10°C$ region. More complex versions of this are identified by numerical cloud models (Renick and Maxwell, 1978). Some success is claimed for such techniques, but at-tempts to reproduce the results elsewhere, for example, in Colorado, have not been very successful.

c. Hail and Winds Aloft

Dessens (1960) proposed that hailstorms were strongly fa-vored by the existence of strong winds in the upper tro-posphere. Ratner (1961) examined this hypothesis and concluded that neither strong wind nor wind shear was im-portant to hailstorms. However, Ratner based his study on the occurrence or nonoccurrence of hail or thunderstorms at 42 North American rawinsonde sites, essentially ignoring what has been said above about the spatial variability of hailfall. One should monitor hail occurrence over a large area surrounding the radiosonde site to search properly for any correlation between the sounding parameters and hail occurrence. Ratner's failure to do this probably explains

why his is the only study to deny any importance of winds aloft.

The current thought is that strong winds aloft and strong wind shear through the troposphere do play a role in orga-nizing some of the most severe storms that produce large hail but that many, even most, hailstorms occur without strong winds. Longley and Thompson (1965) found hail in Alberta to be somewhat associated with strong SW winds at 500 mb ($\sim$6,000 m).

Strong winds aloft are generally associated with the jet stream, as are the vertical motion systems that modulate air-mass stability. There is thus an intercorrelation problem in assessing the role and relative importance of winds aloft to hailstorms.

Fawbush and Miller (1953) emphasized the importance of winds exceeding 35 knots (18 m s^{-1}) in the middle tropo-sphere for the occurrence of tornado-bearing severe storms. Darkow and Fowler (1971) compared a set of proximity soundings with a set of check soundings and documented the existence of strong winds aloft in tornado situations, which often produce large hail.

Others have supported theoretically and empirically the role of strong winds in the environment of severe hail-storms. Among these are Schleusener (1962), Das (1962), Frisby (1962), and Modahl (1969).

Ludlam (1963) stressed the association between very se-vere thunderstorms and hailstorms and the jet stream, show-ing several examples (Fig. 11.14) from Europe in which the storms occurred on the anticyclonic side of a large-scale jet maximum. Figure 11.14 shows relationships between thun-derstorms and the jet stream. The isotachs are actually of wind shear between a low level and 500 mb, but this strongly reflects the wind maximum of the jet. Ludlam also showed the global correspondence between areas subject to severe squall thunderstorms and the mean position of the jet stream during the months of peak storminess in each area (Fig. 11.15).

Thompson and Summers (1970) showed that upper winds strongly influence the spatial distributions of hail in Al-berta. Hail in long, well-organized swaths occurred most frequently with strong westerly winds aloft and a reversal of wind shear about 1,000 ft above the ground, while poorly organized swaths and scattered hail patterns occurred with light winds aloft and no shear reversal. The average swath orientation was about 25° to the right of the midtropo-spheric wind flow.

Newton and Newton (1959) proposed that the importance of strong winds aloft and the accompanying strong wind shear lies in the dynamic pressure fields generated by the wind blowing against the storm column. The shear deter-mines the vertical gradients of these pressures. When the wind increases with height, these gradients cause negative vertical accelerations upwind and positive downwind. For a typical severe-storm wind profile these forces favor devel-opment and propagation of the storm on its front right flank.

The importance of the strong winds and wind shears was explained by Browning and Ludlam (1962) as providing a

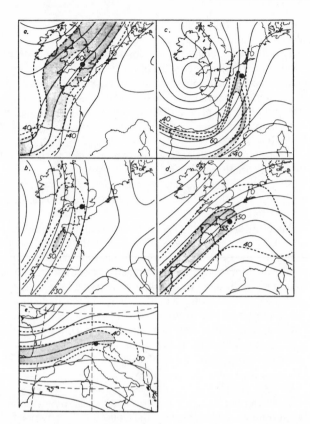

Figure 11.14. Maps showing the relationship between five severe thunderstorms in Western Europe and wind-shear structure. The continuous lines are 500-mb contours at 40-m intervals. Dashed lines are isotachs of the wind shear between the surface and 500 mb with the strongest areas stippled. The location of the maximum hailstorm intensity is shown by the black dot (Ludlam, 1963).

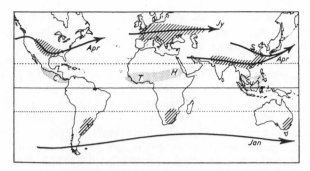

Figure 11.15. Worldwide distribution of areas subject to severe squall thunderstorms. In middle latitudes the areas (hatched) are closely related to the mean monthly position of the 500-mb jet and often produce large hail. In the tropics the squall thunderstorms (stippled) occur where the monsoonal circulations generate a well-defined intertropical convergence zone, and these are not accompanied by large hail (Ludlam, 1963).

setting for the maintenance of what they termed a *supercell*. The sheared-wind structure causes low-level air to approach the storm from the front with considerable speed. This air rises into the storm along sloped trajectories that allow rain forming within it to fall out, thereby enhancing its buoyancy and allowing it to achieve strong vertical velocities. At middle and upper levels the strong winds blowing against the back of the storm create dynamic pressure forces that deviate the streamlines into the vertical and then downwind, creating the familiar "anvil" or "plume" that can often be seen stretching hundreds of kilometers downwind of large thunderstorms. Some of the rain falling out of the sloping updraft at lower and middle levels falls into very dry air overtaking the storm from its rear. Evaporation of the rain into this air chills it (in the same way that air flowing over a wet-bulb thermometer cools it below the air temperature), and it becomes cold and negatively buoyant. A coherent downrush or downdraft of air thus formed spreads forward under the sloping updraft. At its leading edge this downdraft acts somewhat like a snowplow, thrusting up the warm inflowing air it displaces. The storm thus contains a positive

feedback loop: the rising warm air produces falling rain that evaporates to produce cold air that functions to thrust up more warm air, and so forth. Such a storm can persist for many hours. The energy gained by the chilled downdraft constitutes one of the most damaging aspects of severe storms; surface winds in excess of 40 m s^{-1} often occur over long paths from such storms.

There are two schools of thought on hail growth. One maintains that hail grows in a once-up, then-down fashion, the other, that hail "recirculates," making several up-and-down trips. There is evidence for both, and both probably occur. The layered structure of hailstones was ascribed to up-and-down excursions of the stone in the cloud at least as early as Volta, but it has been shown (see Chap. 12) that layered structure can also occur without it. The rare occurrences of giant hailstones have lent strength to the recirculation theories.

In addition to playing a role in determining the intensity and lifetime of severe thunderstorms, wind shear and strong upper winds affect the shape of the airflow in storms, and this is felt to be important to large-hail growth. Browning and Ludlam (1962) analyzed radar and radiosonde observations of a severe traveling storm in England and concluded that, owing to strong winds aloft, the streamlines of the updraft (inflow) air were inclined toward (from front to back) the storm in the low levels and away from it (downwind) at high levels. This allowed small hailstones in the upper part of the storm to descend at the front of the storm column and be swept back into the storm for continued growth. This is the much-discussed recirculation model of large-hailstone growth. Morgan (1972) has calculated trajectories of growing hailstones in a simplified numerical model of the hailstorm airflow. These show that, given the proper initial size, growth rate, and position in the airflow, a hailstone can float at constant level, perform loops, or be thrown out of the storm. In particular instances hailstones can be retained for hours, since they move toward regions of stronger updraft as their fallspeeds increase. There is thus sufficient time for the growth of hailstones to the maximum size supportable by the updraft and no need for explosive growth rates. The rarity of the combination of conditions—a persistent, strong updraft and the proper range of temperatures in a region of the cloud where the airflow has the proper configuration—may account for the rarity of large hail.

d. The General Problem of Forecasting Hail

The preceding discussion has concerned partial approaches to hail forecasting. In practice an integrated approach is required. A number of factors must be considered simultaneously, and it is possible that nonlinear combinations of parameters will be required. For example, wind shear plays a role in the organization of the most severe hailstorm, but it is likely that, if shear is too strong, storm development will be inhibited. A major source of nonlinearity in the forecast problem is the existence of several distinct types of hailstorms (Marwitz, 1972a,b,c). Some principal defined types are these: (1) an air mass or pulsating, multiple-bubble storm (Ludlam, 1959); (2) a "multicell" storm (Renick, 1971); and (3) a large, severe supercell storm (Browning and Ludlam, 1962). The first requires great thermal instability and occurs in the absence of wind shear or strong winds. It is not often associated with heavy or widespread crop damage. The second requires moderate-to-strong instability and a proper vertical wind profile. It is responsible for substantial crop damage because of the quantity, and occasionally size, of hail produced. The role of the downdraft in this type of storm has not been extensively explored. The third may occur without great instability, requires strong winds with a properly organized vertical profile, and is associated with a strong, organized downdraft fed by rain-cooled air from the middle troposphere. It can produce very large stones, great crop damage, and severe wind damage. It seems to be a type of storm associated with tornadoes (Browning and Donaldson, 1963).

Nelson and Young (1978) analyzed observers' reports from the National Severe Storms Laboratory network in Oklahoma and determined that hailstones are on the average larger there than those in South Africa, and hailfall areas in Oklahoma are larger than those in either South Africa or Illinois. This was attributed to a high relative frequency of supercell storms in Oklahoma, where 24% of the sample of observed storms were supercells. In contrast, no such storms have been observed in South Africa, and 10% of Illinois storms are supercells. Definitions of these types of storms are rather subjective, and on some occasions it may be difficult to associate a given hail occurrence with one type or the other.

Adequate forecasting must deal with predicting which storm type will occur, then with the probability of hail occurrence, and then with details of hail size, amount, location, and timing. Medium-range forecasting (3 to 12 h) will require considerable advancement in our understanding of relationships between the hailstorm and its environment. At the shortest time ranges storm motion can be extrapolated from meteorological radar data, though interpretation of radar information is not without its share of serious problems.

At this writing, the state of hailstorm forecasting is not among the brighter spots in meteorology. It is difficult to forecast thunderstorms adequately, and it is even more difficult to forecast the occurrence of hail, not to mention details of time, place, duration, and intensity.[1]

[1]The authors thank L. Wojtiw, of the Alberta Research Council, for providing the raw hailpad data from the Alberta networks used in Sec. 2a. The hailpad data for the 1976 Colorado network were provided by R. Matson. Nancy Knight wrote Sec. 2e on hailstone embryos. Finally, our thanks go to Barbara Strand for typing the manuscript.

12. Properties and Growth of Hailstones

Roland List

1. Introduction

Hailstones are products of many thunderstorms in which they can grow to large size, provided sufficiently large updrafts allow the ice meteors to stay long enough in cloud regions where icing takes place. Hail occurs in many parts of the world, and it is no surprise that people have been interested in hailstones for a long time, not only because of their beauty but also because of the damage they produce. The Po Valley, in Italy, has always experienced much hail—Leonardo da Vinci proposed that the city of Verona fight hail with mortars—and the first known drawing of a layered hailstone originates from the same region and goes back to Alessandro Volta (Weickmann, 1953). Observations of hailstones were numerous in the nineteenth century, particularly in the region surrounding the Alps. Trabert (1896) gave an extensive survey including theories on hail formation. In England, where hail occurs occasionally, Reynolds (1877) was able to establish that hailstones grow by accretion of droplets, and Bilham and Relf (1937) addressed themselves to aerodynamic questions. Schumann (1938) formulated the first mathematical theory on hail formation and, after moving to South Africa, initiated hail research continued there by Mossop and Kidder (1961) and Carte (1961). Ludlam (1958), involved in the Italian hail problem, produced a new, comprehensive hail theory on the basis of observations and scientific deduction. His work with Macklin and Browning was extended later by Macklin with his group in Australia.

The Swiss Hail Commission initiated in 1952 (parallel to the hail-suppression experiment at the southern slope of the Alps, the Grossversuche I–III) the first extensive laboratory studies of hailstones, including the building of wind tunnels in which hailstone growth could be simulated. This work was carried out by R. List, who was later joined by Aufdermaur. In 1963, List started his new group in Canada.

Argentina, with its own hail-suppression experiment, also felt a need for scientific backup. Thus Iribarne and de Pena (1962) began the numerical modeling of hailstones that grow by competing for available water; Levi is known for her work on ice structures (Levi and Aufdermaur, 1970).

Abich (1869) investigated hailstones in the Caucasus, another area with frequent hail. Recent hailstone research in the USSR is summarized by Sulakvelidze et al. (1967).

In the United States, Knight and Knight initiated research on hailstones at NCAR, specializing in structure and growth. The Illinois State Water Survey (Changnon and colleagues) concentrated on climatological aspects at the ground associated with hail.

The following sections indicate our knowledge of the properties and growth of hailstones, outlining the achievements of the past and pointing out their implications for the future (for a more extensive treatment of hail, see Foote and Knight, 1977).

2. Description of Hailstones and Their Evolution

a. Definitions

The major types of ice particles involved in the growth of hailstones can be defined as follows (List, 1965):

(1) Graupel: *Graupel*, or soft hail, are white, opaque, conical (but sometimes dendritic, rounded, or irregular) pellets with diameters up to 0.005 m and densities up to 800 kg m^{-3}. The pellets consist of a central ice crystal that has accreted supercooled water droplets that freeze after impact; growth may also be initiated by frozen droplets. The ice framework of graupel consists of a few single crystals of ice. In the conical shapes the cone surface may sometimes exhibit a feathery structure, indicating growth by sublimation (deposition) from the gaseous phase. The main growth, however, occurs at the base by droplet accretion. Graupel is compressible and rebounds on a hard surface. The expression "snow pellet," i.e., a particle consisting of agglomerates of frozen cloud droplets but no discernible ice crystals, should not be used for graupel; it grows under different, wintertime conditions. The worldwide finding of mostly conical hailstone centers supports this distinction. A typical early state of a graupel with the initial dendritic crystal still clearly recognizable is shown in Fig. 12.1; a larger, "mature" graupel is depicted in Fig. 12.2.

(2) Small Hail: *Small hail* (or ice pellet type *b*, according to the *Glossary of Meteorology*, Huschke, 1959) is generally semitransparent and rounded, often with conical tips, diameters up to 0.005 m, and densities ranging from about

Figure 12.1. A rimed dendrite, diameter 1.45 mm, thickness 0.7 mm (List, 1958a).

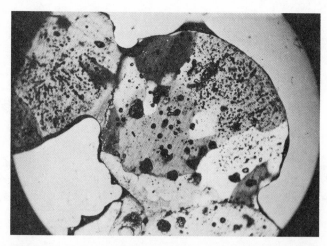

Figure 12.3. Thin section (thickness 0.35 mm) through a small hail particle, diameter 4.2 mm. Small hail particles are always wet and freeze together with others; hence the two other attached particles under polarized light, with individual single crystals indicated by varying grayness. (List, 1958a).

Figure 12.2. Thin section (thickness 0.35 mm) through the main axis of conical graupel, height 4.5 mm (List, 1958a).

800 to ~990 kg m⁻³ (for comparison, the density of ice is 917 kg m⁻³; higher densities imply inclusion of water, with the water density at 1,000 kg m⁻³). Small, growing hail consists partly of liquid water; an outer shell may be frozen. These particles generally consist of a few ice single crystals. They grow from graupel by intake of liquid water into the air capillaries of their ice framework (spongy-ice type II, as opposed to type I, which grows directly). The water can be produced either by accretion of cloud droplets that do not

freeze completely or by partial melting of the original graupel.

Small-hail particles represent an intermediate stage between graupel and hailstones. They are distinguished from graupel by their higher density and an at least partly glazed surface and from hailstones by size (limitation to 0.005 m). A cut through a typical small-hail particle in polarized light is shown in Fig. 12.3.

(3) Ice Pellets: *Ice pellets*, or sleet, are transparent, globular, or irregular grains of ice with diameters of less than 0.005 m and densities nearly equal to ice density or higher (indicating the presence of liquid water), but < 1,000 kg m⁻³. The structure is mono- or multicrystalline. Their interiors may be partly liquid, in which case they may break when they hit a hard surface. They are produced by freezing of raindrops or refreezing of partly melted snowflakes; they may also grow from fragments of drops that have broken up while freezing. What may be a frozen drop forming a hailstone center is shown in Fig. 12.4. The origin of essentially single crystalline hailstone centers (diameters up to 0.014 m) occasionally observed is still unknown. Such particles would certainly fall into the class of ice pellets.

(4) Hailstones: *Hailstones* are lumps of ice or ice and water, with air inclusions and diameters > 0.005 m. Partially or completely opaque, they exhibit mostly a layered, shell-like arrangement of air bubbles. Shapes are usually roughly spherical or conical (diameters 0.005a–0.01 m); ellipsoidal or conical (0.01–0.02 m); ellipsoidal, often with small lobes or knobs and indentations along the shortest axis (0.01–0.05 m); and roughly spherical or irregular, with small or large protuberances (0.04–0.10 m). Other shapes,

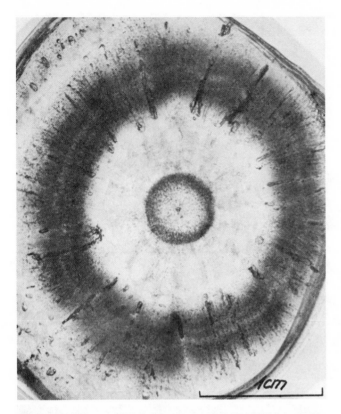

Figure 12.4. Section of hailstone 57.22, showing what is probably a frozen 5.5-mm raindrop (List 1958b).

Figure 12.5. Sample of mostly ellipsoidal hailstones of the hailstorm in Fischbach, Switzerland, on 21 June 1957 (List, 1958b).

such as disks, crystals with plane surfaces, and slices of spheres, have also been observed. Hailstones may consist partly of spongy ice (ice-water mixtures). Slushy hail with density limited by the density of water has a particularly high liquid-water content. The density of hailstones stored at temperatures below 0°C before investigation is mostly between 850 and 917 kg m^{-3}, but somewhat less when there are large interior air cavities. The hailstone centers may be either transparent or opaque.

Hailstones grow by accretion of supercooled water droplets or drops, starting mainly from small-hail particles. Sometimes frozen drops may be recognizable as embryos. The crystallographic structure of hailstones is also layered, with shells of small single crystals often being accompanied by shells of air bubbles, and layers of palisadelike big single crystals by clear ice regions.

As a rule, hailstones grow from one single center; clusters of different original particles are very rare. A typical sample of ellipsoidal hailstones is displayed in Fig. 12.5, and unusual shapes are displayed in Fig. 12.6.

The shell-like arrangement of air bubbles with alternating clear and opaque ice can be recognized from the 0.002-m slice of ice from a hailstone (Fig. 12.7). Note the obvious embryo region, representing the original graupel. The same slice, machined to a thickness of 0.00033 m, placed between two crossed polarizing filters, and exposed to light,

gives the crystallographic picture, i.e., the size, shape, and arrangement of single crystals (Fig. 12.8). These descriptions of ice particles could be extended by data such as the small- and large-scale roughness of the outer surface, the large-scale roughness of intermediary shapes, and the isotope contents of hailstone shells.

Selected information leading to these definitions and more detailed descriptions of hailstones can be found in Browning (1966), Carte and Kidder (1970), Douglas (1963), English (1973), Genève (1961), the *Glossary of Meteorology*, Knight and Knight (1971, 1973a and b, 1974), List and de Quervain (1953), List (1958a and b, 1959a, 1960a and b, 1961a and b), List and Schemenauer (1971), List et al. (1970, 1972), Ludlam (1958), Macklin and Ludlam (1961), Macklin (1961, 1963), Macklin and Bailey (1966, 1968), Mason (1971), Mossop and Kidder (1961), Reinking (1975), Sarrica (1959a and b), Schaefer (1960), and Weickmann (1956, 1964).

b. The Growth Stages of Hailstones

The different growth stages are often recognizable from the hailstone structure. However, direct observations in nature from mountain observatories or aircraft of ice particles at different stages of their development more firmly establish the pattern of this evolution.

Figure 12.6. Unusual-shaped hailstones 64.6: C1, C2, and C3, that fell in Root, Switzerland, on 22 July 1964. Diameter of coin, 3.2 cm (photograph Wengi, courtesy A. A. Aufdermaur).

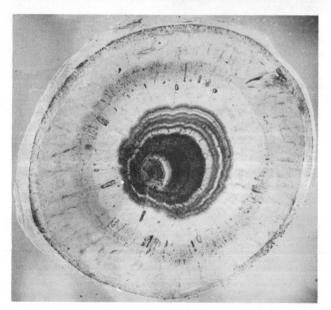

Figure 12.7. Section (thickness 2.0 mm) of hailstone 59.1 in transmittent light; diameter 4.0 cm. Note the conical embryo in the center of the subsequent shells of air bubbles (List, 1960a).

Figure 12.8. Thin section (thickness 0.3 mm) of hailstone 59.1 under polarized light, exposing crystal structure; diameter 4.0 cm. Note that the embryo region consists of larger single crystals and that the air-bubble region (compare with Fig. 12.7) is accompanied by either small or large single crystals (List, 1960a).

The growth of hailstones can be explained with the help of Fig. 12.9. Hail formation generally takes place in a cloud of supercooled water droplets that originated from condensation on cloud condensation nuclei (CCN). Ice requires not only a temperature below 0°C but also a catalyst to trigger the phase transition. The following types of ice nucleation are recognized: deposition of water vapor into the ice phase on particulate matter; condensation of vapor into the liquid phase with subsequent freezing by nucleation; activation of nuclei immersed in water droplets; and contact nucleation, where nuclei collide with droplets and induce them to solidify (Parungo et al., 1976). The relative importance of the different mechanisms is still disputed (Fukuta, 1975). No matter what the effective mechanism of nucleation is in a given situation, deposition of water vapor into the solid phase leads to the growth of ice crystals, at the expense of the omnipresent cloud droplets. Most ice nuclei are 10^{-7} to 10^{-6} m in diameter, but ice crystals will grow to 0.001 m or more. When they reach ~ 0.0003 to 0.001 m, their relative fall velocity is such that they collide with essentially stationary cloud droplets ($\sim 10^{-6}$ to 2×10^{-5} m in diameter, depending on the situation) and capture them (Sasyo, 1971). The heat budget normally allows them to freeze very quickly. This riming process initiates the growth of graupel. The fall velocity increases with increasing particle size, often bringing the graupel into warmer regions of the cloud. The droplet collection rate becomes higher, and the freezing is slower such that the accreted droplets can be sucked into the air capillaries of the graupel, initiating a densification stage. Small hail is a transitory stage that, after densification of the original graupel is completed, automatically leads to a resumption of the volumetric growth. This normally takes place at ~ 0.0005 m. The new growth stage is called *hailstone*.

This evolution from ice nucleus to hailstone is straightforward and represents the most probable development. It is complicated, however, by the possible occurrence of an ice multiplication mechanism (Hallett and Mossop, 1974; Mossop, 1976) that can explain the existence of more ice particles than can be accounted for by the number of ice nuclei.

There is also evidence that frozen drops, rather than ice crystals, can serve as hailstone embryos (see Knight and Knight, 1974). The original drops (diameters 0.0002 to 0.004 m) can be formed directly through the warm-rain mechanism (List, 1974), i.e., without the involvement of ice particles. However, it is unlikely that this process is important for hail formation. It is more likely that drops are produced by smaller ice particles melting in warm parts of a cloud. If such drops fall to the ground, they represent a typical case of cold rain, i.e., rain formed by the Wegener-Bergeron-Findeisen process (see Chap. 16). However, if drops are again swept upward into the cold regions of the cloud, they may freeze, form sleet, and grow into hailstones by accretion of supercooled droplets.

There are two other mechanisms for drop formation accompanying the hail process. Growing hailstones can shed parts of their liquid water skin in the form of large drops, particularly when the growing hailstones rotate or gyrate.

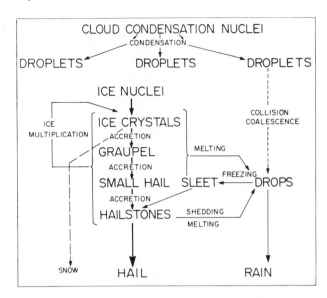

Figure 12.9. Major growth stages of hail in a cloud of supercooled droplets.

When this type of direct conversion of cloud water into raindrops takes place at subzero temperatures, the newly formed larger drops can either freeze and form new hailstone embryos or be captured by other hailstones. Hailstone melting would also produce drops falling as rain or new embryos if the liquid particles were later lifted by updrafts.

The involvement of drops (in addition to droplets) in the formation of hail may be a new key concept in our understanding of hail formation. There is another point to be made. The particles indicated in Fig. 12.9 have distinctive properties by which they can be recognized by the skilled observer, but they are nevertheless labeled hailstones as soon as they surpass 0.005 m, a criterion established by the World Meteorological Organization. There is really no benefit in asking why this cloud produces hail and another similar-looking one does not when both contain ice particles but some in the first cloud happen to be large enough to be called hail. There is also no distinction made in this present treatment of hailstones and their growth in the type of cloud in which they evolve, except that they need to have regions with temperature below 0°C, supercooled water, and updrafts.

c. Spongy Ice

The original justification for building the Swiss hail tunnel (List, 1959b) lay in the recognition that the growth history of hail is imprinted in the shape and structure of the stones and in the possibility of discovering it by proper techniques. In particular, it was believed that the icing conditions that lead to hail growth could be duplicated in the laboratory and that experiments in an icing tunnel with artificial hailstones could reveal the growth history. This thesis has governed research on hailstone growth since the 1950s. It served its purpose well when simplistic assumptions were more than

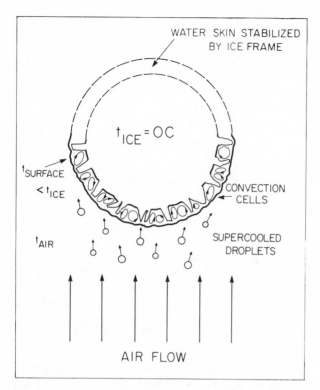

Figure 12.10. Schematic diagram of spongy-ice growth. The ice frame grows from the hailstone center while the latent heat of freezing is removed at the outer surface, where accretion of supercooled cloud droplets take place. If the heat loss at the surface to the air is not sufficient to freeze all the accreted water, then spongy ice is formed.

adequate. Its effective breakdown comes, however, with the steadily increasing recognition of the complexity of hailstone behavior and growth, which, to analyze even one single hailstone, would require technologies and manpower hitherto unheard of in cloud physics.

The first experiment in the Swiss hail tunnel (List, 1959c) showed a completely new type of ice, formed under conditions where the heat transfer to the hailstone is insufficient to freeze all the accreted water. The unfrozen water is built into and stabilized by a growing ice framework, producing *spongy ice* (List, 1960b). Previously Schumann (1938) had assumed—and Ludlam (1958) agreed—that only as much water could be accreted as could be frozen. The rest would be shed into the airstream. But this accretion process turned out to be very complex and not amenable to theoretical solution; experiments are required.

Spongy-ice formation is diagrammed in Fig. 12.10. Figure 12.11 shows the air capillary system in a real spongy-ice deposit after the liquid water was removed in a centrifuge. The ice framework is never allowed to reach the surface and spread, but is always covered with newly incoming droplets.

Spongy ice led to complications, because the growth and properties of an ice layer do not depend on the initial growth conditions alone; they can be substantially altered at a later time. List (1961b) showed how the three types of ice encountered in icing by droplet accretion can be transformed. First, all three ice types—spongy ice, *porous ice* (ice with connecting air capillary systems), and *compact ice* (ice with any occurring air bubbles or air pockets not interconnecting)—can grow directly. Second, each type can also result from one (or both, in the case of compact ice) of the other two as is indicated in Fig. 12.12. No satisfactory way has

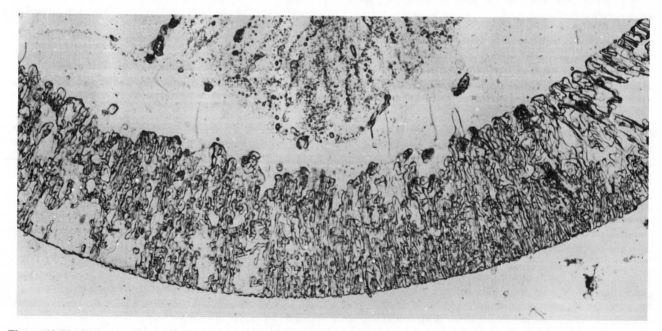

Figure 12.11. Spongy-ice deposit grown in Swiss hail tunnel I on a fixed ice sphere with a diameter of 2 cm. Icing conditions: $T_A = -10°C$, $V = 18$ m s^{-1}, $EW_f = 7$ g m^{-3}, $I = 28\%$. The water that remained liquid after accretion (72%) was removed in a centrifuge before this photograph was taken.

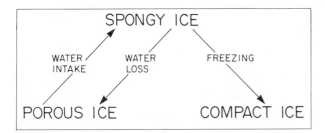

Figure 12.12. Transition of ice types involving spongy, porous, and compact ice. These three types can also grow directly.

yet been found to ascertain the original ice type and to resolve the superposition of growth stages in any given hailstone shell (see also Knight and Knight, 1968).

d. The Growth Mechanisms of Hailstones

(1) Accretion and Loss Mechanisms: Understanding the mechanisms and rate of hailstone growth is the principal objective of hail studies. Reynolds (1876), who resolved the problem of raindrop growth in favor of the coalescence mechanism over growth by condensation, also tackled the hail problem. For this purpose he built the first simulator, as drawn in Fig. 12.13. In this miniature wind tunnel the airflow was produced by bellows and the cloud droplets by injection of a stream of droplets through a needle. Air and droplets were cooled by injected ether. The deposits he produced on splinters of wood were similar to deposits on hailstones, and this convinced him that the governing growth mechanism had to be droplet accretion. More elaborate wind tunnels such as those by List (1959b, 1966), Mossop and Kidder (1962), and Macklin (1977) confirmed and expanded those findings.

The rate of encounter of droplets and hailstones depends primarily on their relative speed or mainly, since droplet speeds are small (R. J. List, 1968), on the speed of the hailstones. Drag coefficients of smooth spheres were first measured in the proper Reynolds number range by Wieselsberger (1923). However, his results were not applied to hailstone fall velocities. When a hailfall in England with ice-particle diameters of up to 0.05 m and more stimulated interest, Bilham and Relf (1937) pulled smooth spheres through the atmosphere with an aircraft and deduced appropriate drag coefficients. These or equivalent values are still used in calculations of hail growth. When and how these values have to be changed is explained below.

A falling hailstone is assumed to sweep out the liquid water in its path. If all the cloud droplets have a total mass concentration of W_f (liquid water content, *LWC*, in kg m^{-3}) and no appreciable fall velocity relative to the surrounding air, and if the hailstone fall velocity is given by V (m s^{-1}), then the mass growth rate, dM/dt, is proportional to $W_f V$. This needs to be multiplied by the hailstone cross section ($\pi D^2/4$ for spherical particles). If only a fraction E of the

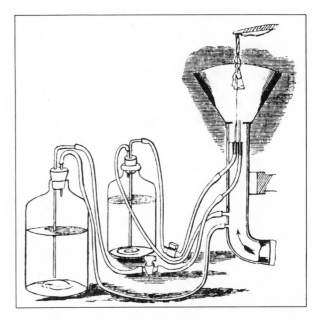

Figure 12.13. The apparatus of Reynolds (1877) for the production of artificial ice deposits.

droplets in the hailstone path is collected, then the mass growth rate of a spherical hailstone is

$$dM/dt = \frac{1}{2}\,\pi D^2 \rho_h\, dD/dt = \pi E D^2\, VW_f/4. \quad (12.1)$$

The middle term is another expression of mass growth in terms of the hailstone diameter D; ρ_h is the hailstone density.

The velocity is dependent on the diameter because both are related through Newton's third law, which equates the total drag force with the weight. For spheres, this leads to

$$V = \sqrt{\frac{4\,\rho_h\, g}{3\,\rho\, c_D}\,D}\,, \quad (12.2)$$

where ρ is the density of the air, g is the gravitational acceleration, and c_D is the drag coefficient. Drag coefficients are normally displayed versus the Reynolds number, $Re = VD/\nu$, where ν is the kinematic viscosity of air. For free fall, it is advisable to use the Best number, $Be = c_D\, Re^2$. This way, no iterative procedures are required to determine drag coefficients.

Substituting Eq. 12.2 in Eq. 12.1 leads to a growth equation:

$$D^{-1/2}\, dD/dt = E\, W_f\, \sqrt{g/(3\rho\,\rho_h\, c_D)}\,. \quad (12.3)$$

An appreciation of growth times can be obtained by assuming typical (constant) values for the following parameters: $E = 0.5$, $W_f = 3 \times 10^{-3}$ kg m^{-3}, $g = 9.81$ m s^{-2}, $\rho = 1$ kg m^{-3}, $\rho_h = 9 \times 10^2$ kg m^{-3}, and $c_D = 0.5$. Integrating Eq. 12.3 then leads to the following estimate:

$$D = 4.09 \times 10^{-9}\, (\Delta t)^2, \quad (12.4)$$

where Δt represents the growth time of a hailstone from 0 to

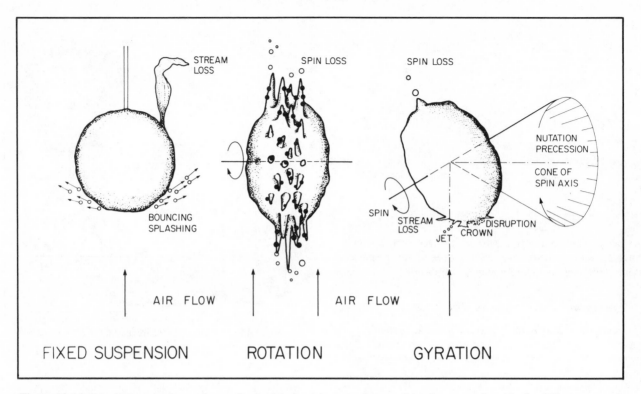

Figure 12.14. Principal types of water losses observed during icing experiments with spheres or spheroids, for different types of suspension systems.

diameter D. Since estimate assumptions are not very good for particles up to $D \sim 0.005$ m, the growth times are best given for diameter growths of $D = 0.005$ to $D = 0.01$ m, where $\Delta t \sim 458$ s; $D = 0.005$ m to 0.02 m, $\Delta t \sim 1106$ s; $D = 0.005$ to 0.05 m, $\Delta t \sim 2,391$ s; $D = 0.005$ to 0.10 m, $\Delta t \sim 3840$ s. These hailstone growth times are within the limits inferred in nature by radar. Δt is particularly sensitive to the liquid water content, W_f, and the collection efficiency, E, to which it is inversely proportional. If W_f were increased by a factor of five (which is still within the bounds of nature), the growth time would be five times faster. For more reliable calculations, however, one must use models that take into account the changes in cloud conditions, the competition of the hailstones for available water, and feedbacks between hailstones and cloud dynamics (see Sec. 4).

Langmuir and Blodgett (1946) showed that E depends on droplet size. Macklin and Bailey (1968) confirmed this through experiments in their tunnel, where the typical droplet size was $\sim 2 \times 10^{-5}$ m. List, in his icing-tunnel work, always used droplet spectra with median droplet diameters of about 7×10^{-5} m, i.e., droplets with an inertia that makes it adequate to assume $E = 1$ (there are no data available yet about droplet spectra in hail growth regions of clouds, but the use of armored aircraft [Musil et al., 1973] may clarify this aspect).

In the standard literature the collection efficiency, E, is normally broken down into a collision efficiency, E_1 (the probability that the droplets in the swept-out volume are

colliding with the hailstone), and the coalescence efficiency, E_2 (the probability that the colliding droplets are incorporated into the hailstone), with $E = E_1 E_2$. Some losses are always observed, but Carras and Macklin (1973) and the experience in the Swiss hail experiments of 1972 and 1974 (List et al., 1976) showed that this concept must be further expanded. In the previous experiments reported in the literature, no bouncing had been explicitly reported. Shedding was certainly present in the fixed-suspension type investigations by List (1960b) and Mossop and Kidder (1962), but this was attributed, at least by List, to the stationary suspension system. While Carras and Macklin (1973) studied shedding of slowly rotating cylinders, List et al. (1976) and List (1977) reported icing experiments with cylinders and fixed spherical and gyrating spheroidal hailstone models, where bouncing and various types of shedding were observed.

The types of shedding observed in different modes of motion of the icing test particles are drawn in Fig. 12.14. Although the final results are still not available, it can be said that 50–80% or more of the accreted water was lost in some way. Bouncing and streaming off (Fig. 12.14, left) seem to be the key mechanisms for ice particles moving without rotational motions. Rotational motion about an axis fixed in space leads to icicle formation with drops ($D \sim 2 - 5 \times 10^{-4}$ m) traveling along the icicles and detaching at the tips (Fig. 12.14, center). Gyrational motions, i.e., rotations (spin) about an axis, which itself moves continuously on a cone surface (the cone traveling with the hailstone and its tips remaining in the particle center), lead also to spinoff in the particle wake where the pressure fields assist detachment (Fig. 12.14, right). Jet and crown formations are also observed, as well as a streaming off in ring form. A complete disruption may be the result of disintegrating crowns.

The key message of these experiments is that the collection concept needs expansion. The events can be divided into two groups:

1. Those where water substance losses are directly caused by specific collisions. Jets and crowns are in this category, with bouncing represented by the former. For jets it can be assumed that the lost water is part of the incoming droplet that directly causes the event. For the crowns, however, the water may come mainly from the water skin resulting from previous water accretions. These loss mechanisms could be represented by a coalescence efficiency, E_2. At this writing, it is still an open question whether more water can be lost through crown formation than gained by the impacting drop.

2. Those where water losses are controlled by the status of the surface water skin covering the hailstone in part or completely. Spinoff and streaming off depend only on the bulk status, not on individual collisions. Here the lost water may have essentially water skin properties. This mechanism seems to account for most of the losses.

These processes led List (1977) to propose a new concept: the net collision efficiency, E_{net}, the ratio of the net or true growth rate, represented by the difference between the initial accretion of droplets and all the losses by shedding and bouncing or similar mechanisms, and the total droplet mass flux in the swept-out air volume.

In summary, the growth mechanisms are more complex than expected when the original bulk growth concept expressed by Eq. 12.1 was formulated. Further, the loss mechanisms involved in the growth of hailstones depend on the hailstones' motions during their fall, and the substantial fractional losses (or small values of E_{net}) will considerably affect the thermodynamic conditions (see Sec. 3c).

(2) Principal Aspects of Heat and Mass Transfer: The heat and mass transfers from a growing hailstone are of interest because they determine the fate of the accreted water (will it contribute to growth or will it be shed at a later time?) and the type of the growing ice deposit, as well as sizes and size distributions of ice single crystals and air bubbles.

This is explained with the help of Fig. 12.15. Let us assume that a hailstone is growing in a cloud with supercooled droplets at a level where the temperature is given by t_A and that the air is saturated with water vapor at pressure e_{sv}. The hailstone, for simplicity, is assumed to have a dry (icy) surface with temperature t_D and vapor pressure e_{sh} over it according to saturation over ice. The hailstone conditions are represented by a point on the curve $e_{sh}(t_D)$. Where it is along the curve depends on (1) cooling by conduction and

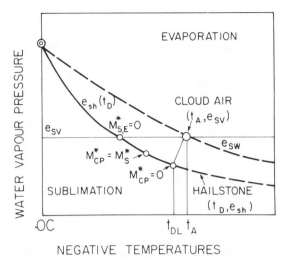

Figure 12.15. Possibilities of hailstone surface conditions and heat and mass transfer for given cloud air characteristics (t_A, e_{sv}) and droplet accretion at water-vapor saturation; sublimation (deposition) with no accretion $M_{CP}^* = 0$; mass growth by droplet accretion equal to growth by sublimation, $M_{CP}^* = M_S^*$; no sublimation or evaporation accompanying accretion, $M_{S,E}^* = 0$; hailstone evaporation for $e_{sh} > e_{sv}$; sublimation for $e_{sh} < e_{sv}$; spongy-ice growth $t_D = 0°C$.

convection through the air, (2) heating or cooling by condensing or evaporating of water molecules, and (3) the heat imparted by the accreted and/or lost water.

Particle size and shape also play considerable roles. Very specific sets of conditions help provide better understanding:

1. If there is no mass accretion of water ($M_{CP}^* = 0$), then the hailstone becomes heated because the H_2O molecules from the air sublimate on it and release latent heat, but the contact with air tends to limit the heating.

2. As soon as some water droplets are captured, they help to heat the hailstone further because their supercooling is inadequate to freeze them completely when contacted by ice (at $-20°C$ supercooling could freeze one-fourth of the water since the latent heat of fusion is one-fourth of the enthalpy).

3. With limited accretion, heating results from the collected drops as well as from sublimation. However, the larger the accretion becomes, the smaller the contribution by sublimation. Thus there is a point where the two mass accretions are equal ($M_S^* = M_{CP}^*$).

4. More accretion moves the growing hailstone to the condition $M_{ES}^* = 0$; i.e., mass accretion through sublimation disappears. Then the hailstone is at a temperature such that the saturation vapor pressure over ice equals the saturation pressure over the droplets, $e_{sh} = e_{sv}$. Further increase of accretion produces evaporation, which contributes to cooling of the growing ice particle.

5. Very special conditions are obtained once the hailstone reaches a temperature of $0°C$. At first, the heat ex-

change is adequate to freeze all or most accreted water. However, with increased cloud liquid water content, more and more water is built into a spongy-ice structure.

Gedanken experiments can be carried out for any hailstone size. However, substantial complications are faced in finding out whether a large particle growing in an identical environment will heat up faster than a smaller one and therefore grow at a slower or faster rate.

3. Behavior and Growth of Hailstones

a. Shape, Density, and Size Distributions

The description of key characteristics and phenomena of hailstones in Sec. 2 helps set the stage for a more specific treatment of hail growth. The question of fall mode depends on size, shape, and density distribution. The first two aspects have already been mentioned. Density measurements were carried out by Vittori and Di Caporiacco (1959), Macklin et al. (1960), Browning et al. (1963), and others. All values found fell within 840–917 kg m^{-3}, with the exception of spongy particles, with an upper bound of 1,000 kg m^{-3}. The investigation by List et al. (1970) is the only one that addresses itself to the density of hailstone shells. The values they found varied from 850 to 900 kg m^{-3}.

Size distributions can be found in the literature (Auer, 1972; Carte and Kidder, 1970; Changnon, 1971; Douglas, 1963; Federer and Waldvogel, 1975). One point may be added here: some authors try to make their values—with some success—conform with Marshall-Palmer (i.e., inverse exponential) distributions, not realizing that these exponential relationships are, as in the case of rain, generally valid only for averaging over many samples.

b. Free-Fall Aerodynamics

If hailstones were smooth spheres, their fallspeeds would be adequately known. However, this is not the case, and complications arise when questions are asked about the largest possible hailstones. Speculations that the considerable reduction of drag for smooth spheres at the critical Reynolds number (where the flow separation point moves upstream and causes a narrower wake) leads to a size limitation seem to be premature, because real hailstones are rarely spherical. Rather, they are both nonspherical and rough, with significant bumps and protuberances. Such elements of roughness not only change the value of Re_{crit}—and thus the limiting size—but also considerably reduce the drop in drag (Young and Browning, 1973; List et al., 1973), and thus the fallspeeds are no longer drastically increased.

How could nature grow a spherical hailstone if accretion occurs on the downward-pointing face? The answer may be that hailstone rotation promotes even growth on all sides. This is highly improbable, and spherically symmetric hailstones are extremely rare in nature.

Encasing of the original embryo in ice implies some kind of hailstone tumbling. List (1959a) studied drags of ellip-soidal hailstones and motions of models of such hailstones and found that the ellipsoidal particles fall mainly in the direction of the shortest axis. He also studied falling spheroids. By measuring not only drag but also lift forces and moments and applying those data in numerical calculations, List et al. (1973) showed that spheroids can oscillate about a horizontal main axis and sometimes commence and carry out continuous rotations. This type of motion is always a possibility; structures of real hailstones do not, however, favor this mode of motion. Kry and List (1974a,b) carried out measurements of torques on rotating spheroids and came up with a general solution to the equation of motion. The key equations treat the falling hailstone like a spinning top, but a top that is not bound by a surface. The most general motion for a smooth spheroid turned out to be a gyration with the spin around the minor axis, whereby this minor axis follows the surface of a cone (Fig. 12.14, right). Macklin (1977) carried out icing experiments with similar forced motions and was able to show that the products have the characteristics of real ellipsoidal hailstones.

It may be added here that Stewart (1977) established the free-fall existence of this mode for the case of disks ($Re <$ 8,000), but attempts with smooth spheroids at similar Re have not shown similar motions. Studies using larger particles may have different results.

There is no indication of how roughness would affect the tumbling motions. One thing is clear: we have a long way to go to understand the aerodynamics of freely falling hailstones. Perhaps one should go back to Knight and Knight's (1970) pioneering attempt and have freely falling particles followed by a parachutist. Unfortunately, this should be done in a hailstorm.

Spin and nutation-precession frequencies of gyrating hailstones are estimated to be up to 50 Hz. This may well have an effect on the approach pattern of cloud droplets and their collection efficiency. However, nothing is known about this aspect except some indication from incompletely evaluated icing experiments (List, 1977), where net collection efficiencies were found to be 0.6 and 0.17 at −20°C for $W_f = 2 \times$ and 30×10^{-3} kg m^{-3} respectively, for 0.02-m spheroids with an axis ratio of 0.66, $f_{spin} = -3.2$ Hz, and $f_{nut/prec} = 16$ Hz. To explain some of the implications of these considerable losses, a new heat balance consideration needs to be made.

c. Heat Balance of Growing Smooth Spherical Hailstones

For simplicity, the following considerations are limited to spheres. Some information is available on the heat transfer of spheroids (Macklin, 1963; List and Dussault, 1967; Hierlihy, 1968; Schuepp and List, 1969) but not yet on gyrating spheroids.

List and Dussault (1967) divided the total heat transfer into four aspects, expressing that the sum of the transfer processes by conduction and convection, Q_{CC}^*, by evaporation, sublimation or condensation, Q_{ESC}^*, and by accretion of supercooled droplets, Q_{CP}^*, is used to freeze (or melt) the accreted water, Q_{FM}^*. Hence,

$$Q_{CC}^* + Q_{ESC}^* + Q_{CP}^* + Q_{FM}^* = 0, \qquad (12.5)$$

where

$$Q_{CC}^* = -1.68\, k\, Re^{1/2}\, D\, (t_D - t_A), \qquad (12.6)$$

$$Q_{ESC}^* = -C_{1,2}\, D_{wa}\, T_A^{-1}\, Re^{1/2} D(e_{sh} - e_v), \qquad (12.7)$$

$$Q_{CP}^* = -0.785\, \nu\, E\, W_f\, D\, Re\, \bar{c}_w\, (t_D - t_A), \qquad (12.8)$$

and

$$Q_{FM}^* = 0.785\, \nu\, E\, W_f\, D\, Re\, L_f\, I. \qquad (12.9)$$

Equations 12.6 and 12.7 are derived for smooth spheres from the definitions of the Nusselt number, Nu, and the Sherwood number, Sh, whereby empirical values are substituted according to Ranz and Marshall (1952):

$$Nu = hD/k = 0.60\, Pr^{1/3}\, Re^{1/2}, \qquad (12.10)$$

and

$$Sh = \beta D/D_{wa} = 0.60\, Sc^{1/3}\, Re^{1/2}. \qquad (12.11)$$

The terms of these new formulas are defined as follows:

k = thermal conductivity (2.28×10^{-2} J m^{-1} s^{-1} K^{-1} at $-20°$C)

D = diameter (m)

C_1 = 8.663×10^3 J K m^{-3} Pa^{-1} for liquid-gas transitions

C_2 = 9.835×10^3 J K m^{-3} Pa^{-1} for solid-gas transitions

D_{wa} = diffusivity of water vapor in air (1.701×10^{-5} m^2 s^{-1} at $-20°$C)

T_A = absolute temperature of air

ν = kinematic viscosity of air (1.15×10^{-5} m^2 s^{-1} at $-20°$C)

$\bar{c}_w$ = specific heat of water averaged over the temperature range (t_D, t_A) (4.265×10^3 J kg^{-1} K^{-1} for $0°$C, $20°$C)

L_f = latent heat of fusion at t_D (3.33×10^5 J kg^{-1} for $t_D = 0°$C)

I = fraction of accreted water that freezes

h = heat transfer coefficient (J m^{-2} s^{-1})

β = mass transfer coefficient (m^3 s^{-1})

Pr = Prandtl number (= 0.71 for air)

Sc = Schmidt number (= 0.616 for air)

Equations 12.6 through 12.9 have been substituted in Eq. 12.5, and general ideas about the conditions for hail formation have been found (List and Dussault, 1967). In expanding the considerations to the atmosphere, adiabatic cloud water contents were assumed. It is clear, however, that those values may be well exceeded (see Chap. 14). There are also findings that give instructions on how to cope with roughness. However, the low net collection efficiency found for gyrating ice particles in the Swiss experiments by List and colleagues makes it imperative to consider also the effect of the substantial losses in the heat balances. Equations 12.8 and 12.9 are expanded because they deal with the accreted drops.

The contribution to the total heat transfer, Q_{CP}^*, can be split into two parts:

1. The contribution by the droplets permanently incorporated in the hailstone is characterized by E_{net} and is given by

$$Q_{CP,1}^* = -0.785\, \nu\, W_f\, D\, Re\, E_{net}\, \bar{c}_w\, (t_D - t_A). \qquad (12.12)$$

2. The fraction of initially collected drops is given by E, the net collected is given by E_{net}, and the fractional lost water substance is given by $E - E_{net}$. Restriction to large cloud droplets allows setting E equal to 1. The lost water has a specific enthalpy of $\bar{c}_w (t_S - t_A)$, where t_S is the temperature of the shed or bounced water. If the fraction I_S of the shed water is frozen, the value of $I_S L_f$ has to be subtracted. Hence,

$$Q_{CP,2}^* = -0.785\, \nu\, W_f\, D\, Re\, (1 - E_{net})$$
$$\times (\bar{c}_w [t_S - t_A] - I_S L_f). \qquad (12.13)$$

E needs to be replaced by E_{net} in Eq. 12.9, and substituting the amended terms in Eq. 12.5 gives, when solved for the ice fraction I in the deposit and conditions $t_A = -20°$C and $t_D = 0°$C,

$$I = 1.19 \times 10^{-3} \frac{1}{E_{net}\, W_f\, (VD)^{1/2}} + 0.256$$
$$+ \frac{1 - E_{net}}{E_{net}} (1.28 \times 10^{-2}[t_S - t_A] - I_S) \qquad (12.14)$$

This equation is valid for kg, m, s, and C.

The effect of the shed water can be studied by considering the three cases with different values for the third term, T_3, on the right side:

Case 1: $T_{31} = 0$, for $t_S = t_A$ and $I_S = 0$. (Shed water has properties of accreted water, i.e., no interaction.)

Case 2: $T_{32} = 0.256 ([1/E_{net}] - 1)$, for the lost water having a temperature $t_S = 0°$C ($= t_D$). (Shed water is warmed up to freezing point.)

Case 3: $T_{33} = -0.744 ([1/E_{net}] - 1)$, for the lost water substance consisting completely of ice, $I_S = 1$, and having a temperature of $t_S = 0°$C. (Shed substance is ice at $0°$C.)

A quick check shows that for $V = 20$ m s^{-1} and $D = 0.02$ m, the terms T_{32} and T_{33} are of the same order of magnitude as the sum of the first and second terms. In other words, the temperature, phase composition, and lost water substance really control the heat transfer, particularly in situations where E_{net} is small. This situation is dealt with in Fig. 12.16, for the case of an icing cylinder (2.2-cm diameter), where the net collision efficiency at $t_A = -20°$C and air density $\rho = 1.29$ kg m^{-3} was found (List et al., 1976) to be represented (in SI units) by

$$E_{net} = 0.13 + 1.18 \times 10^{-4} (2500 - V^2)$$
$$+ \frac{0.87 - 1.18 \times 10^{-4} (2500 - V^2)}{1 + 0.425\, V^2\, W_f}. \qquad (2.15)$$

Figure 12.16. Calculated fractional ice in spongy deposit growing on a rotating (2 Hz) cylinder as function of the liquid water content. Assumptions: surface temperature $t_D = 0°C$, velocities 10 or 32 m s^{-1}.

Case 1: No interaction (*NI*) of shed or bounced water with surface skin, water leaves at supercooling of accreted water ($t_S = t_A$). Case 2: The shed or bounced water has temperature $t_S = 0°C$, and does not contain ice, $I_S = 0$. Case 3: The shed particles consist entirely of ice at $t_S = 0°C$. $I_S = 1$. E_{net} used in the calculations has been measured according to Eq. 12.15. On the basis of present knowledge, the ice fraction in the deposit could be anywhere within the spread of the curves (List, 1977; reproduced from the *Journal of Glaciology* by permission of the International Glaciological Society).

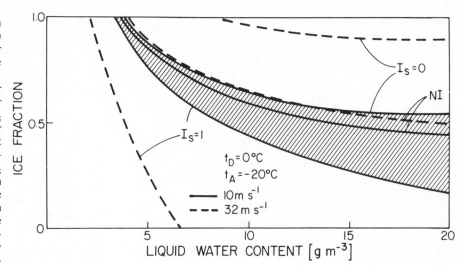

The heat transfer for cylinders is somewhat different than that for spheres. The first term on the right side of Eq. 12.14 needs to be replaced by $6.73 \times 10^{-3} V^{-0.4} (E_{net} W_f)^{-1}$ (List, 1977). The message of Eqs. 12.14 and 12.15 is clear: the thermal properties of the water released by a growing hailstone are of prime importance to the heat transfer. They need to be known (measured); otherwise there is no way to relate structures and surface temperatures with growth conditions.

One other point should be made here. It seems that icing cylinders lose water substance by shedding. Thus the thermal properties of the lost water may be quite different at different modes of motion even under conditions where the net growth is the same.

d. Air-Bubble Size Distributions

The shell-like structure of hailstones is one of the most impressive imprints of the variations in icing conditions during hailstone growth. Often this variation is attributed to a cyclic fall and lift within a storm. However, the available growth times of the order of 600–1,000 s, as determined by radar observations of cloud evolution, would be insufficient for such travel. Hence, let us just state that the shells are products of changing (often cyclically) icing conditions.

Measurement of bubble-size distributions in hailstones have been made by List et al. (1972). They found log-normal distributions with roughly constant slopes. Opaque zones contained higher concentrations of smaller bubbles; transparent zones consisted mostly of larger air inclusions. The mean planar bubble diameter separating the two regions was about 42×10^{-6} m (please note that "opaque" and "transparent" are subjective assessments and are not physically defined). The density of opaque shells was found to be between 810 and 910 kg m^{-3}; for transparent shells the densities were between 900 and 917 kg m^{-3}.

Artificial growth of spherical ice particles with diameters of 0.02 m and rotation about a horizontal axis at 1 Hz (List and Agnew, 1973) also gave log-normal distributions of air-bubble sizes, with opaque and transparent zones separated by the same value as that found by List et al. (1972). However, the bubbles of the opaque shells had much smaller mean diameters. In spongy deposits such a difference could have been caused by a different mode of freezing (Knight et al., 1974). This speed of freezing might also explain the differences in air-bubble distributions observed in raindrops frozen while floating (Murray and List, 1972).

Other authors also studied air-bubble distributions in ice deposits; however, they looked at freezing slabs (Carte, 1961) or at deposits growing on slowly rotating cylinders (Macklin, 1962; Carras and Macklin, 1975). A strict analogy to hailstones is questionable because the heat transfer of cylinders is governed by laws different from the laws for spheres. In real hailstones, which may carry out more complex motions, internal heat conduction from the zones where no accretion takes place to the icing zones also helps freeze uneven or zonal deposits. Those may exhibit completely different relationships between bubble-size distributions (or density) and appearance.

e. Single Crystals in Hailstones

The colored photographs of hailstone thin sections (List, 1958b, 1960a; Knight and Knight, 1971) have always attracted scientists to the intricacies of the crystal matrix in hailstones. Studies on natural hailstones by Aufdermaur et al. (1963) showed that the position of the main crystallographic axis, the *c* axis, of the single crystals is weakly related to the local direction of ice growth. Often it is parallel, in other cases perpendicular, or in between. These authors showed that for artificial hailstones spongy ice grown at low air temperatures ($-30°C$) did not show any preferred *c'*-

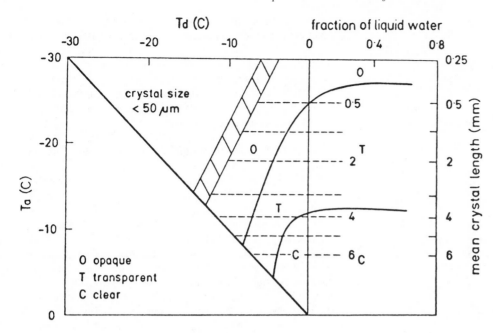

Figure 12.17. Composite diagram of opacity of accreted ice deposits and mean crystal length as a function of deposit (T_d) and ambient (T_a) temperatures in dry growth regime, $T_d < 0°C$, and fraction of unfrozen water in wet growth regime. The curved lines separate opaque from transparent and transparent from clear ice zones. The hailstone is always warmer than the surrounding air during growth ($T_d > T_a$), at low T_d the growing ice crystals in the deposit are quite small ($< 50 \times 10^{-6}$ m), and for crystals with lengths > 0.0005 m, the length is only a function of T_a (Macklin et al., 1975).

axis direction, whereas spongy-ice growth at $-10°C$ resulted in the c' axis being perpendicular to the local growth direction (c' is the c-axis projection in the plane of observation). List and Agnew (1973) concentrated on crystal sizes in artificial hailstones and found that crystal sizes diminish with decreasing temperature and increase with liquid water content. List et al. (1970) found in two samples of natural hailstone that average single crystals larger than 1.7×10^{-6} m^2 occurred in transparent shells, and smaller ones were associated with opaque ones. The knowledgeable student of hailstone structure knows, however, that there are violations of this tentative rule.

Crystal sizes of artificial ice deposits on cylinders were related to hail by Levi and Aufdermaur (1970). Macklin et al. (1976) confirmed the findings and superimposed the ice appearance (see Fig. 12.17). Combining mean crystal length and opacity seems a reasonable approach to identify icing conditions of cylinders. Another word of caution is in order: C. A. Knight (personal communication) drew attention to recrystallization, which he showed to be crucial if icing occurs at 0°C. Hence there is another warning flag against any overzealous desire to interpret hailstone structures in terms of growth history.

f. Other Microphysical Aspects of Hailstone Growth

Hailstones collect aerosol particles during their fall. Their presence or absence may also be indicative of hailstone growth conditions (Rosinski, 1966, 1967; Rosinski et al., 1976). However, much more information about the presence, type, and concentration of the particular aerosols is required to understand this phenomenon.

The isotope composition of hailstone shells has attracted even more attention because the hailstone history may be traceable, like the age of artifacts, by the carbon-14 method. However, the isotope concentration would give not hailstone age but, in an involved way, the temperature at which water is accreted.

Isotope determination was first applied by Facy et al. (1963); a more recent contribution was by Macklin et al. (1977). During condensation H_2O^{18} and HDO molecules (O^{18} is an oxygen isotope, oxygen normally having a molecular weight of 16; D stands for deuterium, which contains one proton and one neutron but, chemically, is hydrogen because it has one electron) are incorporated differently into the liquid phase from regular H_2O; this separation process is dependent on isotope species and temperature. The isotope content of the cloud droplets is assumed to be in equilibrium with the cloud air, which is acceptable because of the short relaxation times involved. The last key assumption is that the ice formed at a given level has the same isotope properties as the collected droplets. If the water substance losses during hail growth are as substantial as expected, then this assumption is in need of careful study in icing experiments.

The application of this method is justifiable if the isotope content of the air flowing into the hailstorm and the local relative humidity are constant, if the ascent of air is adiabatic without mixing (see Chap. 4), and if the incorporation of the isotope into the ice is straightforward.

The argument involving tritium, T, in water (HTO) is somewhat different because the source of T is in the stratosphere (tritium consists of one proton, two neutrons, and one electron; thus it is also hydrogen in the chemical sense). The separation of HTO in relation to H_2O in air depends on hailstone growth conditions and varies with height in the atmosphere; thus its fractional presence could be used to determine the height at which accretion took place. Again

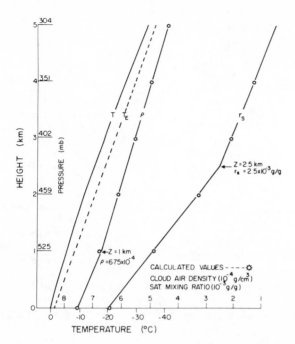

Figure 12.18. Cloud model parameters as functions of height z above freezing level, with T the cloud and T_E the environment temperature. Updraft air density ρ and saturation mixing ratio r_s show linear approximations (Charlton and List, 1972).

there is no room to accommodate evaporation during growth, superposition of growth phases, and diffusion losses of water substances.

Electrification theories and their microphysical aspects are discussed in Chap. 13. To understand fully charge separation and generation, it is necessary to have (1) the measurement in thunderstorms of charge distributions of all types and sizes of cloud and precipitation particles, together with local electrical fields; (2) better and more sophisticated laboratory experiments; and (3) numerical models to study the evolution of charge distributions for growing particles. The hitherto standard assumption of one average charge per size category is not adequate, since the tails in the charge distributions may control the overall charge evolution. Further, it should be added that hail is not always accompanied by lightning (from unpublished surveys of the author). Thus electrical effects may not be that important for hail growth, unless they affect the net collection efficiency.

g. An Attempt at Interpretation of Hailstone History

Macklin et al. (1976) gave the following steps for the identification of icing conditions leading to shells in hailstones:

1. Use both isotopic composition and crystallographic structure (length of crystals) to deduce air temperature T_A and height Z at which the specific growth at diameter D took place, and assume free fall according to size, i.e., $\rightarrow D(T_A) \rightarrow D(Z) \rightarrow dD/dZ$.

2. Use the air-bubble concentration n to deduce T_D (deposit temperature), assuming a given median volume diameter d for the cloud droplets, i.e., $n = n(D, d, T_D, T_A)$. Since D, d, and T_A are known or assumed, $n \rightarrow T_D$.

3. Knowing the heat transfer equations (Eqs. 12.5–12.9), it is now possible to deduce the amount of collected water (no shedding assumed in equations), i.e., given T_A, T_D, D (and implicitly V) $\rightarrow EW_f$.

4. Since E is known as function of D and d, it is now possible to evaluate the liquid water content at which the considered icing took place, i.e., given $E \rightarrow W_f$.

5. Given $dD/dZ \rightarrow (U - V) \rightarrow V$ (from the relationship between $U - V = dZ/dt$ and dD/dZ; V is the updraft speed).

It is seen from the previous discussion of hailstone properties and behavior that this approach by Macklin et al. (1976) is very bold and subject to considerable criticism, because most of the air-bubble and structural relationships have been established from cylinder icing and may not be transferable to hailstones. Also, the isotope argument and the heat and mass transfer situation are not simple. Nevertheless, the applied approach is a start toward developing more trustworthy schemes. A tremendous amount of ingenuity, technology, and labor is involved in the development of this type of procedure for evaluating hailstone history.

4. Hailstone-Hailstone Interactions and Ensemble Behavior

a. Collisions

There is a small probability that hailstones of different sizes collide in the atmosphere. An estimate of the occurrences can be obtained whenever the size distribution and the corresponding free-fall velocities are either known or assumed. A "mean free hailstone path" can then be calculated to estimate the collision rate. No effect is expected for encounters, except that collisions or near misses could result in aerodynamic transitions from oscillatory to gyrational motions (Stewart, 1977).

b. Growth Interference by Competition for Available Cloud Water

Iribarne and Pena (1962) were the first to consider the mass conservation of water substances in hail growth. Prior calculations (see, for example, Ludlam, 1958) considered, without spelling it out, the growth of a single hailstone in a cloud, without paying attention to the depletion of cloud droplets that slows the growth of other hailstones competing for the same water. This competition concept was extended by List et al. (1968) to a cloud environment, representative of hailstorms in Colorado, with a replenishment of droplets in adiabatic lifting. Figure 12.18 shows the changes of the cloud parameters with height. The lifting condensation level of the cloud has a pressure of $P = 67$ kPa (670 mb), a temperature of $T = 5°C$, and a water saturation mixing ratio of $r_s = 0.00822$. The freezing level is at $P = 59.5$ kPa (595 mb), with $W_f = 1.33 \times 10^{-3}$ kg m^{-3}. The cloud was further assumed to be one-dimensional; i.e., its properties changed only with height, and no mixing was allowed. Thus, with ρ for air density and V_z for updraft velocity,

$$\rho \, V_z = \text{const.} = C_A. \qquad (12.16)$$

The adiabatic behavior of the clouds with initial hail growth in Colorado makes Eq. 12.16 quite reasonable.

List et al. further assumed a constant influx of hail embryos of concentration N into the updraft right at the freezing level; i.e.,

$$N \, (V_z - V_t) = \text{const.}, \qquad (12.17)$$

where V_t is the terminal velocity of the embryos and hailstones.

The growth of an infinitesimal ice shell on a spherical hailstone is controlled by the rate of accretion of cloud water (see Eq. 12.1, with $W_f = \rho r$, where r is the liquid water mixing ratio). If growth occurs within an updraft with velocity V_z, and considering $dz/dt = V_z - V_t$, then the growth rate can be expressed by

$$\frac{dD}{dt} = \frac{dD}{dz} \cdot (V_z - V_t). \qquad (12.18)$$

Substituting Eq. 12.1 in Eq. 12.18 leads to

$$\frac{dD}{dz} = \frac{E \, V_t \, r \, \rho}{2\rho_h \, (V_z - V_t)}, \qquad (12.19)$$

where the collection efficiency E is assumed to equal 1 in the following development.

The change in the liquid water mixing ratio Δr over a height interval Δz consists of two parts; the first, $\Delta r_{\rho s}$, is the change of the liquid water mixing ratio caused by condensation while lifting over Δz, and the second is the removal of liquid water by the hailstones present in concentration N. The liquid water is assumed to ascend with the speed of the air; i.e., $\Delta z / \Delta t = V_z$. This leads to the finite difference equation,

$$\frac{\Delta r}{\Delta z} = \frac{\Delta r_{\rho s}}{\Delta z} - \frac{\pi D^2 V_t \, r \, N}{4 V_z}. \qquad (12.20)$$

The calculations in this model in an atmosphere typical of Colorado hailstorms showed that hailstones reach largest sizes if the original embryo concentration is low and embryo size is large. Embryos of 0.005-m diameter (small hail) could grow to 0.025–0.030 m within 480–720 s.

Greater embryo concentrations (≤ 2.35 m^{-3}) are possible in updrafts of 18 m s^{-1} than in drafts of 22 m s^{-1}, where one hailstone per 10 m^3 is the upper limit; otherwise the competition is so strong that the particles do not grow much and are blown out at the top of the cloud.

The study of List et al. (1968) was expanded by Charlton and List (1972) to consider input of embryo spectra into the same cloud. The hailstones, characterized by size groups j, not only were allowed to grow while ascending (representing fallout of a tilted updraft) but also could continue their growth on descent (subscripts a for ascent, d for descent). With $M = (\pi/6) \rho_h D^3$ representing the mass of a spherical

hailstone, the constant mass flux of water substance C_w, which includes the water vapor and liquid water content flux, is represented by

$$(r + r_s) \, \rho \, V_z + \sum_{j = 1, n} [N_{aj} \, (V_z - V_{taj}) \, M_{aj}$$
$$+ N_{dj} \, (V_z - V_{tdj}) \, M_{dj}] = C_w, \qquad (12.21)$$

where r_s is the saturation water vapor mixing ratio.

The constant number flux of hailstones of the jth-size group is expressed for a and d growth as follows:

$$N_{aj} \, (V_z - V_{taj}) = C_j = N_{dj} \, (V_z - V_{tdj}) \qquad (12.22)$$

Substituting Eqs. 12.16 and 12.22 in Eq. 12.21 and combining it with Eq. 12.19 results in

$$\frac{dD_j}{dz} = \frac{\rho \, V_{tj}}{2\rho_h (V_z - V_{tj})} \left[\frac{C_w - \sum_{j = 1, n} (M_{aj} - M_{dj}) \, C_j}{C_A} - r_s \right]. \qquad (12.23)$$

Equation 12.23 requires suitable subscripts a and d on D_j and V_{tj} so that $2n$ simultaneous first-order differential equations are available for the ascent and descent models.

Assuming embryos of one size, the effect of their number concentration and growth is represented in Fig. 12.19, with the depletion in liquid water content. Growth times and icing conditions (surface temperature or fractional ice content at 0°C) are also displayed. Very small concentrations (0.1 m^{-3}) are accompanied by fast growth and short times of residence in the icing regions of the cloud. Thus maximum growth requires maximum residence time, which translates into maximum competition for which descent is still feasible.

A puzzling feature of this type of model is the possible accumulation of hailstones at a so-called balance level, where no growth occurs because all the liquid droplets have been accreted by the hailstones just below. This effect tends to appear when hailstone numbers are such that 30% to 40% of the cloud's liquid water content is depleted.

Charlton and List (1972) demonstrated that this effect is a result of the injection of single-sized embryos. Even a very narrow size spread makes the effect disappear. Their results on the growth of embryos with five size classes of a varying concentration are presented in Fig. 12.20. The two smallest classes are blown out of the top of the cloud and do not return, whereas the 0.005-m embryos (with $N_0 = 1.4$ m^{-3}) reach highest levels and thus stay longer and grow bigger than the two larger categories (it should be pointed out here that the selection of the updraft is crucial to the modeling outcome—a comment that also applies to Fig. 12.19). The dashed curves are for updraft only and demonstrate for the *LWC* that the droplet depletion and growth are greatest during descent. This study also clarified thermodynamic feedback through the creation of thermal buoyancy; this is very important because thermal buoyancy can compensate for the drag forces by the hydrometeors. This display of the hailstone number density clearly demonstrates that growth during descent really favors the formation of larger stones.

One of the most important demonstrations of this model-

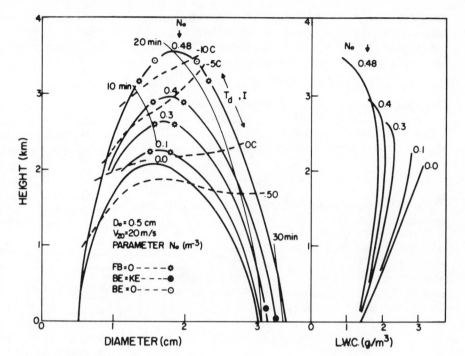

Figure 12.19. Hail growth and liquid water curves for uniform-sized embryos growing during ascent and descent (*a* and *d*) in the same cloud updraft. $D = 0.005$ m, $V = 20$ m s^{-1} and variable concentration N_{oi}. The embryos with the largest concentration ($N_o = 0.48$ m^{-3}) grow into larger hailstones than those with a negligible concentration ($N = 0$) because they stay longer in a growth environment. *FB* = 0 indicates points where the drag force by the water substance is balanced by the thermal buoyancy, BE is the integration of *FB* to level *Z*, *KE* is the air parcel's specific kinetic energy (Charlton and List, 1972).

ing work is the importance of thermodynamic coupling between hail growth and updraft strength. This really points to the need for modeling hail growth in a cloud where the cloud microphysics interacts with the dynamics of the cloud (see Orville and Kopp, 1976).

c. Ensemble Interactions

The bulk dynamic effect of the presence of hailstones on the immediate environment is given by their total drag. The motion of the hailstones is given by the individual speeds. The present practice in modeling is to calculate an average V_T for all the hailstones and let them move as a group at any speed. This does not allow growth during ascent and descent at any given location. It also does not allow the hailstones in a given packet to separate or mix with others. Clark and List (1971) and List and Clark (1973) drew attention to this fact and applied their study to rain. However, the implications are the same as for hail.

These authors stipulated that precipitation particles with size distributions need to be treated by a Lagrangian technique; thereby, marker particles, representative for their size class, are followed individually as a function of time. Figure 12.21 shows how a package of raindrops, homogeneously distributed at time zero, would separate into different groups according to size and, as a whole, occupy a much larger cloud region and fall as precipitation at a reduced rate, over a longer time period, compared with the situation where one single average V_T is assumed. The onset time for precipitation would also be different. In hail, where

size and speed variations are much larger than those in rain, these effects must be considered if a hail and cloud model is to duplicate or re-create natural situations. It is recognized, however, that the corresponding complications are very substantial (see Girard and List, 1974).

5. Final Comments

Considerable progress has been achieved over the past decades in our understanding of hailstone formation. The following points may indicate areas where further attention is needed.

1. Characteristics of hailstones are known to quite some extent, but there are no single hailstone samples from one single storm in which all known structural aspects and the degree of variation have been studied.

2. In most models, the growth of hailstones has been necessarily treated in a simplistic fashion, with the assumption of spherical ice particles and homogeneous growth by bulk accretion of cloud droplets. The modeling results unquestionably help us understand many aspects of hail growth.

3. Growth has been simulated in icing tunnels with spheres and spheroids, but mostly with cylinders. Not enough care has been taken to consider the inherent differences between cylinders and spheres or spheroids.

4. Advances in understanding of hailstone aerodynamics and heat and mass transfer have made it clear that each type

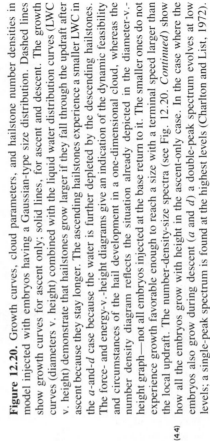

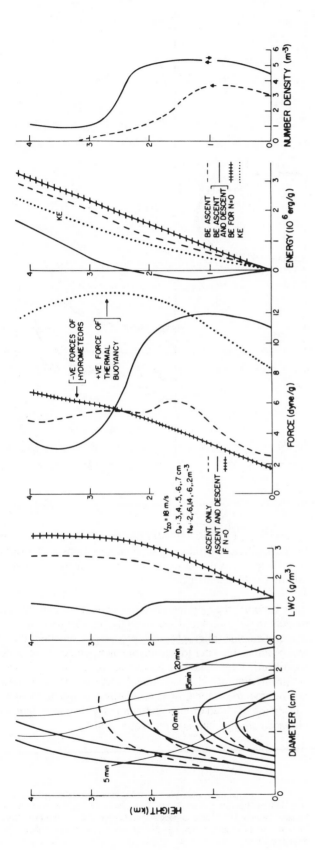

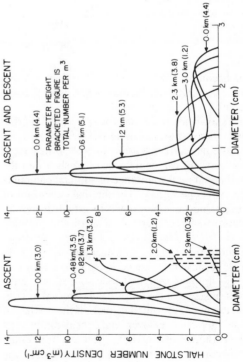

Figure 12.20. Growth curves, cloud parameters, and hailstone number densities in model injected with embryos having a Gaussian-type size distribution. Dashed lines show growth curves for ascent only; solid lines, for ascent and descent. The growth curves (diameters v. height) combined with the liquid water distribution curves (LWC v. height) demonstrate that hailstones grow larger if they fall through the updraft after ascent because they stay longer. The ascending hailstones experience a smaller LWC in the *a*-and-*d* case because the water is further depleted by the descending hailstones. The force- and energy-v.-height diagrams give an indication of the dynamic feasibility and circumstances of the hail development in a one-dimensional cloud, whereas the number density diagram reflects the situation already depicted in the diameter-v.-height graph—not all embryos injected at the base return to it. The smaller ones do not experience growth favorable enough to reach a size with a terminal speed larger than the local updraft. The number-density-size spectra (see Fig. 12.20. *Continued*) show how all the embryos grow with height in the ascent-only case. In the case where the embryos also grow during descent (*a* and *d*) a double-peak spectrum evolves at low levels; a single-peak spectrum is found at the highest levels (Charlton and List, 1972).

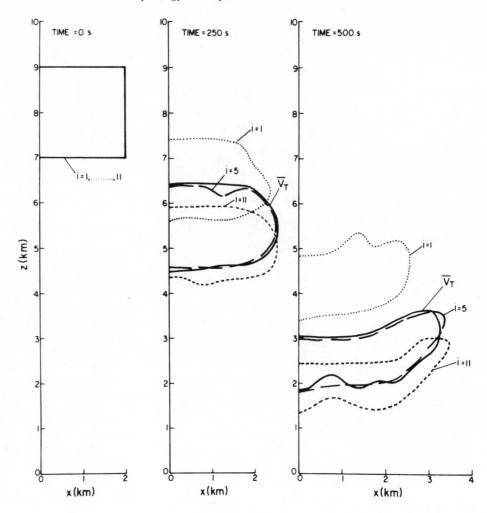

Figure 12.21. Fall of an ensemble of raindrops. Eleven size classes (1 ≤ i ≤ 11) are initially located in the 2 × 2 km region (slab symmetry) at the 8-km level in an atmosphere that is noninteracting in terms of water substances. Marshall-Palmer distribution with $\lambda = 12.23$ m^{-2} and a total mixing ratio of $r_T = 10^{-2}$. Contours represent positions of zones with particles 1, 5, and 11 at three different times. The solid line represents the position of all particles as calculated using a weighted mean terminal velocity.

of hailstone is accompanied by its special motions relative to the air and that growth can be understood only if these circumstances are properly considered.

5. It can be shown for rotational (or spin) motions that the radial inertia forces at the hailstone surface may be sufficient to overcome the surface tension forces, so that large drops (0.001–0.002 m) can be detached and shed into the airstream, conditional on the presence of sufficient amounts of water on the hailstone surface. The thermal conditions of shedding or bouncing must be known to establish the deposit temperature and ice characteristics of the growing particle.

6. This phenomenon forces reconsideration of the bulk growth concept, because there are no longer two sets of particles involved—droplets and hailstones—that are sufficiently different in size that the drops can be treated as continuously contributing to growth. The days of the "bulk and single hailstone" approach are over, and consideration must be given to the evolution of a particle spectrum from cloud droplets to hailstones, with ice particles throughout the spectrum and drops of 0.0002–0.006 m or more in the middle region (similar to List and Gillespie, 1976). Icing

experiments, too, need to adjust to this situation in spite of the difficulties of producing supercooled drops at the right speed relative to the airspeed within the experimental section of a cold chamber or tunnel.

In general, the parameterization of hail growth in hail models may be replaced increasingly by additional details of cumbersome microphysical processes. Whether those will be amenable later to reasonable, new, and more reliable parameterization schemes is still an open question. The possibility that growing, gyrating hailstones represent a direct source for fully grown raindrops through immediate conversion of cloud droplets into rain may shed new light on the mechanics of hail and rain formation.[1]

[1]Most of the author's work referred to has been sponsored by the Canadian National Research Council, the Atmospheric Environment Service of Canada, and the U.S. National Oceanic and Atmospheric Administration, Department of Commerce, through its National Severe Storms Laboratory, Norman, Okla.

13. Storm Electricity and Lightning

E. T. Pierce

1. Introduction

It is universally known that thunderclouds are electrified. It is far less well known that the fair-weather atmosphere is also electrified and that thunderstorms are the generators of this electrification. The association between stormy and fair-weather electrical phenomena, in a kind of global circuit, is the most interesting feature in worldwide atmospheric electricity. Accordingly, we start our review of storm electricity by outlining this global association before proceeding to discussion of cloud electrification, lightning, and atmospherics. Expanded descriptions of some of the topics discussed will be found in good standard texts; these include Chalmers (1967), Uman (1969), Israel (1973), Golde (1973), and Golde (1977). Stow (1969) and Uman et al. (1975) are valuable review articles that include extensive bibliographies. More recent topical reviews and bibliographies are presented by Hallett (1983), Lhermitte and Williams (1983), and Uman (1983).

2. Thunderstorms and Fair-Weather Electricity

a. The Fundamental Problem

In fair weather the atmosphere is at a positive potential, V_h, with respect to the Earth, and this potential increases with height, h, above the Earth's surface. Under these conditions the potential gradient, $\partial V_h / \partial h$, is considered positive. In the past, the electric field, E_h, was commonly used synonymously with potential gradient, but now many investigators are wisely using the proper physical definition of the electric field; i.e., it points in the direction the positive charge moves. The relationship between the vertical field and potential gradient is

$$E_h = -(\partial V_h / \partial h). \qquad (13.1)$$

At the surface of the Earth and under unpolluted conditions, $E_0 \sim -100$ V m^{-1}. The bound charge σ on the Earth's surface corresponding to this vertical field is given by Gauss's theorem, $\varepsilon_0 E_0 = \sigma$. Since ε_0, the permittivity of free space, is 8.854×10^{-12} F m^{-1}, it follows that $\sigma \sim -9 \times 10^{-10}$ C m^{-2}.

The atmosphere is slightly conducting because it contains ions. Near the Earth's surface, and in the absence of pollu-

tion, the conductivity $\lambda_0 \sim 3 \times 10^{-14}$ mho m^{-1}. There is therefore, by Ohm's law, a current density, $j = \lambda_0 E_0 \sim -3 \times 10^{-12}$ A m^{-2}, carrying positive electricity into the Earth. This should neutralize the bound charge σ in only 300 s. Yet the Earth maintains its negative charge. Why it does has been termed the fundamental problem of atmospheric electricity.

b. Conductivity and Columnar Resistance

Ions are generated in the atmosphere by three main agencies: ground radioactivity, radioactive gases in the atmosphere, and cosmic rays. The effects of the first two agencies decrease with increasing altitude h. The cosmic-ray contribution is subject to geomagnetic influences and a solar cyclical variation, but increases as h increases to attain a maximum at $h \sim 15$ km. The combined ionizing effect, q_h, of all three agencies is about $8I$ at 0 km, $4I$ at 1 km, and $30I$ at 15 km, where I is the rate of production of single-ion pairs per cubic centimeter per second.

Initially the ionizing agencies produce a free electron and a positive molecular ion. These original ions and their progeny then undergo many transformations. Eventually two stable or terminal forms of ion emerge: the small cluster ion, consisting of several molecules (often H_2O) clustered around a core molecular ion, and the large ion, formed by attachment of a small ion to an aerosol particle. The mobility, k, of the small ion is about 10^{-4} m^2 V^{-1} s^{-1}; that of the large ion is about 10^{-7} m^2 V^{-1} s^{-1}.

The conductivity of the atmosphere can be generally written as

$$\lambda_h = \Sigma_i \, n_i \, e_i \, k_i, \qquad (13.2)$$

where n_i, e_i, and k_i are the number density, charge, and mobility of type i ions; the summation covers all the types of ions present.

Any precise evaluation of Eq. 13.2 would be intolerably involved. The number density is controlled by the balance of production, aeronomic loss and gain processes, and transport effects; the resulting balance equations yielding n_i can be very complicated. Mobilities are not well known as a function of ion type, while the possibilities of e_i being a multiple of the electronic charge e cannot be eliminated in a rigid treatment.

Fortunately, however, the gross subdivision of ions into

Table 13.1. Representative Values of Fair-Weather Parameters

Altitude h (km)	Conductivity λ_h (mho m^{-1})	Columnar resistance R_h (ohm m^2)	Field E_h (V m^{-1})	Potential V_h (V)
0	3×10^{-14}	0	-100.00	0
2	5×10^{-14}	5×10^{16}	-60.00	1.5×10^5
12	4×10^{-13}	9×10^{16}	-7.50	2.7×10^5
40	10^{-10}	10^{17}	-0.03	3.0×10^5

small and large categories is surprisingly effective in explaining the major phenomena of atmospheric electricity. With this enormous simplification, the small-ion number density, n_h, in static conditions is related to the rate of ion production q_h by

$$q_h \sim \alpha_h \, n_h^2 + \beta_h \, n_h \, Z_h, \qquad (13.3)$$

where α_h is the recombination coefficient between small ions of opposite signs of charge, β_h is the attachment coefficient between small ions and aerosols, and Z_h is the aerosol concentration. Furthermore, measurements show that even in big-city environments N_h, the large-ion concentration, does not exceed 100 n_h. It follows that since the small-ion mobility is 1,000 times as great as that for large ions, the small-ion contribution to the conductivity always dominates, and the conductivity is approximately

$$\lambda_h \sim 2 \, e \, n_h \, k_h. \qquad (13.4)$$

The factor of 2 in Eq. 13.4 assumes equal mobilities for positive and negative small ions.

Table 13.1 gives some respresentative values of λ_h and E_h as functions of height. Also shown are the columnar resistance parameter,

$$R_h = \int_0^h (a/\lambda_h) \, dh, \qquad (13.5)$$

and the potential,

$$V_h = -\int_0^h E_h \, dh. \qquad (13.6)$$

The conductivity increases approximately logarithmically with height up to 40 km. This is primarily because of the change of mobility, k_h (inversely proportional to atmospheric density), with altitude in Eq. 13.4; n_h, on the other hand, varies only from 10^9 to 10^{10} m^{-3} between $h = 0$ and 40 km. Above 40 to 50 km the effects of free electrons become significant, and the increase in conductivity with altitude is even more pronounced; it is again logarithmic, but the scale height is halved.

According to the data in Table 13.1, the magnitude of the air-Earth current (V_h/R_h) is approximately constant with altitude at 3×10^{-12} A m^{-2}, and the major contributions to V_h and R_h are at the lower heights. The overall picture approaches that of the classic spherical capacitor formed by the conducting Earth, a conducting upper atmosphere (the electrosphere), and a leaky dielectric in between (Israel, 1973). The capacitor is charged to a potential of 3×10^5 V, and the leakage current is the air-Earth current.

c. The Thunderstorm Generator and the Global Circuit

We now turn to the fundamental problem: How is the Earth's negative charge maintained? The solution, first advanced by Wilson (1925, 1926), is that thunderstorms feed negative charge (resulting in positive current) into the Earth in an amount sufficient to compensate for the fair-weather current.

Generally a thundercloud is electrified so that the upper portions are positively charged and the lower parts negatively charged. Below the cloud there is an interchange of electricity with the Earth by three main processes (Fig. 13.1):

1. Cloud-to-ground lightning: Over 90% of discharges to Earth carry negative charge from the cloud to the ground. Typically this portion of the current is 0.3 A per storm.

2. Point discharge and conduction currents: The strong fields below a storm cause pointed objects such as trees, buildings, and bushes to go into corona, or point discharge. The corona increases the local ionization and conductivity, and under the influence of the intense positive fields positive ions move upward and negative ions toward the ground. An estimate for the current to ground per storm is 0.9 A.

3. Rain: Falling raindrops reduce the effects of the point discharge currents by capturing some of the upward-moving positive ions and returning them to Earth. The rain is also sometimes positively charged when it leaves the cloud. The rain current per storm is perhaps 0.2 A.

Summing the effects of all three processes suggests that a storm transfers negative electricity to ground at a rate of about 1 A per storm.

Wilson originally considered only conditions below the cloud. However, he later formulated the concept that has become known as the *global circuit*: a thunderstorm transfers positive charge toward the conducting upper atmosphere (Fig. 13.1). Here the charge is redistributed laterally to the fair-weather areas so that the thunderstorms effectively supply the driving potential of 3×10^5 V for the fair-weather currents. The exact morphology of the currents in the upper atmosphere is still somewhat uncertain, but the overall concept of the global circuit is generally accepted.

Measurements above thunderclouds show that the conductivity is not unusually enhanced in comparison with fair-weather conditions. However, the upper positive charge in the cloud creates a strong field, driving positive ions upward. The current per storm is about 0.7 A toward the electrosphere. Note that this is less than the current of 1 A to ground, possibly indicating leakage and losses within the cloud generator. Intracloud lightning and charge transport by air motion within the storm disperse a portion of the charge that remains in the air or attached to cloud particles after the storm ceases to exist. This charge is subsequently neutralized as a result of the conductivity of the air.

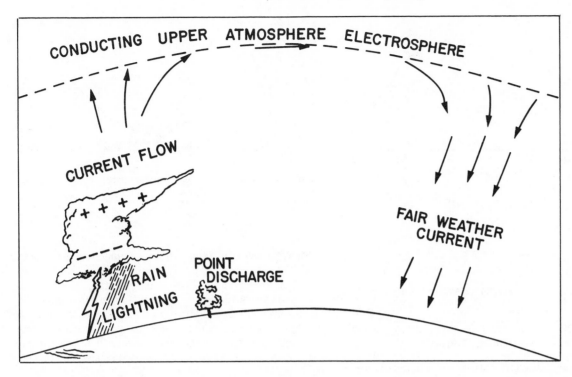

Figure 13.1. Global circuit of atmospheric electricity.

There are three notable tests of the concept that thunderstorms maintain the Earth's negative charge and drive the global circuit:

1. Equivalence of currents: The total fair-weather current should be approximately equal to that from all global thunderstorms. It has been estimated that, on the average, 2,000 storms are active simultaneously over the Earth; with a current of 0.7 to 1 A per storm this yields a total of 1,400 to 2,000 A. A fair-weather current of 3×10^{-12} A m^{-2} integrated over the total global surface gives about 1,500 A.

2. Balance sheets: Several estimates have been made of the flow of positive and negative electricity into the Earth's surface at specific localities. Note that the quantities of the two signs need not necessarily balance everywhere; places with many storms should get an excess of negative charge and places with few storms a positive surplus. The balance sheet information in Table 13.2 for land stations (usually with some storm activity) confirms this, but it is also generally supportive of the global-circuit concept.

3. Diurnal variation: There is a diurnal variation related to universal time (UT) in global-storm activity, because the tropical land masses are not uniformly distributed longitudinally over the world. The peak activity is from 1200 to 2000 UT, corresponding to local afternoon over Africa and South America. Fair-weather parameters such as air-Earth current should reflect the global diurnal thunderstorm variation, if the global-circuit concept is valid. This is approximately the case; Fig. 13.2 illustrates the observed parallelism.

Table 13.2. Representative Balance Sheet

Agent carrying charge	Range of charge density values (C km^{-2} per yr)	Mean (C km^{-2} per yr)
Fair-weather current	+30 to +100	+60
Point discharge current	−30 to −300	−90
Precipitation	+10 to + 40	+20
Lightning	−10 to − 50	−30
Balance	0 to −210	−40

It is worth emphasizing that, contrary to some popular belief, fair-weather electricity fed by the thunderstorm generator is not a significant source of energy. Each of the 2,000 active storms conveys 1 A to the fair-weather areas, but here the available potential is only 3×10^5 V. Thus the power contribution per storm is 300 kW, and the total available power output is only 600 MW, an amount comparable with that produced by only a single, large-scale commercial generating plant!

3. Thunderclouds and Their Electrification

a. Fields and Field Changes

Most of our information on the electrical state of thunderclouds is inferred from ground observations of electric fields and field changes owing to lightning (Chalmers, 1967). Over

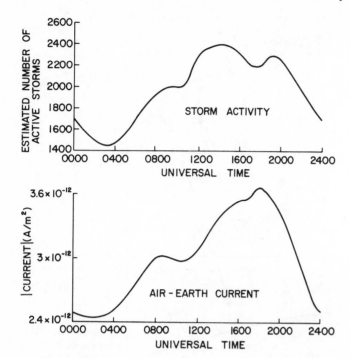

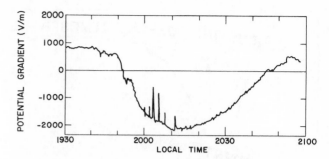

Figure 13.3. Potential-gradient variation during approach and retreat of a very weak thunderstorm.

Figure 13.2. Comparison of diurnal variations with universal time of global thunderstorm activity and of the fair-weather air-Earth current.

land beneath a thundercloud, potential gradient (or field) is directed predominantly vertically, fluctuates in magnitude, and often has a peak magnitude of about 10 kV m^{-1}. The gradient varies in sign but is usually negative, indicating a dominant negative charge in the lower portion of the cloud overhead. As a storm approaches, the positive fair-weather gradient often increases in size, then decreases and passes through zero to become strongly negative when the cloud is overhead.

During the progress of a storm lightning flashes produce pronounced, sudden field changes. Below the cloud these transient excursions may cause temporary reversals of the sign, since the magnitude of the excursions may exceed 50 kV m^{-1}. Within 6 km the changes due to lightning are usually positive (increase the gradient positively). As distance increases, so does the proportion of negative changes, and beyond about 20 km the ratio of positive to negative changes is quasi-constant at about 1.2. Typically, at 20 km the size of a field change is ~100 V m^{-1}.

The field fluctuates so violently during a typical thunderstorm and field changes owing to lightning occur so frequently that some of the generalizations of the preceding two paragraphs are rarely apparent on a record of field versus time. However, Fig. 13.3 illustrates the behavior during a very weak storm that approached within 7 km of the recording site. Two important points are evident in Fig. 13.3: the reversal of the potential gradient from positive to negative as the storm moves nearer and the abrupt positive changes caused by close lightning.

Measurements of fields within a thundercloud are difficult. Nevertheless, the existing information is fairly self-consistent (Winn et al., 1974; Christian et al., 1980). Measurements by several investigators suggest that generally fields within clouds are about 50 to 200 kV m^{-1}, that there is often an increase in field when the cloud is entered, that there are localized regions of extremely high fields in the cloud with dimensions of a few hundred meters, and that the fields may be as great as 400 kV m^{-1}.

b. Models

If we have a charge Q at a height H above the Earth's surface, then the field at the ground at a horizontal distance D is given by

$$E = \frac{2QH}{4\pi\varepsilon_0(H^2 + D^2)^{3/2}}. \tag{13.7}$$

By recognizing that Eq. 13.7 can be extended to include several distributed-charge centers of positive and negative signs, it is possible to deduce models of cloud charges consistent with the information in Sec. 3a.

A simple but typical such model would consist of charges of -20 C and $+20$ C centered at heights of 4 and 8 km, respectively, and laterally displaced by 4 km. With this arrangement the potentials at the charge centers are approximately -10^8 V and $+10^8$ V. The field at the Earth's surface with this model is about 20 kV m^{-1}; this is reduced to the observed 10 kV m^{-1} by ions released at the Earth from point discharge. When a lightning flash to ground occurs, it usually removes negative charge from the cloud and in this case everywhere produces a shift of the potential gradient toward more positive values. Another common form of flash occurs when the two cloud charges attempt to neutralize each other; this intracloud discharge yields positive changes at close distances but negative ones farther away.

A question of much significance in thunderstorm electrification theories is that of the distribution of charge, in magnitude and sign, within a thundercloud from charge carried on precipitation of different sizes. Specifically, it is important to know whether positive- and negative-charge carriers are always present in the same area at comparable strengths so that the net space charge is only the small difference. The alternative of whether the charge carriers are effectively segregated is equally significant.

Unfortunately, the experimental information is very scanty. The maximum space charge within a cloud is about 3×10^{-8} C m^{-3}; by Poisson's equation this corresponds to a potential gradient change of 3 kV m^{-1} at the edge of the regions of extremely high fields. More generally within the cloud the space charge is about 3×10^{-9} C m^{-3}, and the limited information suggests that this sometimes approximates the difference between positive- and negative-space charges of some 10^{-8} C m^{-3} residing on precipitation. However, whether there are often substantial charges on ions and very small particles remains a major uncertainty.

c. Electrification Theories

Many theories and mechanisms have been suggested whereby a thundercloud can become charged. It is now clear that there is no unique mechanism for the charging (Dawson, 1974; Latham, 1981). Several mechanisms probably operate simultaneously within different parts—for some mechanisms in the same part—of the cloud.

The theories can be divided into two categories, gravitational and convective. In the gravitational theories some microscopic mechanism of charge separation places negative charge on large precipitation and positive on smaller particles; these then separate under gravity to produce a charged cloud of the observed polarity (negative toward the base, positive above). With the convective theories, air motions, including shears, updrafts, and downdrafts, are the dominant influences in separating the charge. It is noteworthy that modern models of thundercloud electrification suggest a considerable horizontal separation of the upper positive- and lower negative-charge centers. This implies that both gravity and air motions are active in segregating charge.

The many mechanisms that may contribute to charging before gravitational separation include inductive charging, selective ion capture processes, freezing effects involving impurities, and other miscellaneous phenomena in which ice and water are concerned. Inductive charging occurs as a charge transfer during the collision without coalescence of particles polarized by the field. Ion capture is a special instance of inductive charging when a falling polarized particle attracts and absorbs a particular sign of ion selectively. Freezing potential between ice and water is considerable when the water contains salts in dilution, as is the case in some thunderclouds; the mechanism might be very effective under certain conditions, but it is uncertain whether these apply within storms. Miscellaneous phenomena involving ice and water include riming, evaporation, melting, and splintering on freezing; all produce electrical effects.

The mechanisms specified in the preceding paragraph seem of minor importance, however, compared with the thermoelectric influences that are immensely active when hail, ice crystals, and supercooled droplets are present in the same region of a cloud (Stow, 1969). The mobility of the positive $(OH_3)^+$ defect in ice is greater than that of the negative $(OH)^-$ defect, and the number of defects increases with temperature. Consequently when warm- and cold-ice particles are momentarily in contact, positive charge flows out of the warm particle faster than negative charge in the reverse direction. Typically, a warm hail pellet falling through ice crystals will thus acquire a substantial negative charge. The exact magnitude will depend on time of contact and on temperature difference, which is affected by surface roughness and latent-heat effects.

Although convective theories are not as widely accepted as gravitational theories, they certainly cannot be discounted, particularly when it is realized that air velocities within a thundercloud often considerably exceed those acquired by particles under gravitational or electrical forces. The largest, and therefore fastest, precipitation falls gravitationally at only a few meters per second; this is also the order of speed acquired by the smallest (small ions), and therefore fastest, charged particles in the general electrical fields in clouds. Typically a convective theory starts with the natural positive-space charge of the fair-weather atmosphere (Vonnegut, 1963). This is entrained upward as an updraft develops, so that a convective cloud is initially positively charged. Negative ions are then attracted toward the cloud but are trapped on cloud particles around the edges of the cloud in a screening layer. As the cloud circulation increases, downdrafts develop that strip off the screening layers and convey the negative charge toward the cloud base. Here the negative charge produces high fields that liberate positive ions by corona from the Earth's surface; these ions move under the influence of the field and into the intensifying updraft core, thus perpetuating a kind of feedback cycle. In this cycle the positive cloud core attracts screening negative ions, especially at the side edges of the cloud, and these in turn move in downdrafts to the cloud base, there to intensify the entrainment of positive charge into the core updraft and to increase the development of the cloud electrification.

4. Lightning

a. Flash Development

The most obscure aspect of lightning is the position and manner of its initiation. It seems plausible that the first breakdown occurs in the localized cloud regions of high field ($\sim$400 kV m^{-1}). However, 400 kV m^{-1} is an insufficiently high field to cause breakdown of itself. What may occur is a growing system of corona streamers from precipitation, initiated by the ambient 400-kV m^{-1} field. Calculations suggest that two or three such successive streamers could produce fields of 1 MV m^{-1} over 2–3 m (Griffiths and Phelps, 1976). The resulting potential discontinuity is a few megavolts; with a discontinuity of this size the field at the streamer tip is large enough for it to become self-propagating.

Once launched, the streamer, or *leader*, as it is commonly termed, advances at a speed of some 2×10^5 m s^{-1} as a conducting core surrounded by a sheath of charge caused by corona (Uman, 1969). The core effectively carries the potential of the initiating point with it so that the fields at the tip of the leader increase as it moves, thus facilitating the leader advance. The charge deposited along the leader core and its sheath is some 2 C km^{-1}, while the average leader current is ~100 A. Leader durations range from tens to hundreds of milliseconds.

Most lightning flashes are within the cloud (intracloud). For these discharges the leader, moving steadily toward diffuse centers of charge opposite its sign, is the principal feature in promoting the mutual neutralization of the main cloud charges. However, as the leader progresses, it occasionally encounters localized concentrations of opposite charge rather than diffuse distributions. When this occurs, there is a recoil streamer along the leader; this is often termed a *K process*. The current in a K streamer is several kiloamperes; consequently, there is a significant associated generation of luminosity and of field variations.

Discharges to ground have been studied in more detail than have intracloud flashes. The leader originating within the cloud usually transports negative charge toward the Earth. After it emerges from the cloud base, the leader may have a main and subsidiary branches. These move at an average speed of about 2×10^5 m s^{-1} toward the ground. The associated luminosity is slight, except at intervals of some 50 μs, when the tips and adjoining 50 to 100 m of the channel branches brighten abruptly for perhaps 1 μs. Although the leader advance is probably continuous, because of this intermittent brightening it appears to move in a series of successive "steps"; it is, therefore, often termed a *stepped leader*. The step phenomena involve currents of a few kiloamperes; the luminosity and field variation effects, although significant, are usually rather less than those accompanying K streamers. There is no satisfactory physical expanation, incidentally, of the stepping process.

When the main branch of the leader approaches close enough to the Earth, the high field it induces initiates an upward streamer from the ground. This unites with the leader, and the short circuit between cloud and ground is completed. A very brilliant surge of luminosity known as the *return stroke* now travels up the preionized core of the original leader channel at typically 5×10^7 m s^{-1}. Average currents are 20 kA, and the return stroke channel attains a temperature of 2×10^4 to 3×10^4 K; thus the field variations and luminosity changes are very pronounced. Indeed the return stroke is the only phase of the discharge to ground to which an observer's eye usually responds.

After the passage of the return stroke, the original leader channel is effectively at ground potential. Streamers probe into the cloud from the top of the channel in search of further concentrations of negative charge to bring to Earth. If only a small concentration is encountered, there is a recoil K streamer. However, if the concentration is substantial, the recoil is completed to ground as a so-called dart leader, moving at about 2×10^6 m s^{-1}. Conditions are now appropriate for the development of a second return stroke. There may be several successive dart stroke combinations along the same channel of a flash to ground. The strokes are often

Figure 13.4. A flash to ground showing multiple branching. The most luminous channel indicates the one that connected with the Earth (photograph by David Rust).

sufficiently separated in time to produce the flickering effect familiar to the lightning observer.

b. Forms of Lightning

The discharge to ground is visible as a distinct channel. If the channel is branched, it is *forked lightning* (Fig. 13.4); if not, it is *streak lightning*. When the flash is intracloud, the cloud is diffusely illuminated; this is *sheet lightning*. If the storm is far distant at night, so that no thunder is heard and the lightning luminosity is usually diffuse, we have *heat lightning*.

Two very mysterious and perhaps allied forms of lightning are *bead* and *ball*. In bead lightning the luminosity after a return stroke persists in localized portions of the visible channel; there is thus a decay into an apparent string of beadlike bright areas. Ball lightning, when observed, often follows the occurrence of a close, cloud-to-ground flash. A luminous ball of about 15-cm diameter appears at or near the point of ground contact. This ball persists for a few seconds and may move appreciably during this time. No satisfactory explanation of ball lightning exists.

Triggered lightning is a form of lightning defined by origin and not luminosity. It occurs when a flash is initiated that would not otherwise have taken place. Commonly this initiation is by the intrusion of a long conductor, such as a rocket, large aircraft, or high-rise building, into a thundery environment where the fields are already strong (~10 kV m^{-1}). There is an intensification of field at the tip of the conductor that is sufficient to trigger lightning. Interestingly enough, most instances of triggered lightning suggest, from both measurements and theory, a potential discontinuity of 1 or 2 MV between the tip of the conductor and the ambient atmosphere at the time triggering occurs. This is almost identical with the values envisaged by the corona streamer theories on the initiation of natural lightning (Sec. 4a).

c. Lightning Incidence and Statistics

Assessment of lightning hazards is often important in engineering. Such assessment usually involves an estimate of lightning incidence and also of the likelihood of a given lightning parameter exceeding a critical value.

A day is reported meteorologically as a thunderstorm day if thunder is heard. In many respects the thunderstorm day is an unsatisfactory parameter; nevertheless, until the advent of satellite data it was the only quantity available on a global basis from which lightning incidence can be estimated. If T_y is the number of thunderstorm days per year, then the annual flash incidence is proportional to T_y^b, where b typically lies between 1.5 and 2. The increase is greater than a direct proportionality with T_y because storms tend to be of longer total duration (because there are often more than one in a day) and to have greater flashing rates in the more thundery regions. On a monthly basis,

$$L_m^2 = aT_m + a^2 T_m^4, \qquad (13.8)$$

where T_m is the monthly number of thunderstorm days, L_m is the lightning flash density per km² per month, and the constant, a, is 3×10^{-2}. Equation 13.8 generally cannot be converted into an annual relationship for T_y, since the conversion is dependent on the monthly distribution of thunderstorm days, and this will vary among individual stations. However, for typical areas of moderate-to-high storm activity, Eq. 13.8, when the monthly values are summed to an annual basis, yields annual figures that are quite compatible with the T_y^b variation.

The flash incidence in Eq. 13.8 is for all flashes, intracloud and discharges to Earth, occurring over a 1-km² area. It is often important to consider flashes to ground alone. The proportion, p, of discharges to Earth varies greatly among individual storms and even during different phases of the same storm. However, on the long-term average there is a dependence on T_y and geographical latitude ϕ, so that

$$p^2 = \frac{0.1 \{1 + (\phi/30)^2\}}{2 + 0.05 \, T_y}, \qquad (13.9)$$

where ϕ is in degrees. At a typical middle-latitude station ($T_y = 40$, $\phi = 40°$; Washington, D.C., approximates these values), Eq. 13.9 shows that about one-fourth of the flashes go to ground.

Equation 13.8 essentially incorporates several of the behavioral features of storms, including the flashing rate and storm duration. The average flash rate per storm is about 3 or 4 per min; it rarely exceeds 10 per min. Storm durations range from 1 to more than 3 h; the latter is typical of the more thundery localities.

In some engineering applications the diurnal variation of

Table 13.3. Statistics of Lightning Parameters (Flash to Ground)

Parameter	Median value (Exceeded by 50% of values)	Extreme engineering value (Exceeded by 2% of values)
Number of return strokes	2–3	10–11
Total flash duration (ms)	180	850
Peak return stroke current (kA)	20	140
Total charge transfer per flash (C)	15	200
Return stroke current rate of change (kA μs^{-1})	22	100
Continuing current (A) (when present)	140	520
Continuing current duration (ms) (when present)	160	400
Charge transfer in continuing currents (C) (when present)	26	110
Action integral (A² s)	2×10^4	8×10^5

lightning activity is important. The peak activity at a land station is in the local afternoon (1400–1800). The afternoon maximum is about four times the morning (0400–1000) minimum [see also Chap. 2, Sec. 2c].

We now consider the statistics of individual lightning parameters. It is found that almost all these statistics obey a log-normal relationship to a good approximation. In this case, when the individual values are expressed logarithmically with respect to the median, the distribution of the values is normal. The log-normal distribution is completely defined if the median value is given together with any other value and its associated percentage probability of being exceeded. Table 13.3 shows the median and the extreme (from an engineering viewpoint) values exceeded in only 2% of instances. The information is for a flash to ground; intracloud discharges are less severe in most respects and not more severe in any respect.

There is one apparent discrepancy in Table 13.3; clarification of this and of other features is desirable. Occasionally a conducting connection between the ground and the cloud is maintained for some time after a return stroke; a continuing current then ensues and is responsible for a substantial charge transfer. Since most return strokes do not initiate a continuing current phase, flashes with few return strokes only occasionally include a continuing current. This is why for the median flash the charge transfer specified in continuing currents (only occasionally present, however) exceeds the average total charge transfer.

The parameters listed in Table 13.3 are chosen primarily for their engineering importance. Peak current governs thermal vaporization effects, and rate of current change controls electromagnetic coupling. Burning, erosion, and melting are sensitive to values of charge transfer, continuing current parameters, and the action integral (defined as $\int i^2 \, dt$, where i is current and t is time; the integration is over the entire duration of the flash).

Some energy considerations are of interest. The energy per flash is $1/2\ QV$, where Q is the charge involved and V the potential; with $Q = 20$ C and $V = 10^8$, the energy is 10^9 J. With a flashing rate of 3 per min, it follows that the average power dissipated by lightning per storm is 5×10^7 W. This value is reasonably compatible with the power dissipation per storm estimated for all sources below the cloud; this dissipation is approximately the product of the 1-A current from the three processes of lightning, point discharge, and rain (Sec. 2c) and the available voltage, or 10^8 W in all.

If the lightning flash duration is 200 ms and the total energy is 10^9 J, the mean power output over the flash itself is 5×10^9 W. As much as 10^8 J may be dissipated during the first 10 μs of the return stroke, giving an almost instantaneous power peak of 10^{13} W. This is greater than the entire electrical generating capacity within the United States, a fact that demonstrates the awesome explosive strength of lightning. The key word is, however, explosive; the intermittency of flashing, the very short duration of peak power, and the difficulties of interception preclude any practical use of lightning as a power source.

5. Atmospherics

a. The Source Signals

An *atmospheric* (*sferic*) is the transient electric or magnetic field generated by any feature of a lightning discharge or, in less common definition, by the entire flash. We may distinguish two factors in the formation of an atmospheric received at some distance from a storm: the characteristics of the source disturbance and the modifications introduced during propagation.

During a flash there is a redistribution of charge by a vast multiplicity of gas discharge processes, ranging from the slow movement of charge during leader and continuing current phases, to the abrupt large perturbation of the return stroke, and to the minor sparks of corona. Every process generates signals characteristic of the rapidity and extent of the process; the slower and larger these quantities the lower the dominant frequency of the signal. In a flash the smaller, faster processes that generate high-frequency waveforms tend to occur more often. Thus, as frequency increases, the number of pulses increases. This is indeed shown by experimental observations indicating that the number of separate impulses per discharge increases with increasing frequency, reaching a maximum at about 30 MHz and then decreasing.

The radiated source signals at VLF (3–30 kHz) and at HF/VHF (3–300 MHz) are of particular practical importance in sferics location methods. There are notable differences in the general character of the source signals within these two frequency bands. At VLF only isolated transients are generated during the flash. The strongest of these transients are created by return strokes; K processes also produce VLF signals but at much less intensity. Thus a discharge to Earth gives large pulses separated typically by 50 ms corresponding to the return strokes; there are also small signals associated with K streamers. With an intracloud dis-

charge only weak VLF signals owing to K processes are produced.

At HF and VHF, however, there is little difference between intracloud flashes and discharges to ground. In each case a very large number of pulses, often more than 10,000, is generated. The pulses occur almost continuously throughout the discharge, apart from being "quenched" temporarily for some milliseconds after return strokes and, to a lesser degree, following a K streamer. The HF/VHF pulses last ~ 1 μs and are separated by 20–100 μs. Their origin is obscure, but they appear to be associated with leader processes. Specifically, the steps of the stepped leader certainly generate HF/VHF pulses, but the pulses also occur during almost all other phases of the complete discharge.

The source pulses may be considered as generated by a large number of individual dipole radiators of different dimensions. The field from such a radiator is in the far-field regime for $d > c\ (2\pi f)^{-1}$, where d is the distance to the flash, f the frequency, and c the velocity of light. Under these circumstances the field is radiative or electromagnetic and varies inversely as distance.

Measurements made fairly near a flash, but under far-field circumstances, show that the peak magnitudes of the source signals from the overall discharge depend approximately inversely on frequency. This is so even though many types of pulses are involved. Typically, at $d = 50$ km, a VLF pulse (3–30 kHz) would be 6 V m^{-1}, with a maximum spectral content (at about 5 kHz) within the pulse of 400 mV m^{-1} in a 1-kHz bandwidth. Within a VHF pulse (at 100 MHz), a corresponding spectral content over the same bandwidth would be 20 μV m^{-1}.

b. Propagation

The propagation of radio atmospherics obeys the same laws, of course, as those controlling the propagation of conventional radio signals. Generally speaking, at frequencies below 300 kHz the lower ionosphere is the dominant influence in the propagation. At MF and HF (0.3–30 MHz) it is the middle and upper ionosphere, and at higher frequencies the propagation is effectively line-of-sight.

Propagation at VLF (3–30 kHz) is particularly important because of its intrinsic interest and also because of its practical significance in long-range sferics detection and location of storms. The propagation at VLF and the adjacent ELF (0.03–3 kHz) and LF (30–300 kHz) bands is channeled within the quasi-waveguide formed by the Earth and the lower ionosphere, the D-region—about 70–100 km. Within this waveguide the propagation can be envisaged as occurring in two essentially, although not obviously, equivalent ways. One concept is the ray approach, in which the received sferic is made up of a series of successively arriving rays. These consist of a ground signal from the source, a ray representing a single reflection of the source impulse at the ionosphere, a ray reflected twice at the ionosphere and once at the Earth, and so on. The second concept is the waveguide treatment. The source sferic excites a number of modes in the waveguide; each mode propagates with characteristic frequency-dependent attenuation factors, and the received sferic signal is the vectorial sum of the separate modes of significance. The ray approach is more useful for short distances; the mode approach is usually preferred for long distances when only a single mode is often dominant.

Whether the interpretation of a received sferic is by mode or by ray theory is immaterial to the remarkable efficiency of propagation in the quasi-waveguide. Even at $d = 3,000$ km, the electric field in a VLF return stroke pulse is -100 mV m^{-1}. Since these pulses are discrete and well separated at the source and the temporal stretching of the pulses in progation is limited, return stroke sferics are easily recognized at very great distances.

At MF and HF, groundwave signals are rapidly attenuated, and the reception of sferics at a distance depends on reflections from the higher ionosphere (E and F regions). The characteristics of the propagation such as absorption have marked temporal variations, as with time of day. However, under almost all circumstances the sferic energy can be received by several ionospheric paths. The number of pulses generated at the source is already large, and the propagation path multiplicity is a further complication. Additionally, energy will sometimes be received simultaneously from more than one distant discharge. Because of all these factors it is difficult to relate sferics observations at MF and HF of distant lightning to detailed source properties. The aggregate of the received signals is treated as the radio noise familiar to engineers. Studies of radio noise at MF and HF have the phenomenological orientation usual in areas of practical engineering importance.

At VHF and higher frequencies the ionosphere is essentially transparent, and pulses are strongly received only by line-of-sight paths. Except for satellite observations, this implies a limitation, because of Earth curvature, to ranges of 100 to 200 km, depending on the height of the flash. However, the source structure is largely maintained except for distance attenuation; it follows that useful deductions on the source properties of thunderstorms and lightning can be derived from ground observations of VHF sferics for comparatively short ($\sim$100 km) distances. On the other hand, VLF sferics studies are revealing over distances of thousands of kilometers.

Appendix A

Lightning Hazards and Damage

Lightning is a menace to people and to property. Precise statistics on all lightning-related fatalities are not compiled within the United States. However, it is known that about 100 people are killed annually by direct lightning strikes, and perhaps the same number die as a result of lightning-caused fires and accidents. This total of 200 deaths exceeds that caused by tornadoes. Even considering the direct strikes alone, lightning is still the greater killer; this is illustrated in Table 13A.1. As noted by Weigel (1976), "some overlap occurs in death totals from hurricanes and floods, because most hurricane deaths are drownings, and those occurring in rivers and streams swollen by hurricane rains are also counted as flood deaths."

Table 13.4 and Fig. 13.5 show that lightning-related fatalities caused by direct strikes have decreased steadily in recent years. This is primarily due to the increasing urbanization of the United States. Persons working in the open air are far more likely to be killed by lightning than are those in city buildings. Interestingly enough, the curve of Fig. 13.5 seems to be approaching an asymptotic value of about 100 per annum. This probably reflects a tendency for the annually decreasing number of agricultural workers, exposed to lightning because of their occupation, to be compensated for by the increasing number of outdoor recreationists.

The general principles for minimizing lightning dangers are easily defined. Indoors, proximity to good electrical conductors leading outside should be avoided; typically such conductors might include telephone lines, leads to television antennas, utility installations, soot in the chimney, and so on. Outdoors, also, a person should shun electrical conductors, e.g., metal fences. Isolated objects such as trees are to be avoided; since they project well above the general terrain, they are especially likely to be struck and to produce sideflashes or ground currents affecting persons close by. The same type of "elevated vulnerability" applies to people in bare open country; when a storm is overhead, they should reduce their effective height by crouching.

Injury from lightning may be caused by direct strike, by side flashover from an adjacent struck object, or by ground currents. Direct strikes are the most severe, often producing death by respiratory arrest or by cardiac malfunction, but even in these instances heart massage and mouth-to-mouth resuscitation should be applied (Golde, 1973). Only about

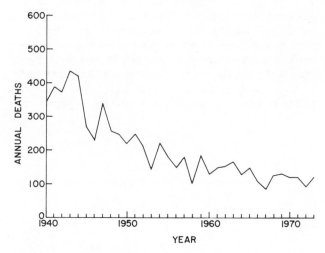

Figure 13.5. Lightning fatalities in the continental United States caused by direct strikes.

one-third of the persons injured by any manner of lightning strike actually die; with the remainder the recovery is usually complete.

Lightning causes property losses approaching $1 billion per annum in the United States. This is so even though modern steel-framed buildings are far less vulnerable than are older structures. Whatever the type of building, however, the general principle of lightning protection applies: use lightning conductors that intercept the lightning stroke current and convey it harmlessly to ground. In a good protective conducting system, the conductors will have few bends; the resistance to ground will be low; and the system will be bonded to the accessible large metal parts of the structure. Failure to follow these last two requirements can result in high voltages developing between the conductor system and independently grounded metallic parts of the structure. Side flashover can then occur; it is the most common reason why damage occurs in a nominally protected building.

Fire is the major cause of lightning damage to structures. In monetary terms fire losses exceed those from mechanical damage by a factor of about 20. Lightning fires are not usually set by the violent surge of current accompanying the

Table 13.4. Numbers of Deaths from Lightning, Tornadoes, Floods, and Hurricanes, 1940–1981

Year	Lightning deaths	Tornado deaths	Flood deaths	Hurricane deaths
1940	340	65	60	51
1941	388	53	47	10
1942	372	384	68	8
1943	432	58	107	16
1944	419	275	33	64
1945	268	210	91	7
1946	231	78	28	0
1947	338	313	55	53
1948	256	140	82	3
1949	249	212	48	4
Decadal average	329.3	178.8	61.9	21.6
1950	219	70	93	19
1951	248	34	51	0
1952	212	230	54	3
1953	145	515	40	2
1954	220	36	55	193
1955	181	126	302	218
1956	149	83	42	21
1957	180	191	82	395
1958	104	66	47	2
1959	183	58	25	24
Decadal average	184.1	140.9	79.1	87.7
1960	129	47	32	65
1961	149	51	52	46
1962	153	28	19	4
1963	165	31	39	11
1964	129	73	100	49
1965	149	296	119	75
1966	110	98	31	54
1967	88	114	34	18
1968	129	131	31	9
1969	131	66	297	256
Decadal average	133.2	93.5	75.4	58.7
1970	122	72	135	11
1971	122	156	74	8
1972	94	27	554	121
1973	124	87	148	5
1974	102	361	135	1
1975	91	60	107	4
1976	74	44	176	9
1977	98	43	212	0
1978	88	53	120	36
1979	63	83	108	22
Decadal average	97.8	98.6	176.9	21.7
1980	76	28	100	4
1981	67	24	89	0
1982	77	64	155	0
1983	77	34	204	22
44-year total	7,741	5,268	4,481	1,923
1940–83 44-year annual average	176	120	102	44
1984	NA	122	126	4

Sources: 1940–73 data from Weigel (1976); 1974–79 flood data from *Climatological Data*, National Summary, Annual Summary, Environmental Data Information Service, National Oceanic and Atmospheric Administration; 1974–80 lightning, tornado, and hurricane data from *Storm Data*, Environmental Data Information Service, National Oceanic and Atmospheric Administration; 1980 flood data and other data, 1981–84 from NOAA, Office of Public Affairs and National Weather Service.

return stroke since this is of very short duration. To ignite flammable material it is necessary for the heat source to be maintained for an appreciable time; the long continuing currents that sometimes succeed return strokes provide this time. Breakdown of a protective system possible by side flashover is, of course, a prerequisite for fire setting. In a good system the conductors will be appropriately located and of such dimensions that as long as the lightning currents are confined to the conductors there is no fire hazard.

Appendix B

Some Recent Findings on Lightning and Related Phenomena in Thunderstorms and Squall Lines[1]

Since the mid-1970s there has been an increase in thunderstorm studies, aided greatly by dramatic advances in instrumentation and data processing. As a result we now have better information on storm behavior than was available previously. Some results are presented here to illustrate the progress under way.

1. Lightning in Small Severe Storms

Lightning from four similar severe storms near the National Severe Storms Laboratory on 19 June 1980 was measured with a VHF mapping system and field change instrumentation. Storms were isolated, i.e., not part of a squall line, and the regions of moderate and stronger radar echoes were about 20 km in diameter. Lightning flashes were of three types: (1) frequent minor flashes at rates from 18 to 36 min^{-1} in each storm, confined to volumes of only about 10 km^2 in horizontal extent, centered at 12-km altitude; (2) much less frequent major flashes, at rates of only about 0.5 min^{-1}, occupying volumes about 30 km^2 in horizontal extent, centered near 5-km altitude; (3) even less frequent major cloud-to-ground flashes $(0.1-0.3 \ min^{-1})$ occupying even larger volumes around 50 km^2 in horizontal extent, also centered or originating near 5-km altitude. The designations "major" and "minor" indicate both the volume of the discharge process and the number of VHF pulses recorded by the sensors.

Figure 13.6 shows alternate presentations of the altitude distributions of minor and major flashes in storms I and IV of this date. The location of these sources in plan has been related to Doppler radar data, with results illustrated for storm I in Fig. 13.7. The major lightning flashes conform best with the radar reflectivity at 5 km; the minor flashes conform best to the divergent horizontal wind pattern which surmounts the main updraft at 13 km.

The features described and illustrated above were similar in all the four storms studied; all storms had damaging winds, and two had large hail. Other studies support the idea that these lightning features are fairly representative of such isolated small severe storms in the U.S. central plains. A principal reference to these results, and also to following sections 2 through 6, has been given by Rust et al. (1984).

2. Lightning in a Squall Line, 11 August 1982

The UHF (70.5-cm) radar at the Wallops Flight Facility, Virginia, was used to obtain data on lightning echoes with radar cross sections between 0.1 m^2, the minimum detectable in precipitation regions, and the maximum observed value near 10 m^2. Observations were concentrated in one cell of a squall line south of the Wallops Flight Facility.

As with the isolated small storms discussed above, the presence of two vertically distinct centers of lightning activity was identified. As illustrated in Fig. 13.8, one was at 6–8 km, and the other above 11 km. Lighting density in the lower center was nearly constant, while the density in the upper region was rather variable. The program of which these measurements were a part showed also that lightning strikes to aircraft are unlikely in regions where lightning is frequent; rather, strikes to aircraft are triggered by the aircraft in regions where the natural electric field is apparently strong but not at breakdown levels.

3. Cloud-to-Ground Lightning in a Mesoscale Convective Complex and in a Storm of Autumn in New England

Mesoscale convective complexes (MCCs) are discussed in Chap. 6. The intense MCC of 28 May 1982, shown in Fig. 13.9, contained two clearly identifiable squall lines that moved into Oklahoma from Texas. Records of cloud-to-ground lightning were compared with visual and infrared observations from satellites and with lightning measurements made by a high-flying NASA U-2 aircraft. Over 7 hours the average rate of flashing to ground in the whole MCC was at least 48 min^{-1}, and rates of detected flashes ranged between 38 min^{-1} and 61 min^{-1}. Of course, the intracloud flash rate (not measured) was certainly many times larger, and there were undoubtedly uncounted flashes to ground also. Observations from the overflying aircraft and from satellites indicate that CG lightning flashes have optical signatures at cloud top many tens of kilometers from the ground strike points.

[1] This appendix has been assembled by the editor and by Charles B. Moore, New Mexico Institute of Mining and Technology, Socorro.

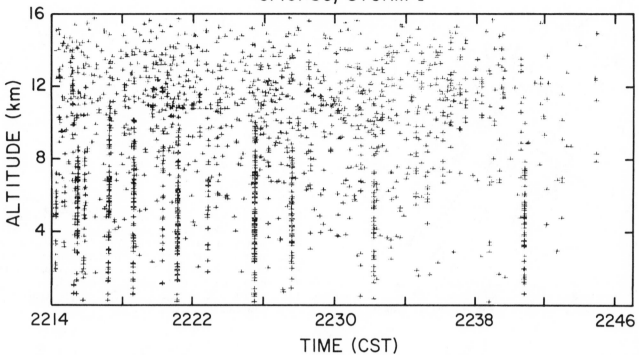

Figure 13.6a. Altitude of all VHF lightning versus time for storm 1 in Oklahoma on 19 June 1980. Vertical arrays indicate major intracloud flashes and flashes to ground.

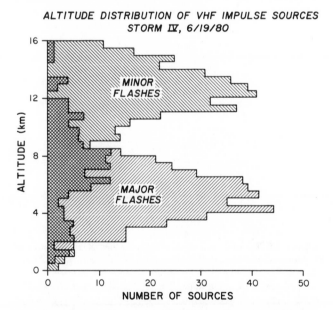

Figure 13.6b. Altitude distributions of VHF lightning impulse sources, 19 June 1980, for storm 4. The total number of impulses is a minimum near 8–10 km. While the total number of sources in major and minor flashes is about the same, the minor flashes are comprised of frequent episodes identified with a few sources, while the major flashes are occasional episodes identified with many sources.

The storm of 8–9 October 1982, in New England, was only weakly manifested in the pressure field, but it produced substantial rain, much more than had been forecasted, and approximately 7,500 CG flashes were recorded in a 10-hr period. The hourly flash rate rose dramatically from zero before 1800 GMT on the eighth to a peak over 1,600 hr^{-1} between 0100 and 0200 of October 9 and then fell again to nearly zero after 1500 GMT. The percentage of flashes that lowered positive charge to ground increased irregularly during the storm and reached 37% in the last hour of significant flash activity, although the average overall was only 4%. The increased flash rate was shown by satellite data to be accompanied by development of an extensive area of deep cloudiness marked by cloud-top temperatures colder than −55°C. As the storm moved offshore, its central pressure deepened substantially, perhaps a response to the widespread deep convection with lightning as its signature (Orville et al., 1982).

4. Screening Layers Around Electrified Clouds and Electric Fields in a Thunderstorm Anvil

Charged layers, known as *screening layers*, at the surface of electrified clouds have become clearly identified by balloon-borne electric field meters, particularly around upper regions of thunderclouds. Screening layers are produced as a result of the discontinuity in electrical conductivity at the

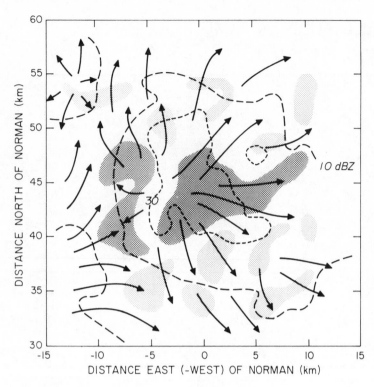

Figure 13.7a. VHF sources of major flashes at all altitudes in storm 1 on 19 June 1980 in Oklahoma are superposed onto the 40 dBZ (long dashed lines) and 50 dBZ (short dashed lines) radar reflectivity contours, and streamlines of Doppler-radar-derived horizontal wind at 5-km altitude. The total shaded area contains 80% of all mapped sources, while 50% are within the darker shading. The radar scan time was 2222–2227 CST, and the lightning occurred between 2219 and 2227 CST.

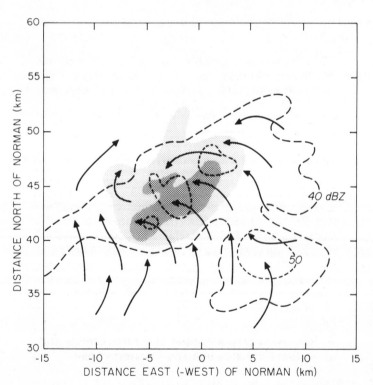

Figure 13.7b. VHF sources of minor flashes at all altitudes are superposed onto the 10 dBZ (long dashed lines) and 30 dBZ (short dashed lines) radar reflectivity contours and horizontal wind streamlines at 13-km altitude. The total shaded areas contain 80% of all mapped sources, while 50% are within the darker shading. The radar scan time and lightning time intervals are the same as in Fig. 13.4a.

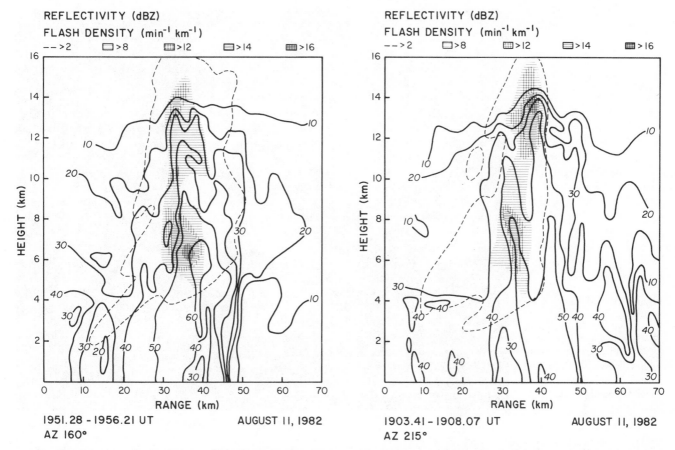

REFLECTIVITY (dBZ)
FLASH DENSITY (min⁻¹ km⁻¹)

1951.28 – 1956.21 UT   AUGUST 11, 1982
AZ 160°

1903.41 – 1908.07 UT   AUGUST 11, 1982
AZ 215°

Figure 13.8. Vertical storm structure and lightning flash density, 11 August 1982, near Wallops Island, Va. Solid lines are radar reflectivity in dBZ from a 10-cm wavelength radar; and lightning densities are based in data obtained with a 70.5-cm wavelength radar. (a) 1403–1408 EST. The azimuth from the radar is 215°. (b) 1451–1456 EST. The azimuth from the radar is 160°.

interface between clear and cloudy air; they may carry several nanocoulombs per cubic meter, the greatest concentrations of charge yet identified in thunderclouds. Charged screening layers have been observed around thunderstorms and in organized downdrafts, and they are observed on most balloon ascents through thundercloud tops.

Studies in Florida before the mid-1970s showed only small electric fields (1–10 kV m⁻¹) even as close as a few kilometers from main storm cores. On 10 May 1982 a much different condition was measured in Oklahoma during the first flight into a severe storm anvil or plume by a free balloon that carried a meter for measuring the vector electric field. The balloon entered cloud base at about 5.5 km MSL, about 65 km from the storm's main precipitation and updraft core. Below cloud base the field was near zero, but its magnitude increased rapidly to −94 kV m⁻¹ as the balloon traversed the negatively charged screening layer about 300 m thick. There was a field reversal at 7.3 km, indicating that within the cloud there was a layer of positive charge about 600 m thick. At 8.6 km, when data transmission ceased above the positive layer, the field was 75 kV m⁻¹. The anvil top exceeded 13 km (Marshall et al., 1984).

5. Positive Cloud-to-Ground Flashes

As noted in the main text of this chapter, lightning flashes to ground (CG's) usually deposit negative charge, but a larger fraction of discharges to very tall structures deposits positive charge; these flashes appear to be triggered by the structures because their leaders propagate upward, not downward as with discharges from the cloud to the ground.

Recent studies of severe storms in Oklahoma have shown that some flashes are positive CG's with downward branching indicative of natural leader propagation downward. TV recordings and photographs show no evidence of upward propagation with either positive or negative flashes to ground. The +CG flashes emanate from the severe-storm regions indicated in Fig. 13.10, which depicts the classical supercell thunderstorm with intense convective region, shear, and large anvil or plume. No positive CG flashes have been observed within heavy precipitation regions of such storms. Flashes from under the upshear anvil on the back of the storm and from the downshear anvil near the main storm tower can lower charge of either polarity; negative charge is usually deposited. In one storm two positive

Figure 13.9. Mesoscale convective complex as depicted by the GOES-5 satellite on 28 May 1982, with locations of 855 cloud to ground lighning flashes (crosses) identified during 20 minutes centered on 0300 GMT (2100 CST, 27 May 1982).

CG flashes were observed to emanate from a mesocyclone region, confirmed by the presence of a rotating wall cloud, but these observations were not repeated among data from several dozen CG's in other mesocyclones. Of the +CG flashes observed, most emerge from high in the storms. Very rarely one severe storm in a group will exhibit a majority of +CG's. In squall lines the typical positive CG flash appears to propagate horizontally for several tens of kilometers before striking the ground.

Positive flashes to ground differ from negative flashes not only in the sign of the charge that is lowered but also in that the vast majority of positives have continuing current and only one return stroke. Figure 13.11 shows records from one of four +CG flashes for which simultaneous electric-field, photographic, and television data were obtained. Note the blurred channel luminosity on the moving-film photograph in Fig. 13.11a, indicative of continuing current during interval *b* of the field change shown in Fig. 13.11b. Continuing current is often associated with lightning-caused fires and with melt-through of materials. The high-time-resolution electric-field waveform shown in Fig. 13.11c was recorded with a bandwidth of 1 MHz and has an initial ramp followed by a fast transition to peak, whose risetime is about 4 μs. Return strokes having fast transition risetimes of less than 1 μs have been observed with +CG flashes. Such short risetimes are indicative of strong inductive effects, particularly dangerous to electronic components in some aircraft and elsewhere where microelectronics susceptible

to induced transients are performing increasingly critical functions and where modern structural materials are of composite construction and do not provide shielding as effective as the conducting metals formerly used.

6. Cloud-to-Ground Lightning and Tornadoes

Collection of comprehensive data from several tornadic storms in Oklahoma has not revealed well-marked or typical associations between flashing rates from the storms as a whole and occurrences of tornadoes on the ground. There is some indication that the proportion of +CG's among all CG's is larger during the pretornadic and tornadic phases than afterward. There are few CG flashes near tornadoes, and the overall flash rate in the mesocyclone area appears to increase during the period when the tornado and mesocyclone are decaying.

7. Lower Positive Charge Centers

Simpson, Scrase, and Robinson (1937, 1940) made electrical soundings through thunderclouds with instrumented meteorological balloons and frequently observed localized volumes of positive charge in the broad, negatively charged bases of thunderclouds. Moore and Vonnegut (1959), using a single electric field meter and a single rain gauge on a mountaintop, noted occasional electric field excursions indicating locally dominant positive charges overhead in the midst of a negative charged cloud base immediately preceding the onset of intense rain on the earth. Subsequently the measuring instrumentation was increased to a net of 75 rain gauges spaced about 300 m apart, with 8 electric field meters over a 2-km meadow and a balloon-borne instrument at cloud base about 4,000 m above sea level. Data from this net showed that the lower positive charge centers appeared immediately after a nearby lightning discharge and indicated that they were caused by lightning. Intense rains frequently formed around these lower positive-charge centers which then dissipated by falling out on the rain or as the result of a neutralizing lightning discharge from that volume. Observations supporting these findings were reported by Holden et al. (1980) and by Jacobsen and Krider (1976).

8. An Index of the Local Rate of Storm Electrification

A local measure of the strength of the electrical generator in thunderclouds has been devised following work by Standler, Winn, Krider, and associates (1979 et seq.), with use of the electric field recovery rate at the ground after occurrence of lightning.

The electric field at the Earth's surface often reverses its polarity immediately after a nearby discharge removes negative charge from the cloud base, leaving a temporary dominant, positive volume of point discharge ions in the subcloud region. After a lightning flash the electric field usually recovers toward its original polarity and intensity as the cloud's generator continues its operation. When the field strength passes through zero during the recovery from reversal, all field-dependent electrical currents temporarily become zero, and the total current flowing is represented by a Maxwellian displacement current, $\varepsilon dE/dt$, where ε is the permittivity of the air.

As the field recovery continues, positive ion point discharge again commences and soon limits any further increase of the surface electric field. At this time, dE/dt approaches zero, and local effects of the generator aloft are matched and canceled by point discharge currents.

The total current density, Σj, therefore, is the sum of those carried by displacement, conduction, and precipitation. Since, from Maxwell, the total current density equals the curl of a magnetic field, its divergence must equal zero, and the total current density is a conservative property representing the current in a circuit tube from the Earth, up through the thundercloud, out into clear air, and back to Earth through the point of observation.

Thus, on occasion, when lightning gives the opportunity, we can estimate the total local current density, Σj, by simultaneous measurements of $\varepsilon dE/dt$ ($E = 0$) and j (rain).

Measurements of dE/dt ($E = 0$) at several field meters in an 1,800-m array (during the absence of precipitation) indicate that the estimated current densities are often related over the array and that they give an index of a storm's local electrical activity. Comparisons of these estimated current

OBSERVED LOCATIONS OF CG'S IN SEVERE STORMS

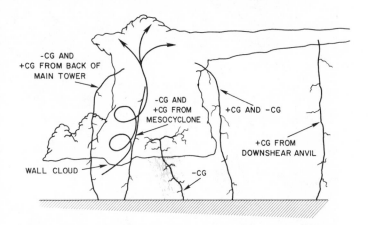

Figure 13.10. Observed locations of CG flashes based on observations of 31 confirmed +CG flashes and numerous −CG flashes in several isolated severe storms.

densities with time-lapse photographs of the cloud tops suggest that the current densities often increase significantly several minutes after a cloud turret has rebounded downward from its apogee. A measure of cloud electrification is now available for comparison with other storm processes.

9. Tests of the Precipitation Hypothesis for Cloud Electrification

For many years the cause of cloud electrification has been assumed to be the fall of charged precipitation, as suggested by Kelvin (1860). Great efforts have since gone into learning how precipitation becomes charged. Observations of thunderclouds, however, show that cloud bases acquire extensive negative charges in regions far removed from the rain shafts, and the most intense rains often fall after electrical discharges rather than before. Despite these apparently conflicting observations, the rain hypothesis is still accepted, and no definitive test of it became available until the advent of Doppler radar for measurements of the fall velocity of precipitation particles. Williams, L'Hermitte, and others have determined the mean velocities of precipitation particles falling from thunderclouds before and after nearby lightning discharges. If the precipitation were carrying charge downward so as to increase the electric field strength in the cloud, the resulting electric forces acting in the precipitation charge should slow the fall of the precipitation. When lightning occurs in the vicinity, it neutralizes some of the charges and thus weakens the electric forces, allowing the precipitation to fall more rapidly.

On the other hand, if the precipitation particles are assembled from charged cloud droplets and have the sum of their masses and charges, the electric forces beneath a charged cloud should act to move the precipitation particles downward faster than their fall under gravitational forces

Figure 13.11a–c. +CG flash recorded at NSSL on 30 May 1982, approximately 2115:30 CST. **13.11a** (above). Streak-film photograph in which continuing current is evident from the smearing of luminosity. Smearing persists for about 60 ms; the associated continuing current field change appears in (b) from R to the first "break" in the curve, labeled interval b.

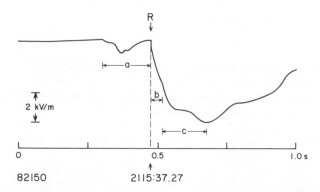

Figure 13.11b. Electrostatic field versus time for the flash shown above. The return stroke is labeled R, and the direction of field change shows that positive charge was lowered. Interval a denotes activity preliminary to the return stroke. Interval b is the confirmed continuing current, and c is either additional continuing current or subsequent intracloud breakdown.

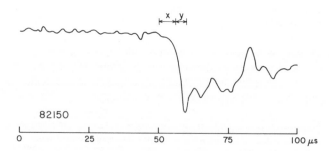

Figure 13.11c. The radiation field versus time, during the moment of the return stroke denoted R in (b) above. Interval x is the slow rise and y the more rapid rise to peak observed in both negative and positive CG flashes. The entire length of this record is just 1/10,000 part of the record shown in (b) above and so corresponds to a time interval much less than the line width in (b). The radiation field is produced primarily by the acceleration of electrons as they take up the new positions productive of the electrostatic field shown in (b).

alone. When lightning occurs in the cloud, these electrical forces should be reduced so that the particles would no longer be repelled by the cloud—then fall velocity should decrease. The role of charged precipitation in the electrification of clouds can therefore be assessed by measurement with vertical pointing Doppler radar of changes in the fall speed of precipitation when lightning is nearby.

Williams (1981) operated such a radar during two summer seasons when more than 30 thunderclouds passed over his radar. Although many hundreds of lightning discharges occurred in his vicinity and many precipitation shafts passed overhead, he found that changes in vertical velocities of precipitation during lightning were rare. The few changes that he did observe indicated that the predischarge particle motion was dissipating electric energy in all cases. The assumption that precipitation motion is contributing to predischarge cloud electrification is not therefore supported by these observations.

10. Lightning on Other Planets

Lightning has been observed in the atmospheres of Venus and Jupiter, where conditions and compositions are greatly different from those on Earth (Williams et al., 1983). It is difficult to speculate meaningfully about the causes of these remote discharges since we know so little about the details of the atmospheres in which they occur and since we have not well identified the causes of lightning in our own atmosphere, but it seems likely that some common features produce the same phenomenon even in widely different situations.

These new observations present many challenges for explanations that will involve a broad spectrum of disciplines and capabilities. This work is just beginning.

14. Model Relationships Among Storm Cloudiness, Precipitation, and Airflow

Edwin Kessler

1. Introduction

Even casual observers sense close connections among cloudiness, precipitation, and airflow. Air cools as it rises, owing to its expansion against the surrounding air in which pressure diminishes with height. Cooling in the rising air leads to water vapor condensation and latent-heat release; thus the cooling rate as moisture condenses may be only about two-thirds as much as in the absence of condensation. Relative warmth and ascent of rising parcels are maintained by the heat of condensation, as first clearly elucidated by Espy (1841), and by a sufficiently rapid decline of temperature with height in the surrounding air. Thus towering clouds mark rising currents—formation of rain depends upon the existence of a sufficiently deep and dense cloud and concurrently on a sufficiently deep, strong, and persistent updraft.

Water vapor and tiny cloud droplets share the motions of the air vertically and horizontally. Thus thunderclouds spread out aloft, because the airstreams that cap updraft columns are necessarily divergent. On the other hand, large raindrops formed from cloud fall through the air at 5 to 10 m s^{-1}, faster than most updrafts, and are subject to both evaporation and horizontal convergence at low altitudes. Thus showers arrive at the ground in narrow shafts. Study reveals other important differences in distributions of cloud and rain that ensue from differences of their fallspeed.

Careful examination of the distributions of clouds and precipitation in relation to airflow on the scale of showers has been undertaken only during the last two decades. While a very interesting subject in its own right, study of moisture distribution on the shower scale has apparently depended on certain stimuli: conventional weather radar, for example, provides data on the three-dimensional development of precipitation in storms—study of these data provides an important avenue toward understanding some physical processes intertwined in storms. Doppler radar presents airflow along with precipitation distribution and provides a much firmer basis for connecting airflow with the distribution of condensation products formed in moist updrafts.

In the following section there is a nonmathematical description of cloud and precipitation in relation to storm airflow. This discussion is principally qualitative, but it is informed significantly by the mathematical approach indi-

cated in Sec. 3. Discussion leads primarily from four papers by the author (Kessler, 1969, 1974, 1975a and b) and represents a great simplification of natural processes. For example, in the real world turbulence is responsible for much irregularity in real wind and water distributions undisclosed by the present treatment but observed, for example, by radar and aircraft.

2. Cloud and Precipitation Density in Updrafts

a. Cloud Profiles

Consider a rising current originating at the Earth's surface. It cools as it rises, and moisture starts to condense on numerous microscopic condensation nuclei at an altitude that is lower with larger moisture content. When drafts do not mix much with their surroundings and air is quite moist, cloud base may be as low as 200 or 300 m.

If parcels that rise to the condensation level find there a warmer environment, they rise only a little farther by virtue of their inertia, but if the parcels are warmer than their surroundings, upward motion may continue and accelerate. Cloud particles, usually numbering at least several hundred per cubic centimeter, then continue to grow, and with condensate so distributed over many particles, their typical diameter is only a few microns (millionths of a meter) (Byers, 1965; Mason, 1971; Rogers, 1979). Since the cloud particles are so fine, they are carried aloft with the rising air, and as condensation continues, the mass of condensate per unit volume increases. If the air parcel rises rapidly, then a larger proportion of the condensation nuclei is activated, the cloud droplets are particularly numerous and hence more uniformly small, and conversion of cloud to precipitation may occur only after the air parcel has risen very high or has even left the rising air column.

When our parcel rises very high, it becomes quite cold, and little moisture remains for further condensation. In other words, most moisture condenses at the lower altitudes and warmer temperatures. At great altitudes, cloud density may even diminish with rising motion, because the cloud expands along with the air, and little new cloud can be created by condensation. Air density is lower at the base of the stratosphere (11,000 m over the United States) than at mid-

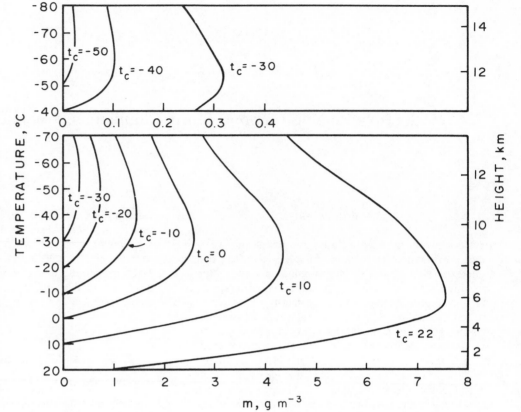

Figure 14.1. Vertical profiles of cloud density in trains of air parcels risen from various condensation levels without precipitation formation and without mixing of ambient air. The temperatures at the condensation level are indicated on the curves and at the intersections of the curves with the left-hand ordinate. The altitude at various temperatures is indicated by the right-hand ordinate. The cloud water content at various heights and temperatures is indicated by the abscissas. Profiles were calculated for a model tropical atmosphere from data in the *Smithsonian Meteorological Tables* (Smithsonian Institution, 1958; see tables 71, 78, 108).

troposphere (5,500 m) by nearly a factor of 2. Our discussion suggests cloud profiles as shown in Fig. 14.1.

In narrow columns, mixing and diffusion are particularly important and lead to diminution or total loss of cloud by evaporation, with termination of ascending mo-evaporation, with termination of ascending motion in part a result of the local cooling that accompanies evaporation.

We note that cloud development must proceed faster with faster airspeed, but the *shape* of steady cloud profiles is unrelated to airspeed in this first approximation. This is so because we have assumed the cloud particles to move with the air in all cases, and we have introduced no other dependencies on airspeed. Such approximate treatment illuminates functions of the central condensation process and of the air density distribution produced by universal gravity.

b. Precipitation Profiles

Precipitation forms from clouds that consist of droplets having different sizes, chemical components, and fallspeeds. Where there is much variety in these qualities, some droplets tend to grow at the expense of others, which evaporate, and the relative motions of cloud droplets produce occasional contacts resulting in fusion. By such processes a few large particles are formed initially. These fall through the cloud, growing further by accretion of the cloud droplets. Much additional important detail has been given, but we are

concerned here only with the concepts that (1) time is taken for precipitation to form from cloud and (2) precipitation formation is fastest where cloud is densest or where the distribution of cloud droplet sizes is broadest.

Consider a cloud column with density distribution represented by an intermediate profile in Fig. 14.1. Somewhere near the dense middle of the cloud, precipitation forms first. Unless the updraft is faster than a few meters per second, the precipitation particles descend to the ground. The tiny cloud particles continue to form and rise, but they are now subject to losses occasioned by their contacts with precipitation. So the precipitation grows during its descent to the ground, while the cloud is thinner than before. Eventually precipitation forms near or at the top of the cloud layer and develops at expense to cloud during its descent to the ground. When precipitation is abundant, the rate of precipitation development at each height during its descent depends mainly on the rate of cloud formation at that height, because the cloud collection process is very efficient and leaves little cloud to be carried by vertical currents to another level.

The rates of condensation and of cloud formation in rising saturated air depend on the product of updraft speed and the diminution of saturation vapor density with height. The latter gradient quantity is largest where the air is warmest, usually at or near the ground; updraft speed is largest at middle altitudes (in any event, updraft is zero at its upper and lower boundaries and has a maximum somewhere be-

298

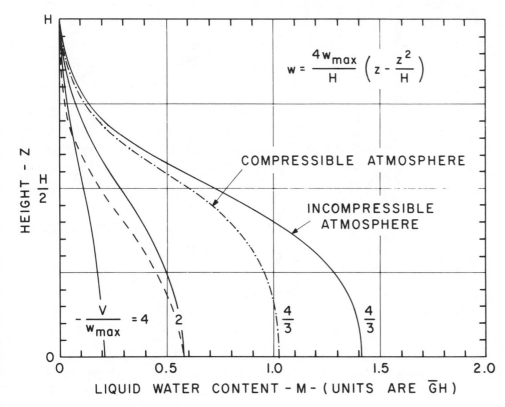

$$w = \frac{4 w_{max}}{H} \left(z - \frac{z^2}{H} \right)$$

COMPRESSIBLE ATMOSPHERE

INCOMPRESSIBLE ATMOSPHERE

$-\dfrac{V}{w_{max}} = 4$ 2 $\dfrac{4}{3}$ $\dfrac{4}{3}$

HEIGHT – Z

LIQUID WATER CONTENT – M – (UNITS ARE $\overline{G}H$)

Figure 14.2. Model steady-state vertical profiles of precipitation content in saturated updrafts whose maximum speeds are different fractions of the constant precipitation fallspeed. The amount of condensation per unit volume per unit vertical displacement of saturated air (G) is constant except with the dashed line. In that case, G declines linearly to zero at height H. Note, for example, that if the height H of the cloud top is 10^4 m and G is 1.5 g m^{-4} then the unit 1 on the abscissa refers to a precipitation content of 1.5 g m^{-3}.

tween). Thus it is probably common to have most rapid development of descending precipitation somewhere in the lower half of the updraft column. These concepts are implicit in the profiles shown in Fig. 14.2, where there is also some additional detail discussed in part below.

We now consider model relationships between vertical profiles of the air's precipitation content and updraft speed. We deal here with considerable complexity. Remember that the condensation rate in a moist updraft is proportional to the updraft speed and that the cloud content (density) is suppressed by its collection by precipitation. Suppose the updraft speed doubles from a prior value. Since this doubles condensation rate, cloud content tends at first to double, as does the rate of precipitation development, since precipitation formation is proportional to the product of cloud and precipitation. As both precipitation and cloud contents are doubled, the accretion rate approaches four times its original value. The cloud content is reduced again by the faster accretion process to approximately its former value, since this maintains a balance between the larger rate of cloud formation and depletion of cloud in the presence of the doubled precipitation amounts. Thus in weak updrafts the model steady precipitation rate is proportional to updraft speed, but the cloud content accompanying steady precipitation is hardly dependent on updraft speed.

Actually the development of precipitation depends not only on the rate at which vapor is transformed to conden-

sate but also on the time interval available for precipitation development during its descent to the ground. As long as updraft speeds are quite small (for example, less than 0.5 m s^{-1}) compared with precipitation fallspeed (about 6–8 m s^{-1}), time taken for precipitation to descend to the ground is only slightly affected by variations of updraft speed. But when the updraft speed is considerably faster than fallspeed, substantially more time passes during precipitation descent as the updraft increases. This means, for example, that a doubling of maximum updraft speed from 1 to 2 m s^{-1} may associate with increased precipitation rate at the ground by a factor, for example, of about 2.5, and not simply 2. In this case, increased updraft speed contributes significantly to both the rate of development of a precipitation packet and the time interval available for its development before it reaches the ground. Horizontal convergence and divergence that necessarily accompany vertical currents are crucial elements in satisfying considerations of mass balance (see Sec. 3).

Strong updrafts are of special interest here because they are characteristic of intense thunderstorms. We define a strong updraft as one whose peak speed is about 50% or more faster than the fallspeed of typical precipitation particles. In such a case both precipitation and cloud are borne upward to near the top of the updraft column. Of course, precipitation is always falling with respect to cloud, and the same kind of collection process operates, as in the weak up-

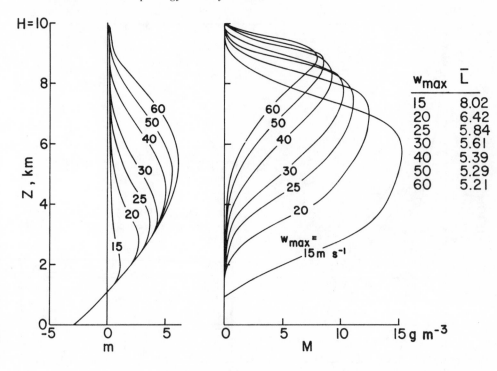

w_{max}	$\bar{L}$
15	8.02
20	6.42
25	5.84
30	5.61
40	5.39
50	5.29
60	5.21

Figure 14.3. Model steady-state profiles of cloud density (m) and precipitation density (M) for various speeds of strong updrafts. The updraft profile is parabolic with maximum at 5 km, zeros at 0 and 10 km. The condensation level is near 1 km. Note that for the whole updraft column the average content of cloud plus precipitation, L, declines slowly with updraft speed and becomes practically invariant for the fastest speeds.

draft case, to build precipitation at a loss to cloud. When the updraft is strong, the cloud particles rise farther before they are converted to precipitation. This means that the cloud content tends to be greater as updraft increases. But when conversion to precipitation starts, there is a larger amount of cloud to change to precipitation, and hence a larger amount of precipitation in the upper part of the column, where it is very effective in reducing the amount of cloud by accretion. Thus, in the upper part of the updraft column, the precipitation density becomes greater and the cloud density becomes less as the updraft speed increases. Such profiles of cloud and precipitation are shown in Fig. 14.3.

In a strong updraft, precipitation cannot descend to the ground through the rising current. What happens to it? In some cases it may descend to the ground in adjacent descending currents, especially if there is substantial horizontal wind at altitude. Then the precipitation is subject to large losses by evaporation, because the distance to the ground may be far and descending currents are usually dry. In other cases the upward transport of water vapor and condensate may be balanced for some time by the horizontal spreading of a great storm anvil or plume at high altitudes.

When the updraft is very strong, the precipitation transport process closely resembles the cloud transport process. In other words, the fallspeeds of both precipitation and cloud may be negligible compared with the updraft speed. In this case, the content of combined cloud and precipitation is close to that of cloud alone and is independent of the updraft speed. This finding, implicit in the governing equations, has interesting implications for thunderstorm behavior. Independence of water load and updraft speed means

that perturbations in one parameter do not affect the other and in particular do not stimulate oscillations. On the other hand, in the regime of weak updrafts, as already noted, precipitation content is a strong function of updraft speed. Therefore, coupled oscillations could characterize this regime. In fact, weak and moderate convective clouds represent showers or intermittent pulsations of rain, while the intense local storms not uncommon in the U.S. Mississippi Valley have often been associated with quasi-steady behavior (see Chap. 7).

3. Mathematical Development

a. Derivation of Equations of Continuity

Consider an elementary volume in the form of a cube with sides dx, dy, and dz in conventional Cartesian coordinates as shown in Fig. 14.4. Let air density be ρ, and let the windspeed components in the directions of x, y, and z be u, v, and w, respectively.

The rate of airmass flow into the left face of the cube is $\rho u\,dy\,dz$. The flow out of the right side is $[\rho + (\partial/\partial x)(\rho u)dx]dy\,dz$. The difference represents the net rate of accumulation or depletion in the volume owing to the horizontal wind parallel to the page:

$$\frac{\partial \rho}{\partial t}\,dx\,dy\,dz = \rho u\,dy\,dz - \left[\rho u + \frac{\partial}{\partial x}(\rho u)dx\right]dy\,dz$$

$$= \left[-\frac{\partial}{\partial x}(\rho u)\right]dx\,dy\,dz. \qquad (14.1)$$

Consideration of the vertical flow and of the component

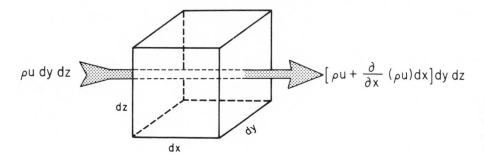

$$\rho u \, dy \, dz \qquad \left[\rho u + \frac{\partial}{\partial x}(\rho u)dx \right] dy \, dz$$

Figure 14.4. Illustration of the physical basis for the equation of continuity. The difference between mass inflow and outflow is the net change of interior mass.

of horizontal flow through the front face of the cube in Fig. 14.4, i.e., into the page, leads to two other terms of identical form on the right side. Dividing both sides by *dxdydz* yields

$$\frac{\partial \rho}{\partial t} = - \left[\frac{\partial(\rho u)}{\partial x} + \frac{\partial(\rho v)}{\partial y} + \frac{\partial(\rho w)}{\partial z} \right]$$

$$= -\rho \left[\frac{\partial u}{\partial x} + \frac{\partial v}{\partial y} + \frac{\partial w}{\partial z} \right] - u \frac{\partial \rho}{\partial x} - v \frac{\partial \rho}{\partial y} - w \frac{\partial \rho}{\partial z} .$$
(14.2)

This general equation of continuity can be simplified for our use. Observations in the real atmosphere show that terms $\partial \rho / \partial t$, $u(\partial \rho / \partial x)$, and $v(\partial \rho / \partial y)$ are much smaller than the others. Although thermodynamics teaches that these terms are of great significance in equations describing the forces that accelerate the air motion, they are of little significance in describing velocity relationships among existing flow components. Henceforth we use the continuity equation in the form

$$\frac{\partial u}{\partial x} + \frac{\partial v}{\partial y} + \frac{\partial w}{\partial z} + w \frac{\partial ln\rho}{\partial z} = 0. \qquad (14.3)$$

This is an anelastic continuity equation, widely used in mathematical studies of atmospheric phenomena (Ogura and Phillips, 1962).

Exactly the same method is used to derive a continuity equation for $\mathfrak{M}$, the density of all the water substance (cloud and vapor) that fully shares the air motion. Our method leads to

$$\frac{\partial \mathfrak{M}}{\partial t} = - u \frac{\partial \mathfrak{M}}{\partial x} - v \frac{\partial \mathfrak{M}}{\partial y} - w \frac{\partial \mathfrak{M}}{\partial z}$$

$$- \mathfrak{M} \left[\frac{\partial u}{\partial x} + \frac{\partial v}{\partial y} + \frac{\partial w}{\partial z} \right], \qquad (14.4)$$

analogous to Eq. 14.2 and the bracketed expression can be replaced by a single term through substitution from Eq. 14.3. We have then

$$\frac{\partial \mathfrak{M}}{\partial t} = - u \frac{\partial \mathfrak{M}}{\partial x} - v \frac{\partial \mathfrak{M}}{\partial y} - w \frac{\partial \mathfrak{M}}{\partial z}$$

$$+ \mathfrak{M} w \frac{\partial ln\rho}{\partial z} . \qquad (14.5)$$

This equation tells us that the local density of all water sub-

stance that fully shares the air motion changes as a result of horizontal advection (the first two terms on right-hand side), vertical advection (the third term), and the expansion or contraction that accompanies rising or descending motion in the compressible atmosphere.

Since the distinction between cloud and vapor must be made here, we write

$$\mathfrak{M} = m + Q_s, \qquad (14.6)$$

where Q_s is the saturation vapor density, positive m is the cloud density, and negative m is the density of water vapor needed to saturate the air. We assume that when $\mathfrak{M} < Q_s$, there is no cloud, and that when $\mathfrak{M} > Q_s$, the air is saturated. Then in this model, cloud must condense (evaporate) instantly as Q_s declines (increases), which Q_s does rapidly with strong upward (downward) air motion. This seems appropriate for revealing working relationships, since it has been shown that vapor supersaturation or undersaturation in the presence of cloud is limited to about 1% under extreme conditions (i.e., strong vertical motions). Substitution of Eq. 14.6 into Eq. 14.5 gives

$$\frac{\partial Q_s}{\partial t} + \frac{\partial m}{\partial t} = - u \left[\frac{\partial Q_s}{\partial x} + \frac{\partial m}{\partial x} \right] - v \left[\frac{\partial Q_s}{\partial y} + \frac{\partial m}{\partial y} \right]$$

$$- w \left[\frac{\partial Q_s}{\partial z} + \frac{\partial m}{\partial z} \right] + (m + Q_s)w \frac{\partial ln\rho}{\partial z} .$$
(14.7)

Some terms in this equation can be dropped because observations show them to be relatively small. Thus Q_s is related to air temperature and density, and radiosonde data show that the principal variation of Q_s is along the vertical. Since, in addition, Q_s varies only slowly with time, the major parameter relationships are given by

$$\frac{\partial m}{\partial t} = - u \frac{\partial m}{\partial x} - v \frac{\partial m}{\partial y} - w \frac{\partial m}{\partial z} + mw \frac{\partial ln\rho}{\partial z}$$

$$+ w \left[Q_s \frac{\partial ln\rho}{\partial z} - \frac{\partial Q_s}{\partial z} \right] . \qquad (14.8)$$

The term in brackets accounts for cloud condensation and evaporation that accompany vertical air motion in the compressible atmosphere, and we sometimes denote it by G. Its units are g m^{-4}, referring under saturated conditions to the amount of moisture condensed or evaporated per meter of ascent or descent in one cubic meter of air. Under unsaturated conditions the departure from saturation is changed at the same rate. In an atmosphere typical of summer in the United States a rough approximation is $G = 3 \times 10^{-3} - 3 \times 10^{-7} z$, and this relationship is used here except where otherwise indicated.

An equation for precipitation, M, is derived similarly, but we must note that the vertical motion of precipitation particles is not simply w but $V + w$, where V, a negative quantity, may be the average terminal velocity of precipitation particles of different sizes. Then:

$$\frac{\partial M}{\partial t} = - u \frac{\partial M}{\partial x} - v \frac{\partial M}{\partial y} - (w + V) \frac{\partial M}{\partial z}$$

$$- M \frac{\partial V}{\partial z} + Mw \frac{\partial ln\rho}{\partial z}. \qquad (14.9)$$

b. Microphysical Processes

In neither Eq. 14.8 nor Eq. 14.9 is there any provision for several essential processes:

1. Conversion of cloud to precipitation (*cc*).
2. Accretion of cloud particles by precipitation once formed (*ac*).
3. Evaporation of precipitation in unsaturated air (*ep*).
4. Mixing and diffusion.

We represent the *cc* process by

$$\frac{\partial m}{\partial t} = - k_1 (m - \alpha) \quad [\text{for } m > \alpha]. \quad (14.10)$$

Here k_1 is the reciprocal of a characteristic conversion time, and α is a threshold below which there is no conversion. A wide range of natural conditions can be crudely simulated by appropriate choices of k_1 and α; in some applications α has been spatially variable. Of course, the conversion of cloud to precipitation is manifested as a loss in the cloud equation and as an equal gain in the precipitation equation.

Our consideration of the accretion process starts from observations by Marshall and Palmer (1948), who proposed that observations of raindrop distributions may be represented approximately by the inverse exponential function,

$$N = N_0^{-\lambda D}, \qquad (14.11)$$

where N is the number of drops per unit volume per unit size range of the distribution, D is drop diameter, and λ is a parameter related to water content or rainfall rate. The parameter N_0 is approximately constant for most rains and is near 10^7 m^{-4}; it tends to be larger in drizzle and smaller in hail and snow.

Raindrop fall velocity in relation to drop size was examined carefully by Gunn and Kinzer (1949), and an equation that fits their data closely for diameters larger than 1 mm is $V = -130 D^{1/2}$ m s^{-1}. Each raindrop sweeps out the much smaller cloud droplets in its path in a cross-sectional area, $\pi D^2/4$. Of course, the efficiency of catch is not generally

unity, but we here consider it to be so. The rate of accumulation of cloud by a single raindrop is then

$$\frac{\delta M}{\delta t} = \frac{\pi D^2}{4} (130 \, D^{1/2}) \text{ m}. \qquad (14.12)$$

It remains to integrate Eq. 14.12 over the distribution of sizes represented by Eq. 14.11:

$$\frac{\partial M}{\partial t} = \int_0^\infty \frac{\delta M}{\delta t} NdD = \int_0^\infty N_0 \exp(-\lambda D) \frac{130\pi}{4} D^{5/2} \text{ m } dD$$

$$= \frac{130\pi}{4} N_0 \int_0^\infty \exp(-\lambda D) D^{5/2} \, dD. \qquad (14.13)$$

The inverse exponential distribution not only is a fair model of raindrop sizes but also has nice properties of mathematical manipulation. Thus

$$\int_0^\infty \exp(-\lambda D)D^n dD = \frac{\Gamma(n + 1)}{\lambda(n + 1)}, \qquad (14.14)$$

where Γ is the gamma function, available in tabulations. When n is an integer, tables are not needed, since $\Gamma(n + 1) = n!$ The result of integration between limits $0 \rightarrow \infty$ is usually less than 15% larger than when limits are taken corresponding to real raindrop distributions. In the case of Eq. 14.13, we have

$$\frac{\partial M}{\partial t} = 6.96 \times 10^{-4} N_0^{1/8} m M^{7/8} \text{ (g m}^{-3} \text{ s}^{-1}). \qquad (14.15)$$

In deriving Eq. 14.15, we have made use of

$$\lambda = 42.1 N_0^{1/4} M^{-1/4}, \qquad (14.16)$$

obtained by integrating raindrop mass over the distribution function (Eq. 14.11). As with cloud conversion represented by Eq. 14.10, the accretion of cloud is manifested as a loss in the cloud equation and an equal gain in the precipitation equation.

The evaporation of precipitation has been modeled by reference to the evaporation rates of individual drops in a fashion that somewhat resembles the treatment above accorded to accretion. The result is

$$\frac{\partial M}{\partial t} = 1.93 \times 10^{-6} N_0^{7/20} m M^{13/20} \text{ (g m}^{-3} \text{ s}^{-1}). \quad (14.17)$$

This term appears as a deficit in the precipitation equation and as an equal gain in the cloud-plus-vapor equation. Our complete system of modeling equations thereby becomes

$$\frac{\partial m}{\partial t} = - u \frac{\partial m}{\partial x} - v \frac{\partial m}{\partial y} - w \frac{\partial m}{\partial z} + wG$$

$$+ mw \frac{\partial ln\rho}{\partial z}$$

$$- k_1 (m - \alpha) - k_2 N_0^{1/8} m M^{7/8}$$

$$- k_3 N_0^{7/20} m M^{13/20}, \qquad (14.18a)$$

and

$$\frac{\partial M}{\partial t} = - u \frac{\partial M}{\partial x} - v \frac{\partial M}{\partial y} - (w + V) \frac{\partial M}{\partial z}$$

$$- M \frac{\partial V}{\partial z} + Mw \frac{\partial ln\rho}{\partial z} + k_1(m - \alpha)$$

$$+ k_2 N_0^{1/8} m M^{7/8} + k_3 N_0^{7/20} m M^{13/20}, \qquad (14.18b)$$

where k_1 is about 10^{-4} s^{-1} when $m > \alpha$; otherwise $k_1 = 0$; α is about 1 g m^{-3}; $k_2 = 6.96 \times 10^4$ when $m > 0$; otherwise $k_2 = 0$; and $k_3 = 1.93 \times 10^6$ when $m < 0$; otherwise $k_3 = 0$. We may also take

$$V = V_0 = -38.3 \, N_0^{-1/8} \, M^{1/8} \, (\rho/\rho_0)^{1/2}$$

and

$$(\rho/\rho_0)^{1/2} \sim \exp(-10^{-4} \, z/2),$$

in order to relate vertical flux of raindrops to the fall velocity V_0 of the median volume diameter and to vertical variations of air density. The air-density factor ranges from near unity to about 1.4. It may be omitted without much loss to understanding of basic working relationships. When it is included in the V equation, it should be multiplied into the coefficient of the accretion term (Eq. 14.15) also. Then k_2 becomes a function of altitude.

It should be noted that in spite of some apparent complexity, Eqs. 14.18a and b do not include terms descriptive of mixing and diffusion, and our model in this form does not embrace fallspeed transitions characteristic of melting snow or mixtures of disparate precipitation types, such as rain and hail. The cloud physics parameterizations are gross simplifications of real process, and there is no mechanism here for interaction between the field of water substance and the field of motion. Nevertheless, various forms of these equations, considered with particular assumed wind fields, give substantial insights into cloud and precipitation processes.

c. Application of the Equations

(1) Precipitation Rate at the Ground in the Steady Case: Addition of Eqs. 14.18a and 18b yields a continuity equation for total water substance:

$$\frac{\partial(m + M)}{\partial t} = -\left[u \frac{\partial(m + M)}{\partial x} + v \frac{\partial(m + M)}{\partial y} \right.$$

$$\left. + w \frac{\partial(m + M)}{\partial z} \right] - \frac{\partial}{\partial z}(MV)$$

$$+ (m + M) w \frac{\partial ln\rho}{\partial z} + wG. \qquad (14.19)$$

Consider the case where horizontal advection is zero and conditions are steady state as in the core of a steady-updraft column. Then

$$\frac{\partial}{\partial z}(MV) = - w \frac{\partial(m + M)}{\partial z}$$

$$+ (m + M) w \frac{\partial ln\rho}{\partial z} + wG. \qquad (14.20)$$

The quantity $-MV$ is the precipitation rate, provided $w = 0$. Thus in order to relate rainfall rate at the ground to other parameters, we integrate from the ground, where $w = 0$, to the top of updraft column, where $w = M = 0$. Then

$$-MV\Big|_0 = R_0 = - \int_0^H w \frac{\partial(m + M)}{\partial z} \, dz$$

$$+ \int_0^H (m + M) \, w \, \frac{\partial ln\rho}{\partial z} \, dz + \int_0^H wG dz.$$

$$(14.21)$$

Notice that

$$- w \frac{\partial(m + M)}{\partial z} = - \frac{\partial}{\partial z}\Big[w(m + M) \Big] + (m + M) \frac{\partial w}{\partial z}.$$

Integration of the total derivative between our limits yields zero, and the term $(m + M) \, \partial w / \partial z$ can be replaced by others indicated by our equation of continuity for air. Then

$$R_0 = \int_0^H wG dz - \int_0^H (m + M)\left(\frac{\partial u}{\partial x} + \frac{\partial v}{\partial y} \right) dz. \qquad (14.22)$$

The first term on the right is the rate of condensation through the whole depth of the air column. Equation 14.22 tells us that even under steady-state nonadvective conditions the rainfall rate is generally not equal to the rate of condensation overhead. Thus, if $m + M$ is larger near the base of the updraft column than aloft and the horizontal divergence is symmetrically distributed, then the precipitation rate at the ground is larger than the rate of condensation vertically overhead. On the other hand, with strong updrafts, the profile of $m + M$ may resemble that of cloud alone, i.e., the magnitude of $m + M$ is larger aloft, and then the second integral contributes negatively to R_0 and may even cancel it completely, as it must in a steady case without precipitation at the ground. Examples of geometrical interpretations of Eq. 14.22 are illustrated by Fig. 14.5.

(2) Development of Vertical Profiles with Time: Our continuity equations are in the Eulerian form; i.e., they describe relationships among spatial distributions. Lagrangian forms descriptive of the development of individual packets can be derived by using the mathematical identities

$$\frac{dm}{dt} = \frac{\partial m}{\partial t} + u \frac{\partial m}{\partial x} + v \frac{\partial m}{\partial y} + w \frac{\partial m}{\partial z}, \qquad (14.23a)$$

and

$$\frac{dM}{dt} = \frac{\partial M}{\partial t} + u \frac{\partial m}{\partial x} + v \frac{\partial M}{\partial y} + (w + V) \frac{\partial M}{\partial z}. \qquad (14.23b)$$

Figure 14.5. Role of horizontal divergence in the precipitation process. As an extreme example, consider condensing, upward-moving air (in entire area interior to the streamlines of air motion) that is depleted of cloud by descending precipitation near altitude $z = H/2$. Thus cloud exists only below height $z = H/2$. As precipitation descends farther, it is funneled into the smaller cross section B by horizontal convergence demanded at low altitudes by continuity. Thus the volume of air contributing precipitation in an area at the ground suggested by cross section B can be much larger (by the diagonal shading C plus vertically shaded A) than the volume of the shaft B vertically overhead.

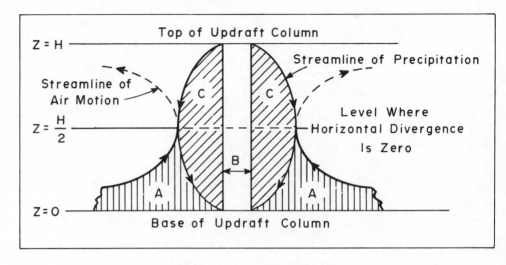

Substituting Eqs. 14.23a and b into their respective counterparts, Eqs. 14.18a and b, yields

$$\frac{dm}{dt} = mw \frac{\partial ln\rho}{\partial z} + w\left[Q_s \frac{\partial ln\rho}{\partial z} - \frac{\partial Q_s}{\partial z} \right]$$
$$- \text{ microphysical processes} \qquad (14.24a)$$

and

$$\frac{dM}{dt} = Mw \frac{\partial ln\rho}{\partial z} - M \frac{\partial V}{\partial z} + \text{ microphysical processes.}$$
$$(14.24b)$$

Equations 14.24a and b describe the development of packets of m and M as they move with or through the air at velocities u, v, and w or $(w + V)$.

A time-dependent process is clearly illuminated by a model without horizontal advection (updraft core) that omits compressibility and takes the fallspeed V relative to air as constant. With these simplifications the sum of Eqs. 14.24a and b is

$$\frac{d(m + M)}{dt} = wG. \qquad (14.25)$$

Consider first a saturated updraft in which cloud is changed instantly to precipitation falling relative to the air at speed V. In this instance we use the set of equations

$$\frac{dM}{dt} = wG, \qquad (14.26a)$$

$$\frac{dz}{dt} = w + V. \qquad (14.26b)$$

Equation 14.26a tells us how rapidly the concentration of precipitation in each packet increases while descending along the vertical path defined by Eq. 14.26b. To accom-

plish the required integration, note from Eq. 14.23b that without horizontal advection $dM/dt = (w + v) (dM/dz)$, where $dM/dz = \partial m/\partial z$ is the steady-state vertical profile of M. Therefore, we can identify the magnitude of increase of an M packet that accompanies its displacement from z_i to z_f during the time interval $t_f - t_i$ from the integrals

$$M_f - M_i = \int_{z_i}^{z_f} \frac{wG}{w + V} dz \qquad (14.27a)$$

and

$$t_f - t_i = \int_{z_i}^{z_f} \frac{dz}{w + V} . \qquad (14.27b)$$

Construction of time-dependent profiles is reasonably accomplished graphically through use of plots of M versus z and t versus z, as defined by Eq. 14.27. The right side of Fig. 14.6 shows time-dependent profiles so determined, for indicated values of K in $t = K(H/w_{max})$, and with a steady-state parabolic vertical profile of updraft w and the fallspeed V set to twice the maximum value of the updraft.

The left side of Fig. 14.6 represents time-dependent distributions of vapor deficit m in a downdraft. These plots lead from assumptions that M and V are zero.

Now return to Eq. 14.24a and consider a more general case. If we trace the development of a packet of m in a moist updraft from a starting condition when $m = 0$, we have first a growth of m owing to condensation, then as m increases, an increasing tendency of expansion to offset the condensation rate. Microphysical processes, first cloud conversion and then accretion, manifest themselves at some time after cloud is formed and act to deplete cloud. If the microphysical processes are so rapid that m remains small, then the expansion term does not significantly affect m. On the other hand, we know that conversion of cloud to pre-

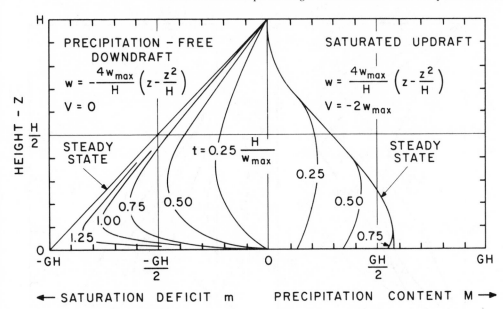

Figure 14.6. Time-dependent and steady vertical profiles of water substance in downdrafts (left) and updrafts (right), when the condensation function G is constant.

cipitation is much more rapid in the presence of precipitation than without it; therefore, the onset of rain may be marked by a starting gush that reflects the rapid deposition of condensation accumulated as cloud over a relatively long period. This is illustrated in Fig. 14.7, which portrays the result of numerical marching calculations for Eqs. 14.18a and b simplified by omission of the horizontal advection terms and the terms in $\partial ln\rho/\partial z$. Rain gushes have also been attributed to electrical effects (Moore et al., 1962; Moore, 1965), but this analysis shows that the gush phenomenon may have a simple kinematic basis.

(3) Steady-State Vertical Profiles of Cloud and Precipitation: To facilitate illustration, consider relatively simple conditions: constant fallspeed V; no horizontal advection (e.g., updraft core); and rapid microphysical processes with condensation appearing immediately as precipitation M, i.e., no cloud. Then the sum of Eqs. 14.18a and 14.18b is simply

$$\frac{\partial M}{\partial z} = \frac{Mw\,\frac{\partial ln\rho}{\partial z} + wG}{w + V}.$$ (14.28)

Now consider two extremes. In the first the magnitude of w is small compared with the fallspeed of condensate, and so we omit w from the denominator. Then Eq. 14.28 becomes

$$\frac{\partial M}{\partial z} = \frac{w}{V}\Big(M\,\frac{\partial ln\rho}{\partial z} + G\Big) \qquad \Big[\Big|\frac{w}{V}\Big| \ll 1\Big].$$ (14.29)

Now, since w/V is small, M is itself small, and in particular $M(\partial ln\rho/\partial z)$ is small compared with G. The first term in parentheses on the right side may be omitted, as we chose to do in the treatment leading to Fig. 14.6. Thus $\partial M/\partial z \sim$

wG/V. So, subject to our constraint on the magnitude of w/V, $\partial M/\partial z$ and M increase nearly linearly with w. Since $w = 0$ necessarily at the ground and at the top of the updraft column, $\partial M/\partial z = 0$ at the same places, and we are led to steady-state vertical profiles shaped as in Fig. 14.2 and on the right side of Fig. 14.6.

When $w \gg |V|$, we drop V in the denominator of Eq. 14.28 and have

$$\frac{\partial M}{\partial z} = M\,\frac{\partial ln\rho}{\partial z} + G.$$ (14.30)

Then the steady-state profiles are shaped as for cloud in Fig. 14.1. The profile shape for precipitation is independent of updraft speed *if that speed is sufficiently large*. It should be noted that if there is no conversion of cloud to precipitation then M and $\partial M/\partial t$ are zero, and the sum of Eq. 14.18a and b is identical to Eq. 14.30 with M replaced by m. Thus this equation also describes cloud profiles in the absence of precipitation.

Figure 14.3 illustrates some profiles calculated on a large computer for the full set of processes, as represented in Eqs. 14.18a and b for a range of strong updrafts. Note that the precipitation maximum is at higher elevations with stronger air currents and that the lower elevations are marked by denser cloud as updraft speed increases. Both of these features reflect the higher altitude to which cloud is carried by stronger updrafts before the cloud has time to change to rain. The average cloud amount increases and the average precipitation amount decreases with increased updraft speed, while the sum of cloud and precipitation changes only quite slowly. This means that stronger updraft columns are expected to be darker, because a given water mass obscures more light when the droplets that constitute that mass are smaller and, therefore, constitute a larger cross-sec-

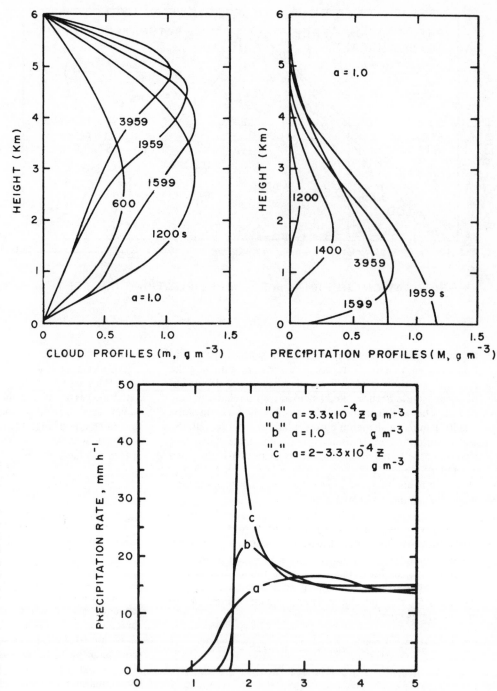

Figure 14.7. (Above) Transient vertical profiles of cloud and precipitation for a case in which precipitation begins near the middle of the cloud column. The maximum updraft is held at 0.5 m s^{-1} throughout, and the condensation function, the bracketed term in Eq. 14.8, is $G = 3 \times 10^{-3} - 3 \times 10^{-7} z$ (g m^{-4}).
(Below) Time history of model rainfall at the ground for cases in which the autoconversion threshold α is manipulated to force initial precipitation formation near the top (curve c), middle, and base of the model cloud column.

tional area. Thus it seems likely that the relative darkness that accompanies thunderstorm gust fronts relates to the strong updraft and thick cloud above, with numerous small cloud droplets. As a storm passes overhead and rain begins with the aggregation of cloud droplets into larger particles, the sky lightens. Our theory relates also to the weak radar-echo region in strong thunderstorms, as discussed by Browning in Chap. 7. Since radar reflectivity is proportional to the summation of sixth powers of drop diameters, the dense cloud in strong updrafts gives only weak radar return, but the weak-echo region is bounded (usually on three sides, occasionally all around) by strong echoes from the resulting rain and hail.

Where $(w + V) \sim 0$, and where horizontal advection is also weak and cloud content small, i.e., cloud collection is practically complete in the presence of heavy precipitation, the governing steady-state equation for precipitation density is

$$M = - \frac{G}{\partial ln\rho / \partial z} . \qquad (14.31)$$

Since G increases with temperature, this equation indicates larger values in warmer atmospheres and at lower altitudes. In fact, in the real atmosphere moderate updrafts never possess the buoyancy required to sustain the amount of precipitation indicated by this equation at low altitudes. This suggests that precipitation production may be necessarily oscillatory when buoyancy tends to drive moderate updrafts in a moist warm atmosphere. However, if the updraft is so strong at low altitudes that any precipitation there is swept upward, precipitation may find a high-level float altitude where G is small and the equilibrium precipitation content is correspondingly small. Then the accompanying strong updraft could be maintained by its thermal buoyancy derived from the stratification of the airmass (see Chap. 4). Discussion of this point is extended to Sec. (6) below.

(4) Precipitation Development in Relation to Updraft Strength and Duration: A given amount of condensation may be produced by a slow updraft operating over a long period of time or by a stronger updraft operating for a proportionately shorter period. The period of condensation is followed or overlapped by a stage of cloud conversion and then by precipitation at the ground. The amount of condensate that arrives at the ground as precipitation beneath the updraft column depends on whether the vertical displacement of air is large enough and completed rapidly enough to carry cloud out of the updraft column before microphysical processes have time to change the cloud to precipitation. Thus precipitation at the ground is expected to be proportional to the amount of small vertical displacements, but with large displacements to depend on both the air's displacement and its velocity. The indeterminacy of rain-gage data in relation to the causative updrafts under many observed conditions is suggested by Fig. 14.8a, b, derived from matching calculations.

(5) Two-Dimensional Model Distributions of Cloud and Precipitation: General and obvious features of precipita-

ting weather systems are reproduced in a numerical model (Kessler, 1969) involving Eqs. 14.18a and b with the model wind field shown in Fig. 14.9. The development of vapor, cloud, and precipitation distributions was calculated by a marching process with the aid of a large computer. In Fig. 14.10 we have development of water distributions starting from initial vapor saturation and maximum updrafts and downdrafts of 2.5 m s^{-1} comparable with a mild shower. The cloud content passes through a dense transient stage, then thins in response to accretion. Substantial overturning of the air has occurred at the time represented at lower left in Fig. 14.10. At this time, T_1, winds are equated to zero, and subsequent calculations follow the fallout of precipitation in still air. Note that the cloud base lifts rapidly after updrafts cease, a response to the accretion process when it is no longer balanced by condensation. The high cloud that persists after updrafts cease seems analogous to conditions that follow many natural shower events. About 80% of the moisture condensed in this model reaches the ground as precipitation; this is about 30% of all the moisture originally present as vapor.

Moisture development in an initially unsaturated case with stronger updrafts and downdrafts (10 m s^{-1}) is shown in Fig. 14.11. Only 53% of the moisture that condenses in this model reaches the ground as precipitation, because the stronger circulation carries condensate out of the moist updraft column, and the condensate is more subject to evaporation in the drier environment. Less moisture condenses also, because there is less to begin with; thus the ratio of precipitation on the ground in the two cases is only 35%, though the drier case has 76% as much moisture as the moister case. These numerical data suggest a remarkable sensitivity of natural precipitation to atmospheric moisture content and stability.

(6) Interaction Between Updraft and Water Load: The analyses presented above have been extended with two equations that help clarify the dynamical coupling between vertical air motion and water loading. The acceleration of vertical motion, dw/dt, is aided by a buoyancy force B and is retarded by a frictional force roughly proportional to the updraft speed itself, and retarded also by the condensed water load L. Thus

$$\frac{dw}{dt} = B - K_1 w - K_2 L. \qquad (14.32)$$

For a typical updraft cell it can be shown that K_1 is probably in the range 10^{-4} to 10^{-3} s^{-1}, the larger value corresponding to stronger updrafts (see Kessler, 1969, p. 73), and K_2 is roughly approximated by 10^{-2} m^4 g^{-1} s^{-2}.

Recall that for updrafts up to a few m s^{-1} our analysis shows that the water load tends to increase or decrease in proportion to the vertical airspeed, at least during a transient period determined roughly by H/w and $H/(V + w)$. The former ratio represents the time it takes for an air parcel to ascend at rate w to the top of the active layer of depth H; the latter represents the time it takes for precipitation to fall

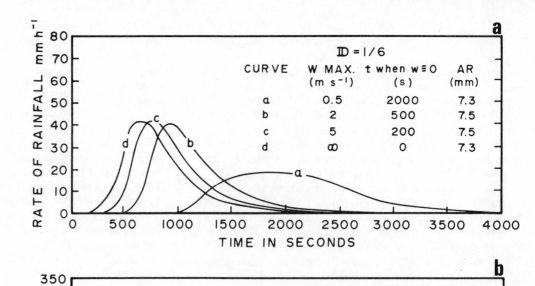

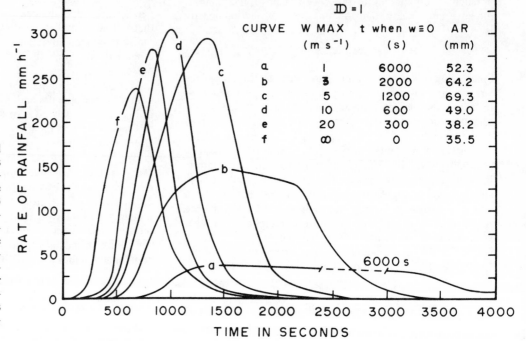

Figure 14.8. (a) Surface rainfall rates versus time for various rates of displacement in a saturated air column 6 km high. The condensation function is $G = 3 \times 10^{-3} - 3 \times 10^{-7}\, z$. The displacement $D = w_{max}\, t/H$ is completed at the time listed in the third column; AR is the accumulated rainfall. (b) Vertical displacement is six times larger. For rapid displacements the precipitation trace at the ground yields little information about the updraft intensity.

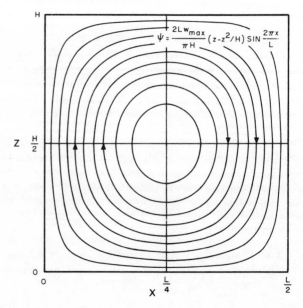

Figure 14.9. Streamlines of the model wind field used in calculations that lead to Figs. 14.10 and 14.11.

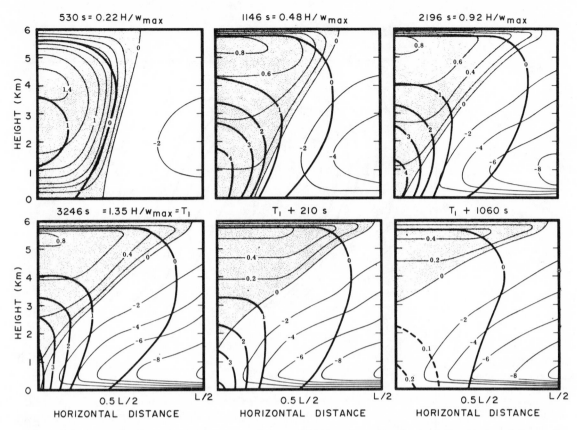

Figure 14.10. Distribution of condensate (g m^{-3}) in an initially saturated weak circulation ($w_{\max} = 2.5$ m s^{-1}). Heavy lines are isopleths of precipitation content, light lines in stippled areas mark cloud, and light lines in the unshaded areas refer to saturation deficit.

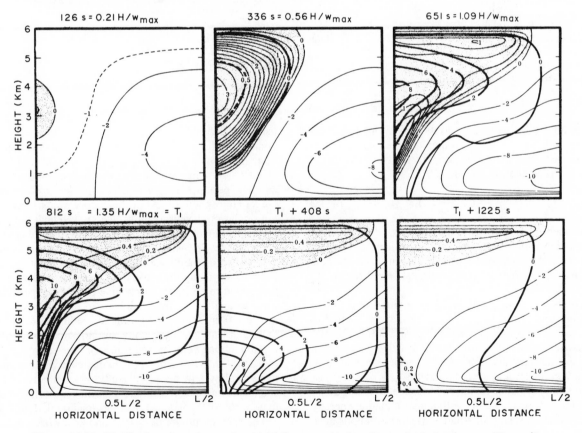

Figure 14.11. Distribution of condensate in an initially unsaturated moderate circulation ($w_{\max} = 10$ m s^{-1}).

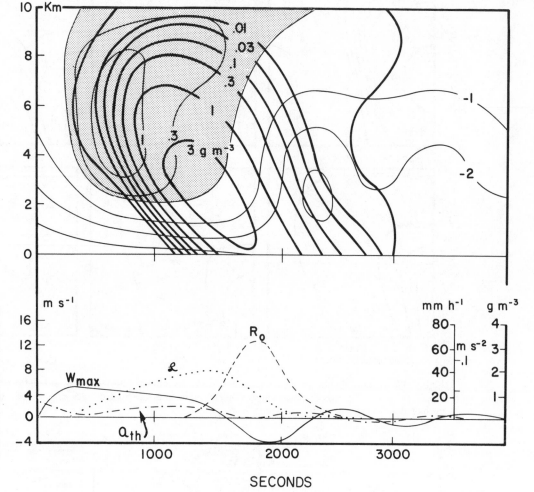

Figure 14.12. Development of vertical velocity, cloud, precipitation, and buoyancy in a weakly perturbed, conditionally unstable model air column. The thermal component of buoyancy a_{th} is given in m s^{-2}. The average columnar burden of cloud plus precipitation is given by the dotted line L. Isopleths in the upper part of the figure define precipitation, cloud, and saturation deficit in g m^{-3}.

from the top of the active layer to its base. Since precipitation tends to fall out of an air column at a rate that increases with its mass, we attempt to account for this also in the companion precipitation equation,

$$\frac{dL}{dt} = C_1 w - C_2 L. \qquad (14.33)$$

Here we identify C_1 with G in the preceding discussion. A representative value for C_1 in a summer airmass is 1.5×10^{-3} g m^{-4}. We identify C_2 with $-V/H$ in weak updrafts and with $-w(\partial ln\rho/\partial z)$ in strong updrafts. In either case $C_2 \sim 10^{-3}$ s^{-1}.

Although Eqs. 14.32 and 14.33 are written in terms of parcels and individual derivatives, they may be applied to average conditions through the depth of an updraft column, this because $dw/dt = (\partial w/\partial t) + (1/2) \partial(w^2)/\partial z$, and, when vertical averages are taken, $\partial(w^2)/\partial z$ vanishes since w^2 vanishes on both upper and lower boundaries.

The quantity L can be eliminated between Eqs. 14.32 and 14.33, and the second-order differential equation thereby obtained has both steady-state and oscillatory solutions. The

oscillatory solutions occur when $(K_1 - C_2)^2 < 4 K_2 C_1$. Analysis indicates that this is practically always well satisfied; the length of the period is about $2\pi/(K_2 C_1)^{1/2}$, or about 1,600 s, in fair agreement with observations in showers. The period is longer as K_1 is smaller, i.e., longer in a colder atmosphere (a test of this theory might be developed with radar observations on showers). The analysis complements the model proposed by Byers and Braham (1949) and amplified by Srivastava (1969), wherein a cycle in vertical velocity accompanies development of precipitation.

In the strong updraft case our kinematic model shows the water load to be rather insensitive to updraft speed. Therefore, to analyze updraft behavior in this situation, we set $dL/dt = 0$ in Eq. 14.33 and find that solutions of the set are then characterized by monotonic adjustment toward equilibrium among velocity and forces of buoyancy, water load, and drag. Thus this simple mathematical representation of a dynamical system based on study of kinematical relationships indicates that oscillatory behavior of real updrafts may relate to dependence of water load on updraft speed.

The skeletal model described above has been developed

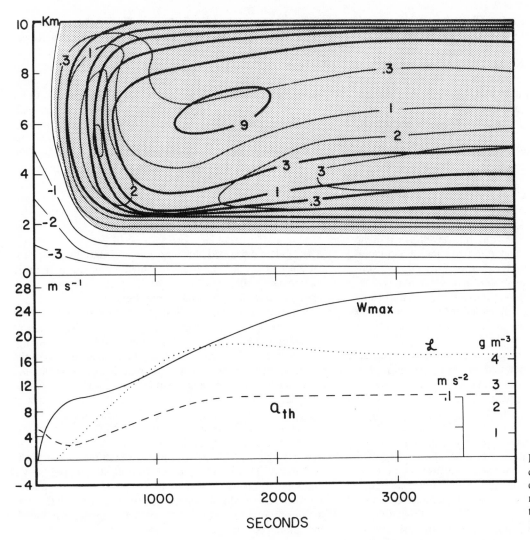

Figure 14.13. Meteorological parameters in a model air column with a starting thermal perturbation of 1.4°C, twice as large as that in Fig. 14.12.

further in an effort to define some probable working relationships among various processes (Kessler, 1974). In this expanded vertical profile model, which may be regarded as a moist version of an earlier study by Priestley (1953), terms to describe a mixing process, adjustable to simulate a range of scales, are added to the continuity equations (Eqs. 14.18a and b). These equations, without the horizontal advection terms, are solved numerically in conjunction with (1) an equation that constrains the vertical profile of vertical velocity to a parabolic shape, with zeros at base and top of the updraft and maximum halfway between; (2) an equation that defines the rate of change of the magnitude of vertical current in terms of thermal buoyancy, water load, and mixing between the rising current and its (stationary) environment; and (3) an equation that relates the thermal buoyancy itself to environmental parameters, vertical displacement in the air column of interest, heat of condensation, evaporation of precipitation, and mixing. Figures

14.12 and 14.13 show contrasting model results suggestive of showers and intense, quasi-steady thunderstorms, where the only difference at the start is in the strength of an initiating perturbation.

Thus at the top of Fig. 14.12 is a time-height portrayal of the development of cloud, precipitation, and vapor distributions in a weak-perturbation case. Beneath that, on the same time scale, the magnitudes of the maximum updraft, average condensed water load, and rainfall rate at the ground are plotted with the thermal component of buoyancy.

In physical terms, the development of updrafts and hydrometeors shown in Fig. 14.12 is regulated as follows: an upward air current develops immediately after the start in response to an input perturbation thermal buoyancy. The thermal buoyancy immediately starts to decline, partly as a result of mixing of updraft air with environmental air but more because the environmental lapse rate is stable for vertical motions of dry air; i.e., the airmass is only conditionally unstable, as discussed in Chap. 4. As saturation is attained, condensation occurs. Thermal buoyancy then declines less rapidly and, indeed, the thermal component increases again after 300 seconds. The increase corresponds to a rapid addition of heat from condensation, exceeding the rate of loss of sensible heat by mixing of ambient and environmental air and evaporation of cloud.

Meanwhile, however, condensation products accumulate in the updraft column, and because the effective buoyancy is related to both its thermal component and its water load, this increase of condensation products also affects the updraft. In Fig. 14.12, the rate of increase of condensation products is shown to overwhelm the rate of increase of thermal buoyancy, and after 300 seconds there is a net decrease of effective buoyancy and diminishing updraft speed. By then substantial amounts of precipitation have formed in the updraft column, and as the updraft weakens, precipitation descent is hastened. When precipitation falls into the subcloud layer, its partial evaporation there substantially contributes to negative thermal buoyancy. The downdraft starting at about 1,600 seconds is attributable to dominant water load effects, in the presence of a small residual positive thermal buoyancy.

As precipitation falls rapidly out of the descending air column and the cloud evaporates, we have descending dry motion in a stable environment, and an upward buoyancy again increases. The subsequent record shows a variation known as a Brunt-Vaisala oscillation.

We note in passing that in such cases one effect of hastened transformation of cloud to precipitation in the model is a reduction of the total amount of precipitation deposited on the ground. The reduction occurs because the updraft, the ultimate source of precipitation in the model, suffers an earlier reduction of buoyancy owing to precipitation evaporating in the subcloud layer. We infer that stimulation of the cloud conversion process in an effort to increase rainfall might actually have the opposite effect unless the effort is carefully timed.

The early developments illustrated in Fig. 14.13 are similar to those shown in Fig. 14.12. Because of the stronger starting thermal perturbation, however, the vertical velocity is larger in Fig. 14.13 when condensation begins. The faster rate at which latent heat is released produces a more rapid recovery of thermal buoyancy, which now increases faster than the contrary tendency of the increasing water load. Therefore, the updraft continues to increase, precipitation is held aloft, and the high-speed steady updraft develops. The precipitation aloft diverges there, and descent toward the ground is implied in regions where the updraft is not as strong.

4. Outlook

The models discussed above represent essential working relationships among important parameters, including the role of buoyancy effects produced by water condensation, storage, and evaporation in the atmosphere.

Recently acquired capabilities to observe fields of velocity, precipitation, and electricity in great detail represent a challenge to match such observations with corresponding theories. Modeling studies utilize comprehensive systems of equations to seek numerical simulation of observations, as described in the next chapter. Somewhat conversely, Doppler radar observations of reflectivity and velocity at different times provide a basis for deducing the forces and processes which must act to produce the observations, as discussed in Vol. 3, Chap. 13. Such studies lead to new insights and to improvements in both theories and observations. There will be more exciting discoveries as we continue to measure and examine the electrical, microphysical, and hydrodynamical processes that regulate interactions among the coevolving weather elements that constitute thunderstorms.

15. Mathematical Modeling of Convection

Richard A. Anthes, Harold D. Orville, and David J. Raymond

1. Introduction

Mathematical modeling of atmospheric phenomena forms an important part of our total understanding of physical processes that govern the phenomena. Modeling enhances our perception of cause and effect and reveals the role of complicated interactions and feedbacks among the motion fields, the temperature and pressure structure, and the hydrometeors in thunderstorms. In this chapter we first consider simple analytic models of convection and then discuss more realistic, but also more complicated, models, for which analytic solution is impossible. These models rely on computers to obtain approximate solutions to a system of equations describing the behavior of thunderstorms. Finally we consider how thunderstorms affect the larger scale environment and how their effect may be incorporated into models of atmospheric circulations much larger than individual thunderstorms.

a. Basic Equations

Quantitative study of the dynamics of weather systems, whether small-scale cumulus clouds or Earth-encircling planetary waves, begins with a fundamental set of equations based on Newton's second law, the first law of thermodynamics, the equation for the continuity of mass, the equation of state for an ideal gas, and the equations of continuity for the various phases of water. We present them here as an introduction to analytical modeling and the numerical simulation of thunderstorms; their derivation may be found in many texts, e.g., Haltiner and Martin (1957), Holton (1972), and Dutton (1976).

We consider a moist parcel of air that may contain liquid or frozen water as well as water vapor. The variables that completely describe this parcel of air are pressure p, temperature T, density ρ, water vapor, liquid water, frozen water, and velocity components parallel to all three orthogonal coordinate axes. The content of water vapor, liquid water, and ice may be expressed as the ratio of the mass of water substance present per mass of dry air, or the mixing ratios q, q_l, and q_i. The equation of state for this parcel of air is

$$p = \rho R T_v, \tag{15.1}$$

where R is the gas constant for dry air, and T_v, the virtual temperature, is a function of the amount of water vapor present:

$$T_v = T(1 + 1.61q)/(1 + q) \sim T(1 + 0.61q). \tag{15.2}$$

Newton's second law, that force equals mass times acceleration, may be applied to this parcel of air on the rotating Earth to yield the equation of motion:

$$\frac{d\mathbf{V}}{dt} = -\frac{1}{\rho}\nabla p - 2\,\mathbf{\Omega} \times \mathbf{V} - g(1 + q_l + q_i)\mathbf{k} + \mathbf{F}, \tag{15.3}$$

where $\mathbf{V}$ is the three-dimensional vector wind, $\mathbf{\Omega}$ is the angular velocity of the Earth, g is the acceleration of gravity, $\mathbf{k}$ is the vertical unit vector, and $\mathbf{F}$ is the frictional force owing to viscous stresses. Equation 15.3 states that the acceleration of an air parcel is determined by the pressure gradient force, the Coriolis force (caused by the rotation of the Earth), gravity, and friction. The terms involving q_l and q_i in Eq. 15.3 represent downward accelerations caused by the weight of the liquid and solid water in the parcel. These hydrometeors are assumed to be falling at their terminal velocity.

Equation 15.3 may be broken down into three scalar equations that describe the acceleration of the W–E component u, the S–N component v, and the vertical component w of the wind.

$$\frac{du}{dt} = -\frac{1}{\rho}\frac{\partial p}{\partial x} + (2\Omega \sin\phi)v - (2\Omega\cos\phi)w + F_x, \tag{15.4}$$

$$\frac{dv}{dt} = -\frac{1}{\rho}\frac{\partial p}{\partial y} - (2\,\Omega\sin\phi)u + F_y, \tag{15.5}$$

and

$$\frac{dw}{dt} = -\frac{1}{\rho}\frac{\partial p}{\partial z} - g(1 + q_l + q_i) + (2\Omega\cos\phi)u + F_z, \tag{15.6}$$

where Ω is the magnitude of the Earth's angular velocity, ϕ is latitude, and F_x, F_y, and F_z are the frictional components in the x, y, and z directions respectively. In most theoretical studies on any scale we may neglect $(2\,\Omega\cos\phi)w$ in Eq. 15.4 and $(2\,\Omega\cos\phi)u$ in Eq. 15.6. For motions in which the horizontal scale is much larger than the vertical scale,

Eq. 15.6 may be approximated by the hydrostatic equation,

$$\frac{1}{\rho} \frac{\partial p}{\partial z} = - g(1 + q_l + q_i). \qquad (15.7)$$

On the other hand, for small-scale motions such as thunderstorms, the terms involving the Earth's rotation may be dropped from all three component equations, but vertical accelerations must be retained.

The first law of thermodynamics may be written in a number of useful ways. In terms of temperature, T, for example, it is

$$c_p \frac{dT}{dt} = Q + \frac{1}{\rho} \frac{dp}{dt}, \qquad (15.8)$$

where Q is the diabatic heating rate per unit mass and c_p is the specific heat of air at constant pressure. For dry air, c_p = 1004.8 J kg^{-1} K^{-1}. Another useful form of the first law is given in terms of potential temperature, θ:

$$c_p \frac{d\theta}{dt} = \frac{\theta}{T} Q, \qquad (15.9)$$

where θ is related to temperature and pressure by

$$\theta = T\left(\frac{p_{oo}}{p}\right)^{R/c_p} \qquad (15.10)$$

In Eq. 15.10, p_{oo} is 1,000 mb. The potential temperature is the temperature air would have if it were taken to a pressure of p_{oo} (1,000 mb) without heat being added or subtracted. (The wet-bulb potential temperature, mentioned in Sec. 4 below, involves adiabatic expansion to a saturation condition and recompression to 1,000 mb via a saturation adiabatic process; see Chap. 4.) Equation 15.10 provides a very useful simple expression for how temperature changes in an adiabatic process, because θ is conserved in such a process.

The conservation of mass in a compressible fluid is given by the continuity equation and relates changes of density to the divergence of the wind field:

$$\frac{d\rho}{dt} = -\rho \nabla \cdot \mathbf{V}. \qquad (15.11)$$

The continuity equations for the three phases of water are given by

$$\frac{dq}{dt} = -C - D + F_q, \qquad (15.12)$$

$$\frac{dq_l}{dt} = C + M - P_l + F_{ql}, \qquad (15.13)$$

and

$$\frac{dq_i}{dt} = D - M - P_i + F_{qi}. \qquad (15.14)$$

Equation 15.12 states that the water vapor of a parcel of air is changed by condensation C, deposition D, and molecular diffusion F_q. The mixing ratio of liquid water is changed by condensation, melting M, precipitation P_l, and diffusion F_{ql}. Finally, the mixing ratio of ice changes by deposition, melting, precipitation of ice P_i, and diffusion. P_l and P_i may take on either sign depending on whether precipitation is falling into or out of the parcel, and evaporation, sublimation, and freezing are represented by negative values of C, D, and M.

We now have a complete set of equations describing a moist atmospheric system. In principle they describe what would happen to all air parcels with dimensions somewhat larger than the molecular scale given an initial state of all of the variables. In reality, however, it is impossible to consider all of these scales of motion simultaneously. Therefore, the first simplification necessary when trying to apply the above set to an atmospheric problem is to average the equations over spatial and temporal scales appropriate to the problem. These averaging intervals vary greatly; for synoptic-scale flows typical spatial and temporal averaging intervals may be 100 kilometers and 1 hour. On the other hand, the resolution of thunderstorms requires averaging intervals of about 100 meters and 30 seconds.

An example of the use of the averaging procedure to derive equations relevant to the desired scales of motion is presented in Sec. 4. The equations for the average motion, in addition to containing all of the terms shown so far, also contain various "eddy" terms that result from correlations between the variables on scales smaller than the averaging interval. Their effect is often important in changing the large-scale averages, and the representation of the effects in the large-scale equations is sometimes known as parameterization.

Even if the eddy terms can be related to the large-scale variables, or neglected entirely, the system of equations presented above is still astonishingly complicated, permitting a variety of nonlinear feedbacks among the motion, thermodynamic field, and water substances. Analytic models, therefore, are based on a greatly simplified set of equations in order that solutions may be obtained in closed form. An alternative approach, requiring fewer physical approximations, is to write approximations to the derivatives in the basic set and solve the resulting set of finite difference equations on a computer.

b. Numerical Modeling: General Concepts

Numerical weather prediction, which involves forecasting meteorological variables with computer solutions of the mathematical equations that represent the physics of the atmosphere, has been routine in the United States for more than 20 years. Numerical models have been applied operationally to the prediction of large-scale, or synoptic-scale, atmospheric circulation systems, i.e., those systems that span horizontal distances of several thousand kilometers and persist as identifiable perturbations of the atmospheric flow for one to four days. Encouraged by the success of these models, meteorologists have recently begun experiments with numerical models of atmospheric phenomena on much smaller space and shorter time scales. It is in this middle range, the mesoscale, where many severe-weather phenomena such as hurricanes, tornadoes, ice and snow storms, and severe air pollution occur.

The essential components of any numerical model are outlined in Fig. 15.1. To properly model any atmospheric phenomenon, whether the broad belt of upper-level westerlies that meanders around the globe or an intense, hail- and tornado-producing thunderstorm that covers only a few square kilometers, the first step is the identification and understanding of the important physical processes that affect the feature during its lifetime.

These important processes next must be represented by mathematical equations that can be solved by computers. This second step nearly always requires some simplification, for the finite size and speed of any computer limit the physical and mathematical sophistication allowed. Mathematical representation of the physical relationships produces a set of prediction equations for temperature, pressure, winds, and usually moisture. These equations are solved at many points over a horizontal array (grid) and at several levels in the atmosphere.

A large three-dimensional (3-D) grid in a numerical model might consist of a 50×50 horizontal array applied at 10 levels in the atmosphere, yielding a total of 25,000 model data points. If the 9 variables introduced earlier (temperature, 3 phases of water, pressure, density, and 3 components of velocity) are defined at each data point, there are 225,000 numbers representing the state of the atmosphere at a given moment.

Obtaining an accurate initial analysis of the 3-D atmosphere is the third important aspect of the overall numerical-modeling problem, and it is a major obstacle to the modeling of small-scale and severe-weather phenomena. The initialization phase consists of observation and analysis. Observations are expensive, and so there are never as many observations as there are data points in the model. Therefore, 3-D analyses of all the variables at all the grid points must be made from a limited number of observations. Errors and unrepresentative features in the observations and resulting analyses contaminate the subsequent forecasts.

The traditional source of data for the operational large-scale models has been the rawinsonde, which provides temperature, wind, and humidity data at many levels in the atmosphere. The average horizontal spacing between rawinsonde stations in the United States is about 400 kilometers; as a result, important weather-producing systems with horizontal dimensions less than 400 kilometers are either missed entirely or grossly misrepresented by the conventional network. Recently satellites have provided relatively inexpensive and very detailed observations of clouds, temperatures, moisture, and, to a lesser extent, winds.

The fourth step in the numerical modeling problem is the generation of the forecast itself by solution of the mathematical equations derived in the second step. Given the initial structure of the atmosphere, the prediction equations may be used to obtain the state of the atmosphere in the immediate future. When this process is repeated again and again, a picture of the 3-D structure of the atmosphere for a day or more in advance can be obtained. A typical 24-hour forecast with a large-scale model requires approximately

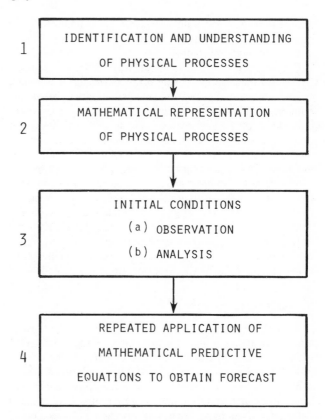

Figure 15.1. Components of numerical models.

100 successive solutions for each equation at each point, or for the model above without liquid and frozen water, a total of 15 million solutions. Clearly, only the most powerful computers are capable of dealing with such sophisticated models.

The basic equations for the temporal rates of change of the variables given above are written in Lagrangian form; i.e., they state how the variables representative of a parcel of air will change in time as the parcel moves about in all three dimensions. Because the parcels diverge and become irregularly spaced, it is useful to rewrite the equations in their Eulerian form. The thermodynamic equation, Eq. 15.9, may be rewritten in Eulerian form to illustrate this difference:

$$\frac{\partial \theta}{\partial t} = -\mathbf{V}_H \cdot \nabla \theta - w \frac{\partial \theta}{\partial z} + \frac{\theta}{c_p T} Q, \quad (15.15)$$

where $\mathbf{V}_H$ is the horizontal wind. The left side of Eq. 15.15 describes how the potential temperature changes at a fixed point in space rather than how the potential temperature of a moving parcel of air is changed. Therefore, the Eulerian form is better suited for models that employ grids to represent the 3-D structure of the atmosphere. The price for this simplification is the appearance of the nonlinear horizontal and vertical advection terms on the right side. These represent the advection or transport of air of different potential temperature past the point in space. Their nonlinearity is one of the main reasons why analytic solutions are difficult in meteorological problems.

Before ending the introduction to numerical modeling, we should mention the vexing problem of lateral boundary conditions when limited domains are treated. There are both physical and mathematical problems to consider on the boundaries of limited regions. Physically, air of varying properties is always being carried into the domain from the outside, where no information is available. Mathematically, the finite difference equations can contain waves that propagate across the boundaries, either into or out of the grid. Inaccurate numerical treatment of these waves can cause a spurious reflection of energy at the boundaries and contaminate the solution. Various techniques have been developed to treat the problem, such as smoothing the solutions near the boundary, but it is unlikely that the problem will ever be completely solved for all classes of limited-area models.

c. Laboratory Modeling [1]

Our current understanding of the fundamental elements of buoyant convection and cloud dynamics owes much to the insights developed from laboratory models. Although it is probably not practical to simulate the evolution of large convective clouds in the laboratory, modeling research continues to contribute to the understanding of several areas of convective dynamics, notably of tornado vortices and of some aspects of buoyant boundary layers. This section introduces the field of laboratory modeling of convection (see Turner's [1973] comprehensive treatment of the subject).

In general, laboratory modeling has contributed most substantially to geophysical fluid dynamics in the early stages of development of a field, when limited amounts of observational data are at hand and one is seeking conceptual understanding and contact with other areas of physics. As the field matures, the perceived complexities in physical processes or boundary conditions become excessively difficult to simulate in the laboratory, but may be accessible to numerical simulation. Even then certain important processes may be more easily simulated and measured in the laboratory than on the computer or in the field.

The key to successful simulation and interpretation of the results usually lies in identifying several dimensionless parameters of the geophysical problem and matching as many as possible in the laboratory analog. The appropriate dimensionless parameters are usually identified in the process of solving, or attempting to solve, the governing fluid equations, but they may also be identified in the formal processes of scale analysis (e.g., Dutton, 1976). For buoyant-convection problems one typically is concerned with the following dimensional quantities: a vertical and a horizontal length scale, H and L; a buoyancy scale, $g' = g\Delta\rho/\bar{\rho}$, where g is the acceleration of gravity, $\bar{\rho}$ is the mean density, and $\Delta\rho$ is a density fluctuation magnitude; a mean flow ve-

locity, U, and/or a mean vertical shear, $\partial U/\partial z$; coefficients of kinematic viscosity, ν, and thermal diffusion, κ. The above six or seven quantities contain two independent dimensions, length and time, so that four or five dimensionless numbers can be defined from them. Though the particular five chosen for listing are arbitrary, a typical set might be (1) an aspect ratio, H/L; (2) the Prandtl number ν/κ; (3) a Reynolds number, HU/ν; (4) a Froude number, $U^2/g'H$; and/or (5) a Richardson number $g'/[H(\partial U/\partial z)^2]$.

Typically the dimensionless parameter most difficult to simulate in the laboratory is the Reynolds number, because the laboratory length scale is almost invariably much smaller than the geophysical scale, the velocity scale is also usually smaller, and few fluids have viscosities more than an order of magnitude smaller than that of air. Thus many laboratory experiments contain frictional and diffusive effects substantially stronger than, or at least different from, their atmospheric analogs.

The observations by Bénard (1900) of cellular structure in a liquid heated from below led to important early work by Lord Rayleigh (1916) on the theory of thermal convection and to the recognition of the significance of the dimensionless number that bears his name. The classic theoretical formulation and most laboratory experiments involve the motions of a fluid between two parallel horizontal plates, the lower being heated and the upper cooled (though Bénard's original experiment had an upper free surface). If the initial heating and cooling are done very slowly and uniformly, diffusion will create a uniform temperature (and density) gradient in the intervening fluid, so that $\partial\rho/\partial z = \Delta\rho/H$. No motions are generated, and preexisting motion fields are damped by viscosity, until the magnitude of the mean density gradient reaches a critical value, expressed in terms of the Rayleigh number as

$$Ra = g'H^3/\nu\kappa, \qquad (15.16)$$

where the critical Rayleigh number is 1,708 (from theory) for the physically realistic case of no-slip surfaces on the plates. The critical Rayleigh number is accompanied by an optimal horizontal cell size, given approximately by

$$L_x^{-2} + L_y^{-2} = (2H)^{-2}, \qquad (15.17)$$

where L_x and L_y are wavelengths in orthogonal horizontal directions. Linear theory gives no information on the optimal form of the cells, however, so that the above relation can be equally well satisfied by horizontal rolls with wavelength $2H$ or by square cells with dimension $(8)^{1/2}H$, or other possibilities, including the hexagonal cells initially observed by Bénard.

Experiments simulating buoyancy have been conducted using one or several sources of buoyant fluid beneath or above a homogeneous or stably stratified fluid. A well-defined convective element is usually produced in the form of a vertical plume if buoyancy is released continuously, or as a bubble or "thermal" if the buoyancy release is sporadic. These experiments have often been regarded as plausible models for convective-cloud elements. This view is not universally accepted, but the general theoretical ap-

---

[1] This section was written by Douglas K. Lilly.

proach developed for convective plumes and thermals is the foundation for most of the one-dimensional (1-D) cloud models used today (see Sec. 2).

The buoyant elements produced in laboratory experiments are obviously turbulent and have an irregular fluctuating outer boundary that expands downstream. The expansion is caused by entrainment of the ambient fluid through the sides and, and in the case of the thermal, through the top and bottom of the turbulent element. Measurements of plumes and thermals have mostly been restricted to their visible properties, principally the geometry, the rates of upward and outward growth, and sometimes velocity fields determined by particle trajectories. Usually a rather large number of experimental realizations should be assessed in the case of the thermals, because a large spread of characteristics exists between realizations.

The theoretical analysis of laboratory experiments usually relies heavily on similarity assumptions, i.e., that the buoyant element attains a certain mean structure early in its development and tends to retain that structure downstream except for changes in size and intensity that can be predicted by dimensional analysis. The most fundamental and critical of the similarity assumptions is associated with entrainment. The entrainment velocity is usually assumed to be proportional to the mean vertical velocity in the buoyant element, or in more sophisticated treatments, to its turbulent intensity or Reynolds stress. There are always one or more arbitrary constants that the theory does not predict, except perhaps to order of magnitude. These constants are related to those that appear in various turbulence parameterizations, and as with those one must remain skeptical about their universality with changing environmental or initial conditions.

2. Theoretical Models of Thunderstorms

The numerical and laboratory simulation techniques introduced above are valuable approaches to understanding thunderstorms. A third technique that is often useful in informing the intuition is the analytic application of the laws of physics in highly simplified ways to arrive at general rules governing storm behavior.

Some of the questions that have been asked are as follows: Why do thunderstorms form? Why do they attain the size and shape that they do? Why do they tend to cluster or form lines on certain days and not others? Why do certain storms produce damaging wind, hail, and tornadoes? What factors control storm movement? Complete answers for a few of these questions, and partial answers for many, may be derived from relatively simple physical arguments.

a. Convective Instability

Thunderstorms occur because the atmosphere becomes unstable to overturning through a deep layer. Much may be learned about convective overturning by analyzing the behavior of an incompressible fluid of variable density, with

the higher density fluid being initially on top. The fluid is constrained between two horizontal plates of separation h, and the time evolution of the fluid flow is computed.

The inviscid flux form of the Euler equation (another form of Eq. 15.3) may be written

$$\frac{\partial \mathbf{U}}{\partial t} + \nabla \cdot (\mathbf{UV}) + \nabla p + g\rho \mathbf{k} = 0, \quad (15.18)[2]$$

where $\mathbf{U} = \rho \mathbf{V}$ is the mass current. An incompressible fluid obeys

$$\nabla \cdot \mathbf{V} = 0, \quad (15.19)$$

and the density satisfies the continuity equation

$$\frac{\partial \rho}{\partial t} + \nabla \cdot \mathbf{U} = 0. \quad (15.20)$$

If $\mathbf{V} = 0$ initially, and if $\rho = \rho_0(z)$ and $p = p_0(z)$ satisfy the hydrostatic equation, Eq. 15.7,

$$\frac{\partial p_0}{\partial z} = -g\rho_0, \quad (15.21)$$

then Eqs. 15.18–15.20 are satisfied for all time by $\mathbf{V} = 0$, i.e., no flow. This is true regardless of the sign of $\partial \rho_0/\partial z$. However, if $\partial \rho_0/\partial z > 0$, we will show that the slightest motion in the fluid will be amplified exponentially with time until it is large in magnitude.

For weak motions, $\nabla \cdot (\mathbf{UV})$ is very small and will be dropped. Likewise, $\rho' = \rho - \rho_0$ will be small for weak motions, allowing the approximation $\mathbf{V} \cdot \nabla \rho = \mathbf{V} \cdot \nabla \rho_0$ in Eq. 15.20. Thus Eqs. 15.18–15.20 become linear in perturbation quantities when the perturbation is weak. Under these circumstances, $\mathbf{V}$, ρ', and p' may be resolved into a Fourier series in space variables, and, most important, the components of the series do not interact with each other but evolve independently. It is therefore sufficient to consider each Fourier component individually. If any component should exhibit an exponential growth rate, then the perturbation as a whole is proved unstable.

Let us assume a solution of the form

$$(u, w, p', \rho') \propto \exp(ikx + \sigma t). \quad (15.22)$$

Substitution into Eqs. 15.18–15.20 yields four equations in four unknowns:

$$\sigma \rho_0 u + ikp' = 0, \quad (15.23a)$$

$$\sigma \rho_0 w + \frac{\partial p'}{\partial z} + g\rho' = 0, \quad (15.23b)$$

$$iku + \frac{\partial w}{\partial z} = 0, \quad (15.23c)$$

and

$$\sigma \rho' + w \frac{\partial \rho_0}{\partial z} = 0. \quad (15.23d)$$

---

[2]For those unfamiliar with tensors, $\nabla \cdot (\mathbf{UV})$ is a vector with components $\nabla \cdot (\rho u \mathbf{V})$, $\nabla \cdot (\rho v \mathbf{V})$, and $\nabla \cdot (\rho w \mathbf{V})$ in the x, y, and z directions, respectively. See, for example, W. M. Lai, D. Rubin, and E. Krempl, *Introduction to Continuum Mechanics*, rev. ed. (Pergamon Press, Elmsford, N.Y., 1978).

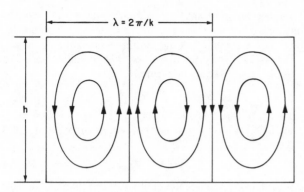

Figure 15.2. Streamlines predicted by a simple, linearized model of convection between two horizontal plates separated by distance h.

By assuming ρ_0 constant except where differentiated in Eq. 15.23d (valid if $h\,|\partial\rho_0/\partial z| \ll \rho_0$), Eqs. 15.23a–d are easily reduced to a single equation in w, the vertical velocity component:

$$\frac{\partial^2 w}{\partial z^2} + k^2\left(\frac{g}{\sigma^2\rho_0}\frac{\partial\rho_0}{\partial z} - 1\right)w = 0. \quad (15.24)$$

In deriving Eq. 15.24 from Eqs. 15.23a–d, we have neglected the term $(1/\rho_0)(\partial\rho_0/\partial z)(\partial w/\partial z)$. If we define $\sigma_0^2 = (g/\rho_0)\,(\partial\rho_0/\partial z)$ and take σ_0 to be constant, the function

$$w = w_0 \sin(\pi z/h), \quad (15.25)$$

where w_0 is a constant, satisfies Eq. 15.24 and the conditions $w = 0$ at the upper and lower plates as long as

$$\sigma^2 = \frac{k^2\sigma_0^2}{k^2 + \pi^2/h^2}. \quad (15.26)$$

Thus we have proved our earlier assertion that exponential growth occurs when $\partial\rho_0/\partial z \propto \sigma_0^2 > 0$.

What can be learned from the above analysis of convection? Figure 15.2 shows the form of a convective cell that results from Eq. 15.23. The width of the cell is $\lambda = 2\pi/k$, and the depth is h. For a given h, Eq. 15.26 shows that the growth rate σ is linear with k for small k, and approaches σ_0 asymptotically for large k. Regardless of the form of the initial perturbation, the pattern that eventually results will be that of the mode with the greatest growth rate. This is easily seen by comparing two modes with initial amplitudes A_1 and A_2 and growth rates σ_1 and σ_2. After a time t, the amplitude ratio will be $R = (A_1/A_2)\exp[(\sigma_1 - \sigma_2)t]$. If $\sigma_1 > \sigma_2$, this will exceed unity for some time t, even if $R \ll 1$ initially. Loosely speaking, the modes with the greatest growth rate are those with $\lambda \leq 2h$. This explains why the horizontal dimensions of thunderstorms are generally of the same magnitude as the depth of the convectively unstable layer, roughly 10 kilometers. The physical reason why the shorter waves grow the fastest is that for a given amplitude of temperature the horizontal density gradient, and hence the buoyancy, is maximized for short waves.

Lord Rayleigh (1916) originally analyzed the above problem, including in addition the effects of viscosity and heat conductivity. When these latter effects are included, the peak growth rate occurs for finite rather than infinite k. However, the direct effects of these molecular processes are negligible in thunderstorms. Presumably turbulent momentum and heat transfer play a similar role, but since turbulent density is coupled to the convective motion by nonlinear terms that have been omitted, our perturbation analysis can supply us with no details. As one might expect, a linear model does not describe strong circulations adequately.

Omission of the term $\partial p'/\partial z$ in Eq. 15.23b considerably simplifies the fluid equations. Under these conditions one easily shows that Eq. 15.26 reduces to $\sigma^2 = \sigma_0^2$. Since this is the asymptotic limit for the unmodified set when $\lambda \ll h$, it is valid to ignore the pressure perturbation in this limit. This opens the way for a whole new class of convection models called *plume models*. The simplification induced by omitting the pressure term in the vertical component of the Euler equation is sufficient to allow a tractable, approximate treatment of turbulence and nonlinear terms. Envisioned are convective updrafts and downdrafts much taller than they are broad. The various conservation equations are integrated over the horizontal cross section of each draft, resulting in ordinary differential equations in the independent variable z.

We now investigate the problem of a time-independent, buoyant plume in an incompressible fluid. Our treatment roughly follows that of Morton et al. (1956). Certain important limitations are discussed when the plume model is applied to moist convection in the real atmosphere.

The key to plume models is the manner in which mixing of the turbulent plume with the environment is treated. When a turbulent fluid is in contact with a quiescent fluid, the latter becomes mixed in with the former, and not vice versa. In this one-way process the turbulent fluid is said to entrain the quiescent fluid. The volume of the turbulent part is thus increased, and its properties are thereby altered by this mixing process.

For a cylindrically symmetric, time-independent plume, the mass continuity equation, Eq. 15.20, can be written

$$\frac{\partial u_z}{\partial z} + \frac{1}{r}\frac{\partial(ru_r)}{\partial r} = 0, \quad (15.27)$$

where r and z are the radial and vertical position coordinates and u_z and u_r are the mass fluxes in the vertical and radial direction. Assuming that the plume has a radius $b(z)$, we can integrate Eq. 15.27 over the plume cross section, resulting in

$$\frac{d}{dz}(\pi b^2 \bar{u}_z) + 2\pi b \tilde{u}_r = 0, \quad (15.28)$$

where the overbar indicates an average over the cross section and the tilde an average over the plume boundary. The quantity $-\tilde{u}_r$ is the environmental mass flux being entrained into the plume. The simplest way to treat $\tilde{u}_r$ is to assume that $-\tilde{u}_r = \alpha\bar{u}_z$, where α is an empirically determined constant of proportionality. This is a plausible hypothesis, since the turbulence that causes the entrainment is presumably generated by the shear between the environment and the plume, which in turn is proportional to $\bar{u}_z$ (however, see Telford [1966] for a critique of this assumption). With the above hypothesis, Eq. 15.28 becomes

$$\frac{d}{dz}(b^2\bar{u}_z) = 2\alpha b\bar{u}_z. \qquad (15.29)$$

Laboratory experiments show that $\alpha \simeq 0.1$ (Turner, 1962, 1963).

Similar arguments applied to the vertical component of the Euler equation yield

$$\frac{d}{dz}(b^2\overline{wu_z}) + gb^2\bar{\rho}' = 0. \qquad (15.30)$$

This equation has no entrainment term, since u_z is assumed zero in the inflowing air at the boundary of the plume.

One can obtain the continuity equation for density excess $\rho' = \rho - \rho_0(z)$ by combining Eqs. 15.19 and 15.20 while ignoring the time derivative:

$$\nabla \cdot (\mathbf{V}\rho') + w\frac{d\rho_0}{dz} = 0. \qquad (15.31)$$

Integration as before yields an ordinary differential equation in z:

$$\frac{d}{dz}(b^2\overline{\rho'w}) + b^2\bar{w}\frac{d\rho_0}{dz} = 0. \qquad (15.32)$$

Terms like $\overline{\rho'w}$ must now be related to $\bar{\rho}'$ and $\bar{w}$. This requires an assumption to be made about the plume cross section. If we assume that all quantities are constant across the plume, then all overbars become redundant, and we obtain

$$\frac{d}{dz}(b^2u_z) = 2\alpha bu_z, \qquad (15.33)$$

$$\frac{d}{dz}(b^2u_zw) = -gb^2\rho', \qquad (15.34)$$

and

$$\frac{d}{dz}(b^2w\rho') = -b^2w\frac{d\rho_0}{dz} \qquad (15.35)$$

for the unknowns w, u_z, ρ', and b. To an excellent approximation, we may let $u_z = \rho_0 w$, thus completing the definition of a closed set of equations.

Figure 15.3 shows the results of integrating Eqs. 15.33 and 15.35 for various initial values of b, with w and ρ' initially fixed at 2 m s^{-1} and 0. In order to mimic deep atmospheric instability, a density profile of

$$\rho_0(z) = \rho_c[1 - \varepsilon(1 - z/h)^2] \qquad (15.36)$$

was assumed, with $\rho_c = 1$ kg m^{-3}, $\varepsilon = 0.008$, and $h = 4$ km. This yields a positive (and hence unstable) vertical density gradient in the lowest 4 km, with a negative gradient above. All plumes, no matter how narrow initially, ascend well beyond the locally neutral stability level of 4 km. However, entrainment of higher-density fluid causes the narrower plumes to cease rising at some level below the 11.6

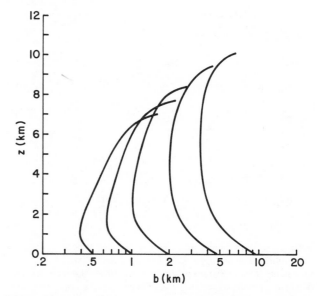

Figure 15.3. Plume radii as a function of height for the dry, incompressible flow case. The initial upward velocity and density perturbation were set to 2 m s^{-1} and 0, respectively.

km attained in undiluted ascent. Because of their inertia plumes actually reach a height in excess of that level at which the plume density equals the density of the surrounding fluid (8 km for undiluted ascent). The plume then falls back and spreads out horizontally at this equilibrium level. This overshooting process is not described by this simple plume model.

Application of the model to moist plumes in the atmosphere requires modification of only the buoyancy equation, Eq. 15.35. The specific entropy, given approximately by

$$s = c_v \ln p - c_p \ln \rho + qL/T_L, \qquad (15.37)$$

is conserved, and obeys a continuity equation similar to Eq. 15.35. In Eq. 15.37, c_v is the specific heat of air at constant volume, L is the latent heat of condensation of water, and T_L is the temperature at which condensation takes place for an initially unsaturated parcel upon adiabatic expansion. In a moist updraft where q is maintained quite near its saturation value, T_L simply becomes the temperature of the parcel.

A related variable more familiar to meteorologists is the equivalent potential temperature θ_e, which is related to s by $c_p\,d\theta_e/\theta_e = ds$. This variable is the temperature one obtains by moist-adiabatically expanding a parcel until all water is condensed, and then dry-adiabatically compressing it to 1,000 mb. Both s and θ_e are conserved in dry or moist adiabatic processes.

Figure 15.4 shows a vertical profile of temperature and relative humidity not unlike that found near many thunderstorms. Very moist air is found in the lowest few kilometers, with dry air above. The temperature difference from the environment of a nonentraining parcel ascending from cloud base is also shown. The parcel temperature exceeds that of

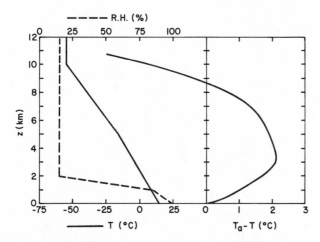

Figure 15.4. Ambient temperature and humidity profiles used for moist plume calculations. $T_a - T$ is temperature excess exhibited by a nonentraining parcel for moist ascent from cloud base at $z = 0$. The temperature sounding was selected to yield a buoyancy profile similar to that for the dry, incompressible case.

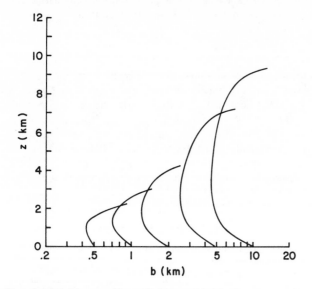

Figure 15.5. Plume radii as a function of height for moist plumes with the ambient conditions illustrated in Fig. 15.4. Note how the plumes of smaller radii are suppressed relative to the dry, incompressible case in Fig. 15.3.

the environment up to about 8.6 km, resulting in a density deficit and upward acceleration. The parcel overshoots this equilibrium level by 2.5 km to a peak altitude of 11.2 km before falling back.

The characteristics of nonentraining plumes for the dry and moist cases were intentionally made similar to highlight the difference between the effects of entrainment in the two cases. Figure 15.5 shows the behavior of moist, entraining plumes with various initial radii and identical initial condi-

tions to those in Fig. 15.3. For the broader plumes there is very little difference between the dry incompressible and moist cases. However, for an initial plume radius of 500 m, the dry plume ascends to 7 km, while the moist plume barely exceeds 2 km.

The difference results primarily from the peculiar nature of the mixing process between dry and saturated air. Unlike the case of an incompressible fluid, mixing dry air and air containing liquid water can result in air with a density greater than that of either initial constituent. This occurs because the dry air evaporates the water, resulting in cooling and an increase in density.

On the basis of measurements in small, nonprecipitating clouds in a shallow maritime layer topped by dry air, Warner (1970) concluded that serious deficiencies existed in moist-plume models of convection, since such models are unable to predict cloud-top height and liquid water content simultaneously. In particular, to reach the observed height, the model needed to have a very low entrainment rate. As a consequence the liquid water content was far in excess of that measured. Conversely, if entrainment was adjusted (for instance by varying the initial cloud radius) so as to yield the correct water content, the model cloud stopped ascending well below the observed tops.

Telford (1975) has proposed that the dilemma is a direct result of the singular nature of the mixing process in moist convection. An essential approximation in plume theory is that mixing occurs only horizontally. No provision is made for mixing between the top of the plume and the quiescent fluid at that level—indeed, since a plume is assumed to be tall and skinny, one might expect this process to be no more than locally important. However, since evaporation can cause a mixture of moist and dry air to attain strong negative buoyancy, such mixed parcels could conceivably penetrate downward through the plume for a considerable distance—a possibility absent in the case of dry convection (see Squires, 1958). If this occurs, the conceptual model of a cumulus cloud as a turbulent plume is incorrect.

Following Telford (1975), we mix varying proportions of air brought moist-isentropically from cloud base with environmental cloud-top air. How far will the resulting mixture sink before it is in density equilibrium with the environment? The magnitude of this distance relative to the depth of the cloud will indicate the importance of topside mixing.

The calculation is easily performed. The moist plume with an initial radius of 500 m ceases rising at somewhat less than 2.3 km. If low-level air is mixed with 2.3-km environmental air, mixtures containing less than 26% of upper-level air continue to have positive buoyancy. Mixtures containing 26% or more become negatively buoyant, and the critical 26% mixture sinks 1.7 km, or about 75% of depth of the cloud before attaining neutral buoyancy.

The result is very different for plumes that reach a high altitude. In the nonentraining case, pure cloud-base air sinks back to 8.6 km from the peak altitude of 11.2 km, or only 25% of cloud depth. All mixtures of cloud-base air with 11.2-km environmental air come to equilibrium at an elevation higher than 8.6 km. There is thus a qualitative difference in behavior; the deep moist plume behaves like a dry plume, in that mixing at the top does not result in great negative buoyancy. Equivalent mixing in a shallow, moist plume results in negatively buoyant downward flux through nearly the entire depth of the cloud. The reason for the difference is that dry, midlevel air has a tremendous capacity for evaporating cloud, whereas high-level air is simply too cold to absorb much water vapor.

From the above arguments, we see that plume theory is more applicable to tall clouds than to short clouds. This model thus gives a better understanding of larger clouds of apparently greater complexity than their small precursors. As often happens in science, the outwardly simple process turns out to be fundamentally complex, and vice versa.

An additional problem arises with deep, moist plumes. As Fig. 15.5 shows, these plumes tend to be about as fat as they are tall, in part because of the dry, marginally unstable environmental profile that was used. Nevertheless, under these conditions the assumptions behind plume theory become somewhat dubious; in particular, ignoring the pressure term is no longer strictly valid. Thus we cannot say that idealized models have led us to a quantitatively accurate understanding of convective instability, but we would be less well prepared to interpret numerical models without having investigated the simpler approach.

b. Plume Tilt and Rotation

The development of plume theory in the previous section is based on the implicit assumption that the environment is stationary. This condition is rare in the atmosphere under any circumstances, and particularly so during conditions favoring severe convection. One generally finds not only strong winds but also, and more important, strong variations in the wind with height.

Material in a plume tends to retain its initial horizontal momentum as it ascends. However, the impingement of the ambient flow upon a plume bends the plume over in the direction of the relative wind. In addition, the plume entrainment process can be altered, and in extreme cases the plume is completely destroyed.

Bates developed a method of calculating the bending of a nonentraining plume in an ambient wind field (Newton, 1966), in which the laws of aerodynamic drag are applied to a horizontal slice or wafer of ascending air in a steady, circular plume. Warner (1972) extended Bates's method to include entrainment of environmental momentum into the plume. The resulting equation that combines the two effects is

$$\frac{d\mathbf{V}_h}{dz} = B(\mathbf{V} - \mathbf{V}_h) + \frac{C}{\pi bw}(\mathbf{V} - \mathbf{V}_h)|\mathbf{V} - \mathbf{V}_h|, \quad (15.38)$$

where $B = M^{-1}dM/dz$ is the logarithmic rate of increase of mass flux in the plume with height due to entrainment, C is the drag coefficient of the plume, $\mathbf{V}(z)$ is the ambient wind as a function of height, and $\mathbf{V}_h$ is the horizontal component of velocity of material forming the plume. As before, w and b are vertical plume speed and plume radius. It is simplest

to assume that the plume pattern is stationary, thus allowing the position of the plume axis as a function of height to be found by the following integration:

$$\frac{d\mathbf{x}_h}{dz} = \frac{\mathbf{V}_h}{w}. \quad (15.39)$$

Noting that $M = \pi b^2 \rho w$ in terms of plume theory, we find through Eq. 15.29 that $B = 2\alpha/b$. Applying this to Eq. 15.38 yields

$$\frac{d\mathbf{V}_h}{dz} = \frac{(\mathbf{V} - \mathbf{V}_h)}{b}\left[2\alpha + \frac{C|\mathbf{V} - \mathbf{V}_h|}{\pi w}\right], \quad (15.40)$$

which may be combined with plume theory to get the tilt of a plume as a function of height. This, of course, may be done only if plume tilt remains small enough for conventional plume theory to be approximately valid. A simpler approach will be used here by specifying a constant plume radius b and an updraft profile of the form

$$w = w_0 + 4(w_m - w_0)(1 - z/z_0)(z/z_0), \quad (15.41)$$

where $w = w_0$ at $z = 0$ and z_0, and $w = w_m$ at $z = z_0/2$.

The entrainment coefficient α will again be set to 0.1. The drag coefficient C is more difficult to specify. For high Reynolds number flow about a smooth cylinder, $C = 0.3$ (Prandtl and Tietjens, 1934). There is some doubt about the applicability of that figure to the present situation, however, since Warner (1972) found it necessary to take C as large as 3 to reproduce observed storm behavior. For purpose of illustration, we will take $C = 1$.

Figure 15.6 shows the behavior of plumes representing two extreme cases. Shear in both is 5 m s^{-1} km^{-1}. Plume A is a weak plume that moves with the ambient wind at $z = 0$. The constants are $b = 1$ km, $w_0 = 2$ m s^{-1}, $w_m = 10$ m s^{-1}, and $z_0 = 10$ km. Because this plume is stationary with respect to the low-level air, material entering at this level initially has a net horizontal momentum of zero. The plume is rapidly bent over, acquiring a downshear tilt.

Plume B moves with the air at 3 km, and thus the surface inflow has a relative speed of 15 m s^{-1} in a direction opposite the shear vector. Assuming this to be a much stronger plume, we let $b = 3$ km, $w_0 = 5$ m s^{-1}, $w_m = 30$ m s^{-1}, and $z_0 = 10$ km. This plume maintains its upshear momentum to high levels, resulting in a predominantly upshear tilt.

Experimenting with different combinations of constants shows that, though all are significant in influencing plume tilts, the most important single factor is the plume-relative inflow velocity at the surface. This velocity is, of course, a reflection of plume motion. If the plume pattern moves rapidly downshear, then the plume will tend to tilt upshear, and vice versa. Narrow plumes with weak updrafts will be bent downshear more than their stronger and broader counterparts, because they have a greater surface-to-volume ratio and because the plume material remains exposed to aerodynamic forces for a longer period of time.

The tilt of a plume is of great interest from the point of view of precipitation production. For a plume with no tilt, precipitation must fall out directly through the rising updraft. If updraft velocity exceeds particle fall velocity, then

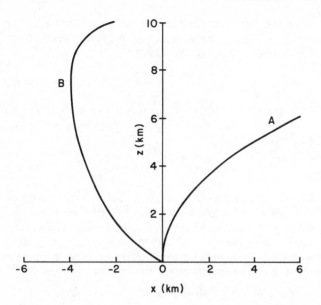

Figure 15.6. Computed plume shapes in linear shear of 5 m s^{-1} km^{-1} for (*A*) a weak plume moving with the low-level wind, and (*B*) a strong plume moving with the wind at $z = 3$ km. The latter case tilts upshear (i.e., to the left) primarily because the incoming low-level air has considerable upshear momentum with respect to the plume.

precipitation-sized particles will be suspended aloft, eventually killing the updraft by virtue of their weight. The only way this stress may be relieved is by slow drift of the precipitation to the plume edge and subsequent fallout.

In a tilted plume, on the other hand, precipitation will fall out on the side to which the plume is tilted. This may be either upshear or downshear; the former corresponds to the classical severe-storm pattern hypothesized by Browning and Ludlam (1962), in which the precipitation falls into dry air on the upshear side of the plume, forming an evaporatively cooled downdraft there. The downshear precipitation fallout is seen frequently as virga falling out of a thunderstorm anvil—the anvil being considered a highly tilted extension of the original updraft plume.

It has been speculated that aerodynamic life forces may also act on plumes (Fujita and Grandoso, 1968). Such forces would be normal to the relative wind and thus could cause plume tilt normal to the shear. For lift to be nonzero, the plume must either have an asymmetric structure or rotate. The latter possibility is generally the only one considered, and it is clearly related to the question of tornado formation. We will now examine the conditions promoting the rotation of a plume.

For air motions in a neutrally stable atmospheric boundary layer, the vorticity equation may be written

$$\frac{d\boldsymbol{\zeta}}{dt} = (\boldsymbol{\zeta} \cdot \nabla)\mathbf{V}, \qquad (15.42)$$

where the vorticity is defined by $\boldsymbol{\zeta} = \nabla \times \mathbf{V}$. The z component of this equation is

$$\frac{d\zeta_z}{dt} = \zeta_z \frac{\partial w}{\partial z} + \boldsymbol{\zeta}_h \cdot \nabla_h w, \qquad (15.43)$$

where the vorticity vector has been split into horizontal $\boldsymbol{\zeta}_h$ and vertical ζ_z components. The vorticity defines the rotational properties of a fluid, and Eq. 15.43 shows that the fluid in a plume may come to rotate by two mechanisms. The first term corresponds to vertical stretching of preexisting vertical vortex lines in the fluid and is a consequence of the conservation of angular momentum. The second term is called the *twisting* or *tilting term*, and it corresponds to the bending of horizontal vortex lines associated with wind shear into the vertical.

Rotation is, of course, an essential characteristic of tornadoes. The great majority of tornadoes exhibit cyclonic rotation (and hence cyclonic vorticity), as does the severe-storm environment as a whole. Recent three-dimensional cloud model simulations (Klemp and Wilhelmson, 1978b) suggest that the Coriolis force is not directly responsible for this cyclonic bias. Supercell storm simulations (discussed in Sec. 3i), both with and without the Coriolis force present in the model equations, produce qualitatively similar results. Rather, the characteristically observed clockwise turning of the environmental wind shear causes preferential development of the right-moving, cyclonically rotating supercell storm. Rotunno (1981) has demonstrated how a storm's vorticity develops as horizontal environmental vorticity is tilted into the vertical and then strongly amplified by vortex stretching. Barnes (1970) has also discussed the relative importance of twisting and stretching to thunderstorm vorticity. This subject is also addressed in Chap. 10.

c. Thunderstorm Movement and Collective Effects

Knowledge of translational velocity is necessary for the computation of plume tilt, but no means for calculating it were advanced in the previous section. This question is addressed here.

Numerous qualitative ideas have been introduced to explain why thunderstorms move. The first idea that comes to mind is simply that thunderstorms must move with the wind. This hypothesis gains encouragement from the observation that many types of clouds appear to do so. However, since thunderstorms extend through a very deep layer of the atmosphere, one is immediately confronted with the question, the wind at which level? Since the wind may vary from 0 m s^{-1} at the surface to 50 m s^{-1} or more at 10 km, this is clearly an important question. If a thunderstorm does indeed move with the wind at some level, this is called the *steering level*. Many thunderstorms, particularly weak storms, do have a steering level, which is typically 3 to 6 km above the surface. However, the most severe storms tend to move with a velocity unequal to the wind at any height, and thus they lack a steering level.

Evidently the approximations that lead to plume theory preclude a determination of the speed of plume movement in shear. As shown earlier, the key approximation for plume theory is the exclusion of the vertical pressure gradient term in the Euler equation. Since convective cells do not spring to life with full intensity but must evolve through a growth stage in which they are initially weak, reversion to something like our initial, linearized model of convection that retains this term may be of value. If perturbations of the form $\exp[ik(x - ct)]$ on a sheared, saturated environment are investigated, one obtains an equation similar in spirit to Eq. 15.24:

$$\frac{\partial^2 w}{\partial z^2} + \left[\frac{1}{c - u} \frac{d^2 u}{dz^2} + \frac{N^2}{(c - u)^2} - k^2 \right] w = 0. \quad (15.44)$$

Here $u(z)$ is the x component of the ambient wind, and $N^2 = (g/c_p)\partial s/\partial z$ is the square of the Brunt-Vaisala frequency (the frequency of vertical gravitational oscillations in a statically stable atmosphere) in a saturated environment. The entropy profile $s(z)$ is given by Eq. 15.37, with q set to its saturation value. N^2 will be negative in convectively unstable regions. For simplicity, scale height effects have been omitted in the derivation.

Solution of Eq. 15.44 satisfying the proper boundary conditions is only possible for certain values of the complex eigenvalue c. The real part of c gives the propagation speed of the perturbation; the growth rate is given by $kIm(c)$.

This approach has not been extensively pursued for the case of moist convection. This is somewhat surprising, because the analogous equation for dry processes has been used for many years, and the techniques for solving it are well known. It is hoped that this neglect will be rectified in the near future.

Moncrieff and Green (1972) have developed a theory of steady, 2-D convective overturning. Such a theory could provide a description of the lines of thunderstorms that sometimes occur in both the tropics and middle latitudes. The assumption of steady flow and strict two-dimensionality imposes surprisingly strong constraints upon such storms. In addition, these authors assume no entrainment, which seems roughly consistent with the behavior of strong cumulonimbus.

Bernoulli's equation is one of the two legs upon which the analysis stands. This equation is essentially a statement of enthalpy conservation for air along a steady fluid streamline, and may be written

$$v^2/2 + gz + \int dp/\rho = \text{const}, \quad (15.45)$$

where v is the magnitude of the velocity. The left side of Eq. 15.45 may be evaluated for a parcel before it enters the updraft at low levels and after it leaves, having been ejected at a high level. Equating these two results, we get

$$|\mathbf{V}_i - \mathbf{c}|^2 = |\mathbf{V}_0 - \mathbf{c}|^2 - 2W. \quad (15.46)$$

Equation 15.46 reduces to

$$2\mathbf{c} \cdot (\mathbf{V}_0 - \mathbf{V}_i) = v_0^2 - v_i^2 - 2W, \quad (15.47)$$

where

$$W = -g(z_0 - z_i) - \int_{p_i}^{p_0} dp/\rho \quad (15.48)$$

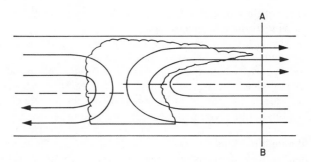

Figure 15.7. Schematic illustration of 2-D storm flow. In this case all air flowing into the front of the storm at low levels is ejected from the front at high levels. Thus, in the frame of the moving storm, the mass flux F through the line AB must be zero. The steering level is simply the level that separates inflow from outflow, and is denoted by a horizontal dashed line. Separate steering levels are indicated on the updraft and downdraft sides.

is the net energy release in the convective ascent and is easily calculable using standard meteorological charts. The subscripts i and 0 denote values taken for inflow and outflow, and a propagation velocity vector $\mathbf{c}$ has been subtracted from $\mathbf{V}_i$ and $\mathbf{V}_0$ to transform Eq. 15.46 to the more familiar Earth reference frame.

The second leg supporting the analysis is simply mass continuity. If we define a vertical plane parallel to the line of storms at some distance x from the line, the mass flux through this plane (in the reference frame of the moving storm) is

$$F = \int_0^h \rho[\mathbf{V}(x, z) - \mathbf{c}] \cdot \hat{\mathbf{n}} dz, \quad (15.49)$$

where $\mathbf{V}$ is the wind velocity, $\hat{\mathbf{n}}$ is a horizontal unit vector normal to the line, and ρ is the density. Since density variations with x will be small, ρ may be replaced by some mean $\rho_0(z)$ with little approximation. By mass continuity, F clearly cannot be a function of x.

For the case of monolithic convective overturning shown in Fig. 15.7, F will be zero, since air entering the storm on one side exits on that same side. This is consistent with Browning and Ludlam's (1962) conceptual model of a severe storm. The steering level on such a storm divides inflowing air at low levels from high-level outflow.

Conceptually, it is possible to see how Bernoulli's equation and the condition $F = 0$ fix the speed of such a storm. If the storm speed is given, then Bernoulli's equation predicts the windspeed for every outgoing streamline, provided the speed on the incoming streamline is known. The storm speed is not known a priori. However, the continuity condition $F = 0$ provides one additional constraint that serves to determine the only remaining variable, c (the line orientation, and hence the direction of $\mathbf{c}$, is assumed known). In summary, if the thermodynamic characteristics and wind profile of the inflowing air are known, the speed of movement of the convective line and the wind profile in the outflowing air may be determined.

The above-described model is subject to a number of problems. First, the argument obtaining the speed of the storm derives exclusively from consideration of the updraft. A completely analogous argument may be made for the downdraft (which is presumably driven by evaporative cooling from precipitation), with a resulting storm speed that will only by rare coincidence equal that derived from the updraft. This constitutes an inconsistency in the model and perhaps explains why gust fronts often run away from their parent storm. Another difficulty recently uncovered by Moncrieff (1977) is that the tilt of the updraft-downdraft interface tends to be such that precipitation falls back into the updraft rather than the downdraft. The conceptual model of Browning and Ludlam (1962), in which evaporating precipitation drives the downdraft, thus appears to be dynamically impossible in a strictly 2-D steady framework. However, as shown in the next section, 2-D nonsteady numerical models do quite well in simulating many of the observed features of thunderstorms in a sheared environment.

The difficulties inherent in a monolithic overturning model of squall line convection lead one to question the assumptions behind such a model. Furthermore, the closer one looks at a squall line, the less monolithic it generally appears. Moncrieff and Miller (1976) have developed a model in which strict two-dimensionality is relaxed in the immediate vicinity of a squall line. Unfortunately, the ability to explicitly determine line propagation speed is lost in this model.

A different class of models has arisen that takes account of the 3-D unsteady nature of the interior flow of a storm in a statistical fashion. In essence, a storm is supposed to consist of numerous plumes or convective elements that coexist with the storm scale flow in a symbiotic manner. The storm flow supplies the plumes with fuel, while the bulk heating and momentum transfer caused by the plumes in turn drive the storm. If the growth stage is considered, a linearized treatment suffices, and an equation of the form

$$\frac{d^2w}{dz^2} + Q(c, z)w = S(c, z) \frac{dw}{dz}\bigg|_{z=0} \quad (15.50)$$

is obtained in analogy to Eq. 15.44, except that w now represents storm scale vertical motion, i.e., with plume-scale fluctuations smoothed out. The function $Q(c, z)$ is identical to the quantity in brackets in Eq. 15.44, except that the Brunt-Väisälä frequency N^2 is evaluated for the dry process, i.e., with $q = 0$ in Eq. 15.37. The primary difference between Eqs. 15.44 and 15.50 is the presence of a nonzero term on the right size of Eq. 15.50, which represents the averaged contribution of the plumes. The proportionality of this term to $dw/dz|_{z=0}$ results from the hypothesized dependence of plume effects on storm scale convergence and upward motion. The form $S(c, z)$ is difficult to obtain, and various models, using different formulations of S, have been proposed.

Matsumoto and Ninomiya (1969) developed a model of winter squall lines that typically form in extreme shear over the Sea of Japan. The plume scale forcing was supposed to consist of vertical momentum transfer, with resulting Reynolds's stresses acting on the storm scale flow. Since the stress is variable in space because of variations in low-level convergence and the resulting plume population, positive feedback is clearly possible. Matsumoto and Ninomiya indeed found amplifying disturbances with propagation speeds that agreed qualitatively with their observations.

One objection to this model is that thermodynamic (buoyancy), as opposed to dynamic (shearing), forces are ignored. The ratio of the two approximates the Richardson number, $Ri = N^2(\delta|V|/\partial z)^{-2}$, of the free atmosphere. Because Ri almost always exceeds unity by a large amount through the depth of the troposphere, one would expect heating to be generally more important than momentum transfer as a plume-induced feedback mechanism.

Lindzen (1974) investigated the effect of such heating in an environment with no ambient wind and found that instability can exist. Raymond (1975; 1976) has developed a similar model, except that realistic ambient profiles of wind and temperature are included. This model is reasonably successful in predicting the early evolution and movement of severe convective storms of the type that lack a steering level but deviate to the left or right of the mean wind.

d. Summary

Though idealized models have not led to a complete understanding of thunderstorms, they have provided answers in certain areas and have defined important questions in others. Some of the more significant insights are these:

1. Deep convective clouds are easier to understand in terms of entity models, such as simple plume models, than their shallower and ostensibly simpler cousins.
2. Strictly 2-D, steady-state models of convection are apparently dynamically inconsistent with the class of thunderstorms most likely to be represented by them. In particular, the predicted tilt of the updraft is in disagreement with the observed ability of such storms to create an upshear downdraft cooled by precipitation. Thunderstorms thus appear to be irredeemably 3-D, unsteady, or both.
3. The main kinematic features of a storm, such as updraft tilt and downdraft location, are determined primarily by the speed of movement of the storm and only to a smaller degree by other factors.
4. Calculation of storm motion is approachable through models that consider a thunderstorm to be an aggregate of convective elements. That thunderstorms generally consist of many cells or plumes is well known. The success of such models suggests that this clustering is in some ways essential to thunderstorm existence.

In the next section we consider more complicated models of convection that permit varied nonlinear feedbacks between the thermodynamic and dynamic fields and the precipitation. These models use the numerical modeling approach introduced at the beginning of this chapter.

3. Numerical Simulation of Thunderstorms

Analytical models of thunderstorm processes stress the fundamental nature of the storms, while numerical simulations attempt to mold the more complex features of the storms into a reproducible, reasonable facsimile. Once this is done, many tests of the sensitivity of various processes to the storm development may be made or other storm-related processes examined. For example, the growth of large hail or the electrification of thunderstorms may be explained eventually through numerical simulations in association with observations.

The equations of motion, of state, of air and water continuity, of ions, and of charge on the cloud and precipitation particles are all needed to simulate a thunderstorm and are extremely complex in interaction. The work is very much in a developmental stage at present, with some scientists concentrating on dynamics, some on microphysics, and some on electrical aspects of thunderstorms. This section concentrates on the results from recent 2-D simulations of severe storms. Most 3-D, time-dependent models are being run now with only limited resolution (grid interval 1 km or so). Finer-mesh 3-D models await extensive testing on next-generation computers.

a. Basic Equations

Equations for deep convection are given by Schlesinger (1973), Hane (1973), Wilhelmson and Ogura (1972), and Cotton (1975). The general equations in Sec. 1a are averaged over appropriate spatial scales for thunderstorm simulations in this section. An approximate form of the continuity equation is used in some cloud models, which assumes that the air density is a function of height alone. In addition, the density variations are retained only where they are multiplied by gravity in the equation of motion, an assumption called the *Boussinesq approximation*. The dynamic set of equations that is based on the Boussinesq approximation is often characterized as being "anelastic," i.e., not admitting sound waves, which allows longer time steps and less computer time to be used. The anelastic equations were first used by Ogura and Charney (1962) and were derived by scale analysis by Ogura and Phillips (1962).

Specializing the general set of averaged equations to two dimensions leads most often to a formulation based on the vorticity and stream function, although Hill (1974) has integrated the primitive (unmodified) set of equations. The following development pertains to the 2-D model described by Orville and Kopp (1977), but development is similar in many 2-D models. Differentiating the first equation of motion (Eq. 15.4) with respect to z and the third equation of motion (Eq. 15.6) with respect to x, subtracting the results, and using the Boussinesq approximation yield a vorticity equation,

$$\frac{\partial \eta}{\partial t} = - \mathbf{V} \cdot \nabla \eta + \frac{2w}{\rho_0} \frac{\partial \rho_0}{\partial z}\left(\eta + u \frac{\partial \rho_0}{\partial z}\right) - uw \frac{\partial^2 \rho_0}{\partial z^2}$$

$$+ \frac{\rho_0 g}{\theta} \frac{\partial \theta'}{\partial x} + 0.61\rho_0 g \frac{\partial q'}{\partial x} - \rho_0 g \frac{\partial l}{\partial x} + F(K_m)$$

$$+ \left[\frac{\partial \rho_e E_z}{\partial x} - \frac{\partial \rho_e E_x}{\partial z}\right], \tag{15.51}$$

where the vorticity about the S–N horizontal axis is

$$\eta \equiv \frac{\partial \rho_0 w}{\partial x} - \frac{\partial \rho_0 u}{\partial z} \tag{15.52}$$

and

$$\nabla^2 \Psi = \eta. \tag{15.53}$$

The horizontal and vertical velocity components are related to the stream function by

$$u = -\frac{1}{\rho_0} \frac{\partial \Psi}{\partial z} \tag{15.54a}$$

and

$$w = \frac{1}{\rho_0} \frac{\partial \Psi}{\partial x}. \tag{15.54b}$$

In Eqs. 15.51–15.54, Ψ is the stream function, θ is the base state potential temperature (normally about 290 K), θ' the deviation from the base state, l the mixing ratio of the total water in liquid and solid phase, and q' the deviation in water vapor mixing ratio. The first term on the right side of Eq. 15.51 is the familiar nonlinear advection term; the second and third terms arise because of the density variation in the z direction and have their origin in the density-weighted nonlinear advection terms in the equations of motion. The fourth and fifth terms are in essence the Boussinesq approximation and embody the assumption that the base state is in hydrostatic equilibrium.

To show how the fourth and fifth terms are derived, recall that the pressure gradient and part of the gravitational acceleration in the third equation of motion, (Eq. 15.6), are

$$-\frac{1}{\rho} \frac{\partial p}{\partial z} - g = -\alpha \frac{\partial p}{\partial z} - g, \tag{15.55}$$

where α is the specific volume. Breaking the variables into a base state portion and a deviation from that base state leads to

$$-(\alpha_0 + \alpha') \frac{\partial}{\partial z} (p_0 + p') - g = -\alpha_0\left(1 + \frac{\alpha'}{\alpha_0}\right)$$

$$\times \left(\frac{\partial p_0}{\partial z} + \frac{\partial p'}{\partial z}\right) - g$$

$$= -\alpha_0 \frac{\partial p'}{\partial z} + \frac{\alpha'}{\alpha_0} g,$$

$$= -\frac{\partial}{\partial z} (\alpha_0 p')$$

$$+ g\left\{\frac{\alpha'}{\alpha_0} + (1 - \kappa) \frac{p'}{p_0}\right\} \tag{15.56}$$

where products of deviations are neglected, $\kappa = R/c_p$, and

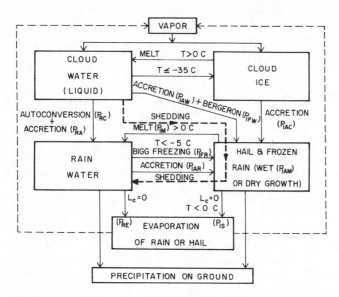

Figure 15.8. Cloud physics processes simulated in a 2-D cloud model.

the base state is assumed to be hydrostatic (i.e., $\alpha_0 \, (\partial p_0/\partial z)$ $= -g$) and adiabatic. In the above the primes stand for deviations and the subscript 0 for the base state. The buoyancy term in brackets is transformed into potential temperature and water vapor deviations by recalling the equation of state in the form given by Eq. 15.1 and using Eqs. 15.2 and 15.10:

$$p\alpha = R \left(\frac{p}{p_{00}} \right)^{\kappa} \theta \, (1 + 0.61 \, q). \qquad (15.57)$$

Differentiating logarithmically and identifying a differential with a deviation quantity lead to

$$\frac{\alpha'}{\alpha_0} + (1 - \kappa) \, \frac{p'}{p_0} = \frac{\theta'}{\theta_0} + 0.61 \, q'. \qquad (15.58)$$

Substitution of the above into Eq. 15.56 and then substitution of that result into the third equation of motion lead to the buoyancy terms in Eq. 15.51.

The sixth term in Eq. 15.51 represents the drag force of the liquid and solid particles in the atmosphere and its effect in creating vorticity. This term arises from the fact that particles falling at their terminal velocities in a fluid medium impart their weight to a fluid parcel.

The turbulence term $F(K_m)$ arises from eddy-mixing terms in the equations of motion and is taken from Drake et al. (1974). The term includes the nonlinear effects of wind shear and thermal instability in affecting greater mixing (see also Hill, 1974).

The term in brackets represents effects of electrical forces in the creation of vorticity. It arises because of a term, $\rho_e \mathbf{E}$, added to the equations of motion, where ρ_e is the electrical space charge density and $\mathbf{E}$ is the electric field, with components E_x and E_z in 2-D models. The term is normally very small, except in localized, highly charged regions in lightning-producing clouds.

b. Cloud Physics

The physical processes in the clouds are governed by the equations in the 1-D cloud model of Wisner et al. (1972) and the parameterized technique of Liu and Orville (1969), Kessler (1969), Srivastava (1967), and Orville and Kopp (1977). Five classifications of water are considered and are usually referred to as *bulk water contents*: water vapor (q), cloud water (q_c), cloud ice (q_i), rain (l_R), and precipitating ice (l_I). The q_i is not as general as that in Eq. 15.14, representing here only the nonprecipitating ice particles. The cloud water and the cloud ice particles are assumed to be small enough that their terminal velocities can be neglected compared with the velocity of air, rain, and hail. The rain and the precipitating ice are assumed to be distributed in a particular manner specified below and to consist of liquid drops and ice particles with appreciable terminal velocities. A mass-weighted mean terminal velocity is used to describe the fallout of the water (Srivastava, 1967; Kessler, 1969). The interaction of these water substances is shown in Fig. 15.8.

An alternative to treating just five water substances is to "discretize" the water and ice particles (Berry, 1967). One equation is needed for each size category and type of particle, whether liquid or ice. Fifty categories require 100 equations. The type and evolution of the particle size distributions are important predictions of these models. The mixing ratios q_l or q_i are obtained by summing over all the appropriate size categories; e.g.,

$$q_l = \sum_{j=1}^{J} n_j \, \frac{4}{3} \, \pi \, r_j^3 \, \rho_l, \qquad (15.59a)$$

where n_j is the number of liquid particles in the jth category per unit mass or air, r_j is the mean radius of the drops in the category, and ρ_l is the density of water. A similar equation applies for q_i. Examples of this work in 1-D cloud models are given by Danielsen et al. (1972) and Silverman and Glass (1973). Clark (1973) and Takahashi (1976) and others have pursued this line of attack in 2-D cloud models.

Observations within thunderstorms have indicated different but characteristic size distributions for the rain and hail particles. One such example is shown in Fig. 15.9. The observations have been used to devise a parameterization of the microphysics as used by several investigators (Murray, 1970; Soong and Ogura, 1973; Hill, 1974), as first suggested by Kessler (1969). The distributions are given as

$$n_R(D_R) = n_{OR} e^{-\lambda_R D_R} \quad \text{and} \quad n_I(D_I) = n_{OI} e^{-\lambda_I D_I},$$
$$(15.59b, c)$$

where n_R is the number of raindrops of diameter D_R per unit volume of air per unit diameter of drop, $n_I(D_I)$ is the number of ice particles of diameter D_I per unit volume of air per unit diameter of particle, and n_{OR}, n_{OI}, λ_R, and λ_I are parameters in the exponential size distributions.

The distributions given by Eq. 15.59b, c are shown as the dashed lines in Fig. 15.9 for an appropriate rain content, and for a hail content of 1.0 g kg^{-1}. The rain distribution was first determined by Marshall and Palmer (1948).

The terminal velocities V_t and U_t for water and ice are

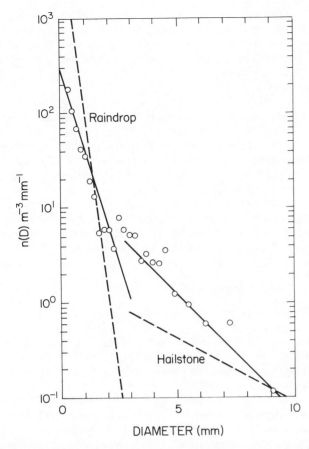

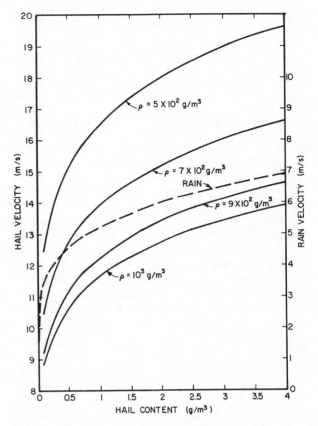

Figure 15.9. Precipitation particle size distribution observed with a foil impactor in the updraft region of a mature cell penetrated at about 7.2 km MSL on 9 July 1973 near Sterling, Colo. The broken lines represent Marshall-Palmer raindrop and Douglas hailstone size distribution functions corresponding to the precipitation concentrations for particles smaller and larger than 3 mm, respectively. The solid lines represent exponential function fits (Smith et al., 1976).

Figure 15.10. Mass-weighted terminal fall velocities for hail and rain. The density of the ambient air is designated by ρ.

then computed as mass-weighted mean velocities (Srivastava, 1967):

$$V_t = \frac{a\,\Gamma\,(4 + b)}{6\lambda_R^b} \quad \text{and} \quad U_t = \frac{\Gamma\,(4.5)}{6\lambda_I^{0.5}}\left(\frac{4g\rho_I}{3C_D\rho}\right)^{0.5},$$
$$(15.60a, b)$$

where the constants a and b are 2,115 cm s^{-1} and 0.8 (Liu and Orville, 1969), Γ is the gamma function, and λ_R and λ_I are given by

$$\lambda_R = \left(\frac{\pi\,\rho_w\,n_{OR}}{\rho l_R}\right)^{0.25} \quad \text{and} \quad \lambda_I = \left(\frac{\pi\,\rho_I\,n_{OI}}{\rho l_I}\right)^{0.25}.$$
$$(15.61a, b)$$

Representative terminal velocities are shown in Fig. 15.10 for several air densities. In Eqs. 15.60 and 15.61 ρ_w and ρ_I are densities of water and ice, ρ is the density of air, C_D is a drag coefficient, and π is 3.14. . . . . Marshall and

Palmer (1948) give a value for n_{OR} of 8×10^{-2} cm^{-4}. Observations of hail distributions by Douglas (1960), Battan (1973, p. 46), and Federer and Waldvogel (1975) indicate a value of about 4×10^{-4} cm^{-4} for n_{OI}, although more study is required to fix the optimum value, particularly since this value for n_{OI} leads to excessive dBZ values (a measure of radar reflectivity) for moderate and large amounts of hail when compared with observations (dBZ $\equiv 10$ log [$Z_e/$ 1 mm^6 m^{-3}], where Z_e is a function of precipitation content [Smith et al., 1975]).

c. Water Conservation Equations

In Orville and Kopp's (1977) model, the predictive equations for the types of water are

$$\frac{\partial q_t}{\partial t} = -\mathbf{V} \cdot \nabla q_t + \nabla \cdot K_h \nabla q_t - P_R - P_I$$

$$\qquad - \left[\frac{1}{\rho_0} \nabla \cdot \rho_0 l_c \mathbf{V}_c\right], \qquad (15.62)$$

$$\frac{\partial l_R}{\partial t} = -\mathbf{V} \cdot \nabla l_R + \nabla \cdot K_m \nabla l_R + P_R - \frac{1}{\rho_0} \nabla \cdot (\rho_0 l_R \mathbf{V}_R),$$
$$(15.63)$$

and

F 15.

$$\frac{\partial l_I}{\partial t} = - \mathbf{V} \cdot \nabla l_I + \nabla \cdot K_m \nabla l_I + P_I - \frac{1}{\rho_0} \nabla \cdot (\rho_0 l_I \mathbf{V}_I),$$
(15.64)

where q_t is the sum of cloud water, cloud ice, and vapor mixing ratios:

$$q_t = q_c + q_i + q.$$
(15.65)

P_R represents the production of rain from cloud, hail, and vapor; P_I represents the production of hail from cloud, rain, and vapor. These water conservation equations are more complex and offer more detail than Eqs. 15.13 and 15.14. Equations 15.62–15.64 allow for interactions between precipitating and nonprecipitating particles; Eqs. 15.12–15.14 refer primarily to phase changes of water.

In addition to the terms representing the advection, the diffusion, and the production of water, the last terms in Eqs. 15.63 and 15.64 denote the fallout of rain and precipitating ice at their terminal velocities defined in Eq. 15.60, if gravitational effects only are considered. In such a case, $\mathbf{V}_c = 0$; i.e., the vapor, cloud water, and cloud ice move with the air. More generally, the quantities $\mathbf{V}_c$, $\mathbf{V}_R$, and $\mathbf{V}_I$, represent both gravitational and electrical forces that act on the averaged-size charged particles of the cloud, rain, and hail fields (in the numerical simulation). The ratio of electrical to gravitational forces on totally charged particles is a function of drop size and electric field (Chiu, 1978). For a drop of 10-μm radius in a 100 V m^{-1} field (a typical fair-weather field), the ratio is about 10^{-5}; for a field of 10^5 V m^{-1}, the ratio is about 8. Drops of 1-mm radius, fully charged, give a ratio of approximately 10^{-1} in a 10^5 V m^{-1} field. Consequently, in large electrical fields, charged particles can deviate substantially from movement with the airflow. These last two terms are explicit forms for P_I and P_i given in Eqs. 15.13 and 15.14.

The fallout terms are always significant in the simulation of the rain and hail fields. They most often lead to loading of the updraft and the eventual formation of a downdraft (see Orville et al., 1975).

See Orville and Kopp (1977) and Wisner et al. (1972) for the derivation of the production terms P_R and P_I. Various processes simulated by these terms include accretion of cloud water by rain and hail and of rain by hail, the freezing of rain (Bigg, 1953), the freezing of cloud water and subsequent riming to form hail, the freezing of cloud water to form cloud ice, the wet and dry growth of hail (Musil, 1970), the shedding of cloud water and rain by hail, evaporation and sublimation, and the melting of hail. These interactions are illustrated in Fig. 15.8.

d. Thermodynamic Energy Equation

Various thermodynamic energy equations appropriate to convection may be derived from the first law of thermodynamics, Eq. 15.8. The major diabatic-heating term Q is associated with changes of phase of water. Some cloud modelers choose to separate the water vapor, cloud water, and temperature fields in model calculations (Soong and Ogura, 1973; Murray, 1970). Others treat these fields with equa-

tions for entropy (involving temperature or potential temperature and water vapor) and for total water (vapor, liquid, and ice) as first suggested by Ogura (1963). Orville and Kopp (1977) use Ogura's method as modified for vapor effects on density (Orville, 1965) and extended to ice processes.

The thermodynamics of the Orville and Kopp model treat the processes of expansional cooling (dry adiabatic ascent) or its inverse (compressional heating); nonlinear advection of heat in both air and the particulates; turbulent mixing; and various cloud microphysical changes involved in freezing or melting, evaporation or condensation, and deposition or sublimation.

Instantaneous, isobaric freezing of the cloud water to cloud ice is assumed to occur at about $-35°C$. The temperature change caused by this freezing follows Saunders's methods (1957); also see Orville and Hubbard (1973).

e. Cloud Electrification

Chapter 13 gives basic information on cloud electrification. The electrification of clouds to breakdown potential gradients is a unique feature of cumulonimbus clouds. Some success has been achieved in simulating the electrical-charging processes in cloud models. In addition to the bracketed terms in Eqs. 15.51 and 15.62, the equations needed to add electrical effects to cloud models are equations for free ions and for the charge on cloud and precipitation particles. Pringle et al. (1973), Takahashi (1974, 1978), and Chiu and Klett (1976) presented early results. The work by Chiu (1978) is summarized here for an all-liquid cloud. The thrust of modeling effort is to understand the various charging processes that have been proposed and to identify the most important ones. Polarization or inductive charging (a gravitational process) and convective charging mechanisms are the main theories being tested here. Inductive and noninductive processes involving the ice phase have been studied by Tzur and Levin (1981) and Kuettner et al. (1981). A survey paper on the electrification of thunderstorms by Lathan (1981) is particularly pertinent.

The continuity (conservation) equations for charge (for an all-liquid process only) are

$$\frac{\partial n_{1,2}}{\partial t} = - \nabla \cdot (n_{1,2} \mathbf{V} \pm n_{1,2} \mu_{1,2} \mathbf{E} - K \nabla n_{1,2})$$

$$+ G - \alpha n_1 n_2 - \left(\frac{\partial n_{1,2}}{\partial t}\right)_c - \left(\frac{\partial n_{1,2}}{\partial t}\right)_R, \quad (15.66)$$

$$\frac{\partial Q_c}{\partial t} = - \nabla \cdot (Q_c \mathbf{V} + Q_c \mathbf{V}_c - K \nabla Q_c)$$

$$+ e \left[\left(\frac{\partial n_1}{\partial t}\right)_c - \left(\frac{\partial n_2}{\partial t}\right)_c \right]$$

$$- \left(\frac{\partial Q_c}{\partial t}\right)_{coalescence} - \left(\frac{\partial Q}{\partial t}\right)_{polarization}, \quad (15.67)$$

and

$$\frac{\partial Q_R}{\partial t} = - \nabla \cdot (Q_R \mathbf{V} + Q_R \mathbf{V}_R - K \nabla Q_R)$$

$$+ e\left[\left(\frac{\partial n_1}{\partial t}\right)_R - \left(\frac{\partial n_2}{\partial t}\right)_R\right]$$

$$+ \left(\frac{\partial Q_c}{\partial t}\right)_{\text{coalescence}} + \left(\frac{\partial Q}{\partial t}\right)_{\text{polarization}}, \quad (15.68)$$

where μ_1 (μ_2) is the mobility of small positive (negative) ions n_1 (n_2), G is the rate of ion formation by cosmic rays, α is the ionic recombination coefficient ($\alpha = 1.6 \times 10^{-12}$ m^3 s^{-1}), e is the elementary electric charge, and $\mathbf{E}$ is the electric field. The values of μ_1, μ_2, and G are specified as functions of height. The subscripts 1 and 2 refer to positive and negative ions.

In Eq. 15.66 the current densities for the macroscopic transport of ions are made up of contributions from convection ($n_{1,2}\mathbf{V}$), electrical conduction ($\pm n_{1,2} \mu_{1,2} \mathbf{E}$), and turbulent diffusion ($-K \nabla n_{1,2}$). The term $\mu \mathbf{E}$ is the drift velocity of small ions. Besides these transport terms ions are assumed to be generated by cosmic-ray ionization at various heights (G). The rate of ion loss is controlled by ionic recombination between ions of opposite polarities and also by ion attachments to cloud droplets and raindrops with the rates of $(\partial n_{1,2}/\partial t)_c$ and $(\partial n_{1,2}/\partial t)_R$, respectively. Evaporation of the water particles releases ions back to the atmosphere.

In Eqs. 15.67 and 15.68 the cloud water and rainwater charge densities, i.e., the charges Q_c and Q_R on the cloud and rainwater contents, are transported by air convection, their terminal velocities relative to air, and turbulent diffusion, in keeping with the water substance equations described previously. Both cloud droplets and raindrops can obtain electrical charge through ion attachment. (Droplet and drop sizes [diameters] are taken as the average size particle in the raindrop distribution and as a function of the number of droplets and cloud water content for the cloud droplets. The number of drops is obtained from the average size and the appropriate rain content. The number of droplets is 100, 300, or 500 cm^{-3}, depending on the case.) More important, the cloud and rain particles can also be electrified and charged because of the "polarization charging mechanism" when particles in an electric field collide with each other and then separate. This effect is represented by $(\partial Q/\partial t)_{\text{polarization}}$ in Eqs. 15.67 and 15.68. However, most of the cloud droplets colliding with raindrops result in coalescence. The process of coalescence results in a partial transfer of the charge density related to the cloud water to the charge density associated with the rainwater, according to the number of cloud droplets coalescing with raindrops. This effect is denoted by $(\partial Q_c/\partial t)_{\text{coalescence}}$. The total charge on the cloud or rain mixing ratios is the net charge on the average-sized particle multiplied by the number of such particles. Figure 15.11 illustrates some of these processes.

The electric field is determined from

$$\nabla^2 \phi_e = -\frac{\rho_e}{\varepsilon_0} \quad \text{and} \quad \mathbf{E} = -\nabla\phi_e, \quad (15.69)$$

with ϕ the electrical potential, ε_0 the permittivity of air (about 8.859×10^{-12} F m^{-1}), and with the total space charge density given by

$$\rho_e = e(n_1 - n_2) + Q_c + Q_R \ (\text{C} \ m^{-3}), \quad (15.70)$$

where e is the elementary electrical charge.

The electrical field $\mathbf{E}$ as given by Eq. 15.69 results in a different sign convention from that discussed in Chap. 13. Consequently, when comparing electric fields in Fig. 15.11 (and 15.18) with the electric field in Chap. 13, Fig. 13.3, remember to reverse the sign of the field in one of the figures.

The treatment of ionic attachment to the cloud and rain particles is explained by Chiu (1978). In addition, the simulation of the polarization charging mechanism is described in that paper. Electrical effects also influence certain cloud microphysical processes, such as coalescence, and can be tested in numerical models.

f. Boundary and Initial Conditions and Numerical Techniques

In the Orville and Kopp (1977) model the top boundary is rigid, with all variables temporally constant. At the side boundaries the horizontal gradients are set equal to zero. At the lower boundary the vorticity and stream function are zero at all times. Evaporation and heating rates at the surface are specified, and the water vapor and heat are diffused into the lowest grid points, located 10 m above the surface. This diffusion induces changes in the entropy and water vapor fields (Orville, 1965). These changes at the lower boundary are then advected and diffused into the surrounding grid points, eventually leading to thermals and ultimately clouds if the initial atmospheric sounding is sufficiently unstable and moist. Cloud shadow effects on the surface heating rate are simulated as described by Liu and Orville (1969).

Rawinsonde data are used as initial conditions for temperature, humidity, and pressure heights. In addition, the horizontal wind in the direction of motion of the storm is used in a modified form. The speeds are reduced to allow the storms to remain in the domain of integration longer and to compensate for the exaggerated effect of vertical wind shear in 2-D models. This effect refers to the fact that 2-D models do not allow airflow around the middle levels of an active convective cloud but tend to inhibit convection that protrudes into regions of high wind shear. Normally the windspeeds projected onto the 2-D "storm motion" plane are taken to be 20% of the observed values. When needed, the initial atmospheric electrical conditions are assumed to be fair-weather values.

The equations of the model are solved over a 20-km by 20-km domain with a 200-m grid interval in both the x and z directions. Crowley-Leith advection techniques are used (Crowley, 1968). Following Marchuk and Leith (see Haltiner, 1971, p. 210), a two-step advection scheme is used—the horizontal advection is calculated first, the vertical advection second. The scheme is of first-order accuracy in time, second-order in space. Direct methods (Rognlie and

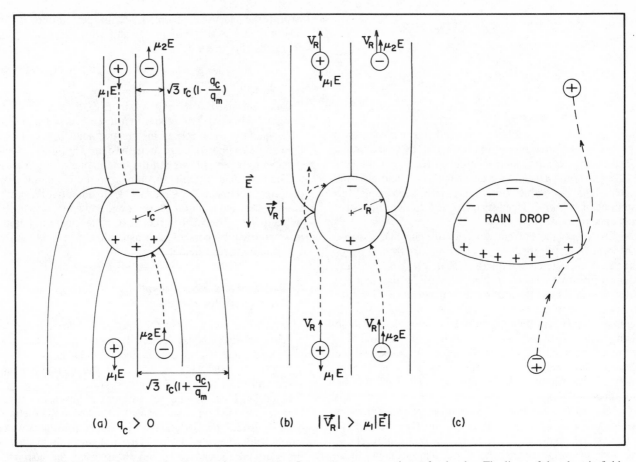

Figure 15.11. (a) Schematic of an ion attachment process. Ion capture cross sections of a droplet. The lines of the electric field around the droplet of radius r_c polarized in an electric field **E** show the radii of the ion capture cross sections of the droplet when it carries a positive net charge. $+$ and $-$ denote certain positive and negative ions that exist at either side of the droplet where the electric field remains uniformly distributed. Dotted lines are the paths of ions that may be attached to the droplet. Short vectors attached to the ions represent the direction of the drift velocity of the ions. (b) Drop of radius r_R has a terminal velocity $\mathbf{V}_R$ with respect to its environment. The directions of $\mathbf{V}_R$ and **E** coincide. The velocity of the ion caused by either airflow or electrical attraction is denoted in vector notation in the uniform electric field region at both sides of the drop. (c) A schematic of the polarization charging mechanism. A small droplet in an electric field (directed as in [a] and [b]) collides with a raindrop and separates, leaving a net positive charge with the droplet, net negative charge with the drop.

Kopp, 1976) for an irregular grid domain are used to solve the Poisson-type equation for the stream function or electrical potential. The diffusion terms are represented in the standard fashion, substituting the second-order approximation for the ∇^2 term and the nonlinear values for K. The precipitation fallout terms are calculated by expanding the flux form of the fallout term to three terms, averaging the coefficients, and differencing (of the form $\bar{V}_t[\partial l_R/\partial z]$, where $\bar{V}_t$ is the average terminal velocity [positive] of the precipitation mass). Tests of the model using 50-m and 100-m grid intervals have been reported elsewhere (Orville, 1968; Orville and Sloan, 1969).

g. Simulation of a Severe Storm

The 2-D model discussed above was initialized with the temperature and dewpoint sounding shown in Fig. 15.12. In this simulation, electrical effects were neglected. Figures 15.13–15.15 illustrate many features of severe storms described in other chapters of this book. Figure 15.13a–h shows the airflow, cloud outline, rain, and hail fields (more than 1 g of precipitation per kilogram of air) of the model storm at 3-min intervals (from 99 to 120 min of simulation time). Integrations were started with a weak flow from right to left in the lower atmosphere, with a slightly stronger flow from left to right in the upper atmosphere. Clouds began forming after about 45 min of heating and evaporation at the Earth's surface. The more organized phase of the storm is represented by the panels in Fig. 15.13.

The common features of the observations and the numerical simulation are the sloping updraft, the diverging flow at the tropopause (Fig. 15.13g in particular), the recycling of hail caused by the diverging flow aloft and the sloping updraft (Figs. 15.13b–d), the pedestal and shelf clouds, the gust front and its movement across the domain (Figs. 15.13a–e), the classic two-cell, severe-storm circulation in the early stages (Fig. 15.13a), and the precipitation cascade and radar overhang (Fig. 15.14b, c).

The movement of the gust front out of the domain at about 113 min signifies the start of the dissipation stage of the storm. Loss of moisture from the lower levels cuts off the energy supply for this model storm. Maximum rain and hail accumulations of 3.0 cm and 2.7 cm occur.

The vertical-velocity panels (Fig. 15.15) show bubbles of updraft maxima. The accelerating updrafts, associated with warm buoyant regions in the model atmosphere, lead to cellular patterns. The larger storm circulation has superimposed on it smaller perturbations that travel up the main sloping updraft and intensify the storm periodically (Fig. 15.15b, d shows maximum speeds). Doppler radar observations have shown this same feature (Battan, 1975).

The features not in agreement with some observations are the strong airflow from behind the gust front (Fig. 13b–d) and the lack of a bounded, weak-echo region in the simulation. The microphysical simplifications for the rain field may be the reason for this last discrepancy. Even small amounts of rain (0.1 g kg^{-1} or less) in the Marshall-Palmer type size distributions have some large particles, so that mass-weighted mean terminal velocities of 1 m s^{-1} or more exist. This allows fallout into the weak-updraft regions and rapid filling in of an echo-weak region.

h. Atmospheric Electricity Effects

Equations similar to Eqs. 15.51–15.70, but without ice processes, were solved by Chiu (1978) in an axisymmetric (radial-height) domain to test the simulation of atmospheric-electricity processes. A sample of the results for the rain water content total charge density, and electric field are shown in Figs. 15.16–15.18.

Figure 15.16 shows the cloud outline and the contoured rain content field at the most active growth period of the model cloud. Only portions of the domain are shown to save space. The cylindrical domain is 12.8 km high with a radius of 6.4 km. The shape of the cloud, with its persistent flat base, is a realistic feature of the axisymmetric type models. Updrafts of 20 m s^{-1} and downdrafts of 5 m s^{-1} occur.

The total charge density field is shown in Fig. 15.17. The classic dipole structure is seen in the 14- and 18-min panels, with negative charges low and positive charges high in the cloud. At 22 min, a positive-charge center shows up at cloud base, a feature sometimes observed in thunderstorms. The total charge density increases by three orders of magnitude from 14 min to 30 min. According to the numerical results, the electrical structure of the cloud depends on the stage of cloud and rain development.

The development of the vertical electric field is shown in Fig. 15.18. The contour interval changes during the development. The maximum field strength in the cloud occurs at 30 min, when a value of 1.2×10^4 V (volt) m^{-1} is present.

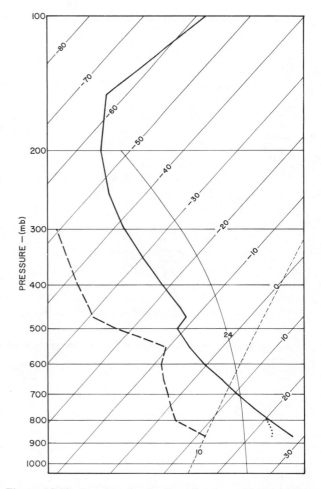

Figure 15.12. Sounding for Sterling, Colo., on 21 June 1972. Dashed and solid lines sloping upward to the left are dew point and temperature observed and used to initialize the numerical model, except that the dotted branch of the temperature plot represents temperatures actually observed in the boundary layer. The 24°C curve of wet-bulb potential temperature and 10 g/kg curve of saturation water vapor mixing ratio are also shown.

The radial electric field has similar values. This is 100 times stronger than the fair-weather potential of 100 V m^{-1} but is still short of lightning potential (10^5 to 10^6 V m^{-1}). However, higher fields should be possible when the ice processes are included in a severe-storm simulation, as discussed in the previous subsection. At 14 min the vertical electric field is downward (negative) throughout the whole cloud. During the active-growth period of the cloud the central electric field between the two main charge centers remains downward with increasing magnitude, while the electrical field in the lower and upper parts of the cloud changes its direction from downward to upward with increasing magnitude. This variation of structure is consistent with the charge centers shown in Fig. 15.17.

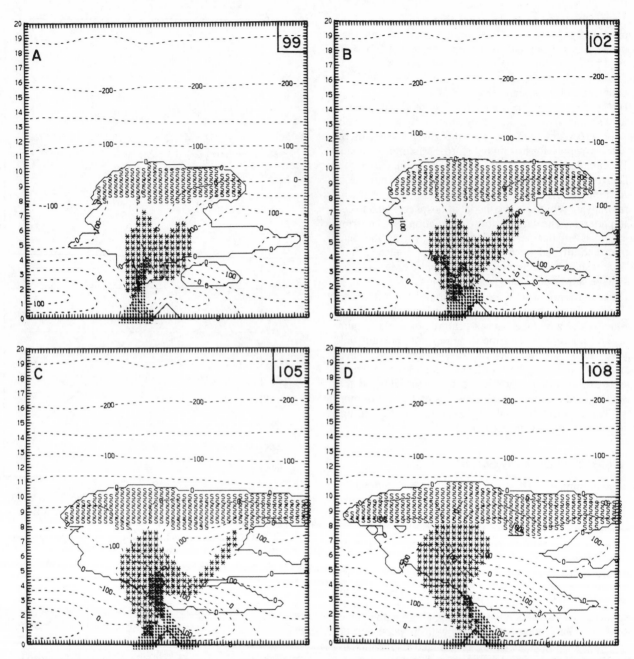

Figure 15.13. Numerical simulation of cloud and precipitation evolution in a vertical cross section of the atmosphere, 20 km on a side. A mountain ridge 1 km high is centered on the lower boundary. Cloud area (100% relative humidity) is outlined by the solid lines; the stream function illustrates the airflow and is given by the dashed lines (contour interval $5 \times 10^3 \, \text{kg m}^{-1} \, \text{s}^{-1}$ except in (F) and (H), where the interval is $1 \times 10^4 \, \text{kg m}^{-1} \, \text{s}^{-1}$). The symbols · and * denote rainwater and graupel or hail contents greater than $1 \, \text{g kg}^{-1}$, respectively, and the S denotes cloud ice regions. (A) is for 99 min of simulated real time; the other figures follow at 3-min intervals, the last being for 120 min. The arrow on the lower border denotes the gust front. Major tick marks are 1 km apart.

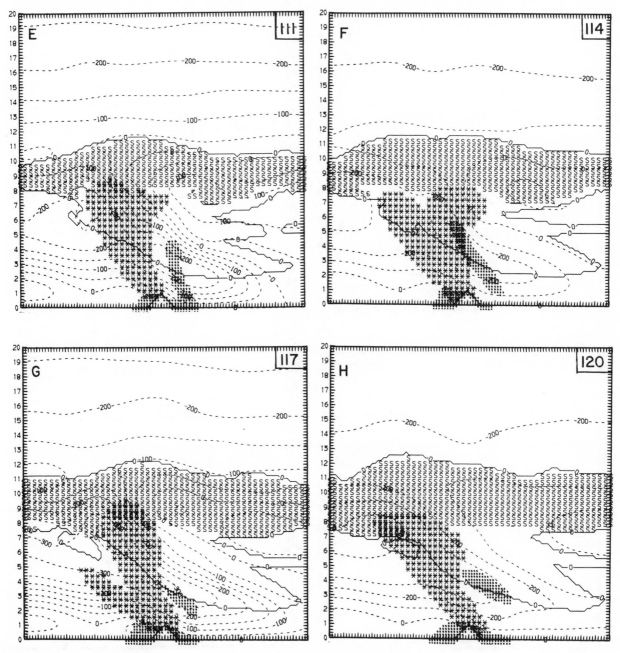

Figure 15.13. *Continued.*

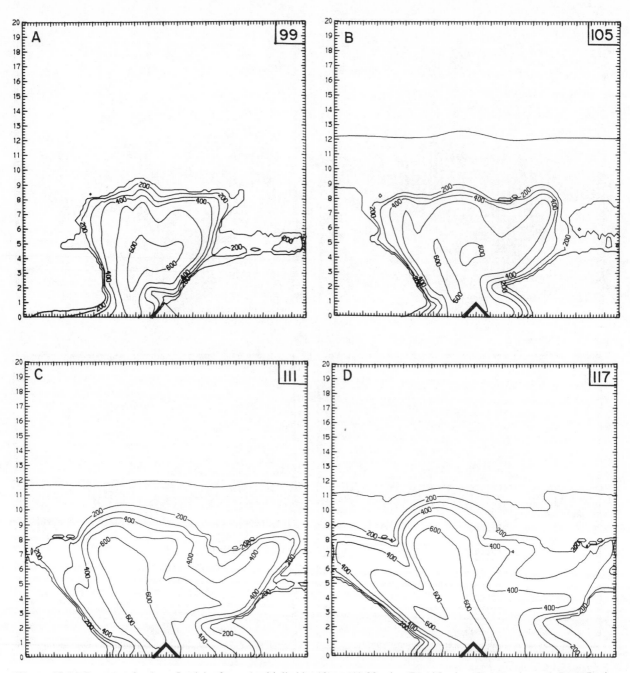

Figure 15.14. Patterns of radar reflectivity factor (multiplied by 10) at (A) 99 min, (B) 105 min, (C) 111 min, and (D) 117 min. The contours are for every 10 dBz starting at 10 dBz.

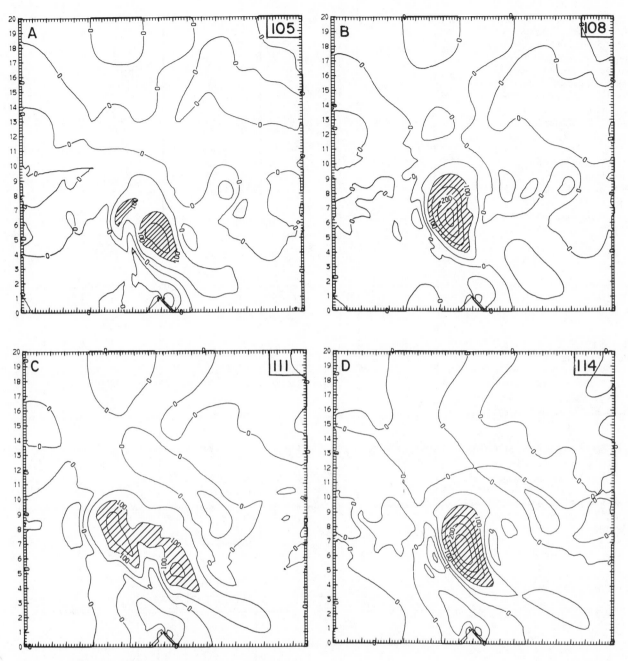

Figure 15.15. The fields of vertical velocity (multiplied by 10) at (A) 105 min; (B) 108 min; (C) 111 min; (D) 114 min. Contour interval is 5 m s^{-1}; values greater than 10 m s^{-1} are shaded.

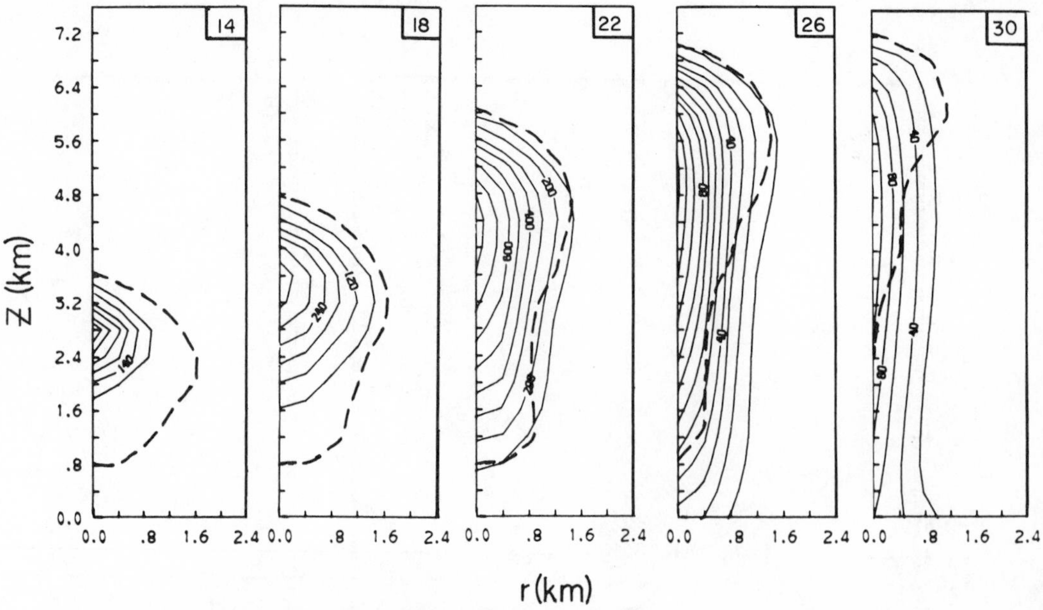

Figure 15.16. The rain content and cloud outline (dashed line) as predicted in an axisymmetric cloud model. At time = 14 min the contour interval Δ is 0.1 g kg^{-1} with a maximum value of 0.63 g kg^{-1}; at $t = 18$ the interval is 0.6 g kg^{-1}, maximum value 4.2 g kg^{-1}; at $t = 22$, $\Delta = 1$ g kg^{-1}, maximum value = 8.6 g kg^{-1}; at $t = 26$, $\Delta = 1$ g kg^{-1}, maximum value = 11.5 g kg^{-1}; at $t = 30$, $\Delta = 1$ g kg^{-1}, maximum value = 12.0 g kg^{-1}.

Figure 15.17. The total electrical charge density. At $t = 14$ min, the contour interval Δ is 10^{-13} C m^{-3}, range is -5×10^{-13} to 4×10^{-13}; at $t = 18$, $\Delta = 10^{-12}$ C m^{-3}, range -5×10^{-12} to 3×10^{-12} C m^{-3}; at $t = 22$, $\Delta = 10^{-11}$ C m^{-3}, range -5×10^{-11} to 2×10^{-11} C m^{-3}; at $t = 26$, $\Delta = 8 \times 10^{-11}$ C m^{-3}, range -2.4×10^{-10} to 1.6×10^{-10} C m^{-3}; at $t = 30$, $\Delta = 10^{-10}$ C m^{-3}, range -5×10^{-10} to 4×10^{-10} C m^{-3}.

Figure 15.18. The evolution of the vertical electric field in the axisymmetric cloud model. At $t = 14$, $\Delta = 10$ V m^{-1}, E_z max $= 1 \times 10^2$ V m^{-1}; at $t = 18$, $\Delta = 40$ V m^{-1}, E_z max $= 2.4 \times 10^2$ V m^{-1}; at $t = 22$, $\Delta = 400$ V m^{-1}, E_z max $= 1.6 \times 10^3$ V m^{-1}; at $t = 26$, $\Delta = 1,000$ V m^{-1}, E_z max $= 6.6 \times 10^3$ V m^{-1}; at $t = 30$, $\Delta = 3,000$ V m^{-1}, E_z max $= 1.2 \times 10^4$ V m^{-1}.

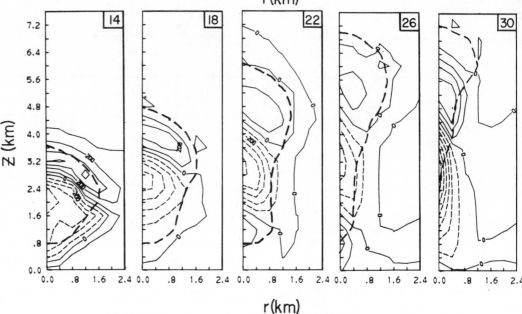

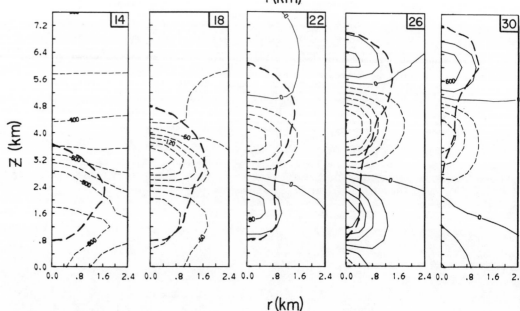

i. Three-Dimensional Modeling Results

Severe storms are basically 3-D in nature. The rotation of the "parent" severe storm is evident in many observations and leads at times to the production of tornadoes. The occurrence of very large hail may require a longer time in the supercooled regions of the cloud than is afforded by the recycling of hailstones in 2-D models. The movements of the storms to the right or left of the winds can be captured only by 3-D storm simulations. The reaction of the storm to the environmental winds with strong vertical shear needs to be understood for accurate forecasting. Consequently, efforts in 3-D modeling of severe storms are an important, vital part of the present numerical modeling effort. Further, they are needed to aid in understanding how the large vertical vorticity associated with tornadoes is generated.

Several 3-D models have appeared in the last few years (e.g., Miller, 1974; Wilhelmson, 1974; Schlesinger, 1975; Moncrieff and Miller, 1976; Schlesinger, 1977; Klemp and Wilhelmson, 1978a; Clark, 1979). These simulations reproduce many of the dynamical features of severe storms. Schlesinger's model uses an anelastic set of equations; Klemp and Wilhelmson employ a compressible set of equations of motion. The latter form allows the pressure to be predicted, eliminating the need to invert an elliptic equation to solve for pressure. The results from either set of equations are essentially identical because the presence of sound waves in the compressible models is of negligible importance energetically.

The model of Klemp and Wilhelmson (1978a) has several unique features, including a time-splitting technique used to reduce computer time in solving the fully compressible equations. Fourth-order spatial derivatives are used for the horizontal advection terms to reduce phase errors associated with a horizontal grid interval that is larger than the vertical one. The turbulence parameterization includes the computation of turbulence energy using the local buoyancy, shear, and dissipation rates, and first-order closure using nearly conservative variables. Lateral boundary conditions are treated with care, and a method that minimizes gravity wave reflections is used. Open boundaries are used to provide appropriate fluxes of moisture and momentum, which allows the reversal of flow at the boundaries as occurs in the 2-D model results reported above. Further, the horizontal flow at the lateral boundaries is quite similar to that from simulations using a larger horizontal domain in two dimensions.

These models have been used to simulate splitting storms. Such storms can occur when sufficient vertical environmental wind shear exists. The splitting process is illustrated by Klemp and Wilhelmson (1978b) in Fig. 15.19, where rainwater contours at the 2.25-km level are shown at 30-min intervals for a simulation that was initialized with a one-directional wind shear. The initial rainwater (and storm) is elongated in time and eventually splits. By 90 min both split storms have developed self-sustaining supercell-like structures. This structure can be inferred from the superimposed plots of horizontal wind vectors, vertical velocities, and rainwater boundaries in Fig. 15.20. The horizontal wind

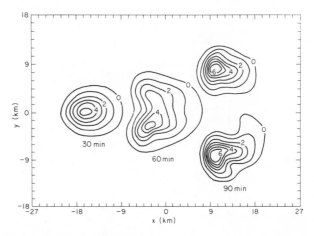

Figure 15.19. Horizontal cross section of rainwater contours at 0.5-h intervals at $z = 2.25$ km. Labeled contours are in units of g kg^{-1}.

vectors are not quite relative to storm motion, since the storms are moving laterally apart at about 5 m s^{-1}. For the right-moving (southern) storm, moisture is supplied through low-level inflow from the east (Fig. 15.20a) and is carried upward through a cyclonically rotating updraft (Figs. 15.20b and c). In the upper part of the storm, outflow from the updraft is swept downstream to the east, producing a pair of merging anvils (Fig. 15.20d) as occasionally observed in split storms (e.g., Fujita and Grandoso, 1968). Although the undisturbed flow is in the E–W plane, the right-moving storm induces a flow at middle levels that passes around the east side of the updraft from the south and feeds into the downdraft located on the north side of the updraft (Fig. 15.20b), as suggested by Browning (1964) from observational analysis. In addition, the downdraft observed in Fig. 15.20b is supplied by flow from the west that develops anticyclonic rotation. The downdraft then spreads out just above the ground to the south and west underneath the updraft, and a gust front is formed (Fig. 15.20a). How this gust front spreads out is important to the continued existence of the storm in that low-level convergence (caused by environmental wind from the east approaching the gust front) must not move away from the storm toward the east.

The left-moving (northern) storm is almost a mirror image of the right-moving one, differing from it only because of Coriolis effects. If the environmental wind-shear vector changes direction with height, one of the two storms will be enhanced while the other is suppressed. Specifically, an environmental wind hodograph that turns clockwise (counterclockwise) with height at low and midlevels favors the selective development of the right- (left-) moving storm. The frequently observed clockwise turning of the environmental wind shear may explain why two self-sustaining split storms are not common and why right-moving, cyclonic supercells predominate (Klemp and Wilhelmson, 1978b).

In Fig. 15.21, W–E vertical cross sections pass through the point of maximum updraft velocity in the right-moving

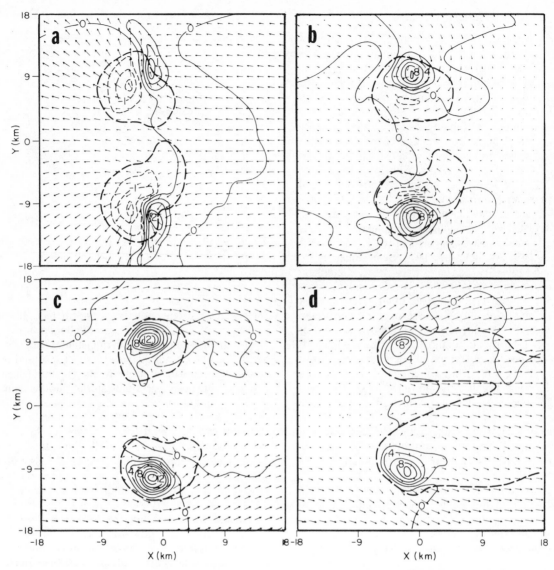

Figure 15.20. Horizontal vector plots with vertical velocity field superimposed in meters per second at 90 min. The right-moving cell is the southern cell. (a) $z = 0.25$ km; (b) $z = 2.25$ km; (c) $z = 3.75$ km; (d) $z = 5.75$ km. Solid line denotes updraft; thin dashed line is downdraft. Heavy dashed line marks the outer boundary of the rainwater field in (a)–(c); in (d) it encloses the cloud-water field.

storm (corresponding to the maximum w in Fig. 15.20c). The vector plot in Fig. 15.21a coupled with Fig. 15.20 reveals that the southern updraft tilts upstream to the west and north with height; at lower levels the rain falls into the downdraft to the north and west of the updraft. An apparent weak-echo region and vault occurs between 0 and 2 km, with the rain field overhanging to the east and south. A hook structure also occurs in the rainwater field (see Fig. 15.19) in this region, apparently caused by a value of the vertical component of vorticity of up to 1.1×10^{-2} s^{-1} in the region.

Schlesinger (1977, p. 261) has also simulated some split-

ting storms and notes the following in these simulations:

1. The updraft column as a whole resists rather than yields to the ambient shear;
2. The cold, moist low-level downdraft is located upshear of the updraft;
3. The respective right and left flanks, looking down the direction of storm motion, show strong cyclonic and anticyclonic vorticity through most of the cloud depth;
4. The storm gradually splits into a slow, right-moving cyclonic cell and a fast, left-moving anticyclonic cell, with the former tending to dominate the latter;
5. Relative to the storm motion, mid-tropospheric airflow is di-

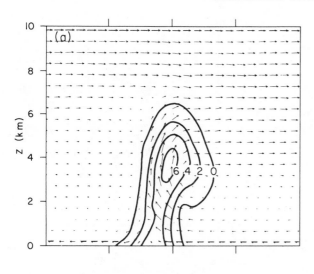
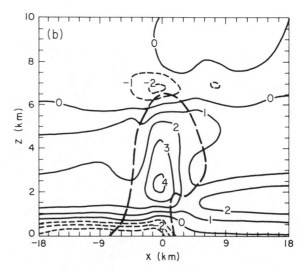

Figure 15.21. W–E cross sections at 90 min taken through the position of maximum updraft velocity in the right-moving storm. (a) Vector plot with rainwater contours superimposed and labeled in units of g kg^{-1}. (b) Perturbation potential temperature in °C. Heavy dashed line is the rainwater boundary.

verted around the storm core, much like potential flow around a cyclindrical obstacle.

More recent 3-D cloud-model simulations have further improved the understanding of the internal structure of supercell storms (Schlesinger, 1980; Klemp et al., 1981). Simulation of a tornadic storm observed near Del City, Okla., on 20 May 1977 suggests that the overall structure of a particular observed supercell storm can be reproduced in a numerical model, using a representative nearby environmental sounding (Klemp et al., 1981). Figure 15.22 illustrates the low- and midlevel structures of the simulated supercell and the observed storm during its mature (1833 CST) and tornadic (1847 CST) phases. Analyses of the model and observational data reveal that the strong low-level cyclonic vorticity is located between the updraft and downdraft and is produced through vertical tilting of horizontal vorticity followed by intense vortex stretching in the low-level inflow.

In its tornadic phase the storm develops finer-scale structure which cannot be resolved with the 1-km horizontal grid in the model. By nesting a higher-resolution (250-m) simulation within the central portion of the storm (denoted by the box in Fig. 15.22a), Klemp and Rotunno (1983) were able to resolve many of the smaller-scale features of the tornadic storm. Figure 15.23 displays a schematic of the low-level flow field which combines the model data from the coarse- and fine-resolution simulations. The observed gust-front occlusion near the center of the mesocyclone is clearly resolved in the simulation. Their analyses indicate that this occlusion is dynamically induced by the strong low-level rotation.

Other recent modeling studies have emphasized the role of mesoscale lifting in supporting convective storms. Trip-

oli and Cotton (1980) simulated thunderstorm development on 17 July 1973 over southern Florida's FACE (Florida Area Cumulus Experiment) area in weak-to-moderate shear (Fig. 15.24). All runs included a central low-level humidity impulse initially. The first run, A, with no initial lifting, produced a vigorous but short-lived single cell, as strong organized entrainment eroded the cloud from the base rapidly upward. Full-area low-level mesoscale ascent w_m was added in the other cases—strongest at the center and trailing off outward in bell-shaped distributions. Runs B and C assumed equal area-averaged w_m profiles but a higher and narrower central peak in C than in B. Cases D and E were like B but with w_m doubled in D and multiplied by 3.5 in E. Case B produced a considerably longer-lived storm than case A, though still falling short of being quasi-steady; B produced a much "firmer" cloud base and nearly three times as much rainfall after 60 min, also generating a transient secondary updraft southeast of the primary one. Storm C was slightly stronger, "wetter," and more persistent than B, although without the secondary updraft. The more intense initial mesoscale lifting in D and E resulted in yet more intense and "wet" counterparts of storm C; a sharper low-level convergence line formed, roughly perpendicular to the updraft inflow, in D and E, with an excessively wide main cloud in E. Time plots showing the increase in cumulative rainfall for each of cases A–E are shown. In simulating an 8 June 1974 supercell storm in central Oklahoma, Schlesinger (1982) found that specification of mesoscale lifting was required to sustain a long-lived storm.

The biggest weaknesses in 3-D models at present are their lack of spatial resolution and their treatment of precipitation processes. Both frailties can be traced to the limitations of computer power: speed and core storage. Grid intervals of 1 km in the horizontal and 0.5 km in the vertical are used

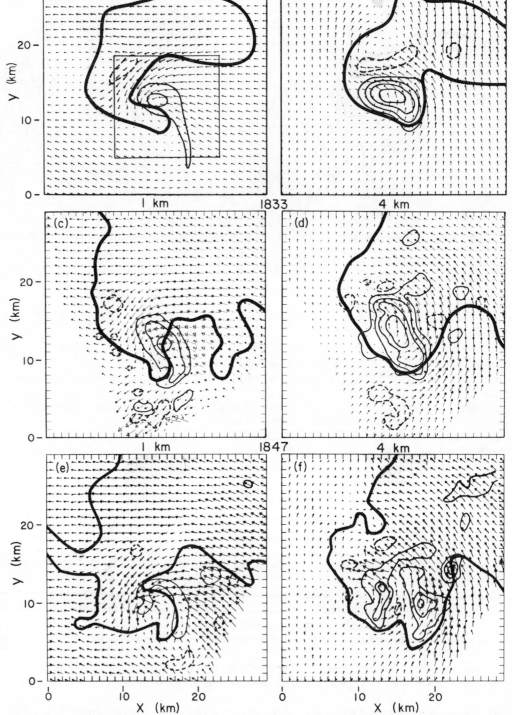

Figure 15.22. (a) and (b) Horizontal cross sections of a model supercell storm 1 km and 4 km above the ground after 2 hours of numerical integration. (c) and (d) Cross sections through storm of 20 May 1977 during its mature stage, as defined by Doppler radar. (e) and (f) Observed cross section through storm of 20 May 1977 during its tornadic phase (Klemp et al., 1981).

for supercell simulations by Klemp and Wilhelmson (1978a) and Klemp et al. (1981), slightly larger ones by Schlesinger (1977, 1982). The domains are 30 to 50 km wide and 10 to 16 km deep. Only cloud liquid and rain processes are treated in both models. The distribution of water substances within a storm influences the circulation in some important ways, through loading, melting of ice, and evaporation of rain and hail, and will require simulation eventually.

Future research in numerical simulation of severe storms will need to define those situations that can be handled most expeditiously by 1-, 2-, or 3-D models. Currently it appears that precipitation initiation and cloud-top predictions are treated appropriately in many cases with 1-D models, that better precipitation simulations are possible with 2-D models, and that the rotation of storms, the development of intense vortices, and the intricate interaction among 3-D flow fields and precipitation can be handled only with the 3-D models.

j. Future of Thunderstorm Modeling

Although exciting results are emerging in the numerical simulations of thunderstorms, much work remains to be done to make the models useful tools in the study and forecasting of severe storms. Boundary conditions are difficult and perplexing problems in these thunderstorm models. Periodic or constant boundary conditions, although neat mathematically, are too restrictive physically. A severe storm draws upon air from the lower boundary layer many tens of kilometers from the storm's primary updraft. Constant boundary conditions cause the return flow to the storm to be cycled from within the domain. This return flow usually consists of dry air that when ingested into the storm causes its demise. Open boundary conditions or conditions slowly varying at large distances from the storm center may suffice, but more study is needed.

The initial conditions from rawinsonde data may not be representative of the time-dependent environment of the storm. Although a time-dependent surface layer has been simulated in cloud models (Orville and Kopp, 1977) the thunderstorms themselves modify the mesoscale structure of the environment, as do synoptic-scale processes. Mesoscale models may provide the necessary changing boundary and initial conditions needed for the cloud scale models.

Representation of microphysical processes can be as complex as our imagination allows; some form of parameterization is required for the models to be integrated in a reasonable amount of computer time. Improved, time-varying size distribution functions for precipitation would probably help in the prediction of rain and hail development and the appearance of echo-weak regions with realistic patterns of radar reflectivity factors.

The potential uses of thunderstorm and cloud scale numerical models are many. Of greatest importance would be the development of forecast models that would not take an inordinate amount of computer time but would be helpful in predicting the amount of rain or hail and the occurrence of high winds or even tornadoes. A major problem is in ini-

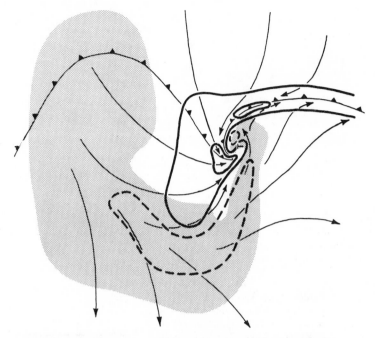

Figure 15.23. Schematic low-level flow field from a composite of the $z = 250$ m fields at 120 min in a storm-scale simulation and at 6 min in a finer-scale resolution simulation. Vertical velocity is contoured approximately at 2 m s^{-1} intervals with the zero line omitted, and the $-1°$C isotherm is denoted by the cold frontal boundary. Flow arrows represent storm relative surface streamlines, and the region in which rainwater exceeds 0.5 g kg^{-1} is shaded. The location of maximum vertical vorticity is marked with a T. Note the storm-scale rear flank downdraft west of the updraft and the small-scale occlusion downdraft near the center of circulation (Klemp and Rotunno, 1983).

tializing the cloud scale models. Perhaps interfacing the cloud models with mesoscale models would provide adequate initialization. Quantitative prediction of convective-cloud characteristics and precipitation amounts and types could be made at selected points where mososcale models indicate atmospheric conditions favorable for severe storms. This approach is speculative, expensive, and not competitive with the statistical forecasts now provided by the National Weather Service and described in Vol. 1, Chap. 8. As computer time becomes less expensive and more computing power becomes available, the full numerical solutions may become more attractive.

There are other applications of the research into the simulation of severe storms. Evaluation of the effects of air pollution on the weather have been made in urban regions and near pulp mills. The variation in surface roughness from rural to city area and the different albedos of the underlying surfaces are easily simulated and the effects quantitatively assessed by cloud models.

The models are also useful in estimating the influence of power plants and cooling towers on weather processes. Heat sources of 10,000 to 50,000 MW have been proposed. The effects of this rate of heat addition on severe storms or local

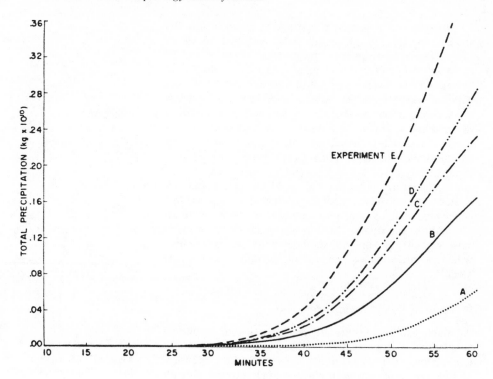

Figure 15.24. Variation of total precipitation fallen within integration domain versus time for numerical experiments A–E (Tripoli and Cotton, 1980).

precipitation have been hypothesized. Cloud scale models provide a means of gaining some insight into the atmospheric effects before unalterable commitments to construction of large power plants have been made.

Intentional weather modification projects are relying more and more on cloud models to help in the planning, operation, and evaluation phases of the research. The models offer insight into appropriate hypotheses regarding the effects of various seeding agents, such as silver iodide, dry ice, and powdered salt on the precipitation processes. Quantitative comparisons can be made of rain or hail amounts from seeded and unseeded model clouds and storms.

The above uses of numerical cloud models demand models that have been extensively tested and compared against observations. During this developmental and testing phase the model simulations themselves may be useful in suggesting hypotheses that can be tested against observations. Through this cooperative process a better understanding of the complicated circulations of many scales that constitute the thunderstorm should emerge.

4. Effect of Thunderstorms on the Larger-Scale Environment

The beginning of this chapter treats some of the fundamental properties of deep convection through some analytic models. These theories help sketch a basic outline of deep cumulus clouds. We saw how nonlinear effects and com-

plicated feedbacks between processes affecting cloud and precipitation development and the larger-scale dynamics combine to fill in the rough outline with intricate details. Although details undoubtedly vary from thunderstorm to thunderstorm, most storms probably contain these same processes in varying degrees. In this last section we visualize the importance of thunderstorms on their environment. Although many scales of the thunderstorm environment could be considered and the effect must vary considerably with scale, we concentrate on horizontal dimensions of several hundred kilometers and periods of about a day. On this space scale we imagine thunderstorms covering a small percent of the area, and we ask how the thunderstorms change the average temperature, moisture, and wind fields in their environment.

a. Qualitative Effects

Before considering the magnitude of changes produced by deep clouds in the average thermodynamic properties of their environment, it is worthwhile to construct a schematic model to illustrate qualitatively how various processes in thunderstorms modify their environment. A schematic 3-D model of a mature thunderstorm is depicted in Fig. 15.25. This model, which represents an extratropical, moderately severe storm, is based on previous models by Browning and Ludlum (1962), Newton (1963), and Fritsch (1975). The prevailing environmental winds show low-level southeasterly flow becoming westerly at high levels. This veering wind profile, which implies large-scale warm advection through the thermal wind relationship, is typical of many thunderstorm environments over North America and often occurs ahead of an upper-level trough.

For convenience we divide the thunderstorm circulation into two parts: the updraft in which condensation takes place and the downdraft in which evaporation occurs. Real thunderstorms, of course, may have multiple updrafts and downdrafts, but many can be described by the single pair drawn here. The updraft is fed by the inflowing branch of southeasterly low-level air and is typically a few degrees warmer than its environment. Above the freezing level, freezing of the liquid cloud and rain droplets begins. At the higher levels of the cloud, where temperatures typically decrease to below $-30°C$, the proportion of ice increases. Finally, the updraft encounters a stable layer (often the stratosphere), and the cloud fans outward downwind to form the characteristic ice anvil.

The downdraft in Fig. 15.25 is fed in part by dry middle-level air that approaches the cloud from the southwest (Newton, 1966). Part of this current is deflected around the storm, but part is incorporated into the cloud. This dry air has a low wet-bulb potential temperature; i.e., it is intrinsically cold. As precipitation falls into this air, it becomes sensibly colder than its environment and negatively buoyant. This air accelerates downward as long as enough precipitation falls into it to maintain evaporation. The relative humidity of this downdraft is less than 100%, and so rain drops evaporate and leave the downdraft cloud free.

As rain falls out of the cloud base, some evaporates in the layer of unsaturated air near the ground. The downdraft spreads horizontally upon hitting the ground, forming a gust front. The evaporation of rain into the subcloud layer next to the ground and the downward flow of air with low wet-bulb potential temperature produce a great stabilizing effect locally; temperature decreases of $10°-15°C$ are not uncommon. However, if the storm is moving, as indicated in Fig. 15.25, this stabilizing effect does not deter this particular storm—it is always moving into a fresh supply of moist, warm air. This point is important, because it illustrates how a stabilization may occur in the mean (area average) but not affect the intensity of the individual thunderstorms, at least temporarily.

In addition to the inflow at cloud base, we have also depicted a mean inflow (entrainment) of environmental air into the updraft. The entrainment concept was first postulated by Stommel (1947). Although it has been very difficult to establish entrainment rates in real thunderstorms, it is commonly believed that the rate of entrainment varies inversely with the horizontal diameter of the cloud. For example, Malkus and Williams (1963) indicated that the vertical mass flux, M, varies with radius R according to

$$\frac{1}{M}\frac{dM}{dz} = \frac{b}{R} \tag{15.71}$$

where

$$M = \pi R^2 \rho w, \tag{15.72}$$

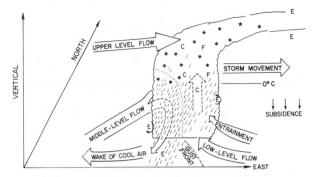

Figure 15.25. Schematic diagram of mature thunderstorm. *E*, *C*, and *F* denote evaporation, condensation, and freezing.

w is vertical velocity, and b is a positive constant. Cloud modelers have found good results for values of b ranging from 0.2 to 0.6 (Cotton, 1975). The increase of mass flux in the vertical requires a mean inflow of air into the cloud above cloud base, which has two main effects on the cloud. First, it dilutes the cloud with drier and usually cooler air, which reduces the bouyancy of the updraft. Second, the entrainment adds water vapor to the updraft. Thus, paradoxically, entrainment acts simultaneously to dry (in a relative sense) and moisten the updraft (by increasing the mass flux).

In addition to the organized entrainment of environmental air, horizontal mixing by small-scale eddies is continuously evaporating water drops from the cloud side. These eddies produce a cooling at the edge of the cloud and may lead to dissipation of small clouds.

With the above conceptual picture in mind, we are now prepared to discuss the energy transfers in the cumulus cloud and show their qualitative effect on the environment. First, there must be a net diabatic heating of the volume that is directly proportional to the precipitation reaching the ground. This should not be confused with a net increase of mean temperature, because the temperature changes depend on the horizontal and vertical motions as well as the diabatic heating (see Eq. 15.15). In this section heating and cooling refer to diabatic effects only (the Q in Eq. 15.15); they do not translate to sensible changes in temperature, which are caused by adiabatic processes as well. However, at any given level there may be either a net heating or cooling, depending on the vertical profiles of condensation, evaporation, freezing, and melting. Of these processes condensation and evaporation are the most important, because the latent heat of condensation is about 7.5 times larger than the latent heat of fusion.

The contribution of evaporation (*E*) and condensation (*C*) to the large-scale heat budget depends simply on the difference between *C* and *E* at any level. If $C > E$, a heating and drying of the environment at that level tends to be produced. Conversely, if $E > C$, there is a cooling and moistening tendency. Although the detailed vertical profiles of $C - E$ vary tremendously from cloud to cloud, positive values of $C - E$ are most likely in the upper troposphere (above the origin of the downdraft), and negative values are most likely in the lower levels of the cloud. Below the cloud base, of course, $C - E$ is always less than or equal to zero; it is here that this term often reaches its maximum negative value. This situation is favored for high cloud bases, low relative humidities near the surface, and strong vertical wind shear near the ground (which ventilates the rain shaft with dry air). These conditions often prevail over the Great Plains.

Thus we see that typical vertical distributions of $C - E$ in deep precipitating clouds tend to warm and dry the upper troposphere while cooling and moistening the lower troposphere. However, we emphasize again that the local changes in temperature and water vapor content depend on horizontal and vertical motions as well as these nonconservative processes, and so the actual environmental changes may be quite different. For example, if the adiabatic cooling owing to upward motion exceeds the diabatic heating owing to condensation, a net sensible decrease in temperature will result at that level. Furthermore, the vertical fluxes of moisture act in an opposite sense from the $C - E$ term, moistening the upper troposphere and drying the lower troposphere.

The above effects of condensation and evaporation, which tend to stabilize the environment, apply only to tall precipitating clouds. In contrast, shallow nonprecipitating clouds may actually destabilize the layers in which they occur if water that condenses in the lower part of the layer is carried upward and evaporates at the higher level. We are not considering this type of cloud in our discussion, however.

Freezing and melting heat levels at which freezing exceeds melting and extracts heat from levels at which the reverse is true. Because all the freezing occurs above the freezing level and all the melting occurs below the freezing level, the net effect must be a transfer of heat upward across the freezing level. This effect also stabilizes the environment, although it is usually minor compared with the effect of condensation and evaporation.

Finally, we consider the qualitative effects of the temperature and moisture of the updraft and rain-cooled downdraft compared with those of the environment. The updraft, being slightly warmer and considerably moister than the large-scale environment, transports heat and moisture upward. The downdraft is usually colder than its environment and so also transfers heat up. The downdraft, however, is also moister than its environment, so it transports moisture downward, opposing the effect of the updraft.

The net effect of the condensation-evaporation and freezing-melting processes and the vertical fluxes of heat and moisture is to heat and moisten the upper troposphere while cooling (or heating less) and drying the lower troposphere. This follows from the fact that the updraft portion of the cloud must dominate the cloud's structure in size and intensity when averaged over the lifetime of the cloud (Newton [1966] estimates that the mass flux in the downdraft of a typical thunderstorm is about 60% that of the updraft), and from the fact that a net overall heating and drying must occur if precipitation reaches the ground. These effects pertain to large-scale averages, not to local points in the vicinity of the individual clouds. Thus the net effect of thunderstorms is to transfer heat and moisture upward. This modification is reflected in a decrease of equivalent potential temperature in the low levels and an increase in the upper levels, as observed in the environment of tropical squall lines (Betts et al., 1976, their Fig. 3). As we shall see in the next section, these transports are large and give the thunderstorms an important role in the modification of the larger-scale environment.

On a global scale, upward transport of heat is compensated by downward transport in subsiding air and by radiation. The upward transport of moisture is compensated by precipitation and the downward transport in sinking air. The upward transport of energy by thunderstorms is the primary driving mechanism for the Hadley cell circulation in the tropics (Simpson, 1973), as well as tropical cyclones (Riehl and Malkus, 1961; Anthes, 1982).

b. Quantitative Effects

In this section we wish to estimate the order of magnitude of the effects of condensation, evaporation, freezing, and melting in thunderstorms on the heat and moisture structure of the environment. To quantitatively represent the effects, we begin with the thermodynamic equation and the continuity equation for water vapor, liquid and solid, and derive expressions for the temporal rates of change of the large-scale averages of these variables. These averages change as a result of the mean (large-scale) motions and the perturbation (cloud scale) motions. We neglect ordinary small-scale turbulence in this discussion.

(1) Derivation of Area-Averaged Equations: The effect of the cloud scale motions on a larger horizontal domain defined by $\Delta x \Delta y$ can be derived by considering the clouds as eddies superimposed on a slowly varying mean flow. The large-scale value of any variable α is defined by the horizontal averaging operator,

$$\bar{\alpha}(x, y) \equiv (\Delta x \Delta y)^{-1} \int_{x - \frac{\Delta x}{2}}^{x + \frac{\Delta x}{2}} \int_{y - \frac{\Delta y}{2}}^{y + \frac{\Delta y}{2}} \alpha \, dy \, dx, \qquad (15.73)$$

where Δx and Δy are the averaging intervals in the x and y directions. In numerical models, Δx and Δy are often taken to be the mesh size in the model. As defined by Eq. 15.73, $\bar{\alpha}$ is a "running mean" in space and varies continuously from point to point. We may now apply the averaging operator, Eq. 15.73, to the equations for the temporal rates of change of potential temperature and the three states of water, after separating each variable into a mean and perturbation part according to

$$\alpha = \bar{\alpha} + \alpha', \qquad (15.74)$$

where α' is considered to be associated with cloud scale perturbations. $\overline{\alpha'}$ does not equal zero exactly, although in most applications this approximation is made. It is a good approximation, provided that the averaging area is larger compared with the size of the perturbations.

The thermodynamic equation, Eq. 15.15, may be written using pressure rather than z as the vertical coordinate:

$$\frac{\partial \theta}{\partial t} + \mathbf{V} \cdot \nabla \theta + \omega \frac{\partial \theta}{\partial p} = \frac{\pi^{-1}}{c_p} Q, \quad (15.75a)$$

where $\omega = dp/dt$, and π is Exner's function $(p/p_{oo})^{R/c_p}$. By use of the continuity equation in pressure coordinates $(\nabla \cdot \mathbf{V} + \partial \omega / \partial p = 0)$, Eq. 15.75a may be expressed as

$$\frac{\partial \theta}{\partial t} + \nabla \cdot \mathbf{V}\theta + \frac{\partial (\omega \theta)}{\partial p} = \frac{\pi^{-1}}{c_p} Q. \quad (15.75b)$$

The variables $\mathbf{V}$, θ, and ω, represented by α, are written in terms of the mean and perturbation parts as defined by Eqs. 15.73 and 15.74 and substituted into Eq. 15.75b. The resulting equation is then averaged according to Eq. 15.73. The result is

$$A^{-1} \int_x \int_y \left[\frac{\partial \overline{\theta}}{\partial t} + \frac{\partial \theta'}{\partial t} + \left(\frac{\partial \overline{u}\overline{\theta}}{\partial x} + \frac{\partial \overline{u}\theta'}{\partial x} + \frac{\partial u'\overline{\theta}}{\partial x} + \frac{\partial u'\theta'}{\partial x} \right) \right.$$
$$+ \left(\frac{\partial \overline{v}\overline{\theta}}{\partial y} + \frac{\partial \overline{v}\theta'}{\partial y} + \frac{\partial v'\overline{\theta}}{\partial y} + \frac{\partial v'\theta'}{\partial y} \right)$$
$$\left. + \left(\frac{\partial \overline{\omega}\overline{\theta}}{\partial p} + \frac{\partial \overline{\omega}\theta'}{\partial p} + \frac{\partial \omega'\overline{\theta}}{\partial p} + \frac{\partial \omega'\theta'}{\partial p} \right) \right] dA = \frac{\overline{\pi^{-1}Q}}{c_p}, \quad (15.76)$$

which may be written

$$A^{-1} \int_x \int_y \left[\frac{\partial \overline{\theta}}{\partial t} + \frac{\partial \theta'}{\partial t} + \nabla \cdot \overline{\mathbf{V}}\overline{\theta} + \nabla \cdot \mathbf{V}'\theta' + \overline{\mathbf{V}} \cdot \nabla \theta' \right.$$
$$+ \theta' \left(\nabla \cdot \overline{\mathbf{V}} + \frac{\partial \overline{\omega}}{\partial p} \right) + \mathbf{V}' \cdot \nabla \overline{\theta} + \overline{\theta} \left(\nabla \cdot \mathbf{V}' + \frac{\partial \omega'}{\partial p} \right)$$
$$\left. + \frac{\partial \overline{\omega}\overline{\theta}}{\partial p} + \overline{\omega} \frac{\partial \theta'}{\partial p} + \omega' \frac{\partial \overline{\theta}}{\partial p} + \frac{\partial \omega'\theta'}{\partial p} \right] dA = \frac{\overline{\pi^{-1}Q}}{c_p}. \quad (15.77)$$

The terms in parentheses in Eq. 15.77 vanish approximately by the continuity equation for the mean and eddy motions. (For the averaging operator given by Eq. 15.73, the continuity equation for the mean motion $\partial \overline{\omega} / \partial p + \nabla_p \cdot \overline{\mathbf{V}} = 0$ is not satisfied exactly; however, it is almost always assumed to hold.) The remaining terms may be written

$$\frac{\partial \overline{\theta}}{\partial t} + \overline{\nabla \cdot \overline{\mathbf{V}}\overline{\theta}} + \overline{\nabla \cdot \mathbf{V}'\theta'} + \frac{\partial \overline{\omega}\overline{\theta}}{\partial p} + \frac{\partial \overline{\omega'\theta'}}{\partial p}$$
$$+ \left[\overline{\overline{\mathbf{V}} \cdot \nabla \theta'} + \overline{\mathbf{V}' \cdot \nabla \overline{\theta}} + \overline{\omega} \frac{\partial \theta'}{\partial p} + \overline{\omega' \frac{\partial \overline{\theta}}{\partial p}} \right] = \frac{\overline{\pi^{-1}Q}}{c_p}, \quad (15.78)$$

which may also be written

$$\frac{\partial \overline{\overline{\theta}}}{\partial t} + \overline{\nabla \cdot \overline{\mathbf{V}}\overline{\theta}} + \overline{\nabla \cdot \mathbf{V}'\theta'} + \frac{\partial \overline{\overline{\omega}\overline{\theta}}}{\partial p} + \frac{\partial \overline{\omega'\theta'}}{\partial p}$$

$$+ \left[\overline{\nabla \cdot \overline{\mathbf{V}}\theta'} + \frac{\partial \overline{\omega}\theta'}{\partial p} + \overline{\nabla \cdot \mathbf{V}'\overline{\theta}} + \frac{\partial \overline{\omega'\overline{\theta}}}{\partial p} \right] = \frac{\overline{\pi^{-1}Q}}{c_p}. \quad (15.79)$$

Equation 15.79 is the exact expression for the area-averaged temporal rate of change of mean θ. Although the terms within brackets in Eqs. 15.78 and 15.79 are often neglected in comparison with the other terms, they are not exactly zero since the mean quantities vary slightly over the averaging area. The other terms in Eq. 15.79 represent the usual horizontal and vertical fluxes of θ by the mean (resolvable) and eddy (subgrid scale) motions.

We do not know to what extent the neglect of terms within brackets in Eq. 15.79 is valid as the averaging interval $\Delta x \Delta y$ is decreased to areas comparable with the area of convective systems such as squall lines or individual thunderstorms. This may be a real problem for mesoscale models in which the grid size is 20 km or less. In this situation terms such as $\overline{\nabla \cdot \overline{\mathbf{V}}\theta'}$ may become significant. To illustrate this fact, consider a simple 1-D case of a cloud being advected into a region Δx (Fig. 15.26) by a constant wind U. Let the potential temperature trace through the cloud resemble the "top-hat" profile as shown in Fig. 15.26b, which depicts a uniform environment and a warmer cloud. Then the average θ profile will appear as shown in Fig. 15.26b, increasing significantly in the center of the cloud because the size of the cloud is a significant fraction of the averaging interval Δx. The θ' profile (Fig. 15.26c) shows small negative values on either side of the cloud and a much larger maximum within the cloud itself. In this example, $\overline{\nabla \cdot \overline{\mathbf{V}}\theta'}$ reduces to

$$- \overline{\nabla \cdot \overline{\mathbf{V}}\theta'} = -U \left[\frac{\theta'\left(x + \frac{\Delta x}{2}\right) - \theta'\left(x - \frac{\Delta x}{2}\right)}{\Delta x} \right] \geq 0. \quad (15.80)$$

Clearly this term represents an important increase in $\overline{\theta}$ over the domain. It is larger than the mean horizontal flux term $\nabla \cdot \overline{\mathbf{V}}\overline{\theta}$, which reduces to

$$\overline{\nabla \cdot \overline{\mathbf{V}}\overline{\theta}} = U \left[\frac{\overline{\theta}\left(x + \frac{\Delta x}{2}\right) - \overline{\theta}\left(x - \frac{\Delta x}{2}\right)}{\Delta x} \right]. \quad (15.81)$$

For larger, 3-D domains it becomes increasingly improbable that the terms in brackets of Eq. 15.79 will be significant. Therefore, even though future mesoscale research should consider their possible importance, we will neglect them here. We will also neglect the horizontal eddy flux divergence term $\overline{\nabla \cdot \mathbf{V}'\theta'}$ in comparison with the diabatic heating and vertical eddy fluxes and make the customary assumption that

$$\overline{\nabla \cdot \overline{\mathbf{V}}\overline{\theta}} = \nabla \cdot \overline{\mathbf{V}}\overline{\theta}. \quad (15.82)$$

These assumptions are probably well justified for $\Delta x \Delta y \geq (100 \text{ km})^2$.

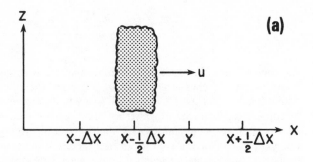

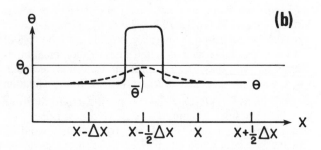

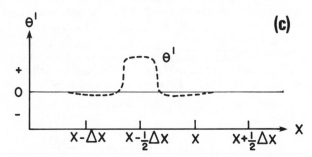

Figure 15.26. How advection of a single cloud into a region changes significantly the area-averaged potential temperature, when the averaging area is not much larger than the area of a cloud. (a) the advection of the cloud into the area; (b) the potential temperature (θ) profile through the cloud and the mean potential temperature, $\bar{\theta}$; and (c) the deviation of potential temperature from the mean.

With the above approximations the thermodynamic equation is

$$\frac{d\bar{\theta}}{dt} = \frac{\pi^{-1}}{c_p} [L_{vl}\bar{C} - L_{il}\bar{M} + L_{vi}\bar{D}] - \overline{\frac{\partial \omega' \theta'}{\partial p}},$$
(15.83)

where C, M, and D are the rates of condensation or evaporation, melting or freezing, and deposition or sublimation, respectively (g H_2O kg^{-1} s^{-1}); L_{vl} is the latent heat of condensation (2.500 × 10^6 J kg^{-1} at 0°C); L_{il} is the latent heat of fusion (0.334 × 10^6 J kg^{-1} at 0°C); and L_{vi} is the latent heat of sublimation (2.834 × 10^6 J kg^{-1} at 0°C). We have neglected radiation in the diabatic heating term and covariance of π^{-1} with C, M, and D.

In a similar manner the approximate equations for the mixing ratio for water vapor q, liquid water q_l, and ice q_i may be derived:

$$\frac{d\bar{q}}{dt} = -\bar{C} - \bar{D} - \overline{\frac{\partial \omega' q'}{\partial p}},$$
(15.84)

$$\frac{d\bar{q_l}}{dt} = \bar{C} + \bar{M} - \bar{P_l} - \overline{\frac{\partial \omega' q_l'}{\partial p}},$$
(15.85)

and

$$\frac{d\bar{q_i}}{dt} = \bar{D} - \bar{M} - \bar{P_i} - \overline{\frac{\partial \omega' q_i'}{\partial p}},$$
(15.86)

where P_l is liquid precipitation fallout ($-P_l$ is precipitation falling into the parcel), P_i is the frozen precipitation fallout, and

$$\frac{d\bar{\alpha}}{dt} = \frac{\partial \bar{\alpha}}{\partial t} + \nabla \cdot \overline{\mathbf{V}\alpha} + \frac{\partial \bar{\omega}\bar{\alpha}}{\partial p}.$$
(15.87)

Except for the vertical eddy fluxes, the temporal rate of change of total water at any level (following the motion) is equal to the net precipitation fallout from the parcel of air:

$$\frac{d(\bar{q} + \bar{q_l} + \bar{q_i})}{dt} = -(\bar{P_l} + \bar{P_i}).$$
(15.88)

Equation 15.83 is equivalent to the thermodynamic equation used in many studies of the interactions between cumulus clouds and the large scale (e.g., Ogura and Cho, 1973; Yanai et al., 1973; Betts, 1975). The right side of Eq. 15.83, with radiation added, is often called the apparent heating (Yanai et al., 1973).

In view of the frequent misconceptions about the relative role of horizontal mixing of warm cloud air and compensating subsidence surrounding the cumulus towers in "heating" the environment, it is worth emphasizing that both effects are present in the diabatic term in brackets on the right side of Eq. 15.83, as noted by Kuo (1974). It is also noteworthy that the contribution to the vertical distribution of convective heat release on the large scale by a single cloud is determined mainly by the vertical distribution in the cloud (the cloud scale heating), but modified somewhat by the vertical eddy flux term. As shown below, this term shifts the maximum convective heating on the large scale upward slightly, but the term is usually smaller than the condensation term. Thus in a region dominated by deep convection, the vertical partitioning of the convective heating to the large scale is close to the vertical partitioning in the deep clouds themselves.

(2) The Vertical Eddy Fluxes by Convection: We now turn our attention to estimating the vertical eddy flux terms on the right-hand sides of Eqs. 15.83–15.86. If the percentage of the large-scale area covered by cloud is denoted by a, we have

$$\bar{\alpha}(x, y) = a\bar{\alpha}^c + (1 - a)\bar{\alpha}^d,$$
(15.89)

where α is any variable and the operators $(\ )^c$ and $(\ )^d$ denote horizontal averages over the cloud and clear regions respectively. If we make the assumption that the mean quantities do not vary appreciably over the averaging interval and use Eq. 15.89, we find

$$\overline{\omega'\alpha'} = \overline{a(\omega_c - \overline{\omega})(\alpha_c - \overline{\alpha})}^c + \overline{(1 - a)(\omega_d - \overline{\omega})(\alpha_d - \overline{\alpha})}^d , \tag{15.90}$$

where the subscripts c and d denote cloud and environmental values. If we substitute for $\overline{\omega}_d^d$ and $\overline{\alpha}_d^d$ from Eq. 15.89 into Eq. 15.90 and make the approximations that

$$\overline{\alpha_c\omega_c}^c = \overline{\alpha}_c^c\overline{\omega}_c^c \tag{15.91}$$
$$\overline{\alpha_d\omega_d}^d = \overline{\alpha}_d^d\overline{\omega}_d^d,$$

we find

$$\overline{\omega'\alpha'} = \frac{a(\overline{\omega}_c^c - \overline{\omega})(\overline{\alpha}_c^c - \overline{\alpha})}{(1 - a)} . \tag{15.92}$$

These approximations imply that we may neglect the covariance of α and ω on small scales of motion within the cloud. They would be least valid if the property α differed greatly in downdrafts compared with updrafts within the cloud. From now on, we will drop the overbar notation on ω_c and α_c for convenience; ω_c will denote the average vertical velocity in the cumulus cloud. Equation 15.92 gives the horizontal average of the vertical eddy flux of any quantity as a function of the large-scale average of that quantity and the average over the cloud.

In the thermodynamic equation, this eddy term results in a diabatic cooling of the lower troposphere and a heating of the upper troposphere when deep convection exists, since the maximum upward eddy flux of heat occurs in the middle troposphere, where the vertical velocity and cloud temperature excess are a maximum. In the water vapor equation, Eq. 15.84, the vertical eddy flux term dries the lower troposphere and moistens the upper troposphere as observed by Betts et al. (1976, their Fig. 4). Thus the eddy fluxes of both heat and moisture transfer energy upward and tend to stabilize the environment.

c. Parameterization of Precipitating Convection

Equations 15.83, 15.84, and 15.92 describe the temporal changes of the large-scale potential temperature and mixing ratio fields owing to deep convection. The goal of many studies, including modeling calculations, is to calculate the effects of convection on the larger scale by relating the terms on the right-hand side of Eqs. 15.83 and 15.84 to the observable large-scale parameters.

Because of the importance of convection to the evolution of the larger scale system, considerable effort has been directed toward developing methods for representing the net effect of the many short-lived convective cells on the thermodynamic, moisture, and momentum structures of the environment. Ooyama (1971), Fraedrich (1973, 1974), and Kreitzberg and Perkey (1976) summarize many of the problems associated with cumulus parameterization. Frank (1983) provides a review of the parameterization of cumulus convection in mesoscale and large-scale numerical models. From a modeling point of view, the problem is to relate the convective transports of heat, moisture, and momentum by the cumulus clouds, which cannot be explicitly resolved by the larger scale model, to the variables predicted by the model. Cumulus parameterization schemes may be divided into two main classes: convective-adjustment and cloud model schemes. In the convective-adjustment type, the effect of the cumulus convection on the environment is considered simply by adjusting the model's moisture and thermodynamic fields toward a moist neutral state in which the equivalent potential temperature is constant with height. An example of this type of parameterization and its use in a hurricane model is given by Kurihara (1973) and Kurihara and Tuleya (1974). The advantages of this type of parameterization are its simplicity and its reliability for representing the gross stabilizing effects of convection on the environment. However, these bulk adjustment schemes contribute little to the understanding of how the convection and the large scale interact, and are probably not capable of representing the variety of subtle feedbacks between the convection and the larger scale structure of the environment.

Cumulus parameterization schemes of the second type consider the effect of subgrid scale penetrative convection on the large-scale equations by a model of the clouds themselves. Once the cloud distribution and the cloud properties (temperature, humidity, momentum) are determined, their effect on their environment may be computed as additional eddy terms in the larger scale equations. Examples of this type are given by Kuo (1974), Ooyama (1971), Ogura and Cho (1973), Arakawa and Schubert (1974), Fraedrich (1974), Kreitzberg and Perkey (1976), and Anthes (1977a). These schemes, because of their additional degrees of freedom compared with the simple adjustment models, are capable of representing more of the details of the cloud-environment interactions.

Within the framework of the development presented so far in this section, the parameterization problem is to determine the total precipitation rate in the grid volume, the vertical distribution of the cloud scale heating, the mean properties of temperature, moisture, and momentum in the clouds, and the percent area covered by cumulus clouds. This information, which may be obtained with the help of a cumulus-cloud model, can then be used to calculate the right-hand terms in Eqs. 15.83 and 15.84. The major problem is to determine the cloud spectrum, which includes the number of clouds of various radii over the domain. In general, the contribution by each cloud size to the condensation and eddy flux terms has to be computed, as discussed by Ooyama (1971) and Arakawa and Schubert (1974). A simpler method is to use a model of single-type cloud (Anthes, 1977a). This simplification may be adequate when a dominant cloud size exists, for example, in disturbed conditions when most of the condensation heating occurs in deep clouds.

We will not go into the details of how the total precipitation rate and the percent area of convective cloud cover have been related to the large-scale variables. In several methods the total rate of precipitation is related to the large-scale

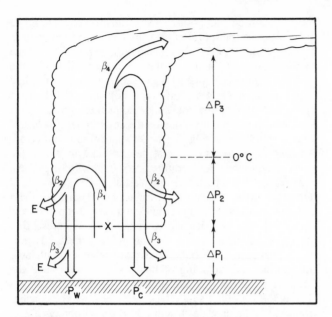

Figure 15.27. Schematic diagram of simplified water budget in mature storm.

variables through an equilibrium assumption between some large-scale process such as moisture convergence (Kuo, 1974; Anthes, 1977a) and rate of large-scale destabilization (Arakawa and Schubert, 1974). There is considerable observational support for relating the precipitation rate to the mesoscale moisture convergence in both the tropics and the extratropics (Syono et al., 1951; Matsumoto et al., 1967; Sasaki and Lewis, 1970; Hudson, 1971; Cho and Ogura, 1974; Krishnamurti et al., 1980, 1983).

Others (for example, Kreitzberg and Perkey, 1976) have related the rate of condensation to the large-scale potential buoyant energy, which represents the positive area between moist-parcel ascent and the environment on a thermodynamic diagram. None of the above assumptions is valid for all situations, because it is possible to find cases in which the condensation heating temporarily exceeds the large-scale convergence of energy or water vapor (Fritsch et al., 1976) or vice versa. Likewise, the amount of positive area on a thermodynamic chart is often a poor measure of the intensity of convection. In the tropics, for example, the most intense convection occurs with the least amount of positive area (see, for example, Betts, 1974). It is almost certain that there is no unique relationship between the instantaneous precipitation rate and the large-scale parameters. Several alternatives also exist for computing a, the percentage of area covered by clouds. Again, the problem has not been solved in general.

In the next section we estimate the order of magnitude of the terms in Eqs. 15.83 and 15.84 for typical situations involving mature thunderstorms. We use some of the results from the numerical models discussed in Sec. 3.

d. Estimates of Thunderstorm Effect on the Large-Scale Environment

At the beginning of this analysis we must emphasize that no single estimate of the terms on the right-hand sides of Eqs. 15.83 and 15.84 can apply to all thunderstorms because of the great variability in size, intensity, and structure of the environment. We will try to point out the parameters that may vary most strongly from one case to another.

(1) Diabatic Effects of Water Phase Change: Let us consider the water budget of a mature thunderstorm as depicted schematically in Fig. 15.27. For convenience we divide the atmosphere into three layers: a subcloud layer of pressure depth Δp_1, the layer between cloud base and the freezing level of depth Δp_2, and the layer from the freezing level to the top of the cloud Δp_3. We estimate the average values of C, M, and D in these three layers and the total rate of precipitation reaching the ground.

Let x be the rate of water vapor addition to a cloud per unit area of cloud base by the upward flux at cloud base and the entrainment of water vapor through the sides of the cloud:

$$x = \rho w q + \varepsilon \quad [\text{g H}_2\text{O m}^{-2}\text{ s}^{-1}], \quad (15.93a)$$

where ρ is density, w is vertical velocity, and ε is the entrainment. The mass of water vapor added to a column of unit area dA per unit time dt is then

$$x' = \int_A \int_t (\rho w q + \varepsilon)\, dt\, dA. \quad (15.93b)$$

A percentage of this water vapor (β_1) is condensed in the layer below the freezing level. A fraction β_2 of this condensed water evaporates around the cloud sides or in a downdraft at more or less the same level at which it condensed, while the remainder falls out of the cloud base. As the remaining precipitation falls through the subcloud layer, a fraction β_3 evaporates before reaching the ground. The portion of the initial water vapor that reaches the ground without going through the freezing process may be called warm precipitation, P_w.

The portion of the water vapor that does not condense below the freezing level is carried up into the subfreezing portion of the cloud. We will not consider any of the details of how the water vapor becomes ice. Even though in reality much of it condenses into water first and then freezes rather than going directly from vapor to solid, the thermodynamics can be accurately represented in this bulk calculation by assuming that only deposition occurs, i.e., by treating the condensation and freezing processes together. We also neglect evaporation above the freezing level completely in order to simplify the analysis. Evaporation above this level is probably small in most cases compared with evaporation below the freezing level because of the lower vapor pressures over ice and water at subfreezing temperatures. Therefore, the term in brackets of Eq. 15.83 for the upper level reduces to simply $L_{vi}\bar{D}$, where $\bar{D}$ represents the total rate of conversion of vapor to ice.

Of the portion of water vapor that is carried above the freezing level, a fraction β_4 is carried out of the cloud in the cirrus anvil. We assume that this amount is lost to the larger scale domain. (If sublimation takes place within the volume of interest, a cooling at the level of sublimation would result, and the following analysis would be modified somewhat.) The remaining precipitation falls back through the freezing level and melts. This portion, which freezes at high levels and melts at middle levels, transports heat upward because of the higher latent heat of sublimation, L_{vi}, compared with the latent heat of melting, L_{vl}. As the melted precipitation falls, the fraction β_2 is evaporated around the cloud sides or in unsaturated downdrafts. This portion also transports heat upward, because the evaporation occurs at a significantly lower level than the condensation. Finally, a fraction β_3 of the remaining precipitation evaporates between the cloud base and the ground. This results in an upward transport of heat. The portion of the original water vapor (now liquid or ice) that reaches the ground after going through the freezing process may be called cold precipitation, P_c.

The above description is summarized in Table 15.1. The net effects of condensation, evaporation, melting, freezing, deposition, sublimation, or precipitation can be estimated by specifying the four β parameters, the water vapor source at cloud base plus entrainment, and the pressure depths of the various layers. Let us consider two types of clouds, a tropical cumulonimbus in a humid environment and an extratropical cumulonimbus in a dry environment. The tropical cloud is representative of a thunderstorm in a disturbed region of the tropics where high relative humidities exist at all levels. The cloud base is low (approximately 900 mb), and evaporation is expected to have a relatively minor effect. Parameters for such a cloud are listed in Table 15.2, with x approximated by the flux of vapor at cloud base; the values of the parameters are arbitrary but reasonable. However, a large variation between thunderstorms is likely, and the reader may wish to experiment with a different set of parameters.

With the assumed water vapor mass flux at cloud base of 20 g H_2O m^{-2} s^{-1} (equivalent to a mean vertical velocity of 1 m s^{-1} and a mixing ratio of 20 g kg^{-1}) and the assumed β percentages listed in Table 15.2, the tropical cloud produces a precipitation rate of 5.6 cm h^{-1}. The precipitation efficiency, defined here as the ratio of precipitation fallout to moisture influx at cloud base, is 78%. Approximately 71% of the precipitation is warm precipitation.

In contrast, the extratropical cloud shows a lower precipitation rate of 1.7 cm h^{-1}, owing to the smaller mixing ratio at the cloud base and a smaller efficiency (47%). The lessened efficiency is a consequence of the higher evaporation rates. Because these rates are not excessively high, some thunderstorms may easily show a considerably lower efficiency. Indeed, storms embedded in a wind shear, which increases evaporation, may show efficiencies as low as 10% (Newton and Fankhauser, 1964; Marwitz, 1972). Also in contrast to the tropical thunderstorm, ice plays a much larger role in the extratropical storm because of the high

Table 15.1. Disposition of Water Vapor Entering Cloud

Quantity*	Disposition
$\beta_1 x'$	Condenses between cloud base and freezing level
$(1 - \beta_1)x'$	Is carried above freezing level and is eventually frozen or exported as water vapor
$\beta_2(\beta_1 x')$	Evaporates around cloud sides or in downdraft in layer from cloud base to freezing level
$(1 - \beta_2)(\beta_1 x')$	Falls through cloud-base level
$\beta_3(1 - \beta_2)(\beta_1 x')$	Evaporates below cloud base
$(1 - \beta_3)(1 - \beta_2)(\beta_1 x')$	Reaches ground as warm precipitation
$\beta_4(1 - \beta_1)x'$	Is carried out of cloud in anvil
$\beta_2(1 - \beta_4)(1 - \beta_1)x'$	Evaporates around cloud sides or in downdraft in layer from cloud base to freezing level
$(1 - \beta_2)(1 - \beta_4)(1 - \beta_1)x'$	Falls through cloud base
$\beta_3(1 - \beta_2)(1 - \beta_4)(1 - \beta_1)x'$	Evaporates below cloud base
$(1 - \beta_3)(1 - \beta_2)(1 - \beta_4)(1 - \beta_1)x'$	Reaches ground as cold precipitation

*x' below, as described in Eq. 15.93b, is the mass of water vapor added to cloud column of unit area over a unit time interval.

cloud base, and cold precipitation accounts for 58% of the total.

These estimates are consistent with the calculations made by Newton (1966) for an extratropical storm. He found that the percentage of initial water vapor transport carried out in the anvil was 14%, the ratio of evaporation to influx was 41%, and the precipitation efficiency was 45%.

The contribution to the large-scale thermodynamic equation by the terms in brackets on the right-hand side of Eq. 15.83 are shown in Fig. 15.28. These values were computed by dividing the rates of addition of water vapor in Table 15.2 by the mass per unit area in each layer ($\Delta p/g$), and

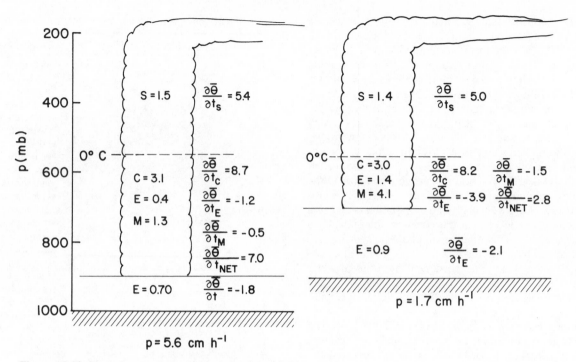

Figure 15.28. Typical area-averaged rates (g kg^{-1} day^{-1}) of deposition (S), condensation (C), evaporation (E), and melting (M) in a tropical (left) and extratropical (right) thunderstorm. P is the precipitation rate. The diabatic rates of change of mean potential temperature $\bar{\theta}$ are given in °C per day under the assumption that the percentage of large-scale area covered by the thunderstorms is 1%.

Table 15.2. Estimates of Typical Parameters for Cumulonimbus Clouds

Parameter	Unit	Tropical	Extratropical
		Value	
β_1	Dimensionless	0.65	0.35
β_2	Dimensionless	0.10	0.20
β_3	Dimensionless	0.05	0.30
β_4	Dimensionless	0.25	0.25
w	m s^{-1}	1.00	1.00
q	g kg^{-1}	20.00	10.00
$x \sim \rho w q$	g H$_2$O m^{-2} s^{-1}	20.00	10.00
ΔP_1	mb	100.00	200.00
ΔP_2	mb	350.00	100.00
ΔP_3	mb	400.00	400.00

Disposition of Water Vapor Entering Cloud	Fraction of x	
Evaporation from cloud sides or in downdraft in layer between cloud base and freezing level	0.0913	0.1675
Evaporation below cloud base	0.0411	0.2010
Advected out in anvil or evaporated within region	0.0875	0.1625
Warm precipitation	0.5558	0.1960
Cold precipitation	0.2244	0.2730
Total	1.0000	1.0000
Precipitation efficiency	0.78	0.47
Precipitation rate: cm/h	5.60	1.70

multiplying by the appropriate latent-heating constant and $(c_p \pi)^{-1}$. The value, which is valid for the cloud, is then converted to an area-averaged value by assuming that the cloud covers 1% of the total area.

The results in Fig. 15.28 show several important points. First, the average temperature change owing to the thunderstorms is positive—this will be true as long as any precipitation reaches the ground. Second, both clouds produce a significant area average cooling in the layer below cloud base. This cooling must occur unless the evaporation below cloud base is zero; that amount can be approached only with low cloud bases and high relative humidities below cloud base.

Another important result in Fig. 15.28 is that the vertical partitioning of the effective heating (the terms in brackets on the right-hand side of Eq. 15.81) is quite different for the two types of clouds. Because of the high cloud base (which reduces the condensation in the low levels) and the greater low-level evaporation in the extratropical cloud, most of the effective heating occurs above the freezing level in the upper troposphere. In contrast, the greatest effective heating occurs below the freezing level in the tropical cloud. This vertical partitioning of heat to the large scale is very important in hurricane development (Yamasaki, 1968; Koss, 1976; Anthes, 1977b).

The effect of the two vertical heating distributions produced here on the large-scale motions would be to induce different large-scale circulations in the tropical and extra-

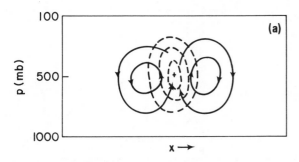 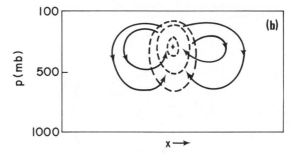

Figure 15.29. Hypothesized heating distribution (dashed lines) and induced large-scale circulation (solid lines) associated with (a) tropical convection and (b) extratropical convection.

tropical environments. The high-level heating distribution would favor a high-level circulation, with inflow into the convective region occurring in the middle troposphere (Fig. 15.29b). The low-level heating distribution would favor a lower-level circulation center, with inflow occurring closer to the surface (Fig. 15.29a). Because of the rapid decrease of moisture with height, the maintenance of the tropical circulation by inflow of moist air would be favored compared with the extratropical system, if the storms in the two environments were similar to the storms analyzed here.

The difference in vertical partitioning of the effective heating on the large scale indicates that extratropical thunderstorms may be more efficient in stabilizing the troposphere. Similar conclusions concerning the differences between tropical oceanic and extratropical continental thunderstorms were reached by Ogura (1975).

The effect of freezing at high levels and melting at middle levels is not entirely negligible in either the tropical or the extratropical cloud. It amounts to $-0.5°C$ d^{-1} (cooling) in the lower part of the tropical cloud and $-1.5°C$ d^{-1} in the extratropical cloud. These rates are comparable with radiative effects. Locally they are considerably greater because the melting occurs in a thin layer below the freezing level rather than uniformly through the thicker layer, as assumed here. Thus local stabilization above the melting layer and destabilization below may be considerably larger than the values in Fig. 15.28 indicate.

In the above examples we have combined entrainment of air into the clouds above cloud base with the cloud-base mass flux. As noted earlier, entrainment increases the total vertical mass flux in the cloud. Thus unless the entrained air is absolutely dry, the total moisture flux also increases. This effect shifts the latent-heating maximum upward and may be significant in tropical clouds that exist in an environment with appreciable moisture. It is probably less important in extratropical clouds that are surrounded by dry air.

It is important to realize that the local thermodynamic effects in the vicinity of the cloud may be quite different from the large-scale averages. On the cloud scale all the terms listed in Fig. 15.28 are 100 times larger. Because the changes cannot be distributed uniformly over the environment instantaneously, large local changes that are quite im-

portant to the details of the cumulus evolution may occur. Under the extratropical cloud, for example, the evaporational cooling amounts to 8.75°C h^{-1}. If this cold air remained under the cloud, the stabilization might kill that particular cloud, while several cloud diameters away there would be no destabilization at all by this effect. Thus the average changes have meaning only over a period of time several times the lifetime of individual thunderstorms (at least several hours).

Finally, we note that the diabatic heating rates shown in Fig. 15.28 are not representative of the observed (local) rates of temperature change. Indeed, almost always opposing tendencies associated with vertical motions develop in response to the mean heating distribution (Fig. 15.29).

(2) Eddy Fluxes of Sensible and Latent Heat: Changes of water phase are not the only mechanisms for redistributing heat and moisture in the vertical. If departures from the large-scale environment of temperature and moisture are correlated with the cloud scale vertical velocities, eddy transports of these quantities occur. The effects of the associated eddy fluxes are represented by the last terms on the right sides of Eqs. 15.83–15.86. We estimate the effect of the eddies on the large-scale temperature and moisture fields using Eq. 15.92, where the average cloud properties, $\bar{\omega}_c^c$ and $\bar{\alpha}_c^c$, represent horizontal averages over the entire cloud. They should also be considered averages over the lifetime of the cloud.

Because the vertical derivatives of the eddy fluxes are important in producing large-scale changes, it is necessary to estimate vertical profiles of $\bar{\omega}_c^c$ and $\bar{\alpha}_c^c$. One way of estimating typical profiles is to use a model of the cloud. However, care must be taken in interpreting the results, because the instantaneous profiles produced by a cloud model may not be appropriate for the averaged quantities required in Eq. 15.91. In this section we compare profiles from a 2-D time-dependent cloud model (Orville and Kopp, 1977) and a 1-D steady-state cloud model (Anthes, 1977a). It is well known that 1-D models cannot simulate properly many of the features in cumulus clouds (Warner, 1970). However, because of their relative simplicity it is important to know how well

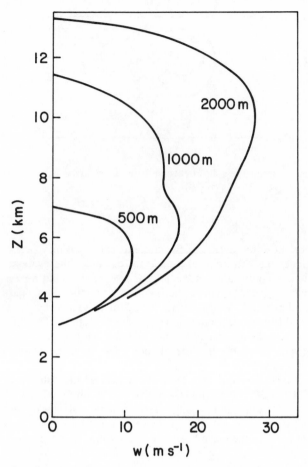

Figure 15.30. Vertical velocity as a function of height as computed from a 1-D cloud model for updraft radii of 500 m, 1,000 m, and 2,000 m.

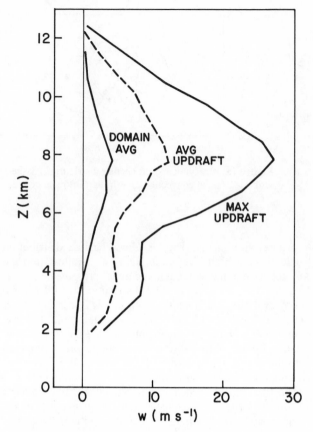

Figure 15.31. Maximum updraft velocity, average updraft velocity, and domain-averaged vertical velocity from a 2-D cloud model.

they can estimate the mean quantities $\bar{\omega}_c^c$, $\bar{\theta}_c^c$, and $\bar{q}_c^c$ required for estimating the eddy fluxes.

The 1- and 2-D cloud models are initialized with a sounding taken from Sterling, Colo., on 21 June 1972 (Fig. 15.12). The hail-producing thunderstorm that occurred on this date is described by Browning and Foote (1976).

One of the more crucial parameters in the 1-D cloud model is the initial updraft radius, because the entrainment rate is inversely proportional to the cloud radius. Therefore, in a dry environment such as that represented in Fig. 15.12, larger clouds grow much more vigorously than do smaller clouds and achieve greater heights. Therefore, we ran the 1-D cloud model for radii of 500, 1,000, and 2,000 m for comparison with the 2-D model cloud.

Figure 15.30 shows the profiles of vertical velocity from the 1-D model. The effect of entrainment in limiting the growth of the smaller clouds is evident. The 500-m cloud cannot penetrate the inversion at 500 mb (Fig. 15.12). The 1,000-m cloud shows evidence of a double maximum caused by this inversion, while the 2,000-m cloud is vigorous

enough to be affected only slightly by this shallow stable layer.

We next computed vertical-velocity profiles from the 2-D model. To obtain representative profiles, we averaged the vertical velocities obtained at 108 and 114 min of the simulation (see Fig. 15.15b, d). The cloud was in a mature stage at this time (Orville and Kopp, 1977). Three vertical-velocity profiles were computed: the maximum updraft velocity, the average velocity in the primary updraft, and the domain-averaged vertical velocity. The last was computed for a 12-km domain and includes the immediate environment of the cloud.

The 2-D vertical-velocity profiles are shown in Fig. 15.31. All three show a maximum updraft at about 8 km MSL. There is not a very good correspondence among any of the 1-D cloud profiles and the 2-D profiles. The greatest similarity occurs between the 2,000-m-radius 1-D cloud and the maximum updraft velocity in the 2-D model, but the shapes of these two profiles are different.

The temperature excesses in the cloud compared with the environment, $T_c - \bar{T}$, for the three 1-D clouds are shown in Fig. 15.32. Again, large differences exist between the different-sized clouds. A double maximum caused by the

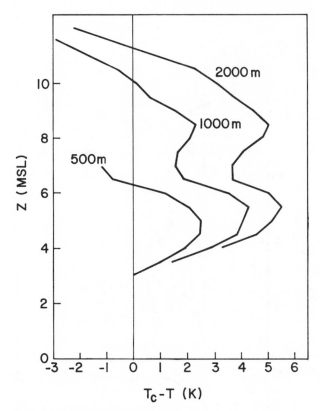

Figure 15.32. Temperature difference $(T_c - T)$ between the updraft and the environment in updrafts of radii 500 m, 1,000 m, and 2,000 m as computed from a 1-D cloud model.

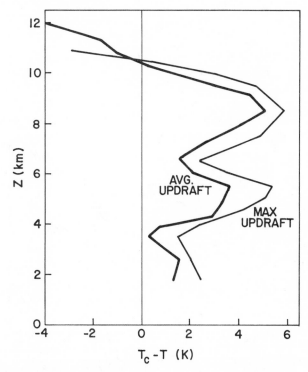

Figure 15.33. Maximum temperature difference between the updraft and the environment and average temperature difference between the updraft and the environment as computed from a 2-D cloud model.

stable layer at 500 mb is characteristic of the two larger clouds.

Two estimates of $T_c - \bar{T}$ from the 2-D cloud are shown in Fig. 15.33, the maximum value of $T_c - \bar{T}$ in the primary updraft and the velocity-weighted average value of $T_c - \bar{T}$ in this updraft. This average is defined by

$$\bar{\alpha} = \sum_{j=1}^{J} w_j \alpha_j \left(\sum_{j=1}^{J} w_j \right)^{-1}, \qquad (15.94)$$

where j is the horizontal grid index and J is the number of grid points in the primary updraft.

Both updraft temperature excesses in the 2-D model are quite similar to the excess computed by the 2,000-m 1-D model (compare Figs. 15.32 and 15.33). Both show maxima between 4° and 5°C at about 5 and 8 km, with a minimum at about 6.5 km. The moisture profiles (q) are also quite similar in the largest 1-D cloud and the 2-D cloud. Therefore, in contrast to the vertical-velocity profiles, the thermodynamic profiles of the 2-D cloud updraft and the 1-D model match well (within 20%). These results suggest that the parameterization of the precipitation loading in the 1-D model is inadequate for this cloud. The vertical-velocity profile in the 1-D model is affected (after the temperature excess) mainly by the precipitation loading, which

is difficult to model in one dimension. It is also probable that the neglect of nonhydrostatic pressure changes in the 1-D model may contribute to the difference (Holton, 1973).

The vertical fluxes of heat, $-(\omega' T')$, in the 1,000-m and 2,000-m 1-D models are shown in Fig. 15.34. In general, there is an upward flux at all levels, with maxima at 5 and 8 km associated with the local maxima in the cloud temperature excesses there.

The corresponding vertical fluxes in the 2-D model were computed for the main updraft, the main downdraft, and the area-weighted average of the main updraft and downdraft. The results, shown in Fig. 15.35, indicate that the cold downdraft is producing a significant upward transport of heat below 7 km. The warm updraft produces an upward transport of heat at all levels with a sharp maximum at about 9 km. The resultant heat flux profile shows a rapid increase in the lowest 500 m, a nearly constant value from 500 m to 5 or 6 km, a rapid increase to a maximum at 9 km, and a steady decrease above this level.

Figure 15.36 shows the vertical profiles of the eddy heating term computed by evaluating $\overline{\partial \omega' T'}/\partial p$, with the help of Eq. 15.92. Here we assumed $a = 0.01$ and $\bar{\omega} = 0$. The assumption of a constant value of $'a'$ regardless of height (and the use of the same value for both the 1-D cloud and the 2-D cloud) is an arbitrary but important one. It is not clear, for example, that the percentage of total area covered by the up-

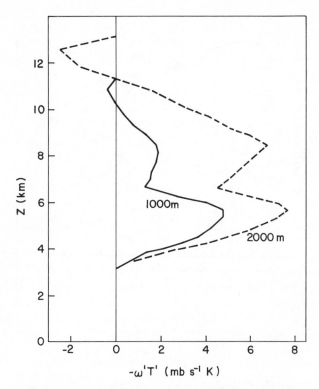

Figure 15.34. Vertical eddy heat flux associated with updrafts of radii 1,000 m and 2,000 m as computed from 1-D cloud model.

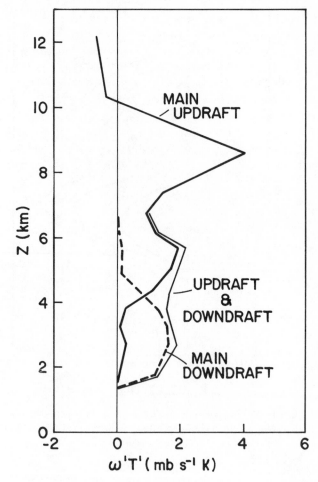

Figure 15.35. Vertical eddy heat flux associated with the main updraft, the main downdraft, and the sum of the updraft and the downdraft as computed from a 2-D cloud model.

draft produced by the 1-D cloud model should be the same as the percentage of area covered by the mean updraft and downdraft pair in the 2-D model. Because the 1-D model profiles most closely resemble the profiles through the core of the 2-D model updraft, the value of *a* associated with the 1-D model should probably be considerably less than that associated with the 2-D model. The width of the 2-D cloud (primary updraft and downdraft) is about 7,200 m. The width of the inner core of the updraft is about 1,800 m. Therefore, the percentage of area covered by the 2-D cloud could be on the order of 16 times greater than the percentage covered by the updraft in the 1-D model. Thus the comparison of numerical values shown in Fig. 15.36 must not be taken literally unless the values are modified by the appropriate values of *a* for each cloud. They do give the heating and cooling rates if 1% of the environment is covered by thunderstorms with the updraft and temperature excess profiles equal to those obtained from these models.

Although the gross characteristics of the total heat flux profiles (Figs. 15.34 and 15.35) obtained from the 1-D and 2-D models are similar (both show positive values with middle or upper tropospheric maxima), there are important differences. The 1-D model produces a vertical heat flux approximately two times that produced in the 2-D model and does not show the effect of the downdraft in the lower troposphere. The resulting eddy heating rate profile (Fig. 15.36), therefore, shows no cooling below cloud base and stronger

cooling in the layer between 3 and 5 km than that in the 2-D model. The role of the downdraft in the cloud, therefore, is to concentrate the eddy cooling very close to the ground.

The double maxima in the heat flux profile from the 1-D model produce a shallow layer of strong warming at 6 km, which is only weakly present in the 2-D results. Both models give cooling at 8 km and warming above this level.

The results shown in Fig. 15.36 indicate that large heating and cooling rates may be generated locally by small-scale features in the vertical profiles of the cloud and by environmental variables. Although such perturbations undoubtedly exist for individual clouds, they are not likely to be persistent in time or widespread in space. Therefore, the relevant eddy heat flux profiles and their associated temperature change profiles are probably highly smoothed versions of those shown in Figs. 15.34–15.36.

Figure 15.37 shows the change of average mixing ratio caused by the vertical divergence of the eddy water vapor flux (the last term in Eq. 15.84). In contrast to the changes

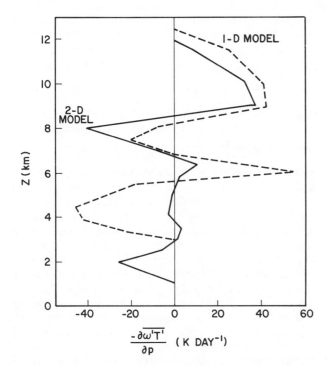

Figure 15.36. Diabatic heating rate associated with the divergence of the vertical eddy heat flux in 1-D and 2-D models.

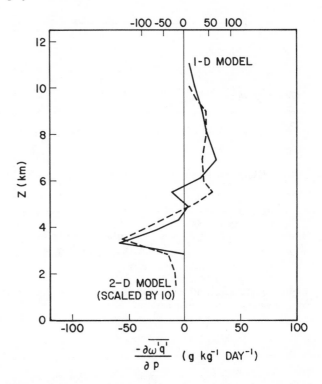

Figure 15.37. Rate of change of average mixing ratio associated with divergence of vertical eddy moisture flux in 1-D and 2-D models. The equivalent diabatic heating rate in °C/*d* is given at the top.

in temperature owing to the eddy sensible heat transport (Fig. 15.36), in which the order of magnitude was the same in both cloud models, the integrated water vapor flux and the corresponding changes of mixing ratio are an order of magnitude less in the 2-D model (note that the profile corresponding to the 2-D model is scaled by 10 in Fig. 15.37). In both models the mixing ratio profiles are very similar—within 1 g kg^{-1}. The difference results from the use of the average vertical velocity in the 2-D cloud model. This average, which is computed over the primary updraft and downdraft (a distance of about 8,000 m), gives a much weaker vertical-velocity profile than that in the 1-D model, and so the vertical flux of q is reduced. A reduction of this magnitud does not occur in the heat flux term because $(T_c - T)$ is positively correlated with the vertical velocities in the cloud. Thus the cold downdraft adds to the effect of the warm updraft.

The shapes of the profiles of $\partial\overline{\omega'q'}/\partial p$ in the 1-D and 2-D clouds are quite similar. Both clouds dry the lower troposphere and moisten the upper troposphere. For the value of a assigned here (0.01), the change in average mixing ratio associated with the 1-D model profile reaches 25 g kg^{-1} d^{-1} in the upper troposphere. The value is sufficient to cause rapid saturation at this level in the absence of a significant moisture sink such as mean subsidence. The equivalent heating rate $(L/c_p)(\overline{\partial\omega'q'}/\partial p)$ in this case reaches 50°C d^{-1}—a value comparable with the condensation and eddy heat flux term.

Because the vertical divergence of the eddy heat and moisture fluxes is very sensitive to small-scale variations in the cloud model profile and the environmental-temperature profile, the details in the profiles depicted in Figs. 15.36 and 15.37 may be quite different for other clouds. However, the following results may be considered to have general applicability:

1. The overall effect of the eddy heat flux term is to transfer heat upward, thereby stabilizing the environment.
2. The role of cold downdrafts is to increase the upward heat flux in the lower troposphere and concentrate the cooling close to the ground.
3. The effect of the eddy moisture flux term is to transfer moisture upward. This process may produce rapid saturation in upper levels, where the saturation vapor pressure deficit is small.
4. For a given assumed value of a, the 1-D and 2-D cloud models can give eddy heat flux profiles of the same order of magnitude, because the downdraft is colder than the average while the updraft is warmer.
5. Because such a strong positive correlation between vertical velocity and moisture does not exist in the 2-D cloud, the eddy vapor flux may be an order of magnitude smaller in the 2-D cloud.

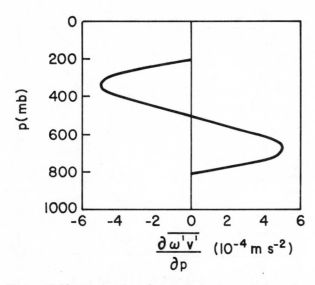

Figure 15.38. Acceleration of mean motion by vertical transport of momentum in model thunderstorm.

(3) Eddy Fluxes of Momentum: The acceleration of the mean motion **V** caused by the eddy stresses associated with the vertical transport of momentum in thunderstorms is

$$\frac{\partial \overline{\mathbf{V}}}{\partial t_c} = - \frac{\overline{\partial \omega' \mathbf{V}'}}{\partial p}, \qquad (15.95)$$

where $\mathbf{V}' = \mathbf{V}_c - \overline{\mathbf{V}}$.

It is difficult to estimate representative horizontal velocities in either the 1-D or the 2-D cloud models. Therefore, we estimate the acceleration given by Eq. 15.95 by specifying a simple yet not unrealistic profile of ω_c and $\mathbf{V}'$. We will consider 2-D flow in the x–z plane and assume that the W-to-E component of the velocity increases with height. The x component of Eq. 15.95 is then

$$\frac{\partial \overline{u}}{\partial t_c} = - \frac{\overline{\partial \omega' u'}}{\partial p}. \qquad (15.96)$$

If we assume that the cumulus cloud tends to conserve its low-level momentum, u' will be negative. For the order of magnitude calculations, we assume that both ω_c and u' are quadratic function of p and are zero at cloud base (p_b) and cloud top (p_t). Similar profiles were calculated by Newton (1966) by considering the drag forces on an updraft. The assumptions yield

$$\omega(p) = \hat{\omega}\, F(p)$$

and

$$u'(p) = \hat{u}\, F(p), \qquad (15.97)$$

where

$$F(p) = \frac{4}{(p_b - p_t)^2} [-p^2 + (p_b + p_t)p - p_b p_t], \quad (15.98)$$

$\hat{\omega}$ is the minimum value of ω, and $\hat{u}$ is the minimum value of u'. The divergence of the eddy flux, $\partial \omega' u' / \partial p$, is then

$$\frac{\partial \omega' u'}{\partial p} = \frac{32\, \hat{\omega}\, \hat{u}}{(p_b - p_t)^4} [-p^2 + (p_b p_t)p - p_b p_t]$$
$$\times [-2p + p_b p_t]. \qquad (15.99)$$

The area-averaged acceleration is obtained by multiplying Eq. 15.99 by a. Figure 15.38 shows the vertical profile of the acceleration caused by the momentum flux in the cumulus clouds for the following values of the parameters: $p_b = 800$ mb, $p_t = 300$ mb, $\hat{\omega} = -3600$ mb h^{-1} (about 13 m s^{-1} at a pressure of 600 mb), $\hat{u} = -10$ m s^{-1}, and $a = 0.01$. These values are not extreme (see Newton, 1966). Because the horizontal momentum in the cloud is less than the environmental momentum, the cloud transports westerly momentum downward, accelerating the lower tropospheric air and decelerating the upper tropospheric air. The maximum acceleration of 5×10^{-4} m s^{-2} is comparable with the Coriolis acceleration for a 5-m s^{-1} wind in middle latitudes, where $f = 10^{-4}$ s^{-1}. Thus moderate thunderstorms may significantly affect the mean motion by transferring horizontal momentum vertically. However, the pressure forces in the convection may also produce large accelerations (Moncrieff and Miller, 1976), and so the net effect of strong convective systems may be to increase rather than decrease the environmental shear, as observed by Betts et al. (1976).

e. Summary

In this section we have considered the effect of moderate thunderstorms on their environment when the thunderstorms occupy a small fraction of the total area. By considering the thunderstorms as eddies superimposed on the mean flow, the area-averaged equation for the potential temperature and mixing ratio were derived. These equations showed that the vertical distribution of the large-scale heating and moistening effects were the same as the cloud scale distributions of these effects, with a correction because of the vertical eddy fluxes of heat and moisture.

The vertical distributions of condensation, evaporation, freezing, and melting were considered in tropical and extratropical thunderstorms. Both clouds produced a net heating of the troposphere. The vertical distribution of the heating functions, however, differed in the two clouds. The dry environment of the extratropical cloud resulted in more evaporation in the low levels, which tended to compensate for the condensation there. The result was a high-level heating maximum. The tropical thunderstorm, on the other hand, released a much larger fraction of the total heat in the low and middle troposphere. Therefore, the extratropical cloud produced a greater stabilization of the atmosphere than did the tropical cloud.

The effect of freezing at high levels and melting at lower levels also stabilized the atmosphere. The heat transfers owing to this process were on the order of 1°C d^{-1} averaged over deep layers—a rate comparable with radiative effects and about 10% of the condensation and evaporation effects for these clouds.

The vertical fluxes of heat and water vapor were estimated for a hail-producing thunderstorm over Colorado using 1-D and 2-D cloud models. The 1-D model considered only an updraft; the 2-D model produced an updraft-downdraft pair. The 1-D model profiles were most like those in the core of the updraft in the 2-D model. When the percentage of the large-scale environment covered by the two clouds was assumed to be equal at 1% (not necessarily a good assumption), the vertical heat flux in the 1-D model was about twice that in the 2-D model, producing average temperature changes of about 10°C d^{-1}. However, the vertical moisture flux was an order of magnitude greater in the 1-D model, which produced changes of mixing ratio on the order of 25 g kg^{-1} d^{-1}. The difference in ratios of heat flux and moisture flux between the 1-D and 2-D models was related to the downdraft properties in the 2-D model. Because the downdraft was cold, it transported heat upward and added to the heat flux of the warm updraft. However, the downdraft was moister than the environment and acted to transport moisture downward, thereby opposing the upward transports in the updraft.

Finally, an order-of-magnitude calculation showed that a moderate thunderstorm could produce significant acceleration of the mean motion by transporting horizontal momentum in the vertical. For the case in which the westerly component of the wind increases upward, the thunderstorm accelerates the lower tropospheric air and decelerates the upper tropospheric air.

In general, the results illustrate the importance of thunderstorms over areas 100 times greater than the area of the thunderstorms themselves. These thunderstorms transport heat and moisture upward, acting to stabilize the environment, while they transport momentum downward (when the wind shear is positive), acting to decrease the wind shear.

16. Modification of Thunderstorms

Louis J. Battan

1. Introduction

Thunderstorms and associated weather events—torrential rain, strong winds, hail, lightning, and tornadoes—do great property damage and can cause injury and death. On the other hand, the rain produced by thunderstorms is essential to almost everyone and particularly to the farmers of the world.

Although recorded history shows that people have tried a great variety of methods—usually religious but sometimes of a martial character—to change the weather, there is little evidence of any success until recent decades. Ceremonial dances, the ringing of church bells, and the firing of cannons may have satisfied people's need to "do something" about storms or droughts or other malevolent aspects of the weather, but for the most part nature has gone its own way, regardless of the human attempts at intervention.

In the late 1940s significant advances in developing a scientific basis for modifying clouds and weather were made by Irving Langmuir and his associates Schaefer (1946) and Vonnegut (1947) at the General Electric Research Laboratories. They carried out a series of experiments in both the laboratory and the atmosphere showing that certain clouds could be modified and that certain crucial experimental results were in agreement with physical theory.

It has long been known that many clouds, particularly during their development, are composed of liquid droplets even at elevations where temperatures are below 0°C. Such water clouds are called *supercooled* because they have temperatures below the nominal freezing temperature of water.

Supercooled clouds composed of nearly uniform droplets tend to be stable in the sense that the droplets generally do not grow large enough to become raindrops. On the other hand, if ice crystals are introduced into a supercooled cloud, the system becomes unstable. Because of the difference between the saturation vapor pressure over water and ice at subfreezing temperatures (Fig. 16.1), the ice crystals grow and the water droplets evaporate. As the crystals grow, they fall with respect to the water droplets and smaller crystals, causing collisions, accretion of the colliding particles, and formation of snowflakes and other frozen hydrometeors. This process of precipitation formation is called the *ice crystal process*, or the *Bergeron-Findeisen process*, after

the scientists who carried out early studies of this precipitation mechanism in the 1930s.

Usually ice crystals form on minute particles called ice nuclei, most of which are thought to be finely divided clay particles blown up from the ground. Sometimes there are so few ice nuclei that a supercooled cloud remains in that state until it ultimately evaporates and disappears.

Langmuir and his associates proved that ice crystals could be made to form in supercooled clouds by introducing particles of frozen carbon dioxide (dry ice) or substances such as silver iodide and lead iodide, whose crystal structures resemble ice. Dry ice produces ice crystals because its temperature is so low—about −78°C—that crystals can be formed directly from water vapor.

The initiation of ice crystal growth by the introduction of a foreign substance is known as *cloud seeding*. Although there has been a great deal of research seeking effective, inexpensive ice-nucleating substances, most often, particularly in the United States, supercooled clouds are seeded with a smoke composed of tiny particles of silver iodide. Figure 16.2 shows a silver iodide seeding generator mounted under an airplane wing. A solution of silver iodide in highly flammable acetone is sprayed and ignited. The burning solution vaporizes the silver iodide, which then recondenses in tiny particles. The number of active nuclei per gram of silver iodide increases from very low values at about −5°C to extremely large values at −20°C (Fig. 16.3).

When ice nuclei composed of silver iodide are introduced into a supercooled cloud, ice crystals are produced, and if the cloud is thick enough, the crystals lead to the formation of precipitation. It should be noted that, as water freezes, latent heat is released to the surroundings and increases its temperature. The latent heat of fusion amounts to about 80 cal g^{-1}, and if enough water is frozen, the quantity of available latent heat can be sufficient to affect cloud buoyancy and cloud growth.

The ice crystal process accounts for much of the precipitation reaching the ground. During cold periods large ice particles and snowflakes are observed. When air temperatures near the ground are above 0°C, the falling ice particles can melt and become raindrops.

Not all rain originates as frozen hydrometeors. Much of it, particularly at lower latitudes and in the summer, grows

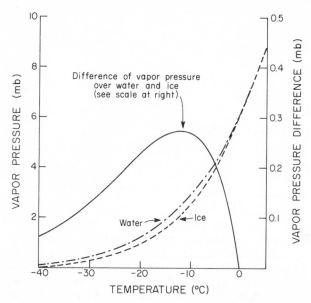

Figure 16.1. Saturation vapor pressure over ice and water at temperatures below 0°C.

by a mechanism known as the *condensation coalescence process*. In many clouds growing in warm, humid air of oceanic origin, the condensation process leads to a wide spectrum of cloud droplet sizes. Although most of the droplets have diameters of less than 30 μm, such clouds can have some droplets as large as 50 to 100 μm in diameter. When this is the case, the larger droplets fall through the ensemble of smaller ones, colliding and coalescing with them. If the cloud is sufficiently large, persistent, and heavy with water, rain showers occur. This sequence of events is sometimes called the *warm-cloud process*. When a warm cloud is deficient in large cloud droplets, the cloud can be seeded with relatively large salt particles (1 to 10 μm in diameter) that can grow first by condensation and then by coalescence. Warm clouds have also been seeded with large water droplets, sometimes containing salt in solution.

Most attempts to influence the behavior of thunderstorms have employed ice-nuclei seeding. The results of a number of well-known programs are discussed below. In the author's judgment they give a reasonably fair picture of the status of the weater modification field in 1983.

Figure 16.2. Silver iodide generator used for cloud seeding (courtesy of Meteorology Research, Inc., Altadena, Calif.). It burns a solution composed of AgI-NH$_4$I in acetone.

2. Modification of Precipitation

In the United States and elsewhere there have been experimental programs designed to learn whether it is possible to increase rainfall by economically significant amounts (about 10% or more) by seeding developing cumuliform and thunderstorm clouds. Some of the work has been summarized by Simpson and Dennis (1974), the National Academy of Sciences (1973), Cleveland et al. (1978), and Dennis (1980).

Experiments conducted on summer cumuliform clouds in southern Arizona (Battan, 1966) and Missouri (Braham, 1966) attempted to blanket a prescribed region with silver iodide nuclei. It was reasoned that many of the clouds were deficient in natural ice nuclei and that, by supplying an adequate number, more precipitation particles and more rain would be produced. The method was to seed all clouds on a randomly selected sample of days and not to seed any clouds on an equal number of randomly selected days. The evidence indicates to this author that rainfall was decreased in Missouri, but the same cannot be said about the Arizona results. There have been strong disagreements among analysts on interpretation of the results. Lovasich et al. (1971) questioned the seeding procedures used in the Missouri experiment and the validity of the conclusion that seeding decreased rainfall. Battan (1966) reported that, even though there was less rain on seeded days than on nonseeded days in the Arizona experiment, the results probably occurred by chance rather than because of seeding. Neyman et al. (1972), who analyzed the data using different criteria from those employed by Battan, concluded that rainfall was decreased by the seeding.

Results of cloud-seeding tests in South Dakota (Dennis and Koscielski, 1969) led to the conclusion that relatively small, isolated cumuliform clouds could be made to yield more rain and that seeding of large, widespread clouds could cause rainfall decreases.

Randomized experiments by Australian scientists (Smith, 1974) showed that rain from individual supercooled cumulus clouds could be increased by seeding them with silver iodide nuclei. In Switzerland, in a program designed to test whether hail could be decreased, it was found that the thunderstorms apparently produced more rain after seeding with silver iodide nuclei (Schmid, 1967). Soviet scientists in the Ukraine have reported that seeding with ice nuclei increased rainfall from cumulonimbus clouds (see Battan, 1977a).

Gagin and Neumann (1976), reporting Israeli experiments involving the silver iodide seeding of convective clouds in winter, concluded that precipitation was increased by about 15%. In 1976 the Israeli government decided to begin operational seeding of the clouds over the drainage basin for Lake Tiberias. The clouds in Israel responding favorably to seeding are characterized as being "continental"; they are composed of large concentrations of small droplets. They differ from most cumulonimbus clouds observed over the United States in the summer, which usually have smaller droplet concentrations and larger droplets and are said to be "maritime" in character.

In summary, the experimental evidence suggests that, ex-

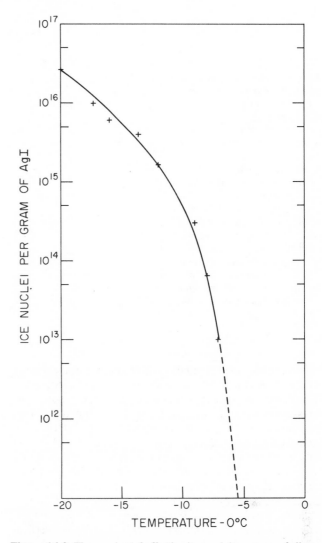

Figure 16.3. The number of effective ice nuclei per gram of silver iodide produced by a generator such as the one shown in Fig. 16.2. The dashed line is an extrapolation by the present author (Langer et al., 1974).

cept possibly in regions dominated by continental clouds composed of large concentrations of small, supercooled droplets, the effects of widespread seeding of all cumulus clouds over an area cannot be predicted adequately. When ice nuclei are seeded into clouds forming in moist air originating over oceans or heavily polluted air, the effects may be positive, negative, or nonexistent.

A second procedure for seeding convective clouds has been called *dynamic seeding* by Simpson et al. (1965). It is an extension of a procedure first tested by Kraus and Squires (1947) and Langmuir (1950) and operates on the hypothesis that, if the temperature within certain cumuliform clouds can be increased by small amounts, the clouds can be made to grow more than they are naturally inclined to do.

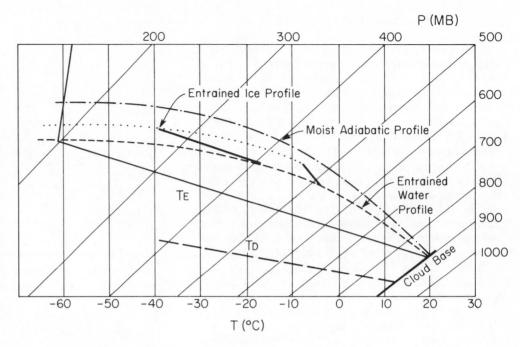

Figure 16.4. An illustration of the principle of "dynamic cumulus seeding." T_E and T_D represent environmental temperature and dew point, respectively. The heavy solid line extending from −15°C to −40°C is the postulated effect of natural ice nucleation. The shorter, heavy dark line extending from −4°C to −8°C represents the postulated effect of heavy ice nucleus seeding. Note that between the pressure levels 520 and 260 mb a seeded cloud would be expected to be warmer and more buoyant than a non-seeded cloud (McCarthy, 1972).

A cumulus cloud continues to grow as long as the density of cloud air is less than the density of the surrounding air. The cloud density depends on the temperature and vapor pressure of the air as well as on the mass of liquid or frozen hydrometeors per unit volume. Relatively simple theoretical models have been developed by Simpson et al. (1965) and others, allowing calculations of the vertical extent of a convective cloud as a function of its diameter for any given vertical distribution of temperature and dewpoint. On some occasions, in the middle layers of the atmosphere, there is a shallow, stable layer through which the temperature increases with height. The layer serves as a lid for vertical growth. In some circumstances increasing the cloud temperature only a few tenths of a degree Celsius raises the cloud buoyancy enough to allow the cloud to penetrate the stable layer and grow to greater altitude (Fig. 16.4). The dynamic-seeding technique seeks to do this by heavily seeding the supercooled part of the cloud in order to convert the cloud particles to ice and release large amounts of latent heat of fusion. Calculations show that this can raise the cloud temperature by as much as 1°C.

Simpson and Woodley (1971) and their associates carried out many experiments in Florida to test these ideas. Experimental clouds were selected after first calculating, for any day, which ones would respond favorably to seeding. The term *seedability* was used to represent the additional vertical growth that was predicted to occur as a result of seeding. After a cloud likely to be affected by seeding was identified, a random decision was made about whether to seed it or use it as a control cloud. The seeding was done by flying over a cloud and dropping into it flares containing silver iodide. Figure 16.5 presents the results of experiments conducted in 1965. They indicate that the seeding produced the expected augmentation of cloud growth. It was also concluded that more rain fell from seeded clouds as a result of the seeding.

Although the case is strong that individual cumuliform clouds can be made to yield more rain, the question of interest to agriculturalists and water engineers is whether significantly more rain can be made to fall over a fixed area. Specifically, can rainfall be increased by 10% or more during the summer over an area of about 2,000 km^2 by the selective seeding of cumuliform clouds indicated to be favorable by the latest mathematical model for predicting cloud growth? From 1970 to 1976, Simpson and her colleagues carried out the Florida Area Cumulus Experiment (FACE) to answer this question. From estimates provided by rain-gauge network and radar it was reported by Woodley et al. (1982) that over a fixed area in Florida there was more rain on seeded periods, but the differences between seeded and nonseeded days might reasonably have occurred by chance. On the other hand, other related analyses suggest that rainfall was increased because of the seeding.

During the summers of 1978 through 1980 a second series of cloud-seeding experiments was carried out to confirm or refute the results of the first FACE. According to Woodley et al. (1983), the new experiments gave indications that the seeding might have increased rainfall over the target area, but the results did not prove that the seeding increased the rainfall. In other words, the results did not confirm earlier evidence that rainfall over the target area could be increased significantly.

3. Hail-Damage Suppression

As noted in Chap. 11, hail does enormous damage to vegetation in many countries, particularly when it is accompanied by strong winds. For almost three decades cloud seeding has been employed in attempts to reduce the fall of damaging hail. Atlas (1977), Changnon (1977), Sulakvelidze et al. (1974), NAS (1973), Cleveland et al. (1978), and Dennis (1980) present surveys of hail modification research. Three fundamental approaches have been tried in hail modification programs:

1. The *glaciation hypothesis* proposes that, if virtually all the supercooled droplets in a cloud could be converted to ice crystals, hail would not form. There would be no way for collisions and accretion of supercooled droplets if none existed. Glaciation requires the appropriately timed and placed introduction of very large numbers of nuclei. Even if the seeding logistics could be worked out, the cost of seeding over the hail-prone regions of the United States or any other country would be impractically large.

2. The *beneficial-competition hypothesis* proposes that, by producing many more hailstones than would occur naturally, one can reduce the average size (Sulakvelidze et al., 1974). This concept assumes that there is, in any cloud, a nearly fixed supply of supercooled water available for the growth of hailstones. If this were the case, the average diameter would vary approximately as the cube root of the number of stones per unit volume. Various investigators, notably Browning and Foote (1976) and Young (1977), have argued that this concept of hailstone development is not valid in the Colorado supercell hailstorms. According to the competition hypothesis, relatively small amounts of seeding material are needed provided the material is inserted into a supercooled cloud at altitudes at which temperatures are between about $-5°$ and $-10°C$.

3. The *trajectory-lowering hypothesis* proposes that, by introducing large condensation nuclei (e.g., large salt particles) into the lowest part of the updraft of potential hailstorms, the average hailstone size can be reduced. Analyses show that large hailstones are almost accidental occurrences in the sense that of perhaps 10^4 growing hail embryos perhaps one follows a trajectory in a cloud that takes the stone through regions of sufficient supercooled liquid water to allow it to grow to large size (Young, 1977). The trajectory-lowering hypothesis calls for the production of many large water drops in a growing thunderstorm with the expectation that as they freeze and become large hailstone embryos they follow a low trajectory in the storm. There should be more hailstones, but the maximum sizes should be diminished.

Over the years there have been many hailstorm-seeding programs. Most were operational, i.e., all potential storms were seeded, and it is virtually impossible to determine unequivocally whether the seeding had any effect. The few programs designed as experiments to find out whether hail could be suppressed have given inconclusive results.

A randomized experiment known as Grossversuch III in Switzerland, carried out from 1957 to 1963 and seeding with silver iodide from the ground, failed to show that hail could be decreased (Schmid, 1967). In fact, a higher fraction of the seeded days had hail than did the nonseeded

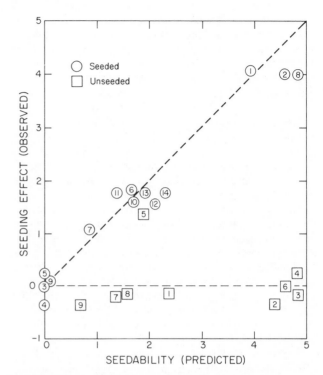

Figure 16.5. Seedability versus seeding effects for 14 seeded clouds (circles) and 9 control (squares) clouds in southern Florida in 1965. The data show that the clouds behaved mostly as they were predicted to behave (Simpson and Dennis, 1974).

days, and there is evidence for believing that this may have been caused by the seeding. There is no way of knowing whether there were significant differences in crop damage on seeded and nonseeded days. The amount of seeding material employed was small and certainly not enough to glaciate the storms.

An ice nucleus seeding experiment in Argentina, which involved randomization, gave mixed results (Grandoso and Iribarne, 1963). When the data were stratified according to whether the storms were associated with cold fronts or not, the first group of days showed 79% less hail damage on seeded days than on nonseeded days. When storms were not associated with cold fronts, there was 43% more damage on seeded days.

A randomized seeding project aimed at reducing hail was conducted in North Dakota over four seasons (Miller et al., 1975). It was reported that hail was generally less severe on seeded than on nonseeded days. Analyses of crop data led to the conclusion that seeding was responsible for the reduction in damage.

Interpretation of nonrandomized hail-suppression operations is difficult. Changnon (1977) summarized analyses of a number of hail-seeding projects and reported that estimated reductions of hail damage to crops amounted to 20 to 50% but that the results were "largely not significant at the 5% level."

Since the early 1960s, Soviet scientists have been carrying out hailstorm-seeding operations over increasingly large agricultural regions (Sulakvelidze et al., 1974; Sedunov, 1974). During 1976 about 12 million acres of farmland were subject to hail-suppression activities. Most Soviet programs work on the basis of the competition hypothesis. Lead iodide or silver iodide nuclei are introduced into the supercooled regions of potential hailstorms by rockets or exploding artillery shells. In part of the Republic of Georgia storms are seeded by firing projectiles containing about 230 g of sodium chloride into the warm part of the cloud (Battan, 1977a). About 2 to 3 min later, ice nuclei are fired into the supercooled region of the cloud.

Stantchev and Simeonov (1981) reported that more than 9,000 km^2 of farmland in Bulgaria have been covered by a hail-suppression program that involves seeding with lead iodide dispersed by rockets. They stated that the seeding "coincided with a reduction of crop losees due to hail amounting to 50–60 percent each year, or a cost-benefit ratio of 1:3." At the same time they reported that there had been "relatively little success in seeding severe supercell storms which occur on the average about once every four years."

According to Sulakvelidze et al. (1974) and Sedunov (1974), the seeding operations in the USSR have been reducing crop damage by 50 to 95%. It is virtually impossible to interpret satisfactorily the claims made by Soviet and Bulgarian scientists. Notwithstanding the analyses of Changnon (1977), the same can be said about the generally optimistic reports of commercial cloud seeders who have carried out hail-suppression operations without randomization or other suitable controls.

To determine whether the Soviet seeding techniques are as good as they are reported to be, appropriately designed tests must be conducted. The National Hail Research Experiment was established, in part, for such a purpose (Atlas, 1977).[1] Unfortunately, the seeding techniques were not equivalent to those used in the USSR. After 3 years of seeding it was found that hail occurrence or intensity had not been decreased. As a matter of fact, Atlas (1977) concluded that the seeding probably increased the number of hailstones, but the case certainly is not strong, and Knight et al. (1979) concluded that, because of the high degree of uncertainty in the statistical analyses, "no conclusion about a seeding effect can be drawn."

A joint Swiss-French-Italian group has carried out Grossversuch IV, a program for testing Soviet seeding rockets and procedures in a hail-suppression experiment in Switzerland (Federer et al., 1979). According to unpublished reports presented at the Conference-Workshop on Hailstorms and Hail Prevention held in Sofia, Bulgaria, September 20–25, 1982, the seeding tests carried out during Grossversuch IV did not show that the fall of damaging hail could be reduced.

Recent research (e.g. Nelson, 1983) suggests that perhaps the formation of large hail depends at least as much on

[1] See also the nine papers that appear in *Journal of Applied Meteorology* 18:1526–1639.

the dynamical structure of clouds as on their microphysics. If this were the case, it might explain why seeding with ice nuclei has not demonstrably modified hailstorms.

Questions are sometimes raised about the possibility that seeding for the purpose of reducing hail might also reduce rainfall. If the quantities of ice nuclei are at the levels used on the basis of the competition hypothesis, rainfall decreases are not likely but cannot be ruled out. In the Swiss experiment (Schmid, 1967) it appeared that more rain occurred as a result of the seeding. However, this point has not been given adequate attention.

In summary, evidence that cloud seeding can decrease hail and hail damage is conflicting. In theory it may be possible, but acceptable scientific evidence still does not exist.

4. Reduction of Lightning

Lightning is the greatest single cause of forest and grassland fires. It also causes extensive damage to property as well as injuries and deaths. For these reasons and because of a continuing interest in learning about electrical aspects of thunderstorms and lightning, there have been several attempts to modify lightning storms.

Underlying the experiments dealing with lightning reduction is the general hypothesis that by increasing the electrical conductivity of cumulonimbus clouds one can reduce the quantities of electric charge accumulated in the clouds.

The U.S. Forest Service carried out two sets of experiments in Montana, each during two summer periods, in which they tested the effects of ice-nuclei seeding. It was reasoned that an increase of ice crystals in the clouds would mean additional sources of corona currents and an increase in the leakage current between electric charge centers and the ground. On the basis of experiments in 1965 and 1967, Fuquay (1974) concluded from a comparison of lightning over the test area, during specific time periods when effects of seeding might be expected, that the data failed to show that seeding influenced lightning occurrence. On the other hand, when individual seeded thunderstorms were compared with nonseeded ones, it was found that there were fewer lightning strokes from seeded storms and that they had shorter durations than the lightning discharges from nonseeded storms. Fuquay (1974) has stated that the results strongly suggest that, "in some instances, lightning can be modified [by silver iodide seeding] in a beneficial manner."

Battan (1967) observed cloud-to-ground lightning frequency from randomly seeded and nonseeded clouds in southeastern Arizona and did not detect a seeding effect.

A second approach to the modification of lightning storms, changing the leakage currents, has been tested by Kasemir et al. (1976). The technique involves the dispersal, by means of an airplane, of huge numbers of 10-cm-long electrically conducting fibers at the base of a developing cumulonimbus cloud. After comparing 10 seeded and 18 nonseeded storms, Kasemir et al. concluded that the conducting fibers caused a reduction in lightning activity. These conclusions were questioned by Battan (1977b) and Griffiths (1977) and defended by Kasemir et al. (1977).

It appears that it might be possible to reduce cloud-to-ground lightning, but this has not yet been demonstrated conclusively.

5. Wind Reduction

Strong winds generated by thunderstorms are damaging to most forms of vegetation. Grains are blown over, and fruit trees can be stripped.

A characteristic feature of a thunderstorm is a downdraft transporting cool, moist air from aloft. In a mature, intense thunderstorm large masses of air descend, strike the ground, and spread outward. This accounts for the cool, gusty winds experienced as thunderstorms approach. The speed of the wind depends on the quantity of descending air and, perhaps more important, on the strength of the winds through the cloud layer. When the winds are strong, the downdraft air has a great deal of horizontal momentum that is mostly preserved as it descends.

When a line of severe thunderstorms occurs, the combined downdrafts can lead to strong outflowing winds at the ground. Sometimes they blow in a narrow zone in one direction and do substantial damage. When this happens, they are called *plow winds*.

It would be desirable to reduce the occurrence and strength of plow winds, but no one has yet proposed a scientifically proven method for doing so. Ice nucleus seeding was tried in Panama, on an operational basis, for the purpose of reducing wind damage to banana trees (Crow, 1959). The seeding was supposed to lead to a "reduction or suppression of the vertical development of cumulus clouds." It is doubtful that silver iodide seeding could accomplish this result. As noted earlier, it can be argued that ice crystal production can sometimes stimulate the growth of convective clouds.

In the Soviet Union there has been considerable work on the dissipation of growing convective clouds by artificial means. It is reasoned that if a downdraft can be initiated in a convective cloud, even a growing one, the downdraft will spread through the cloud and lead to its dissipation (Vul'fson et al., 1970; Vul'fson and Levin, 1972). It has been proposed that downdrafts can be initiated in several ways: by the introduction of several kilograms of powder such as cement into the upper part of the cloud, by the downwash of an airplane flying at a steep rate of climb through the cloud top, and by means of an explosive charge in the cloud top. There are serious questions about the theoretical foundation for these methods as they apply to vigorous convection leading to thunderstorms. There is only weak experimental evidence for the claims that the methods work. It cannot be concluded that, if the dissolution of small cumulus can be accelerated, the same procedure can inhibit cumulonimbus growth.

Presumably, if it were possible to destroy vigorous, growing cumulus, it would be possible to prevent the formation of thunderstorms. If this could be done, one could reduce thunderstorm-generated winds and reduce rainfall over regions where it was not wanted. It has yet to be shown, however, that the growth of thunderstorms can be prevented by artificial means.

6. Tornado Modification

It certainly would be desirable to find a way to prevent the formation of, or hasten the dissipation of, tornadoes. A typical tornado has a total energy equal to only about a thousandth that of an average thunderstorm. Unfortunately, the energy tends to be dissipated in a matter of minutes, and therefore the power for destruction is great. Nevertheless, the relatively low energy level of a tornado lends encouragement to those few scientists concerned with finding a procedure for tornado modification. Unfortunately, no one has come up with a promising, practical scheme for achieving this goal.

Davies-Jones and Kessler (1974) have summarized much of what is known about tornadoes and the suggestions for modifying them. They note that it has been proposed that, on days when tornadoes are expected, one might conceivably initiate the formation of many convective clouds in order to prevent any potential tornado-producing storm from getting the needed inflow air. Presumably the storms might be triggered by stimulated updrafts by means of the heat-generating meteotron (Dessens, 1960) or an array of jet engines used to produce a hot stream of rising air (Vul'fson et al., 1972; see also Battan, 1977a). The practical aspects of this procedure, even if it were theoretically valid, pose insurmountable difficulties.

It has been speculated that cloud seeding might be used to increase rainfall in order to increase the amount of outflowing cool air at the cloud base. The aim of this approach would be to cut off the air flowing into a tornado vortex. Still another suggestion is that explosive charges might be fired in tornado funnels with the hope that they would somehow disrupt the airflow in the vortex (see Chapter 10).

It seems clear that at this time there is no sound basis for tornado modification. It should also be noted that this problem has received very little attention. Most meteorologists take the position that, because of the ephemeral nature of tornadoes and the inadequate understanding of the physical processes involved, it is premature to give serious attention to tornado modification, but in view of the deadly and destructive character of tornadoes I take the contrary view and believe that it is important to intensify investigations of possible techniques for mitigating tornado hazards.

7. Certain General Problems

In any program to change any feature of the weather, particularly if the goal is to increase precipitation or decrease hail by means of cloud seeding, it is necessary to give consideration to possible effects outside the primary area of interest (the so-called target area). Evidence indicates that rainfall might be increased or decreased (Neyman et al., 1973). This possibility has led to legal actions by property owners who feel deprived of their natural rainfall. The courts have also heard claims that hail suppression has caused rain suppression. The absence of facts about what cloud seeding can or cannot do has not prevented the institution of lawsuits.

There are many legal, economic, ecological, and other social questions associated with weather modification. An interested reader may wish to refer to Sewell (1966), Fleagle (1968), Taubenfeld (1970), Haas (1974), and Cleveland et al. (1978).

8. Summary

This brief review of the progress and problems in the modification of thunderstorms does not support the view of some investigators that a practical weather modification technology exists. The evidence indicates that in certain meteorological situations thunderstorm rainfall might be increased but that in other circumstances it might be decreased.

Although the Hydrometeorological Services of the USSR and Bulgaria appear convinced that ice nuclei seeding by means of artillery and rockets can reduce hail damage to agriculture, and a number of commercial cloud seeders believe that seeding from airplanes can do likewise, the scientific evidence does not yet support that position.

The evidence that lightning can be reduced is meager but encouraging. At this time ideas on reducing wind damage or mitigating tornado hazards are in the realm of speculation.

In view of the enormous potential benefits of thunderstorm modification technologies and the fact that the available evidence offers some basis for optimism, additional research is urgently needed.

References

Chapter 2

Alexander, W. H., 1915, 1924, 1935. Distribution of thunderstorms in the United States. *Mon. Weather Rev.* 44:322–40; 52:337–48; 63:157–58.

Baldwin, J. F., 1968. *Climatic Atlas of the United States*. Environmental Data Service, Environmental Science Services Administration.

———, 1973. *Climates of the United States*. Environmental Data Service, NOAA.

Baliles, M., 1958. *History of Observational Instructions as Applied to Thunderstorms*. Key to Meteorological Records Documentation 3.12, Office of Climatology, U.S. Weather Bureau.

Brooks, C. F., A. J. Connor, et al., 1936. *Climatic Maps of North America*. Harvard University Press, Cambridge, Mass.

Bureau of Meteorology (Australia), 1929. *Results of Rainfall Observations Made in Western Australia*. Government Printer, Melbourne, Victoria, pp. 108–13.

Carte, A. R., 1967. Areal hail frequency. *J. Appl. Meteorol.* 6:336–38.

———, and I. L. Basson, 1970. Hail in the Pretoria-Witwatersrand area, 1962–1969. CSIR Res. Rep. No. 293, Pretoria, South Africa.

Changnon, S. A., 1957. Thunderstorm-precipitation relations in Illinois. Illinois State Water Survey Report of Investigation 34.

Changnon, S. A., Jr., 1973. Secular trends in thunderstorm frequencies. Preprints, Eighth Conference on Severe Local Storms, Denver, Colo., October 15–17, 1973. American Meteorological Society, Boston, pp. 115–21.

———, 1977. The scales of hail. *J. Appl. Meteorol.* 16:626–48.

Climatological Services Division, 1952. Mean number of thunderstorm days in the United States. U.S. Weather Bureau Tech. Paper 19.

Court, A., 1960. Thunderstorm frequency in northern California. *Bull. Am. Meteorol. Soc.* 41:406–409.

———, 1970. Tornado incidence maps. ESSA Research Laboratories, Natl. Severe Storms Lab., Tech. Memo. ERLTM NSSL-49.

———, 1974. The climate of the conterminous United States. In *Climates of North America*, World Survey of Climatology, Vol. 11, Elsevier, New York, pp. 193–343.

Crichlow, W. Q., R. C. Davis, R. T. Disney, and M. W. Clark, 1971. Hourly probability of world-wide thunderstorm occurrence. U.S. Office of Telecommunications, Institute for Telecommunication Sciences, Research Report 12.

Crow, L. W., 1969. Relationship between hail and rain in Kansas, Nebraska and eastern Colorado. Final Report, Contract No. NSF C-522.

Environmental Data Service, 1966. *Selected Climatic Maps of the United States*. Environmental Science Services Administration.

Flores, J. F., and V. F. Balagot, 1969. Climate of the Philippines. In *Climates of Northern and Eastern Asia*, World Survey of Climatology, Vol. 8, Elsevier, New York, pp. 159–213.

Frisby, E. M., and H. W. Sansom, 1967. Hail incidence in the tropics. *J. Appl. Meteorol.* 6:339–54.

Fujita, T. T., 1973. Tornadoes around the world. *Weatherwise* 26:56–62, 78–83.

Garnier, B. J., 1967. *Weather Conditions in Nigeria*. Climat. Res. Series, Vol. 2, McGill University, Department of Geography, Toronto.

Gentilli, J., 1971. The main climatological elements. In *Climates of Australia and New Zealand*, World Survey of Climatology, Vol. 13, Elsevier, New York, pp. 119–88.

Gisborne, H. T., 1927. The objectives of forest fire-weather research. *J. Forestry* 25:452–56.

Gokhale, N. R., 1975. *Hailstorms and Hailstone Growth*. State University of New York Press, Albany.

Grandoso, H. N., 1966. Distribución temporal y geográfica del granozo en la provincia de Mendoza y su relación con algunos parametros meteorológicos. Universidad de Buenos Aires, Facultad de Ciencias Exactas y Naturales, Contribuciones Científicas Serie Meteorología, Vol. 1 (7).

Greely, A. W., 1888. *American Weather*. Dodd, Mead & Co., New York.

Gregg, W. R., 1930. *Aeronautical Meteorology*. 2d ed. Ronald Press Co., New York.

Harrington, M. W., 1894. Rainfall and snow of the United States. U.S. Weather Bureau, Bulletin C.

Henderson, T. J., R. E. Rinehart, W. J. Carley, and J. M. Hansom, 1970. Physical studies of thunderstorms and evaluations related to the effectiveness of an operational hail suppression program near Kericho, Kenya. Final Report, Contract NSF C-548, Atmospherics Inc., Fresno, Calif.

Henry, A. J., 1906. Climatology of the United States. U.S. Weather Bureau Bulletin Q.

Henry, W. K., J. F. Griffiths, L. G. Cobb, and J. S. Cornett, 1966. Research on tropical rainfall and associated mesoscale systems. U.S. Army Electronics Command, Fort Monmouth, N.J., DA 36039, Rep. No. 11.

Humphreys, W. J., 1914. The thunderstorm and its phenomena. *Mon. Weather Rev.* 42:348–80.

———, 1920, 1929. *Physics of the Air*. Franklin Institute, Philadelphia.

Kessler, E., and J. T. Lee, 1978. Distribution of the tornado threat in the United States. *Bull. Am. Meteorol. Soc.* 59:61–62.

Kincer, J. B., 1922. *Atlas of American Agriculture*. Part 2, *Climate*, Sec. A, Precipitation and Humidity. U.S. Dept. of Agriculture, Washington, D.C.

Lumb, F. E., 1970. Topographic influences on thunderstorm activity near Lake Victoria. *Weather* 25:404–409.

Lydolph, P. E., 1977. *Climates of the Soviet Union*. World Survey of Climatology, Vol. 7, Elsevier, New York.

Lyman, H., 1915. Percentage frequency of thunderstorms in the United States, 1904–1913. *Mon. Weather Rev.* 44:619–20.

Maunder, W. J., 1971. Elements of New Zealand's climate. In *Climates of Australia and New Zealand*, World Survey of Climatology, Vol. 13, Elsevier, New York, pp. 229–63.

Mills, W. C., and H. B. Osborn, 1973. Stationarity in thunderstorm rainfall in the southwest. Proceedings, 1973 Meeting Arizona Section, American Water Resources Association, Tucson, Vol. 3, pp. 26–31.

Morgan, G. M., Jr., 1973. A general description of the hail problem in the Po Valley of northern Italy. *J. Appl. Meteorol.* 12:335–53.

National Weather Service, 1977. Climatology of heavy summer precipitation in eight states. NWS Central Region, Tech. Attachment 74-9.

Papee, H. M., E. G. Gori, A. C. Montefinale, and G. L. Petriconi, 1974. Comments on "A General Description of the Hail Problem in the Po Valley of Northern Italy." *J. Appl. Meteorol.* 13:182–84.

Paul, A. H., 1968. Regional variation in two fundamental properties of hailfalls. *Weather* 23:424–29.

Pautz, M. E. (ed.), 1969. Severe local storm occurrences, 1955–1967. U.S. Weather Bureau, ESSA Tech. Memo., WBTM FCST-12.

Portig, W. H., 1963. Thunderstorm frequency and amount of precipitation in the tropics, especially in the African and Indian monsoon regions. *Arch. Meteorol.*, Geophys. Bioklimatol. Ser. B, 13:21–35.

———, 1976. The Climate of Central America. In *Climates of Central and South America*, World Survey of Climatology, Vol. 12, Elsevier, New York, pp. 405–78.

Ramdas, L. A., V. Satakopan, and S. G. Rao, 1938. Frequency of days with hailstorms in India. *India J. Agri. Sci.* 8:787.

Rasmusson, E. M., 1971. Diurnal variation of summertime thunderstorm activity over the United States. U.S.A.F. Environmental Technical Applications Center, Tech. Note 71-4.

Schloemer, R. L., 1956. Thunderstorm Days in the United States. Map prepared in Climatological Services Division, U.S. Weather Bureau (unpublished).

Shands, A. L., 1947. Thunderstorm climatology. Thunderstorm rainfall, Hydrometeorological Rep. No. 5, U.S. Weather Bureau and Corps of Engineers, Vicksburg, Miss., pp. 81–233.

———, 1948. Thunderstorm probabilities in the United States. *Bull. Am. Meteorol. Soc.* 29:270–74.

Skaggs, R. H., 1974. Severe hail in the United States. Proceedings, Association of American Geographers, 6:43–46.

Smith, L., and E. C. Thom, 1941. *Airway Meteorological Atlas for the United States*. U.S. Weather Bureau, No. 1314.

Stout, G. E., and S. A. Changnon, Jr., 1968. Climatography of hail in the central United States. Crop Hail Insurance Actuarial Association, Research Rep. 38.

Sulakvelidze, A. K., 1969. *Rainstorms and Hail*. Trans. by Israel Program for Scientific Translation (National Technical Information Service, Springfield, Va., TT68-50466).

Takeuchi, T., and M. Nagatani, 1974. Oceanic thunderstorms in the tropical and subtropical Pacific. *J. Meteorol. Soc. Japan* 52(6):509–11.

Trent, E. M., and S. G. Gathman, 1972. Oceanic thunderstorms. *Pure Appl. Geophys.* 100(8):60–69.

U.S. Army Engineer Topographic Labs, 1974. Weather extremes around the world. ETL-TR-74-5.

USDA (U.S. Department of Agriculture), 1941. *Climate and Man*. Washington, D.C.

USGS (U.S. Geological Survey), 1971. *National Atlas of the United States*.

U.S. Naval Weather Service, 1969– . *World-Wide Airfield Summaries*. Vols. 1–11.

Vigansky, H., 1975. General summary of tornadoes, 1975. U.S. Department of Commerce, NOAA, *Climatological Data, National Summary* 26(13).

Visher, S. S., 1948. Thunderstorms. *Sci. Mon.* 64:335–40.

———, 1954. *Climatic Atlas of the United States*. Harvard University Press, Cambridge, Mass.

Wallace, J. M., 1975. Diurnal variations in precipitation and thunderstorm frequency over the conterminous United States. *Mon. Weather Rev.* 103:406–19.

Ward, R. D., and C. F. Brooks, 1936. *Climates of North America: Mexico, United States, Alaska*. Handbuch der Klimatologie, W. Köppen and R. Geiger (eds.), Vol. 2. Borntrager, Berlin.

Watts, I. E. H., 1969. Climates of China and Korea. In *Climates of Northern and Eastern Asia*, World Survey of Climatology, Vol. 8, Elsevier, New York, pp. 1–117.

Weigel, E. P., 1976. Lightning: the underrated killer. *NOAA Mag.* 6(2):4–11.

Weikinn, C., 1967. Bermerkenswerte Hydrometeorologische Erscheinungen früherer Jahrhunderte in Europa, Teil I. Sehr starke bzw. verbreitete Hagelfälle in den Jahren 1100–1400 (Remarkable hydrometeorological phenomena of earlier centuries in Europe, Pt. 1. Very intensive or excessive hail during 1100 to 1400). *Acta Hydrophys.* 11(3):181–206.

Williams, L., 1973. Hail and distribution. Special Report of the Engineer Topographic Laboratories, Ft. Belvoir, Va., ETL-SR-73-3.

WMO (World Meteorological Organization), 1953. *World Distribution of Thunderstorm Days*, WMO No. 21, TP. 6 and Supplement (1956), Geneva.

Zegel, F. H., 1967. Lightning deaths in the United States; a seven-year survey from 1959 to 1965. *Weatherwise* 20:169–73, 179.

Chapter 3

Bretschneider, C., 1967. Maximum sea state for the North Atlantic hurricane belt. *Ocean Eng.* 2:43–52.

Golden, J. H., 1974a. The life of Florida Keys waterspouts, I. *J. Appl. Meteorol.* 13:676–92.

———, 1974b. Scale interaction implications for the waterspout life cycle, II. *J. Appl. Meteorol.* 13:693–709.

Mason, B. J., 1972. The Bakerian Lecture, 1971: The physics of the thunderstorm. *Proc. R. Soc. London A* 327:433–66.

Moore, C. B., B. Vonnegut, B. A. Stein, and J. H. Survilas, 1960. Observations of electrification and lightning in warm clouds. *J. Geophys. Res.* 65:1907–10.

Newell, R. E., 1979. Climate and the ocean. *Am. Sci.* 67(4):405–16.

Pierson, W. J., Jr., L. J. Tick, and L. Baer, 1966. Computer based procedures for preparing global wave forecasts and wind field analyses capable of using wave data obtained by a spacecraft. Proceedings, Sixth Symposium Naval Hydrodynamics, 28 September–4 October 1966. Office of Naval Research, Washington, D.C.

Sanders, F., 1972. Meteorological and oceanographic conditions during the 1970 Bermuda yacht race. *Mon. Weather Rev.* 100: 597–606.

Trent, E. M., and S. G. Gathman, 1972. Oceanic thunderstorms. *Pure Appl. Geophys.* 100:60–69.

U.S. Weather Bureau, 1968. Synoptic code: standards and procedures for the coding of synoptic reports. Federal Meteorological Handbook No. 3, Depts. of Commerce, Defense, and Transportation, Washington, D.C.

WMO (World Meteological Organization), 1953. *World Distribution of Thunderstorm Days. Part 1: Tables.* WMO No. 21, TP. 6.

————, 1956. *World Distribution of Thunderstorm Days. Part 2: Tables of Marine Data and World Maps.* WMO No. 21, TP. 21.

Chapter 4

Betts, A. K., 1974. Further comments on "A comparison of the equivalent potential temperature and static energy." *J. Atmos. Sci.* 31:1713–15.

————, 1975. Parametric interpretation of trade wind cumulus budget studies. *J. Atmos. Sci.* 32:1934–45.

————, R. W. Grover, and M. W. Moncrieff, 1976. Structure and motion of tropical squall-lines over Venezuela. *Q. J. R. Meteorol. Soc.* 102:395–404.

Browning, K. A., 1964. Airflow and precipitation trajectories within severe local storms which travel to the right of the winds. *J. Atmos. Sci.* 21:634–39.

————, and F. H. Ludlam, 1962. Airflow in convective storms. *Q. J. R. Meteorol. Soc.* 88:117–35.

Byers, H. R., and R. R. Braham, 1949. *The Thunderstorm.* U.S. Government Printing Office, Washington, D.C.

Darkow, G. L., 1968. The total energy environment of severe storms. *J. Appl. Meteorol.* 7:199–205.

————, and R. L. Livingston, 1975. Hourly surface static energy analysis as a delineator of thunderstorm outflow areas. *Mon. Weather Rev.* 103:817–22.

Emanuel, K. A., 1981. A similarity theory for unsaturated downdrafts within clouds. *J. Atmos. Sci.* 38:1541–57.

Fankhauser, J. C., 1971. Thunderstorm-environmental interactions determined from aircraft and radar observations. *Mon. Weather Rev.* 99:171–91.

————, 1976. Structure of an evolving hailstorm. Part 2: Thermodynamic structure and airflow in the near environment. *Mon. Weather Rev.* 104:576–87.

Foote, G. B., and J. C. Fankhauser, 1973. Airflow and moisture budget beneath a northeast Colorado hailstorm. *J. Appl. Meteorol.* 12:1330–53.

Fritsch, J. M., 1975. Cumulus dynamics: local compensating subsidence and its implications for cumulus parameterization. *Pure Appl. Geophys.* 113:851–67.

Fujita, T., 1955. Results of detailed synoptic studies of squall lines. *Tellus* 7:405–36.

————, 1959. Precipitation and cold air production in mesoscale thunderstorm systems. *J. Meteorol.* 16:454–66.

Fujita, T. T., 1973. Proposed mechanism of tornado formation from rotating thunderstorm. Preprints, Eighth Conference on Severe Local Storms. American Meteorological Society, Boston, pp. 191–96.

————, D. L. Bradbury, and C. F. Van Thullenar, 1970. Palm Sunday tornadoes of April 11, 1965. *Mon. Weather Rev.* 98: 26–29.

Galway, J. G., 1956. The lifted index as a predictor of latent instability. *Bull. Am. Meteorol. Soc.* 37:528–29.

George, J. J., 1960. *Weather Forecasting for Aeronautics.* Academic Press, New York.

Kiefer, P. J., 1941. The thermodynamic properties of water and water vapor. *Mon. Weather Rev.* 69:329–31.

Krietzberg, C. W., 1964. The structure of occlusions as determined from serial ascents and vertically-directed radar. Air Force Cambridge Research Laboratory, Res. Rep. 64-26.

Levine, J., 1959. Spherical vortex theory of bubble-like motions in cumulus clouds. *J. Meteorol.* 16:653–62.

Malkus, J. S., 1952. The slopes of cumulus clouds in relation to external wind shear. *Q. J. R. Meteorol. Soc.* 78:530–42.

Marwitz, J. D., 1972. The structure and motion of severe hailstorms, Part I: supercell storms. *J. Appl. Meteorol.* 11:166–79.

Miller, R. C., 1972. Notes on analysis and severe storm forecasting procedures of the Air Force Global Weather Control. AFGWC Tech. Rep. 200 (Rev.), Air Weather Service, U.S. Air Force.

Moncrieff, M. W., and J. S. A. Green, 1972. The propagation and transfer properties of steady convective overturning in shear. *Q. J. R. Meteorol. Soc.* 98:336–52.

————, and M. J. Miller, 1976. The dynamics and simulation of tropical cumulonimbus and squall lines. *Q. J. R. Meteorol. Soc.* 102:373–94.

Murray, F. W., 1970. Numercial models of a tropical cumulus cloud with bilateral and axial symmetry. *Mon. Weather Rev.* 98:14–28.

Newton, C. W., 1950. Structure and mechanism of the prefrontal squall line. *J. Meteorol.* 7:210–22.

————, 1963. Dynamics of severe convective storms. In *Severe Local Storms*, Meteorol. Monogr. 5, American Meteorological Society, Boston, pp. 33–58.

————, 1966. Circulations in large sheared cumulonimbus. *Tellus* 180:699–713.

————, and H. R. Newton, 1959. Dynamical interactions between large convective clouds and environment with vertical shear. *J. Meteorol.* 16:483–96.

Normand, W. W. B., 1946. Energy in the atmosphere. *Q. J. R. Meteorol. Soc.* 72:145–67.

Paluch, I. R., 1979. The entrainment mechanism in Colorado cumuli. *J. Atmos. Sci.* 36:2462–78.

Prosser, N. E., and D. S. Foster, 1966. Upper air sounding analysis by use of an electronic computer. *J. Appl. Meteorol.* 5: 296–303.

Purdom, J. F. W., 1973. Picture of the month: meso-highs and satellite imagery. *Mon. Weather Rev.* 101:180–81.

————, 1976. Some uses of high resolution GOES imagery on the mesoscale forecasting of convection and its behavior. *Mon. Weather Rev.* 104:1474–83.

Riehl, H., and J. S. Malkus, 1958. On the heat balance of the equatorial trough zone. *Geophysica* 6:503–37.

Showalter, A. K., 1953. A stability index for thunderstorm forecasting. *Bull. Am. Meteorol. Soc.* 34:250–52.

Simpson, J., G. Van Helvort, and M. McCumber, 1982. Three dimensional simulations of cumulus congestus clouds on Gate day 261. *J. Atmos. Sci.* 39:126–45.

Squires, P., 1958. Penetrative downdrafts in cumuli. *Tellus* 10: 381–89.

Stommel, H., 1947. Entraining of air into a cumulus cloud. *J. Meteorol.* 4:91–94.

Zipser, E. J., 1969. The role of organized unsaturated convective downdrafts in the structure and rapid decay of an equatorial disturbance. *J. Appl. Meteorol.* 8:799–814.

————, 1977. Mesoscale and convective-scale downdrafts as distinct components of squall-line structure. *Mon. Weather Rev.* 105:1568–89.

Chapter 5

Anthes, R. A., 1983. Regional models of the atmosphere in middle latitudes. *Mon. Weather Rev.* 111:1306–35.

————, Y.-H. Kuo, S. G. Benjamin, and Y.-F. Li, 1982. The evolution of the mesoscale environment of severe local storms: Preliminary modeling results. *Mon. Weather Rev.* 110:1187–1213.

Austin, J. M., 1951. Cumulus convection and entrainment. In *Compendium of Meteorology*, T. F. Malone (ed.), American Meteorological Society, Boston, pp. 694–704.

Barnes, S. L., 1970. Some aspects of a severe right-moving thunderstorm deduced from mesonetwork rawinsonde observations. *J. Atmos. Sci.* 27:634–48.

————, and S. P. Nelson, 1978. Oklahoma thunderstorms on 29–30 April 1970: IV, Study of a dissipating severe storm. *Mon. Weather Rev.* 106:704–712.

Bates, F. C., 1961. The Great Plains squall-line thunderstorm—a model. Ph.D. diss., St. Louis University. 164 pp. (available from University Microfilms, Ann Arbor, Mich.).

Beebe, R. G., 1955. Types of airmasses in which tornadoes occur. *Bull. Am. Meteorol. Soc.* 36:349–50.

————, 1958. Tornado proximity soundings. *Bull. Am. Meteorol. Soc.* 39:195–201.

————, and F. C. Bates, 1955. A mechanism for assisting in the release of convective instability. *Mon. Weather Rev.* 83:1–10.

Bellamy, J. C., 1949. Objective calculations of divergence, vertical velocity and vorticity. *Bull. Am. Meteorol. Soc.* 30:45–49.

Bjerknes, J., 1951. Extratropical cyclones. In *Compendium of Meteorology*, T. F. Malone (ed.), American Meteorological Society, Boston, pp. 577–98.

————, and J. Holmboe, 1944. On the theory of cyclones. *J. Meteorol.* 1:1–22.

Blackadar, A. K., 1957. Boundary layer wind maxima and their significance for the growth of nocturnal inversions. *Bull. Am. Meteorol. Soc.* 38:283–90.

Bonner, W. D., 1968. Climatology of the low level jet. *Mon. Weather Rev.* 96:833–50.

Bradbury, D. L., 1957. Moisture analysis and water budget in three different types of storms. *J. Meteorol.* 14:599–65.

Brenner, I. S., 1974. A surge of tropical air—Gulf of California to the Southwestern United States. *Mon. Weather Rev.* 102:375–89.

Brooks, H. B., 1946. A summary of some radar thunderstorm observations. *Bull. Am. Meteorol. Soc.* 27:557–63.

Browning, K. A., 1964. Airflow and precipitation trajectories within severe local storms which travel to the right of the winds. *J. Atmos. Sci.* 21:634–39.

————, 1968. The organization of severe local storms. *Weather* 23:429–34.

————, and G. B. Foote, 1976. Airflow and hail growth in supercell storms and some implications for hail suppression. *Q. J. R. Meteorol. Soc.* 102:499–533.

————, and F. H. Ludlam, 1962. Airflow in convective storms. *Q. J. R. Meteorol. Soc.* 88:117–35.

Byers, H. R., and R. R. Braham, Jr., 1949. *The Thunderstorm.* U.S. Government Printing Office, Washington, D.C.

Carlson, T. N., S. G., Benjamin, G. S. Forbes, and Y.-F. Li, 1983. Elevated mixed layers in the regional severe storm environment:

Conceptual model and case studies. *Mon. Weather Rev.* 111:1453–73.

————, and F. H. Ludlam, 1968. Conditions for the occurrence of severe local storms. *Tellus* 20:203–26.

Charba, J. P., 1975. Operational scheme for short range forecasts of severe local weather. Preprints, Ninth Conference on Severe Local Storms. American Meteorological Society, Boston, pp. 51–57.

————, 1979. Two to six hour severe local storm probabilities: an operational forecasting system. *Mon. Weather Rev.* 107:268–82.

Chisholm, A. J., 1973. Radar case studies and airflow models. In *Alberta Hailstorms*, Meteorol. Monogr. 14, American Meteorological Society, Boston, pp. 1–36.

Cooley, J. R., 1978. Cold air funnel clouds. *Mon. Weather Rev.* 106:1368–72.

Crutcher, H. L., 1959. *Upper Wind Statistics Charts of the Northern Hemisphere.* NAVAER 50-1C-535, Vol. 1, Office of Chief of Naval Operations, Washington, D.C.

Das, P., and M. C. Subba Rao, 1972. The unsaturated downdraught. *Ind. J. Meteorol. Geophys.* 23:135–44.

David, C. L., 1976. A study of upper air parameters at the time of tornadoes. *Mon. Weather Rev.* 104:546–51.

Davies-Jones, R. P., and J. H. Henderson, 1975. Updraft properties deduced statistically from rawin soundings. *Pure Appl. Geophys.* 113:787–801.

Desai, B. N., and S. Mal, 1938. Thundersqualls of Bengal. *Gerlands Beitr. Geophys.* 53:285–304.

Dines, W. H., 1912. The vertical temperature distribution in the atmosphere over England, with some remarks on the general and local circulation. *Geophys. Mem.* No. 1.

————, 1919. The characteristics of the free atmosphere. *Geophys. Mem.* No. 13.

Djurić, D., and M. S. Damiani, Jr., 1980. On the formation of the low-level jet over Texas. *Mon. Weather Rev.* 108:1854–65.

Fankhauser, J. C., 1965. Water budget considerations in an extensive squall-line development. Tech. Note 4-NSSL-25, U.S. Weather Bureau, Washington, D.C.

————, 1971. Thunderstorm environment interactions determined from aircraft and radar observations. *Mon. Weather Rev.* 99:171–92.

Fawbush, E. J., and R. C. Miller, 1953. A method for forecasting hailstone size at the earth's surface. *Bull. Am. Meteorol. Soc.* 34:235–44.

————, and ————, 1954. A basis for forecasting peak gusts in non-frontal thunderstorms. *Bull. Am. Meteorol. Soc.* 35:14–19.

————, R. C. Miller, and L. G. Starrett, 1951. An empirical method of forecasting tornado development. *Bull. Am. Meteorol. Soc.* 32:1–9.

Fawcett, E. B., and H. K. Saylor, 1965. A study of the distribution of weather accompanying Colorado cyclogenesis. *Mon. Weather Rev.* 93:359–67.

Foote, G. B., and J. C. Fankhauser, 1973. Airflow and moisture budget beneath a northeast Colorado hailstorm. *J. Appl. Meteorol.* 12:1330–53.

Fritsch, J. M., and D. M. Rodgers, 1981. The Ft. Collins hailstorm—An example of the short-term forecast enigma. *Bull. Am. Meteorol. Soc.* 62:1560–69.

————, C. F. Chappell, and L. R. Hoxit, 1976. The use of large-scale budgets for convective parameterization. *Mon. Weather Rev.* 104:1408–18. (Corrected figures, 105:1063–66.)

Fujita, T., 1955. Results of detailed synoptic studies of squall lines. *Tellus* 7:405–36.

————, 1959. Precipitation and cold-air production in mesoscale thunderstorm systems. *J. Meteorol.* 16:454–66.

———, and H. R. Byers, 1977. Spearhead echo and downdraft burst in the crash of an airliner. *Mon. Weather Rev.* 105:129–46.

Fulks, J. R., 1951. The instability line. In *Compendium of Meteorology*, T. F. Malone (ed.), American Meteorological Society, Boston, Mass., pp. 647–52.

Galway, J. G., 1958. Composite charts for tornado situations under northwest flow aloft. General Meeting, American Meteorological Society, Kansas City, Mo.

Hales, J. E., Jr., 1974. Southwestern United States summer monsoon source—Gulf of Mexico or Pacific Ocean? *J. Appl. Meteorol.* 13:331–42.

Haltiner, G. J., and F. L. Martin, 1957. *Dynamical and Physical Meteorology*. McGraw-Hill, New York.

Hamilton, R. A., and J. W. Archbold, 1945. Meteorology of Nigeria and adjacent territory. *Q. J. R. Meteorol. Soc.* 71:231–64.

Harrison, H. T., and W. K. Orendorff, 1941. Pre-coldfrontal squall lines. United Air Lines Transport Corp. Meteorol. Circ. No. 16.

Henderson, J. H., 1971. The internal structure of a thunderstorm as revealed by θ_w surfaces. Preprints, Seventh Conference on Severe Local Storms. American Meteorological Society, Boston, pp. 234–39.

Hess, S. L., 1959. *Introduction to Theoretical Meterology*. Holt, Rinehart and Winston, New York.

Hitschfeld, W., 1960. The motion and erosion of convective storms in severe vertical wind shear. *J. Meteorol.* 17:270–82.

Hoecker, W. H., Jr., 1963. Three southerly low-level jet streams delineated by the Weather Bureau special pibal network of 1961. *Mon. Weather Rev.* 91:573–82.

House, D. C., 1963. Forecasting tornadoes and severe thunderstorms. In *Severe Local Storms*, Meteorol. Monogr. 5, American Meteorological Society, Boston, pp. 141–55.

Hoxit, L. R., and C. F. Chappell, 1975. Tornado outbreak of April 3–4, 1974; synoptic analysis. Tech. Rep. ERL 338-APCL 37, NOAA Environmental Research Laboratories, Boulder, Colo.

Huff, F. A., and S. A. Changnon, Jr., 1964. A model 10-inch rainstorm. *J. Appl. Meteorol.* 3:587–99.

Humphreys, W. J., 1914. The thunderstorm and its phenomena. *Mon. Weather Rev.* 42:348–80.

Johns, R. H., 1977. A climatology of northwest flow severe weather outbreaks. Preprints, Tenth Conference on Severe Local Storms. American Meteorological Society, Boston, pp. 174–79.

———, 1982. A synoptic climatology of northwest flow severe weather outbreaks. Part I: Nature and significance. *Mon. Weather Rev.* 110:1653–63.

Kamburova, P. L., and F. H. Ludlam, 1966. Rainfall evaporation in thunderstorm downdraughts. *Q. J. R. Meteorol. Soc.* 92:510–48.

Karr, T. W., and R. L. Wooten, 1976. Summer radar echo distribution around Limon, Colorado. *Mon. Weather Rev.* 104:728–34.

Kelly, D. L., J. T. Schaefer, R. P. McNulty, C. A. Doswell III, and R. F. Abbey, Jr., 1978. An augmented tornado climatology. *Mon. Weather Rev.* 106:1172–83.

Kessler, E., 1969. *On the Distribution and Continuity of Water Substance in Atmospheric Circulations*. Meteorol. Monogr. 10, American Meteorological Society, Boston.

Kocin, P. J., L. W. Uccellini, and R. A. Petersen, 1982. The role of jet streak "coupling" in the development of the 10–11 April 1979 Wichita Falls tornado outbreak. Preprints, Twelfth Conference on Severe Local Storms. American Meteorological Society, Boston, pp. 560–63.

Kropfli, R. A., and L. J. Miller, 1975. Thunderstorm flow patterns in three dimensions. *Mon. Weather Rev.* 103:70–71.

Krumm, W. R., 1954. On the cause of downdrafts from dry thunderstorms over the plateau area of the United States. *Bull. Am. Meteorol. Soc.* 35:122–25.

Lemon, L. R., 1976. The flanking line, a severe thunderstorm intensification source. *J. Atmos. Sci.* 33:686–94.

McDonald, W. F., 1938. *Atlas of Climatic Charts of the Oceans*. W. B. No. 1247, U.S. Government Printing Office, Washington, D.C.

McNab, A. L., and A. K. Betts, 1978. A mesoscale budget study of cumulus convection. *Mon. Weather Rev.* 106:1317–31.

McNulty, R. P., 1978. On upper tropospheric kinematics and severe weather occurrence. *Mon. Weather Rev.* 106:662–72.

Maddox, R. A., 1976. An evaluation of tornado proximity wind and stability data. *Mon. Weather Rev.* 104:133–42.

———, C. F. Chappell, and L. R. Hoxit, 1979. Synoptic and meso-α scale aspects of flash flood events. *Bull. Am. Meteorol. Soc.* 60:115–23.

———, L. R. Hoxit, C. F. Chappell, and F. Caracena, 1978. Comparison of meteorological aspects of the Big Thompson and Rapid City flash floods. *Mon. Weather Rev.* 106:375–89.

Marwitz, J. D., 1972a. The structure and motion of severe hailstorms: I, Supercell storms. *J. Appl. Meteorol.* 11:166–79.

———, 1972b. Precipitation efficiency of thunderstorms on the high plains. *J. Rech. Atmos.* 6:367–70.

———, 1973. Trajectories within the weak echo regions of hailstorms. *J. Appl. Meteorol.* 12:1174–82.

Means, L. L., 1944. The nocturnal maximum occurrence of thunderstorms in the midwestern states. University of Chicago, Department of Meteorology, Misc. Rep. No. 16.

———, 1952. On thunderstorm forecasting in the central United States. *Mon. Weather Rev.* 80:165–89.

———, 1954. A study of the mean southerly wind maximum in low levels associated with a period of summer precipitation in the Middle West. *Bull. Am. Meteorol. Soc.* 35:166–70.

Miller, J. E., 1955. Intensification of precipitation by differential advection. *J. Meteorol.* 12:472–77.

Miller, R. C., 1972. Notes on analysis and severe-storm forecasting procedures of the Air Force Global Weather Central. Tech. Rep. 200 (Rev.), Air Weather Service, Scott Air Force Base, Ill.

Mintz, Y., and G. A. Dean, 1952. The observed mean field of motion of the atmosphere. *Geophys. Res. Papers* 17:1–65.

Nelson, S. P., and R. R. Braham, Jr., 1975. Detailed observational study of a weak echo region. *Pure Appl. Geophys.* 113:735–46.

Newton, C. W., 1950. Structure and mechanism of the prefrontal squall line. *J. Meteorol.* 7:210–22.

———, 1963. Dynamics of severe convective storms. *Meteorol. Monogr.* 5(27):33–58.

———, 1966. Circulations in large sheared cumulonimbus. *Tellus* 18:699–713.

———, 1968. Convective cloud dynamics—a synopsis. Proceedings, International Conference on Cloud Physics, Toronto. American Meteorological Society, Boston, pp. 487–98.

———, and J. C. Fankhauser, 1964. On the movements of convective storms, with emphasis on size discrimination in relation to water-budget requirements. *J. Appl. Meteorol.* 3:651–68.

———, and ———, 1975. Movement and propagation of multicellular convective storms. *Pure Appl. Geophys.* 113:747–64.

———, and H. R. Newton, 1959. Dynamical interactions between large convective clouds and environment with vertical shear. *J. Meteorol.* 16:483–96.

Normand, C. W. B., 1938. On instability from water vapor. *Q. J. R. Meteorol. Soc.* 64:47–69.

———, 1946. Energy in the atmosphere. *Q. J. R. Meteorol. Soc.* 72:145–67.

Notis, C., and J. L. Stanford, 1973. The contrasting synoptic and physical character of northeast and southeast advancing tornadoes in Iowa. *J. Appl. Meteorol.* 12:1163–73.

———, and ———, 1976. The synoptic and physical character of Oklahoma tornadoes. *Mon. Weather Rev.* 104:397–406.

Ogura, Y., and M.-T. Liou, 1980. The structure of a midlatitude squall line: A case study. *J. Atmos. Sci.* 37:553–67.

Palmén, E., and C. W. Newton, 1969. *Atmospheric Circulation Systems.* Academic Press, New York.

Pearson, A., and S. J. Weiss, 1979. Some trends in forecast skill at the National Severe Storms Forecast Center. *Bull. Am. Meteorol. Soc.* 60:319–26.

Perkey, D. J., 1976. A description and preliminary results from a finemesh model for forecasting quantitative precipitation. *Mon. Weather Rev.* 104:1513–26.

Petterssen, S., 1956. *Weather Analysis and Forecasting.* 2d ed. Vols. 1 and 2. McGraw-Hill, New York.

Porter, J. M., L. L. Means, J. E. Hovde, and W. B. Chappell, 1955. A synoptic study on the formation of squall lines in the north central United States. *Bull. Am. Meteorol. Soc.* 36:390–96.

Ramaswamy, C., 1956. On the sub-tropical jet stream and its role in the development of large-scale convection. *Tellus* 8:26–60.

Rasmusson, E. M., 1967. Atmospheric water vapor transport and the water balance of North America: I, Characteristics of the water vapor flux field. *Mon. Weather Rev.* 95:403–26.

———, 1971. Diurnal variation of summer-time thunderstorm activity over the United States. USAFETAC TN 71-4, U.S. Air Force Environmental Technical Applications Center, Washington, D.C.

Reap, R. M., and D. S. Foster, 1975. New operational thunderstorm and severe storm probability forecasts based on model output statistics (MOS). Preprints, Ninth Conference on Severe Local Storms. American Meteorological Society, Boston, pp. 58–63.

Rhea, J. O., 1966. A study of thunderstorm formation along dry lines. *J. Appl. Meteorol.* 5:58–63.

Riehl, H., 1954. *Tropical Meteorology.* McGraw-Hill, New York.

Roach, W. T., 1967. On the nature of the summit areas of severe storms in Oklahoma. *Q. J. R. Meteorol. Soc.* 93:318–36.

Sanders, F., and K. A. Emanuel, 1977. The momentum budget and temporal evolution of a mesoscale convective system. *J. Atmos. Sci.* 34:322–30.

———, and R. J. Paine, 1975. The structure and thermodynamics of an intense mesoscale convective storm in Oklahoma. *J. Atmos. Sci.* 32:1563–79.

Saucier, W. J., 1955. *Principles of Meteorological Analysis.* University of Chicago Press, Chicago.

Showalter, A. K., and J. R. Fulks, 1943. Preliminary report on tornadoes. U.S. Weather Bureau, Washington, D.C.

Stout, G. E., and S. A. Changnon, Jr., 1968. Climatography of hail in the central United States. Res. Rep. No. 38, Crop Hail Insurance Actuarial Association, Chicago.

———, and H. W. Hiser, 1955. Radar scope interpretations of wind, hail, and heavy rain storms between May 27 and June 8, 1954. *Bull. Am. Meteorol. Soc.* 36:519–27.

Uccellini, L., and D. R. Johnson, 1979. The coupling of upper and lower tropospheric jet streaks and implications for the development of severe convective storms. *Mon. Weather Rev.* 107:682–703.

U.S. Weather Bureau, 1956. Forecasting tornadoes and severe thunderstorms, Forecasting Guide No. 1. J. S. Winston (ed.), U.S. Department of Commerce, Washington, D.C.

Wallace, J. M., 1975. Diurnal variations in precipitation and thunderstorm frequency over the conterminous United States. *Mon. Weather Rev.* 103:406–19.

Walters, G. W., 1975. Severe thunderstorm wind gusts. S.M. thesis, Dept. of Atmospheric Science, Colorado State University, Fort Collins.

Weaver, J. F., 1979. Storm motion as related to boundary-layer convergence. *Mon. Weather Rev.* 107:612–19.

Weickmann, H. K., 1953. Observational data on the formation of precipitation in cumulonimbus clouds. In *Thunderstorm Electricity,* H. R. Byers (ed.), University of Chicago Press, Chicago, pp. 66–138.

———, 1964. The language of hailstorms and hailstones. *Nubila* 6:7–51.

Weisman, M. L., and J. B. Klemp, 1982. The dependence of numerically simulated convective storms on vertical wind shear and buoyancy. *Mon. Weather Rev.* 110:504–20.

Whitney, L. F., Jr., 1977. Relationship of the subtropical jet stream to severe local storms. *Mon. Weather Rev.* 105:398–412.

Williams, R. J., 1976. Surface parameters associated with tornadoes. *Mon. Weather Rev.* 104:540–45.

WMO (World Meteorological Organization), 1953. *World Distribution of Thunderstorm Days.* WMO No. 21, TP. 6 and Supplement (1956). World Meteorological Organization, Geneva, Switzerland, 204.

Zehr, R. M., and J. F. W. Purdom, 1982. Examples of a wide variety of thunderstorm propagation mechanisms. Preprints, Twelfth Conference on Severe Local Storms. American Meteorological Society, Boston, pp. 499–502.

Chapter 6

Ackerman, B., and H. Appleman, 1974. Boundary layer program. Interim report of METROMEX studies, 1971–73, Illinois State Water Survey, pp. 121–24.

Angell, J. K., W. H. Hoeker, L. R. Dickson, and D. H. Pack, 1973. Urban influence on a strong daytime air flow as determined from tetroon flights. *J. Appl. Meteorol.* 12:924–36.

Atkinson, B. W., 1981. *Meso-scale atmospheric circulation systems.* Academic Press, London.

Beebe, R. G., 1958. Tornado proximity soundings. *Bull. Am. Meteorol. Soc.* 39:195–201.

———, and F. C. Bates, 1955. A mechanism for assisting in the release of convective instability. *Mon. Weather Rev.* 83:1–10.

Benjamin, S. G., and T. N. Carlson, 1983. Effects on stability, winds and surface pressure due to surface heating and topography in the regional severe storm environment. Preprints, Thirteenth Conference on Severe Local Storms. American Meteorological Society, Boston, pp. 332–35.

Berggren, R., 1952. The distribution of temperature and wind connected with active tropical air in the higher troposphere and some remarks concerning clear air turbulence at high altitudes. *Tellus* 4:43–54.

Berry, E., and H. B. Bluestein, 1982. The formation of severe thunderstorms at the intersection of a dryline and a front: the role of frontogenesis. Preprints, Twelfth Conference on Severe Local Storms. American Meteorological Society, Boston, pp. 597–602.

Blackadar, A. K., 1957. Boundary layer wind maxima and their significance for the growth of nocturnal inversions. *Bull. Am. Meteorol. Soc.* 38:283–90.

Bleeker, W., and M. J. Andre, 1951. On the diurnal variation of precipitation, particularly over central U.S.A. and its relations to large-scale orographic circulation systems. *Q. J. R. Meteorol. Soc.* 77:260–71.

Blumen, W., 1980. A comparison between the Hoskins-Bretherton model of frontogenesis and the analysis of an intense surface frontal zone. *J. Atmos. Sci.* 37:64–77.

Bolin, B., 1953. The adjustment of a nonbalanced velocity field tornado geostrophic equilibrium in a stratified fluid. *Tellus* 5:373–85.

Bonner, W. D., 1966. Case study of thunderstorm activity in relation to the low-level jet. *Mon. Weather Rev.* 94:167–78.

———, 1968. Climatology of the low-level jet. *Mon. Weather Rev.* 96:833–50.

———, S. Esbensen, and R. Greenburg, 1968. Kinematics of the low-level jet. *J. Appl. Meteorol.* 7:339–47.

———, and J. Paegle, 1970. Diurnal variations in boundary layer winds over the south-central United States in summer. *Mon. Weather Rev.* 98:735–44.

Bosart, L. F., and F. Sanders, 1981. The Johnstown flood of July 1977: a long-lived convective system. *J. Atmos. Sci.* 38:1616–42.

Brown, R. A., 1972. On the inflection point instability of a stratified Ekman boundary layer. *J. Atmos. Sci.* 29:850–59.

Brunk, I. W., 1949. The pressure pulsation of 11 April 1944. *J. Meteorol.* 6:181–87.

Buajitti, K., and A. K. Blackadar, 1957. Theoretical studies of diurnal wind structure variations in the planetary boundary layer. *Q. J. R. Meteorol. Soc.* 83:486–500.

Businger, J. A., J. C. Wyngaard, Y. Izumi, and E. F. Bradley, 1971. Flux profile relationships in the atmospheric surface layer. *J. Atmos. Sci.* 28:181–89.

Cahir, J. J., 1971. Implications of circulations in the vicinity of jet streaks at subsynoptic scales. Ph.D. diss., Pennsylvania State University.

Carlson, T. N., S. G. Benjamin, and G. S. Forbes, 1983. Elevated mixed layers in the regional severe storm environment: conceptual model and case studies. *Mon. Weather Rev.* 111:1453–73.

———, R. A. Anthes, M. Schwartz, S. G. Benjamin, and D. G. Baldwin, 1980. Analysis and prediction of severe storms environment. *Bull. Am. Meteorol. Soc.* 61:1018–32.

Chang, L. A., 1979. A two-dimensional numerical simulation of the dryline environment and its role in the development of mesoscale convective systems. Ph.D. diss., University of Oklahoma.

Chang, L. W., 1976. A numerical study of the diurnal variation of the low-level jet. Ph.D. diss., University of Oklahoma.

Changnon, S. A., Jr., R. G. Semonin, and F. A. Huff, 1976. A hypothesis for urban rainfall anomalies. *J. Appl. Meteorol.* 15:544–60.

Charba, J., and Y. Sasaki, 1971. Structure and movement of the severe thunderstorms of 3 April 1964 as revealed from radar and surface mesonetwork data analysis. *J. Meteorol. Soc. Japan* 49:191–213.

Charney, J. C., 1948. On the scale of atmospheric motions. *Geophys. Pub.* 17:3–17.

Chu, P. S., 1975. A mesosynoptic analysis of convective thunderstorms and an associated dryline in south-central Brazil. Preprints, Ninth Conference on Severe Local Storms. American Meteorological Society, Boston, pp. 181–86.

Cunningham, R. M., 1959. Cumulus circulation. In *Recent Advances in Atmospheric Electricity*, Pergamon Press, New York, pp. 361–67.

Danielson, E. F., 1975. A conceptual theory of tornado genesis based on macro-, meso- and microscale processes. Preprints, Ninth Conference on Severe Local Storms. American Meteorological Society, Boston, pp. 376–83.

Davies-Jones, R. P., and J. H. Henderson, 1975. Updraft properties deduced statistically from rawinsondings. *Pure Appl. Geophys.* 113:787–801.

Defant, F., 1951. Local winds. In *Compendium of Meteorology*, T. F. Malone (ed.), American Meteorological Society, Boston, pp. 655–72.

Doswell, C. A., 1976. The use of filtered surface data to reveal subsynoptic scale dynamics. Ph.D. diss., University of Oklahoma.

Einaudi, F., and D. P. Lalas, 1975. Wave induced instabilities in an atmosphere near saturation. *J. Atmos. Sci.* 32:536–47.

Eldridge, R. H., 1957. A synoptic study of west African disturbance lines. *Q. J. R. Meteorol. Soc.* 83:303–14.

Eliassen, A., 1962. On the vertical circulation in frontal zones. *Geofys. Publ.* 24:147–60.

Emanuel, K. A., 1979. Inertial instability and mesoscale convective systems. Part I: Linear theory of inertial instability in rotating viscous fluids. *J. Atmos. Sci.* 36:2425–49.

———, 1978. Inertial instability and mesoscale convective systems. Ph.D. diss., Massachusetts Institute of Technology.

Fankhauser, J. C., 1971. Thunderstorm-environment interactions determined from aircraft and radar observations. *Mon. Weather Rev.* 99:171–92.

Fawbush, E. J., and R. C. Miller, 1954. The types of airmasses in which North American tornadoes form. *Bull. Am. Meteorol. Soc.* 35:154–65.

Feteris, P. J., 1968. Statistical analysis of sub-synoptic meteorological patterns. Final Report, NSF GA-1321, Illinois State Water Survey, pp. 9–21.

———, 1961. The influence of the circulation around cumulonimbus clouds on the surface humidity pattern. *Aero-Revue* 36:626–30.

Fritsch, J. M., 1975. Cumulus dynamics local compensating subsidence and its implications for cumulus parameterization. *Pure Appl. Geophys.* 13:851–67.

———, C. F. Chappell, and L. R. Hoxit, 1976. The use of large-scale budgets for convective parameterization. *Mon. Weather Rev.* 104:1408–18.

Fuelberg, H. E., and J. R. Scoggins, 1978. Kinetic energy budgets during the life cycle of intense convective activity. *Mon. Weather Rev.* 106:637–53.

Fujita, T. T., and D. L. Bradbury, 1969. Determination of mass airflow from a thunderstorm complex using ATS III pictures. Satellite and Mesometeorology Research Project Paper No. 79, University of Chicago.

———, H. Newstein, and M. Tepper, 1956. Mesoanalysis—an important scale in the analysis of weather data. Research Paper 39, U.S. Weather Bureau, Washington, D.C.

Fulks, J. R., 1951. The instability line. In *Compendium of Meteorology*, T. F. Malone (ed.), American Meteorological Society, Boston, pp. 647–52.

Gall, R., 1976. A comparison of linear baroclinic instability theory with eddy statistics of a general circulation model. *J. Atmos. Sci.* 33:349–73.

Gedzelman, S. D., and R. A. Rilling, 1978. Short-period atmospheric gravity waves: a study of their dynamic and synoptic features. *Mon. Weather Rev.* 106:196–210.

Gidel, L. T., 1978. Simulation of the differences and similarities of warm and cold surface frontogenesis. *J. Geophys. Res.* 83:915–28.

Goldie, A. H. R., 1925. Waves at an approximately horizontal surface of discontinuity in the atmosphere. *Q. J. R. Meteorol. Soc.* 51:239–46.

Golus, R. E., and S. E. Koch, 1983. Gravity wave initiation and modulation of strong convection in a CCOPE case study. Preprints, Thirteenth Conference on Severe Local Storms. American Meteorological Society, Boston, pp. 105–108.

Gossard, E. E., and W. H. Hooke, 1975. *Waves in the Atmosphere, Atmospheric Intrasound and Gravity Waves—Their Generation and Propagation*. Elsevier Scientific Publishing Co., Amsterdam.

Gray, W. M., 1973. Cumulus convection and larger scale circulations, I. Broadscale and mesoscale consideration. *Mon. Weather Rev.* 101:839–55.

Gurka, J. J., 1976. Satellite and surface observations of strong wind zones accompanying thunderstorms. *Mon. Weather Rev.* 104:1484–93.

Haltiner, G. J., 1971. *Numerical Weather Prediction*. John Wiley & Sons, New York.

———, and F. L. Martin, 1957. *Dynamical and Physical Meteorology*. McGraw-Hill, New York.

Haurwitz, B., 1947. Comments on the sea breeze circulation. *J. Meteorol.* 4:1–8.

Hering, W. S., and T. R. Borden, Jr., 1962. Diurnal variations in the summer wind field over the central United States. *J. Atmos. Sci.* 19:81–86.

Hoecker, W. H., Jr., 1963. Three southerly low-level jet systems delineated by the Weather Bureau special pibal network of 1961. *Mon. Weather Rev.* 11:573–82.

Holton, J. R., 1967. The diurnal boundary layer wind oscillation above sloping terrain. *Tellus* 19:199–205.

———, 1972. *An Introduction to Dynamic Meteorology*. Academic Press, New York.

Hoskins, B. J., and F. P. Bretherton, 1972. Atmospheric frontogenesis models: mathematical formulation and solution. *J. Atmos. Sci.* 29:11–37.

House, D. C., 1959. The mechanics of instability line formation. *J. Meteorol.* 16:108–20.

Hoxit, L. R., 1973. Variability of planetary boundary layer winds. Atmos. Sci. Paper No. 199, Colorado State University, Fort Collins.

———, 1975. Diurnal variations in planetary boundary-layer winds over land. *Boundary Layer Meteorol.* 8:21–38.

———, C. F. Chappell, and J. M. Fritsch, 1976. Formation of mesolows or pressure troughs in advance of cumulonimbus clouds. *Mon. Weather Rev.* 104:1419–28.

Hsu, S. A., 1969. Mesoscale structure of the Texas coast sea breeze. Report No. 16, NSF Grant GA-367Z, University of Texas at Austin, College of Engineering, Atmospheric Science Group.

Iwashima, T., and R. Yamamoto, 1974. Large-scale topography effects on the planetary-scale motions—a role of the Ekman boundary layer above sloping terrian. *J. Meteorol. Soc. Japan* 52:512–16.

Johnson, R. H., 1977. Effects of cumulus convection on the structure and growth of the mixed layer over South Florida. *Mon. Weather Rev.* 105:713–24.

Kaylor, R., and A. J. Faller, 1972. Instability of the stratified Ekman boundary layer and generation of internal waves. *J. Atmos. Sci.* 29:497–509.

Keyser, D., and R. A. Anthes, 1982. The influence of planetary boundary layer physics on frontal structure in the Hoskins-Bretherton horizontal shear model. *J. Atmos. Sci.* 39:1783–1802.

Koch, S. E., 1982. The role of apparent gravity waves as a triggering mechanism for severe thunderstorms along a dryline. Preprints, Twelfth Conference on Severe Local Storms. American Meteorological Society, Boston, pp. 573–76.

———, and J. McCarthy, 1982. The evolution of an Oklahoma dryline. Part II: Boundary layer forcing of mesoconvective systems. *J. Atmos. Sci.* 39:237–57.

Kocin, P. J., L. W. Uccellini, and R. A. Peterson, 1982. The role of jet streak "coupling" in the development of the 10–11 April 1979 Wichita Falls tornado outbreak. Preprints, Twelfth Conference on Severe Local Storms. American Meteorological Society, Boston, pp. 560–63.

Kuettner, J. P., 1971. Cloud bands in the earth's atmosphere—observations and theory. *Tellus* 23:404–26.

Kung, E. C., and T. L. Tsui, 1975. Subsynoptic scale kinetic energy balance in the storm area. *J. Atmos. Sci.* 32:729–40.

Landsberg, H. E., and T. N. Maisel, 1972. Micrometeorological observations in an area of urban growth. *Boundary Layer Meteorol.* 2:365–70.

Lanicci, J. M., and T. N. Carlson, 1983. Three-dimensional numerical simulations of dryline and elevated mixed layer evolution as related to soil moisture distribution. Preprints, Thirteenth Conference on Severe Local Storms. American Meteorological Society, Boston, pp. 328–31.

LeMone, M. A., 1973. The structure and dynamics of horizontal roll vortices in the planetary boundary layer. *J. Atmos. Sci.* 30:1077–91.

Lilly, D. K., 1966. On the instability of Ekman boundary flow. *J. Atmos. Sci.* 23:481–94.

Lindzen, R. S., and K. K. Tung, 1976. Banded convective activity and ducted gravity waves. *Mon. Weather Rev.* 104:1602–17.

Livingston, R. L., 1983. On the subsynoptic pre-tornado surface environment. Ph.D. diss., University of Missouri.

Lopez, R. E., 1973. Cumulus convection and larger scale circulations, II. Cumulus and mesoscale interactions. *Mon. Weather Rev.* 101:856–70.

McCarthy, J., and S. E. Koch, 1982. The evolution of an Oklahoma dryline. Part I: A meso- and subsynoptic-scale analysis. *J. Atmos. Sci.* 39:225–36.

McGinley, J. A., and Y. K. Sasaki, 1975. The role of symmetric instabilities in thunderstorm development on drylines. Preprints, Ninth Conference on Severe Local Storms. American Meteorological Society, Boston, pp. 173–80.

McGuire, E. L., 1962. The vertical structure of three drylines as revealed by aircraft traverses. National Severe Storms Project Report No. 7, Norman, Okla.

McNulty, R. P., 1978. On upper tropospheric kinematics and severe weather occurrence. *Mon. Weather Rev.* 106:662–72.

Maddox, R. A., 1980a. Mesoscale convective complexes. *Bull. Am. Meteorol. Soc.* 61:1374–87.

———, 1980b. An objective technique for separating macroscale and mesoscale features in meteorological data. *Mon. Weather Rev.* 108:1108–21.

———, 1983. Large-scale meteorological conditions associated with midlatitude, mesoscale convective complexes. *Mon. Weather Rev.* 111:1475–93.

———, and W. Dietrich, 1981. Synoptic conditions associated with the simultaneous occurrence of significant severe thunderstorms and flash floods. Preprints, Fourth Conference on Hydrometeorology. American Meteorological Society, Boston.

———, D. J. Perkey, and J. M. Fritsch, 1980. The evolution of upper-tropospheric features during the development of a midlatitude, mesoscale convective complex. Preprints, Eighth Conference on Weather Casting and Analysis. American Meteorological Society, Boston, pp. 233–39.

Magor, B. W., 1958. A meso-low associated with a severe storm. *Mon. Weather Rev.* 86:81–90.

———, 1959. Mesoanalysis: some operational analysis techniques utilized in tornado forecasting. *Bull. Am. Meteorol. Soc.*

40:499–511.

———, 1971. Statistics of selected surface conditions found within the hour preceding tornado occurrence, having identified a mesolow. Preprints, Seventh Conference on Severe Local Storms. American Meteorological Society, Boston, pp. 17–22.

Mahrt, L., 1976. Mixed layer moisture structure. *Mon. Weather Rev.* 104:1403–1407.

Marwitz, J. D., 1973. Non-hydrostatic pressures in severe thunderstorms. Preprints, Eighth Conference on Severe Local Storms. American Meteorological Society, Boston, pp. 14–17.

Mastrantonio, G., F. Einaudi, and D. Fua, 1976. Generation of gravity waves by jet streams in the atmosphere. *J. Atmos. Sci.* 33:1730–38.

Means, L. L., 1954. A study of the mean southerly wind maximum in low levels associated with a period of summer precipitation in the Middle West. *Bull. Am. Meteorol. Soc.* 35:166–70.

Miller, D. A., and F. Sanders, 1980. Mesoscale conditions for the severe convection of 3 April 1974 in the east central United States. *J. Atmos. Sci.* 37:1041–55.

Miller, J. E., 1948. On the concept of frontogenesis. *J. Meteorol.* 5:169–71.

Miller, R. C., 1972. Notes on analysis and severe storm forecasting procedures of the military weather warning center. Tech. Report 200 (Rev.), Air Weather Service (M AC), Belleville, Ill.

Moore, J. T., and M. F. Squires, 1982. Ageostrophic winds and vertical motion fields accompanying upper level jet streak propagation during the Red River Valley tornado outbreak. Preprints, Ninth Conference on Weather Forecasting and Analysis. American Meteorological Society, Boston, pp. 424–29.

Newton, C. W., 1950. Structure and mechanism of the prefrontal squall line. *J. Meteorol.* 7:210–22.

———, 1963. Dynamics of severe convective systems. *Severe Local Storms*, Meteorol. Monogr. 5, American Meteorological Society, Boston, pp. 33–58.

———, 1966. Circulations in large sheared cumulonimbus. *Tellus* 18:699–712.

———, and H. R. Newton, 1959. Dynamical interactions between large convective clouds and environment with vertical shear. *J. Meteorol.* 16:483–96.

Ninomiya, K., 1971a. Mesoscale modification of synoptic situations from thunderstorm development as revealed by ATS III and aerological data. *J. Appl. Meteorol.* 10:1103–21.

———, 1971b. Dynamic analysis of outflow from tornado-producing thunderstorms as revealed by ATS III pictures. *J. Appl. Meteorol.* 10:275–94.

O'Brien, J. J., 1970. A note on the vertical structure of the eddy exchange coefficient in the planetary boundary layer. *J. Atmos. Sci.* 27:1213–15.

Ogura, Y., and D. Portis, 1982. Structure of the cold front observed in Sesame-Ave III and its comparison with the Hoskins-Bretherton frontogenesis model. *J. Atmos. Sci.* 39:2773–92.

Økland, H., 1970. On the adjustment toward balance in primitive equation weather prediction models. *Mon. Weather Rev.* 98:271–79.

Orlanski, I., 1975. A rational subdivision of scales for atmosphere processes. *Bull. Am. Meteorol. Soc.* 56:527–30.

Orville, H. D., and L. J. Sloan, 1970. A numerical simulation of the life history of a rainstorm. *J. Atmos. Sci.* 27:1148–59.

Paegle, J., and G. E. Rasch, 1973. Three-dimensional characteristics of the diurnally varying boundary-layer flows. *Mon. Weather Rev.* 101:746–56.

Palmén, E., and C. W. Newton, 1969. *Atmospheric Circulation Systems—Their Structure and Physical Interpretation.* Academic Press, New York.

Peterson, R. E., 1983. The west Texas dryline: Occurrence and behavior. Preprints, Thirteenth Conference on Severe Local Storms. American Meteorological Society, Boston, pp. J9–J11.

Petterssen, S., 1956. *Weather Analysis and Forecasting, Vol. I—Motion and Motion Systems.* 2d ed. McGraw-Hill, New York.

Pitchford, K. L., and J. London, 1962. The low-level jet as related to nocturnal thunderstorms over midwest United States. *J. Appl. Meteorol.* 1:43–47.

Pielke, R. A., 1973. A three-dimensional model of the sea breeze. Tech. Memo. ERL WMPO-2, NOAA Environmental Research Laboratories, Boulder, Colo.

Plutarch (A.D. 100). *Plutarch*, Langhorne and W. Langhorne (trans.), 1832. 7 vols. A. J. Valpy, London.

Purdom, J. F. W., 1976. Some uses of high-resolution GOES imagery in the mesoscale forecasting of convection and its behavior. *Mon. Weather Rev.* 104:1474–83.

Raymond, D. J., 1978. Instability of the low level jet and severe storm formation. *J. Atmos. Sci.* 35:2274–80.

Reed, R. J., and E. F. Danielson, 1959. Fronts in the vicinity of the tropopause. *Arch. Meteorol. Geophys. Bioklim.* A11:1.

Riehl, H., J. Badner, J. E. Hovde, N. E. LaSeur, L. L. Means, W. C. Palmer, M. J. Schroeder, L. W. Snellman, et al., 1952. *Forecasting in Middle Latitudes.* Meteorol. Monogr. 1(5), American Meteorological Society, Boston.

Ross, B. B., and I. Orlanski, 1978. The circulation associated with a cold front. Part II: Moist case. *J. Atmos. Sci.* 35:445–65.

———, and ———, 1982. The evolution of an observed cold front. Part I: Numerical simulation. *J. Atmos. Sci.* 39:296–327.

Sanders, F., 1955. An investigation of the structure and dynamics of an intense surface frontal zone. *J. Meteorol.* 12:542–52.

———, and K. A. Emanuel, 1977. The momentum budget and temporal evolution of the mesoscale convective system. *J. Atmos. Sci.* 34:322–30.

———, and R. J. Paine, 1975. The structure and thermodynamics of an intense mesoscale convective system in Oklahoma. *J. Atmos. Sci.* 32:1563–79.

Sangster, W. E., 1958. An investigation of nighttime thunderstorms in the United States. Tech. Report No. 5, Contract No. AF 19 (604)-2179, University of Chicago, Department of Meteorology.

———, 1967. Diurnal surface geostrophic wind variations over the Great Plains. Preprints, Fifth Conference on Severe Local Storms. American Meteorological Society, Boston, pp. 146–54.

Sasaki, Y., 1973. Mechanism of squall-line formation as suggested from variational analysis of hourly surface observations. Preprints, Eighth Conference on Severe Local Storms. American Meteorological Society, Boston, pp. 300–307.

———, and S. A. Tegtmeier, 1974. An experiment of subjective tornado forecasting using hourly surface observations. Preprints, Fifth Conference of Weather Forecasting and Analysis. American Meteorological Society, Boston, pp. 276–79.

Sawyer, J. S., 1956. The vertical circulation at meteorological fronts and its relation to frontogenesis. *Proc. Ry. Soc.*, A234:956–64.

Schaefer, J. T., 1973. The motion and morphology of the dryline. Tech. Memo. ERL NSSL-66, NOAA Environmental Research Laboratories, Boulder, Colo.

———, 1974. A simulative model of dryline motion. *J. Atmos. Sci.* 31:956–64.

———, 1975. Nonlinear biconstituent diffusion: a possible trigger of convection. *J. Atmos. Sci.* 32:2278–84.

———, 1976. Moisture features of the convective boundary layer in Oklahoma. *Q. J. R. Meteorol. Soc.* 102:447–51.

———, and C. A. Doswell III, 1980. The theory and practical

application of antitriptic balance. *Mon. Weather Rev.* 108: 746–56.

Scofield, R. A., V. J. Oliver, and L. Spayd, 1982. Preliminary efforts in developing a technique that uses satellite data for analyzing precipitation from extra tropical cyclones. Preprints, Ninth Conference on Weather Forecasting and Analysis. American Meteorological Society, Boston, pp. 235–49.

Shapiro, M. A., 1976. A mechanism for the generation of potential vorticity in the vicinity of upper-level jet stream frontal-zone systems. Preprints, Sixth Conference on Weather Forecasting and Analysis. American Meteorological Society, Boston, pp. 297–304.

————, 1981. Frontogenesis and geostrophically forced secondary circulations in the vicinity of jet stream-frontal zone systems. *J. Atmos. Sci.* 38:954–73.

Showalter, A. K., and J. R. Fulks, 1943. Preliminary report on tornadoes. U.S. Weather Bureau, Washington, D.C.

Simpson, J., and A. S. Dennis, 1974. Cumulus clouds and their modification. In *Weather and Climate Modification*, W. N. Hess (ed.). John Wiley & Sons, New York, pp. 552–95.

Sinclair, P. C., 1973. Severe storm air velocity and temperature structure deduced from penetrating aircraft. Preprints, Eighth Conference on Severe Local Storms. American Meteorological Society, Boston.

Staff, NSSP, 1963. Environmental and thunderstorm structures as shown by National Severe Storms Project observations in spring 1960 and 1961. *Mon. Weather Rev.* 91:271–92.

Stone, P. H., 1966. Frontogenesis by horizontal deformation fields. *J. Atmos. Sci.* 23:455–65.

Sun, W. Y., and Y. Ogura, 1979. Boundary-layer forcing as a possible trigger to a squall-line formation. *J. Atmos. Sci.* 36: 235–54.

Takeda, T., 1965. The downdraft in convective shower cloud under vertical wind shear and its significance for the maintenance of convective systems. *J. Meteorol. Soc. Japan* 43:302–309.

Tegtmeier, S. A., 1974. The role of the surface subsynoptic, low pressure system in severe weather forecasting. Master's thesis, University of Oklahoma, Norman.

Tracton, M. S., 1972. The role of cumulus convection in the development of extratropical cyclones. Ph.D. diss., Massachusetts Institute of Technology.

Tsui, T. L., and E. C. Kung, 1977. Subsynoptic-scale energy transformations in various severe storm situations. *J. Atmos. Sci.* 34:98–110.

Turner, J. S., 1973. *Buoyancy Effects of Fluids*. Cambridge University Press, Cambridge.

Uccellini, L. W., 1975. A case study of apparent gravity wave initiation of severe convective storms. *Mon. Weather Rev.* 103: 497–513.

————, 1980. On the role of upper tropospheric jet streaks and leeside cyclogenesis in the development of low-level jets in the Great Plains. *Mon. Weather Rev.* 108:1689–96.

————, and D. R. Johnson, 1979. The coupling of upper and lower tropospheric jet streaks and implications for the development of severe convective storms. *Mon. Weather Rev.* 107: 682–703.

Wallace, L. M., 1975. Diurnal variations in precipitation and thunderstorm frequency over the conterminous United States. *Mon. Weather Rev.* 103:406–19.

Ward, N. B., 1967. The effect of rotation on a buoyant convective column. Preprints, Fifth Conference on Severe Local Storms. American Meteorological Society, Boston, pp. 368–73.

Weiss, C. E., and J. F. W. Purdom, 1974. The effect of early morn-

ing cloudiness on squall line activity. *Mon. Weather Rev.* 102: 400–402.

Weldon, R., 1979. Satellite training course notes. Part IV: Cloud patterns and the upper air wind field. Applications Division, NESDIS/NOAA, Camp Springs, Md.

Weston, K. J., 1972. The dryline of northern India and its role in cumulonimbus convection. *Q. J. R. Meteorol. Soc.* 98:519–31.

Wexler, H., 1961. A boundary layer interpretation of the low-level jet. *Tellus* 13:369–78.

Williams, R. J., 1967. Atmospheric frontogenesis: A numerical experiment. *J. Atmos. Sci.* 25:1157–59.

Wu, S. S., 1965. A study of heat transfer coefficients in the lowest 400 meters of the atmosphere. *J. Geophys. Res.* 70:1801–1807.

Zipser, E. J., 1969. The role of organized unsaturated convective downdrafts in the structure and rapid decay of an equatorial disturbance. *J. Appl. Meteorol.* 8:799–814.

————, 1977. Mesoscale and convective-scale downdrafts as distinct components of squall line structure. *Mon. Weather Rev.* 105:1568–89.

Chapter 7

Achtemeier, G. L., 1969. Some observations of splitting thunderstorms over Iowa on August 25–26, 1965. Preprints, Sixth Conference on Severe Local Storms. American Meteorological Society, Boston, pp. 89–94.

Ackerman, B., 1969. The "near" environment of cloud turrets. Preprints, Sixth Conference on Severe Local Storms. American Meteorological Society, Boston, pp. 85–88.

Auer, A. H., Jr., and J. D. Marwitz, 1968. Estimates of air and moisture flux into hailstorms on the high plains. *J. Appl. Meteorol.* 7:196–98.

————, and W. Sand, 1966. Updraft measurements beneath the base of cumulus and cumulonimbus clouds. *J. Appl. Meteorol.* 5:461–66.

————, D. L. Veal, and J. D. Marwitz, 1969. Updraft deterioration below cloud base. Preprints, Sixth Conference on Severe Local Storms. American Meteorological Society, Boston, pp. 16–19.

Barge, B. L., and F. Bergwall, 1976. Fine scale structure of convective storms associated with hail production. Preprints, International Conference on Cloud Physics, Boulder, Colo. American Meteorological Society, Boston, pp. 341–48.

Barnes, S. L., 1970. Some aspects of a severe, right-moving thunderstorm deduced from mesonetwork rawinsonde observations. *J. Atmos. Sci.* 27:634–48.

————, 1974. Mesonetwork observations and analyses. Papers on Oklahoma thunderstorms, Tech. Memo. ERL NSSL-69, NOAA Environmental Research Laboratories, Boulder, Colo., pp. 17–88.

————, 1976. Severe local storms: concepts and understanding. *Bull. Am. Meteorol. Soc.* 57:412–19.

————, 1978. Oklahoma thunderstorms on 29–30 April 1970. Part 1: Morphology of a tornadic storm. *Mon. Weather Rev.* 106:673–84.

Battan, L. J., 1975. Doppler radar observations of a hailstorm. *J. Appl. Meteorol.* 14:98–108.

————, 1980. Observations of two Colorado thunderstorms by means of a zenith-pointing Doppler radar. *J. Appl. Meteorol.* 19:580–92.

———, and J. B. Theiss, 1966. Observations of vertical motion and particle sizes in a thunderstorm. *J. Atmos. Sci.* 23:78–87.

Bluestein, H. B., and C. J. Sohl, 1979. Some observations of a splitting severe thunderstorm. *Mon. Weather Rev.* 107:861–73.

Bonesteele, R. G., and Y. J. Lin, 1978. A study of updraft-downdraft interaction based on perturbation pressure and single-Doppler radar data. *Mon. Weather Rev.* 106:62–68.

Brandes, E. A., 1977a. Flow in severe thunderstorms observed by dual-Doppler radar. *Mon. Weather Rev.* 105:113–20.

———, 1977b. Gust front evolution and tornado genesis as viewed by Doppler radar. *J. Appl. Meteorol.* 16:333–38.

Brown, R. A., and K. C. Crawford, 1972. Doppler radar evidence of severe storm high-reflectivity cores acting as obstacles to airflow. Preprints, Fifteenth Radar Meteorological Conference. American Meteorological Society, Boston, pp. 16–21.

Browning, K. A., 1962. Cellular structure of convective storms. *Meteorol. Mag.* 91:341–50.

———, 1964. Airflow and precipitation trajectories within severe local storms which travel to the right of the winds. *J. Atmos. Sci.* 21:634–39.

———, 1965a. A family outbreak of severe local storms—a comprehensive study of the storms in Oklahoma on 16 May 1963: Part 1. AFCRL-65-695 (1) Special Report No. 32.

———, 1965b. The evolution of tornadic storms. *J. Atmos. Sci.* 22:664–68.

———, 1965c. Some inferences about the updraft within a severe local storm. *J. Atmos. Sci.* 22:669–77.

———, 1968. The organization of severe local storms. *Weather* 23:429–34.

———, 1977. The structure and mechanism of hailstorms. *Meteorol. Monogr.* 16, American Meteorological Society, Boston, pp. 1–39.

———, and R. J. Donaldson, Jr., 1963. Airflow and structure of a tornadic storm. *J. Atmos. Sci.* 20:533–45.

———, J. C. Fankhauser, J-P. Chalon, P. J. Eccles, R. C. Strauch, F. H. Merrem, D. J. Musil, E. L. May, and W. R. Sand, 1976. Structure of an evolving hailstorm. Part 5: Synthesis and implications for hail growth and hail suppression. *Mon. Weather Rev.* 104:603–10.

———, and G. B. Foote, 1976. Airflow and hail growth in supercell storms and some implications for hail suppression. *Q. J. R. Meteorol. Soc.* 102:499–533.

———, and C. R. Landry, 1963. Airflow within a tornadic storm. Preprints, Tenth Weather Radar Conference. American Meteorological Society, Boston, pp. 116–22.

———, and F. H. Ludlam, 1960. Radar analysis of a hailstorm. Tech. Note 5, Department of Meteorology, Imperial College, London.

———, and ———, 1962. Airflow in convective storms. *Q. J. R. Meteorol. Soc.* 88:117–35.

Burgess, D. W., and R. P. Davies-Jones, 1979. Unusual tornadic storms in eastern Oklahoma on 5 December 1975. *Mon. Weather Rev.* 107:451–57.

———, R. Lemon, and G. L. Achtemeier, 1976. Severe storm splitting and left-moving storm structure: the Union City, Oklahoma Tornado of 24 May 1973, R. A. Brown (ed.), NOAA Tech Memo. ERL-NSSL-80, 53-66 [NTIS.PB 269443/AS].

———, ———, and R. A. Brown, 1975. Evolution of a tornado signature and parent circulation as revealed by a single Doppler radar. Preprints, Sixteenth Radar Meteorological Conference. American Meteorological Society, Boston, pp. 99–106.

Burnham, J., and J. T. Lee, 1969. Thunderstorm turbulence and its relation to weather radar echoes. *J. Aircraft* 6(5):438–45.

Bushnell, R. H., 1973. Dropsonde measurements of vertical winds in the Colorado thunderstorm of 22 July 1972. *J. Appl. Meteorol.* 12:1371–74.

Byers, H. R., and L. J. Battan, 1949. Some effects of vertical wind shear on thunderstorm structure. *Bull. Am. Meteorol. Soc.* 30:168–75.

———, and R. R. Braham, Jr., 1949. *The Thunderstorm.* U.S. Government Printing Office, Washington, D.C.

Carlson, T. N., S. G. Benjamin, G. S. Forbes, and Y.-F. Li, 1983. Elevated mixed layers in the regional severe storm environment: conceptual model and case studies. *Mon. Weather Rev.* 111:1453–73.

———, and F. H. Ludlam, 1968. Conditions for the occurrence of severe local storms. *Tellus* 20:203–26.

Charba, J., and Y. Sasaki, 1971. Structure and movement of the severe thunderstorms of 3 April 1964 as revealed from radar and surface mesonetwork data analysis. *J. Meteorol. Soc. Japan* 49:191–214.

Chisholm, A. J., 1970. Alberta hailstorms: a radar study and model. Ph.D. diss., Department of Meteorology, McGill University.

———, 1973. Part I: Radar case studies and airflow models. In *Alberta Hailstorms*, Meteorol. Monogr. 14, American Meteorological Society, Boston, pp. 1–36.

———, and J. H. Renick, 1972. The kinematics of multicell and supercell Alberta hailstorms. Alberta Hail Studies, 1972, Research Council of Alberta Hail Studies Rep. No. 72-2, pp. 24–31.

———, and C. Warner, 1969. Radar and stereo photo measurements. Part 2: the hailstorms of 29 June 1967. Sci. Rep. MW-59, Stormy Weather Group, McGill University, Montreal, pp. 8–16.

Clark, T. L., 1979. Numerical simulations with a three-dimensional cloud model: lateral boundary condition experiments and multicellular severe storm simulations. *J. Atmos. Sci.* 36:2191–2215.

Cooper, L. W., 1970. Reports on hailstorm models project—1969. Part 2: Updraft study of the Black Hills hailstorm. Rep. 70-6, Institute of Atmospheric Science, South Dakota School of Mines and Technology, Rapid City.

———, D. C. Hall, and D. R. Booker, 1969. Report on hail models project. Vol. 4: Updraft mapping and balloon-transponder tracking. Rep. 69-1, Institute of Atmospheric Science, South Dakota School of Mines and Technology, Rapid City.

Davies-Jones, R. P., 1974. Discussion of measurements inside high-speed thunderstorm updrafts. *J. Appl. Meteorol.* 13:710–17.

———, and J. H. Henderson, 1975. Updraft properties deduced statistically from rawin soundings. *Pure Appl. Geophys.* 113:787–801.

———, D. W. Burgess, and L. R. Lemon, 1976. An atypical tornado-producing cumulonimbus. *Weather* 31:337–47.

Dennis, A. S., 1971. Final report on hailstorm models project. Rep. 71-11, Institute of Atmospheric Science, South Dakota School of Mines and Technology, Rapid City.

———, C. A. Schock, and A. Koscielski, 1970. Characteristics of hailstorms of western South Dakota. *J. Appl. Meteorol.* 9:127–35.

Donaldson, R. J., Jr., 1965. Methods for identifying severe thunderstorms by radar: a guide and bibliography. *Bull. Am. Meteorol. Soc.* 46:174–93.

———, A. C. Chmela, and C. R. Shackford, 1960. Some behaviour patterns of New England hailstorms. In *Physics of Pre-*

cipitation, Geophys. Monogr. 5, American Geophysical Union, Washington, D.C., pp. 354–68.

Douglas, R. H., 1963. Recent hail research: a review. In *Severe Local Storms*, Meteorol. Monogr. 5, American Meteorological Society, Boston, pp. 157–67.

Dye, J. E., B. E. Martner, and L. J. Miller, 1983. Dynamical-microphysical evolution of a convective storm in a weakly-sheared environment. Part 1: Microphysical observations and interpretation. *J. Atmos. Sci.* 40:2083–96.

Eagleman, J. R., and W. C. Lin, 1977. Severe thunderstorm internal structure from dual-Doppler radar measurements. *J. Appl. Meteorol.* 16:1036–48.

Ellrod, G. P., and J. D. Marwitz, 1976. Structure and interaction in the subcloud region of thunderstorms. *J. Appl. Meteorol.* 15:1083–91.

Emanuel, K. A., 1981. A similarity theory for unsaturated downdrafts within clouds. *J. Atmos. Sci.* 38:1541–57.

Fankhauser, J. C., 1971. Thunderstorm-environment interactions determined from aircraft and radar observations. *Mon. Weather Rev.* 99:171–92.

Fawbush, E. J., and R. C. Miller, 1953. A method of forecasting hailstone size at the earth's surface. *Bull. Am. Meteorol. Soc.* 34:235–44.

Foote, G. B., and J. C. Fankhauser, 1973. Airflow and moisture budget beneath a northeast Colorado hailstorm. *J. Appl. Meteorol.* 12:1330–53.

———, and H. W. Frank, 1983. Case study of a hailstorm in Colorado. Part 3: Airflow from triple-Doppler measurements. *J. Atmos. Sci.* 40:686–707.

———, and C. G. Wade, 1982. Case study of a hailstorm in Colorado. Part 1: Radar echo structure and evolution. *J. Atmos. Sci.* 39:2828–46.

———, ———, and K. A. Browning, 1975. Air motion and hail growth in supercell storms. Preprints, Ninth Conference on Severe Local Storms. American Meteorological Society, Boston, pp. 444–51.

Frisch, A. S., and R. G. Strauch, 1976. Doppler radar measurements of turbulent kinetic energy dissipation rates in a northeastern Colorado convective storm. *J. Appl. Meteorol.* 15:1012–17.

Fritsch, J. M., 1975. Cumulus dynamics: local compensating subsidence and its implications for cumulus parameterization. *Pure Appl. Geophys.* 113:851–67.

Fujita, T., 1963. Analytical mesometeorology: a review. In *Severe Local Storms*, Meteorol. Monogr. 5, American Meteorological Society, Boston, pp. 77–125.

Fujita, T. T., 1981. Tornadoes and downbursts in the context of generalized planetary scales. *J. Atmos. Sci.* 38:1511–34.

———, and H. R. Byers, 1977. Spearhead echo and downbursts in the crash of an airliner. *Mon. Weather Rev.* 105:129–46.

———, and G. Caracena, 1977. An analysis of three weather-related aircraft accidents. *Bull. Am. Meteorol. Soc.* 58:1164–81.

———, and H. Grandoso, 1968. Split of a thunderstorm into anticyclonic and cyclonic storms and their motion as determined from numerical model experiments. *J. Atmos. Sci.* 25:416–39.

Goyer, G. G., 1970. The hailstorm of July 6, 1969. Tech. Rep. of the Joint Hail Research Project, NCAR, April 1970.

———, W. E. Howell, V. J. Schaefer, R. A. Schleusener, and P. Squires, 1966. Project hailswath. *Bull. Am. Meteorol. Soc.* 47:805–809.

Grandia, K. L., and J. D. Marwitz, 1975. Observational investigations of entrainment within the weak echo region. *Mon. Weather Rev.* 103:227–34.

Haman, K. E., 1973. On the updraft-downdraft interaction in convective clouds. *Acta Geophys. Pol.* 21:215–33.

———, 1975. On the airflow and motion of quasi-steady convective storms. *Mon. Weather Rev.* 104:49–56.

———, 1978. On the motion of a three-dimensional quasi-steady convective storm in shear. *Mon. Weather Rev.* 106:1622–27.

Hammond, G. R., 1967. Study of a left moving thunderstorm of 23 April 1964. ESSA Tech. Memo. IERTM-NSSL 31, U.S. Department of Commerce, National Severe Storms Laboratory, Norman, Okla.

Hart, H. E., and L. W. Cooper, 1968. Thunderstorm airflow studies using radar transponder and superpressure balloons. Preprints, Thirteenth Radar Meteorological Conference. American Meteorological Society, Boston, pp. 196–201.

Hauser, D., and P. Amayenc, 1981. Drop-size distributions and vertical air motions in a thunderstorm as inferred from Doppler radar observations at vertical incidence, Tech. Note CRPE/96, CNET-CNRS, Issy-les-Moulineaux, France.

Henderson, T. J., and D. W. Duckering, 1970. Reports on hailstorm models project—1969. Part 1: Thunderstorm inflow measurements by aircraft and related time-lapse photography. Rep. 70-6, Institute of Atmospheric Science, South Dakota School of Mines and Technology, Rapid City.

Heymsfield, A. J., P. N. Johnson, and J. E. Dye, 1978. Observations of moist adiabatic ascent in Northeast Colorado cumulus congestus clouds. *J. Atmos. Sci.* 35:1689–1703.

———, and D. J. Musil, 1982. Case study of a hailstorm in Colorado. Part 2: Particle growth processes at mid-levels deduced from in-situ measurements. *J. Atmos. Sci.* 39:2847–66.

Heymsfield, G. M., 1976. Statistical objective analysis of dual-Doppler radar data from a tornadic storm. *J. Appl. Meteorol.* 15:59–68.

———, 1978. Kinematic and dynamic aspects of the Harrah tornadic storm analyzed from dual-Doppler radar data. *Mon. Weather Rev.* 106:233–54.

———, 1981. Evolution of downdrafts and rotation in an Illinois thunderstorm. *Mon. Weather Rev.* 109:1969–88.

Hookings, G. A., 1965. Precipitation-maintained downdrafts. *J. Appl. Meteorol.* 4:190–95.

Hoxit, L. R., C. F. Chappell, and J. M. Fritsch, 1976. Formation of mesolows or pressure troughs in advance of cumulonimbus clouds. *Mon. Weather Rev.* 104:1419–28.

Kamburova, P. L., and F. H. Ludlam, 1966. Rainfall evaporation in thunderstorm downdraughts. *Q. J. R. Meteorol. Soc.* 92:510–18.

Kessler, E., 1969. *On the Distribution and Continuity of Water Substance in Atmospheric Circulations*. Meteorol. Monogr. 10, American Meteorological Society, Boston.

———, 1974. Model of precipitation and vertical air currents. *Tellus* 26:519–42.

———, 1975a. Condensate content in relation to sloping updraft parameters. *J. Atmos. Sci.* 32:443–44.

———, 1975b. On the condensed water mass in rising air. *Pure Appl. Geophys.* 113:971–81.

Klemp, J. B., and R. Rotunno, 1983. A study of the tornadic region within a supercell thunderstorm. *J. Atmos. Sci.* 40:359–77.

———, and R. B. Wilhelmson, 1978a. The simulation of three dimensional convective storm dynamics. *J. Atmos. Sci.* 35:1070–96.

———, and ———, 1978b. Simulations of right- and left-moving storms produced through storm splitting. *J. Atmos. Sci.* 35:1097–1110.

———, ———, and P. S. Ray, 1981. Observed and numerically

simulated structure of a mature supercell thunderstorm. *J. Atmos. Sci.* 38:1558–80.

Knupp, K. R., and W. R. Cotton, 1982a. An intense, quasi-steady thunderstorm over mountainous terrain. Part 2: Doppler radar observations of the storm morphological structure. *J. Atmos. Sci.* 39:343–58.

———, and ———, 1982b. An intense, quasi-steady thunderstorm over mountainous terrain. Part 3: Doppler radar observations of the turbulent structure. *J. Atmos. Sci.* 39:359–68.

Kropfli, R. A., and L. J. Miller, 1976. Kinematic structure and flux quantities in a convective storm from dual-Doppler radar observations. *J. Atmos. Sci.* 33:520–29.

Kyle, T. G., 1975. Turbulence in convective storms. Unpublished manuscript.

———, W. R. Sand, and D. J. Musil, 1976. Fitting measurements of thunderstorm updraft profiles to model profiles. *Mon. Weather Rev.* 104:611–17.

Lemon, L. R., 1976a. Wake vortex structure and aerodynamic origin in severe thunderstorms. *J. Atmos. Sci.* 33:678–85.

———, 1976b. The flanking line, a severe thunderstorm intensification source. *J. Atmos. Sci.* 33:686–94.

———, D. W. Burgess, and R. A. Brown, 1978. Tornadic storm airflow and morphology derived from single-Doppler radar measurements. *Mon. Weather Rev.* 106:48–61.

———, and C. A. Doswell III, 1979. Severe thunderstorm evolution and mesocyclone structure as related to tornado-genesis. *Mon. Weather Rev.* 107:1184–97.

Lilly, D. K., 1983. Helicity as a stabilizing effect on rotating convective storms. Preprints, Thirteenth Conference on Severe Local Storms. American Meteorological Society, Boston, pp. 219–22.

Ludlam, F. H., 1959. Hailstorm studies, 1958. *Nubila* 2(2): 7–27.

———, 1963. Severe local storms: a review. In *Severe Local Storms*, Meteorol. Monogr. 5, American Meteorological Society, Boston, pp. 1–30.

MacCready, P. B., Jr., 1964. Standardization of gustiness values from aircraft. *J. Appl. Meteorol.* 3:439–49.

Mahrt, L., 1975. The influence of low level vertical gradients of moisture on parcel stability. Preprints, Ninth Conference on Severe Local Storms. American Meteorological Society, Boston, pp. 40–44.

Malkus, J. S., 1960. Recent developments in studies of penetrative convection and its application to hurricane cumulonimbus towers. In *Cumulus Dynamics*, C. E. Anderson (ed.), Pergamon Press, New York, pp. 65–84.

Marroquin, A., and D. J. Raymond, 1982. A linearized convective overturning model for prediction of thunderstorm movement. *J. Atmos. Sci.* 39:146–51.

Marwitz, J. D., 1972a. The structure and motion of severe hailstorms. Part 1: Supercell storms. *J. Appl. Meteorol.* 11:166–79.

———, 1972b. The structure and motion of severe hailstorms. Part 2: Multicell storms. *J. Appl. Meteorol.* 11:180–88.

———, 1973. Trajectories within the weak echo regions of hailstorms. *J. Appl. Meteorol.* 12:1174–82.

———, and E. X. Berry, 1971. The airflow within the weak echo region of an Alberta hailstorm. *J. Appl. Meteorol.* 10:487–92.

———, A. H. Auer, Jr., and D. L. Veal, 1972. Locating the organized updraft on severe thunderstorms. *J. Appl. Meteorol.* 11:236–38.

———, A. J. Chisholm, and A. H. Auer, Jr., 1969. The kinematics of severe thunderstorms sheared in the direction of motion. Preprints, Sixth Conference on Severe Local Storms.

American Meteorological Society, Boston, pp. 6–12.

Miller, L. J., 1975. Internal airflow of a convective storm from dual-Doppler radar measurements. *Pageoph.* 113:765–85.

———, J. E. Dye, and B. E. Martner, 1983. Dynamical-microphysical evolution of a convective storm in a weakly-sheared environment. Part 2: Airflow and precipitation trajectories from Doppler radar observations. *J. Atmos. Sci.* 40:2097–2109.

———, F. I. Harris, and J. C. Fankhauser, 1982. The 22 June 1976 case study: structure and evolution of internal airflow. In Hailstorms of the Central High Plains, Vol. 2. *Case Studies of the National Hail Research Experiment* (C. A. Knight and P. Squires, eds.), Colorado Associated University Press, Boulder, pp. 35–59.

Miller, M. J., 1978. The Hampstead storm: a numerical simulation of a quasi-stationary cumulonimbus system. *Q. J. R. Meteorol. Soc.* 104:413–27.

Moncrieff, M. W., and J. S. A. Green, 1972. The propagation and transfer properties of steady convective overturning in shear. *Q. J. R. Meteorol. Soc.* 98:336–52.

———, and M. J. Miller, 1976. The dynamics and simulation of tropical cumulonimbus and squall lines. *Q. J. R. Meteorol. Soc.* 102:373–94.

Nelson, S. P., 1976. Characteristics of multicell and supercell hailstorms in Oklahoma. Preprints, International Conference on Cloud Physics, Boulder, Colo. American Meteorological Society, Boston, pp. 335–40.

———, 1983. The influence of storm flow structure on hail growth. *J. Atmos. Sci.* 40:1965–83.

———, and R. R. Braham, Jr., 1975. Detailed observational study of a weak echo region. *Pure Appl. Geophys.* 113:735–46.

———, and S. K. Young, 1979. Characteristics of Oklahoma hailfalls and hailstorms. *J. Appl. Meteorol.* 18:339–47.

Newton, C. W., 1963. Dynamics of severe convective storms. In *Severe Local Storms*, Meteorol. Monogr. 5, American Meteorological Society, Boston, pp. 33–58.

———, 1966. Circulations in large sheared cumulonimbus. *Tellus* 18:699–713.

———, 1968. Convective cloud dynamics—a synopsis. Proceedings, International Conference on Cloud Physics, Toronto, 26–30 August 1968. American Meteorological Society, Boston, pp. 487–98.

———, and J. C. Fankhauser, 1975. Movement and propagation of multicellular convective storms. *Pure Appl. Geophys.* 113: 747–64.

———, and H. R. Newton, 1959. Dynamical interactions between large convective clouds and environment with vertical shear. *J. Meteorol.* 16:483–96.

Normand, Sir Charles, 1946. Energy in the atmosphere. *Q. J. R. Meteorol. Soc.* 72:145–67.

Pakiam, J. E., and J. Maybank, 1975. The electrical characteristics of some severe hailstorms in Alberta, Canada. *J. Meteorol. Soc. Japan* 53:363–83.

Paul, A. H., 1973. The heavy hail of 23–24 July 1971 on the western prairies of Canada. *Weather* 28:463–71.

Piggott, D., 1955. A flight in a thunderstorm. *Weather* 10: 304–307.

Ray, P. S., R. J. Doviak, G. B. Walker, D. Sirmans, J. Carter, and B. Bumgarner, 1975. Dual-Doppler observation of a tornadic storm. *J. Appl. Meteorol.* 14:1521–30.

———, B. C. Johnson, K. W. Johnson, J. S. Bradberry, J. J. Stephens, K. K. Wagner, R. B. Wilhelmson, and J. B. Klemp, 1981. The morphology of several tornadic storms on 20 May 1977. *J. Atmos. Sci.* 38:1643–63.

Raymond, D., 1978. Pressure perturbations in deep convection: an experimental study. *J. Atmos. Sci.* 35:1704–11.

Renick, J. H., 1966. Stereoscopic cloud photography and measurements. Master's thesis, McGill University.

———, 1971. Radar reflectivity profiles of individual cells in a persistent multicellular Alberta hailstorm. Preprints, Seventh Conference on Severe Local Storms. American Meteorological Society, Boston, pp. 63–70.

———, A. J. Chisholm, and P. W. Summers, 1972. The seedability of multicell and supercell storms using droppable pyrotechnic flares. Preprints, Third Conference on Weather Modification. American Meteorological Society, Boston, pp. 272–78.

Roach, W. T., 1967. On the nature of the summit areas of severe storms in Oklahoma. *Q. J. R. Meteorol. Soc.* 93:318–36.

Rotunno, R., 1981. On the evolution of thunderstorm rotation. *Mon. Weather Rev.* 109:577–86.

———, and J. B. Klemp, 1982. The influence of the shear-induced pressure gradient on thunderstorm motion. *Mon. Weather Rev.* 110:136–51.

Sand, W. R., 1976. Observations in hailstorms using the T-28 aircraft system. *J. Appl. Meteorol.* 15:641–50.

———, D. J. Musil, and T. G. Kyle, 1974. Observations of turbulence and icing inside thunderstorms. Preprints, Sixteenth Conference on Aerospace and Aeronautical Meteorology. American Meteorological Society, Boston, pp. 299–304.

Saunders, P. M., 1961. An observational study of cumulus. *J. Meteorol.* 18:451–67.

———, 1962. Penetrative convection in stably stratified fluids. *Tellus* 14:177–94.

Schlesinger, R. E., 1975. A three-dimensional numerical model of an isolated deep convective cloud: preliminary results. *J. Atmos. Sci.* 32:934–57.

———, 1978. A three-dimensional numerical model of an isolated thunderstorm. Part 1: Comparative experiments for variable ambient wind shear. *J. Atmos. Sci.* 35:690–713.

———, 1980. A three-dimensional numerical model of an isolated thunderstorm. Part 2: Dynamics of updraft splitting and mesovortex couplet evolution. *J. Atmos. Sci.* 37:395–420.

Sinclair, P. C., 1969. Vertical motion and temperature structure of severe convective storms. Preprints, Sixth Conference on Severe Local Storms. American Meteorological Society, Boston, pp. 346–50.

———, 1973. Severe storm air velocity and temperature structure from penetrating aircraft. Preprints, Eighth Conference on Severe Local Storms. American Meteorological Society, Boston, pp. 25–32.

Srivastava, R. C., 1967. A study of the effect of precipitation on cumulus dynamics. *J. Atmos. Sci.* 24:36–45.

Steiner, R., and R. H. Rhyne, 1962. Some measured characteristics of severe storm turbulence. National Severe Storms Project, Rep. No. 10, U.S. Weather Bureau, Washington, D.C.

Strauch, R. G., and F. H. Merrem, 1976. Structure of an evolving hailstorm. Part 3: Internal structure from Doppler radar. *Mon. Weather Rev.* 104:588–95.

Sulakvelidze, G. K., N. Sh. Bibilashvili, and V. F. Lapcheva, 1967. *Formation of Precipitation and Modification of Hail Processes.* Israel Program for Scientific Translation (trans.), National Technical Information Service, Springfield, Va.

Summers, P. W., G. K. Mather, and D. S. Treddenick, 1972. The development and testing of a droppable pyrotechnic flare system for seeding Alberta hailstorms. *J. Appl. Meteorol.* 11:695–703.

Thorpe, A. J., and M. J. Miller, 1978. Numerical simulations showing the role of the downdraught in cumulonimbus motion and splitting. *Q. J. R. Meteorol. Soc.* 104:873–93.

Toutenhoofd, V., and J. B. Klemp, 1983. An isolated cumulonimbus observed in northeastern Colorado: comparison of field observations with results of a three-dimensional simulation. *Mon. Weather Rev.* 111:468–78.

Vonnegut, B., and C. B. Moore, 1958. Giant electrical storms. In *Recent Advances in Atmospheric Electricity,* L. C. Smith (ed.), Pergamon Press, New York, pp. 399–411.

Warner, C., 1976. Wave patterns with an Alberta hailstorm. *Bull. Am. Meteorol. Soc.* 57:780–87.

———, 1981. Comments following "Observations of two Colorado thunderstorms by means of a zenith-pointing Doppler radar": a wall chart of a severe storm. *J. Appl. Meteorol.* 20:214–16.

Wichmann, H., 1951. Über das vorkommen und verhalten des hagels in gewitterwolken. *Ann. Meteorol.* 4:218–25.

Wilhelmson, R. B., and J. B. Klemp, 1978. A numerical study of storm splitting that leads to long-lived storms. *J. Atmos. Sci.* 35:1974–86.

———, and ———, 1981. A three-dimensional numerical simulation of splitting severe storms on 3 April 1964. *J. Atmos. Sci.* 38:1581–1600.

Wills, P. A., 1939. Account by Mr. Philip Wells of his flight of July 1, 1939. *Q. J. R. Meteorol. Soc.* 65:508–10.

Chapter 8

Adedokun, J. A., 1978. West African precipitation and dominant mechanisms. *Arch. Met. Geoph. Biokl.* 28:289–310.

Agee, E. M., 1982. An introduction to shallow convective systems. In *Cloud Dynamics,* ed. E. M. Agee and T. Asa. Reidel, Hingham, Mass.

———, T. S. Chen, and K. E. Dowell, 1973. A review of mesoscale cellular convection. *Bull. Am. Meteorol. Soc.* 54:1004–12.

Albignat, J. P., and R. J. Reed, 1980. The origin of African wave disturbances during Phase III of GATE. *Mon. Weather Rev.* 108:1827–39.

Anthes, R. A., 1982. *Tropical Cyclones.* Am. Meteorol. Soc., Boston.

Aspliden, C. I., Y. Tourre, and J. B. Sabine, 1976. Some climatological aspects of West African disturbance lines during GATE. *Mon. Weather Rev.* 104:1029–35.

Balogun, E. E., 1981. Convective activity over Nigeria. Report, International Conference on Early Results of FGGE and Large-Scale Aspects of Its Monsoon Experiments. ICSU/WMO GARP, Geneva, pp. 8–22.

Barrett, E. C., and D. W. Martin, 1981. *The Use of Satellite Data in Rainfall Monitoring.* Academic Press, New York.

Betts, A. K., R. W. Grover, and M. W. Moncrieff, 1976. Structure and motion of tropical squall-lines over Venezuela. *Q. J. R. Meteorol. Soc.* 102:395–404.

Bhalme, H. N., and Parasnis, 1975. 5–6 day oscillations in the pressure gradients over India during SW monsoon. *Ind. J. Meteorol. Geophys.* 26:77–80.

Brode, R. W., and M.-K. Mak, 1978. On the mechanism of the monsoonal midtropospheric cyclone formation. *J. Atmos. Sci.* 35:1473–84.

Brown, J. M., 1979. Mesoscale unsaturated downdraft driven by rainfall evaporation: a numerical study. *J. Atmos. Sci.* 36:313–38.

Burpee, R. W., 1972. The origin and structure of easterly waves in the lower troposphere of North Africa. *J. Atmos. Sci.* 29:77–90.

———, 1975. Some features of synoptic-scale waves based on compositing analysis of GATE data. *Mon. Weather Rev.* 103:921–25.

———, and R. J. Reed, 1982. Synoptic-scale motions. In *The GARP Atlantic Tropical Experiment (GATE) Monograph.* GARP Publication Series No. 25, pp. 63–120.

Byers, H. R., and R. R. Braham, 1949. *The Thunderstorm Project.* U.S. Weather Bureau, U.S. Department of Commerce, Washington, D.C. [NTIS PB 234515].

Carlson, T. N., 1968. Structure of a steady-state cold low. *Mon. Weather Rev.* 96:763–77.

———, 1969a. Synoptic histories of three African disturbances that developed into Atlantic hurricanes. *Mon. Weather Rev.* 97:256–76.

———, 1969b. Some remarks on African disturbances and their progress over the tropical Atlantic. *Mon. Weather Rev.* 97:716–26.

Chang, C.-P., J. E. Erickson, and K. M. Lau, 1979. Northeasterly cold surges and near-equatorial disturbances over the winter MONEX are during December 1974. Part 1: Synoptic aspects. *Mon. Weather Rev.* 107:812–29.

———, V. F. Morris, and J. M. Wallace, 1970. A statistical study of easterly waves in the western Pacific: July–Dec., 1964. *J. Atmos. Sci.* 27:195–201.

Chen, Y.-L., and Y. Ogura, 1982. Modulations of convective activity by large-scale flow patterns observed in GATE. *J. Atmos. Sci.* 39:1260–79.

Churchill, D. D., 1982. Development and structure of winter monsoon cloud clusters. M.S. thesis, University of Washington.

———, and R. A. Houze, Jr., 1984a. Development and structure of winter monsoon cloud clusters on 10 December 1978. *J. Atmos. Sci.* 41:933–60.

———, and ———, 1984b. Mesoscale updraft magnitude and cloud-ice content deduced from the ice budget of the stratiform region of a tropical cloud cluster. *J. Atmos. Sci.* 41:1717–25.

Erickson, C. O., 1971. Diagnostic study of tropical disturbance. *Mon. Weather Rev.* 99:67–79.

Estoque, M. A., and M. Douglas, 1978. Structure of the intertropical convergence zone over the GATE area. *Tellus* 30:55–61.

Fein, J. S., and J. P. Kuettner, 1980. Report on the Summer MONEX field phase. *Bull. Am. Meteorol. Soc.* 61:461–74.

Fortune, M., 1980. Properties of African disturbance lines inferred from time-lapse satellite imagery. *Mon. Weather Rev.* 108:153–68.

Frank, W. M., 1978. The life-cycle of GATE convective systems. *J. Atmos. Sci.* 35:1256–64.

———, 1983. The structure and energetics of the east Atlantic Intertropical Convergence Zone. *J. Atmos. Sci.* 40:1916–29.

Fujita, T. T., 1971. Application of ATS III photographs for determination of dust and cloud velocities over the northern tropical Atlantic. *J. Meteorol. Soc. Japan* 49:818–20.

Gamache, J. F., and R. A. Houze, Jr., 1982. Mesoscale air motions associated with a tropical squall line. *Mon. Weather Rev.* 110:118–35.

———, and ———, 1983. Water budget of a mesoscale convective system in the tropics. *J. Atmos. Sci.* 40:1835–50.

Godbole, R. V., 1977. The composite structure of the monsoon depression. *Tellus* 29:25–40.

Goswami, B. N., V. Satyan, and R. N. Keshavamurty, 1981. Growth of monsoon disturbances over western India. In *Monsoon Dynamics*, ed. J. Lighthill and R. P. Pearce. Cambridge University Press, Cambridge, pp. 415–28.

Gray, W. M., 1965. Calculation of cumulus vertical draft velocities in hurricanes from aircraft observations. *J. Appl. Meteorol.* 4:47–53.

Griffith, C. G., W. L. Woodley, J. S. Griffin, and S. C. Stromatt, 1980. Satellite-derived precipitation atlas for GATE. Division of Public Documents, U.S. Government Printing Office, Washington, D.C.

Hamilton, R. A., and J. W. Archbold, 1945. Meteorology of Nigeria and adjacent territories. *Q. J. R. Meteorol. Soc.* 71:231–35.

Houze, R. A., Jr., 1977. Structure and dynamics of a tropical squall-line system. *Mon. Weather Rev.* 105:1541–67.

———, and A. K. Betts, 1981. Convection in GATE. *Rev. Geophys. Space Phys.* 129:541–76.

———, and P. V. Hobbs, 1982. Organization and structure of precipitating cloud systems. *Adv. Geophys.* 24:225–315.

———, and E. N. Rapaport, 1984. Air motions and precipitation structure of an early summer squall line over the eastern tropical Atlantic. *J. Atmos. Sci.* 41:553–74.

———, S. G. Geotis, F. D. Marks, Jr., and A. K. West, 1981. Winter monsoon convection in the vicinity of North Borneo. Part 1: Structure and time variation of the clouds and precipitation. *Mon. Weather Rev.* 109:1595–1613.

Hubert, L. F., 1966. Mesoscale cellular convection. Meteorological Sattelite Laboratory, *Report No. 37*, Washington, D.C.

Ilesanmi, O. O., 1971. An empirical formulation of an ITD rainfall model for the tropics: a case study of Nigeria. *J. Appl. Meteorol.* 10:882–90.

International Council of Scientific Unions/World Meteorological Organization [ICSU/WMO], 1970. The planning of GARP tropical experiments. *GARP Rep. 4*, Geneva.

———, 1976. The monsoon experiment. *GARP Pub. Ser. No. 18*, Geneva.

Ireland, A. W., 1962. The little dry season of southern Nigeria. *Nigerian Meteorological Service Technical Note No. 24*.

Johnson, R. H., and D. C. Kirete, 1982. Thermodynamic and circulation characteristics of winter monsoon tropical mesoscale convection. *Mon. Weather Rev.* 110:1898–1911.

———, and D. L. Priegnitz, 1981. Winter monsoon convection in the vicinity of north Borneo. Part 2: Effects on large-scale fields. *Mon. Weather Rev.* 109:1615–26.

Keshavamurty, R. N., 1973. Power spectra of large-scale disturbances of the Indian southwest monsoon. *Indian J. Meteorol. Geophys.* 24:117–35.

———, G. C. Oshnani, P. V. Pillai, and S. K. Das, 1978. Some studies of the growth of monsoon disturbances. *Proc. Indian Acad. Sci.* 87A:61–75.

Krishnamurti, T. N., and H. N. Bhalme, 1976. Oscillations of a monsoon system. Part 1: Observational aspects. *J. Atmos. Sci.* 33:1947–54.

———, and R. S. Hawkins, 1970. Mid-tropospheric cyclones of the southwest monsoon. *J. Appl. Meteorol.* 9:442–58.

———, M. Kanamitsu, R. Godbole, C. B. Chang, F. Carr, and J. H. Chow, 1975. Study of a monsoon depression (1), synoptic structure. *J. Meteorol. Soc. Japan* 53:227–40.

———, P. Ardanuy, Y. Ramanathan, and R. Pasch, 1981. On the onset vortex of the summer monsoon. *Mon. Weather Rev.* 109:344–63.

———, R. J. Pasch, H.-L. Pan, S.-H. Chu, and K. Ingles, 1983. Details of low latitude medium range numerical weather prediction using a global spectral model. Part 1: Formation of a monsoon depression. *J. Meteorol. Soc. Japan* 61:188–206.

Leary, C. A., 1981. The precipitation spectrum of a mesoscale feature in a tropical cloud cluster. Preprints, Twentieth Conference on Radar Meteorology. American Meteorological Society, Boston, pp. 358–63.

———, and R. A. Houze, Jr., 1979. The structure and evolution of convection in a tropical cloud cluster. *J. Atmos. Sci.* 36:

437–57.

——, and ——, 1980. The contribution of mesoscale motions to the mass and heat fluxes of an intense tropical convective system. *J. Atmos. Sci.* 37:784–96.

LeMone, M. A., and E. J. Zipser, 1980. Cumulonimbus vertical velocity events in GATE. Part 1: Diameter, intensity, and mass flux. *J. Atmos. Sci.* 37:2444–57.

Liebmann, B., and D. L. Hartman, 1982. Interannual variations of outgoing IR associated with tropical circulation changes during 1974–78. *J. Atmos. Sci.* 39:1153–62.

Lindzen, R. S., B. Farrell, and A. J. Rosenthal, 1983. Absolute barotropic instability and monsoon depressions. *J. Atmos. Sci.* 40:1178–84.

Lorenz, E. N., 1967. The nature and theory of the general circulation of the atmosphere. World Meteorological Organization, No. 218.TP.115.

McBride, J. L., and W. M. Gray, 1980. Mass divergence in tropical weather systems. Paper 2: Large-scale controls on convection. *Q. J. R. Meteorol. Soc.* 106:517–38.

Madden, R. A., and P. R. Julian, 1971. Detection of a 40–50 day oscillation in the zonal wind in the tropical Pacific. *J. Atmos. Sci.* 28:702–708.

——, and ——, 1972. Description of global scale circulation cells in the tropics with a 40–50 day period. *J. Atmos. Sci.* 29:1109–23.

Maddox, R. A., 1980. Mesoscale convective complexes. *Bull. Am. Meteorol. Soc.* 61:1374–87.

Mak, M.-K., 1975. The monsoonal mid-tropospheric cyclogenesis. *J. Atmos. Sci.* 32:2246–53.

——, and C.-Y J. Kao, 1982. An instability study of the onset-vortex of the southwest monsoon, 1979. *Tellus* 34:358–68.

Malkus, J. S., and H. Riehl, 1964. Cloud structure and distributions over the tropical Pacific Ocean. *Tellus* 16:275–87.

Mandal, G. S., S. C. Gupta, and S. K. Saha, 1984. Kinetic energy budget of an Arabian Sea cyclone in June 1979. *Mausam* (Meteorological Department of India) 35:145–51.

Martin, D. W., 1975. Characteristics of west African and Atlantic cloud clusters. GATE Rep. No. 14, Vol. 1, WMO, pp. 182–90.

——, and A. J. Schreiner, 1981. Characteristics of west African and east Atlantic cloud clusters: A survey from GATE. *Mon. Weather Rev.* 109:1671–88.

Mass, C., 1979. A linear primitive equation model of African wave disturbances. *J. Atmos. Sci.* 36:2075–92.

Miller, F. R., and R. N. Keshavamurty, 1968. *Structure of an Arabian Sea Summer Monsoon System.* East-West Center Press, Honolulu.

Murakami, M., 1976. Analysis of summer monsoon fluctuations over India. *J. Meteorol. Soc. Japan* 54:15–31.

——, 1983. Analysis of the deep convective activity over the western Pacific and southeast Asia. Part 1: Diurnal variation. *J. Meteorol. Soc. Japan* 61:60–75.

Murakami, T., 1980a. Temporal variations of satellite-observed outgoing longwave radiation over the winter monsoon region. Part 1: Long-period (15–30 day) oscillations. *Mon. Weather Rev.* 108:408–26.

——, 1980b. Temporal variations of satellite-observed outgoing longwave radiation over the winter monsoon region. Part 2: Short-period (4–6 day) oscillations. *Mon. Weather Rev.* 108:427–44.

Nitta, T., 1970. Statistical study of tropospheric wave disturbances in the tropical Pacific region. *J. Meteorol. Soc. Japan* 48:47–60.

——, and K. Masuda, 1981. Observational study of a monsoon depression developed over the Bay of Bengal during summer MONEX. *J. Meteorol. Soc. Japan* 59:672–82.

Norquist, D. C., E. E. Recker, and R. J. Reed, 1977. The energetics of African wave disturbances as observed during Phase III of GATE. *Mon. Weather Rev.* 105:334–42.

Obasi, G. O. P., 1965. Atmospheric, synoptic, and climatological features of the west African region. *Nigerian Meteorological Service Technical Note No. 28.*

Ogura, Y., 1982. A modeling study of mesoscale convective storms. *Proc. CIMMS 1982 Symposium*, University of Oklahoma, pp. 83–126.

——, and Y.-L. Chen, 1977. A life history of an intense mesoscale convective storm in Oklahoma. *J. Atmos. Sci.* 33:1458–76.

——, and M. T. Liou, 1980. The structure of a mid-latitude squall line: a case study. *J. Atmos. Sci.* 37:553–67.

——, and K. S. Tai, 1984. Easterly waves over the eastern Pacific in Northern Hemisphere summer as revealed by FGGE Level III-data. FGGE Newsletter No. 6, pp. 2–8.

——, Y.-L. Chen, J. Russell, and S.-T. Soong, 1979. On the formation of organized convective systems observed over the eastern Atlantic. *Mon. Weather Rev.* 107:426–41.

Ooyama, K. V., 1982. Conceptual evolution of the theory and modeling of the tropical cyclone. *J. Meteorol. Soc. Japan* 60:369–80.

Palmer, C. P., 1952. Tropical meteorology. *Q. J. R. Meteorol. Soc.* 78:126–63.

Payne, S. W., and M. W. McGarry, 1977. The relationship of satellite inferred convective activity to easterly waves over West Africa and the adjacent ocean during Phase III of GATE. *Mon. Weather Rev.* 105:413–20.

Ramage, C. S., 1971. *Monsoon Meteorology.* Academic Press, New York.

Raman, C. R. V., Y. P. Rao, S. K. Subramanian, and Z. E. Sheikh, 1978. Wind shear in a monsoon depression. *Nature* 275:51–53.

Rao, Y. P., 1976. Southwest monsoon. In *Meteor. Monogr. Synoptic Meteorol.*, No. 1. Indian Meteorology Department, New Delhi, pp. 107–85.

Reed, R. J., 1978. The structure and behavior of easterly waves over west Africa and the Atlantic. In *Meteorology over the Tropical Oceans*, ed. D. B. Shaw, Royal Meteorological Society, Bracknell, Berkshire, pp. 57–71.

——, and E. E. Recker, 1971. Structure and properties of synoptic-scale wave disturbances in the equatorial western Pacific. *J. Atmos. Sci.* 28:1117–33.

——, D. C. Norquist, and E. E. Recker, 1977. The structure and properties of African wave disturbances as observed during Phase III of GATE. *Mon. Weather Rev.* 105:317–33.

Riehl, H., 1945. Waves in the easterlies and the polar front in the tropics. Misc. Rept. No. 17, Dept. of Meteorology, University of Chicago.

——, 1948. On the formation of typhoons. *J. Meteorol.* 5:247–64.

——, 1954. *Tropical Meteorology.* McGraw-Hill, New York.

——, 1979. *Climate and Weather in the Tropics.* Academic Press, New York.

——, and J. S. Malkus, 1958. On the heat balance in the equatorial trough zone. *Geophysica* 6:503–38.

——, and ——, 1961. Some aspects of Hurricane Daisy, 1958. *Tellus* 13:181–213.

——, and J. Simpson, 1979. The heat balance of equatorial trough zone, revisited. *Contr. Atmos. Phys.* 52:287–305.

Rosenthal, S., 1960. Some estimates of the power spectra of large-scale disturbances in low latitudes. *J. Meteorol.* 17:259–63.

Sadler, J. C., 1975. The monsoon circulation and cloudiness over the GATE area. *Mon. Weather Rev.* 103:369–87.

———, 1976. A role of the tropical upper tropospheric trough in early season typhoon development. *Mon. Weather Rev.* 104:1266–78.

———, 1978. Mid-season typhoon development and intensity changes and the tropical upper tropospheric trough. *Mon. Weather Rev.* 106:1137–52.

Saha, K., F. Sanders, and J. Shukla, 1981. Westward propagating predecessors of monsoon depressions. *Mon. Weather Rev.* 109:330–43.

Sanders, F., 1984. Quasi-geostrophic diagnosis of the monsoon depression of 5–8 July 1979. *J. Atmos. Sci.* 41:538–52.

———, and K. A. Emanuel, 1977. The momentum budget and temporal evolution of a mesoscale convective system. *J. Atmos. Sci.* 34:322–30.

———, and R. J. Paine, 1975. The structure and thermodynamics of an intense mesoscale convective storm in Oklahoma. *J. Atmos. Sci.* 32:1563–79.

Shimamura, M., 1981. The upper-tropospheric cold lows in the northwestern Pacific as revealed in the GMS satellite data. *Geophys. Mag.* (Japan Meteorological Agency, Tokyo) 39:119–56.

———, 1982. An application of GMS satellite data in the analysis of the upper cold low in the western north Pacific. *Geophys. Mag.* (Japan Meteorological Agency, Tokyo) 40:113–51.

Shin, K.-S., and M.-K Mak, 1983. Aircraft measurements of the subsynoptic-scale properties of the monsoonal onset-vortex of 1979. *Mon. Weather Rev.* 111:1587–98.

Shukla, J., 1977. Barotropic-baroclinic instability of mean zonal wind during summer monsoon. *Pure Appl. Geophys.* 115:1449–61.

———, 1978. CISK-barotropic-baroclinic instability and the growth of monsoon depressions. *J. Atmos. Sci.* 35:495–508.

Sikka, D. R., 1977. Some aspects of the life history, structure and movement of monsoon depressions. *Pure Appl. Geophys.* 115:1501–29.

Soong, S.-T., and S. C. Chen, 1984. The effect of wind shear and ice phase on the structure of a tropical cloud cluster. Fifteenth Conference on Hurricanes and Tropical Meteorology. American Meteorological Society, Boston, pp. 181–82.

Surgi, N., 1984. The structure and dynamics of a monsoon depression. Fifteenth Conference on Hurricanes and Tropical Meteorology. American Meteorological Society, Boston, pp. 354–58.

Tai, K. S., 1980. Vertical coupling of synoptic-scale disturbances in the tropics. M.S. thesis, University of Illinois.

Thompson, R. M., S. W. Payne, E. E. Recker, and R. J. Reed, 1979. Structure and properties of synoptic-scale wave disturbances in the Intertropical Convergence Zone of the eastern Atlantic. *J. Atmos. Sci.* 36:53–72.

Ulanski, S. L., and M. Garstang, 1978. The role of surface divergence and vorticity in the life cycle of convective rainfall. Part 2: Descriptive model. *J. Atmos. Sci.* 35:1063–69.

Vincent, D. G., 1981. Kinematic analysis of the large-scale mean state during Phases I, II and III of GATE. *Q. J. R. Meteorol. Soc.* 107:899–917.

———, 1982. Circulation features over the South Pacific during 10–18 January 1979. *Mon. Weather Rev.* 110:981–93.

Walker, G. T., 1924. Correlations in seasonal variations of weather. 9: A further study of world weather. *Mem. India Meteorol. Dept.* 24:275–332.

Walker, H. O., 1960. The monsoon in West Africa. In *Monsoons of the World*. India Meteorological Department, New Delhi, pp. 35–42.

Wallace, J. M., and C.-P. Chang, 1969. Spectrum analysis of large-scale wave disturbances in the tropical lower troposphere. *J. Atmos. Sci.* 26:1010–25.

Warner, C., 1981. Photogrammetry from aircraft side camera movies: Winter MONEX. *J. Appl. Meteorol.* 20:1516–26.

———, 1982. Mesoscale features and cloud organization on 10–12 December 1978 over the South China Sea. *J. Atmos. Sci.* 39:1619–41.

———, 1984. Core structure of a Bay of Bengal monsoon depression. *Mon. Weather Rev.* 112:137–52.

———, and R. H. Grumm, 1984. Cloud distributions in a Bay of Bengal monsoon depression. *Mon. Weather Rev.* 112:153–72.

Woodley, W., C. G. Griffith, J. S. Griffin, and S. C. Stromatt, 1980. The inference of GATE convective rainfall from SMS-1 images. *J. Appl. Meteorol.* 19:388–408.

Yanai, M., 1961. A detailed analysis of typhoon formation. *J. Meteorol. Soc. Japan* 39:187–214.

Zipser, E. J., 1969. The role of organized unsaturated convective downdrafts in the structure and rapid decay of an equatorial disturbance. *J. Appl. Meteorol.* 8:799–814.

———, 1977. Mesoscale and convective-scale downdrafts as distinct components of squall-line structure. *Mon. Weather Rev.* 105:1568–89.

———, and M. A. LeMone, 1980. Cumulonimbus vertical velocity events in GATE. Part 2: Synthesis and model core structure. *J. Atmos. Sci.* 37:2458–69.

———, R. J. Meitin, and M. A. LeMone, 1981. Mesoscale motion fields associated with a slowly moving GATE convective band. *J. Atmos. Sci.* 38:1725–50.

Chapter 9

Brandes, E. A., 1977. Gust front evolution and tornado genesis as viewed by Doppler radar. *J. Appl. Meteorol.* 16:333–38.

Charba, J., 1974. Application of gravity current model to analysis of squall-line gust front. *Mon. Weather Rev.* 102:140–56.

———, and Y. Sasaki, 1971. Gravity current model applied to analysis of squall-line gust-front. Preprints, Seventh Conference on Severe Local Storms, Kansas City, Missouri. American Meteorological Society, Boston, pp. 277–83.

Goff, R. C., 1975. Thunderstorm-outflow kinematics and dynamics. Tech. Memo. ERL NSSL-75, NOAA Environmental Research Laboratories, Boulder, Colo.

———, J. T. Lee, and E. A. Brandes, 1977. Gust front analytical study. Report No. FAA-RD-77-119, prepared for U.S. Dept. of Transportation, Federal Aviation Administration, Washington, D.C. (available through the National Technical Information Service, Springfield, Va.).

Hane, C. E., 1973. The squall-line thunderstorm: numerical experimentation. *J. Atmos. Sci.* 30:1672–90.

Hess, S. L., 1959. *Introduction to Theoretical Meteorology*. Holt, Rinehart and Winston, New York.

Kessler, E., 1969. *On the Distribution and Continuity of Water Substance in Atmospheric Circulations*. Meteorol. Monogr. 10(32), American Meteorological Society, Boston.

Klemp, J. B., and R. Wilhelmson, 1978. Simulations of right- and left-moving storms through storm splitting. *J. Atmos. Sci.* 35:1097–1110.

Malkus, J. S., and G. Witt, 1959. The evolution of a convective element: a numerical calculation. In *The Atmosphere and the*

Sea in Motion, B. Bolin (ed.), Rockefeller Institute Press, New York, pp. 425–39.

Margules, M., 1905. Zur Sturmtheorie. *Meteorol. Zeit.* 23: 481–97.

Miller, M. J., 1978. The Hampstead storm: a numerical simulation of a quasi-stationary cumulonimbus system. *Q. J. R. Meteorol. Soc.* 104:351–65.

Mitchell, K. E., and J. B. Hovermale, 1977. A numerical investigation of the severe thunderstorm gust front. *Mon. Weather Rev.* 105:657–75.

Ogura, Y., 1963. The evolution of a moist convective element in a shallow, conditionally unstable atmosphere: a numerical calculation. *J. Atmos. Sci.* 20:407–24.

Orville, H. D., and L. J. Sloan, 1970. A numerical simulation of the life history of a rainstorm. *J. Atmos. Sci.* 27:1148–59.

Saski, Y., 1973. Mechanism of squall-line formation as suggested from variational analysis of hourly surface observations. Preprints, Eighth Conference on Severe Local Storms. American Meteorological Society, Boston, pp. 300–307.

Steiner, J. T., 1973. A three-dimensional model of cumulus cloud development. *J. Atmos. Sci.* 30:414–35.

Thorpe, A. J., and M. J. Miller, 1978. Numerical simulations showing the role of the downdraft in cumulonimbus motion and splitting. *Q. J. R. Meteorol. Soc.* 104:873–93.

Wilhelmson, R., and C. S. Chen, 1982. Cell development along cold outflow boundaries. Preprints, Twelfth Conference on Severe Local Storms, January 12–15, 1982. American Meteorological Society, Boston, pp. 127–30.

Chapter 10

Abbey, R. F., 1976. Risk probabilities associated with tornado windspeeds. Proceedings, Symposium on Tornadoes: Assessment of Knowledge and Implications for Man, Lubbock, Texas. Texas Tech University, Lubbock, pp. 177–236.

Agee, E. M., J. T. Snow, and P. R. Clare, 1976. Multiple vortex features in the tornado cyclone and the occurrence of tornado families. *Mon. Weather Rev.* 104:552–63.

Atkinson, B. W., 1981. *Meso-scale Atmospheric Circulations.* Academic Press, New York.

Baker, D., E. Agee, G. Baker, and R. Pauley, 1982. The Rush County, Indiana, tornado of 9 July 1980. Preprints, Twelfth Conference on Severe Local Storms, San Antonio, Texas. American Meteorological Society, Boston, pp. 379–82.

Baker, G. L., and C. R. Church, 1979. Measurements of core radii and peak velocities in modeled atmospheric vortices. *J. Atmos. Sci.* 36:2413–24.

Barnes, S. L., 1968. On the source of thunderstorm rotation. Tech. Memo. ERLTM NSSL-38, NOAA Environmental Research Laboratories, Boulder, Colo.

———, 1970. Some aspects of a severe, right-moving thunderstorm deduced from mesonetwork rawinsonde observations. *J. Atmos. Sci.* 27:634–48.

Bates, F. C., 1968. A theory and model of the tornado. Preprints, International Conference on Cloud Physics, Toronto, Canada. American Meteorological Society, Boston, pp. 559–63.

Bedard, A., and C. Ramzy, 1983. Surface meteorological observations in severe thunderstorms. Part 1: Design of TOTO. *J. Climate Appl. Meteorol.* 22:911–18.

Beebe, R. G., 1958. Tornado proximity soundings. *Bull. Am. Meteorol. Soc.* 39:195–201.

Bengtsson, L., and M. J. Lighthill, eds., 1982. *Intense Atmospheric Vortices.* Springer-Verlag, Berlin.

Blechman, J. B., 1975. The Wisconsin tornado event of April 21, 1974: observations and theory of secondary vortices. Preprints, Ninth Conference on Severe Local Storms, Norman, Okla. American Meteorological Society, Boston, pp. 344–49.

———, 1981. Vortex generation in a numerical thunderstorm model. *Mon. Weather Rev.* 109:1061–71.

Bluestein, H. B., 1983. Surface meteorological observations in severe thunderstorms. Part 2: Field experiments with TOTO. *J. Climate Appl. Meteorol.* 22:919–30.

Bode, L., L. M. Leslie, and R. K. Smith, 1975. A numerical study of boundary effects on concentrated vortices with applications to tornadoes and waterspouts. *Q. J. R. Meteorol. Soc.* 101: 313–24.

Brandes, E. A., 1977. Gust front evolution and tornado genesis as viewed by Doppler radar. *J. Appl. Meteorol.* 16:333–38.

———, 1978. Mesocyclone evolution and tornadogenesis: some observations. *Mon. Weather Rev.* 106:995–1011.

———, 1981. Fine structure of the Del City–Edmond tornado mesocirculation. *Mon. Weather Rev.* 109:635–47.

———, 1984. Relationships between radar derived thermodynamic variables and tornadogenesis. *Mon. Weather Rev.* 112: 1033–52.

Brooks, E. M., 1949. The tornado cyclone. *Weatherwise* 2:32–33.

Brown, J. M., and K. R. Knupp, 1980. The Iowa cyclonic-anticyclonic tornado pair and its parent thunderstorm. *Mon. Weather Rev.* 108:1626–46.

Brown, R. A., D. W. Burgess, and K. C. Crawford, 1973. Twin tornado cyclones within a severe thunderstorm: single Doppler radar observations. *Weatherwise* 26:63–71.

———, L. R. Lemon, and D. W. Burgess, 1978. Tornado detection by pulsed Doppler radar. *Mon. Weather Rev.* 106:29–38.

Browning, K. A., 1964. Airflow and precipitation trajectories within severe local storms which travel to the right of the winds. *J. Atmos. Sci.* 21:634–39.

———, and C. R. Landry, 1963. Airflow within a tornadic storm. Preprints, Tenth Weather Radar Conference, Washington, D.C. American Meteorological Society, Boston, pp. 116–22.

Burgers, J. M., 1948. A mathematical model illustrating the theory of turbulence. *Advan. Appl. Mech.* 1:197–99.

Burgess, D. W., 1976a. Single Doppler radar vortex recognition: part 1—mesocyclone signatures. Preprints, Seventeenth Conference on Radar Meteorology, Seattle, Wash. American Meteorological Society, Boston, pp. 97–103.

———, 1976b. Anticyclonic tornado. *Weatherwise* 29:167.

———, R. A. Brown, L. R. Lemon, and C. R. Safford, 1977. Evolution of a tornadic thunderstorm. Preprints, Tenth Conference on Severe Local Storms, Omaha, Nebr. American Meteorological Society, Boston, pp. 84–89.

———, V. T. Wood, and R. A. Brown, 1982. Mesocyclone evolution statistics. Preprints, Twelfth Conference on Severe Local Storms, San Antonio, Texas. American Meteorological Society, Boston, pp. 422–24.

Burggraf, O. R., and M. R. Foster, 1977. Continuation or breakdown in tornadolike vortices. *J. Fluid Mech.* 80:685–703.

———, K. Stewartson, and P. Belcher, 1971. Boundary layer induced by a potential vortex. *Phys. Fluids* 14:1821–33.

Chang, C. C., 1976. Preliminary work toward "killing the tornado" laboratory partial simulation experiment. Proceedings, Symposium on Tornadoes: Assessment of Knowledge and Implications for Man, Lubbock, Texas. Texas Tech University, Lubbock, pp. 493–99.

Church, C. R., 1982. An experimental investigation of the factors governing the dynamic structure and intensity of atmospheric vortices. *Cloud Dynamics*, E. M. Agee and T. Asai (eds.),

D. Reidel Publishing Co., Dordrecht, Holland, pp. 329–45.

———, and C. M. Ehresman, 1973. Waterspout research at Purdue University. *Bull. Am. Meteorol. Soc.* 54:687–88.

———, and J. T. Snow, 1979. The dynamics of natural tornadoes as inferred from laboratory simulations. *J. Rech. Atmos.* 12: 111–33.

———, and ———, 1983. Measurements of axial pressures in tornado-like vortices. Preprints, Thirteenth Conference on Severe Local Storms, Tulsa, Oklahoma. American Meteorological Society, Boston, pp. 74–77.

———, ———, and E. M. Agee, 1977. Tornado vortex simulation at Purdue University. *Bull. Am. Meteorol. Soc.* 58: 900–908.

———, ———, G. L. Baker, and E. M. Agee, 1979. Characteristics of tornado-like vortices as a function of swirl ratio: a laboratory investigation. *J. Atmos. Sci.* 36:1755–76.

———, ———, and J. Dessens, 1980. Intense atmospheric vortices associated with a 1000 MW fire. *Bull. Am. Meteorol. Soc.* 61:682–94.

Colgate, S., 1975. Comment on "On the relation of electrical activity to tornadoes," by R. P. Davies-Jones and J. H. Golden. *J. Geophys. Res.* 80:4556.

———, 1982. Small rocket tornado probe. Preprints, Twelfth Conference on Severe Local Storms, San Antonio, Texas. American Meteorological Society, Boston, pp. 396–400.

Connell, J., 1975. A non-thermal mechanism for forcing cumulonimbus cloud. *J. Appl. Meteorol.* 14:1406–10.

Cooley, J. R., 1978. Cold air funnel clouds. *Mon. Weather Rev.* 106:1368–72.

Danielsen, E. F., 1975. A conceptual theory of tornadogenesis based on macro-, meso- and microscale processes. Preprints, Ninth Conference on Severe Local Storms, Norman, Okla. American Meteorological Society, Boston, pp. 376–83.

Darkow, G. L., 1971. Periodic tornado production by long-lived parent thunderstorms. Preprints, Seventh Conference on Severe Local Storms, Kansas City, Mo. American Meteorological Society, Boston, pp. 214–17.

Davies-Jones, R. P., 1973. The dependence of core radius on swirl ratio in a tornado simulator. *J. Atmos. Sci.* 30:1427–30.

———, 1976. Laboratory simulations of tornadoes. Proceedings, Symposium on Tornadoes: Assessment of Knowledge and Implications for Man, Lubbock, Texas. Texas Tech University, Lubbock, pp. 151–74.

———, 1982. Observational and theoretical aspects of tornadogenesis. In *Intense Atmospheric Vortices*, L. Bengtsson and M. J. Lighthill (eds.), Springer-Verlag, Berlin, pp. 175–89.

———, 1983. The onset of rotation in thunderstorms. Preprints, Thirteenth Conference on Severe Local Storms, Tulsa, Okla. American Meteorological Society, Boston, pp. 215–18.

———, and J. H. Golden, 1975a. On the relation of electrical activity to tornadoes. *J. Geophys. Res.* 80:1614–16.

———, and ———, 1975b. Reply. *J. Geophys. Res.* 80: 4557–58.

———, and ———, 1975c. Reply. *J. Geophys. Res.* 80: 4561–62.

———, and E. Kessler, 1974. Tornadoes. In *Weather and Climate Modification*, W. N. Hess (ed.), John Wiley and Sons, New York, pp. 552–95.

———, D. W. Burgess, and L. R. Lemon, 1976. An atypical tornado-producing cumulonimbus. *Weather* 31:336–47.

———, ———, ———, and D. Purcell, 1978. Interpretation of surface marks and debris patterns from the 24 May 1973 Union City, Oklahoma, tornado. *Mon. Weather Rev.* 106:12–21.

Degarabedian, P., and F. Fendell, 1971. A method for rapid estimation of maximum tangential wind speed in tornadoes. *Mon. Weather Rev.* 99:143–45.

Deissler, R. G., 1977. Models for some aspects of atmospheric vortices. *J. Atmos. Sci.* 34:1502–17.

Dessens, J., 1972. Influence of ground roughness on tornadoes: a laboratory simulation. *J. Appl. Meteorol.* 11:72–75.

Donaldson, R. J., R. M. Dyer, and M. J. Kraus, 1975. An objective evaluator of techniques for predicting severe weather events. Preprints, Ninth Conference on Severe Local Storms, Norman, Okla. American Meteorological Society, Boston, pp. 321–26.

Dutton, J. A., 1976. *The Ceaseless Wind*. McGraw-Hill, New York.

Emmons, H. W., and S. J. Ying, 1967. The fire whirl. Proceedings, Eleventh Symposium on Combustion. Combustion Institute, pp. 475–88.

Eskridge, R. E., and P. Das, 1976. Effect of a precipitation-driven downdraft on a rotating wind field: a possible trigger mechanism for tornadoes? *J. Atmos. Sci.* 33:70–84.

Fankhauser, J. C., 1971. Thunderstorm-environment interactions determined from aircraft and radar observations. *Mon. Weather Rev.* 99:171–92.

Ferrel, W., 1893. *A Popular Treatise on the Winds*. John Wiley and Sons, New York, pp. 347–49.

Flora, S. D., 1954. *Tornadoes of the United States*. University of Oklahoma Press, Norman.

Forbes, G. S., 1976. Photogrammetric characteristics of the Parker tornado of April 3, 1974. Proceedings, Symposium on Tornadoes: Assessment of Knowledge and Implications for Man, Lubbock, Texas. Texas Tech University, Lubbock, pp. 58–77.

———, 1978. Three scales of motion associated with tornadoes. *Contract Report* NUREG/CR-0363 RB, U.S. Nuclear Regulatory Commission, Washington, D.C.

Fujita, T. T., 1960. A detailed analysis of the Fargo tornadoes of June 20, 1957. Res. Paper No. 42, U.S. Weather Bureau, Washington, D.C.

———, 1963. Analytical mesometeorology: a review. In *Severe Local Storms*, Meteorol. Monogr. No. 5. American Meteorological Society, Boston, pp. 77–125.

———, 1971. Proposed characterization of tornadoes and hurricanes by area and intensity. SMRP Res. Paper No. 91, Dept. of Geophysical Sciences, University of Chicago.

———, 1973. Proposed mechanism of tornado formation from rotating thunderstorm. Preprints, Eighth Conference on Severe Local Storms, Denver, Colo. American Meteorological Society, Boston, pp. 191–96.

———, 1974. Jumbo tornado outbreak of 3 April 1974. *Weatherwise* 27:116–26.

———, 1975. New evidence from April 3–4, 1974, tornadoes. Preprints, Ninth Conference on Severe Local Storms, Norman, Okla. American Meteorological Society, Boston, pp. 248–63.

———, 1977. Anticyclonic tornadoes. *Weatherwise* 30:51–64.

———, and A. D. Pearson, 1973. Results of FPP classification of 1971 and 1972 tornadoes. Preprints, Eighth Conference on Severe Local Storms, Denver, Colo. American Meteorological Society, Boston, pp. 142–45.

———, D. L. Bradbury, and P. G. Black, 1967. Estimation of tornado wind speeds from characteristic ground marks. SMRP Res. Paper No. 69, Dept. of Geophysical Sciences, University of Chicago.

———, ———, and C. F. Van Thullenar, 1970. Palm Sunday tornadoes of April 11, 1965. *Mon. Weather Rev.* 98:29–69.

———, G. S. Forbes, and T. A. Umenhofer, 1976. Close-up view of 20 March 1976 tornadoes: sinking cloud tops to suction vortices. *Weatherwise* 29:116–31, 145.

————, and R. M. Wakimoto, 1982. Anticyclonic tornadoes in 1980 and 1981. Preprints, Twelfth Conference on Severe Local Storms, San Antonio, Texas. American Meteorological Society, Boston, pp. 401–404.

Fulks, J. R., 1962. On the mechanics of the tornado. Tech. Memo. ERLTM-NSSL 4, NOAA Environmental Research Laboratories, Boulder, Colo.

Gall, R. L., 1982. Internal dynamics of tornado-like vortices. *J. Atmos. Sci.* 39:2721–36.

————, 1983. A linear analysis of the multiple vortex phenomenon in simulated tornadoes. *J. Atmos. Sci.* 40:2010–24.

Galway, J. G., 1975. Relationship of tornado deaths to severe weather watch areas. *Mon. Weather Rev.* 103:737–41.

————, 1977. Some climatological aspects of tornado outbreaks. *Mon. Weather Rev.* 105:477–84.

Gentry, R. C., 1983. Genesis of tornadoes associated with hurricanes. *Mon. Weather Rev.* 111:1793–1805.

Glaser, A. H., 1960. An observational deduction of the structure of a tornado vortex. In *Cumulus Dynamics*, Pergamon Press, New York, pp. 157–66.

Golden, J. H., 1968. Waterspouts at Lower Matecumbe Key, Florida, September 2, 1967. *Weather* 23:103–14.

————, 1973. Some statistical aspects of waterspout formation. *Weatherwise* 26:108–17.

————, 1974a. The life cycle of Florida Keys' waterspouts, Part 1. *J. Appl. Meteorol.* 13:676–92.

————, 1974b. Scale-interaction implications for the waterspout life cycle, Part 2. *J. Appl. Meteorol.* 13:693–709.

————, 1976. An assessment of wind speeds in tornadoes. Proceedings, Symposium on Tornadoes: Assessment of Knowledge and Implications for Man, Lubbock, Texas. Texas Tech University, Lubbock, pp. 5–42.

————, 1977. An assessment of waterspout frequencies along the U.S. east and gulf coasts. *J. Appl. Meteorol.* 16:231–36.

————, and D. Purcell, 1977. Photogrammetric velocities for the Great Bend, Kansas, tornado of 30 August 1974: accelerations and asymmetries. *Mon. Weather Rev.* 105:485–92.

————, and ————, 1978a. Life cycle of the Union City, Oklahoma, tornado and comparison with waterspouts. *Mon. Weather Rev.* 106:3–11.

————, and ————, 1978b. Airflow characteristics around the Union City tornado. *Mon. Weather Rev.* 106:22–28.

Goldman, J. L., 1965. The Illinois tornadoes of 17 and 22 April 1963. SMRP Res. Paper No. 39, Dept. of Geophysical Sciences, University of Chicago.

Hall, M. G., 1966. The structure of concentrated vortex cores. *Prog. Aeronaut. Sci.* 7:53–110.

————, 1972. Vortex breakdown. *Ann. Rev. Fluid Mech.* 4:195–213.

Hardy, R. N., 1971. The Cyprus waterspouts and tornadoes of 22 December 1969. *Meteorol. Mag.* 100:74–82.

Harlow, F. H., and L. R. Stein, 1974. Structural analysis of tornado-like vortices. *J. Atmos. Sci.* 31:2081–98.

Hennington, L., D. Zrnić, and D. Burgess, 1982. Doppler spectra of a maxi-tornado. Preprints, Twelfth Conference on Severe Local Storms, San Antonio, Texas. American Meteorological Society, Boston, pp. 433–36.

Hill, E. J., W. Malkin, and W. A. Schulz, 1966. Tornadoes associated with cyclones of the tropical origin. *J. Appl. Meteorol.* 5:745–63.

Hoecker, W. H., 1960. Wind speed and airflow patterns in the Dallas tornado of April 2, 1957. *Mon. Weather Rev.* 88:167–80.

————, 1961. Three-dimensional pressure pattern of the Dallas tornado and some resultant implications. *Mon. Weather Rev.* 89:533–42.

Houze, R. A., and P. V. Hobbs, 1982. Organization and structure of precipitating cloud systems. *Advances Geophys.* 24:225–315.

Howard, L. N., and A. S. Gupta, 1962. On the hydrodynamic and hydromagnetic stability of swirling flows. *J. Fluid Mech.* 14:463–76.

Isaacs, J. D., J. W. Stork, D. B. Goldstein, and G. L. Wick, 1975. Effect of vorticity pollution by motor vehicles on tornadoes. *Nature* 253:254–55.

Jenson, B., T. P. Marshall, M. A. Mabey, and E. N. Rasmussen, 1983. Storm scale structure of the Pampa storm. Preprints, Thirteenth Conference on Severe Local Storms, Tulsa, Okla. American Meteorological Society, Boston, pp. 85–88.

Keller, D., and B. Vonnegut, 1976. Wind speeds required to drive straws and splinters into wood. *J. Appl. Meteorol.* 15:899–901.

Kelly, D. L., J. T. Schaefer, R. P. McNulty, C. A. Doswell, and R. F. Abbey, 1978. An augmented tornado climatology. *Mon. Weather Rev.* 106:1172–83.

Kessler, E., and J. T. Lee, 1978. Distribution of the tornado threat in the United States. *Bull. Am. Meteorol. Soc.* 59:61–62.

Klemp, J. B., and R. Rotunno, 1983. A study of the tornadic region within a supercell thunderstorm. *J. Atmos. Sci.* 40:359–77.

————, and R. B. Wilhelmson, 1978. Simulations of right- and left-moving storms produced through storm splitting. *J. Atmos. Sci.* 35:1097–1110.

————, ————, and P. S. Ray, 1981. Observed and numerically simulated structure of a mature supercell thunderstorm. *J. Atmos. Sci.* 38:1558–80.

Koscielski, A., 1967. The Black Hills tornado of 23 June 1966 in South Dakota. *Weatherwise* 20:272–74.

Kuo, H. L., 1966. On the dynamics of convective atmospheric vortices. *J. Atmos. Sci.* 23:25–42.

Lee, J. T., R. P. Davies-Jones, D. S. Zrnić, and J. H. Golden, 1981. Summary of AEC-ERDA-NRC supported research at NSSL 1973–1979. Tech. Memo. ERL NSSL-90, NOAA Environmental Research Laboratories, Boulder, Colo.

Leibovich, S., 1969. Stability of density stratified rotating flows. *AIAA J.* 7:177–78.

————, 1978. The structure of vortex breakdown. *Ann. Rev. Fluid Mech.* 10:221–46.

Lemon, L. R., 1977. New severe thunderstorm radar identification techniques and warning criteria: a preliminary report. Tech. Memo. NWS NSSFC-1, National Severe Storms Forecast Center, Kansas City, Mo.

————, and C. A. Doswell, 1979. Severe thunderstorm evolution and mesocyclone structure as related to tornadogenesis. *Mon. Weather Rev.* 107:1184–97.

————, D. W. Burgess, and R. A. Brown, 1975. Tornado production and storm sustenance. Preprints, Ninth Conference on Severe Local Storms, Norman, Okla. American Meteorological Society, Boston, pp. 100–104.

————, ————, and ————, 1978. Tornadic storm airflow and morphology derived from single-Doppler radar measurements. *Mon. Weather Rev.* 106:48–61.

————, ————, and L. D. Hennington, 1982. A tornado extending to extreme heights as revealed by Doppler radar. Preprints, Twelfth Conference on Severe Local Storms, San Antonio, Texas. American Meteorological Society, Boston, pp. 430–32.

Leslie, F. W., 1977. Surface roughness effects on suction vortex formation: a laboratory simulation. *J. Atmos. Sci.* 34:1022–27.

————, 1979. The dependence of maximum tangential velocity

on swirl ratio in a tornado simulator. Preprints, Eleventh Conference on Severe Local Storms. American Meteorological Society, Boston, pp. 361–66.

Leslie, L. M., 1971. The development of concentrated vortices: a numerical study. *J. Fluid Mech.* 48:1–21.

———, and R. K. Smith, 1978. The effect of vertical stability on tornadogenesis. *J. Atmos. Sci.* 35:1281–88.

———, and ———, 1982. Numerical studies of tornado structure and genesis. In *Intense Atmospheric Vortices*, L. Bengtsson and M. J. Lighthill (eds.), Springer-Verlag, Berlin, pp. 205–11.

Leverson, V. H., P. C. Sinclair, and J. H. Golden, 1977. Waterspout wind, temperature and pressure structure deduced from aircraft measurements. *Mon. Weather Rev.* 105:725–33.

Lewellen, W. S., 1976. Theoretical models of the tornado vortex. Proceedings, Symposium on Tornadoes: Assessment of Knowledge and Implications for Man, Lubbock, Texas. Texas Tech University, Lubbock, pp. 107–43.

———, and Y. P. Sheng, 1980. Modelling tornado dynamics. *Contract Report* NUREG/CR-1585, U.S. Nuclear Regulatory Commission, Washington, D.C.

Lewis, W., and P. J. Perkins, 1953. Recorded pressure distribution in the outer portion of a tornado vortex. *Mon. Weather Rev.* 81:379–85.

Lilly, D. K., 1969. Tornado dynamics. NCAR Manuscript 69-117, National Center for Atmospheric Research, Boulder, Colo.

———, 1976. Sources of rotation and energy in the tornado. Proceedings, Symposium on Tornadoes: Assessment of Knowledge and Implications for Man, Lubbock, Texas. Texas Tech University, Lubbock, pp. 145–50.

———, 1982. The development and maintenance of rotation in convective storms. In *Intense Atmospheric Vortices*, L. Bengtsson and M. J. Lighthill (eds.), Springer-Verlag, Berlin, pp. 149–60.

———, 1983. Helicity as a stabilizing effect on rotating convective storms. Preprints, Thirteenth Conference on Severe Local Storms, Tulsa, Okla. American Meteorological Society, Boston, pp. 219–22.

Long, R. R., 1956. Sources and sinks at the axis of a rotating liquid. *Q. J. Mech. Appl. Math.* 9:385–93.

———, 1958. Vortex motion in a viscous fluid. *J. Appl. Meteorol.* 15:108–12.

Lugt, H. J., 1983. *Vortex Flow in Nature and Technology.* John Wiley and Sons, New York.

Magor, B. W., 1959. Mesoanalysis: some operational analysis techniques used in tornado forecasting. *Bull. Am. Meteorol. Soc.* 40:499–511.

Mal'bakhov, V. M., 1972. Investigation of the structure of tornadoes. *Atmos. Oceanic Phys.* 8:8–14.

———, and L. N. Gutman, 1968. A non-stationary problem of a mesoscale atmospheric vortex with vertical axis. *Atmos. Oceanic Phys.* 4:333–40.

Maxworthy, T., 1972. On the structure of concentrated, columnar vortices. *Astronaut. Acta* 17:363–74.

———, 1973. A vorticity source for large-scale dust devils and other comments on naturally occurring columnar vortices. *J. Atmos. Sci.* 30:1717–22.

———, 1982. The laboratory modelling of atmospheric vortices: a critical review. In *Intense Atmospheric Vortices*, L. Bengtsson and M. J. Lighthill (eds.), Springer-Verlag, Berlin, pp. 229–46.

Mehta, K. C., 1976. Windspeed estimates: engineering analyses. Proceedings, Symposium on Tornadoes: Assessment of Knowledge and Implications for Man, Lubbock, Texas. Texas Tech University, Lubbock, pp. 89–103.

———, J. E. Minor, J. R. McDonald, B. R. Manning, J. J. Abernethy, and U. F. Koehler, 1975. Engineering aspects of the tornadoes of April 3–4, 1974. A report for Committee on Natural Disasters, National Academy of Sciences, Washington, D.C.

Michaud, L. M., 1977. On the energy and control of atmospheric vortices. *J. Rech. Atmos.* 11:99–120.

Miller, R. C., 1972. Notes on analysis and severe-storm forecasting procedures of the military weather warning center. Tech. Rep. 200 (rev.), Air Weather Service, U.S. Air Force (available Scott AFB, Illinois).

Morton, B. R., 1966. Geophysical vortices. In *Progress in Aeronautical Sciences*, Vol. 7, Pergamon Press, New York, pp. 145–93.

———, 1969. The strength of vortex and swirling core flows. *J. Fluid Mech.* 38:315–33.

———, 1970. The physics of fire whirls. *Fire Res. Abstr. Rev.* 12:1–19.

———, 1983. The generation and decay of vorticity. G.F.D.L. report, Monash University, Clayton, Victoria, Australia.

National Committee for Fluid Mechanics Films, 1972. *Illustrated Experiments in Fluid Mechanics.* MIT Press, Cambridge, Mass.

National Oceanic and Atmospheric Administration (NOAA), 1974. Scientists study role of cirrus clouds as severe storm inhibitors. *NOAA Week* 5(22):3.

Novlan, D. J., and W. M. Gray, 1974. Hurricane spawned tornadoes. *Mon. Weather Rev.* 102:476–88.

Orton, R., 1970. Tornadoes associated with Hurricane Beulah on September 19–23, 1967. *Mon. Weather Rev.* 98:541–47.

Pauley, R. L., C. R. Church, and J. T. Snow, 1982. Measurements of maximum surface pressure deficits in modeled atmospheric vortices. *J. Atmos. Sci.* 39:369–77.

Pearson, A., and S. J. Weiss, 1979. Some trends in forecast skill at the National Severe Storms Forecast Center. *Bull. Am. Meteorol. Soc.* 60:319–26.

Peterson, R. E., 1979. Horizontal funnels—a historical note. *Bull. Am. Meteorol. Soc.* 60:795.

Purdom, J. F. W., 1976. Some uses of high-resolution GOES imagery in the mesoscale forecasting of convection and its behaviour. *Mon. Weather Rev.* 104:1474–83.

Ray, P. S., 1976. Vorticity and divergence fields within tornadic storms from dual-Doppler observations. *J. Appl. Meteorol.* 15:879–90.

———, C. E. Hane, R. P. Davies-Jones, and R. L. Alberty, 1976. Tornado-parent storm relationship deduced from a dual-Doppler radar analysis. *Geophys. Res. Lett.* 3:721–23.

Rayleigh, Lord, 1916. On the dynamics of revolving fluids. *Proc. R. Soc.* A93:148–54.

Raymond, W. H., and H. L. Kuo, 1982. Simulation of laboratory vortex flow by axisymmetric similarity solutions. *Tellus* 34:588–600.

Rossmann, F. O., 1960. On the physics of tornadoes. In *Cumulus Dynamics*, Pergamon Press, New York, pp. 167–74.

Rossow, V., 1970. Observations of waterspouts and their parent clouds. NASA Tech. Note D-5854, National Aeronautics and Space Administration, Washington, D.C.

Rott, N., 1958. On the viscous core of a line vortex. *Z. Angew. Math. Physik* 96:543–53.

Rotunno, R., 1977. Numerical simulation of a laboratory vortex. *J. Atmos. Sci.* 34:1942–56.

———, 1978. A note on the stability of a cylindrical vortex sheet. *J. Fluid Mech.* 87:761–71.

———, 1979. A study in tornado-like vortex dynamics. *J. Atmos. Sci.* 36:140–55.

————, 1981. On the evolution of thunderstorm rotation. *Mon. Weather Rev.* 109:577–86.

————, 1982. A numerical simulation of multiple vortices. In *Intense Atmospheric Vortices*, L. Bengtsson and M. J. Lighthill (eds.), Springer-Verlag, Berlin, pp. 215–28.

————, and J. B. Klemp, 1982. The influence of the shear-induced pressure gradient on thunderstorm motion. *Mon. Weather Rev.* 110:136–51.

Ruskin, R. E., and W. D. Scott, 1974. Weather modification instruments and their use. In *Weather and Climate Modification*, W. N. Hess (ed.), John Wiley and Sons, New York, pp. 136–205.

Sarpkaya, T., 1971. On stationary and travelling vortex breakdowns. *J. Fluid Mech.* 45:545–59.

Sasaki, Y., and S. A. Tegtmeier, 1974. An experiment of subjective tornadic storm forecasting using hourly surface observations. Preprints, Fifth Conference on Weather Forecasting and Analysis, St. Louis, Mo. American Meteorological Society, Boston, pp. 276–79.

Schlesinger, R. E., 1978. A three-dimensional numerical model of an isolated thunderstorm: part 1. *J. Atmos. Sci.* 35:690–713.

Schwiesow, R. L., 1981. Horizontal velocity structure in waterspouts. *J. Appl. Meteorol.* 20:349–60.

————, R. E. Cupp, P. C. Sinclair, and R. F. Abbey, 1981. Waterspout velocity measurement by airborne Doppler lidar. *J. Appl. Meteorol.* 20:341–48.

SELS Staff, 1956. Forecasting tornadoes and severe thunderstorms. *Forecasting Guide No. 1*, U.S. Weather Bureau, Kansas City, Mo.

Serrin, J., 1972. The swirling vortex. *Phil. Trans. R. S. London,* A 271:325–60.

Shapiro, J. H., 1962. Bathtub vortex. *Nature* 196:1080–81.

Shultz, W. A., and D. L. Smith, 1972. Powerline breaks: potential aid in tornado identification and tracking. *Mon. Weather Rev.* 100:307–308.

Simpson, J., 1982. Cumulus rotation: model and observation of a waterspout-bearing cloud systems. In *Intense Atmospheric Vortices*, L. Bengtsson and M. J. Lighthill (eds.), Springer-Verlag, Berlin, pp. 161–73.

Skaggs, R. H., 1969. Analysis and regionalization of the diurnal distribution of tornadoes in the United States. *Mon. Weather Rev.* 97:103–15.

Smith, R. K., 1980. Untwisting the mysteries of tornadoes. *New Scientist* 85:650–52.

————, and L. M. Leslie, 1978. Tornadogenesis. *Q. J. R. Meteorol. Soc.* 104:189–99.

————, and ————, 1979. A numerical study of tornadogenesis in a rotating thunderstorm. *Q. J. R. Meteorol. Soc.* 105:107–27.

————, J. V. Mansbridge, and L. M. Leslie, 1977. Comments on "Effect of a precipitation-driven downdraft on a rotating wind field: a possible trigger mechanism for tornadoes?" by R. E. Eskridge and P. Das. *J. Atmos. Sci.* 34:548–49.

Snow, J. T., 1978. On the inertial instability as related to the multiple vortex phenomena. *J. Atmos. Sci.* 35:1660–77.

————, 1982. A review of recent advances in tornado vortex dynamics. *Rev. Geophys. Space Phys.* 20:953–64.

————, C. R. Church, and B. J. Barnhart, 1980. An investigation of the surface pressure fields beneath simulated tornado cyclones. *J. Atmos. Sci.* 37:1013–26.

Staley, D. O., and R. L. Gall, 1979. Barotropic instability in a tornado vortex. *J. Atmos. Sci.* 36:973–81.

Starr, V. P., 1974. The tornado mechanism and its possible artificial duplication. *Rev. Ital. Geofis.* 23:267–71.

————, N. E. Gaut, and R. D. Rosen, 1974. An angular momentum theorem for tornadoes and related topics. *Rev. Ital. Geofis.* 23:317–28.

Sullivan, R. D., 1959. A two-cell vortex solution of the Navier-Stokes equations. *J. Aerosp. Sci.* 26:767–68.

Taylor, W. I., 1975. Detecting tornadic storms by the burst rate nature of electromagnetic signals they produce. Preprints, Ninth Conference on Severe Local Storms, Norman, Okla. American Meteorological Society, Boston, pp. 311–16.

Tornado Forum, 1976. *Nature* 260:457–61.

Turner, J. S., and D. K. Lilly, 1963. The carbonated water tornado vortex. *J. Atmos. Sci.* 20:468–71.

Vaughan, D. H., and B. Vonnegut, 1976. Luminous electrical phenomena associated with nocturnal tornadoes in Huntsville, Alabama, 3 April 1974. *Bull. Am. Meteorol. Soc.* 57:1220–24.

Vonnegut, B., 1960. Electrical theory of tornadoes. *J. Geophys. Res.* 65:203–12.

————, 1975. Comment on "On the relation of electrical activity to tornadoes" by R. P. Davies-Jones and J. H. Golden. *J. Geophys. Res.* 80:4559–60.

Wakimoto, R. M., 1983. The West Bend, Wisconsin, storm of 4 April 1981: a problem in operational meteorology. *J. Climate Appl. Meteorol.* 22:181–89.

Ward, N. B., 1964. The Newton, Kansas tornado cyclone of May 24, 1962. Preprints, Eleventh Weather Radar Conference, Boulder, Colo. American Meteorological Society, Boston, pp. 410–15.

————, 1972. The exploration of certain features of tornado dynamics using a laboratory model. *J. Atmos. Sci.* 29:1194–1204.

Watkins, D. C., J. D. Cobine, and B. Vonnegut, 1978. Electrical discharges inside tornadoes. *Science* 199:171–74.

Weisman, M. L., and J. B. Klemp, 1982. The dependence of numerically simulated convective storms on vertical wind shear and buoyancy. *Mon. Weather Rev.* 110:504–20.

Widnall, S. E., and D. B. Bliss, 1971. Slender-body analysis of the motion and stability of a vortex filament containing axial flow. *J. Fluid Mech.* 50:335–53.

Wilk, K. E., and R. A. Brown, 1975. Applications of conventional and Doppler radar measurements in severe storm research. Preprints, Third Symposium on Meteorological Observations and Instrumentation, Washington, D.C. American Meteorological Society, Boston, pp. 165–74.

Wilkins, E. M., Y. Sasaki, R. L. Inman, and L. L. Terrell, 1974. Vortex formation in a friction layer: a numerical simulation. *Mon. Weather Rev.* 102:99–114.

Wilson, J. W., and G. M. Morgan, 1971. Long-track tornadoes and their significance. Preprints, Seventh Conference on Severe Local Storms, Kansas City, Mo. American Meteorological Society, Boston, pp. 183–86.

Wolford, L. V., 1960. Tornado occurrences in the United States. Tech. Paper No. 20, rev. ed., U.S. Weather Bureau, Washington, D.C.

Ying, S. J., and C. C. Chang, 1970. Exploratory model study of tornado-like vortex dynamics. *J. Atmos. Sci.* 27:3–14.

Zrnić, D. S., 1976. Magnetometer data acquired during nearby tornado occurrences. *J. Geophys. Res.* 81:5410–12.

————, and R. J. Doviak, 1975. Velocity spectra of vortices scanned with a pulse-Doppler radar. *J. Appl. Meteorol.* 14:1531–39.

————, ————, and D. W. Burgess, 1977. Probing tornadoes with a pulse-Doppler radar. *Q. J. R. Meteorol. Soc.* 103:707–20.

————, and M. Istok, 1980. Wind speeds in two tornadic storms and a tornado, deduced from Doppler spectra. *J. Appl. Meteorol.* 19:1405–15.

Chapter 11

Admirat, P., 1973. Natural hail cores and their ability to estimate the efficiency of hail prevention systems. Proceedings, WMO/IAMAP Scientific Conference on Weather Modification, Tashkent. WMO No. 399, pp. 197–206.

Appleman, H., 1959. An investigation into the formation of hail. *Nubila* 2(1):28–37.

Atlas, D., 1976. The present and future of hail suppression. Proceedings, Second WMO Scientific Conference on Weather Modification, Boulder, Colo. WMO No. 443, Geneva, pp. 207–19.

———, M. Kerker, and W. Hitschfeld, 1953. Scattering and attenuation by nonspherical atmospheric particles. *J. Atmos. Terrest. Phys.* 3:109–19.

Barge, B. L., and G. A. Isaac, 1973. The shape of Alberta hailstones. *J. Rech. Atmos.* 7:11–20.

Battan, L. J., 1975. Doppler radar observations of a hailstorm. *J. Appl. Meteorol.* 14:198–208.

Beckwith, W. B., 1960. Analysis of hailstorms in the Denver network. *J. Meteorol.* 23:348–53.

Bilham, E. G., and E. F. Relf, 1937. The dynamics of large hailstones. *Q. J. R. Meteorol. Soc.* 63:149–62.

Blifford, I. H., Jr., R. L. Patterson, Jr., L. B. Lockhart, Jr., and R. A. Bans, 1957. On radioactive hailstones. *Bull. Am. Meteorol. Soc.* 38:139–41.

Boone, L. M., 1974. Estimating crop losses due to hail. Agr. Econ. Rep. 267, U.S. Department of Agriculture, Washington, D.C.

Boyden, C. J., 1963. A simple instability index for use as an synoptic parameter. *Meteorol. Mag.* 92:198–210.

Bradley, M. M., 1977. A preliminary investigation of the applicability of a one-dimensional, time dependent cloud model to operational forecasting. Rep. 77-7, Subcontract NCAR S5011. Inst. Atmos. Sci., South Dakota School of Mines and Tech., Rapid City.

Briggs, G. A., 1968. Hailstones, starfish and daggers—spiked hail falls at Oak Ridge, Tennessee. *Mon. Weather Rev.* 96:744–45.

Brooks, C. E. P., 1944. The frequency distribution of hailstone sizes. *Q. J. R. Meteorol. Soc.* 70:227–28.

Browning, K. A., and R. J. Donaldson, Jr., 1963. Airflow and structure of a tornadic storm. *J. Atmos. Sci.* 20:533–45.

———, and G. B. Foote, 1976. Airflow and hail growth in supercell storms and some implications for hail suppression. *Q. J. R. Meteorol. Soc.* 102:499–533.

———, and F. H. Ludlam, 1962. Airflow in convective storms. *Q. J. R. Meteorol. Soc.* 88:117–35.

Byers, H. R., and R. R. Braham, 1949. *The Thunderstorm.* U.S. Government Printing Office, Washington, D.C.

———, H. Moses, and P. J. Harney, 1959. Measurement of rain temperature. *J. Meteorol.* 6:51–55.

Carte, A. E., and I. L. Basson, 1970. Hail in the Pretoria-Wilwatersrand area, 1962–68. C.S.I.R. Research Rep. No. 293, Pretoria, South Africa.

———, and R. E. Kidder, 1966. Transvaal hailstones. *Q. J. R. Meteorol. Soc.* 92:382–91.

———, and ———, 1970. Hailstones from the Pretoria-Wilwatersrand area, 1959–1969. C.S.I.R. Res. Rep. No. 297, Pretoria, South Africa.

———, and G. Held, 1978. Variability of hailstorms on the South African plateau. *J. Appl. Meteorol.* 17:365–73.

———, R. H. Douglas, R. C. Srivastava, and G. N. Williams, 1963. Alberta hail studies. Rep. MW-36, McGill University, Montreal.

Changnon, S. A., Jr., 1966. Note on recording hail occurrences. *J. Appl. Meteorol.* 5:899–901.

———, 1970. Hailstreaks. *J. Atmos. Sci.* 27:109–25.

———, 1971. Note on hailstone size distributions. *J. Appl. Meteorol.* 10:168–70.

———, 1973. Hail sensing and small-scale variability of windblown hail. *J. Weather Modif.* 5:30–42.

———, 1977. The scales of hail. *J. Appl. Meteorol.* 16:626–48.

———, and N. A. Barron, 1971. Quantification of crop-hail losses by aerial photography. *J. Appl. Meteorol.* 10:86–96.

———, and G. M. Morgan, Jr., 1976. Design of an experiment to suppress hail in Illinois. Bulletin 61, Illinois State Water Survey, Urbana.

———, et al., 1977. Hail suppression, impacts and issues. Final Report, Technology Assessment of the Suppression of Hail, ERP75-09980, Office of Exploratory Research and Problem Assessment Research Applied to National Needs Program, National Science Foundation. Illinois State Water Survey, Urbana.

Chisholm, A. J., 1967. Small-scale radar structure of Alberta hailstorms. Rep. MW-49, Stormy Weather Group, McGill University, Montreal.

———, 1969. Observations by 10 cm radar of the hailstorm of 29 June 1967. The hailstorm of 29 June 1964, Rep. MW-59, McGill University, Montreal.

———, and M. English, 1973. *Alberta Hailstorms.* Meteorol. Monogr. 14, American Meteorological Society, Boston.

Crow, E. L., P. W. Summers, A. B. Long, C. A. Knight, G. B. Foote, and J. E. Dye, 1976. National hail research experiment randomized seeding experiment, 1972–1974. Part 1, experimental results and overall summary. National Center for Atmospheric Research, Boulder, Colo.

Danielsen, E. F., 1978. Inherent difficulties in hail probability predictions. In *Hail: A Review of Hail Science and Hail Suppression,* Meteorol. Monogr. 16, American Meteorological Society, Boston, pp. 135–44.

Darkow, G. L., and M. G. Fowler, 1971. Tornado proximity sounding wind analysis. Preprints, Seventh Conference on Severe Local Storms, Kansas City, Mo. American Meteorological Society, Boston, pp. 148–51.

Das, P., 1962. Influence of wind shear on the growth of hail. *J. Atmos. Sci.* 19:407–14.

Dennis, A. S., and D. J. Musil, 1973. Calculations of hailstone growth and trajectories in a simple cloud model. *J. Atmos. Sci.* 30:278–88.

Dessens, H., 1960. Severe hailstorms are associated with strong winds between 6,000 and 12,000 meters. In *Physics of Precipitation,* American Geophysical Union, Washington, D.C., pp. 333–36.

Diebert, R. J. (ed.), 1976. Alberta hail project field program. Rep. No. 2, Alberta Weather Modif. Board, Three Hills, Alberta.

Donaldson, R. J., Jr., 1965. Methods for identifying severe thunderstorms by radar: a guide and bibliography. *Bull. Am. Meteorol. Soc.* 46:174–93.

Douglas, R. H., 1963. Recent hail research: a review. In *Severe Local Storms,* Meteorol. Mongr. 5, American Meteorological Society, Boston, pp. 157–67.

———, 1965a. Intermittency in western Canadian hailfall. Proceedings, International Conference on Cloud Physics, Tokyo, May 1965, pp. 291–95.

———, 1965b. Size distribution of Alberta hail samples. Alberta hail studies, 1962–63. Rep. MW-36, McGill University, Montreal, pp. 55–70A.

English, M., 1969. Hail growth in the storm of 29 June 1967. The hailstorm of 29 June 1967, Rep. MW-59, McGill University,

Montreal.

———, 1973. The growth of large hail: studies derived from Alberta and Montreal hailstorms. Rep. MW-78, McGill University, Montreal.

———, and C. Warner, 1970. Observations and theory of a Montreal hailstorm. Preprints, Conference on Cloud Physics, Ft. Collins, Colo. American Meteorological Society, Boston, pp. 57–58.

Eng Young, R., and K. A. Browning, 1967. Wind tunnel tests of simulated spherical hailstones with variable roughness. *J. Atmos. Sci.* 24:58–62.

Facy, L., L. G. Merlivat, G. Nief, and E. Roth, 1963. The study of the formation of a hailstone by means of isotopic analysis. *J. Geophys. Res.* 58:3841–48.

Favreau, R. F., and G. Goyer, 1967. The effect of shock waves on a hailstone model. *J. Appl. Meteorol.* 6:326–35.

Fawbush, E. J., and R. C. Miller, 1953. A method for forecasting hailstone size at the earth's surface. *Bull. Am. Meteorol. Soc.* 34:235–44.

———, ———, and L. G. Starrett, 1957. Severe local storms and mid-tropospheric flow patterns. *Bull. Am. Meteorol. Soc.* 38:115–23.

Federer, B., 1978. Methods and results of hail suppression in Europe and the USSR. In *Hail: A Review of Hail Science and Hail Suppression*, Meteorol. Monogr. 16, American Meteorological Society, Boston, pp. 215–24.

———, and A. Waldvogel, 1975. Hail and raindrop size distributions from a Swiss multicell storm. *J. Appl. Meteorol.* 14:91–97.

Flora, S. D., 1956. *Hailstorms of the United States*. University of Oklahoma Press, Norman.

Foote, G. B., and C. A. Knight (eds.), 1978. *Hail: A Review of Hail Science and Hail Suppression*. Meteorol. Monogr. 16, American Meteorological Society, Boston.

Fort, C., 1919. *The Book of the Damned*. Boni and Liveright, New York.

Frisby, E. M., 1962. Relationship of ground hail damage patterns to features of the synoptic map in the upper Great Plains of the United States. *J. Appl. Meteorol.* 1:348–52.

———, and H. W. Sansom, 1967. Hail incidence in the tropics. *J. Appl. Meteorol.* 6:399–54.

Galway, J. E., 1956. The lifted index as a predictor of latent instability. *Bull. Am. Meteorol. Soc.* 37:528–29.

Genève, R., 1961. La grêle [hail]. Memo. 48, Météorologie Nationale, Paris (NCAR Library Translation No. 157).

Gibson, W. S., 1861. *Hailstorms and Their Phenomena, in Miscellanies Historical and Biographical*. Longham, Roberts and Green (1863), pp. 279–91.

Gitlin, S. N., H. Fogler, and G. G. Goyer, 1966. A calorimetric method for measuring water content of hailstones. *J. Appl. Meteorol.* 5:715–21.

Gokhale, N. R., and K. M. Rao, 1969. Theory of hail growth. *J. Rech. Atmos.* 4:153–78.

Grosh, R., and G. M. Morgan, Jr., 1975. Radar-thermodynamic hail day determination. Preprints, Ninth Conference on Severe Local Storms. American Meteorological Society, Boston, pp. 454–59.

Hallet, J., 1967. Charge separation and the growth of hail. *Weather* 22:80.

Harrison, H. T., and W. B. Beckwith, 1959. Studies on the distribution and forecasting of hail in the western United States. *Bull. Am. Meteorol. Soc.* 32:119–31.

Heymsfield, A. J., A. R. Jameson, and H. W. Frank, 1980. Hail growth mechanisms in a Colorado storm. Part 2: Hail formation processes. *J. Atmos. Sci.* 37:1779–1807.

Hitschfeld, W., 1971. Hail research at McGill, 1956–1971. Sci. Rep. MW-68, Stormy Weather Group, McGill University, Montreal.

———, and R. H. Douglas, 1963. A theory of hail growth based on studies of Alberta storms. *Z. Angew. Math. Phys.* 14:554–62.

———, and M. Stauder, 1965. The temperature of hailstones. Alberta Hail Studies, 1964, Sci. Rep. MW-42. Stormy Weather Group, McGill University, Montreal.

Hoerner, S. F., 1965. *Fluid Dynamic Drag*. 2d ed., published by the author, Dr. Ing. S. F. Hoerner, 148 Busteed Drive, Midland Park, N.J. 07432.

Huff, F. A., 1964. Correlation between summer hail patterns in Illinois and associated climatological events. *J. Appl. Meteorol.* 3:240–46.

Humphreys, W. J., 1964. *Physics of the Air*. 3d ed., Dover, New York.

Huschke, R. E. (ed.), 1959. *Glossary of Meteorology*. American Meteorological Society, Boston.

Jaffe, G., W. Wittmann, and C. C. Bates, 1954. Radioactive hailstones in the District of Columbia area, May 26, 1953. *Bull. Am. Meteorol. Soc.* 35:245–49.

Jean, C., J. L. Tondut, and D. Tena, 1976. Programme "Languedoc" été 1975. Groupement Interdépartemental D'Etudes des Fleaux Atmosphériques, Rapport Technique No. 24, Montpellier, France.

Kämtz, L. F., 1840. *Vorlesungen über Meteorologie*. Halle.

Knight, C. A., and N. C. Knight, 1973. Quenched, spongy hail. *J. Atmos. Sci.* 30:1665–71.

———, and ———, 1976. Hail embryo studies. Preprints, International Conference on Cloud Physics, Boulder, Colo. American Meteorological Society, Boston, pp. 222–26.

———, D. H. Ehalt, N. Roper, and N. C. Knight, 1975. Radial and tangential variation of deuterium in hailstones. *J. Atmos. Sci.* 32:1990–2000.

———, N. C. Knight, and K. A. Kime, 1980. Deuterium contents of storm inflow and hailstone growth layers. *J. Atmos. Sci.* 30:2485–99.

Knight, N. C., and C. A. Knight, 1978. Some observations on foreign materials in hailstones. *Bull. Am. Meteorol. Soc.* 59:282–86.

Landry, C. R., and K. Hardy, 1970. Fall speed characteristics of simulated ice spheres: a radar experiment. Preprints, Fourth Radar Meteorology Conference, Tucson, Ariz. American Meteorological Society, Boston, pp. 27–30.

Larson, H. R., 1973. Studies of thunderstorms by spherics and radar. Rep. MW-79, McGill University, Montreal.

List, R., 1961. On the growth of hailstones. *Nubila* 4:29–38.

———, 1963. On the effect of explosion waves on hailstone models. *J. Appl. Meteorol.* 2:494–97.

Longley, R. W., and C. E. Thompson, 1965. A study of the causes of hail. *J. Appl. Meteorol.* 4:69–82.

Ludlum, D. (ed.), 1971. The "New Champ" hailstone. *Weatherwise* 24:151.

Ludlam, F. H., 1959. Hailstorm studies, 1958. *Nubila* 2:7–27.

———, 1963. Severe local storms: a review. In *Severe Local Storms*, Meteorol. Monogr. 5, American Meteorological Society, Boston, pp. 1–30.

Macklin, W. C., C. A. Knight, H. E. Moore, N. C. Knight, W. H. Pollock, J. N. Carras, and S. Thwaites, 1977. Isotopic, crystal and air bubble structures of hailstones. *J. Atmos. Sci.* 34: 961–67.

Mandrioli, P., G. L. Puppi, and N. Bagni, 1973. Distribution of microorganisms in hailstones. *Nature* 246:416–17.

Marshall, J. S., and W. McK. Palmer, 1948. The distribution of raindrops with size. *J. Meteorol.* 5:165.

Marwitz, J. D., 1972a. The structure and motion of severe hailstorms. Part 1: Supercell storms. *J. Appl. Meteorol.* 11: 166–79.

———, 1972b. The structure and motion of severe hailstorms. Part 2: Multicell storms. *J. Appl. Meteorol.* 11:180–88.

———, 1972c. The structure and motion of severe hailstorms. Part 3: Severely sheared storms. *J. Appl. Meteorol.* 11: 189–201.

Miller, R. C., 1972. Notes on analysis and severe storm forecasting procedures of the Air Force Global Weather Central. TR 200 (Rev.), Air Weather Service (MAC), U.S. Air Force.

Modahl, A. C., 1969. The influence of vertical wind shear on hailstorm development and structure. Colorado State University, Atmos. Sci. Paper 137, Fort Collins.

Mollo-Christensen, E., 1962. The distribution of raindrops and gusts in showers and squalls. *J. Atmos. Sci.* 19:191–92.

Morgan, G. M., Jr., 1970. An examination of the wet-bulb-zero as a hail forecasting parameter in the Po Valley, Italy. *J. Appl. Meteorol.* 9:537–40.

———, 1972. On the growth of large hail. *Mon. Weather Rev.* 100:196–205.

———, 1973. A general description of the hail problem in the Po Valley of northern Italy. *J. Appl. Meteorol.* 12:338–53.

———, and N. G. Towery, 1974. Small-scale variability of hail and its significance for hail prevention experiments. *J. Appl. Meteorol.* 14:763–70.

———, and ———, 1975. On the role of strong winds in damage to crops by hail and its estimation with a simple instrument. *J. Appl. Meteorol.* 15:891–98.

Mossop, S. C., 1971. Some hailstones of unusual shape. *Weather* 26:222.

Nelson, L., 1976. Numerical simulation of natural and seeded hail-bearing clouds. Proceedings, Second WMO Scientific Conference on Weather Modification, Boulder, Colo. WMO No. 443, Geneva, pp. 371–80.

Nelson, S. P., 1983. The influence of storm flow structure on hail growth. *J. Atmos. Sci.* 40:1965–83.

———, and S. K. Young, 1978. Characteristics of Oklahoma hailfalls (unpublished manuscript).

Newton, C. W., 1950. Structure and mechanism of the prefrontal squall line. *J. Meteorol.* 7:210–22.

———, and H. R. Newton, 1959. Dynamical interactions between large convective clouds and environment with vertical shear. *J. Meteorol.* 16:483–96.

Orville, H. D., 1978. A review of hailstone-hailstorm simulations. In *Hail: A Review of Hail Science and Hail Suppression*, Meteorol. Monogr. 16, American Meteorological Society, Boston, pp. 49–62.

Pappas, J. J., 1962. A simple yes-no hail forecasting technique. *J. Appl. Meteorol.* 1:353–54.

Paul, A. H., 1968. Regional variation of two fundamental properties of hailfalls. *Weather* 23:424–29.

Pell, J., 1967. Computer analysis of intermittency in Alberta point hailfall. Preprints, Fifth Conference on Severe Local Storms, St. Louis, Mo., October 1967. American Meteorological Society, Boston, pp. 307–14.

———, 1970. The interactions and radar detectability of hail cells aloft as inferred from surface data. Preprints, Fourteenth Radar Meteorology Conference, Tucson, Arizona, November 1970. American Meteorological Society, Boston, pp. 13–18.

Prandtl, L., 1914. Uber der Luftwiderstand von Kugeln. *Goettingen Nachr.*, pp. 177–82.

Prodi, F., 1974. Climatologia della grandine nella Valle Padona (1968–1972). [Climatology of hail in the Po Valley (1968–1972)]. *Rivista Italiana di Geofisica* 23(516):283–90.

———, and C. T. Nagamoto, 1971. Chloride segregation along grain boundaries in ice. *J. Glaciol.* 10:299–308.

Prohaska, K., 1907. Die hagelfalle des 6 Juli 1905 in Ostalpen. *Meteorol. Zeit.* 24(5):13–201.

Ratner, B., 1961. Do high-speed winds aloft influence the occurrence of hail? *Bull. Am. Meteorol. Soc.* 42:443–46.

Renick, J. H., 1971. Radar reflectivity profiles of individual cells in a persistent multicellular Alberta hailstorm. Preprints, Seventh Conference on Severe Local Storms. American Meteorological Society, Boston, pp. 63–70.

———, and J. B. Maxwell, 1978. Forecasting hailfall in Alberta. In *Hail: A Review of Hail Science and Hail Suppression*, Meteorol. Monogr. 16, American Meteorological Society, Boston, pp. 145–51.

Roos, D., 1972. A giant hailstone from Kansas in free fall. *J. Appl. Meteorol.* 11:1008–11.

Rosinki, J., 1966. Solid water-insoluble particles in hailstones and their geophysical significance. *J. Appl. Meteorol.* 5:481–92.

———, 1974. Role of aerosol particles in formation of precipitation. *Rev. Geophys. Space Phys.* 12:129–34.

Sansom, H. W., 1966a. A possible effect of lightning on hail. *Weather* 21:315.

———, 1966b. The use of explosive rockets to suppress hail in Kenya. *Weather* 21:86–91.

Schaefer, V. J., 1946. The production of ice crystals in a cloud of supercooled water droplets. *Science* 104:457.

Schleusener, R. A., 1962. On the relation of the latitude and strength of the 500 mb west wind along 110° W. longitude to the occurrence of hail in the lee of the Rocky Mountains. Colorado State University, Atmos. Sci. Tech. Paper 26, Fort Collins.

Shands, A. L., 1944. The hail-thunderstorm ratio. *Mon. Weather Rev.* 72:71–73.

Showalter, A. K., 1953. Stability index for forecasting thunderstorms. *Bull. Am. Meteorol. Soc.* 34:250–52.

Spahn, J. F., and P. L. Smith, Jr., 1976. Some characteristics of hailstone size distributions inside hailstorms. Preprints, Seventeenth Weather Radar Conference, Seattle, Wash. American Meteorological Society, Boston, pp. 187–91.

Strong, G. S., 1974. The objective measurement of Alberta hailfall. M.S. thesis, University of Alberta, Edmonton.

Sulakvelidze, G. K., 1967. *Rainstorms and Hail.* Trans. by Israel Program for Scientific Translation (National Technical Information Service, Springfield, Va., NTIS TT-68-50466), 1969.

———, H. S. Bibilashvili, and O. F. Lapcheva, 1967. *Formation of Precipitation and Modification of Hail Processes.* Trans. by Israel Program for Scientific Translation (National Technical Information Service, Springfield, Va.).

Summers, P. W., 1968. Soft hail in Alberta hailstorms. Proceedings, International Conference on Cloud Physics, Toronto, Canada, August 1968, pp. 455–59.

———, 1972. The silver fallout patterns in precipitation from seeded convective storms. Preprints, Third Conference on Weather Modification, Rapid City, S. Dak. American Meteorological Society, Boston, pp. 279–86.

———, and B. Hitchon, 1973. Source and budget of sulfate in precipitation from Central Alberta, Canada. *J. Air Pollut. Control Assoc.* 23(3):194–99.

———, J. C. Fankhauser, G. M. Morgan, Jr., G. B. Foote, and A. C. Modahl, 1979. Results of a randomized hail suppression experiment in northeast Colorado. Part 8: The representative draw analysis. *J. Appl. Meteorol.* 18:1618–28.

Talman, C. F., 1936. Ice from thunderclouds. *Nat. Hist.* 38: 109–19.

Thompson, W., and P. W. Summers, 1970. The influence of upper winds on hailfall patterns in central Alberta. Presented at the Fourth Annual Congress of the Canadian Meteorological Society, Winnipeg, Manitoba (unpublished manuscript).

Tomassimi, G., and G. M. Morgan, Jr., 1968. Prova di un apparato per la misura della temperatura della pioggia in regime temporalesco [Trials of apparatus for measuring the temperature of thunderstorm rain]. XVIII Convegno della Associazione Geofisica Italiana, Rome.

Towery, N. G., and G. M. Morgan, Jr., 1977. Hailstripes. *Bull. Am. Meteorol. Soc.* 58:588–91, cover photograph.

———, G. M. Morgan, Jr., and S. A. Changnon, Jr., 1976. Examples of the wind factor in crop hail damage. *J. Appl. Meteorol.* 15:1116–20.

Vali, G., 1970. Entry of freezing nuclei into precipitation. In *Precipitation Scavenging*, U.S. Atomic Energy Commission Symposium, Series No. 22, pp. 49–68.

———, 1971. Freezing nucleus content of hail and rain in Alberta. *J. Appl. Meteorol.* 10:73–78.

Vento, D., and G. M. Morgan, Jr., 1976. Statistical evaluation of energy imparted to hail by wind in Europe and United States. Proceedings, Second WMO Scientific Conference on Weather Modification, Boulder, Colo. WMO No. 443, Geneva, pp. 281–85.

Vittori, O., 1960. Preliminary note on the effects of pressure waves on hailstones. *Nubila* 3:34–52.

———, and G. di Caporiacco, 1959. The density of hailstones. *Nubila* 2:51–57.

———, F. Prodi, G. Morgan, and G. Cesari, 1969. Natural tracer distribution in hailstones. *J. Atmos. Sci.* 26:148–52.

Vogel, J., 1974. Synoptic analyses. In *Interim Report of Metromex Studies, 1971–73*, F. A. Huff (ed.), National Science Foundation, GI-38317, pp. 6–16.

Volta, A., 1806. Sopra la grandine [On hail]. Memorie dell'Instituto Nazionale Italiano. Fratelli Mesi e Compagno, Bologna.

Warner, C., 1969. Photographic, surface and pilot balloon observations of low altitude phenomena of the hailstorm. The hailstorm of 29 June 1967, Rep. MW-59, McGill University, Montreal.

Wegener, A., 1911. *Thermodynamik der Atmosphäre*, Leipzig.

Weickmann, H. K., 1953. Observational data on the formation of precipitation in cumulonimbus clouds. In *Thunderstorm Electricity*, H. R. Byers (ed.), University of Chicago Press, Chicago, pp. 66–138.

———, 1964. The language of hailstorms and hailstones. *Nubila* 4:7–50.

Willis, J. T., K. A. Browning, and D. Atlas, 1964. Radar observations of ice spheres in free fall. *J. Atmos. Sci.* 21:103–108.

Wojtiw, L., 1975. Climatic summaries of hailfall in central Alberta. Atmos. Sci. Rep. 75-1, Res. Council of Alberta, Edmonton.

———, and G. Lunn, 1977. Hailfall studies. Atmos. Sci. Rep. 77-3, Res. Council of Alberta, Edmonton, pp. 43–62.

Wood, C. P., 1955. A theory of hail formation. M.S. thesis, Massachusetts Institute of Technology, Cambridge.

Young, K. C., 1978. A numerical examination of some hail suppression concepts. In *Hail: A Review of Hail Science and Hail Suppression*, Meteorol. Monogr. 16, American Meteorological Society, Boston, pp. 195–224.

Ziegler, C. L., P. S. Ray, and N. C. Knight, 1983. Hail growth in an Oklahoma multicell storm. *J. Atmos. Sci.* 40:1768–91.

Chapter 12

Abich, H., 1869. Zwei denkwürdige Hagelfälle in Georgien. *Z. Österr. Ges. Meteorol.* 4:417–21.

Auer, A. H., 1972. Distribution of graupel and hail with size. *Mon. Weather Rev.* 100:325–28.

Aufdermaur, A. N., R. List, W. C. Mayes, and M. de Quervain, 1963. Kristallachsenlagen in Hagelkoernern. *Z. Angew. Math. Phys.* 14(5):574–89.

Bilham, E. G., and E. F. Relf, 1937. The dynamics of large hailstones. *Q. J. R. Meteorol. Soc.* 63:149–62.

Browning, K. A., 1966. The lobe structure of giant hailstones. *Q. J. R. Meteorol. Soc.* 92:1–14.

———, F. H. Ludlam, and W. C. Macklin, 1963. The density and structure of hailstones. *Q. J. R. Meteorol. Soc.* 89:75–84.

Carras, J. N., and W. C. Macklin, 1973. The shedding of accreted water during hailstone growth. *Q. J. R. Meteorol. Soc.* 99: 639–48.

———, and ———, 1975. Air bubbles in accreted ice. *Q. J. R. Meteorol. Soc.* 101:127–46.

Carte, A. E., 1961. Air bubbles in ice. *Proc. Phys. Soc. London* 77:757–69.

———, and R. E. Kidder, 1970. Hailstones from the Pretoria-Witwatersrand area, 1959–1969. CSIR Research Rep. 297, Pretoria, South Africa.

Changnon, S. A., 1971. Note on hailstone size distributions. *J. Appl. Meteorol.* 19:168–70.

Charlton, R. D., and R. List, 1972. Hail size distribution and accumulation zones. *J. Atmos. Sci.* 29(6):1182–93.

Clark, T. L., and R. List, 1971. Dynamics of a falling particle zone. *J. Atmos. Sci.* 28:718–27.

Douglas, R. H., 1963. Recent hail research: a review. In *Severe Local Storms*, Meteorol. Monogr. 5, American Meteorological Society, Boston, pp. 157–67.

English, M., 1973. Growth of large hail in the storm. In *Alberta Hailstorms*, Meteorol. Monogr. 14, American Meteorological Society, Boston, pp. 37–91.

Facy, L., L. Merlivat, G. Nief, and R. Roth, 1963. The study of formation of hailstones by isotopic analysis. *J. Geophys. Res.* 68:3841–48.

Federer, B., and A. Waldvogel, 1975. Hail and raindrop size distributions from a Swiss multicell storm. *J. Appl. Meteorol.* 14:91–97.

Foote, G. B., and C. A. Knight (eds.), 1977. *Hail: A Review of Hail Science and Hail Suppression*. Meteorol. Monogr. 16, American Meteorological Society, Boston, Mass.

Fukuta, N., 1975. Comments on "A possible mechanism for contact nucleation." *J. Atmos. Sci.* 32:2371–73.

Genève, R., 1961. La grêle. *Mém. de Météorol. Natl.* Paris, No. 48, pp. 1–75.

Girard, C., and R. List, 1974. The fall of precipitation particle zones. Preprints, Conference on Cloud Physics, Tucson, Ariz., 23–24 October. American Meteorological Society, Boston, pp. 223–26.

Hallet, J., and S. C. Mossop, 1974. Production of secondary ice particles during the riming process. *Nature* 249:26–28.

Hierlihy, R. D., 1968. Measurements of the mass transfer of spheroidal hailstone models. M.S. thesis, University of Toronto.

Huschke, R. E. (ed.), 1959. *Glossary of Meteorology*. American Meteorological Society, Boston.

Iribarne, J. V., and R. G. de Pena, 1962. The influence of particle concentrations on the evolution of hailstones. *Nubila* 5:7–30.

Knight, C. A., and N. C. Knight, 1968. The final freezing of spongy ice: hailstone collection techniques and interpretation of structures. *J. Appl. Meteorol.* 7:875–81.

———, and ———, 1970. The falling behaviour of hailstones. *J. Atmos. Sci.* 27:672–81.

———, and ———, 1971. Hailstones. *Sci. Am.* 224:96–104.

———, and ———, 1973a. Conical graupel. *J. Atmos. Sci.* 30:118–24.

———, and ———, 1973b. Quenched, spongy hail. *J. Atmos. Sci.* 30:1665–71.

———, and ———, 1974. Drop freezing in clouds. *J. Atmos. Sci.* 31:1174–76.

———, C. E. Abbott, and N. C. Knight, 1974. Comments on "Air bubbles in artificial hailstones." *J. Atmos. Sci.* 31:2236–38.

Kry, P. R., and R. List, 1974a. Aerodynamic torques on rotating oblate spheroids. *Phys. Fluids* 17:1087–92.

———, and ———, 1974b. Angular motions of freely falling spheroidal hailstone models. *Phys. Fluids* 17:1093–1102.

Langmuir, I., and K. B. Blodgett, 1946. Mathematical investigations of water droplet trajectories. G. E. Rep. RL-224. In *Collected Works of Dr. I. Langmuir*, Vol. 10, Pergamon Press, New York, pp. 335–95.

Levi, L., and A. N. Aufdermaur, 1970. Crystallographic orientation and crystal size in cylindrical accretions of ices. *J. Atmos. Sci.* 27:443–52.

List, R., 1958a. Kennzeichen atmosphaerischer Eispartikeln, 1. Teil. *Z. Angew. Math. Phys.* 9a:180–92.

———, 1958b. Kennzeichen atmosphaerischer Eispartikeln, 2. Teil. *Z. Angew. Math. Phys.* 9a:280–92.

———, 1959a. Zur Aerodynamik von Hagelkoernern. *Z. Angew. Math. Phys.* 10:143–59.

———, 1959b. Der Hagelversuchskanal. *Z. Angew. Math. Phys.* 10:381–415.

———, 1959c. Wachstum von Eis-Wassergemischen im Hagelversuchskanal. *Helv. Phys. Acta* 32:293–96.

———, 1960a. Growth and structure of graupel and hailstones. In *Physics of Precipitation*, Geophys. Monogr. 5, American Geophysical Union, Baltimore, Md., pp. 317–24.

———, 1960b. Zur Thermodynamik teilweise waessriger Hagelkoerner. *Z. Angew. Math. Phys.* 11:273–306.

———, 1961a. Physical methods and instruments for characterizing hailstones. *Bull. Am. Meteorol. Soc.* 42:452–66.

———, 1961b. On the growth of hailstones. *Nubila* 4:29–38.

———, 1965. The mechanism of hailstone formation. Proceedings, International Conference on Cloud Physics, Tokyo and Sapporo, 24 May–1 June, pp. 481–91.

———, 1966. A hail tunnel with pressure control. *J. Atmos. Sci.* 23:61–66.

———, 1974. The warm-rain mechanism—its modelling and modifications. Proceedings, WMO Technological Conference on Typhoon Modification, Manila, 15–18 October. WMO No. 408, pp. 1–8.

———, 1977. Ice accretions on structures. *J. Glaciol.* 19:451–65.

———, and T. A. Agnew, 1973. Air bubbles in artificial hailstones. *J. Atmos. Sci.* 30:1158–65.

———, and T. L. Clark, 1973. The effect of particle size distributions on the dynamics of falling precipitation zones. *Atmosphere* 11:179–88.

———, and M. de Quervain, 1953. Zur Struktur von Hagelkoernern. *Z. Angew. Math. Phys.* 4:3–7.

———, and J-G. Dussault, 1967. Quasi steady state icing and melting conditions and heat and mass transfer of spherical and spheroidal hailstones. *J. Atmos. Sci.* 24:522–29.

———, and J. R. Gillespie, 1976. Evolution of raindrop spectra with collision-induced breakup. *J. Atmos. Sci.* 33:2007–13.

———, and R. S. Schemenauer, 1971. Free fall behavior of planar snow crystals, conical graupel and small hail. *J. Atmos. Sci.* 28:110–15.

———, J-C. Cantin, and M. G. Farland, 1970. Structural properties of two hailstone samples. *J. Atmos. Sci.* 27:1080–90.

———, R. B. Charlton, and P. I. Buttuls, 1968. A numerical experiment on the growth and feedback mechanisms of hailstones in a one-dimensional steady state model cloud. *J. Atmos. Sci.* 25:1061–74.

———, W. A. Murray, and C. Dyck, 1972. Air bubbles in hailstones. *J. Atmos. Sci.* 29:916–20.

———, U. W. Rentsch, A. C. Byram, and E. P. Lozowski, 1973. On the aerodynamics of spheroidal hailstone models. *J. Atmos. Sci.* 30:653–61.

———, P. I. Joe, G. Lesins, P. R. Kry, M. R. de Quervain, J. D. McTaggart-Cowan, P. W. Stagg, E. P. Lozowski, E. Freire, R. E. Stewart, C. G. List, M. C. Steiner, and J. von Niederhausern, 1976. On the variation of the collection efficiencies of icing cylinders. Proceedings, International Cloud Physics Conference, Boulder, Colo., July, 1976, pp. 233–39.

List, R. J., 1968. *Smithsonian Meteorological Tables*. Smithsonian Institution Press, Washington, D.C.

Ludlam, F. H., 1958. The hail problem. *Nubila* 1:12–96.

Macklin, W. C., 1961. Accretion in mixed clouds. *Q. J. R. Meteorol. Soc.* 87:413–24.

———, 1962. The density and structure of ice formed by accretion. *Q. J. R. Meteorol. Soc.* 88:30–50.

———, 1963. Heat transfer from hailstones. *Q. J. R. Meteorol. Soc.* 89:360–69.

———, 1977. The characteristics of natural hailstones and their interpretation. In *Hail: A Review of Hail Science and Hail Suppression*, Meteorol. Monogr. 16, American Meteorological Society, Boston, pp. 65–88.

———, and I. H. Bailey, 1966. On the critical liquid water concentrations of large hailstones. *Q. J. R. Meteorol. Soc.* 92:297–300.

———, and ———, 1968. The collection efficiencies of hailstones. *Q. J. R. Meteorol. Soc.* 94:393–96.

———, and F. H. Ludlam, 1961. The fallspeeds of hailstones. *Q. J. R. Meteorol. Soc.* 87:72–81.

———, J. N. Carras, and P. J. Rye, 1976. The interpretation of the crystalline and air bubble structures of hailstones. *Q. J. R. Meteorol. Soc.* 102:25–44.

———, E. Strauch, and F. H. Ludlam, 1960. The density of hailstones collected from a summer storm. *Nubila* 3:12–17.

———, C. A. Knight, H. E. Moore, N. C. Knight, W. H. Pollock, J. N. Carras, and S. Thwaites, 1977. Isotopic crystal and air bubble structures of hailstones. *J. Atmos. Sci.* 34:961–67.

Mason, B. J., 1971. *The Physics of Clouds*. Clarendon Press, London.

Mossop, S. C., 1976. Production of secondary ice particles during the growth of graupel by riming. *Q. J. R. Meteorol. Soc.* 102:45–57.

———, and R. E. Kidder, 1961. Hailstorm at Johannesburg on 9th November 1959. Part 2: Structure of hailstones. *Nubila* 4:74–86.

———, and ———, 1962. Artificial hailstones. *Bull. Obs. Puy de Dôme* 2:65–80.

Murray, W. A., and R. List, 1972. Freezing of waterdrops. *J. Glaciol.* 11:415–29.

Musil, D. J., W. R. Sand, and R. A. Schleusener, 1973. Analysis of data from T-28 aircraft penetration of a Colorado hailstorm. *J. Appl. Meteorol.* 12:1364–70.

Orville, H. D., and F. J. Kopp, 1976. The numerical simulation of a hailstorm. Proceedings, International Cloud Physics Conference, July, Boulder, Colo., pp. 349–56.

Parungo, F. P., B. P. Patten, and F. F. Pueschel, 1976. AgI ice nuclei: their properties and effectiveness. Proceedings, Second WMO Scientific Conference on Weather Modification, Boulder, Colo., August, 1976. WMO No. 443, pp. 505–12.

Ranz, W. A., and W. R. Marshall, 1952. Evaporation from drops. *Chem. Eng. Prog.* 48:141–80.

Reinking, R. F., 1975. Formation of graupel. *J. Appl. Meteorol.* 14:745–54.

Reynolds, O., 1877. On the manner in which raindrops and hailstones are formed. *Proc. Manchester Lit. Phil. Soc.* 16:23–33.

Rosinski, J., 1966. Solid water-insoluble particles in hailstones and their geophysical significance. *J. Appl. Meteorol.* 5:481–92.

———, 1967. Insoluble particles in hail and rain. *J. Appl. Meteorol.* 6:1066–74.

———, K. A. Browning, G. Langer, and C. G. Nagamoto, 1976. On the distribution of water-insoluble aerosol particles in hailstones and its possible value as an indication of the hail growth history. *J. Atmos. Sci.* 33:530–36.

Sarrica, O., 1959a. Varie conformazioni presentate dai chicci di grandine. Assoc. Geof. Italiana, VIII Convegno, Rome, February, pp. 165–72.

———, 1959b. Struttura cristallina della grandine. Assoc. Geof. Italiana, VIII Convegno, Rome, February, pp. 173–76.

Sasyo, Y., 1971. Study of the formation of precipitation by the aggregation of snow particles and the accretion of cloud droplets on snowflakes. *Pap. Meteorol. Geophys.* 22:69–142.

Schaefer, V. J., 1960. Hailstorms and hailstones of the western great plains. *Nubila* 3:18–29.

Schuepp, P. H., and R. List, 1969. Mass transfer of rough hailstone models in flows of various turbulence levels. *J. Appl. Meteorol.* 8:254–63.

Schumann, T. E. W., 1938. The theory of hailstone formation. *Q. J. R. Meteorol. Soc.* 64:3–21.

Stewart, R. E., 1977. Experimental investigation of the aerodynamics of freely falling disks. Ph.D. diss., University of Toronto.

Sulakvelidze, G. K., N. Sh. Bibliashvili, and V. F. Lapcheva, 1967. *Formation of Precipitation and Modification of Hail Processes.* Trans. by Israel Program for Scientific Translation (National Technical Information Service, Springfield, Va.).

Trabert, W., 1896. Die Bildung des Hagels. *Meteorol. Z.* 10:433–47.

Vittori, O., and G. di Caporiacco, 1959. The density of hailstones. *Nubila* 1:51–57.

Weickmann, H. K., 1953. Precipitation in observational data on the formation of cumulo-nimbus clouds. In *Thunderstorm Electricity*, University of Chicago Press, Chicago, pp. 66–138.

———, 1964. The language of hailstorms and hailstones. *Nubila* 6:7–51.

Wieselsberger, C., 1923. Versuche über den Luftwiderstand ge-

rundeter und kantiger Körper. Ergebnisse der Aerodynamischen Versuchsanstalt Göttingen, 2:29–32.

Young, R. G., and K. A. Browning, 1967. Wind tunnel tests of simulated spherical hailstones with variable roughness. *J. Atmos. Sci.* 24:58–62.

Chapter 13

Chalmers, J. A., 1967. *Atmospheric Electricity*. Pergamon Press, New York.

Christian, H., C. R. Holmes, J. W. Bullock, W. Gaskell, A. J. Illingworth, and J. Latham, 1980. Airborne and ground-based studies of thunderstorms in the vicinity of Langmuir Laboratory. *Q. J. R. Meteorol. Soc.* 106(447):159–74.

Dawson, G. A., 1974. An introduction to atmospheric electricity. In *Weather and Climate Modification*, W. N. Hess (ed.), John Wiley, New York, pp. 596–604.

Golde, R. H., 1973. *Lightning Protection*. Edward Arnold, London.

——— (ed.), 1977. *Lightning*, vols. 1 & 2. Academic Press, London.

Griffiths, R. F., and C. T. Phelps, 1976. A model for lightning initiation arising from positive corona streamer development. *J. Geophys. Res.* 81:3671–76.

Hallett, J., 1983. Progress in cloud physics. In *Contributions in Meteorology: U.S. National Report, 1979–1982*. American Geophysical Union, Washington, D.C., pp. 965–84.

Israel, H., 1973. *Atmospheric Electricity*. 2 vols. Trans. by U.S. Department of Commerce, National Technical Information Service TT67-51394/2.

Latham, J., 1981. The electrification of thunderstorms. *Q. J. R. Meteorol. Soc.* 107(452):277–98.

Lhermitte, R., and E. Williams, 1983. Cloud electrification. In *Contributions in Meteorology: U.S. National Report, 1979–1982*. American Geophysical Union, Washington, D.C., pp. 984–92.

Stow, C. D., 1969. Atmospheric electricity. *Rep. Progr. Phys.* 32:1–67.

Uman, M. A., 1969. *Lightning*. McGraw-Hill, New York.

———, 1983. Lightning. In *Contributions in Meteorology: U.S. National Report, 1979–1982*. American Geophysical Union, Washington, D.C., pp. 992–97.

———, G. A. Dawson, and W. A. Hoppel, 1975. Progress in atmospheric electricity. *Rev. Geophys. Space Phys.* 13:760–65, 849:53.

Vonnegut, B., 1963. Some facts and speculations concerning the origin and role of thunderstorm electricity. In *Severe Local Storms*, Meteorol. Monogr. 5, American Meteorological Society, Boston, pp. 224–41.

Weigel, E. P., 1976. Lightning—the underrated killer. *NOAA* 6(2):4–11.

Wilson, C. T. R., 1925. The electric field of a thundercloud and some of its effects. *Proc. Phys. Soc. London* 37:32D–37D.

———, 1926. Discussions of the electrical state of the upper atmosphere. *Proc. R. Soc. London* 3:1–13.

Winn, W. P., G. W. Schwede, and C. B. Moore, 1974. Measurements of electric fields in thunderclouds. *J. Geophys. Res.* 79:1761–67.

Appendix 2

Holden, D. N., C. R. Holmes, C. B. Moore, W. P. Winn, J. W. Cobb, J. E. Griswold, and D. M. Lytle, 1980. Local charge concentrations in thunderclouds. In Lothar Runnke and John Latham, eds., *Proceedings in Atmospheric Electricity*. A. Deepak Pubs., Hampton, Va., 1983, pp. 179–83.

Jacobson, E., and E. P. Krider, 1976. Electrostatic field changes produced by Florida lightning. *J. Atmos. Sci.* 33:103–17.

Kelvin, Lord, 1860. Atmospheric electricity. Royal Inst. Lecture. In *Papers on Electrostatics and Magnetism*, pp. 208–26.

Krider, E. P., and J. A. Musser, 1982. Maxwell currents under thunderstorms. *J. Geophys. Res.* 87:11171–76.

Marshall, T. C., W. D. Rust, and W. P. Winn, 1984. Screening layers at the surface of thunderstorm anvils. Preprints, Seventh International Conference on Atmospheric Electricity, Albany, N.Y., June 3–8, pp. 246–47. American Meteorological Society, Boston.

Moore, C. B., and B. Vonnegut, 1959. Observations of thunderstorms in New Mexico. Report to Office of Naval Research, Contract NONR, 1684.

Orville, R. E., R. W. Henderson, and L. F. Bosart, 1983. An East Coast lightning detection network. *Bull. Am. Meteorol. Soc.* 9:1029–37.

Rust, W. D., W. L. Taylor, D. R. MacGorman, E. Brandes, V. Mazur, R. Arnold, T. Marshall, H. Christian, and S. J. Goodman, 1984. Lightning and related phenomena in thunderstorms and squall lines. Paper no. 0467, AIAA, Twenty-second Aerospace Sciences Meeting, Reno, Nev., Jan. 9–12.

Simpson, G. C., and F. J. Scrase, 1937. The distribution of electricity in thunderclouds. *Proc. R. Soc.* A 161:309–52.

———, and G. D. Robinson, 1940. The distribution of electricity in thunderclouds. Pt. 2. *Proc. R. Soc.* A 177:281–329.

Standler, R. B., and W. P. Winn, 1979. Effects of coronae in electric fields beneath thunderstorms. *Q. J. R. Meteorol. Soc.* 105:285–302.

Williams, E. R., 1981. Thunderstorm electrification: precipitation versus convection. Ph.D. diss., Massachusetts Institute of Technology, pp. 44, 70.

Williams, M. A., E. P. Krider, and D. M. Hunter, 1983. Planetary lightning: Earth, Jupiter, and Venus. *Rev. Geophys. Space Phys.* 21:892–902.

Chapter 14

Byers, H. R., 1965. *Elements of Cloud Physics*. University of Chicago Press, Chicago.

———, and R. R. Braham, 1949. *The Thunderstorm*. U.S. Government Printing Office, Washington, D.C.

Espy, J. P., 1841. *The Philosophy of Storms*. Little and Brown, Boston.

Gunn, R., and G. D. Kinzer, 1949. The terminal velocity of fall for water droplets in stagnant air. *J. Meteorol.* 6:243–48.

Kessler, E., 1969. *On the Distribution and Continuity of Water Substance in Atmospheric Circulations*. Meteorol. Monogr. 10, American Meteorological Society, Boston.

———, 1974. Model of precipitation and vertical air currents. *Tellus* 26:519–42.

———, 1975a. Condensate content in relation to sloping updraft parameters. *J. Atmos. Sci.* 32:443–44.

———, 1975b. On the condensed water mass in rising air. *Pure Appl. Geophys.* 113:971–81.

Marshall, J. S., and W. McK. Palmer, 1948. The distribution of raindrops with size. *J. Meteorol.* 5:165–66.

Mason, B. J., 1971. *The Physics of Clouds*. 2d ed., Clarendon Press, Oxford.

Moore, C. B., 1965. Lightning discharge and precipitation. *Q. J. R. Meteorol. Soc.* 91:368.

———, B. Vonnegut, J. A. Machado, and H. J. Survilas, 1962. Radar observation of rain gushes following overhead lightning strokes. *J. Geophys. Res.* 67:207–20.

Ogura, Y., and N. A. Phillips, 1962. Scale analysis of deep and shallow convection in the atmosphere. *J. Atmos. Sci.* 19:173–79.

Priestley, C. H. B., 1953. Buoyant motions in a turbulent environment. *Aust. J. Phys.* 6:270–90.

Rogers, R. R., 1979. *A Short Course in Cloud Physics*. Pergamon Press, New York.

Smithsonian Institution, 1958. *Smithsonian Meteorological Tables*. Vol. 114 in Smithsonian Miscellaneous Collections (Pub. 4014).

Srivastava, R. C., 1969. A study of the effect of precipitation on cumulus dynamics. *J. Atmos. Sci.* 24:36–45.

Chapter 15

Anthes, R. A., 1977a. A cumulus parameterization scheme utilizing a one-dimensional cloud model. *Mon. Weather Rev.* 105:270–86.

———, 1977b. Hurricane model experiments with a new cumulus parameterization scheme. *Mon. Weather Rev.* 105:287–300.

———, 1982. Tropical cyclones—their evolution, structure and effects. *Meteorol. Monogr.* 41, American Meteorological Society, Boston.

Arakawa, A., and W. H. Schubert, 1974. Interaction of a cumulus cloud ensemble with the large-scale environment. Part 1. *J. Atmos. Sci.* 31:674–701.

Barnes, S., 1970. Some aspects of a severe, right-moving thunderstorm deduced from mesonetwork rawinsonde observations. *J. Atmos. Sci.* 27:634–48.

Battan, L. J., 1973. *Radar Observation of the Atmosphere*. University of Chicago Press, Chicago.

———, 1975. Doppler radar observations of a hailstorm. *J. Appl. Meteorol.* 14:98–108.

Bénard, H., 1900a. Les tourbillons cellulaires dans une nappe liquide. *Rev. Gén. Sci.* 11:1261–71, 1309–28.

———, 1900b. *Rev. Gén. Sci.* 12:1261, 1309.

Berry, E. X., 1967. Cloud droplet growth by collection. *J. Atmos. Sci.* 24:688–701.

Betts, A. K., 1974. Thermodynamic classification of tropical convective soundings. *Mon. Weather Rev.* 102:760–64.

———, 1975. Parametric interpretation of trade-wind cumulus budget studies. *J. Atmos. Sci.* 32:1934–45.

———, R. W. Grover, and M. W. Moncrieff, 1976. Structure and motion of tropical squall-lines over Venezuela. *Q. J. R. Meteorol. Soc.* 102:395–404.

Bigg, E. K., 1953. The supercooling of water. *Proc. Phys. Soc. London* 66:669–94.

Browning, K. A., 1964. Airflow and precipitation trajectories within severe local storms which travel to the right of the winds. *J. Atmos. Sci.* 21:634–39.

———, and G. B. Foote, 1976. Airflow and hail growth in supercell storms and some implications for hail suppression. *Q. J. R. Meteorol. Soc.* 89:75–84.

———, and F. H. Ludlam, 1962. Airflow in convective storms. *Q. J. R. Meteorol. Soc.* 88:117–35.

Chiu, C. S., 1978. Numerical study of atmospheric electricity in an axisymmetric time-dependent warm cloud model. *J. Geophys. Res.* 83:5025–49.

———, and J. D. Klett, 1976. Convective electrification of clouds. *J. Geophys. Res.* 81:1111–24.

Cho, H. R., and Y. Ogura, 1974. A relationship between the cloud activity and the low-level convergence as observed in Reed-Recker's composite easterly waves. *J. Atmos. Sci.* 31:2058–65.

Clark, T. L., 1973. Numerical modeling of the dynamics and microphysics of warm cumulus convection. *J. Atmos. Sci.* 30:857–78.

———, 1979. Numerical simulations with a three-dimensional cloud model: Lateral boundary condition experiments and multicellular severe storm simulations. *J. Atmos. Sci.* 36:2191–2215.

Cotton, W. R., 1975. Theoretical cumulus dynamics. *Rev. Geophys. Space Phys.* 13:419–48.

Crowley, W. P., 1968. Numerical advection experiments. *Mon. Weather Rev.* 96:1–11.

Danielsen, E. F., R. Bleck, and D. A. Morris, 1972. Hail growth by stochastic collection in a cumulus model. *J. Atmos. Sci.* 29:135–55.

Douglas, R. H., 1960. Size distributions, ice contents and radar reflectivities of hail in Alberta. *Nubila* 3:5–11.

Drake, R. L., P. D. Coyle, and D. P. Anderson, 1974. The effects of nonlinear eddy coefficients on rising line thermals. *J. Atmos. Sci.* 31:2046–57.

Dutton, J. A., 1976. *The Ceaseless Wind.* McGraw-Hill, New York.

Federer, B., and A. Waldvogel, 1975. Hail and raindrop size distributions from a Swiss multicell storm. *J. Appl. Meteorol.* 14:91–97.

Fraedrich, K., 1973. On the parameterization of cumulus convection by lateral mixing and compensating subsidence. Part 1. *J. Atmos. Sci.* 30:409–13.

———, 1974. Dynamic and thermodynamic aspects of the parameterization of cumulus convection. Part 2. *J. Atmos. Sci.* 31:1838–49.

Frank, W. M., 1983. The cumulus parameterization problem. *Mon. Weather Rev.* 111:1859–71.

Fritsch, J. M., 1975. Cumulus dynamics: local compensating subsidence and its implications for cumulus parameterization. *Pure Appl. Geophys.* 113:851–67.

———, C. F. Chappell, and L. R. Hoxit, 1976. The use of large-scale budgets for convective parameterization. *Mon. Weather Rev.* 104:1408–18.

Fujita, T., and H. Grandoso, 1968. Split of a thunderstorm into anticyclonic and cyclonic storms and their motion as determined from numerical model experiments. *J. Atmos. Sci.* 25:416–39.

Haltiner, G. J., 1971. *Numerical Weather Prediction.* John Wiley & Sons, New York.

———, and F. L. Martin, 1957. *Dynamical and Physical Meteorology.* McGraw-Hill, New York.

Hane, E. C., 1973. The squall line thunderstorm numerical experimentation. *J. Atmos. Sci.* 30:1672–90.

Hill, G. E., 1974. Factors controlling the size and spacing of cumulus clouds as revealed by numerical experiments. *J. Atmos. Sci.* 31:646–73.

Holton, J. R., 1972. *An Introduction to Dynamic Meteorology.* Academic Press, New York.

———, 1973. A one-dimensional cumulus model including pressure perturbations. *Mon. Weather Rev.* 101:201–205.

Hudson, H. R., 1971. On the relationship between horizontal moisture convergence and convective cloud formation. *J. Appl. Meteorol.* 10:755–62.

Kessler, E., III, 1969. *On the Distribution and Continuity of Water Substance in Atmospheric Circulations.* Meteor. Monogr. 10, American Meteorological Society, Boston.

Klemp, J. B., and R. Rotunno, 1983. A study of the tornadic region within a supercell thunderstorm. *J. Atmos. Sci.* 40:359–77.

———, and R. B. Wilhelmson, 1978a. The simulation of three-dimensional convective storm dynamics. *J. Atmos. Sci.* 35:1070–96.

———, and ———, 1978b. Simulations of right- and left-moving storms produced through storm splitting. *J. Atmos. Sci.* 35:1097–1110.

———, ———, and P. S. Ray, 1981. Observed and numerically simulated structure of a mature supercell thunderstorm. *J. Atmos. Sci.* 38:1558–80.

Koss, W. J., 1976. Linear stability of CISK-induced disturbances: Fourier component eigenvalue analysis. *J. Atmos. Sci.* 33:1195–1222.

Kreitzberg, C. W., and D. J. Perkey, 1976. Release of potential instability: part 1. *J. Atmos. Sci.* 33:456–75.

Krishnamurti, T. N., S. Low-Nam, and R. Pasch, 1983. Cumulus parameterization and rainfall rates, part 1. *Mon. Weather Rev.* 111:815–28.

———, Y. Ramanathan, N.-L. Pan, R. J. Pasch, and J. Molinari, 1980. Cumulus parameterization and rainfall rates, part 2. *Mon. Weather Rev.* 108:465–72.

Kuettner, J. P., Z. Levin, and J. D. Sartor, 1981. Thunderstorm electrification—inductive or noninductive? *J. Atmos. Sci.* 38:2470–84.

Kuo, H. L., 1974. Further studies of the parameterization of the influence of cumulus convection on large-scale flow. *J. Atmos. Sci.* 31:1232–40.

Kurihara, Y., 1973. A scheme of moist convective adjustment. *Mon. Weather Rev.* 101:547–53.

———, and R. E. Tuleya, 1974. Structure of a tropical cyclone developed in a three-dimensional numerical simulation model. *J. Atmos. Sci.* 31:893–919.

Latham, J., 1981. The electrification of thunderstorms. *Q. J. R. Meteorol. Soc.* 107:277–98.

Lindzen, R. S., 1974. Wave-CISK in the tropics. *J. Atmos. Sci.* 31:156–79.

Liu, J. Y., and H. D. Orville, 1969. Numerical modeling of precipitation and cloud shadow effects on mountain-induced cumuli. *J. Atmos. Sci.* 26:1283–98.

Malkus, J. S., and R. T. Williams, 1963. On the interaction between severe storms and large cumulus clouds. In *Severe Local Storms,* Meteorol. Monogr. 5, American Meteorological Society, Boston.

Marshall, J. S., and W. McM. Palmer, 1948. The distribution of raindrops with size. *J. Meteorol.* 5:165–66.

Marwitz, J. D., 1972. Precipitation efficiency of thunderstorms on the high plains. *J. Rech. Atmos.* 6:367–70.

Matsumoto, S., and K. Ninomiya, 1969. On the role of convective momentum exchange in the mesoscale gravity wave. *J. Meteorol. Soc. Japan* 47:75–85.

———, ———, and T. Akiyama, 1967. Cumulus activities in relation to the meso-scale convergence field. *J. Meteorol. Soc. Japan* 45:292–305.

Miller, M. J., 1974. On the use of pressure as vertical coordinate in modeling convection. *Q. J. R. Meteorol. Soc.* 100:155–62.

Moncrieff, M. W., 1978. The dynamical structure of two-dimensional steady convection in constant vertical shear. *Q. J. R. Meteorol. Soc.* 104:543–67.

———, and J. S. A. Green, 1972. The propagation and transfer properties of steady convective overturning in shear. *Q. J. R. Meteorol. Soc.* 98:336–52.

———, and M. J. Miller, 1976. The dynamics and simulation of tropical cumulonimbus and squall lines. *Q. J. R. Meteorol. Soc.* 102:373–94.

Morton, B. R., G. I. Taylor, and J. S. Turner, 1956. Turbulent gravitational convection from maintained and instantaneous sources. *Proc. R. Soc. London* A234:1–23.

Murray, F. W., 1970. Numerical models of a tropical cumulus cloud with bilateral and axial symmetry. *Mon. Weather Rev.* 98:14–28.

Musil, D. J., 1970. Computer modeling of hailstone growth in feeder clouds. *J. Atmos. Sci.* 27:474–82.

Newton, C. W., 1963. Dynamics of severe convective storms. In *Severe Local Storms*, Meteorol. Monogr. 5, American Meteorological Society, Boston, pp. 33–58.

———, 1966. Circulations in large sheared cumulonimbus. *Tellus* 18:699–713.

———, and J. C. Fankhauser, 1964. On the movements of convective storms with emphasis on size discrimination in relation to water budget requirements. *J. Appl. Meteorol.* 3:651–68.

Ogura, Y., 1963. The evaluation of a moist convection element in a shallow, conditionally unstable atmosphere: a numerical calculation. *J. Atmos. Sci.* 20:407–24.

———, 1975. On the interaction between cumulus clouds and the larger scale environment. *Pure Appl. Geoph.* 113:869–89.

———, and J. Charney, 1962. A numerical model of thermal convection in the atmosphere. Proceedings, International Symposium on Numerical Weather Prediction, Tokyo, Japan, 7–13 November 1960. Meteorological Society of Japan, Tokyo, pp. 431–51.

———, and H. R. Cho, 1973. Diagnostic determination of cumulus cloud populations from observed large-scale variables. *J. Atmos. Sci.* 30:1276–86.

———, and N. A. Phillips, 1962. Scale analysis of deep and shallow convection in the atmosphere. *J. Atmos. Sci.* 19:173–79.

Ooyama, K., 1971. A theory on parameterization of cumulus convection. *J. Meteorol. Soc. Japan* 39:744–56.

Orville, H. D., 1965. A numerical study of the initiation of cumulus clouds over mountainous terrain. *J. Atmos. Sci.* 22:684–99.

———, 1968. Grid interval effects on a numerical model of upslope winds and mountain-induced cumulus. *J. Atmos. Sci.* 25:1164–67.

———, and K. G. Hubbard, 1973. On the freezing of liquid water in a cloud. *J. Appl. Meteorol.* 12:671–76.

———, and F. J. Kopp, 1977. Numerical simulation of the life history of a hailstorm. *J. Atmos. Sci.* 34:1596–1618.

———, and L. J. Sloan, 1969. Effects of higher order advection techniques on a numerical cloud model. *Mon. Weather Rev.* 98:7–13.

———, F. J. Kopp, and C. G. Myers, 1975. The dynamics and thermodynamics of precipitation loading. *Pure Appl. Geophy.* 113:983–1004.

Prandtl, L., and O. G. Tietjens, 1934. *Applied Hydro- and Aero-Mechanics.* 1957 ed., Dover Publications, New York.

Pringle, J. E., H. D. Orville, and T. D. Stechmann, 1973. Numerical simulation of atmospheric electricity effects in a cloud model. *J. Geophys. Res.* 78:4508–14.

Rayleigh, Lord, 1916. On convection currents in a horizontal layer of fluid when the higher temperature is on the underside. *Philos. Mag.* 6th ser., 32:529–46.

Raymond, D. J., 1975. A model for predicting the movement of continuously propagating convective storms. *J. Atmos. Sci.* 32:1308–17.

———, 1976. Wave-CISK and convective mesosystems. *J. Atmos. Sci.* 33:2392–98.

Riehl, H., and J. S. Malkus, 1961. Some aspects of Hurricane Daisy, 1958. *Tellus* 13:181–213.

Rognlie, D. M., and F. J. Kopp, 1976. Application of direct Poisson solvers to time-dependent numerical cloud models. *Mon. Weather Rev.* 104:953–60.

Rotunno, R., 1981. On the evolution of thunderstorm rotation. *Mon. Weather Rev.* 109:577–86.

Sasaki, Y., and J. M. Lewis, 1970. Numerical variation objective analysis of the planetary boundary layer in conjunction with squall line formation. *J. Meteorol. Soc. Japan* 48:381–99.

Saunders, P. M., 1957. The thermodynamics of saturated air: a contribution to the classical theory. *Q. J. R. Meteorol. Soc.* 83:342–50.

Schlesinger, R. E., 1973. A numerical model of deep moist convection. Part 1. *J. Atmos. Sci.* 30:835–56.

———, 1975. A three-dimensional numerical model of an isolated deep convective cloud: preliminary results. *J. Atmos. Sci.* 32:934–57.

———, 1977. A three-dimensional numerical model of an isolated large-diameter thunderstorm: results of an experiment with directional ambient wind shear. Preprints, Tenth Conference on Severe Local Storms, Omaha, Nebr., 18–21 October 1977. American Meteorological Society, Boston, pp. 255–62.

———, 1980. A three-dimensional numerical model of an isolated thunderstorm: Part 2. Dynamics of updraft splitting and mesovortex couplet evolution. *J. Atmos. Sci.* 37:395–429.

———, 1982. Effects of mesoscale lifting, precipitation and boundary layer shear on severe storm dynamics in a three-dimensional numerical modeling study. Preprints, Twelfth Conference on Severe Local Storms, 12–15 January 1982, San Antonio, Texas. American Meteorological Society, Boston, pp. 536–41.

Silverman, B. A., and M. Glass, 1973. A numerical simulation of warm cumulus clouds: part 1. *J. Atmos. Sci.* 30:1620–37.

Simpson, J., 1973. The global energy budget and the role of cumulus clouds. Tech. Memo. ERL WMPO-8, NOAA Environmental Research Laboratories, Boulder, Colo.

Smith, P. L., Jr., D. J. Musil, S. F. Weber, J. F. Spahn, G. N. Johnson, and W. R. Sand, 1976. Raindrop and hailstone size distributions inside hailstorms. Preprints, International Conference on Cloud Physics, Boulder, Colo. American Meteorological Society, Boston, pp. 252–57.

———, C. G. Myers, and H. D. Orville, 1975. Radar reflectivity factor calculations in numerical cloud models using bulk parameterization of precipitation. *J. Appl. Meteorol.* 14:1156–65.

Soong, S. T., and Y. Ogura, 1973. A comparison between axisymmetric and slab-symmetric cumulus cloud models. *J. Atmos. Sci.* 30:879–93.

Squires, P., 1958. Penetrative downdraughts in cumuli. *Tellus* 10:381–89.

Srivastava, R. C., 1967. A study of the effects of precipitation on cumulus dynamics. *J. Atmos. Sci.* 24:36–45.

Stommel, H., 1947. Entrainment of air into a cumulus cloud. *J. Meteorol.* 4:91–94.

Syono, Y., Y. Ogura, K. Gambo, and A. Kasahara, 1951. On the negative vorticity in a typhoon. *J. Meteorol. Soc. Japan* 29: 397–415.

Takahashi, T., 1974. Numerical simulation of warm cloud electricity. *J. Atmos. Sci.* 31:2161–81.

———, 1976. Hail in an axisymmetric cloud model. *J. Atmos. Sci.* 33:1579–1601.

———, 1978. Riming electrification as a charge generation mechanism in thunderstorms. *J. Atmos. Sci.* 35:1536–48.

Telford, J. W., 1966. The convective mechanism in clear air. *J. Atmos. Sci.* 23:652–66.

———, 1975. Turbulence, entrainment, and mixing in cloud dynamics. *Pure Appl. Geophys.* 113:1067–84.

Tripoli, G. J., and W. R. Cotton, 1980. A numerical investigation of several factors contributing to the observed variable intensity of deep convection over south Florida. *J. Appl. Meteorol.* 19:1037–63.

Turner, J. S., 1962. The starting plume in neutral surroundings. *J. Fluid Mech.* 13:356–68.

———, 1963. The motion of buoyant elements in turbulent surroundings. *J. Fluid Mech.* 16:1–16.

———, 1973. *Buoyancy Effects in Fluids*. Cambridge University Press, New York.

Tzur, I., and Z. Levin, 1981. Ions and precipitation charging in warm and cold clouds as simulated in one-dimensional, time-dependent model. *J. Atmos. Sci.* 38:2444–61.

Warne, J., 1970. On steady-state one-dimensional models of cumulus convection. *J. Atmos. Sci.* 27:1035–40.

Warner, C., 1972. Calculations of updraft shapes in storms. *J. Atmos. Sci.* 29:1516–19.

Wilhelmson, R., 1974. The life cycle of a thunderstorm in three dimensions. *J. Atmos. Sci.* 31:1629–51.

———, and Y. Ogura, 1972. The pressure perturbation and numerical modeling of a cloud. *J. Atmos. Sci.* 29:1295–1307.

Wisner, C. E., H. D. Orville, and C. G. Myers, 1972. A numerical model of a hail-bearing cloud. *J. Atmos. Sci.* 29:1160–81.

Yamasaki, M., 1968. Numerical simulation of tropical cyclone development with the use of primitive equations. *J. Meteorol. Soc. Japan* 46:178–201.

Yanai, M., S. Esbensen, and J. Chu, 1973. Determination of bulk properties of tropical cloud clusters from large-scale heat and moisture budgets. *J. Atmos. Sci.* 30:611–27.

Chapter 16

Atlas, D., 1977. The paradox of hail suppression. *Science* 195:139–45.

Battan, L. J., 1966. Silver-iodide seeding and rainfall from convective clouds. *J. Appl. Meteorol.* 5:669–83.

———, 1967. Cloud seeding and cloud-to-ground lightning. *J. Appl. Meteorol.* 6:102–104.

———, 1977a. Weather modification in the Soviet Union—1976. *Bull. Am. Meteorol. Soc.* 58:4–19.

———, 1977b. Comment on "Lightning suppression by chaff seeding at the base of thunderstorms." *J. Geophys. Res.* 82:1977.

Braham, R. R., Jr., 1966. Final Report of Project Whitetop. Parts 1 and 2. Mimeographed report to the National Science Foundation. Printed by Department of Geophysical Sciences, University of Chicago, August 1966.

Browning, K. A., and G. B. Foote, 1976. Airflow and hail growth in supercell storms and some implications for hail suppression. *Q. J. R. Meteorol. Soc.* 102:499–533.

Changnon, S. A., Jr., 1977. On the status of hail suppression. *Bull. Am. Meteorol. Soc.* 58:20–28.

Cleveland, H., et al., 1978. The management of weather resources. Report to the Secretary of Commerce from the Weather Modification Advisory Board, Vols. 1 and 2. U.S. Government Printing Office, Washington, D.C.

Crow, L., 1959. Final Report of Project "Wind Control." Mimeographed report, Weather Engineers, Inc., Loomis, Calif.

Davies-Jones, R., and E. Kessler, 1974. Tornadoes. In *Weather and Climate Modification*, W. N. Hess (ed.), John Wiley & Sons, New York, pp. 552–95.

Dennis, A. S., 1980. *Weather Modification by Cloud Seeding*. Academic Press, New York.

———, and A. Koscielski, 1969. Results of a randomized cloud seeding experiment in South Dakota. *J. Appl. Meteorol.* 8:556–65.

Dessens, H., 1960. A project for a formation of cumulonimbus by artificial condensation. In *Physics of Precipitation*, Geophys. Monogr. 5, American Geophysical Union, pp. 396–98.

Federer, B., A. Waldvogel, W. Schmid, F. Hampel, E. Rosini, D. Vento, P. Admirat, and J. F. Mezeix, 1979. Plan for the Swiss Randomized Hail Suppression Experiment. Design of Grossversuch IV. *Pure Appl. Geophys.* 117:548–71.

Fleagle, R. G. (ed.), 1968. *Weather Modification and Public Policy*. University of Washington Press, Seattle.

Fuquay, D. M., 1974. Lightning damage and lightning modification caused by cloud seeding. In *Weather and Climate Modification*, W. N. Hess (ed.), John Wiley & Sons, New York, pp. 604–12.

Gagin, A., and J. Neumann, 1976. The second Israeli cloud seeding experiment—the effect of seeding in varying cloud populations. Papers presented at Second WMO Scientific Conference on Weather Modification, WMO No. 443, World Meteorological Organization, Geneva, pp. 195–206.

Grandoso, H. N., and J. V. Iribarne, 1963. Evaluation of the first three years in a hail prevention experiment in Mendoza (Argentina). *Z. Angew. Math. Phys.* 14:549–53.

Griffiths, R. F., 1977. Comments on "Lightning suppression by chaff seeding at the base of thunderstorms." *J. Geophys. Res.* 82:1801–1802.

Haas, J. E., 1974. Sociological aspects of weather modification. In *Weather and Climate Modification*, W. N. Hess (ed.), John Wiley & Sons, New York, pp. 787–812.

Kasemir, J. W., F. J. Holitza, W. E. Cobb, and W. D. Rust, 1976. Lightning suppression by chaff seeding at the base of thunderstorms. *J. Geophys. Res.* 81:1965–70.

———, ———, ———, and ———, 1977. Reply. *J. Geophys. Res.* 82:1800, 1803–1806.

Knight, C. A., G. B. Foote, and P. W. Summers, 1979. Results of a randomized hail suppression experiment in northeast Colorado. Part 9: Overall discussion and summary in the context of physical research. *J. Appl. Meteorol.* 18:1629–39.

Kraus, E. B., and P. Squires, 1947. Experiments on the stimulation of clouds to produce rain. *Nature* 159:489–91.

Langer, G., C. T. Nagamoto, J. Rodgers, and J. Rosinski, 1974. Evaluation of the seeder for the NHRE hail suppression rocket. Preprints, Fourth Conference on Weather Modification. American Meteorological Society, Boston, pp. 236–41.

Langmuir, I., 1950. Control of precipitation from cumulus clouds by various seeding techniques. *Science* 112:35–41.

Lovasich, J. L., J. Neyman, E. L. Scott, and M. A. Wells, 1971. Hypothetical explanations of the negative apparent effects of cloud seeding in the Whitetop experiment. *Proc. Nat. Acad. Sci.* 68:2643–46.

McCarthy, J., 1972. Computer model determination of convective cloud seeded growth using Project Whitetop data. *J. Appl. Meteorol.* 5:818–22.

Miller, J. R., E. I. Boyd, R. A. Schleusener, and A. S. Dennis, 1975. Hail suppression data from western North Dakota. *J. Appl. Meteorol.* 14:755–62.

NAS (National Academy of Sciences), 1973. Weather and climate modification: problems and progress. Committee on Atmospheric Sciences, National Research Council, National Academy of Sciences.

Nelson, Stephan P., 1983. The influence of storm flow structure on hail growth. *J. Atmos. Sci.* 40:1965–83.

Neyman, J., H. B. Osborn, E. L. Scott, and M. A. Wells, 1972. Re-evaluation of the Arizona cloud-seeding experiment. *Proc. Nat. Acad. Sci.* 69:1348–52.

———, E. L. Scott, and M. A. Wells, 1973. Downwind and upwind effects in the Arizona cloud-seeding experiment. *Proc. Nat. Acad. Sci.* 70:357–60.

Schaefer, V. J., 1946. The production of ice crystals in a cloud of supercooled water droplets. *Science* 104:457–59.

Schmid, P., 1967. On "Grossversuch III," a randomized hail suppression experiment in Switzerland. Proceedings of the Fifth Berkeley Symposium on Math. Stat. and Probability, Vol. 5. University of California Press, Berkeley, pp. 141–59.

Sedunov, Y., 1974. Weather by order. *Izvestiia*, Moscow, 23 Feb. 1974, p. 5.

Sewell, W. R. D. (ed.), 1966. Human dimensions of weather modification. University of Chicago Res. Paper 105, Chicago.

Simpson, J., and A. S. Dennis, 1974. Cumulus clouds and their modification. In *Weather and Climate Modification*, W. N. Hess (ed.), John Wiley & Sons, New York, pp. 229–81.

———, and Woodley, 1971. Seeding cumulus in Florida: new 1970 results. *Science* 172:117–26.

———, R. H. Simpson, D. A. Andrews, and M. A. Eaton, 1965. Experimental cumulus dynamics. *Rev. Geophys.* 3:387–431.

Smith, E. J., 1974. Cloud seeding in Australia. In *Weather and Climate Modification*, W. N. Hess (ed.), John Wiley & Sons, New York, pp. 432–53.

Stantchev, K., and P. Simeonov, 1981. Hail suppression—research and operations in Bulgaria. *WMO Bull.* 30:182–84.

Sulakvelidze, G. K., B. I. Kiziriya, and V. V. Tsykunov, 1974. Progress of hail suppression work in the U.S.S.R. In *Weather and Climate Modification*, W. N. Hess (ed.), John Wiley & Sons, New York, pp. 410–31.

Taubenfeld, H. J. (ed.), 1970. *Controlling the Weather.* Dunellen Co., Inc., Port Washington, N.Y.

Vonnegut, B., 1947. The nucleation of ice formation by silver iodide. *J. Appl. Phys.* 18:593–95.

Vul'fson, N. I., and L. M. Levin, 1972. Destruction of developing cumulus clouds by explosions. *Izvest. Akad. Nauk SSSR, Fiz. Atmos. i Okeans* 8:156–66.

———, A. V. Kondratora, A. G. Laktionov, L. M. Levin, V. I. Skatskii, and Ye. P. Cherenkova, 1972. Modification of convective clouds by jets. *Trudy V Vses. Meteor. S"yeda*, No. 4, Gidrometeoizdat, Leningrad, pp. 62–78.

———, L. M. Levin, and Ye. P. Cherenkova, 1970. Destruction of developing cumulus clouds by artificially created descending currents. *Izvest. Akad. Nauk SSSR, Fiz. Atmos. i Okeans* 6:14–28.

Woodley, W. L., A. Barnston, J. A. Flueck, and R. Biondini, 1983. The Florida Area Cumulus Experiment's Second Phase (FACE-2). Part 2: Replicated and confirmatory analyses. *J. Climate Appl. Meteorol.* 22:1529–40.

———, J. Jordan, J. Simpson, A. Biondini, J. Flueck, and A. Barnston, 1982. Rainfall results of the Florida Area Cumulus Experiment, 1970–1976. *J. Appl. Meteorol.* 21:139–64.

Young, K. C., 1977. A numerical examination of some hail suppression concepts. In *Hail: A Review of Hail Science and Hail Suppression*, Meteorol. Monogr. 16, American Meteorological Society, Boston, pp. 195–214.

The Authors

Richard A. Anthes is Director of the Atmospheric Analysis and Prediction Division at the National Center for Atmospheric Research, Boulder, Colorado. Previously he was Professor of Meteorology in Pennsylvania State University. He holds B.S., M.S., and Ph.D. degrees in meteorology from the University of Wisconsin. His specialties are numerical modeling of atmospheric flows on synoptic and mesoscales; his many papers and several books include a study of tropical cyclones published as a monograph by the American Meteorological Society in 1982. He is a member of the National Academy of Science Committee on Atmospheric Sciences and is a consultant to several government organizations. In 1980 he received the Meisinger Award of the American Meteorological Society.

Stanley L. Barnes is a Senior Scientist in the Weather Research Program in NOAA's Environmental Research Laboratories, Boulder, Colorado. His current work involves diagnostic studies on the relationship between short waves and mesoscale convective systems, empirical-theoretical studies of objective interpolation schemes. From 1950 to 1954 he was a weather observer in the U.S. Navy. He studied meteorology at Oklahoma State University and Texas A&M University, receiving B.S. and M.S. degrees from the latter in 1958 and 1959. He received the Ph.D. degree from the University of Oklahoma and joined the National Severe Storms Laboratory in 1967. Subsequently, until 1974, he was Chief of the Severe Storm Morphology and Dynamics Project at NSSL. From 1974 to 1981 he served as Meteorologist and Office Manager for the Severe Environmental Storms and Mesoscale Experiment (Project SESAME) and as Deputy Director of Operations during its 1979 field program.

Louis J. Battan, who received the Ph.D. degree from the University of Chicago in 1953, is Professor in the Institute of Atmospheric Physics at the University of Arizona and formerly Director of that institute. He is the author or coauthor of more than a dozen books and many articles. He is consultant to various U.S. government agencies and was President of the American Meteorological Society and of the Meteorology Section of the American Geophysical Union. He received the Meisinger, Brooks, and Second Half

Century awards from the American Meteorological Society and has been a member and chairman of the Committee on Atmospheric Sciences of the U.S. National Academy of Science. He is Chairman of the Planning Commission of the American Meteorological Society.

Thomas L. Baxter graduated from the University of Oklahoma in 1967 and received an M.S. in meteorology from Saint Louis University in 1972. From 1967 to 1974 he was at various times a forecaster and research meteorologist at several facilities of the U.S. Air Force and the U.S. Navy. During 1974–75 he was a research meteorologist for Ocean Data Systems, Inc., Monterrey, California. At his death in 1982 he was President of the Weather Station, Inc., which sold forecast services, and of the Atmospheric Research Corporation, both of Norman, Oklahoma.

Keith A. Browning is Deputy Director (Physical Research) in the British Meteorological Office. He has a Ph.D. degree in meteorology from Imperial College, London, and is a Fellow of the Royal Society. He is also a Fellow of the American Meteorological Society and of the Royal Meteorological Society and is a recipient of some of their awards. His specialties are in the application of radar techniques in the study of the physics of precipitation and the dynamical structure of mesoscale phenomena. For a number of years he worked in the field of severe local storms and hail growth, most recently as Chief Scientist with the National Hail Research Experiment. Since 1967 he has been carrying out research in the structure and mechanism of mesoscale weather systems in the British Isles, and he has established a project to develop ways of using radar and satellite data together to improve short-period forecasts.

Charles F. Chappell is Director of the Weather Research Program in the Environmental Research Laboratories, Boulder, Colorado. He holds a B.S. degree in electrical engineering from Washington University (Saint Louis) and M.S. and Ph.D. degrees in atmospheric science from Colorado State University. His specialties include severe-local-storm prediction, thunderstorm-environmental interactions, and weather modification. He is a member of the Precipitation Commissdion of the Hydrology Section of the American

Geophysical Union and is an associate editor of the *Journal of Atmospheric Sciences*.

Arnold Court is Professor Emeritus of Climatology in California State University, Northridge (Los Angeles). He has published more than 100 papers on meteorology, climatology, streamflow and rainfall, and weather-modification evaluation. He has been a newspaper reporter and editor, meteorologist at Little America, and wartime weather officer in Alaska, and has been employed as meteorologist and climatologist by the Army Quartermaster Corps, the University of California at Berkeley, the U.S. Forest Service, the U.S. Air Force Cambridge Research Laboratories, and the Lockheed-California Company. He remains a consultant to Lockheed, as he has been to other industrial firms and government agencies. He received degrees in geography from the University of Oklahoma (A.B., 1934) and the University of California at Berkeley (Ph.D., 1956), and an M.S. in meteorology and climatology from the University of Washington. He is a member or fellow of many scientific societies and is active on their committees.

Grant L. Darkow is Professor of Atmospheric Sciences in the University of Missouri—Columbia. He holds the B.S. degree in mathematics and M.Sc. and Ph.D. degrees in meteorology from the University of Wisconsin. His areas of specialization are the dynamics of mesoscale systems, with emphasis on severe local storms and storm forecasting. He has served as Chairman of the Committee on Severe Local Storms of the American Meteorological Society and on the Board of Trustees of the University Corporation for Atmospheric Research.

Robert Davies-Jones completed undergraduate work in physics at Birmingham University, England, received a Ph.D. degree in astrogeophysics from the University of Colorado, and during 1969–70 held a postdoctoral research appointment at the National Center for Atmospheric Research. His specialties are the fluid dynamics of tornadoes and severe thunderstorms. Now at the National Severe Storms Laboratory, he directs work of the Tornado Dynamics Unit and of the Tornado Intercept Project to observe severe storms in the field. He also holds an adjunct appointment at the University of Oklahoma and is a consultant on tornadoes to the Nuclear Regulatory Commission and other agencies.

John C. Freeman founded the Institute for Storm Research of Houston, Texas, where he is now Director of Research. The institute conducts basic studies and provides forecasting support to weather-dependent operations, especially in the petroleum industry. He is also Professor of Physics and Meteorology in the University of Saint Thomas, in Houston. He majored in mathematics at Rice Institute and received S.M. and Ph.D. degrees in meteorology from the California Institute of Technology and the University of Chicago, respectively. During World War II he was a weather officer in the U.S. Air Force and later conducted research at

the Princeton University Institute for Advanced Study. He received the Meisinger Award from the American Meteorological Society in 1951 and shared in that society's Award for Outstanding Achievement in 1961. During the mid-1970s he was Chairman of the Industrial Meteorology Committee of the AMS and President of the National Council of Industrial Meteorologists.

John F. Griffiths is Professor of Meteorology in Texas A&M University and also State Climatologist for Texas. His degrees in mathematics, theology, physics, and meteorology were obtained from London University in 1947 and 1948. He served in various positions in Africa and Europe, including 4 years in charge of meteorological research in Her Majesty's Colonial Scientific Service in East Africa. He has also been a consultant for the United Nations in Spain, Greece, and Southeast Asia. He was elected a member of the World Academy of Art and Science in 1970, received awards from the Rockefeller Foundation and the Munitalp Foundation, and was awarded the Drew Gold Medal for mathematics by London University. He has written 5 books on instrumentation, climatology, and tropical meteorology and many papers and is an editor of the *International Journal of Environmental Studies*.

L. Ray Hoxit is a consulting meteorologist with Climatological Consulting Corporation, Asheville, North Carolina. He received B.S. and M.S. degrees from Florida State University and the Ph.D. in atmospheric science from Colorado State University. From 1967 through 1974 he was employed at the National Climatic Center in Asheville, where he studied tropical cyclone development and movement and analyzed diurnal variations in stratospheric temperatures. From 1974 to 1981 he was a research meteorologist in the Office of Weather Research and Modification, Environmental Research Laboratories, Boulder, Colorado, where he examined interactions between convective clouds and their environment and meteorological conditions associated with extreme precipitation. In 1981 he returned to the National Climatic Data Center, where he was Deputy Director in 1981–82 and Acting Director from 1982 to 1984.

Edwin Kessler has been Director of NOAA/ERL's National Severe Storms Laboratory, Norman, Oklahoma, since 1964 and is Adjunct Professor of Meteorology in the University of Oklahoma. A graduate of Columbia College, New York City, he received the Sc.D. in meteorology from the Massachusetts Institute of Technology in 1957. His meteorological papers have dealt mainly with applications of weather radar and with distributions of water substance in relation to coevolving distributions of wind. He has been a Councilor of the American Meteorological Society and has served on numerous boards and committees.

Roland List has been Professor of Physics (Meteorology) in the University of Toronto, Toronto, Canada, since 1963, with the exception of the period 1982–84, when he served as the Deputy Secretary-General of the World Meteorological Organization, in Geneva, Switzerland. He received M.Sc. and Ph.D. degrees from the Swiss Federal Institute of Technology, Zurich. In 1952 he took charge of the section on Atmospheric Ice Formation of the Swiss Federal Institute of Snow and Avalanche Research in Davos. In 1963 he moved to Toronto and expanded his work to include the physics of rain formation, cloud dynamics, and weather modification, as demonstrated in more than 150 papers. From 1970 to 1982 he was Chairman of the Executive Committee Panel on Weather Modification of the World Meteorological Organization, where he initiated and guided the International Precipitation Enhancement Project in Spain. He has also served in many other national and international agencies and has chaired international conferences on cloud physics, weather modification, and typhoon moderation. He is a member of the Royal Society of Canada and its Academy of Sciences.

Frank H. Ludlam was Professor of Meteorology in the Imperial College of the University of London. He obtained the D.Sc. degree in meteorology in that university. He specialized in the physics of clouds, and wrote extensively on this subject. (Editor's note: This characteristically modest autobiographical sketch was prepared by Dr. Ludlam shortly before his death in 1977.)

Griffith M. Morgan, Jr., is Field Manager for the Program for Atmospheric Water Supply undertaken by Simpson Weather Associates, Inc., for the Water Research Commission of the Republic of South Africa. He is in South Africa during a six-month operational period each year. He received the B.A. degree in physics from Northwestern University in 1955 and the M.S. degree in meteorology from New York University in 1961. On graduation from Northwestern he received a commission in the U.S. Air Force and served as a weather forecaster in Europe and North Africa. He received a Fulbright Study Grant in 1962 to study hailstorms in Italy. Subsequently he became Director of the Observatory for Hailstorm Research in Verona, Italy, was a senior meteorologist at the Illinois State Water Survey, and from 1976 to 1983 was Head of the Design and Evaluation Group of the Convective Storms Division at the National Center for Atmospheric Research in Boulder, Colorado. He is the author of more than 60 papers and reports, mainly on hailstorms, cloud physics, and synoptic meteorology.

Chester W. Newton is Head of the Empirical Studies Group of the Climate Project at the National Center for Atmospheric Research, Boulder, Colorado. Following two years at Phoenix Junior College, he was an Air Corps Aviation Cadet at the University of Chicago, where he later received the B.S., M.S., and Ph.D. degrees. His research as a synoptic meteorologist has been mainly in the areas of thunderstorms and squall lines, fronts and jetstreams, cyclone structure and mechanics, and the energy and angular momentum balance of the Earth's atmosphere. He taught meteorology at the University of Chicago and was Chief Scientist of the U.S. Weather Bureau National Severe Storms Project from 1961 to 1963, when he joined NCAR. With Erik Palmén he is coauthor of *Atmospheric Circulation Systems*. He served as editor of *Monthly Weather Review* in 1974–77 and as President of the American Meteorological Society in 1979.

Yoshi Ogura is Professor of Meteorology and Director of the Laboratory for Atmospheric Research of the University of Illinois, Urbana-Champaign. He received the B.S. and Ph.D. degrees in geophysics from the University of Tokyo. His research interests include atmospheric turbulence, planetary boundary layers, dynamics of atmospheric convection, and marine meteorology. He has served on many international and national committees and panels, including the WMO/ICSU Joint Organizing Committee for the Global Atmospheric Research Programmes (GARP).

Harold D. Orville is Professor and Head of the Department of Meteorology, South Dakota School of Mines and Technology, Rapid City. He holds the B.A. degree in political science from the University of Virginia, the M.S. degree in meteorology from Florida State University, and the Ph.D. in meteorology from the University of Arizona. His specialities are in cloud physics and the numerical modeling of clouds. He is an editor of the *Journal of the Atmospheric Sciences* and a member of the International Commission on Cloud Physics of the International Union of Geodesy and Geophysics.

Edward T. Pierce was a graduate of the University of Wales and received a doctorate in atmospheric physics from Cambridge University, England, in 1951. After more than a decade of teaching and research at Cambridge in solar and meteorological research, he was employed for high-voltage research by Vickers, Ltd., and for research in geophysics by AVCO Corporation. During 1960–76 he was employed at Stanford Research Institute, Stanford, California, and became widely known as an authority on atmospheric electricity and the hazardous effects of electric fields and lightning on aircraft, supertankers, and rockets. During 1976–77, he worked at NOAA's National Severe Storms Laboratory in Norman, Oklahoma. His professional career produced more than 150 reports and publications. He was Honorary President of the International Commission on Atmospheric Electricity from 1975 until his death in 1978.

David J. Raymond is Professor of Physics in the New Mexico Institute of Mining and Technology, Socorro. He obtained the B.S. in physics from Rensselaer Polytechnic Institute in 1965 and the Ph.D. in high-energy physics from Stanford University in 1970. He studied mountain lee waves and trade cumuli and taught physics while at the Cloud Physics Observatory, University of Hawaii in Hilo, and is well known for his work on wave-CISK models of severe thunderstorms. His current research is with aircraft observations of mountain-induced thunderstorms in New Mexico.

Frederick Sanders is Professor Emeritus of Meteorology in the Massachusetts Institute of Technology and an experienced sailor. His education at Amherst College, emphasizing mathematics, musical composition, and political science, was interrupted by World War II, and he was introduced to meteorology as a weather officer in the U.S. Air Force, with a tour of duty in Greenland. Following graduation from Amherst in the late 1940s, he was a forecaster with the U.S. Weather Bureau and then entered MIT for graduate study, which led to the doctorate in meteorology and his main career at the same school. In 1977 he received the National Weather Association Award for outstanding contributions to applied meteorology. He has held several posts in the American Meteorological Society, including that of National Councilor.

Yoshi K. Sasaki received the Ph.D. in meteorology from Tokyo University in 1955. From 1956 to 1960 he did meteorological research at Texas A&M University. Since 1960 he has been associated with the University of Oklahoma and was appointed George Lynn Cross Research Professor there in 1975. In 1980 he was appointed Director of the Cooperative Institute for Mesoscale Meteorological Studies. He is widely known for original and important work in squall-line theory and in variational optimization of meteorological analysis and prediction. He received a Japan Meteorological Society Award in 1955 for the investigation of typhoons and an Outstanding Educator of America Award in 1974.

Joseph T. Schaefer is Chief of the Scientific Services Division in the National Weather Service Central Region, Kansas City, Missouri. The SSD transfers advances in theoretical meteorology to operationally useful forecast methods. From 1976 to 1984 he was Chief of the Techniques Development Unit of the National Severe Storms Forecast Center at Kansas City. He received B.S. and Ph.D. degrees from Saint Louis University, was a staff meteorologist at several National Weather Service offices, and conducted research with the Naval Weather Research Facility in Norfolk, Virginia. His studies of the dryline and its relationship to thunderstorm development were undertaken while he worked at the National Severe Storms Laboratory, Norman, Oklahoma, from 1971 to 1976.

Peter W. Summers is a Senior Research Scientist with the Canadian Atmospheric Environment Service, Downsview, Ontario. He returned in 1980 after two years with the weather-modification program of the World Meteorological Organization, in Geneva, Switzerland. Previously he spent two years as a visiting scientist with the National Hail Research Experiment at the National Center for Atmospheric Research, Boulder, Colorado. During 1964–73 he was at first coordinator and subsequently director of the Alberta Hail Studies Project. He holds the B.Sc. degree in mathematics from Nottingham University, England, a postgraduate diploma in meteorology from Imperial College, England, the Ph.D. (1964) in meteorology from McGill University, Montreal. His specialties include hailstorms, weather modification, and air pollution, and he developed the "on-top" technique for seeding hailstorms, which has been used in several projects.

Index

Accretion process: 263, 265–66, 302, 328
Adiabatic processes: 60–62, 156
Advection: differential, 89–91; and stability change, 90; and squall-line formation, 91
Ageostrophic winds: effects on differential advection, 90; vertical motions associated with, 96; relationship to frictional retardation, 117
Air bubbles in hailstones: 253, 270
Air-mass (thunder)storms: 5, 133
Anelastic continuity equation: 301, 325, 337
Angular momentum: 197, 224; eddy transport of, 219, 227
Anticyclonic tornado: 197, 203, 206, 219
Arabian Sea disturbances: 162, 166–68
Atmospherics: 284–85
Available potential energy: 68, 176

Balance level: 273
Ball lightning: 282
Baroclinic flow and vorticity: 218
Baroclinic instability: 125; in summer monsoon over Asia, 169–70
Barotropic conversion process: 175–76
Barotropic flow and vorticity: 215, 216, 218
Barotropic instability in summer monsoon over Asia: 162, 169
Barotropic stability in tornadoes: 227
Bay of Bengal cyclogenesis: 168–70
Bead lightning: 282
Beneficial competition hypothesis: 363
Bergeron-Findeisen process: 263, 359
Bernoulli's equation: 323
Boundary conditions in numerical cloud models: 329–30, 337, 341
Boundary layer processes: 114ff.; instabilities, 121
Bound charge: 277
Boussinesq approximation: 325
Breakdown field: 281
Brunt-Vaisala oscillation: 312, 322
Bubble high: 127
Buoyancy: term for, in momentum equation, 63, 192, 225, 320, 326; role of, in generation of gust front, 192–93, 195–96; energy contained in, 193, 348; growth

rate of waves due to, 318; in plumes, 320
Burgers-Rott vortex: 226

Capping inversions: 91–92
Charge transfer by lightning: 283
Circulation: 114; rate of change of, 119–20; definition of, 114, 197, 215; of a tornado, 217
Clear slot in clouds around tornado: 205
Climatology: of thunderstorms, 9ff.; of hail, 24–25, 34–37, 237; of tornadoes, 37–39, 206–207; of oceanic thunderstorms, 41ff.; of thunderstorms in relation to prevailing winds, 75–76; of thunderstorms in relation to season, 76–78
Cloud bands: 121
Cloud clusters in the tropics: 156; squall, 177–80; non-squall, 180–86
Cloud density: vertical profiles of, 298, 300, 305
Cloud electrification: 281, 293–94, 328ff.
Cloud physics processes: numerical modeling of, 302, 326–28, 341
Cloud seeding: possible effect of, 312; principle of, 359–60; evaluation of, 361–62
Cloud-to-ground lightning: transfer of negative charge to ground by, 278; transfer of positive charge to ground by, 291–92
Cold-air tornado funnels: 208
Cold surges: 159
Collection efficiency: 265–66, 273, 302
Columnar electrical resistance: 277
Condensation, heat of: 59, 297; loading of updraft by, 71, 144–46
Condensation coalescence process: 360
Conditional instability: 65
Conditional instability of the second kind (CISK): 159, 169–70
Conductivity: 277
Conservation equations for water: 300ff., 327–28
Continuing current: 283
Continuity, equations of: 300ff., 314, 327–28
Convection: 3, 59; cumulus, 2–4, 7, 59; tropical, 4, 153ff.; in middle latitudes, 4–6; parcel theory of, 5; energetics of, 59ff.; forced, 105; feedbacks of, to

Thunderstorm Morphology and Dynamics,

designed by Ed Shaw and Bill Cason, was set in various sizes of Times Roman by G & S Typesetters and printed offset on fifty-pound Cougar Opaque by the University of Oklahoma Printing Services, with case binding by John H. Dekker & Sons.